ENGLISH PLACE-NAME SOCIETY. VOLUME LXXXIV
FOR 2006

GENERAL EDITOR

RICHARD COATES

PRODUCTION EDITOR

PAUL CAVILL

THE PLACE-NAMES OF LEICESTERSHIRE

PART IV

THE SURVEY OF ENGLISH PLACE-NAMES
UNDERTAKEN WITH THE APPROVAL AND SUPPORT OF
THE ARTS AND HUMANITIES RESEARCH COUNCIL
AND
THE BRITISH ACADEMY

THE PLACE-NAMES OF
LEICESTERSHIRE

BY

BARRIE COX

PART FOUR

GARTREE HUNDRED

NOTTINGHAM
ENGLISH PLACE-NAME SOCIETY
2009

Published by the English Place-Name Society,
School of English Studies, University of Nottingham,
Nottingham NG7 2RD.

Registered Charity No. 257891

ISBN-10: 0 904889 82 3
ISBN-13: 978 0 904889 82 6

Typeset by Paul Cavill & Printed in Great Britain
by 4Word, Bristol.

CONTENTS

PREFACE

This fourth volume of *The Place-Names of Leicestershire* follows the format which I adopted for my three previous volumes, in that each is largely self-contained and, I trust, user-friendly. It has been long in the making.

The Gartree Hundred is fortunate in having three important local sources of medieval documents relating to it, namely the Peake MSS (Nevill of Holt), the Market Harborough Parish Records and the Shangton Records. My collections from these and other medieval sources were undertaken in the late 1960s when I was preparing a doctoral thesis on the place-names of Leicestershire and Rutland. My very belated thanks must be extended to the staffs of the former Leicestershire Record Office and the Leicester Archives Department, Leicester Museum, both of New Walk, Leicester, who gave me so much help with the medieval documents during this period.

The seventeenth- and eighteenth-century Glebe Terriers for the Leicestershire parishes are housed for the most part in Lincolnshire Archives, Lincoln. My thanks are due to its staff for their assistance in making available this material from which I extracted in the later 1990s.

Eighteenth-, nineteenth- and twentieth-century estate maps, deeds, surveys, miscellaneous terriers and Tithe Apportionment documents for the Gartree Hundred parishes are preserved in The Record Office for Leicestershire, Leicester and Rutland, Wigston Magna. Its staff has been of the greatest help in making accessible such items for my examination during the past four years. For this, my sincerest thanks.

Dr Anne Tarver produced the parish map of the Gartree Hundred for the volume. Her cartography is invariably splendid.

Finally (and yet again) I must extend my best thanks to Dr Paul Cavill of the English Place-Name Survey for his typesetting of this volume which, as always, is meticulously presented.

Barrie Cox September 2008

INTRODUCTION TO THE PLACE-NAMES OF GARTREE HUNDRED

The Gartree Hundred occupies the majority of the south-east quarter of the county, extending from Leicester to the borders of Northamptonshire and Rutland. It comprises two separate areas of High Leicestershire, together with the South-East Lowland and the eastern half of the Lutterworth Upland. Except in the east, its land rarely rises above 500 ft. Much of it overlies the Lower Lias clays which stretch eastwards from Leicester to the Middle and Upper Lias of High Leicestershire. A large part of the Hundred is covered with glacial drift which produces soils suitable for the growth of good quality grass and thus the region is now devoted in large measure to livestock farming of sheep and cattle. It is an undulating landscape of small villages, often located on patches of gravel by large springs in the valleys of two systems of streams. These streams are tributaries of the river Soar which flow north-westwards and those of the river Welland which flow south-eastwards.

A ridge forms the watershed between these two systems of streams and marks the line of a Bronze Age trackway which forded the river Wreake at Melton Mowbray and ran south through Illston on the Hill, Kibworth Harcourt, Saddington and Mowsley. It was known to the Anglo-Saxons as *le Ferdgate* 'the army road'. It crossed the later major Roman *Via Devana* (Gartree Road) which ran south-eastwards from Leicester, at a spot in Shangton parish almost in the geographical centre of the Hundred. Here at *Gartree Bush* was the Hundred's moot-site, earlier called *Mathelou* 'the assembly (or speech) headland'.

The *Via Devana* from Leicester survives for much of its length to Medbourne in the far south-east of the Hundred where there was a Romano-British town of up to sixty hectares in area, as well as three villas, plus at least three non-villa farmsteads. The town and the villas have produced early Anglo-Saxon pottery which suggests that occupation continued without dislocation of the settlement pattern hereabouts. A pagan Anglo-Saxon inhumation cemetery has also been discovered at Medbourne. A villa site is known a little to the east-south-east of nearby Hallaton, another at East Langton and yet another at West

Langton, while a Roman site which may have been a villa is located at Shangton. Pagan Anglo-Saxon cemeteries are known at West Langton and Foxton beside Langton Brook, which also suggests continuity of occupation here. From the *Via Devana* just south-east of Medbourne, another Roman road (Margary 571) branched east through Drayton, Great Easton (where its route is recorded as *Barnsdale strete*), Caldecott and King's Cliffe to meet Ermine Street at *Durobrivae* (Water Newton).

These three principal early routes within Gartree Hundred were used in the Middle Ages as saltways, as local names with *salt* and *saltere* in Billesdon, Tur Langton, Cranoe, Slawston, Drayton and Nevill Holt parishes indicate.

Unlike in Framland Hundred and in East Goscote Hundred to the north, the settlement names in Gartree Hundred are overwhelmingly of Old English origin. A strip of later Scandinavian names with *-by*, perhaps signalling in part the eventual break-up of former English estates, lies north-east of the Gartree Road. It comprises Thurnby, Bushby, Galby, Frisby and Goadby. Only in the south-east of the Hundred in a small area at Slawston and Blaston is there evidence of the probable appropriation of former English settlements by Scandinavians of the great Viking army which disbanded in the region in 877. This echoes and accords with the limited early Scandinavian settlement in Rutland at Glaston, some six miles to its north-east.

There are 62 major township-names in Gartree Hundred (this counting the three Langtons, the two Kibworths, the two Strettons and the two Bowdens as one name each). If one treats Blaston, Illston and Rolleston as wholly English, 51 or 82% of these township-names are of Old English formation. The pre-English Glen may be added to these non-Scandinavian toponyms. Early Scandinavian settlements signalled by the so-called Grimston-hybrid type of name are limited to Slawston plus the possible Blaston, Illston and Rolleston. There are six names only with *-by*. Of these Frisby has an Old English specific and Westerby is a late minor adjunct to Smeeton, while the specifics in the names Thurnby, Bushby and Galby suggest later exploitation of poorer soils. To such settlements on once marginal land may be added Scraptoft. There are three names with the later *-thorpe*: the simplex Thorpe (Langton) and Hothorpe and Othorpe, each of which may have an Old English specific.

It is unsurprising that this early and densely English settled area of the county bears numerous traces in its minor toponymy of the ancient superstitions of its peasant inhabitants. Many names of springs and wells relate to the desire for fertility. These include *Our Lady's Well* (earlier *Maidewell'*) in Nevill Holt, Lady Well in Market Harborough,

Maidenewell in Husbands Bosworth, St Ann's Well in Church Langton, which may remember the Celtic mother goddess Anu, and perhaps Birdwell in Theddingworth, a sacred well to be visited by new brides. *Seaven Wells* in Lubenham, *Seuenewell* in Great Bowden and the unlocated *Sevenewelles* also in this region may have originated as pre-Christian sacred springs. Seven is nowadays still regarded as a lucky number. The pre-Christian site of Holyoaks (early *Haliach* 'the sacred oak-tree') in well-wooded Stockerston no doubt prompted the establishment there of the hermitage of *Mirabel* to counter surviving superstitions among the country folk. A demon was thought by them to lurk in *Thyrspyt* in Nevill Holt and on *Shuggborowe* in Burton Overy. Perhaps a hobgoblin haunted *Tommor* in Great Easton and maybe another at *Grimeslade* in Glooston. In addition to those wells restyled as Lady Well, *Our Lady's Well* and *Holiewell* (in Cranoe), from the period after the conversion to Christianity is *St Morrills Well* in Hallaton. This spring, also known as *Stowe Welle* (with **stōw** 'a holy place'), is presumably named after a locally-esteemed Anglo-Saxon named Merewala (or Merewald) and recalls the well of the Anglo-Saxon St Tibba in Ryhall, Rutland, whose sacred spring lies in land associated historically with Merewala, brother of Wulfhere of Mercia.

Major religious houses of the Middle Ages have left only a limited mark on the names of the Hundred. There were two important sites here, Owston Abbey, a foundation for Augustinian Canons which came into being c.1160 and Bradley Priory, also for Augustinian Canons, founded c.1200. Sulby Abbey across the county boundary in Northamptonshire farmed an important grange in Husbands Bosworth, while the lost *Prestgrave* in Nevill Holt parish probably became a grange of Peterborough Abbey.

The last major impact on the toponyms of Gartree Hundred was provided by the developing canal system at the end of the eighteenth century and that of the railways in the second half of the nineteenth. From 1792 to 1797, the Union Canal was cut south-eastwards from Leicester, stopping short for some years at Debdale Wharf in Gumley parish because of financial problems and the war with France. A further section of canal south-eastwards from it to Market Harborough was completed by 1809, while the combined Grand Union Canal opened in 1814, with the well-known staircase of ten locks at Foxton built in 1812. These canals have left their marks in the names of their bridges, their locks, their wharfs and their taverns for the bargemen. By 1850, the Midland Railway from Leicester was pushing through Gartree Hundred to Market Harborough en route to Kettering, while the Rugby and

Stamford Railway from Market Harborough passed through Drayton, Bringhurst and Great Easton parishes on its way north-eastwards through Rutland. At the end of the nineteenth century, a Great Central Railway line was opened southwards through Hallaton, Medbourne and Slawston parishes. The tracks of both the Rugby and Stamford and the Great Central have been long dismantled, but the names of the cuttings, the embankments and stations of all three railways have contributed significantly to the local toponymy of the Hundred. Such informative canal and railway names, as well as those of inns and taverns throughout the region, are frequently disregarded or undervalued in our toponymic searches beyond their eras into a more distant past.

NOTES ON ARRANGEMENT

1. The Gartree Hundred name is discussed first. After this, the place-names are treated within the civil parishes. Within each civil parish, the townships are dealt with in alphabetical order. For each township, the township name is followed by names of primary historical or etymological interest, also arranged in alphabetical order. At the end of these sections, all the remaining names related to the township appearing on the 1956–67 O.S. 6" maps, on the 1951–66 O.S. 2½" maps and on the 1967–8 O.S. 1" maps (and any names recorded only locally) are listed with such early forms and etymological comment as can be provided. These names, however, are sometimes of obvious origin or are ones about whose history it is unwise to speculate. The forms of all names in the above sections are presented in the order: spelling, date, source. The final section for each township lists field-names, divided into modern (i.e. post-1750) and earlier. The pre-1750 field-names are printed in italic.

2. Place-names believed to be no longer current are marked '(lost)', e.g. 'PRESTGRAVE (lost)'. This does not necessarily mean that the site to which the name was once applied is unknown. We are dealing primarily with names and it is the names which are lost. Such names are printed in italic in the index. Place-names marked '(local)' are believed to be current locally.

3. In explaining the various toponyms, summary reference is always made, by printing the elements in bold type, to the analysis of elements at the end of this volume and to the more extended treatment of these in *English Place-Name Elements* (EPNS 25 and 26), in the *Addenda and Corrigenda* to these volumes in JEPNS 1 and in *The Vocabulary of English Place-Names*, in progress: e.g. '*Wyndmylnhyl* 1410 (*v.* **wind-mylne**, **hyll**)'.

4. Manuscript sources of early spellings of the names are indicated by printing the abbreviations for the sources in italic. The abbreviations for published sources are printed in roman type.

5. Where two dates are given for a spelling, e.g. '1189 (1332)' or '1477 (e.16)', the first date is the date at which the document purports to

have been composed, the second the date of the copy that has come down to us. Sources whose dates cannot be fixed to a particular year are dated by century, e.g. '12', '13', '14' etc. (often more specifically 'e.13', 'm.13', 'l.13' etc., early, mid and late thirteenth century respectively); by regnal date, e.g. 'Hy 2', 'Edw 1', 'Stephen' etc.; or by a range of years, e.g. '1209 × 35', such a date meaning that the form belongs to a particular year within those limits but cannot be more precisely fixed.

6. The sign '(p)' after a source indicates that the particular spelling given appears in that source as a person's surname, not primarily as a reference to a place; thus '*Fleckenai* 1166 LN (p)' refers to one *Ricardus de Fleckenai*, bearing *Fleckenai* as his surname.

7. When a letter or letters (sometimes words or phrases) in an early place-name form are enclosed in parentheses, it means that spellings with and without the enclosed letter(s) occur; e.g. '*Bryn(n)ynghurst*' means that the forms *Brynynghurst* and *Brynnynghurst* are found. When only one part of a place-name spelling is given as a variant, preceded or followed by a hyphen or tilde, it means that the particular spelling only differs in respect of the cited part from the preceding or following spelling, e.g. '*Goltropp ~*, *Golthorpe Close*'.

8. When an entry reads, e.g. 'HARE PIE BANK, 1846 White', the name appears in its modern spelling in the source quoted.

9. Names presented in capital letters are those which appear on the Ordnance Survey maps used in preparing the Leicestershire survey.

10 Cross references to other names are sometimes given with *supra* or *infra*, the former referring to a name already dealt with, the latter to a name dealt with later in the text.

11. When a place-name is compared with an example from another county, that county is indicated; e.g. 'Bozenham (Nth 100)' which refers to Bozenham in Northamptonshire and to a specific page in the EPNS survey *The Place-Names of Northamptonshire*.

12. In order to save space in presenting early spellings of a name, *et passim* and *et freq* are sometimes used to indicate that the preceding form occurs from time to time or frequently from the date of the last quoted source to that of the following one.

13. Hypothetical forms of place-name elements which appear asterisked in the analysis of elements at the end of this volume are not asterisked in the text, although the discussion will often make it clear which are on independent record and which are inferred.

ABBREVIATIONS AND BIBLIOGRAPHY

Abbreviations printed in roman type refer to printed sources and those in italic to manuscript sources.

a.	*ante.*
AAS	Reports and Papers of the Associated Architectural Societies.
Abbr	*Placitorum Abbrevatio* (RC), 1811.
acc.sg.	accusative singular.
Acct	Account Books in private collections.
AD	*Catalogue of Ancient Deeds* (PRO), in progress.
AddCh	Additional Charters in the British Library, London.
adj.	adjective, adjectival, adjectivally.
adv.	adverb.
Æthelweard	*The Chronicle of Æthelweard*, ed. A. Campbell, 1962.
AFr	Anglo-French.
AILR	Auditors' Inrolements – Land Revenues, in various publications.
AllS	Manuscripts in the Muniments Room of All Souls' College, Oxford.
AN	Anglo-Norman.
Angl	Anglian dialect of Old English.
Anglo-Scand	Anglo-Scandinavian.
ASC	*The Anglo-Saxon Chronicle*, ed. B. Thorpe (RS), 1861.
Ass	Assize Rolls in various publications.
ASWills	*Anglo-Saxon Wills*, ed. D. Whitelock, 1930.
Banco	*Index of Placita de Banco 1327–28* (PRO Lists and Indexes 32), 1909; De Banco Rolls in Farnham.
BCS	*Cartularium Saxonicum*, ed. W. de G. Birch, 3 vols., 1885–93.
BelCartA	Small Cartulary of Belvoir Priory (Add MS 98), Duke of Rutland's Muniments Room, Belvoir Castle, Leics.
BelCartB	Large Cartulary of Belvoir Priory (Add MS 105), Duke of Rutland's Muniments Room, Belvoir Castle, Leics.
Berkeley	*Catalogue of the Charters at Berkeley Castle*, ed. I. H. Jeayes, 1892.
Bewicke	Bewicke MSS, The Record Office for Leicestershire, Leicester and Rutland, Wigston Magna.
Bk	*The Place-Names of Buckinghamshire* (EPNS 2), 1925.
BL	British Library, London.
Blore	T. Blore, *History and Antiquities of the County of Rutland*, 1811.
BM	*Index to the Charters and Rolls in the Department of Manuscripts, British Museum*, 1900–12.
BNF	*Beiträge zur Namenforschung.*

BodCh *Calendar of Charters and Rolls preserved in the Bodleian Library*, ed. W. H. Turner and H. O. Coxe, 1878.
BPR *The Register of Edward the Black Prince* (PRO), 4 vols., 1930–3.
Bracton *Henricus de Bracton*, *Note Book*, ed. F. W. Maitland, 1887.
Brai Cartularium Familiae Braibroc (BL MS Sloane 986).
Braye Braye MSS, The Record Office for Leicestershire, Leicester and Rutland, Wigston Magna.
Brit British.
Brk *The Place-Names of Berkshire* (EPNS 49–51), 1973–6.
Bru Brudenell MSS, Northamptonshire Record Office, Northampton.
Burton W. Burton, *The Description of Leicestershire*, 1622.
c. *circa*.
Ca *The Place-Names of Cambridgeshire* (EPNS 19), 1943.
Campbell A. Campbell, *Old English Grammar*, 1959.
CDEPN Victor Watts, *The Cambridge Dictionary of English Place-Names*, 2004.
CENS Publications of the Centre for English Name Studies, University of Nottingham, Nottingham.
Census Censuses variously published.
cent. century.
cf. compare.
Ch *Calendar of Charter Rolls* (PRO), 6 vols., 1903–27.
Ch *The Place-Names of Cheshire* (EPNS 44–7), 1970–2, (EPNS 48, 54), 1981, (EPNS 74), 1997.
ChancP *Calendar of Proceedings in Chancery in the Reign of Queen Elizabeth*, 3 vols., 1827–32; *Index of Chancery Proceedings* (series ii) (PRO Lists and Indexes 7, 24, 30).
ChancR Chancellor's Rolls (as footnotes to *Pipe Rolls* (PRS), in progress).
ChancW *Calendar of Chancery Warrents* (PRO), in progress.
Chap *Chapter Acts, Lincoln Cathedral* (LRS 12, 13, 15).
Charyte Charyte's Novum Rentale of Leicester Abbey, incorporating Geryn's Rental (Bodleian Laud Misc 625), Bodleian Library, Oxford.
Chas 1 Regnal date, t. Charles 1.
ChR *Rotuli Chartarum* (RC), 1837.
ChronPetr *Chronicon Petroburgense* (Camden Society 47), 1849.
Cl *Calendar of Close Rolls* (PRO), in progress.
Clayton Clayton MSS in The Record Office for Leicestershire, Leicester and Rutland, Wigston Magna.
ClR *Rotuli Litterarum Clausarum* (RC), 1833–44.
Cl(s) Close(s) (in field-names).
CN *Carte Nativorum, a Peterborough Abbey Cartulary* (NRS 20), 1960.
Coleman Coleman Estate Documents in The Record Office for Leicestershire, Leicester and Rutland, Wigston Magna.
Comp Compotus Rolls, Duke of Rutland's Muniments Room, Belvoir Castle, Leics.; The Record Office for Leicestershire, Leicester and Rutland, Wigston Magna; in the Middleton MSS, Nottingham University Archives, Nottingham.
comp. comparative.

comp.adj. comparative adjective.
Conant Conant MSS, The Record Office for Leicestershire, Leicester and Rutland, Wigston Magna.
cons. consonant.
ContGerm Continental Germanic.
CoPleas Common Pleas in various publications.
Cor Coroners' Rolls in various publications.
Coram Coram Rege Rolls in various publications.
Cox[1] Barrie Cox, *English Inn and Tavern Names*, 1994.
Cox[2] Barrie Cox, *A Dictionary of Leicestershire and Rutland Place-Names*, 2005.
CRCart Roll Cartulary of Croxton Abbey (II 29 iii), Duke of Rutland's Muniments Room, Belvoir Castle, Leics.
Crox The Large Cartulary of Croxton Abbey (Add. MS 70), Duke of Rutland's Muniments Room, Belvoir Castle, Leics.
Ct Court Rolls in the Ferrers MSS, the Hazlerigg MSS, the Rothley Temple Deeds and the Winstanley MSS, The Record Office for Leicestershire, Leicester and Rutland, Wigston Magna.
Cu *The Place-Names of Cumberland* (EPNS 20–22), 1950–52.
Cur *Curia Regis Rolls* (PRO), in progress.
Curtis J. Curtis, *A Topographical History of the County of Leicester*, 1831.
CustRo The Custumary of the Manor and Soke of Rothley, ed. G. T. Clark, *Archaeologia* 47 (1882).
d. died.
Dan Danish.
Dane F. M. Stenton, *Documents illustrative of the Social and Economic History of the Danelaw*, 1920.
dat.pl. dative plural.
dat.sg. dative singular.
DB Domesday Book; *Domesday Book: Leicestershire*, ed. P. Morgan, 1979.
Db *The Place-Names of Derbyshire* (EPNS 27, 28, 29), 1959.
DBPN A. D. Mills, *A Dictionary of British Place-Names*, 2003.
Deed Miscellaneous published deeds.
Deed Miscellaneous deeds in The Record Office for Leicestershire, Leicester and Rutland, Wigston Magna; in Lincolnshire Archives Office, Lincoln; in private collections.
def.art. definite article.
DEPN E. Ekwall, *The Concise Oxford Dictionary of English Place-Names*, 4th edn, 1960.
Depos Exchequer Special Depositions in PRO.
DI *The Domesday of Inclosures 1517–1518*, ed. I. S. Leadam, 2 vols., 1897; repr. New York 1971.
dial. dialect(al).
DKR *Reports of the Deputy Keeper of the Public Records* (PRO).
DLPN K. Cameron with J. Insley, *A Dictionary of Lincolnshire Place-Names*, 1998.

Do	*The Place-Names of Dorset* (EPNS 52, 53, 59, 60), 1977–1989, in progress.
DS	*Danmarks Stednavne*, Copenhagen 1922 ff.
Du	Dutch.
Dugd	W. Dugdale, *Monasticon Anglicanum*, 6 vols. in 8, 1817–30.
Durham	V. Watts, *A Dictionary of County Durham Place-Names*, 2002.
e.	early.
ECP	*Early Chancery Proceedings* (PRO Lists and Indexes 1–12).
ed.	edited by.
edn	edition.
Edw 1, Edw 2	Regnal date, t. Edward I, t. Edward II etc.
EETS	Early English Text Society.
el.	place-name element.
eModE	early Modern English.
EnclA	Enclosure Awards in various publications.
EnclA	Unpublished Enclosure Awards, The Record Office for Leicestershire, Leicester and Rutland, Wigston Magna.
EngFeud	F. M. Stenton, *The First Century of English Feudalism, 1066–1166*, 1932.
EpCB	*An Episcopal Court Book for the Diocese of Lincoln 1514–20* (LRS 61), 1967.
EPNS	Publications of the English Place-Name Society.
esp.	especially.
Ess	*The Place-Names of Essex* (EPNS 12), 1935.
et freq	*et frequenter* (and frequently (thereafter)).
et passim	and occasionally (thereafter).
ExchSpC	Exchequer Special Commissions in PRO.
FA	*Feudal Aids* (PRO), 6 vols., 1899–1920.
Farnham	G. F. Farnham, *Leicestershire Medieval Village Notes*, 6 vols., 1929–33.
Farnham	Transcriptions by G. F. Farnham, The Record Office for Leicestershire, Leicester and Rutland, Wigston Magna.
Fd	Field (in field-names).
Fees	*The Book of Fees* (PRO), 3 vols., 1921–31.
Feilitzen	O. von Feilitzen, *The Pre-Conquest Personal Names of Domesday Book*, Uppsala 1937.
fem.	feminine.
FF	Feet of Fines in various publications.
FH	Finch-Hatton MSS, Northamptonshire Record Office, Northampton.
Field	J. Field, *A History of English Field-Names*, 1993.
Fine	*Calendar of Fine Rolls* (PRO), in progress.
FineR	*Excerpta e rotulis finium* (RC), 2 vols., 1835–6.
Fm	Farm.
f.n(s).	field-name(s).
For	*Select Pleas of the Forest* (Seld 13), 1901.
For	Forest Proceedings in PRO.
Forssner	T. Forssner, *Continental-Germanic Personal Names in England*, Uppsala, 1916.

France *Calendar of Documents preserved in France* (RS), 1899.
freq. frequently.
GarCart Cartulary of Garendon Abbey (BL Lansdowne 415), British Library, London.
gen.pl. genitive plural.
gen.sg. genitive singular.
Germ German.
GildR Merchant Gild Rolls in RFL and RBL.
Hastings *The Manuscripts of the late Reginald Rawdon Hastings of the Manor House, Ashby de la Zouch*, vol. 1 (HMC), 1928.
Hazlerigg Hazlerigg MSS, The Record Office for Leicestershire, Leicester and Rutland, Wigston Magna.
HCand *The Chronicle of Hugh Candidus*, ed. W. T. Mellows, 1949.
HMC Historical Manuscripts Commission.
Ho. House.
HP Hall Papers in RBL.
Hy 1, Hy 2 Regnal date, t. Henry I, t. Henry II etc.
ib, *ib* *ibidem*.
Inqaqd *Inquisitiones ad quod Damnum* (RC), 1803.
Ipm *Calendar of Inquisitions post mortem* (PRO), in progress.
IpmR *Inquisitiones post mortem* (RC), 4 vols., 1802–28.
ISLR F. A. Greenhill, *The Incised Slabs of Leicestershire and Rutland*, 1958.
JEPNS Journal of the English Place-Name Society.
John Regnal date, t. John.
KCD *Codex Diplomaticus Aevi Saxonici*, ed. J. M. Kemble, 6 vols., 1839–48.
Kelly *Kelly's Directory of the Counties of Leicester and Rutland*, 1925.
L *The Place-Names of Lincolnshire* (EPNS 58, 64–6, 71, 73, 77), 1985–2001, in progress.
l. late.
LAS Transactions of the Leicestershire Archaeological Society, later Leicestershire Archaeological and Historical Society.
Lat Latin.
Laz Cartulary of Burton Lazars (BL Cotton Nero C XII), British Library, London.
LCDeeds Leicester Corporation Deeds, The Record Office for Leicestershire, Leicester and Rutland, Wigston Magna.
LCh Leicestershire Charters, The Record Office for Leicestershire, Leicester and Rutland, Wigston Magna.
Lei *The Place-Names of Leicestershire* (EPNS 75, 78, 81), 1998–2004, in progress.
LeicSurv *The Leicestershire Survey*, ed. C. F. Slade, 1956.
LeicW *Leicester Wills*, ed. H. Hartopp, 2 vols., 1902–20.
Leland *The Itinerary of John Leland*, ed. L. Toulmin-Smith, 5 vols., 1907–10.
LEpis *Lincoln Episcopal Records* (LRS 2), 1912.
LGerm Low German.
Lib *Calendar of Liberate Rolls* (PRO), in progress.

LibCl Liber Cleri in *The State of the Church*, vol. 1 (LRS 23), 1926.
Lindkvist H. Lindkvist, *Middle English Place-Names of Scandinavian Origin*, Uppsala 1912.
LinDoc *Lincoln Diocese Documents 1450–1544*, ed. A. Clark (EETS, Original Series 149), 1914.
LML *Leicestershire Marriage Licences 1570–1729*, ed. H. Hartopp, 1910.
LN *Liber Niger Scaccarii*, 1774.
LNPetr *Liber Niger Monasterii S. Petri de Burgo* in ChronPetr.
LP *Letters and Papers Foreign and Domestic, Henry VIII* (PRO), 1846–1933.
LRoll The Lincoln Roll – a Noseley Cartulary in the Hazlerigg MSS, The Record Office for Leicestershire, Leicester and Rutland, Wigston Magna.
LRS Publications of the Lincoln Record Society.
LTD Liber de terris Dominicalibus of Leicester Abbey (BL Cotton Galba B III), British Library, London.
m. mid.
Map Various printed maps.
Map Unpublished maps in local and private collections.
Margary I. D. Margary, *Roman Roads in Britain*, revised edn, 1967.
masc. masculine.
Mdw(s) Meadow(s) (in field-names).
ME Middle English.
MemR *Memoranda Rolls* (PRS NS 11, 21, 31).
MHG Middle High German.
MHW The Matriculus of Hugh of Wells in *Rotuli Hugonis de Welles* (LRS 3), 1912.
MiD Middleton MSS, University of Nottingham Archives, Nottingham.
MinAccts *Ministers' Accounts: List of the Lands of Dissolved Religious Houses* (PRO Lists and Indexes, Supplementary Series III, vols. 1–4).
MinAccts Unpublished Ministers' Accounts, The Record Office for Leicestershire, Leicester and Rutland, Wigston Magna.
Misc *Calendar of Inquisitions Miscellaneous* (PRO), in progress.
MiscAccts Miscellaneous accounts in various publications.
MiscAccts Miscellaneous accounts in local and private collections.
MktHPR Market Harborough Parish Records, The Record Office for Leicestershire, Leicester and Rutland, Wigston Magna.
MLat Medieval Latin.
MLG Middle Low German.
ModE Modern English.
ModEdial. Modern English dialect(al).
Moulton *Palaeography, Genealogy and Topography: Selections from the collection of H. R. Moulton*, 1930.
MS(S) manuscript(s).
n.d. not dated.
neut. neuter.
Nf *The Place-Names of Norfolk* (EPNS 61, 72, 79), 1989–2002, in progress.

Nichols	J. Nichols, *The History and Antiquities of the County of Leicester*, 4 vols. in 8, 1795–1811.
nom.pl.	nominative plural.
Norw	Norwegian.
NRS	Publications of the Northamptonshire Record Society.
NS	New series in a run of publications.
Nt	*The Place-Names of Nottinghamshire* (EPNS 17), 1940.
Nth	*The Place-Names of Northamptonshire* (EPNS 10), 1933.
O	First edition O.S. 1" maps.
OblR	*Rotulis de Oblatis* (RC), 1835.
obl.sg.	oblique singular.
ODan	Old Danish.
OE	Old English.
OED	*A New English Dictionary*, ed. J. A. H. Murray *et al.*, 1884–1928; re-issued with a supplement in 1933 as *The Oxford English Dictionary*.
OFr	Old French.
OIcel	Old Icelandic.
ON	Old Norse.
ONFr	Old Norman French.
Ord	Ordericus Vitalis, *Ecclesiasticae Historiae*, vols. 2, 3, Paris 1840, 1845.
O.S.	The Ordnance Survey.
OScand	Old Scandinavian.
OSut	*The Rolls and Registers of Bishop Oliver Sutton* (LRS 39, 43, 48, 52, 60), 1948–65.
OSwed	Old Swedish.
OWScand	Old West Scandinavian.
Ox	*The Place-Names of Oxfordshire*, (EPNS 23, 24), 1953–4.
p.	*post*.
P	*Pipe Rolls* (PRS), in progress.
(p)	place-name used as a personal name or surname.
Palmer	The Palmer MSS, The Record Office for Leicestershire, Leicester and Rutland, Wigston Magna.
Pap	*Calendar of Entries in the Papal Registers* (PRO), in progress.
pa.part.	past participle.
Pat	*Calendar of Patent Rolls* (PRO), in progress.
Pat	Patent Rolls in the Public Record Office.
Peake	Peake MSS (Nevill of Holt), The Record Office for Leicestershire, Leicester and Rutland, Wigston Magna.
perh.	perhaps.
pers.comm.	personal communication.
pers.n(s).	personal name(s).
P.H.	Public House.
PK	Powys-Keck Estate Documents, The Record Office for Leicestershire, Leicester and Rutland, Wigston Magna.
Plan	Unpublished plans in The Record Office for Leicestershire, Leicester and Rutland, Wigston Magna.
p.n(s).	place-name(s).

PN -ing	E. Ekwall, *English Place-Names in -ing*, 2nd edn, Lund 1962.
Polyolbion	M. Drayton, *Polyolbion*, ed. J. W. Hebel, 1961.
poss.	possible, possibly.
Potter	Potter MSS, University of Nottingham Archives, Nottingham.
ppl.adj.	participial adjective.
PR	Parish Registers in various publications.
PRep	*The Register of Bishop Philip Repingdon* (LRS 57–8), 1963.
prep.	preposition.
pres.part.	present participle.
presum.	presumably.
PRO	Records preserved in or published by the Public Record Office.
prob.	probable, probably.
PRS	Publications of the Pipe Roll Society.
PrW	Proto-Welsh.
q.v.	*quod vide.*
R.	River.
Rams	*Cartularium monasterii de Rameseia* (RS 79), 1884.
RB	Romano-British.
RBE	*Red Book of the Exchequer* (RS 99), 1896.
RBL	*Records of the Borough of Leicester*, vols. 1–3, ed. M. Bateson 1899–1905; vol. 4, ed. H. Stocks 1923; vols. 5–6, ed. G. A. Chinnery 1965–7.
RC	Publications of the Record Commission.
Rd	Road (in street-names).
Reaney	P. H. Reaney, *A Dictionary of English Surnames*, revised by R. M. Wilson, 3rd edn with appendix by D. Hey, 1995.
Redin	M. Redin, *Uncompounded Personal Names in Old English*, Uppsala 1915.
Reeve	Documents in the Reeve Collection, Lincolnshire Archives Office, Lincoln.
Reg	*Regesta Regum Anglo-Normannorum*, 1913–68.
RegAnt	*Registrum Antiquissimum of the Cathedral Church of Lincoln* (LRS 27–9, 51), 1931–58.
Rental	Various published rentals.
Rental	Various unpublished rentals in local and private collections.
Req	Court of Requests Rolls, in *Farnham*.
RFinib	Rotuli de Finibus in *Rotuli de Oblatis et Finibus in Turri Londinensi* (RC), 1835.
RFL	*Register of the Freemen of Leicester*, ed. H. Hartopp, 2 vols., 1927–33.
RGrav	*Rotuli Ricardi Gravesend Episcopi Lincolniensis* (LRS 20), 1925.
RGros	*Rotuli Roberti Grosseteste Episcopi Lincolniensis* (LRS 11), 1914.
RH	*Rotulis Hundredorum* (RC), 1812–18.
RHug	*Rotuli Hugonis de Welles Episcopi Lincolniensis* (LRS 3, 6), 1912–13.
Ric 1, Ric 2	Regnal dates, t. Richard I, t. Richard II etc.
RotNorm	*Rotuli Normanniae in Turri Londiniensi* (RC), 1835.
RS	Rolls Series.

RTemple	Rothley Temple Deeds, The Record Office for Leicestershire, Leicester and Rutland, Wigston Magna.
Ru	*The Place-Names of Rutland* (EPNS 67–9), 1994.
Rut	Duke of Rutland's MSS, Muniments Room, Belvoir Castle, Leics.
RydCart	*The Rydware Cartulary* (Salt 16), 1895.
S	P. H. Sawyer, *Anglo-Saxon Charters*, 1968.
Sa	*The Place-Names of Shropshire* (EPNS 62–3, 70, 76, 80) 1990–2004, in progress.
s.a.	*sub anno*.
Sale	Particulars of sales in local and private collections.
Salt	Publications of the William Salt Society.
Sandred	K. I. Sandred, *English Place-Names in -stead*, Uppsala 1963.
Saxton	Christopher Saxton, *Atlas of England and Wales*, 1576.
sb.	substantive.
Scand	Scandinavian.
Searle	W. G. Searle, *Onomasticon Anglo-Saxonicum*, 1897.
Selby	*The Selby Abbey Cartulary* (YAA 10, 13), 1891–3.
Seld	Publications of the Selden Society.
Sf	Suffolk.
Sherrard	Sherrard Estate Documents in The Record Office for Leicestershire, Leicester and Rutland, Wigston Magna.
ShR	Shangton Records, The Record Office for Leicestershire, Leicester and Rutland, Wigston Magna.
SlCart	Slawston Cartulary, The Record Office for Leicestershire, Leicester and Rutland, Wigston Magna.
Sloane	Sloane MSS, The British Library, London.
s.n(n).	*sub nomine, sub nominibus*.
Speed	J. Speed, *The Theatre of the Empire of Great Britain*, 1610.
SPNLY	G. Fellows Jensen, *Scandinavian Personal Names in Lincolnshire and Yorkshire*, Copenhagen 1968.
SR	Subsidy Rolls in various publications.
SSNEM	G. Fellows Jensen, *Scandinavian Settlement Names in the East Midlands*, Copenhagen 1978.
St	*The Place-Names of Staffordshire* (EPNS 55), 1984, in progress.
St	Street (in street-names).
Star	Star Chamber Proceedings, in *Farnham*.
Stephen	Regnal date, t. Stephen.
StH	D. Horovitz, *The Place-Names of Staffordshire*, Brewood 2005.
Studies[2]	E. Ekwall, *Studies on English Place-Names*, Stockholm 1936.
Studies[3]	E. Ekwall, *Etymological Notes on English Place-Names*, Lund 1959.
surn(s).	surname(s).
Surv	Surveys in local and private collections.
Swed	Swedish.
s.v.	*sub voce*.
t.	*tempore*.
TA	Various published Tithe Awards.
TA	Tithe Awards, The Record Office for Leicestershire, Leicester and Rutland, Wigston Magna.

Tax *Taxatio Ecclesiastica* (RC), 1802.
Terrier Various published terriers.
Terrier Terriers in local and private collections.
TRE *tempore Regis Edwardi*, the DB term for 'on the day that King Edward the Confessor was alive and dead'.
v. *vide.*
Val *The Valuation of Norwich*, ed. W. E. Lunt, 1926.
Valuation Valuations in local and private collections.
vb. verb.
vbl.sb. verbal substantive.
VCHL *Victoria County History of Leicestershire*, in progress.
VE *Valor Ecclesiasticus* (RC), 1810–34.
VEPN *The Vocabulary of English Place-Names* (CENS), in progress.
Visit *Visitations of Religious Houses in the Diocese of Lincoln* (LRS 14, 21, 33, 35, 37), 1918–47.
W *The Place-Names of Wiltshire* (EPNS 16), 1939.
Wa *The Place-Names of Warwickshire* (EPNS 13), 1936.
We *The Place-Names of Westmorland* (EPNS 42–3), 1967.
White *History, Gazetteer and Directory of Leicestershire and Rutland*, ed. W. White, 1846, 1863, 1877.
Will Wills in various publications.
Will Unpublished wills in local and private collections.
Win Winstanley MSS, The Record Office for Leicestershire, Leicester and Rutland, Wigston Magna.
wk.obl. weak oblique.
Wm 1, Wm 2 Regnal date, t. William I, t. William II.
WoCart John de Wodeford's Cartulary (BL Claudius A XIII), British Library, London.
Wyg Wyggeston Hospital MSS, The Record Office for Leicestershire, Leicester and Rutland, Wigston Magna.
YAA Publications of the Yorkshire Archaeological Association; Record Series.
YCh *Early Yorkshire Charters*, ed. W. Farrer and C. T. Clay, 10 vols., 1914–55.
YE *The Place-Names of the East Riding of Yorkshire and York* (EPNS 14), 1937.
YN *The Place-Names of the North Riding of Yorkshire* (EPNS 5), 1928.
YW *The Place-Names of the West Riding of Yorkshire* (EPNS 30–7), 1961–3.
* a postulated form.
1" O.S. 1" maps, editions of 1967–8.
2½" O.S. 2½" maps, editions of 1951–66.
6" O.S. 6" maps, editions of 1956–67.
(×2), (×3) Two instances of a particular name; three instances etc.

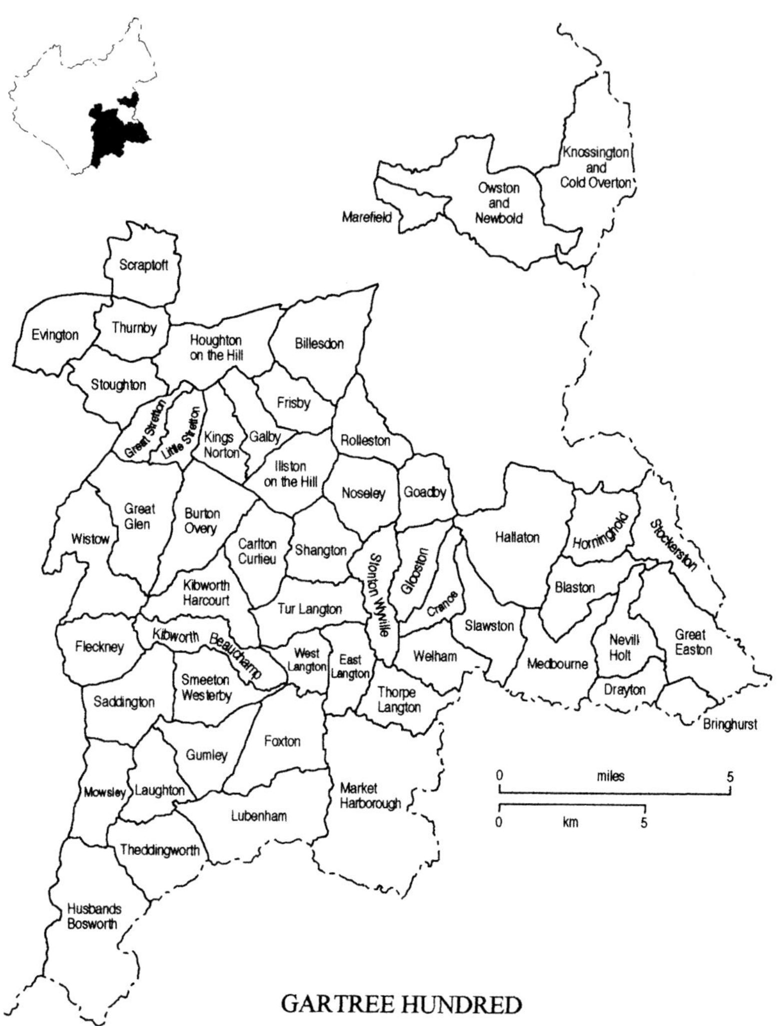

GARTREE HUNDRED

Gartree Hundred

GARTREE HUNDRED

Geretrev 1086 DB (×13), *Geretre* 1186, 1187, 1188, 1190 P
Geretrevves 1086 DB
Gertrev 1086 DB (×5), *Gertre* c.1130 LeicSurv (×2), 1175 P, 1177 ChancR *et passim* to e.14 *BelCartA*, 1227 Fees *et freq* to 1413 Pat *et passim* to 1428 FA, *Gertree* 1260 Ass, 1279 Fine, 1316 FA, 1336 Inqaqd, *Gertrie* 1166, 1195 P *et passim* to 1202 ib, *Gertru* 1176 ChancR, 1177, 1178, 1180 P
Gairtrie 1203 P, *Gayretre* 1247 Fees
Gartre 1285 Cl, c.1291 Tax, 1330 Fine *et passim* to 1443 Pat *et freq* to 1576 LibCl, *Gartrey* 1601 ib, 1604 SR, 1610 Speed

The division is styled:
wapentac, *-tak*, *-taco*, *-tacum*, *-tagio* 1086 DB (freq), c.1130 LeicSurv, 1166 P *et freq* to 1227 Fees
hundred, *-o*, *-um* c.1130 LeicSurv, 1186 P, 1247 Fees *et freq*

v. **vápnatak**, **hundred**.

John Nichols in his *History and Antiquities of the County of Leicester*, Vol. **2**, Part 2, *s.n.* Shangton, states that the county courts used to be held at *Gartree Bush* and gives a detailed description of the site which was on the Roman *Via Devana* (now Gartree Road), about a half mile north of Shangton village. No doubt this was originally the moot-site of the Gartree Wapentake or Hundred. The earliest record of the moot-site is *Mathelou* l.13 *ShR*, and later *Gartre hill* 1477 (e.16) *Charyte*. There was also a Gartree Wapentake in Lincolnshire in the South Riding of Lindsey, but its moot-site is unknown (*v.* DLPN 49).

The name common to both these wapentakes is an ON compound *geirtré*. In Scandinavia, the word appears in place-names only in Sweden, such as *Gertre* in the parish of Kärnbo, Selebo Hundred and *Gärtre* in the parish of Kloster, Eskilstuna. The precise meaning of the compound is uncertain.

H. Lindkvist, *Middle English Place-Names of Scandinavian Origin*, 49, relates the first element of *geirtré* partly to OIcel *geirr* 'a spear' and partly to its derivative *geiri* 'a wedge-shaped piece' (as of a spear-head) but offers no opinions as to its meaning. O. S. Anderson, *The English Hundred Names*, 53, points to the occurrence of the first element with a word for 'pole' twice and with one for 'tree' twice, suggesting that 'these compounds may have had some technical sense now lost'.

The Icelandic *Ragnarssaga loðbroks* contains a documented instance of *geirtré* in a skaldic verse:

gret eigi mik modir
menn ok eptir avaldrekka
ok geir tré i gegnum
geirr latið mic standa

This may be translated: 'No mother will weep for me. I am ready to die fighting at the last. Let the spear-shafts pierce me.' Here *geirtré* specifically images the spear-head with wooden shaft, but in this context it is perhaps a skaldic nonce-word.

Gösta Franzén, 'Svensk Gertre och Engelsk Gartree', *Orter och Namn, Festskrift till Valter Jansson* (1967), 175, suggests that *geirtré* referred to trees that particularly functioned as landmarks and believes that the compound is based on *geiri* 'a wedge-shaped piece' (cf. OE *gāra* 'a piece of ground shaped like the head of a spear, a gore' and Swed dial. *gere* 'something wedge-shaped'). He points out that Ivar Aarsen, *Norsk Ordbog*, 213, notes that in Telemark the word *geire* is used to mean 'a longish patch on a tree as of incipient decay' and that in the Norwegian Dictionary collection, *geire* is also recorded as meaning 'the wood along an overgrown gash in a birch stem'. Franzén concludes that a *geirtré* was 'a tree with a barked and subsequently overgrown gash in the stem'. He comments that 'a tree with an obvious defect of this kind would clearly be an excellent landmark'.

The Leicestershire Gartree Wapentake or Hundred (with its *Gartre hill*) and that in Lincolnshire confirm that in these counties at least the *geirtré* indeed functioned as a landmark for travellers to a moot. The tree was in some way associated with the spear, perhaps either having overall the wedge-like shape of a spear-head (such as the Lombardy Poplar has) or bearing a wedge-shaped scar, maybe the result of the loss of a branch, or with a trunk barked distinctively and deliberately with a wedge-shaped gash for the purpose of providing a landmark. Whether such a gash would have been obviously visible to the uninitiated traveller to the moot-site is, however, problematical. A further possibility is that a *geirtré* was such a tree as the distinctive and stately ash, the wood of which we know from Old English poetry was regularly used for the shafts of spears, *v.* **geirr**, **geiri**, **tré**.

Billesdon

BILLESDON

Billesdone 1086 DB, Hy 2 Dugd, 1274 (1579) (p), 1276 (1579) *LRoll* (p), l.13 *Peake*, *Billesdon* 1156 (1318) Ch, 1190 (p), 1191 P (p), 1196 ChancR *et freq*, *Billesdun* 1203 FF, 1229 Bracton, *Billesdoun* 1360 Ipm, 1394, 1395, 1412 Cl
Bilesdon 1196 ChancR (p), 1203 (p), 1206 (p), 1261 Cur
Billisdon 1253 × 58 RHug, Hy 3 *Crox*, 1275 Ipm *et passim* to 1364 *Wyg* (p), *Billisdona* e.13 (1404) (p), p.1250 (1404) *Laz*
Byllesdon 1257 (1404) *Laz*, 1278 IpmR (p) *et passim* to 1516 *LCh*, 1571 LEpis, *Byllesdoun* 1395 Cl
Billesden 1546 AAS, 1550 BodlCh, 1580 LEpis, *Byllesden* 1466 Pat, 1550 Pat
Bilsdon 1576 Saxton, 1631 LML, *Bylsdon* 1576 LibCl

Probably 'Bil(l)'s hill', *v.* **dūn**. The OE masc. pers.n. *Bil(l)* is either a short form of compound pers.ns. such as *Bilfrið*, *Bilheard*, or *bill* 'a sword' originally used as a by-name. OE *bill* could also mean 'a promontory', a topographical extension of the meaning 'sword'. In the case of Billesdon, the hill-formation here seems to preclude the presence of the sb. *bill* in its sense 'promontory' or 'sword-shaped hill' and the evidence of the surviving forms points to a pers.n. in the possessive case as the first element. It is possible that *bill* became a generic term for 'hill', but it is difficult to conceive this as such in compound with *dūn*. However, J. McN. Dodgson was suspicious of the numerous place-names interpreted as containing the pers.n. *Bil(l)*. For his extended discussion of OE *bill* as 'a hill, a promontory', *v.* BNF iii.

BAPTIST CHAPEL, built 1812. BILLESDON BROOK, *Bilsdon brooke* 1625 *Terrier*, *Billesdon brook* 1798 Nichols, 1925 Kelly, *v.* **brōc**; forms the parish boundary to the south-west. BILLESDON COPLOW, 1798 Nichols, 1835 O, 1925 Kelly; the name of a country house, *v.* The Coplow *infra*. BILLESDON COPLOW LODGE, *v.* **loge**. BROAD ACRES, *v.* **æcer**. BROOK LANE, crosses Billesdon Brook *supra*. CHURCH ST, leading to St John the

Baptist's Church *infra*. THE COPLOW, 1863, 1877 White, 1925 Kelly, *Coppelowe* 1335 GildR, *Coplow* 1514 Ipm, 1806 Map, 'the hill with a crest-like top', *v.* **copp**, **hlāw**; also called *Cophul(l)* Edw 1 (1467 × 84) *LTD*, *Coplow Hill* 1765 *EnclA*, *v.* **hyll**. COPLOW BROOK, 1968 *Surv*, *v.* **brōc**. COPLOW FM, *Coplow farm* 1925 Kelly. COPLOW HO., *Coplow House* 1846 White. COPLOW LANE. COPLOW LODGE, 1877 White, *v.* **loge**. THE DALES, *v.* Wooldales *infra*. GLEBE FM, *v.* **glebe**. GREEN HILL, *Grenehil* p.1250 (1404) *Laz*, *Grenehull* Edw 1 (1467 × 84) *LTD*, *Greenhill* 1765 *EnclA*, *Green Hill* 1792 *Map*, 1826 *Surv*, 1842 *Map*, 1969 *Surv*, *Nethere Grenehil* p.1250 (1404) *LTD* (*v.* **neoðera**), *v.* **grēne**[1], **hyll**. GREEN LANE, *v.* **grēne**[1]. HILLCROFT HOLT, 1969 *Surv*; cf. *Holt Hill* 1826 *ib*, *v.* **hyll**, **croft**, **holt**. HOME CL, *Home Close* 1826 *Surv*, *Old Home Close* 1969 *ib*, *v.* **home**. HOME FM, *v.* **home**. KATES HILL, 1826, c.1930 *Surv*; prob. with the surn. *Kates*, which may be either from the ON pers.n. *Káti* or from ODan *Kati*, although either Scand pers.n. is also possible here. KATES HILL FM, *Kates Hill Farm* 1877 White. LARCH PLANTATION, *v.* **larch**, **plantation**. LEICESTER RD, *Leicester road* 1877 White, *v.* Port Bridge *infra*. LIFE HILL, 1826 *Surv*, 1835 O, cf. *Vnderlith* Edw 1 (1467 × 84) *LTD* (*v.* **under**), *v.* **hlið**[1], **hlíð**[2]; the site of an Iron Age hill-fort, partly obliterated by quarrying. LIFEHILL SPINNEY, *v.* **spinney**. LODGE FM (BILLESDON LODGE SOUTH 2½"), *v.* **loge**. LONG LANE, 1765 *EnclA*, 1877 White, *v.* **lang**[1], **lane**. MILL HO., cf. *Mill Field* 1765 *EnclA*, *Mill Hill* 1826 *Surv*, *v.* **myln**; the site of a windmill. THE MOUNT, 1877 White, *v.* **mont**. NETHER COURT FM (BILLESDON LODGE 2½"), *v.* **court**, **loge**. NEW GREYHOUND (P.H.), *New Greyhound* 1846, 1877 White, 1925 Kelly. OLD GREYHOUND (P.H.) (lost), *Old Greyhound* 1846, 1863, 1877 White. OLD HILL, 1826 *Surv*, *Oldhull* Edw 1 (1467 × 84), *v.* **wald**, **hyll**. PORT BRIDGE, 1925 Kelly, cf. *Portbridge Field* 1765 *EnclA*, *v.* **port**[2], **brycg**; on the main road to the market town of Leicester. The road is *Portgate* Edw 1 (1467 × 84), Edw 3 (1467 × 84) *LTD*, *Portisgate* Edw 3 (1467 × 84) *ib* (*v.* **gata**), *le Portwey* Edw 3 (1467 × 84) *ib* (*v.* **port-wey**). THE QUADRANT HO., *The Quadrant* 1877 White, *The Quadrant house* 1925 Kelly; a fourth side of what were once the stables and kennels building of the Quorn Hunt. QUEEN'S HEAD (P.H.), *Queen's Head* 1846, 1863, 1877 White, 1925 Kelly. ROLLESTON RD, Rolleston lying 2 miles to the south-east. ST JOHN THE BAPTIST'S CHURCH, *Church (St John the Baptist)* 1846, 1877 White, 1925 Kelly; it is earlier recorded as *ecclesia de Billesdon* 1220 MHW, 1253 × 58 RTAL, 1351 *Pat*, cf. *at the Kyrke*, *atte Kyrke* Edw 1 (1467 × 84) *LTD* (p), *atte Kirke* 1363 Pat (p) (*v.* **atte**, **kirkja**), *atte Chirche* 1360 ib (p) (*v.* **chirche**, **churche**). Note also *the Churchyard* 1625 *Terrier*, *the Church Yard* 1674, 1679, 1708 *ib*, *v.* **churchyerd**. SELDOM SEEN FM. SHERWOOD RISE, *v.* **rise**. TILTON LANE, Tilton lying 2 miles to the north-east; it is *Tiltonegat'* e.14 (1404) *Laz*, *Tiltongate* Edw 1 (1467 × 84), *Tyltongate* Edw 3 (1467 × 84) *LTD*, *Tilton Gate* 1826 *Surv*, 1847 *Map*, *v.* **gata**. UNION WORKHOUSE (lost), *Union Workhouse* 1846 White, 1847 *Map*, 1863, 1877 White, *v.* **workhouse**; a Poor Law institution. THE VICARAGE, 1925 Kelly; it is *the Vicaridge house* 1601, 1674 *Terrier et passim* to 1724 *ib*, *the Vicarige House* 1745 *ib*, *Parsonage House* 1821 *ib* (*v.* **personage**), *v.* **vikerage**. VICARAGE FM, *Vicarage farm* 1877 White. WEST LANE, 1877 White; leading westwards from the village centre. WHITE HALL, *v.* **hall**. WHITE HART (P.H.), *White Hart* 1846, 1863, 1877 White, 1925 Kelly.

FIELD-NAMES

In (a), forms presented without dates are 1969 *Surv*; those dated 1765 are *EnclA*; 1792, 1842 and 1847 are *Map*; 1821 are *Terrier*; 1826, 1907, 1920 and c.1930 are *Surv*; 1848 are *Rental*; 1850 are *TA* and 1935 are Sale. Forms throughout dated a.1250 (1404), p.1250 (1404), l.13 (1404) and e.14 (1404) are *Laz*; those dated Edw 1 (1467 × 84) and Edw 3 (1467 × 84) are *LTD*; 1293 and 1330 are Banco; 1477 (e.16) are *Charyte*; 1601, 1625, 1674, 1679, c.1680, 1703, 1708, 1724 and 1725 are *Terrier*; 1685 are *Deed*.

(a) Abbotts Cl 1792, 1847 (poss. with the common Leics. surn. *Abbott*; but note that Leicester Abbey once owned a grange and various small properties in Billesdon, hence also *v.* **abbat**); Above Town 1845 (*v.* **aboven**, **tūn**); One Acre 1969, The Two Acres 1826, Three Acres, Wards Three Acre (cf. *William Ward* 1765), (The) Four ~, Five Acres, Six ~, Wards Six Acre, (The) Six ~, Seven Acres 1969, The Eight ~ 1826, Eight Acres 1969, Eight Acre Cl 1826, Wards Eight Acre Mdw, Nine Acres, Ten ~, Bottom Eleven Acre (*v.* **bottom**), Twelve ~, Fourteen ~, Fifteen ~, Sixteen ~, Twenty Acres 1969 (*v.* **æcer**); Far ~ 1821, Old Allotment c.1930, 1969 (*v.* **allotment**); Andrews Moor 1848 (*v.* **mōr**[1]; with the surn. *Andrews*; cf. Andrews West Cl *infra*); Arnolds Cl 1826 (cf. *Thomas Arnolds Land* 1792, *v.* **land**); Bagbeare Down 1848 (*v.* **bagga**, **bearu**, **dūn**); Ballards, ~ Mdw (with the surn. *Ballard* in the possessive case); The Bank 1826, 1847 (*v.* **banke**); Barley Cl 1826 (*v.* **bærlic**); Barn Cl 1826, c.1930, 1969, Over Barn Cl 1826 (*v.* **ofer**[3]), Close Below (the) Barn 1826, 1842, Barn Fd 1969, Barn Hill 1848, Barn's Orchard 1848 (*v.* **orceard**) (*v.* **bern**); Bay Fd 1969 (prob. with ME **bay** in its sense 'an embankment to divert or dam a stream to form a pond for cattle or to serve a mill', *v.* OED bay sb.[5]); Beacon Hill 1765, 1826, Beaconhill Common 1765 (*v.* **commun**) (*v.* **(ge)bēacon**); Bean Cl (*v.* **bēan**); Lower ~ ~, West ~ ~, Berry Moor, Berry Moor Bottom 1826 (*v.* **botm**) (*v.* **berige**, **mōr**[1]); (The) Big Fd c.1930, 1969; Binneys 1848 (the surn. *Binney* in the possessive case); Botany Bay Cl 1826, 1842, Botany Bay Fox Cover 1826 (*v.*

cover(t)) (a transferred name for a remote piece of land and referring to the penal settlement established at Botany Bay in New South Wales, Australia, in 1788; note Vandeman Cl *infra*); Bottom Cl 1826 (*v.* **bottom**); Bradley's Cl, Great ~ ~, Little Bradley's Mdw 1826 (with the surn. *Bradley*); Brick Kiln Cl 1826, Brick Hill 1920 (*v.* **brike-kiln**); Nether ~ ~, Brook Cl 1826, 1935, Brook Fd 1969, Brook Mdw 1826 (*v.* **brōc**); Burnt Cl 1826, Burnt Ground 1969 (*v.* **grund**) (*v.* **brend**; used of land cleared by burning or on which a fire has taken place); Calves Cl 1826, Calves Pasture 1765, 1826, 1969 (*v.* **pasture**), Calves Plot 1848 (*v.* **plot**) (*v.* **calf**); Cemetery Fd 1969 (adjacent to a cemetery); Coalpit Cl 1826, 1842, Coalpits 1969 (*v.* **col-pytt**; a place where charcoal was made); Church Mdw (*v.* St John the Baptist's Church *supra*); Cleave Orchard 1826 (*v.* **orceard**), Higher ~, Home Cleaves 1848 (*v.* **home**) (*v.* **clif**); Clod Leys 1826, c.1930 (*v.* **clodd**, **leys**); Collins, ~ Mdw (with the surn. *Collins* in the possessive case); Colt's Plot 1848 (*v.* **plot**; prob. referring to land on which young horses were kept, *v.* **colte** and cf. Pony's Fd *infra*, but the surn. *Colt* may be present); Bottom ~ ~ 1842, Coplow Cl, Coplow Mdw 1826 (*v.* The Coplow *supra*); Cow Cl 1969, Cow Lane 1765 (*v.* **lane**), Cow Layer 1826 (*v.* **lair**) (*v.* **cū**); Corner Fd 1969 (*v.* **corner**); The Cricket Fd 1969 (for the game of cricket); The Cross Road Big Fd 1969 (*v.* **cross-road(s)**); Crow Hill 1826, 1969 (*v.* **crāwe**, **hyll**); Dairy Cl 1792, ~ Mdw 1842 (*v.* **deierie**); Drany Moor 1850 (*v.* **mōr**[1]; either with the surn. *Draine* (from ME *dreine* 'a drain, a ditch') or referring to some aspect of drainage); Higher ~ ~, Little ~ ~, Lower ~ ~, East Cl, Great ~ ~, Little East Fd, East Hill 1848 (*v.* **ēast**); Ell Cl 1826 (an L-shaped enclosure); The Far Mdw 1969; First Cl 1826; Lower ~ ~, Float Mdw 1848 (perh. 'land subject to flooding', *v.* **flot**[1]; otherwise **flǫt**[2]); Fore of Life 1969 (*v.* **fore** and Life Hill *supra*); Forman's Cl 1826 (cf. *Wm. Forman* 1764); Forsell 1969 ('furze hill', *v.* **fyrs**, **hyll**); Fox Cover 1842 (*v.* **fox**, **cover(t)**); Front Mdw 1920 (*v.* **front**); Furzedike Cl 1826 (*v.* **fyrs**, **dík**); Garden Cl 1848 (*v.* **gardin**; land used for horticulture); Gibbins Cl c.1930 (with the surn. *Gibbins*); Gorse Hill 1826, Under (the) Gorse 1826, 1848 (*v.* **gorst**); Top ~ ~ 1826, Gravel Hole c.1930, Gravel Hole Cl, Gravel Pit Cl 1826 (*v.* **gravel**, **hol**[1], **pytt** and The Top Mdw *infra*); Great ~, Higher ~, Lower Ham 1848 (*v.* **hamm**); Harry's Orchard 1848 (*v.* **orceard**; with the pet-form *Harry* of the pers.n. *Henry*); Hayse 1848 (*v.* **(ge)hæg**); Higher Down 1848 (*v.* **dūn**); Hill Cl, Hill Fd, Top ~ ~, Lower Hill Side 1969 (*v.* **sīde**); Home Fd 1969, Homes Down 1848 (*v.* **dūn**) (*v.* **home**); Far ~ ~, Middle ~ ~, Near ~ ~, Nether ~ ~, Upper Horse Pasture 1826 (*v.* **pasture**), Old Horse Cl 1842 (*v.* **hors**); Old House Cl 1792, 1826, House Cl 1826, 1969, House Fd 1920, 1969 (*v.* **hūs**); Hovel Cl 1826, 1848, ~ Fd c.1930, 1969, ~ Mdw 1826, 1848, 1969 (*v.* **hovel**); Hunts or Jickins Cl (with the surns. *Hunt* and *Jickins*); James' Cl 1826 (with the surn. *James*); King's Cl, ~ Piece (*v.* **pece** and cf. *Richard King* 1764); Knight Paddock 1847 (*v.* **paddock**), Knights (with the surn. *Knight* in the possessive case); Kuffers Bottom, ~ Top 1969 (with the surn. *Kuffer*, not found in England until the mid 19th cent. and originally Swiss, *v.* **botm**, **topp**); Landry Fd 1969 (with the surn. *Landry*); The Lane, Lane Piece 1826 (*v.* **pece**) (*v.* **lane**); The Lawn 1842 (*v.* **launde**; in late f.ns. referring to grass ground); The Leas 1969 (*v.* **leys**); Life Hill Cl, ~ ~ Fds, ~ ~ Mdw, ~ ~ Top 1969 (*v.* **topp**) (*v.* Life Hill *supra*); Little Cl 1826, ~ Fd 1969, ~ Mdw 1848; Lodge Cl 1826 (*v.* **loge**); Long Cl 1792, 1926, 1847, 1969; Long Dale 1826 (*langdayle* 1601, *v.* **lang**[1]; with **dalr** or **deill**); Long Dyke 1765, c.1930, 1969, ~ Dike 1795, 1848, 1935, Long Dike Mdw 1826 (*v.* **dík**); Long Lane Cl 1826 (*v.* Long Lane *supra*); (The) Long Mdw 1826, 1920, 1969; Longwood Park 1848 (*v.*

lang[1], **wudu**, **park**); Lower Cl 1848; Lower Hill 1848; Mann's Cl 1826 (with the surn. *Mann*); Manton's Mdw 1826 (with the surn. *Manton* of a family poss. originally from Manton, 12 miles to the east in Rutland); The Meadow 1826, 1969, Great Mdw 1850; Far ~ ~, Middle Cl 1826, c.1930; Bottom ~ ~, Top Mill Cl 1826 (*v*. **myln**); The Mires 1826 (*v*. **mýrr**); Miry ~ 1826, Mery Cl 1969, Miry Mdw 1826 (*v*. **myry**); Moor Plot 1848 (*v*. **plot**) (*More*, *Ouermore* Edw 1 (1467 × 84) (*v*. **uferra**), *v*. **mōr**[1]); Mowhay 1848 (either literally a close with good mowing grass (*v*. **hēg**) or if an early name, then 'the moor enclosure', *v*. **mōr**[1], **(ge)hæg**, cf. The Mowwell in Illston on the Hill f.ns. (a)); Narrow Cl 1826 (*v*. **nearu**); Neal's Cl 1826 (with the surn. *Neal*); Nepwell Cl 1850 (cf. *Gnypwelleslade* l.13 (1404) (*v*. **slæd**), 'the spring on or stream from a steep slope', *v*. **gnípa**, **wella**); New Cl 1765, 1935, 1969; New Moor 1848 (*v*. **mōr**[1]); Newton Gate 1826 (*v*. **gata**), Bottom ~ ~ ~, Long ~ ~ ~, Top Newton Road Cl 1826 (Cold Newton lies 5 miles to the north); Ogden's, ~ Mdw (cf. *Wm. Ogden* 1821); Old Hall Orchard 1765 (*v*. **ald**, **hall**, **orceard**); Bottom ~ ~, Top Old Hill, Old Hill Big Fd 1969, Bottom ~ ~ ~, Far ~ ~ ~, Near Old Hill Cl 1826 (cf. *le Oldhulmedewe* Edw 1 (1467 × 84) (*v*. **mēd** (**mēdwe** obl.sg.)), *le Oldhullsike* Edw 1 (1467 × 84) (*v*. **sík**), *v*. Old Hill *supra*); Orchard Moor 1848 (*v*. **orceard**, **mōr**[1]); The Paddock, The Bottom ~, The Little Paddock 1969 (*v*. **paddock**); The Bottom Palletts 1969 (with the surn. *Pallett* in the possessive case); East ~, Little ~, Park 1848, East ~ ~, West Higher Park 1826, The Park 1969 (*v*. **park**); Partridge's Cl 1826 (with the surn. *Partridge*); Peggs Cl c.1930 (with the surn. *Pegg*); Pen Cl 1826 ('enclosure with or by a fold', *v*. **penn**[2]); The Piece 1969 (*v*. **pece**); Pigs Park 1848 (*v*. **pigga**, **park**); Pingle, ~ Mdw 1826, Pinole Mdw (sic) 1969 (*v*. **pingel**); Plow ~ 1792, Plough Cl 1969, Top Plough Cl c.1930 (*v*. **plōg**); Pony's Fd 1920 (*v*. **pony**); Poors Cl, ~ Piece 1826 (*v*. **pece**) (*v*. **pouer(e)**; land dedicated to poor relief or charity); Port Bridge Cl, ~ ~ Mdw 1826 (*v*. Port Bridge *supra*); Potatoe Plot 1848 (*v*. **potato**, **plot**); Little ~ ~, Quarry Cl 1826, Quarry Mdw 1848 (*v*. **quarrere**); Ratcliffe Cl 1826, 1969 (poss. with the surn. *Ratcliffe* of a family originally from Ratcliffe on the Wreake, 9 miles to the north-west; otherwise *v*. **rēad**, **clif**); Higher ~ ~, Lower Reap Park 1848 (prob. with reference to harvesting, *v*. **ripe**, **park**; if not, *v*. **rip**); Road Cl 1969 (a roadside enclosure); Rofers Mdw, Top Rofer Cl (sic) 1969 (*v*. Roper's Mdw *infra*); Rolleson Meer 1826 (with typical Leics. late loss of *t* from the group *-ston*, *v*. **(ge)mǣre**; Rolleston parish adjoins to the south-west); Roper's Mdw, Top Roper's Cl 1826 (with the surn. *Roper*); Rough Piece 1935 (*v*. **rūh**, **pece**); Rushy Ham 1826 (*v*. **riscig**, **hamm**); Sand Acres 1765, Top ~, Bottom Sandacre 1969, Sandacre Mdw 1826 (*Sandakyr* Edw 3 (1467 × 84), *v*. **sand**, **æcer**); Scamwell Sike 1850 ('the piece of meadow beside Scamwell (i.e. the short stream)', *v*. **skammr**, **wella**, **sík**); Big ~, Little Seeds 1920, First ~, Second Seeds, The Old Seeds 1969 (*v*. **sǣd**; used of grasses sown for one year's mowing or grazing, as distinguished from permanent pasture); Sheep Skirt Cl 1792, Sheep Skirt's Cl, ~ ~ Mdw 1826, Sheep Skirts 1969 (*v*. **scēp**, **skirt**); Sheffields Cl 1969 (with the surn. *Sheffield*); Shellaker's Big Fd 1969 (with the surn. *Shellaker*); Shippen Park 1826 (*v*. **scypen**, **park**); Shoulder of Mutton 1920 (a close shaped like a shoulder of mutton; a common modern f.n.); The Slang 1969 (*v*. **slang**); Slawson's 1969 (the surn. *Slawson* in the possessive case of a family originally from Slawston, 3 miles to the south-east; with typical Leics. late loss of *t* from the group *-ston*); Small Park 1848 (*v*. **smæl**, **park**); Sow Sick 1826, 1969, ~ ~ Mdw 1969 (*Suthsike* Edw 1 (1467 × 84), *Suthsyke* 1477 (e.16), *v*. **sūð**, **sík**); Spells Furze 1765 (*Spells Furzes* 1685, *v*. **fyrs**; with the surn.

Spell); Spinney Cl 1935, ~ Mdw 1935, 1969 (*v.* **spinney**); Spring Fd 1969 (*v.* **spring**[1]); Great ~, Little Starter, Starter Mdw 1835, Big Sturter, Sturter Mdw 1935, The Great Sturta, Sturta Mdw 1969 (perh. with **steort** and a reduced second el. **hōh**; but note *Strutthou* in f.ns. (b) of which this may be a late reflex with metathesis); Far ~, Near Stockwell 1907 (*v.* **stocc**, **wella**); Stone Hole 1969 (*v.* **stān**, **hol**[1]); Stonepit 1848, ~ Cl 1826, 1969, Stonepitt Fd 1765 (*v.* **stān-pytt**); Sturgess Cl 1969 (cf. *F.W. Sturgess* 1969, farmer); Summers Land 1848 (land used only in summer, *v.* **sumor**, **land**); Thornwood 1848 (*v.* **þorn**, **wudu**); Three Corner Fd c.1930 (*v.* **three-corner**); Three-Cornered Fd 1848 (*v.* **three-cornered**); Tilton Lane Cl 1826, Tilton Road Fd 1969 (*v.* Tilton Lane *supra*); Toll Bar 1969 (*v.* **toll-bar**), Tollgate Cl 1826 (*v.* **toll-gate**); First ~ ~, Second Toone's Cl 1826, Toones, ~ Mdw, Top Toones 1969 (cf. *John Toone* and *William Toone* 1841 Census); The Top Mdw or Gravelpit Cl 1826, The Top Mdw 1969 (*v.* Gravel Hole *supra*); Town Park 1848 (*v.* **tūn**, **park**); Town's ~ 1826, Town Hill c.1930 (*Tounhul(l)* Edw 1 (1467 × 84), Edw 3 (1467 × 84), *v.* **tūn**, **hyll**); Turnpike Cl, ~ Mdw 1826, 1842, c.1930, Turnpike Hill Cl 1792 (*v.* **turnepike**; fields adjacent to the Leicester–Uppingham road); Vandeman Cl 1969 (with *Van Diemen*, a transferred name for a piece of land remote from the village. The Dutch navigator and explorer Abel Tasman, having been sent in quest of the 'Great Southern Land' by Antony van Diemen, then Governor-General of Batavia, in 1642 discovered the island of Tasmania (so called since 1855), which he named Van Diemen's Land. It became the site of a British penal colony, cf. Botany Bay *supra*); Ward's Cl 1826 (cf. *William Ward* 1765); Bottom ~, Top Watts 1969 (with the surn. *Watts*); Websters Piece 1826, 1847 (*v.* **pece**; with the surn. *Webster*); Andrews ~ ~, Higher ~ ~, Lower West Cl 1848 (*v.* **west**; with the surn. *Andrews*); Lower ~ ~, West Hill 1848, West Mdw 1826 (*v.* **west**); Higher ~ ~, Lower West Moor 1848 (*le Westmoor* Edw 1 (1467 × 84), *v.* **west**, **mōr**[1]); Wheat Fd 1969, Wheat Hill 1826, 1969 (*Whetehull* Edw 3 (1467 × 84), *v.* **hyll**) (*v.* **hwǣte**); Far ~, Near Whitwell 1826 (cf. *Dorothy Whitwell* 1765); Williams Fd, ~ Mdw 1969 (with the surn. *Williams*); Wood Marsh 1848 (*v.* **wudu**, **mersc**); Wooldales 1920 (*Hyewulledale* Edw 1 (1467 × 84) (*v.* **hēah**[1]) (*v.* **wald**; with **dalr** or **deill**); Would ~ 1765, Wold Hedge 1850 (*v.* **wald**, **hecg**); The Bottom ~, The Top Wrights, Wrights Cl 1969 (with the surn. *Wright*).

(b) *Arnaws* Edw 1 (1467 × 84) (*v.* **haga**[1], either with the OE masc. pers.n. *Earna*, or with **ēaren**); *Balhul* Edw 3 (1467 × 84), *Biforbalhul* Edw 1 (1467 × 84) (*v.* **beforan**), *Balhulgate* Edw 1 (1467 × 84) (*v.* **gata**) ('the rounded hill', *v.* **ball**, **hyll**); *Banlond* Edw 1 (1467 × 84) (*v.* **bēan**, **land**); *Banslade* p.1250 (1404), Edw 1 (1467 × 84), 1330, *Baneslade* l.13 (1404) (*v.* **bēan**, **slæd**); (*les*) *Baukes* l.13 (1404), Edw 1 (1467 × 84), *le Netherbaukes* Edw 1 (1467 × 84) (*v.* **neoðera**) (*v.* **balca**); *Bissopescroft* 1477 (e.16) (*v.* **croft**; with the surn. *Bishop*); *Blacthorne hole*, *Blacthornholl* Edw 1 (1467 × 84) (*v.* **blæc-þorn**, **hol**[1]); *Blakemilde*, *Hyeblakemylde* Edw 1 (1467 × 84) (*v.* **hēah**[1]) (*v.* **blæc**, **mylde**); *Bradelandes* l.13 (1404) (*v.* **brād**, **land**); *Brakendale* Edw 1 (1467 × 84) (*v.* **braken**, **dalr**); (*le*) *Breche* l.13 (1404), Edw 1 (1467 × 84), Edw 3 (1467 × 84), 1477 (e.16), *Brechefurlong* p.1250 (1404) (*v.* **furlang**) (*v.* **brēc**); *Brethornhil* l.13 (1404) (*v.* **breiðr**, **þorn**, **hyll**); *Breycliue*, *Breyklif* p.1250 (1404), *Breyclif* l.13 (1404), *Breyclyf* Edw 3 (1467 × 84); *West Breyclif* l.13 (1404), *Westbreyclyff* Edw 1 (1467 × 84) (*v.* **west**), *Breyclyffront* Edw 1 (1467 × 84) (*v.* **front**) (*v.* **breiðr**, **clif**); *le Brodedole* Edw 1 (1467 × 84), *Broddole* Edw 3 (1467 × 84) (*v.* **brād**, **dāl**); *le Broderodes* Edw 1 (1467 × 84), *Brodrodis* Edw

3 (1467 × 84) (*v.* **brād**, **rōd**[3]); *Brosebrocfurlong* p.1250 (1404) (*v.* **brēosa**, **brōc**, **furlang**); *Bruhawes* Edw 3 (1467 × 84) (*v.* **brū**, **haga**[1]); *Burdettisland* 1477 (e.16) (*v.* **land**; with the surn. *Burdett*); *les Buttes* 1293 (*v.* **butte**); *Cheredik* Edw 1 (1467 × 84) ('drainage channel with a bend', *v.* **cerr**, **dík**); *Collecroft* e.14 (1404), Edw 3 (1467 × 84) (prob. 'the cabbage enclosure', *v.* **cole**, **croft**; but the ME surn. *Colle* or one of its sources such as the masc. pers.ns. ON, ODan *Kolli* or OE *Cola* are also poss. as the first el.); *Crathornehull* Edw 3 (1467 × 84) ('hill with thorn-trees frequented by crows', *v.* **crāwe**, **þorn**, **hyll**); *Croumbehalfrodes* Edw 1 (1467 × 84) (*v.* **crumb**, **half**, **rōd**[3]); *le Dikes* Edw 1 (1467 × 84) (*v.* **dík**); *Dik*(*e*)*dole* l.13 (1404) (*v.* **dík**, **dāl**); *the East feild* 1601 (*v.* **ēast**, **feld**; one of the great open-fields of the township); *Erdenothull* Edw 1 (1467 × 84), *Ernotil* Edw 3 (1467 × 84), *Hernotehull*, *Hernotehulsyke* 1477 (e.16) (*v.* **sík**) ('hill where pig-nuts abound', *v.* **eorð-hnutu**, **hyll**); *le Estbreche* Edw 3 (1467 × 84) (*v.* **ēast**, **brēc**); *Estbryge* Edw 1 (1467 × 84) (*v.* **ēast**, **brycg**); *Estwelle* Edw 3 (1467 × 84) (*v.* **ēast**, **wella**); *le Falshalfrodes* Edw 1 (1467 × 84), *Falsalfrodes* Edw 3 (1467 × 84) (*v.* (**ge**)**fall**, **half**, **rōd**[3]); *Felinnges* Edw 1 (1467 × 84) (*v.* **felging**); *Flaxlandsyke* Edw 1 (1467 × 84) (*v.* **sík**), *Flaxlondhyll* Edw 3 (1467 × 84) (*v.* **hyll**) (*v.* **fleax**, **land**); *Flitenewong* l.13 (1404), Edw 1 (1467 × 84), *Flitynwong* Edw 3 (1467 × 84) (*v.* **fliten**, **vangr**); *Flitlond'* Edw 1 (1467 × 84) (*v.* (**ge**)**flit**, **land**); *Folewell* Edw 3 (1467 × 84) (*v.* **fūl**, **wella**); *Fouldale*, *Fowledale* Edw 1 (1467 × 84), *Fouledale* Edw 3 (1467 × 84) (*v.* **fūl**; with **dalr** or **deill**); *le Frontgore* Edw 1 (1467 × 84) (*v.* **front**, **gāra**); *Galutresike* p.1250 (1404), *Galtresike* 1477 (e.16) (*v.* **galg-trēow**, **sík**); *les Garbrodrodes* Edw 1 (1457 × 84) (*v.* **gorebrode**, **rōd**[3]); *Gardisty* Edw 3 (1467 × 84) (*v.* **garðr**, **stīg**); *Gaulond'* Edw 3 (1467 × 84) ('land(s) growing with bog-myrtle', *v.* **gagel**, **land**); *Ghendirismore* Edw 3 (1467 × 84) (prob. 'wasteland where ganders are kept', *v.* **gandra**, **mōr**[1], cf. *Ghonderesyke* e.13 in Wymeswold, Lei **3** 281; but the surn. *Gender* may pertain); *Gosinges* Edw 1 (1467 × 84) (*v.* **gōs**, **eng**); *Goswong* Edw 1 (1467 × 84) (*v.* **gōs**, **vangr**); *Gowyneyerdeland* 1477 (e.16) (*v.* **yerdland**; with the ME pers.n. *Gawain*); *Grauesyke* 1477 (e.16) (*v.* **grāf**, **sík**); *les Grenegatis* Edw 1 (1467 × 84) (*v.* **grēne**[1], **gata**); *le Hallemedowe* 1477 (e.16) (*v.* **hall**, **mēd** (**mēdwe** obl.sg.)); *le Hirnefurlongis* Edw 1 (1467 × 84) (*v.* **hyrne**, **furlang**); *le Holmeswro* Edw 1 (1467 × 84) (*v.* **holmr**, **vrá**); *Hopynges* Edw 3 (1467 × 84), *Hoppers hill* 1601 (these forms appear to belong together, *v.* **hopping** and Hoppers Hill in Goadby f.ns. (a)); *Hwerluedale*, *Huuerewluedale* 1477 (e.16) (*v.* **hwerfel**; with **dalr** or **deill**); *Ingwardbysti* Edw 1 (1467 × 84), *Yngwarbysty* 1477 (e.16) (*v.* **stīg**; Old Ingarsby lies 3 miles to the north-west); *le Kyrkekroft* p.1250 (1404), (*le*) *Kirkcroft* Edw 1 (1467 × 84), Edw 3 (1467 × 84), *le Kyrkcroft* Edw 1 (1467 × 84) (*v.* **kirkja**, **croft** and St John the Baptist's Church *supra*); *Knapcotes*, *Knapcotehull* Edw 1 (1467 × 84) (*v.* **hyll**) (*v.* **cot**; prob. with **cnapa**, but a masc. pers.n. such as OE *Cnapa* or ON *Knapi* may rather feature); *Lituldalhull* Edw 1 (1467 × 84) (*v.* **hyll**), *littledale hill furlong*(*e*) 1601, 1625, *little dale furlong* 1674, 1679, 1708, 1724 (*v.* **furlang**), *Litteldalesouerhende* Edw 1 (1467 × 84) (*v.* **uferra**, **ende**) (*v.* **lȳtel**, **dalr**); *Longhedole* p.1250 (1404), *le Longedole* Edw 1 (1467 × 84), *Langdole* Edw 3 (1467 × 84) (*v.* **lang**[1], **dāl**); *les Longrodes* Edw 1 (1467 × 84) (*v.* **lang**[1], **rōd**[3]); *le Middelstimoorsyke* Edw 1 (1467 × 84) (*v.* **middel**, **stīg**, **mōr**[1], **sík**); *le Midelmoorsyke* Edw 1 (1467 × 84) (*v.* **middel**, **mōr**[1], **sík**); *molendinum de Bilsdon* 1477 (e.16) (with MLat *molendinum* 'a mill'); *Neutoneforthe* l.13 (1404) (a ford on the road to Newton Harcourt, 6 miles to the south-west, *v.* **ford**; *-forth* spellings for *-ford* may have

arisen from the late ME development of *-rd* to *-rth* in unstressed syllables); *Northfeld* Edw 1 (1467 × 84), *the northe fielde* 1601, *the North field* 1625, 1708, 1724 (*v.* **norð**, **feld**; one of the great open-fields); *Orlokisseik* 1477 (e.16) (*v.* **sík**; with the ME surn. *Horloc*, the modern *Horlock*); *Osgotebreche* Edw 1 (1467 × 84), *Osgodisbrech'* Edw 3 (1467 × 84) (*v.* **brēc**; with the late OE masc. pers.n. *Ōsgot*, *Ōsgod* (anglicized ON *Ásgautr* (ODan *Asgot*)), cf. the pers.n. in Osgathorpe, West Goscote Hundred, Cox[2] 77); *le Osiereswell* Edw 1 (1467 × 84) (*v.* **oyser**, **wella**); *the ould bridg* 1601 (*v.* **ald**, **brycg**; in the great North Fd); *the ould feild* 1601 (*v.* **ald**, **feld**); *Pecocroft'* Edw 1 (1467 × 84) (*v.* **pecok**, **croft**; cf. *Pecokcroft* 1275, Lei **2** 9); *Peislond*, *Peysland* Edw 3 (1467 × 84), *Schortpeselonde* Edw 3 (1467 × 84) (*v.* **sc(e)ort**) (*v.* **pise**, **land**); *Pippiswell* Edw 3 (1467 × 84), *Pippeswellhull* Edw 1 (1467 × 84) (*v.* **hyll**), *Pippiswellemore* l.13 (1404) (*v.* **mōr**[1]) (*v.* **pīpe**, **wella**); *le Prestisbring'* Edw 1 (1467 × 84), *Prestisbrynk'* Edw 3 (1467 × 84) (*v.* **prēost**, **brink**); *Prestemor* 1293, *le Prestes more* Edw 1 (1467 × 84) (*v.* **prēost**, **mōr**[1]); *le Redehalfacris* Edw 1 (1467 × 84) (*v.* **half-aker**; either with **rēad** 'red' alluding to the colour of the soil or with **hrēod** 'reed'); *Rolston brooke* 1601 (*v.* **brōc**; Rolleston parish adjoins to the south-east); *Salgate* 1601 (×2) (*v.* **salt**[1], **gata**; a medieval salt-way, running south from the ford at Melton Mowbray); *Scortlondes* Edw 1 (1467 × 84) (*v.* **sc(e)ort**, **land**); *Selesyerd*, *Selisgerth* 1477 (e.16) (*v.* **geard**, **garðr**) (cf. *Johannes de Seles* 1477 (e.16)); *Sidlyng'* Edw 3 (1467 × 84) (*v.* **sīdling**); *le Skarthe*, *by fore the Scarth* Edw 3 (1467 × 84) (*v.* **beforan**) (*v.* **skarð**); *Skeftingtongate* Edw 1 (1467 × 84), Edw 3 (1467 × 84) (*v.* **gata**), *Skeftington strete* Edw 1 (1467 × 84) (*v.* **strǣt**) (the road to Skeffington which lies 2 miles to the east); *Smerclif'* Edw 1 (1467 × 84), *Smerclyf* Edw 3 (1467 × 84), *Biforesmereclif'*, *Byforsmereclif'* Edw 1 (1467 × 84) (*v.* **beforan**) (*v.* **smeoru**, **clif**; a hillside pasture used in summer for the production of butter); *Smethemedwe* Edw 1 (1467 × 84) (*v.* **smēðe**[1], **mēd** (**mēdwe** obl.sg.)); *Souelbrod* l.13 (1404), *Shouelbrodemoor* Edw 1 (1467 × 84) (*v.* **mōr**[1]) (*v.* **scofl-brǣdu**); *Stainingges* Edw 1 (1467 × 84) (*v.* **steinn**, **eng**); *Stanbrynk'* Edw 3 (1467 × 84) (*v.* **stān**, **brink**); *Stocdole* p.1250 (1404), Edw 1 (1467 × 84), Edw 3 (1467 × 84), *Stokdolebring'* Edw 1 (1467 × 84) (*v.* **brink**) (*v.* **stocc**, **dāl**); *le Storth* Edw 1 (1467 × 84) (*v.* **storð**); *Strutthou*, *Struthowslade* Edw 1 (1467 × 84), *Struthouslade* e.14 (1404) (*v.* **slæd**) (*v.* **strūt**, **hōh** and Starter in f.ns. (a)); *le Suthbreche* Edw 1 (1467 × 84), *le Sowebrech'* Edw 3 (1467 × 84) (*v.* **sūð**, **brēc**); *Suthfeld* Edw 1 (1467 × 84) (*v.* **sūð**, **feld**; one of the great open-fields); *Swelles* Edw 3 (1467 × 84) (*v.* **swelle**); *Thornygore* Edw 3 (1467 × 84) (*v.* **þornig**, **gāra**); *le Threstonkys* Edw 1 (1467 × 84), *Threstong'* 1477 (e.16) (*v.* **þrēo**, **stǫng**); *Thwerhull*, *Thewrhul* Edw 1 (1467 × 84) (*v.* **þverr**, **hyll**); *Toftes* Edw 1 (1467 × 84) (*v.* **toft**); *Townforth* 1477 (e.16) (*v.* **tūn**, **ford**); *Trumpeshou* l.13 (1404) (×2), Edw 1 (1467 × 84) (*v.* **hōh**; with the OE masc. pers.n. *Trump*; cf. the pers.n. in Trumpington, Ca 91); *Tythesykys* 1477 (e.16) (*v.* **tēoða**, **sík**); *le Waterfall* Edw 1 (1467 × 84) (*v.* **wæter-(ge)fall**); *the water furrowes* 1601 (*v.* **wæter**, **furh**; prob. 'furrows where water tends to lie'; Field 50 argues that these were deeper furrows so ploughed in order to carry off surface water, but such furrows appear to be called alternatively *Wet furrowes* in Coston (Lei **2** 155–6) and *Watriforowis* in Eaton (Lei **2** 121)); *Welhil* l.13 (1404), *Welhull* Edw 1 (1467 × 84) (*v.* **wella**, **hyll**); *Well Sicke* 1601 (*v.* **wella**, **sík**); *Wellespring* Edw3 (1467 × 84) (*v.* **wella**, **spring**[1]); *Westfeld* Edw 1 (1467 × 84) (*v.* **west**, **feld**; one of the great open-fields, also recorded as *(in) campo occident'* 1477 (e.16), with MLat *campus* 'a field' and *occidentalis* 'west, western'); *Whitleyes* 1601 (*v.* **hwīt**, **leys**; in eModE, *white* 'infertile, dry' may be contrasted with *black* 'fertile', but the reference here may rather be to dry, open pasture, cf. *White leyes* in Goadby f.ns. (b)); *Willow lees* 1601 (*v*. **wilig**, **leys**); *Wilughnegate* Edw 3 (1467 × 84) (*v*. **gata**; with **wiligen** or **wilign**); *le Wold* l.13 (1404), Edw 1 (1467 × 84), *Wold(e)gate* l.13 (1404) (*v*. **gata**), *les Woldfurlonges* Edw 1 (1467 × 84), *le Woldfurlong* p.1250 (1404), *Woldfurlong'* Edw 3 (1467 × 84) (*v*. **furlang**) (*v*. **wald**); *Woodsike* 1601 (*v*. **wudu**, **sík**); *Wronghenges* p.1250 (1404) (*v*. **wrang**, **vrangr**, **eng**); *Wronglond'* Edw 1 (1467 × 84), *Wranglandes* Edw 3 (1467 × 84), *Wronglondys* 1477 (e.16) (*v*. **wrang**, **land**); *Wythenbuske* l.13 (1404), (*le*) *Wythenebusk'* l.13 (1404), Edw 1 (1467 × 84) (*v*. **wīðign**, **buskr**); *Wulmereswell* Edw 1 (1467 × 84) (*v*. **wella**; with the OE masc. pers.n. *Wulfmǣr*); *Wyndeshers* Edw 3 (1467 × 84) (a name which occurs elsewhere in Leics. as early as the lost *Windesers* 1086 DB (in Long Whatton, West Goscote Hundred) and *Windisers*, *Windsers* 1467 × 84 in Thorpe Arnold (Lei **2** 281); perh. literally 'the wind's arse', *v*. **wind**[1], **ears**, used of a conformation of hills resembling buttocks lying in an exposed situation and which funnelled the wind, but the generic could be **herse** 'a hill-top'); *ynnefurlong* e.14 (1404) (*v*. **in**, **furlang**).

Blaston

BLASTON

Bladestone 1086 DB, *Bladeston'* 1227 Fees
Blatheston' 1254 Val, c.1291 Tax, *Blacheston* (rectius *Blatheston*) 1302 Ipm, *Blathiston* 1254 Val, *Blathyston'* 13 *Deed*, *Blatherston'* 1254 Val, *Blathston* 1344 Nichols
Blauestone 1086 DB
Blastone 1086 DB, 1224 RHug, 13 *Peake*, 1302 Ipm, *Blastona* 1224 RHug, *Blaston* 1190, 1191, 1192 P *et freq* to 1465 *Wyg*, 1478 *Peake et passim* to 1526 *ib et freq*, *Blastun'* e.13 *ib*, 1427 Pap
Blaeston' 1165, 1166 P *et freq* to 1174 ib *et passim* to 1423 *Rut*, 1473 *Peake*, *Blaestona* 1167, 1168, 1169, 1173 P
Blayston 1507 Pat, 1509 LP *et passim* to 1537 MinAccts, 1557 Pat
Blason 1594 Fine, 1610 Speed, 1611 LML

Possibly 'Blað's village, estate', *v.* **tūn**. Ekwall DEPN suggests for the specific an unrecorded OE masc. pers.n. *Blēað*, a by-name formed from OE *blēað* 'gentle, timid, sluggish' and showing early shortening of *ēa*. Fellows-Jensen SSNEM 188 rejects this since she believes that shortening of *ēa* in a stressed syllable would have been hardly likely by the compilation of the Domesday Survey. She tentatively suggests, rather, the Scand appellative *blað* 'a leaf, a blade', probably used as a by-name *Blað*. Watts CDEPN, following Fellows-Jensen, interprets the place-name as an OE/Scand hybrid meaning 'Blath's estate'. An unrecorded *Blað* as a by-name is likely to be early and to signify 'a blade' in its sense 'the blade of a weapon' (cf. ON *knífs-blað* 'blade of a knife'). As with nearby Slawston, the place-name may record appropriation by a warrior from the Viking army which disbanded in the region in 877 rather than represent a later manorial creation.

Note the typical later 16th- and 17th-cent. Leics. loss of *t* from the group *-ston* in the *Blason* spellings, while the *d* of *Bladestone* 1086 DB clearly represents *th* [ð].

BLASTON HALL (lost), *Blaston Hall* 1846 White, *The Hall* 1877 ib, v. **hall**; demolished c.1930. BLASTON HILL. BLASTON HOLLOWS, 1968 *Surv*, v. **holh**. BLASTON LODGE, v. **loge**. BLASTON PASTURES, 1824 O, 1968 *Surv*, *Blaston Pasture* 1867 *ib*, v. **pasture**. CHAMBERLAYNE ARMS (P.H.) (lost), *Chamberlayne Arms* 1839 *TA*, 1846 White; *Thomas Chamberlayne* 1846 ib of Horninghold was a major landowner here. CRANESCLOSE SPINNEY is *Cranes Close Plantation* 1839 *TA*, v. **spinney**, **plantation**; with the surn. *Crane*. DENT'S SPINNEY, v. **spinney**; with the surn. *Dent*; this spinney lies partly in Medbourne parish. HALLATON RD, Hallaton lying one mile to the north-west. HIGHLAND SPINNNEY, cf. *Irelands Meadow* 1742 *Map*, *Island Meadow* 1839 *TA*, v. **spinney**; poss. originally with the surn. *Ireland*, otherwise v. **island**. HOME FM, v. **home**. HORNINGHOLD LANE, Horninghold lying one mile to the north. HOVEL BUILDINGS, v. **hovel**. LEWIN'S HOOK, 1863, 1877 White, *Lavin's Hook* (sic) 1839 *TA*, v. **hōc**; with the surn. *Lewin*. MANOR FM. MANOR HO., *Manor house* 1925 Kelly, v. **maner**. OVERCLOSE SPINNEY, *Over Close* 1839 *TA*, *Bottom ~ ~*, *Top Over Close* 1968, v. **uferra**, **clos(e)**, **spinney**. PASTURES LODGE (NEW LODGE 2½"), v. **loge** and Blaston Pastures *supra*. RED HOVEL, cf. *Red Hovel Field* 1968 *Surv*, v. **rēad**, **hovel**. ST GILES'S CHURCH, *St Giles* 1824 O, *St Giles' Church* 1846, 1863 White, *Church (St Giles)* 1925 Kelly. The present church was built in 1878, replacing a small church of 1714; in origin the *capella de Blathiston* 1220 MHW (with MLat *capella* 'a chapel'). Note *the Chapel Close* 1745 *Terrier* and *Chapel Yard* 1839 *TA* (v. **geard**), v. **chapel(e)**). ST MICHAEL'S CHURCH, *St Michael* 1824 O, *St Michael's Church* 1846, 1863, 1877 White, *The Church of St Michael* 1925 Kelly. This church was rebuilt 1867–68, but largely demolished in 1967. STOCKERSTON CROSS ROADS, Stockerston lying two miles to the north-east, v. **cross-road(s)**. STURRAD SPINNEY, *Starwood* 1663 *Conant*, *Starrard* 1839 *TA*, cf. *Starard Close*, *~ Mead* 1742 (v. **mēd**); either 'the wood where starlings roost' (with **stær(e)**) or 'the wood where poles or stakes are got' (with a reduced **stæfer**), v. **wudu**. UPPINGHAM RD, Uppingham in Rutland lying four miles to the north-east. THE WHITE HO. (lost), *The White House* 1642 *Conant*; demolished 1958.

FIELD-NAMES

In (a), forms presented without dates are 1968 *Surv*; those dated 1839 are *TA*; 1867 are *Surv*; 1942 are Sale. Forms throughout dated 1289 are Coram; those dated 1292 are Banco; 1537 are MinAccts; 1601, 1606 and

1704 are *Terrier*; 1642, 1645 and 1663 are *Conant*; 1645, 1677, 1690 and 1735 are *Deed*; 1701 are Nichols; 1709 are AAS; 1742 are *Map*.

(a) Nine ~, Seventeen ~, Nineteen Acres (*v.* **æcer**); Allens Cl 1839, 1847, 1968 (with the surn. *Allen*); Ashbys Cl 1839 (with the surn. *Ashby*); Baker's Cl (with the surn. *Baker*); Banks 1867, ~ Plantation 1839 (*v.* **plantation**), Banks Mdw 1839, 1867, 1968, Hollow Banks 1839, 1968 (*v.* **holh**) (*v.* **banke**); Barkers Cl 1839 (with the surn. *Barker*); Belchers Cl (with the surn. *Belcher*); Bolt Cl (beside Bolt Wood in Stockerston); Borsden's Cl 1867, Borsdens Little Cl, ~ Pasture Cl 1839 (*v.* **pasture**), Borsden's ~, 1867, Bawsdonds Mdw (sic) 1968 (cf. *George Borsden* 1831 Census and *Herbert Borsden* 1870 ib); Bottom Cl 1839; Bradshaws Cl 1839, 1968 (with the surn. *Bradshaw*); Broadholm Mdw, Great Broadholm 1839 (*v.* **brād**, **holmr**); Brook Spinney 1839 (*v.* **brōc**, **spinney**); Bushawe 1839 (*v.* **busc**, **haga**[1]); Calf Cl 1968, ~ Mdw 1839 (*v.* **calf**); Carrs Cl 1839 (with the surn. *Carr*); Church Fd (*v.* St Giles' Church *supra*); Cliffs Cl 1839 (at this date, the surn. *Cliff* belonged largely to the north-west of Leics., so poss. here is **clif** 'a bank, the steep slope of a hillside'); Coles Cl 1839, 1968, Coles' Mdw 1867 (with the surn. *Coles*); Great ~, Little Conery 1839, Great ~, Little Cunnery 1968, Conery ~ 1839, Cunnery Hill 1968 (*v.* **coningre**); Great ~ ~, Coningsgrave Hill 1867 (*v.* **hyll**; with **coning-erth** or **coning**, **græf**); Copy, Bottom ~, Top Coppy 1839, Bottom ~, Long Copey 1968 (*v.* **copis**; the spelling *copy* is due to the popular reconstruction of a 'singular' form); Cow Common 1839 (*v.* **commun**), Cow Pasture 1839 (it is *the neates pasture* 1601, *v.* **nēat**, **pasture**) (*v.* **cū**); Cranes Cl or Nobles Cl 1839, Cranes Cl 1968 with the surns. *Crane* and *Noble*, *v.* Cranesclose Spinney *supra*); Bottom ~ ~, Top Dents Cl 1839, Upper ~ ~, Dent's Cl 1867, Dents Paddocks 1968 (*v.* **paddock**) (with the surn. *Dent*); Dock Cl 1839, 1867, Bottom ~ ~, Top Dock Cl 1942 (*v.* **docce**); Draycotts Cl 1839 (prob. with the surn. *Draycott*, although this was largely limited to the Borough of Leicester at this date; otherwise *v.* **dræg**, **cot**); Bottom ~, Top Dungeon 1839, Big ~, Top Dungen 1968, Dungeon Plantation 1839, ~ Spinney 1942 (*v.* **plantation**, **spinney**) (cf. *Dungeon Close* 1742, *Dungeon Pit* 1709, 1742 (*v.* **pytt**) (*v.* **dyncge** 'manured land' and Dungeon Mdw, Lei **3** 115); Top Far Mdw 1839 (*v.* **feor**); Foot Ball Cl (for the game of football); Franeys 1968, Franeys Far Cl and Bog 1839 (*v.* **feor**, **bog**) (with the surn. *Franey*); Franks Hill 1839, 1968 (with the surn. *Frank*(*s*)); Gibbins's Footbridge Cl 1839 (*v.* **fote-brydge**; with the surn. *Gibbins*); Gilsons Cl 1839 (with the surn. *Gilson*); Bottom ~, Top Glebe 1839 (*v.* **glebe**); Gold Thorpe (*Goulthrop* 1606), Great Goldthorpe 1839, ~ ~ Cl 1867 (*Goltropp* ~ 1645, *Golthorpe Close* 1701), Goldthorpe Mdw (*Golthorpe Meadow* 1701) (*v.* **þorp**; earlier forms are needed to interpret the name of this farmstead which lay at the edge of the great South Fd of Blaston, but poss. as its first el. is the ON masc. pers.n. *Gulli*, or if created late, then ME **goule** (from OE **gūl*) 'a stream, a channel', perh. referring to one of the water-courses which form lengths of the south-western and western bounds of the parish; the *d* of the 19th-cent. spellings appears to be intrusive, but if not, then **golde** '(marsh) marigold' may also be thought of, or much less likely, the OE masc. pers.n. *Golda* (*v.* Goldthorpe, YW **1** 83)); Great Cl 1968, Nether ~ ~, Upper Great Cl 1839 (*Great*(*e*) *Close* 1642, 1742, *Great Close Meadow* 1742, *v.* **grēat**); Great Mdw 1839; Hare Croft 1839, 1867 (*Harecroft* 1606, *v.* **hār**[2], **croft**; a name found also in Hallaton, Slawston and Smeeton Westerby); Herricks (the surn. *Herrick* in the possessive case); High Land Cl (*v.* Highland Spinney *supra*);

Highways ~ 1867, Highway Cl 1968 (*v.* **hēah-weg**); Hill Cl 1839, 1968 (1642); Hill End 1839, 1968 (1742), Hill End Plantation 1839 (*v.* **plantation**) (*v.* **hyll**, **ende**); Hollow Cl 1839, 1968 (*Nether* ~, *Upper Hollow Close* 1742, *v.* **holh** and Blaston Hollows *supra*); Home Cl 1839, 1867, 1968 (1742, *v.* **home**); Bottom ~ ~, Top Hop Yard 1839 (*v.* **hop-yard**); Horse Cl 1839 (1677, 1701, *v.* **hors**); Hovell Cl, Long Hovell (*v.* **hovel**); Hudsons Cl 1839 (with the surn. *Hudson*); Ivy Cl 1839 (*v.* **īfig**); Kingstons Cl 1839 (with the surn. *Kingston*); Land Cl 1839 (*v.* **land**; a close formed from an unspecified number of selions of a former great open-field); Little Cl 1839, 1867, 1968, Little Fd 1867, 1968, Little Mdw, ~ ~ Plantation 1839 (*v.* **plantation**); Long Cl 1839, 1867; Masons Cl 1839, 1968, Thorny Mason's Cl 1867 (*v.* **þornig**), Masons Close Plantation 1839 (*v.* **plantation**), Masons Paddocks 1968 (*v.* **paddock**) (with the surn. *Mason*); Maydwells Homestead 1839 (*v.* **hām-stede**; with the surn. *Maydwell* of a family originally from Maidwell, 12 miles to the south-west in Northants.); Bottom ~ ~, Mill Fd 1839, 1968 (*Mill Feild* 1606, *Millfield* 1663, 1677, 1735), Mill Field Spinney 1839 (*v.* **spinney**) (*v.* **myln**, **feld**; one of the great open-fields of the township, also called the North Fd); Mirabell 1839 (*Meribell Close* 1663; adjacent to Great ~ ~, Little Merrible Wood in Stockerston); Muggletons Cl, ~ Homestead 1839 (*v.* **hām-stede**) (with the surn. *Muggleton*, common in south-east Leics. and Rutland); Needhams Cl 1839 (with the surn. *Needham*); New Lodge Cl 1968 (*v.* **loge**); Nobles Cl 1839 (*v.* Cranes Cl *supra*); Old Road 1839 (*v.* **ald**; a roadside close); The Paddocks (*v.* **paddock**); Palmers Piece 1839 (*v.* **pece**; with the surn. *Palmer*); Parsons Cl (cf. *the Parsons plott* 1645, *v.* **persone**, **plot**); Pasture Mdw 1867 (*v.* Blaston Pastures *supra*); Porters Cl, ~ Hovel (*v.* **hovel**), ~ Spinney 1839 (*v.* **spinney**) (with the surn. *Porter*); Railway, ~ Fd 1968 (beside a dismantled railway track); Seaton Poor Cl 1839 (*v.* **pouer(e)**; land endowed for the poor folk of Seaton in Rutland); Skeffington's Gorse 1867 (*v.* **gorst**; cf. *Reuben Skeffington* 1867 of Blaston, whose family came originally from Skeffington, 5 miles to the north-west); Smock Cl 1839 (*the Smock Close* 1704, ~ *Smook* ~ l.18; prob. referring to land originally held by payment of the money tax known as *smoke-penny* or *smoke-silver* in place of tithewood; but note ModE dial. *smock*, used of both the Greater Bindweed (*Convolvulus sepium*) and the Ladysmock or Cuckoo Flower (*Cardamine pratensis*) which may rather pertain here); Top Stocks, Bottom Stocks Spinney 1839 (*v.* **spinney**), Little ~ ~, Stocks Cl (*v.* **stocc**); Stone Bridge 1867, 1968, ~ ~ Cl 1839 (*v.* **stān**, **brycg**); Store Cl 1839 (*v.* **stor**, used early of livestock; from the 16th cent., also indicating 'abundance'(of food etc.)); Stripe 1839 (*v.* **strīp**); Tea Cl 1839, Tea Browns (with the surn. *Brown* in the possessive case), Tee Close East, ~ ~ West 1968 (originally a T-shaped enclosure); Thorn(e)y Cl 1839, 1867, Little ~, Long ~, Middle Thorney 1968 (*Thorney close* 1537, *v.* **þornig**, **clos(e)**); Turnip Cl 1839 (*v.* **turnepe**); Wadlands Cl 1839 (*v.* **wād**, **land**); Wad Orchard, ~ ~ Mdw, ~ ~ Plantation 1839 (*v.* **plantation**), Woad Orchard, ~ ~ Mdw 1867 (*v.* **wād**, **orceard**); Watsons Acre, ~ ~ Mdw, ~ ~ Plantation 1839 (*v.* **æcer**; with the surn. *Watson*); Wood Cl 1839 (1677, *v.* **wudu**).

(b) *Blaston parsonage* 1601 (*v.* **personage**); *Brechewod* 1289 (*v.* **brēc**, **wudu**); *Bridge Close* 1663, *Bridge furlonge* 1606 (*v.* **furlang**) (*v.* **brycg**); *Browns 12 Acres* 1742 (*v.* **æcer**; with the surn. *Brown*); *Cockshote* (*v.* **cocc-scēte**); *dead more* 1601 (*v.* **dēad**, **mōr**[1]; with reference to infertile wasteland); *fullwell* 1601, *Fulwell* 1606 (*v.* **fūl**, **wella**); *gallow(e) hill* 1601, *Gallow hill* 1606 ('bare hill', *v.* **calu**, **hyll**); *greene hades* 1601 (*v.* **grēne**[1], **hēafod**); *Hall closes* 1677 (*v.* **hall**); *halloughton home* 1601,

Hallaton Home 1606 (*v.* **holmr**), *Haloughton Sties* 1606 (*v.* **stīg**) (Hallaton parish adjoins to the north-west); *Holt sicke* 1601 (*v.* **sík**), *Holt Meadow* 1701; meadowland lying towards Nevill Holt which adjoins to the south-east); *Hunts lane* 1606 (*v.* Hunt's Lane in adjoining Hallaton); *hushome* 1601 (*v.* **hūs**, **holmr**); *Lads willows* 1601 (*v.* **wilig**; prob. with the surn. *Ladd* (note *Ricardus Ladde* c.1175 of nearby Northants.) rather than with its source ME **ladde** 'a servant, a man of low birth' or **lād** 'a water-course'); *maid landes* 1601 (*v.* **land**; with **mægd**, a shortened form of **mægden**, poss. alluding to a young unmarried woman); *Medburne furlonge* 1606 (*v.* **furlang**), *medburn waie* 1601, *Medburne way* 1606 (*v.* **weg**) (Medbourne parish adjoins to the south-east); *the Mill Close* 1701 (*v.* **myln**); *the North Close* 1701; *the North feild* 1601 (*v.* **norð**, **feld**; one of the great open-fields, also known as the Mill Fd *supra*); *Peck feild* 1601, *Pecke field* 1606 (*v.* **pēac**, **feld**; one of the great open-fields); *Ryecroft* 1292 (*v.* **ryge**, **croft**); *Slawston gate* 1601 (*v.* **gata**; the road to Slawston which lies 2 miles to the south-west); *the South feild* 1601 (*v.* **sūð**, **feld**; one of the great open-fields); *Spinney Close* 1663 (*v.* **spinney**); *the Upper Ground* 1701 (*v.* **upper**, **grund**); *Watts close* 1537 (*v.* **clos(e)**; with the surn. *Watt(s)*).

Bringhurst

BRINGHURST

Bruningehurst 1211 ChancR, 1220 Cur
Briningehurst' 1220 Cur (p), *Brinningehurste* 1229 RHug, *Brinegehurst* 1279 Ipm
Breningehurst 1199 FF, 1220 Cur, *Brenningeherst* 1200 ib, *Bremingeherst* 1214 ib (p), *Bremingehurst* 1236 Fees (p)
Bruninghyrst 1189 (1332) Ch, *Bruninghurst* 1220 Cur (p), 1276 Misc (p), *Brunanghurst* 1262 Fine (p)
Brin(n)inghurst m.12 HCand, e.13 *Peake*, 1231 Fine (p), 1264 RGrav, 1293 Ass (p), *Brininghyrst* m.12 HCand, *Brinhinkhirst* c.1150 *Peake*, *Brinningherst* 1231 Fine, *Brin(n)inghirst'* 1275 RGrav, 1292, 1299 *Wyg*, *Bryn(n)ynghurst* 1252 Fine (p), l.13 *Peake*, 1290 (p), 1308 Ipm, *Briminghyrst* 1189 (1332) Ch, *Brimingherst* 1214 Cur (p)
Brenninghurst 1275 (e.15) *BelCartB*, 1293 OSut, 1310 *Rut*, *Brennynghirst* c.1291 Tax, *Bremyngherste* c.1291 ib
Brinegherst, *Brinigherst*, *Brinighurst* 12 *Peake*, *Brinighirst* e.13 *ib*
Brinihirst 1125 × 28 LN, 1293 (p), 1294 *Wyg* (p), 1320 *Peake*, *Brynehyrst* m.13 HCand, *Brinehyrst* l.13 *Peake*
Brinkeherst 1214 Cur (p), *Bryngeherst* 1321 Misc, 1427 *Peake*, *Bryngehirst* 1369, 1428 *ib*, 1429 *Conant*
Brinchirst 1221 RHug (p), *Bringherst(e)* 1254 Val, 1312, 1321, 1382 *Peake*, *Bringhirst* m.13 CN (p), 1291 OSut (p) *et passim* to 1336, 1351 *Peake et freq* to 1394, 1395 *ib*, 1428 FA, *Bringhyrst'* 1317 *LCh* (p) *et passim* to 1444 *Peake*, *Brynghirst* 1336, 1346 *ib et freq* to 1384 *ib*, 1428 FA, *Brynghurst* 1321 Cl, 1330 Pat *et freq* to 1430, 1443 *Peake et passim* to 1518 Visit, 1553 Pat, *Brynghyrst* 1410 *Conant*, 1444 *Peake*, *Bringhurst(e)* 1450, 1457 *Conant et passim* to 1583, 1601 LibCl *et freq*
Bringest 1312 *Peake et passim* to 1604 SR, *Bringeast* 1576 Saxton, 1610 Speed, 1729 LML

'The wooded hill belonging to Brȳni's people', *v.* **-inga-**, **hyrst**. The OE masc. pers.n. *Brȳni* is also to be found in Brineton St **1** 129, Brington Nth 79 and Brinnington Ch **1** 268. The township is sited on a small hill overlooking the river Welland in what was once heavily wooded countryside.

DRAYTON RD is *Westgate* 1347 CN, *v.* **west**, **gata**. RED LION (P.H.) (lost), *Red Lion* 1863, 1877 White. ST NICHOLAS'S CHURCH, *Church (St Nicholas)* 1846, 1863 White, 1925 Kelly; it is earlier recorded as *ecclesie de Brunghurst* 1220 MHW, ~ *de Bryngheurst* 1330, 1336 *Pat*, 1375 *Deed*, ~ *de Brynghirst* 1353, 1355 *Pat*, *ecclesiam de Brynghurst alias Eston* 1486 *ib* (with reference to adjacent Great Easton); note *the Church yeard* 1601 *Terrier*, *v.* **churchyerd**. Also recorded is *the vickerig house* 1674 *Terrier*, *the Vicarige house* 1679 *ib*, *v.* **vikerage**.

FIELD-NAMES

In (a), forms dated 1804 and 1826 are *Plan*; those dated 1805 are *Surv*. Forms throughout dated c.1250 and 1347 are CN; those dated 1302 are Ipm; 1674, 1679, 17, 1712 and m.18 are *Terrier*.

(a) Bluegate Cl 1826 (presum. a close beside 'the cold, cheerless road', *v.* **blár**, **gata**); *Bridge* Fd 1805 (1712, *le Briggefeld* 1347, *v.* **brycg**, **feld**; one of the great open-fields of the township, later also called *the South feild*, *infra*); Grove Hill 1804, Grove Fd 1805 (1712, *v.* **feld**; another of the great open-fields, also called *the East feild*, *infra*) (*v.* **grāf**); Home Cl 1826 (*v.* **home**); Little Cl 1804; Middle Cl 1804; Pasture Cl 1804 (*v.* **pasture**); Savie Fd 1805 (a late name for one of the great fields, early called *le Moorfeld* and later *the West feild*, both *infra*; prob. with dial. **seavy** 'sedge, rush' (from ON **sef**)); Three Quicks Mdw 1826 (*v.* **quyk**; a meadow bordered by three quickset hedges); Westgate Cl 1826 (*v.* **west**, **gata**).

(b) *Brinynghurst Brende* 1302 (*v.* **brende**); *Brinynghurst Stubbyng* 1302 (*v.* **stubbing**); *crucem de Brynghirst* c.1250 (with MLat *crux* (*crucem* acc.sg.) 'a cross'); *the East feild* 17 (*v.* **ēast**, **feld**; one of the great open-fields, later called Grove Fd *supra*); *Fyuerodesty* 1347 (*v.* **fīf**, **rōd**[3], **stīg**); *Garbidg* 1712 (*v.* **gorebrode**); *the Hall Close* 1712 (*v.* **hall**; either the township's hall or *the Vicaridge house* (*supra*) is recorded as *the Mansion house* 17, *v.* **mansion-house**); *Holm* n.d. *Deed* (*v.* **holmr**); *Lammas Close* 17 (*v.* **lammas**); *Long Fern* 1712 (*v.* **lang**[1], **fearn**); *Meadow furlong* m.18 (*v.* **furlang**); *Middelfurlong* 1347 (*v.* **middel**, **furlang**); *Mikelacr'* 1347 (*v.* **micel**, **mikill**, **æcer**); *le Moorfeld* 1347 (*v.* **mōr**[1], **feld**; one of the early great open-fields, later called *the West feild*, *infra* and also Savie Fd *supra*); *the North hill* 1712; *Porters hill* 1712 (*v.* **hyll**; ostensibly with the surn. *Porter*; but poss. is either an original **Potters hill* with ME **pottere** 'a pot-maker' (and *Porters hill* may be a late reflex of the 13th-cent. *potteres hul* recorded for adjacent Great Easton), hills often being the locations of medieval pottery kilns, cf. *Potterhill*, Lei **2** 248, Potter Hill,

Lei **2** 257 and Lei **3** 18), or a **Porthill*, sometimes a shortening of **Portway hill* (ME **port-wey** 'a road to a (market-) town, a road to a market'), referring to the lost route hereabouts of the Roman Gartree Road (*Via Devana*) on its way to Leicester, cf. Porter's Lodge, Lei **3** 169 and Portels Fm, Lei **3** 173; however, **Porthill* may simply be formed with **port**[2] 'a market' and thus refer to an early hill-top market site; but for a reconsideration of such names, *v.* Cox[2] 81); *the South feild* 17 (*v.* **sūð**, **feld**; one of the great open-fields, also called Bridge Fd *supra*); *the Upper meadow* 1713; *the West hades* 1712 (*v.* **west**, **hēafod**); *the West feild* 17, m.18 (*v.* **west**, **feld**; one of the great open-fields, earlier called *le Moorfeld* and later Savie Fd, both *supra*).

Burton Overy

BURTON OVERY

Burtone 1086 DB (×2), 1229 RHug, 1277 Hastings, *Burtona* 1156 (1318) Ch, *Burthona* c.1200 BM, *Burton* 1220 RHug, 1227 Cur *et freq*, *Burtun* c.1220 *Hazlerigg*, *Burtoun* 1360 Ipm
Bocton' c.1130 LeicSurv
Borton' 13 *Peake*, *Bortona* 1190 × 1204 France
Bourton 1317, 1336 Ipm

Either 'the farmstead, village by a fortification' or 'the fortified farmstead, village', *v.* **burh-tūn**. The affix is added as: ~ *Nouerai* 1259 RGrav, ~ *Noveray* 1260 Ass, ~ *Noverey*(*e*) 1285 *et passim* with various spellings to 1727 LML; and by metanalysis as ~ *Overay* 1317 Cl, ~ *Overey*(*e*) 1333 Ipm *et passim* with various spellings to the modern form ~ *Overy* 1582 LEpis, 1610 Speed *et freq*.

The manor was held by *Radulphus de Noveray* in 1260 Ass, by *Robertus de Noveray* in 1261 Cur and remained in the family as late as *John Noverey* 1389 Cl; the family may have originally come from Nourray, south-west of Orléans and north of Tours. The township lies in a valley between two hill-spurs. Either of these is the possible site of an early fortification but there is no evidence on the ground for such. (However, note *the Arbour* in f.ns. (b)). Earthworks surviving in the village are likely to be the remains of the medieval settlement.

THE BANKS, 1981 *Surv*, *v.* **banke**. BEES WELL LANE, *v.* **bēos**, **wella**. BELL (P.H.), *Bell* 1846, 1863 White, 1925 Kelly. BELL LANE, the site of the Bell (P.H.) *supra*. BURTON BROOK, ~ ~ FM, *v.* **brōc**. BURTON GRANGE, *v.* **grange**. GLEBE FM, *v.* **glebe**. THE LODGE, 1877 White, *v.* **loge**. MAINS LANE, *Mayns Lane* 1981 *Surv*, cf. *Wm. Mayn*, *farmer* 1846 White. MAIN ST. MANOR HOUSE FM, *Manor house* 1925 Kelly, *v.* **maner**. MOUNT PLEASANT, 1925 Kelly; Mount Pleasant is for the most part a complimentary name for a location, but occasionally may be bestowed ironically. NEW CROWN (P.H.) (lost), *New Crown* 1846, 1877 White, 1925 Kelly. OLD CROWN (P.H.) (lost), *Old Crown* 1846 White.

THE RECTORY, 1877 White, *The Old Rectory* 1981 *Surv*, *v.* **rectory**; note also *the Parsonage house* 1606, 1707, 1707 (18) *Terrier* (*v.* **personage**), which is called *the mansion howse* 1601 *ib*, ~ ~ *house* 1674, 1700 *ib* (*v.* **mansion-house**). ST ANDREW'S CHURCH, *Church (St Andrew)* 1846, 1863 White, 1925 Kelly; it is earlier recorded as *ecclesie de Burton* 1220 MHW, ~ *de Burton Noveray* 1331, 1355 *Pat et passim* to 1403 *ib*, ~ *de Burton Nover(e)y* 1339, 1343, 1388 *ib*, ~ *de Burton Offray* 1355 *ib*, ~ *de Burton Overay* 1390 *ib*. SCOTLAND, cf. *Scotland Lane* 1981 *Surv*, *v.* **scot**, **land**; land once subject to the payment of a tax. TOWN CLOSE, (*the*) *Town Close* 1707, 1707 (18) *Terrier*, 1800 *Valuation*, 1846, 1863 White, 1981 *Surv*, *v.* **tūn**, **clos(e)**. WASHBROOK LANE, 1981 *Surv*, *v.* **wæsce**, **brōc**.

FIELD-NAMES

In (a), forms presented without dates are 1981 *Surv*; those dated 1765, 1785 and 1856 are *Deed*; 1766 are *EnclA*; 1795 are *Map*; 1864, 1918 and 1928 are Sale. Forms throughout dated 1307 and 1621 are Ipm; those dated 1467 × 84 are *LTD*; 1584 are Moulton; 1601, 1606, 1638, 1674, 1679, 17, 1700, 1707 (18) and 1749 are *Terrier*; 1609 are *Deed*.

(a) Five Acre, Six ~, Seven ~, Eight ~, Nine ~, Ten ~, Thirteen ~, Twenty Acre (*v.* **æcer**); New ~, Old Allotments (*v.* **allotment**); First ~, Second Ashby's (with the surn. *Ashby*); Ayre's Cl (with the surn. *Ayre*); Bailey's Lane (with the surn. *Bailey*); Banham Mdw 1766 (*Banam* 1467 × 84, *Bannum* 1674, *Bannom* 1749, *v.* **bēan**, **hamm**); Barn Fd 1928, 1981 (*v.* **bern**); Bates's Cl 1856 (with the surn. *Bates*); Bell Pool (*Bell Poole* 1749, *v.* **pōl**[1]; the first el. is prob. **belle** in its sense 'a knoll'); Best Cl 1918, 1981, ~ Mdw 1981 (*v.* **best**; complimentary names for very fertile land); 1st ~ ~, 2nd Big Fd; Bird's Cl (with the surn. *Bird*; cf. *Birds peice* 1707, 1707 (18), *Birds Piece Close* 1749, *v.* **pece**); Bluepott Cl 1800, Blue Potts 1981 (1749) (if an early name, then 'cold, cheerless pool' may be thought of, *v.* **blár**, **potte**; if late, the name may have referred to broken shards of blue-glazed pottery in the soil); Bottom Cl (*v.* **bottom**); Brick Kiln Cl (*v.* **brike-kiln**); the Brickyard 1800 (*v.* **brike-yard**); Brook Fd 1766 (*Brokfelde* 1467 × 84, *the brooke feild* 1601, *Brooke feild* 1606, *the Brooke feilde* 1609, 1674, *the broke feilde alias west feilde* 1638, *the Brook feeld* 1700, 1707, *The Brook Field* 1707 (18), 1749, *v.* **brōc**, **feld**; one of the great open-fields of the township); Burton Willow Bed 1835 O (*v.* **wilig**, **bedd**); Bushy Cl (*v.* **busshi**); Butcher's Cl (with the surn. *Butcher*); Carlton Mdw 1766, Carlton Rd 1981, Carlton Sick 1918 (*v.* **sík**) (Carlton Curlieu parish adjoins to the south-east); Carter's Cl (with the surn. *Carter*); Carver's Mdw (with the surn. *Carver*); First Case 1918 (of uncertain meaning; *Case* may be a surn. here); Catwell (1601, 1606, 1674, 1679, *Catell* 1638, *Catwall* 1700, 1707, *v.* **cat(t)**, **wella**, cf. *Catwelle* Lei **3** 117); Charity Cl (the rent of the land provided funds for a charitable purpose); Cheese Worms (sic) (*Cheeseonnge* 1601, 1606, *Chesong(e)* 1638, 17, *Chesewong* 1679, *Cheeswong* 1700,

1707, 1707 (18), *v.* **cis**, **vangr**); Clay Pit Lane Cl 1766, Clay Pits (*v.* **cley-pytt**); Clover Cl 1864 (*v.* **clāfre**; grown as a fodder crop); Coverdale (*Corfe* 1467 × 84, *v.* **corf** 'a gap'; with **dalr**); Bottom ~ ~, Cow Cl 1928, 1981; Cricket Mdw 1928 (for the game of cricket); Cricks (the surn. *Crick*, in the possessive case, of a family originally from Crick, 17 miles to the south-west in Northants.); Crowd Hayes (*v.* **(ge)hæg**); a late form, but perhaps with **crȳde**); Dairy Ground 1928, 1981 (*v.* **deierie**, **grund**); Deacon's Cl 1856 (with the surn. *Deacon*); Ditch End Cl 1795, 1981 (*Dikes end* 1749, *v.* **dík**, **dīc**, **ende**); Eassom's Mdw, Eassom's Top Fd (with the surn. *Eassom*); Elms Lane (*v.* **elm**); The Far Cl 1864; Farthings (*v.* **fēorðung**); First Mdw; Fishponds (*v.* **fisshe-ponde**); Foot Road Fd (*v.* **foot-road**); First ~ ~, Second Fox Holes 1928, First ~, Foxholes 1981 (*v.* **fox-hol**); Frying Pan (alluding to the shape of the close); Gambles Lane 1766 (with the surn. *Gamble*, a reflex of the ON masc. pers.n. *Gamall*); Gartree Fd, Gartree Rd (two fields beside the Roman Gartree Road in the north-east of the parish); Glen Mdw 1928, 1981 (adjacent to Great Glen parish which adjoins to the west); Goose Pits (*v.* **pytt**; the first word is poss. dial. *gosse* 'gorse' rather than **gōs**, with reference to early excavations filled with gorse-bushes, *v.* **gorst**); Gowertons Cl 1856 (with a surn. in the possessive case, presum. once *Goverton*, of a family originally from the village of this name, 32 miles to the north in Notts.); Gravel Hole(s) (*v* **hol**[1]), Gravel Pit Cl, Old Gravel Pits (*Gravel Pitts*, *Gravel Pit hill* 1749, *v.* **pytt**) (*v.* **gravel**); Great Cl 1800, 1981, Great Mdw 1800; Close next Mr Haynes 1795; Hog Bank Cl 1795, 1981 (*v.* **hogg**, **banke**); Hog Lane 1766 (1700, 1707 (18), *Hogg Lane* 1707, *v.* **hogg**, **lane**); First ~ ~, Second Home Bank 1928, 1981 (*v.* **holmr**, **banke**; the earthworks to the west of the parish church are presum. the remains of the medieval settlement); Home Cl 1928, 1981 (*v.* **home**); Homestead 1795 (*the Homsted* 1707, *The Hamestead* 1707 (18), *v.* **hām-stede**); Hooks Cl 1766 (perh. cf. *Hookes Lane* 1601, *Hooks Lane* 1606, *v.* **lane**; a *Thomas Hook* is recorded in the parish in 1601 and 17 and prob. gave his name to the lane; but note *the Cunstables Hooks* and *Mill Dam Hooks* in f.ns. (b), with **hōc**); Jack's Cl 1981, ~ Mdw 1795 (*Jacks medew* 1700, ~ *medow* 1707, ~ *Meadow* 1707 (18); *Jack* is either the common pet-name of *John*, or the surn. *Jack* derived from it); Kibworth or Burton Bridge 1766 (*v.* **brycg**; Kibworth Harcourt parish adjoins to the south); London Rd; First ~ ~, Second Long Leys 1981, Long Leys Cl 1795 (*Long Lays* 1749, *v.* **lang**[1], **leys**); Leys Bridge Lane 1766 (*v.* **leys**, **brycg**, **lane**); Manor Fd (*v.* Manor House Fm *supra*); The Meadow 1864, 1928, 1981 (1749), Little Mdw 1928; Mill Fd (1626, 1749, *the Mylne feilde* 1609, *the Mill feild toward Carleton* 1674, *Carlton feeld called the mill feeld* 1700, 1707, *v.* **myln**, **feld**; one of the great open-fields of the township, Carlton Curlieu parish adjoining to the south-east); Moor Cl 1795 (*Moore close* 1626), Moor(e) Hill Cl 1795 (*la more* 1307, *the Moores* 1679, *v.* **mōr**[1]); Little Morgan 1795, ~ Morgans 1981, Morgan's Mdw 1795 (with the surn. *Morgan*); Morrils ~ 1766, Morrals Cl 1928 (with the surn. *Morrill*); New Cl 1800 (1626); Norton's Lane 1766, Norton Mdw (with the surn. *Norton*); Oaks Cl (cf. *Oacks meadow* 1749; either with the surn. *Oak*(*s*) or with **āc**); Old Hill 1765, 1766, 1785, 1981 (1749, *Woldhyl* 1467 × 84, *v.* **wald**, **hyll**); Orchard Cl (*v.* **orceard**); Over Cl 1766 (1584, *v.* **uferra**, **clos(e)**); Perberdy's Cl (with the surn. *Perberdy*, a variant of *Peabody*); Peewit Mdw (a field frequented by the lapwing, also called the pe(e)wit (*pewit* from the 16th cent.)); Pitborough Cl 1800 (if recording an early name, then prob. referring to a hill with excavations for gravel, stone etc., *v.* **pytt**, **berg**); Pressgate Cl 1800 (*Prestgate* 1467 × 84, *Presgate* 1601, 1606, 1638, 1674, *Prisgate*

1679, *Pressgate* 1700, 1707, 1707 (18), *v.* **prēost**, **gata**); Rabbit Holes 1918, 1981 (*v.* **rabet**); Railway (a close beside the former Midland Railway in the extreme south-west of the parish); Round Cl 1766 (an enclosure approximately circular in shape); First ~ ~, Second Rice Piece (*v.* **pece**) (*Respyrys* 1467 × 84, *riche pearse* 1601, *riche perche* 1606, *rich peares* 1638, *rich pearse* 1674, *Ricepeers* 1700, *Rice pears* 1707, 1707 (18); referring to a place where wild raspberries abounded, *v.* **resbery**, **respis**; the earliest OED citation for raspberry is for c.1532); The Sandilands 1918, 1981 (*Sandylandis* 1467 × 84, *Sandy lands* 1749, *v.* **sandig**, **land**); Sea Brook(s) 1928, 1981 ('the rushy brook', *v.* **sef**, **brōc**); Seeders Cl (*v.* **seeder** 'one who sows seed, a sower'); Wards ~, Seeds (*v.* **sǣd**; used of grasses sown for one year's mowing or grazing, as distinguished from permanent pasture; with the surn. *Ward* in the possessive case); Set(t)croft Mdw 1766 (poss. an earlier **set-copp**, otherwise *v.* **(ge)set**, **croft**); Little ~, Long Shinnel 1795, 1981 (earlier forms are needed; poss. is 'the haunted hill', *v.* **scinn(a)** 'a demon, a spectre', **hyll** (cf. Shincliffe (Durham 112) and note the similar *Shuggborowe* in f.ns. (b) *infra*); otherwise 'pebbly place' may be thought of, *v.* **shingel**[2]); The Spinney 1795, Spinney Fd (*v.* **spinney**); Stonehill Cl 1795, East ~ ~ ~, West Stone Hill Cl (*Stonhul* 1467 × 84, *v.* **stān**, **hyll**); Stretton Sic (*Strettonsyke* 1467 × 84, *Stretton sick(e)* 1601, 1606 *et passim* to 1749, *Stratton Sick* 1700, 1707, *v.* **sík**; Little Stretton parish adjoins to the north-west); Thorny Cl 1766 (*Thorney close* 1626, *v.* **þornig**); Tongs (*v.* **tunge**); (The) Top Cl 1864, 1981; The Torves (*v.* **turf**); Two Cl 1795, 1981 ('double close', *v.* **tū**); Wadlands Cl 1800 (*v.* **wād**, **land**); Bottom ~, Top Washpit 1981, Washpit Leys 1765, Great ~ ~, Little Washpitt Leys 1766, 1800 (*Wash Pitt Lays* 1749, *v.* **leys**) (*v.* **wæsce**, **pytt**); West Fd 1766 (*Westfelde* 1467 × 84, *(the) West(e) feild(e)* 1609, 1638, 1674, *the West field* 1626, *v.* **west**, **feld**; one of the early great open-fields); West Mdw 1766 (1601, 1606 *et passim* to 1749, *west medow* 1638, 1707, *West Middow* 1679, *v.* **west**, **mēd** (**mēdwe** obl.sg.)); Wood's Cl (with the surn. *Wood*).

(b) *the Arbour* 1749 (this may represent **eorð-burh**, a former fortified site; otherwise, *v.* **erber**); *bann lands* 1601, 1606, *Bandelands* 1679, 1700, 1707, *Bandlands* 1707 (18), *Bandy Lands* 1749 (*v.* **bēan**, **land**); *banners aker* 1601, 1638, *banvers aker* 1606, *Banners acres* 1674, *Baners acers* 1700, *Boners acres* 1707 (*v.* **æcer**; with the surn. *Banner*); *barlie haden* 1601, 1606, *barley haden* 1638, 1679, 17, *barly haden* 1674, *Barly hadon* 1700, 1707, 1707 (18), *Barley headon* 1707, ~ *headen* 1707 (18) (*v.* **bærlic**, **hēafod**; note the survival of a ME *-en* pl. (**haveden* > *haden*)); *Beyrhill* 1467 × 84, *Berrill* 1601, 1674, 1679, *berill* 1606, 1638 (*v.* **bere**, **hyll**); *Blaktoftes* 1467 × 84 (*v.* **blæc**, **toft**; with reference to the colour of the soil); *Brygehyll* 1467 × 84, *Bridgell* 1601, 1606, 1638, 1674, 1707, 1707 (18), *Bridgill* 1679, *Brig(e)ll* 1700 (*v.* **brycg**, **hyll**; in the old *Estfelde* (*v. infra*), and thus near the stream which forms the parish boundary with Carlton Curlieu); *the Butts* 1749 (*v.* **butte**); *William Campin his mill* 1707 (*v.* **myln**); *Carleton crose* 1467 × 84, *Carleton crosse hill* 1601, *Carlton Cross(e) hill* 1606, 1638, 1674, 1700, 1707, 1707 (18) (*v.* **cros**; a standing cross on a hill at the parish boundary with Carlton Curlieu (note the adjacent *holy roode leyes*, *infra*)); *Clync* 1467 × 84 (*v.* **clinc**); *Colepitt'* 1467 × 84 (*v.* **col-pytt**; a place where charcoal was made); *(the) Cow Pasture* 1601, 1606, 1674, 1707 (18) (*v.* **cū**, **pasture**); *Crook haden* 1749 (*v.* **crōc**, **hēafod** and *barlie haden*, *supra*); *Crowthornis* 1467 × 84 ('the thorn patch frequented by crows', *v.* **crāwe**, **þorn**; cf. *crouthorn* Lei **2** 29); *the Cunstables Hooks* 1700, *Constable Hooks* 1707, 1707 (18) (*v.* **conestable**, **hōc**); *Dykus* 1467 × 84 (*v.* **dík**); *Estfelde* 1467 × 84, *the*

East feild 1601 (*v.* **ēast, feld**; one of the great open-fields, later called *the feild toward Carelton* 1606, *the feilde towards Karlton* 17 and still later *Carlton feeld called the mill feeld* 1700, 1707 (*v.* **myln**); Carlton Curlieu parish adjoins to the south-east); *Flaxlandis, Flaxlondis* 1467 × 84 (*v.* **fleax, land**); *Fletchers close* 1626 (*v.* **clos(e)**; with the surn. *Fletcher*); *Robert Freeman his mill* 1707, *Robert Freeman's Mill* 1707 (18) (*v.* **myln**); *Fulwell* 1467 × 84 (*v.* **fūl, wella**); *the Glebe land* 1749 (*v.* **glebe**); *Grandell* 1467 × 84 (*v.* **grendel**); *Gravelhyll* 1467 × 84 (*v.* **gravel, hyll**); *Grenfurlong'* 1467 × 84 (*v.* **grēne**[1], **furlang**); *Greyshill* 1467 × 84, *gressell* 1601, 1606, 1707, 1707 (18), *grassell* 1638, 1700, *grassill* 1674 (*v.* **græs, hyll**); *Hassacks* 1749 (*v.* **hassuc**); *Hauards dole* 1700, *the hawards dols* 1707, *the Heywards Doles* 1707 (18) (*v.* **heiward, dāl**); *Hawthorngate* 1467 × 84 (*v.* **hagu-þorn, gata**); *the hy way* 1606, *the highway* 1674, 1679, *the Highway close* 1626, 1749 (*v.* **hēah-weg**); *Hog tree* 1749 (*v.* **hogg, trēow**; a place where swine foraged for mast); *Holoforth* 1467 × 84 (*v.* **holh, ford**); *holy roode ley(e)s* 1601, 1606, *holie rode leyes* 1638, *Holy Rood leyes* 1674, *Holy Rood(e) lays* 1700, 1707, *Holyrood Leys* 1707 (18) (*v.* **hālig, rōd**[2], **leys** and *Carleton crose, supra*); *the Homestall* 1606 (*v.* **hām-stall**; of *the Parsonage house*); *Hopreshyll* 1467 × 84, *Hoperhill* 1674, *hopperill* 1679, *hoprell* 1700, *Hoperill* 1707, 1707 (18), *Upper ~ ~, Hopper hill* 1749 (*v.* **hyll**; the first el. appears to be a ME surn. *Hopere*, a reflex of *hōpere* 'a cooper'); *Jud(d)s willows* 1606, 1679, 17, *Juds willowes* 1638, 1674 (*v.* **wilig**; cf. a *William Judd* of both 1606 and 1674); *Knightons sicke* 1601 (*v.* **sík**; with the surn. *Knighton* of a family originally from the township of this name, 4 miles to the north-west); *Kybworth gate* 1467 × 84 (*v.* **gata**; Kibworth Harcourt lies 2 miles to the south); *Ladipole* 1467 × 84 (*v.* **ladi, pōl**[1]); *Lady rodis* 1467 × 84 (*v.* **ladi, rōd**[3]; poss. here with reference to land dedicated to Our Lady, the Virgin Mary, for the maintenance of a chapel or shrine); *Langton medew* 1700, *~ medow* 1707, *~ meadow* 1749 (with the surn. *Langton*); *Leicester way* 1749; *Lituldale* 1467 × 84 (*v.* **lȳtel, dalr**); *Lytlow* 1467 × 84, *littloe sicke* 1601, *litlelo sick* 1606, *littlo sick* 1638, *Little a sick* 1679, 1707 (*v.* **sík**) (*v.* **lȳtel, hlāw**); *Mawkyns leyes* 1606 (*v.* **leys**; with the surn. *Mawkin*); *Middle close* 1626; *Mill Dam* 1749, *mill dam hooks* 1700, *Milldam Hooks* 1707, 1707 (18) (*v.* **hōc**) (*v.* **myln, damme**); *Netherfurlong* 1467 × 84 (*v.* **neoðera, furlang**; of *Estfelde, supra*); *Nogg(e)s forde* 1601, 1606, *Nogs forde* 1638, 17, *Noggs ford* 1674, *Nogs ford* 1679, 1700, 1707, 1707 (18), *~ foard* 1707 (*v.* **ford**), *Noggs home* 1601, *Nogges ~* 1606, *Nogs ~* 1638, 1638 *et passim* to 1707 (*v.* **holmr**) (perh. with the surn. *Nogg*, a shortened reflex of the ContGerm pers.n. *Norgaud*, but more likely is **hogg**, cf. *Hogges Foarde* in Great Bowden f.ns. (b)); *Normanhill* 1467 × 84 (*v.* **hyll**; with the surn. *Norman*); *the North Feild* 1679 (*v.* **norð, feld**; one of the great open-fields); *ouer nynete(e)ne leyes* 1601, 1638, *(on) over ninetine leyes* 1674, *ouer ninteene leese* 1679 (*v.* **ofer**[3], **nyentene, leys**; grassland units of tenure corresponding to *lands* similarly used of arable); *Ortondale* 1601, 1606, 17, *ortendale* 1700, *Horton Dale* 1707, *Ortindale* 1749 (*Orton* is poss. the name of an early farmstead (*v.* **ofer**[2], **tūn**); if so, then with **dalr**, but otherwise the surn. *Orton* with **deill**); *ould meadowe* 1601, *~ medow* 1606, *ould meadow haden* 1674, *old medow hadon* 1700, *~ ~ headon* 1707, *~ ~ headen* 1707 (18) (*v.* **hēafod** and *barlie haden, supra*) (*v.* **ald**); *Oxdall', Oxundal'* 1467 × 84 (*v.* **oxa, oxna** (gen.pl.); with **dalr** or **deill**); *Parsons hedge* 1749 (*v.* **persone, hecg**); *the Pasture* 1749 (*v.* **pasture**); *porte hedge* 1601 (*v.* **hecg**; a hedge lining the Roman Gartree Road), *Porthyll* 1467 × 84, *port hill* 1606, 1638 (*v.* **hyll**; beside the Roman road), *Portwey* 1467 × 84 (*v.* **port-wey**) (*v.* **port**[2]; alluding to Gartree Road, the main route to Leicester); *Quarelpyttes* 1467 × 84 (*v.* **quarrelle**, **pytt**); *Redemore* 1467 × 84, *Redmoore* 1601, 1606, 1638, *redd moore* 1606, *Redmore* 1674, *Read moor*(*e*) 1700, 1707, 1707 (18) (*v.* **hrēod**, **mōr**[1]); *Roger well* 1601, 1606, 1638, 1674, 1679, 17, ~ *wall* 1700, 1707 (*v.* **wella**; with the OFr pers.n. *Roger*; a feature earlier recorded as (*apud*) *fontem Rogeri* 1467 × 84 '(at) the spring or well of Roger', with MLat *fons* (*fontem* acc.sg.) 'a spring, a well'); *Sandihillis* 1467 × 84 (*v.* **sandig**, **hyll**); *the Sands* 1749 (*v.* **sand**); *Shuggborowe leys* 1601, *Shugbor*(*r*)*ow leyes* 1606, 1638, 1674, *Shubborow leise* 1679 (*v.* **scucca**, **berg**, **leys**; and note Shinnel in f.ns. (a)); *Slatborow* 1638, 1679, *Slatboru* 1674 (*v.* **slæget**, **berg**); *Somergate* 1467 × 84, 1601, 1674, *Summer gate* 1679, 1700, 1707 (*v.* **sumor**, **gata**; a track only suitable for use or required in summer); *the South*(*e*) *feild*(*e*) 1601, 1638, 1679, 17, (*the*) *South feeld* 1700, 1707, *the South Field* 1707 (18), 1749 (*v.* **sūð**, **feld**; one of the great open-fields); *Stonpit* 1467 × 84 (*v.* **stān-pytt**); *Swarsell* 1601, 1606, 17, 1707, 1707 (18), *Swarcell* 1749 (*v.* **hyll**; the first el. appears to be either a pers.n. or a surn. in the possessive case, such as ON *Svartr* or its surn. reflex *Swart*); *Theyswong* 1467 × 84 (*v.* **vangr**; the specific may well be the ODan pers.n. *Þerir* (gen.sg. *Þeris*) in what is prob. a scribe's miscopied cartulary form); *the Town Land* 1749 (*v.* **tūn**); *the Watering place* 1749 (*v.* **wateryng**, **place**); *water thorow*(*e*)*s* 1601, 1606, 1638, 1674, *Water thorows* 1679, *waterforrowes* 1700, *water fourrows* 1707, *Water furrows* 1707 (18) (*v.* **wæter**, **furh** and *the water furrowes* in Billesdon f.ns. (b)); *Watho haden* 1606 (*v.* **hēafod** and *barlie haden*, *supra*), *watho meere* 1601, *Water Meere* (sic) 1679 (*v.* **(ge)mǣre**), *Watho Stones* 1601, 1606, *Wathow stones* 1674, *Waterston*(*e*)*s* (sic) 1679, 1700, 1707, 1707 (18) (*v.* **stān**) (poss. 'wet spur of land', *v.* **wēt**, **hōh**, but *Watho* may be a late form of *Wortho*, *infra*); *Waxlandes* 1467 × 84, *wax lands* 1601, 1606, 1638, 1674, 17, 1700, *Waxlands* 1679, *waxs lands* 1707, *Wax's Lands* 1707 (18) (*v.* **weax**, **land**); *the Weyn Way* 1467 × 84, *Weane waie* 1601, ~ *way* 1606, 1638, 1674, *wene way* 1707, 1707 (18), *Wain way* 1749 (*v.* **wægn**, **weg**); *Welhyll* 1467 × 84 (*v.* **wella**, **hyll**); *Whatston haden* 1700, ~ *headon* 1707, 1707 (18) (*v.* **hwet-stān**, **hēafod** and *barlie haden*, *supra*); *Winilondys* 1467 × 84 (*v.* **whinny**, **land**); *Woldmedew* 1467 × 84 (*v.* **wald**, **mēd** (**mēdwe** obl.sg.)); *Worthohyll* 1467 × 84 (*v.* **wyrt**, **hōh**, **hyll** and *Watho*, *supra*); *Wranghaden* 1467 × 84 (*v.* **wrang**, **hēafod** and cf. *barlie haden*, *supra*); *Wranglandis*, *Schortwranglondis* 1467 × 84 (*v.* **sc(e)ort**), *Long Ranglands* 1749 (*v.* **wrang**, **land**).

Carlton Curlieu

CARLTON CURLIEU

Cherlentonæ s.a. 1081 (1131) Ord, *Cheletona* c.1055 (13) Rams
Carlintone 1086 DB, *Carlentona* 1190 × 1204 France
Carletone 1086 DB, *Carleton'* c.1130 LeicSurv, 1220 MHW *et freq* to 1439 *ShR*, 1443 Pat *et passim* to 1576 Saxton, 1627 LML, *Carletone* l.12 *GarCart* (p)
Karletona a.1219 RHug, c.1250 *Rut*, *Karletun'* c.1220 *Hazlerigg* (p), *Karletone* 1234 RHug, *Karleton'* 1240 RGros, 1245 Cl *et passim* to 1280 Coram, 1337 *Rut*, *Kar(r)elton'* e.13 (p), l.13 *Wyg* (p), *Karlton'* l.13 *ib* (p)
Carlton 1351 *Wyg*, 1362 Ipm *et passim* to 1576 LEpis, 1604 SR *et freq*

The affix is added as:
~ *Curly(e)* 1272, 1273 Cur *et freq* to 1457 *Wyg et passim* to 1537 CoPleas, ~ *Kurley* 1426 Banco, ~ *Kirle* 1533 × 38 ECP
~ *Curlu* 1351 *Pat*, 1439 *ShR*, 1519 EpCB, ~ *Corleue* 1410 *Wyg*, ~ *Curluy* 1484 Cl, ~ *Curlew(e)* 1483 *ShR*, 1506 Banco *et passim* to 1576 LEpis, 1604 SR, ~ *Kirlewe* 1627 LML

The name Carlton is a Scandinavianized form of OE **Ceorlenatūn* 'the farmstead, village of the free peasants', *v.* **ceorl** (**ceorla**, **ceorlena** gen.pl.), **karl** (**karla** gen.pl.), **tūn**. The manor was held by *Willielmus de Curly* in 1253 Cur, by *Robertus de Curly* in 1271 ib and remained with this family (which may originally have come from Cully in Normandy) as late as *John Curly* 1327 Banco, ~ *Corlu* 1347 Pat. The feudal affix appears to have been attracted later to the name of the moorland bird, the curlew (recorded as *curlu* a.1340, *corlue* 1377 OED).

CARLTON CLUMP, 1835 O, *v.* **clump**; it is *Carlton Earth* 1806 Map (either with **eorðe** in its sense 'earth or lair', as for the badger or fox, or **erð** 'ploughed land'). CARLTON CURLIEU HALL, 1846, 1863, 1877 White, 1925 Kelly, *Carlton Hall* 1831 Curtis, 1835 O, *v.* **hall**; note a pair of earlier halls evidenced by *atte Uphall* 1456 Fine (p) (*v.* **atte**, **up**), *v.* J. Turville-Petre, 'Overhall and Netherhall', JEPNS 31, 115–17. CARLTON GRANGE, 1972 *Surv*, *v.* **grange**. THE RECTORY, 1877 White, 1925 Kelly, *v.* **rectory**; its predecessor was *the Parsonage house* 1674, 1694, 1704, 1724 *Terrier*, *v.* **personage**. ST MARY'S CHURCH, *Church (St Mary)* 1846, 1863, 1877 White, 1925 Kelly; it is earlier recorded as *ecclesiam de Karletona* a.1219 RHug, ~ *de Carleton* 1220 MHW, ~ *de Karleton* 1240 RGros, *ecclesie de Carleton Curl(e)y* 1350, 1351 *Pat et passim* to 1443 *ib.* Note also *the Churchyard* 1674 *Terrier*, *v.* **churchyerd**. SHEEPTHORNS SPINNEY, *Sheepthorn* 1663 *Palmer*, *Sheep Thorns* 1806 Plan, *Sheepthorne thickett* 1664 *Palmer*, *Sheep Thorns Thicket* 1850 *TA* (*v.* **þiccett**), *Sheep-thorns Spinney* 1835 O (*v.* **spinney**), *Sheephorne Fox Cover* 1972 *Surv* (*v.* **cover(t)**), 'thorn-scrub amongst which sheep are able to graze', *v.* **scēp**, **þorn**.

FIELD-NAMES

In (a), forms presented without dates are 1972 *Surv*; those dated 1756 and 1820 are *Palmer*; 18 are *Plan*; 1821 are *Terrier*. Forms throughout dated 1601 are *Deed*; those dated 1638 are Ipm; 1639, 1643, 1646, 1647, 1650, 1652, 1653, 1657, 1659, 1660, 1663, 1664, 1665, 1667, 1679, 1694, 1700, 1702, 1708, 1709 and e.18 are *Palmer*; 1674, 1679, 1703, 1704 and 1724 are *Terrier*; 1699 are Nichols; 1710 are *EnclA*.

(a) (the) Ash Cl 1820, 1850 (1652, 1663, 1664, 1674, *le Ash close* 1638), (the) Ash Mdw 1820, 1850 (e.18) (*v.* **æsc**); Ashley 1756 (*v.* **æsc**, **lēah**); Bankey Mdw 1850 (*v.* **banke**, **-ig**[3]); Far ~ ~, Baysleys Mdw 1850, Baysley Mdw 1972 (with the surn. *Bazeley*); Big Fd; Birds Mdw 1850 (with the surn. *Bird*); Boothys Mdw 1850 (prob. with the surn. *Booth* in the possessive case; otherwise '(land with) sheds or shelters', *v.* **bothe**); Brick Cl 1821 ((*the*) *Brick(e) Close* 1679, 1694, 1703, 1704, 1724, *the Bricke Close or fielde*, *the Bricke fielde* 1674, 'land on which bricks are made', *v.* **brike**); Brook Fd 1850 (1710, *Brookfields* 1653, 1663, 1664, 1667, *Brookfield Meadow* e.18), Brook Mdw 1850 (*the Brucke* 1601, *v.* **brōc**); Burnett Cl, Burnett Fd 1850, Burny Fd 1972 ((*the*) *Burnett field* 1659, 1660, 1663, 1664, 1708; with the surn. *Burnett*); Busshey Cl 18 (*v.* **busshi**); Butchers Mdw (with the surn. *Butcher*); the Cawdell 1850 (*Cawdewell close* 1638, *Cawdell Seike Close* 1664 (*v.* **sík**), *v.* **cald**, **wella**); Chestnut Fd (prob. with reference to the sweet chestnut tree (*Castanea sativa*), the wood of which was of considerable use in farming, such as for fencing, gate posts, props and poles etc.); the Church Walk 1820 (*v.* **walk** and St Mary's Church *supra*); Clump Fd, Clump Mdw (*v.* Carlton Clump *supra*); the Coombs 1850, the Combs 1972 ((*the*) *Combes closes* 1652, 1663, *Coome Closes* 1664, *v.* **cumb**); Nether ~ ~, Upper Cross Hill 1756, Over Cross Hill Mdw 1850 (*v.* **uferra**), Bottom ~, Top Crawsell 1972 (*Crosehill close* 1660, *Crosse Hill* 1663, *Nether Cross Hill*

1710, *v.* **cros**, **hyll** and *Carleton crose* in adjacent Burton Overy f.ns.(b)); the Croft 1850, 1972 (*v.* **croft**); Dale Fd 1850 (*Dales field(e)* 1659, 1660, 1674, *Dale's Field* 1710), Dale Mdw 1850 (*Dalesfield meadow* 1653) (either with the surn. *Dale* or with **dalr**); Deadmans Cl 1850, The Deadmine, Deadmine Mdw 1972 (*Deadman(s) Close* 1679, 1756, *v.* **dede-man**; at the parish boundary and thus poss. recording the discovery of a pagan Anglo-Saxon inhumation cemetery); Far Mdw 1850; The Glebe 1850 (*v.* **glebe**); Gravel Pit Cl 1820, 1850 (1646, 1663, *The Inward ~ ~ ~*, *The Out Gravel Pit Close* 1710, *Gravell Pits* 1653, *Gravel Pitts* 1657, 1664, 1667, *v.* **gravel**, **pytt**); Great Cl 1850 (18, *Mrs Bates Great Close* e.18); Hall Cl 1850 ((*the*) *Hall Close* 1652, 1653, 1663, 1674, 1710), Hall Fd 1972, Hall Yard 1820, 1850 (*Halleyard* 1359 Banco, *v.* **hall**, **geard**; with reference to a medieval hall, the present hall having been built c.1635, *v.* Carlton Curlieu Hall *supra*); Hill Cl 1850 (1667); Home Cl 1850, 1972 (*v.* **home**); Hop Cl 1820, 1850 (*the Hop close* 1652, 1663, *v.* **hoppe**); Inn Mdw 1850 (1664, 1710, *v.* **in**); Jobs Cl 1850, Jobes Cl 1972, Jobs Mdw 1850 (with the surn. *Job*); Lammas Cl 1850, Lamas ~ 1972 (*Lammas Close* 1638, 1660, 1663, 1664), Lammas Mdw 1850 (*v.* **lammas**); Leeches Mdw (with the surn. *Leach/Leech*, cf. Leaches Cl in neighbouring King's Norton f.ns. (a)); Little Mdw 1821, 1850 ((*the*) *little meadow* 1674, *the Litle Middo* 1679, *Little Medow* 1703, 1704); Long Fd 1972; Long Leys 1850 (1643, 1664, 1665, *West Long Leys* 1664, *v.* **lang**[1], **leys**); Long Mdw 18; Long Old Fd 1850 (1710, *the Long-old field* 1674, *Longold field* 1663, *Long Hold field* 1699 (poss. with **wald**, cf. Old Hill *infra*); Mill Fd 1850, East ~ ~, West Mill Fd 1972 (*the Millfield* 1663, *Little Mill field*, *the Upper Mill Field* 1710, *Millfield meade* 1653 (*v.* **mēd**), *Millfield* (*meadow*) *and windmill* 1663, 1664, 1667 (*v.* **wind-mylne**), *v.* **myln**, **feld**); New Mdw; Old Hill (*v.* **wald** and Long Old Fd *supra*); The Park 1820, 1850 (1694, *v.* **park**); Parson's Mdw 1972 (*v.* **persone**); Far ~ ~, Nether Shankton Leys 1850, Shangton Leys 1972 (*Shangton Cross(e) Leys* 1643, 1660, *Shanckton Crosse Leys* 1663, 1664, 1665 (*v.* **cros**, **leys**; evidently with reference to a standing boundary cross; note Cross Hill *supra*; otherwise *v.* **cross**), Shangton Mere 1972 (*v.* **(ge)mǣre**) (Shangton parish adjoins to the south-east); The Slade 1972, Slady Mdw 1850 (*Lancelades* 1663, *the Land Slade*, *Land Slade Close* 1708 (*v.* **land**), *Middle Land Slade Meadow* 1756, *v.* **slæd**); The Spinney 1820 (*v.* **spinney**); Spring Cl 1850 (*v.* **spring**[1]); Swinnel Cl 1850 (*Swinsell or Swynhill or Great Swinhill and Little Swinhill closes* 1639, *Swinsell or Swynhill or Great Swynhill and Little Swynhill* 1650, *Swinhill or Great Swinhill*, *Little Swinhill*, *Swinhill Close* 1709, *Swinsell or Swynhill Close*, *Little Swynhill Close* 1700, *Swine Hill Close* 1756, *Swine Hill Meadow* 1710, *v.* **swīn**, **hyll**); Tilt Fd 1850, Till Fd 1972, Tilt Mdw 1850 (*Tiltfield Close* 1646, *the Tiltfield* 1663, *Bigger Tell field* 1710, *v.* **tilð**); Tween Dykes, ~ ~ Mdw 1850, Twin Dykes, ~ ~ Mdw 1972 (*Twindicks* 1657, 1660, *Twindickes* 1659, *Twindikes* 1660, 1663, 1708, *v.* **twinn**, **dík**); the Upper Cl 1821 (1674, 1679 *et passim to* 1724; *v. Longhill Close*, *infra*); Upper Fd (1664, 1674, 1710, *Upper Field meadow* 1702, 1710); Warners Cl and Mdw 1821 (*Warners Close* 1674, 1679, 1694, 1703, 1704, 1724; with the surn. *Warner*).

(b) *Brownes closes* 1674, *Brunn's Close* 1710 (with the surn. *Brown*); *Cow close* 1638, 1664; *Hawes close* 1647, *Hawesfield* 1647, 1663, *Hawes's Field*, *Hawes's Meadow* 1710 (with the surn. *Hawes*); *Hecyning* (sic) 1664 (*v.* **hegning**); *Hemmings close* 1638 (with the surn. *Hemming(s)*, a reflex of the ON pers.n. *Hem(m)ingr* (ODan *Hem(m)ing*)); *Ilston gate close* 1638 (*v.* **gata**; Illston on the Hill lies 1½ miles to the north-east); *Kirke Lane* 1533 × 38 ECP (*v.* **kirkja**, **lane** and St Mary's Church *supra*); *the Langmore Closes* 1710 (*v.* **lang**[1], **mōr**[1]); *the Leys* 1660 (*v.* **leys**); *the Longhill Field* 1646, *Longhill Close or the Upper Close* 1710 (*v.* **lang**[1], **hyll** and the Upper Cl *supra*); *Mounthill* 1663 (*v.* **mont**, **hyll**); *Overfield close* 1646 (*v.* **uferra**); *Payretree* ~ 1664, *Peare tree Croft* 1674 (*v.* **pertre**, **croft**); (*the*) *Penn Close* 1643, 1660, 1665 (*v.* **penn**[2]); *the Upper Ground* 1704 (*v.* **upper**, **grund**).

Cranoe

CRANOE

Craweho 1086 DB, *Crauueho* 1295 *Peake* (p)
Craueho 1086 DB
Crowenhou c.1130 LeicSurv, *Crowenhowe* 1241 RGros, *Crowenho* 1247 Ass
Crawenho 1198 P, 1199 FF *et passim* to 1250, 1255 Fine *et freq* to 1326 Banco, 1330 (16) *SlCart et passim* to 1343 Ipm, 1344 Cl, *Crawenhoe* 1285 Banco, c.1291 Tax, 13 (16) *SlCart*, 1328 Ass
Cravenhou 1254 Val, 1257 Ch *et passim* to 1336 Pat (p), *Cravenhowe* 1354 AD (p), *Crauenhou* 1274 RGrav, 1300 ChancW, 1300 Pat, *Crauenhowe* c.1291 Tax
Craunhou 1220 MHW
Cranehou 1306 *Peake*, 1306 (16) *SlCart*, 1342 (1449) *WoCart*, 1349 (16) *SlCart*, *Cranehowe* 1337 *Rut*, 1357, 1375 Pat, 1428 FA, *Craneho(e)* 1369, 1386 Banco, 1519 EpCB, 1524 Ipm *et passim* to 1612, 1626 LML, *Cranehoo* 1518 Visit, 1519 EpCB, 1576 LibCl, 1576 LEpis
Cranhou 1349 Inqaqd, 1350 Pat, *Cranhowe* 1383 ib, 1405 PRep, *Cranho(e)* 1519 EpCB, 1614, 1626 LML
Craynowe 1486 ECP, *Creyno* 1487 Cl
Cranow(e) 1349 (16) *SlCart*, 1350 Banco *et passim* to 1550 *LCh*, 1619 LML, *Crano(e)* 1604 SR, 1606, 1609 *Bru et freq*

'The hill-spur frequented by crows', *v.* **crāwe** (**crāwena** gen.pl.), **hōh**. The township is situated on the side of a small spur of land which rises steeply from the broad valley of the river Welland.

CARDIGAN ARMS (P.H.) (lost), *Cardigan Arms* 1863, 1877 White, 1925 Kelly; named from *the Earl of Cardigan, lord of the manor* 1863 White. CHURCH HILL, *the Church hill* 1606 *Terrier*, cf. *Church Hill Road* 1828 *EnclA*, *v.* St Michael's Church *infra*. CRANOE LODGE, 1846 White, *Cranhoe Lodge* 1824 O, *v.* **loge**. THE GRANGE, *v.* **grange**. HORSE AND TRUMPET (P.H.) (lost), *Horse and Trumpet* 1846 White; may be an earlier name for the Cardigan Arms *supra*. The 7th Earl of Cardigan with his 11th Hussars led the Charge of the Light Brigade at Balaclava in 1854; but otherwise a popular 18th-cent. name from coaching days, *v.* Cox[1]. THE OLD RECTORY is *The Rectory* 1863, 1877 White, 1925 Kelly, *v.* **rectory**; earlier is *the Parsonage house* 1606, 1690 *Terrier* (*v.* **personage**), also called *the mantion house* 1706, *the Mansion House* 1706 (18), 1745 (*v.* **mansion-house**). ST MICHAEL'S CHURCH, *Church (St Michael)* 1846, 1863, 1877 White, 1925 Kelly; it is earlier recorded as *ecclesie de Craunhou* 1220 MHW, *ecclesiam de Crowenhowe* 1241 RGros. Note also *the Church yard* 1606, 1679 *Terrier et passim* to 1821 *ib*, *v.* **churchyerd**. SCHOOL LANE. WELHAM LANE is *Welham Road* 1828 *EnclA*, Welham lying 2 miles to the south.

FIELD-NAMES

In (a), forms presented without dates are 1828 *EnclA*; those dated 1824 are O; 1863 are White. Forms throughout dated 1511, 1587, 1607, 1608, 1609 and 1637 are *Bru*; those dated 1601, 1606, 1679, 1690, 1694, 1706, 1706 (18) and 1745 are *Terrier*.

(a) Allam Cl, ~ ~ Mdw (with the surn. *Allam*; cf. *Ricardus Alum* 1327 SR of Leics.); Church Fd (*v.* St Michael's Church *supra*); Dent's Great Cl (with the surn. *Dent*); East Fd; Fallow Fd 1824 (cf. *Fallow Close* 1637, *v.* **falh**); Far Cl; Goadby Bridle Way (*v.* **brīdel**; Goadby lies 2 miles to the north-west); Hallaton Foot Way (*v.* **fote-waye**; Hallaton lies 2 miles to the north-east); House Cl; Kibworth Rd (Kibworth Beauchamp lies 5 miles to the south-west); Meadow Cl; The Pound (*v.* **pund**); Radley Fd (*Radley feilde* 1637, *the Nether Radley Field* 1679, *v.* **rēad**, **lēah**, **feld** and *Radley gutter*, *infra*); The Saltway 1863 (*v.* **salt**[1], **weg**; it is *Salters gate* 1606, 1679 *et passim* to 1745, *Soltors Gate* 1706, *v.* **saltere**, **gata**; alternative names for the Roman Gartree Road which runs south-east from Leicester towards Medbourne and was used in the Middle Ages as a salters' route); Slawston Bridle Way (*v.* **brīdel**), Slawston Foot Way (*v.* **fote-waye**) (Slawston lies one mile to the south-east); Stone Pit Cl (*v.* **stān-pytt**); Townside Fd (*v.* **tūn**, **sīde**).

(b) (*the furlong*) *Against the Hill* 1601, 1679, 1694, 1706 (18), (*the forlong*) *againest the hill* 1706 (*v.* **furlang**) (*v.* **ageynst**); (*the furlong*) *Beneath the Towne* 1601, *Below the Town* 1745 (*v.* **benethe**, **tūn**); *Josiah Bents hard Layes* 1745 (*v.* **heard**, **leys**); (*the*) *Borrough*(*e*) *fielde* 1601, 1606, *Burrow Feilde* 1637, *Burrough* ~ 1679, 1690, 1694, *Bor*(*r*)*ough Field* 1706, 1706 (18) (*v.* **feld**; one of the great open-fields of the township), *Borrough Hill* 1606, (*the*) *Burrough hill* 1679, 1694, 1706 (18), *Burrowe* ~ 1694, *the Bor*(*r*)*ough hill* 1706, 1706 (18) (*v.* **berg**, **hyll**); *Brode Meadow* 1637 (*v.* **brād**); *the brooke* 1606 (*v.* **brōc**); *Bushy Banks* 1637 (*v.* **busshi**, **banke**); *Cochcraft* 1679, *Cotchcraft* 1694, 1706, *Catch Croft* 1706 (18) (*v.* **cot**, **croft**; with dial. **cotch** 'a cottage', cf. Cotch Ferns, Ru 205 and Cotch Platt, Ru 209); (*the*) *Church lane* 1606, 1745 (*v.* **lane** and St Michael's Church *supra*); *the*

Cow(e) Pasture 1606, 1637, 1745 (*v.* **cū**, **pasture**); *Cranohe* ~ 1606, *Cranoe Close* 1607, 1608, 1609, 1637); *Cranoe Cross* 1637 (*v.* **cros**); *the drift way* 1606 (*v.* **drift**); *greene gate* 1606, *Greengate* 1637 (*v.* **grēne**[1], **gata**); *the Haggs* 1745 (*v.* **hǫgg**); *the Hall Close* 1606, *the Hall yard* 1606 (*v.* **geard**) (*v.* **hall**); *Hallaton Nookes* 1608, 1609 (*v.* **nōk**; Hallaton parish adjoins to the north-east); *Hamsgate* 1679, 1694 *et passim* to 1745 (*v.* **hamm**, **gata**); *Harborough Way* 1606 (*v.* **weg**; Market Harborough lies 5 miles to the south-west); *the highe waie* 1601, *the kings high way* 1606 (*v.* **king**, **hēah-weg**); *the hill furl'* 1601, (*the furlonge*) *on the hill* 1606 (*v.* **furlang**), *the Hill* 1745; *Holiewell furlong* 1606 (*v.* **hālig**, **wella**); *Innam Close* 1637, *the Inhame Close* 1706, 1706 (18), *Innam Leys* 1587 (*v.* **leys**) (*v.* **innām**); *Langham leas* 1601, 1637, 1706, ~ *leies* 1606, ~ *leyes* 1606, 1679, 1694, ~ *Lays* 1745, *Langham leas fielde* 1601, *Langham leies Fielde* 1606, *Langham Lays Field* 1745 (*v.* **feld**; one of the great open-fields), *Langham leas forelong* 1706, *Langham Leys Furlong* 1706 (18) (*v.* **furlang**), *Langham Lays Hill* 1745 (*v.* **lang**[1], **hamm**, **leys**); *the Litle meadowe* 1606, *the Little meadow* 1679, 1694, 1706 (18), 1745, *the Litle Medow* 1706; (*the*) *Long Meadow* 1637, 1745 (*v.* **lang**[1]); *the Mill Field* 1745, *milne hedge furlonge* 1601 (*v.* **furlang**), *the mill hedge* 1606, *the Milne hedge* 1679, *the mill hagg* (sic) 1706, 1706 (18) (evidently a Terrier miscopying and not a reflex of **hǫgg** despite *the Haggs*, *supra*), *Mill Hedge* 1745 (*v.* **hecg**), *the mill moote* 1606, *little Miln moote* 1679, *little mill moote* 1694, *the lit(t)le mill mote* 1706, 1706 (18), *the moote furl'* 1601 (*v.* **mote**) (*v.* **myln**; with reference to a windmill set on an artificially raised mound; note *the Wyndmylle* 1511, *v.* **wind-mylne**); *Nether End* 1745 (*v.* **ende**); (*the*) *Nether feild* 1601, ~ ~ *Field* 1690 *et passim* to 1745, *Neather Feilde* 1637 (*v.* **neoðera**, **feld**; one of the great open-fields); *Nook End* 1745 (*v.* **nōk**, **ende**); *North Feilde* 1637 (*v.* **norð**, **feld**); *Nutts Nook* 1745 (*v.* **nōk**; poss. with the surn. *Nutt* in the possessive case rather than with **hnutu**; the surn. is an original by-name for a man with a round head or with a brown complexion, cf. Nutts Leys in Kibworth Beauchamp f.ns. (a)); *the Old Enclosure* 1690 (*v.* **enclosure**); *the Parsonage ground* 1606 (*v.* **grund**), *the Parsonage meadow* 1606 (*v.* **personage**); *the Pikes* 1601, 1745, *the Pike Furlong* 1679, 1694, 1706 (18), *the pike forelong* 1706 (*v.* **furlang**) (*v.* **pīc**); *Radley gutter* 1637 (*v.* **goter** and Radley Fd *supra*); *Thornie meddowe* 1606, *Thorn(e)y meadow* 1637, 1679, 1694, 1706 (18), 1745, *Thorney Medow* 1706 (*v.* **þornig**); *Thranghlie* 1601, *Thrallie* 1637, *Thrally* 1679, *Thralley* 1694, *Thranghlie field(e)* 1601, 1606, *Thralley* ~ 1690, 1694, *Thrally Field* 1679, 1706, 1706 (18), 1745 (*v.* **feld**; one of the great open-fields) (prob. 'the dense wood', *v.* **þrang**, **lēah**; OE *þrang* is recorded only as a noun meaning 'a throng, a crowd', but here it appears to be used adjectivally in the fashion of its reflex ME *thrang* 'thick, dense'); *Three Roode Riggs* 1637, *Three rood rigg(e)s* 1679, 1694, 1706 (*v.* **þrēo**, **rōd**[3], **hryggr**); *the Town(e)s end* 1679, 1694, 1706 (*v.* **tūn**, **ende**); *Upper Meadow* 1679, 1694, *the uper medow* 1706 (*v.* **upper**); *Wellham hedg* 1679, *Whellham* ~ 1706, *Whelham Hedge* 1706 (18) (*v.* **hecg**; the parish boundary hedge with Welham which adjoins to the south), *Wellham hedg furlong* 1679, *Welham hedge Furlong* 1694 (*v.* **furlang**), *Wellham Nook* 1745 (*v.* **nōk**); *Willow sick Furlong* 1679, *Willoseek forlong* 1706, *Willoseek Furlong* 1706 (18) (*v.* **wilig**, **sík**, **furlang**); *the Wood Close* 1679, *Wood Nook* 1637 (*v.* **nōk**) (*v.* **wudu** and note *Thranghlie*, *supra*); *Wm. Worths Piece* 1745 (*v.* **pece**).

Drayton

DRAYTON

Dreitun 1041 × 57 (m.12) HCand, *Dreiton*' 1186, 1187 P, 1231 Fine, 1209 × 35 RHug, *Dreyton*' Hy 3 *Crox*

Draitone e.12, 13 *Peake*, *Draitun* a.1150 *ib* (p), *Draiton*' 1163, 1166 P *et passim* to 1384 *Peake*, 1394 Ipm, (~ *iuxta Eston* l.13 *Peake*, 1308 Ass), *Draitona* 12 (p), e.13 *Peake*, a.1219 RHug

Draytone m.13 HCand, l.13, 13, 1347 *Peake*, 1391 × 1405 HP, *Drayton* p.1150, 12, e.13 *Peake et freq*, (~ *iuxta Brynghirst* 1381 *ib*, ~ *iuxta Brynghurst* 1453 *ib*), (~ *iuxta Wyland* 1422 *ib*), (~ *iuxta Wyland* 1422 *ib*, ~ *iuxta Wiland* 1466 *ib*), *Draython*' e.13, 1433 *ib*, *Draytune* e.13 *ib*

Draton 1529 *Peake*

'The farmstead, village at the steep slope where hauling is necessary', *v*. **dræg**, **tūn**. The township is at the foot of a hill which rises evenly 250 ft in a half mile. The modern road from Drayton to Nevill Holt takes this gradient directly in two straight stages and probably follows the line of the early trackway. The suffixes refer to neighbouring Great Easton and Bringhurst and to the river Welland.

BROOKFIELD HOUSE FM. DRAYTON HO. GREAT EASTON RD, Great Easton lying one mile to the north-east. THE HALL, a medieval hall recorded in f.ns. (b). HILLSIDE. HOLT YARD. MAIN ST. MANOR FM, *v*. **maner**. MEDBOURNE RD, Medbourne lying 2 miles to the north-west. NEVILL HOLT RD, Nevill Holt lying one mile to the north. PLOUGH (P.H.) (lost), *Plough* 1846 White, 1925 Kelly, *Plough Inn* 1877 White. ST JAMES'S CHAPEL, *Chapel (St James)* 1925 Kelly; earlier is recorded *capella de Drayton* 1330 *Pat* (with MLat *capella* 'a chapel') and *ecclesiam de Draitona* a.1219 RHug (with MLat *ecclesia* 'a church'). Now it is a tiny, one-celled chapel which was out of religious use until remodelled 1878–9. WATSON'S GORSE, *v*. **gorst**; *the Hon. R. Watson* 1846 White was at this date a major landowner in the parish.

FIELD-NAMES

In (a), names presented without dates are 1804 *EnclA*; those dated 1805 are *Surv*; 1806 are *Plan*. Forms throughout dated 12, c.1200, c.1250, l.13, 13, 1312, 1316, 1332, 1335, 1340, 1351, 1358, 1359, 1361, 1368, 1381, 1420, 1425, 1438, 1443 and 1445 are *Peake*; those dated 1312, 1332, 1359, 1375 and 15 are *Deed*; 1578 are Pat; c. 1700 are *Terrier*.

(a) Ashley Mdw (land bordering Ashley parish which lies beyond the river Welland in Northants); Crabtree (*v*. **crabtre**); Cuckoo Cl 1804, 1806 (alluding to the cuckoo bird (*Cuculus canorus*)); Hill Fd 1804, 1805 (*le hilfeld* 1312, *Hill Feild* c.1700, *v*. **hyll**, **feld**; one of the early great open-fields of the township); Holt Bridge, Holt Hedge (*v*. **hecg**; a parish boundary hedge) (Nevill Holt adjoins to the north-west); Meadow Fd 1804, 1805 (*Meadow feild* c.1700; one of the great open-fields); Presgrave Fd 1804, 1805 (*Presgraue feild* c.1700, *v*. **feld**; another of the open-fields, this bordering the deserted village of *Prestgrave*, a site now in Nevill Holt parish; a great field perh. to be identified with (*in*) *campo orientali* 1312 (with MLat *campus* 'a field' and *orientalis* 'eastern')).

(b) *Baneland* 1312 (*v*. **bēan**, **land**); *Barehers* 1332 (poss. 'the bare hill-top', *v*. **bær**[1], **herse**, although a disparaging 'Bare Arse' may also be thought of (with **ears**), referring to unproductive land, as could be the case in the later *Barearse hill* in Goadby f.ns. (b); *v*. *Bareherse*/*Barearse* in Hallaton f.ns. (b)); *Barnakesthyng* 1438 (*v*. **thing**; cf. *Alicia de Bernak* c.1250 and *Hugo de Bernak* l.13, of a family in origin from Barnack in Northants.); *Bascotesthyng* 1381 (*v*. **thing**; with the surn. *Bascote* of a family originally from Bascote, 32 miles to the south-west in Warwks.); *Bersaker* 1351 (*v*. **berse**, **æcer**); *Bowdon londe* 1443, 1445 (*v*. **land**; the first word may be a toponym ('the curving hill', *v*. **boga**, **dūn**) or land in some way connected with Bowden (*Bowdon* 1430), 6 miles to the south-west, or a surn. *Bowdon* derived from the p.n.); *Carltonholm* 1340 (*v*. **holmr**; land beside the river Welland which here borders East Carlton in Northants.); *le Cotch Leys* 1578 (*v*. **cot**, **leys**; here with dial. **cotch**); *Cotes peice furlong* c.1700 (*v*. **cot**, **pece**, **furlang**); *Depedale* c.1200 (*v*. **dēop**, **dalr**); *Dodmerisdale* 1358 (*v*. **dæl**[1], poss. with an unrecorded OE masc. pers.n. *Dodemǣr* (cf. *Dudemǣr*, *v*. Feilitzen 224 n.12); the name is also recorded in adjoining Medbourne as *Dodemersdale* c.1230 and in Nevill Holt as *Dodemeredale* 1334); *Dokholm* 1340 (*v*. **docce**, **holmr**); *le Gatefurlong* 1312 (*v*. **gata**, **furlang**); *Godmanesslad* a.1250 (*v*. **slæd**; with the OE masc. pers.n. *Godmann*); *Goldiuethorn* 12, *Goldiuethornwang* 12, c.1200 (*v*. **vangr**) (*v*. **þorn**; with the OE fem. pers.n. *Goldgifu*); *le halle thing* 1438 (*v*. **hall**, **thing**); *Herewardescroft* 13 (*v*. **croft**), *Herewardissike* 1335, *Herewardisseke* 1345 (*v*. **sík**) (with the OE masc. pers.n. *Hereweard*); *Holefurew* c.1200, *Holuforu* 1335, *Holowforugh* 1425 (*v*. **hol**[2], **furh**); *Howes* 15, *Howeslonde* l.13 (*v*. **land**), *Houwisgate* 1312 (*v*. **gata**) (*v*. **hōh** (**hōs** nom.pl.)); *Howbyescroft* 1420 (*v*. **croft**; with the surn. *Hoby* of a family originally from Hoby, 18 miles to the north-west); *Huntewong* l.13 (*v*. **vangr**; either with the OE masc. pers.n. *Hunta* or with the ME surn. *Hunte* (ModE *Hunt*)); *le Kirkehaued* 1332 (*v*. **kirkja**, **hēafod** and St James's Chapel *supra*); *lusthornebroc* 12, *lusthornbroc* c.1200 (*v*. **lūs-þorn**, **brōc**); *the Moors* c.1700 (*v*. **mōr**[1]); *mylneholm* 1316, *Milneholm* 1335, 1339, 1359 (*v*. **holmr**), *le mylnewong* 1316, *le Milnewong*

1335 (*v.* **vangr**) (*v.* **myln**); *Northlangfurlang* c.1200, *Northlongfurlong* 1358, 1368 (*v.* **norð**, **lang**[1], **furlang**); *Playstowe* 1312, *le Westerplaystowe* 1312 (*v.* **wester**) (*v.* **pleg-stōw**); *Roheheges* 12, *le Rowehegges* a.1250, *Roweheggus* 1333 (*v.* **rūh**, **hecg** (in its sense 'a hedged enclosure')); *Rokeswelle* 1312 (*v.* **wella**; with the OE masc. pers.n. *Hrōc* or **hrōc**); *Saltresgate* c.1200, *Salteresgate* a.1250 (*v.* **saltere**, **gata**; with reference to the lost Roman road (Margary 571) running north-east from Medbourne towards Great Easton and Caldecott to meet Ermine Street at *Durobrivae* (Water Newton), used as a salters' route in the Middle Ages); *le Scharpel* 1312 (*v.* **scearpol**); *Sigrimeswro* c.1200 (*v.* **vrá**; with the ON masc. pers.n. *Sægrímr* (ODan *Segrim*)); *Silkinemede* c.1200 (*v.* **mēd**; poss. with **seolcen** 'silken', used figuratively to indicate the nature and quality of the grassland; or perh. a reduced **sīoluchamm* 'water-meadow with a gulley' (cf. *siolucham*(*m*) 990 (12) KCD 673 (S 874)) may be thought of; otherwise with the surn. *Silkin* (*v.* Reaney *s.n.*), but the date seems very early for such a surn.); *Steinland* c.1200 (*v.* **steinn**, **land**); *Stockes* c.1200 (*v.* **stocc**); *Stockuall Hollow* c.1700 (*v.* **stocc**, **wella**, **holh**); *Stokewong* 1312 (*v.* **stoc**, **vangr**); *Tasholm* 1312 (*v.* **holmr**; more forms are required, but poss. as first el. is the OE masc. pers.n. *Tǣsa*, or **tǣse**, or a reduced **tǣsel**); *Wdgate* c.1200 (*v.* **wudu**, **gata**); *West Willardesdik'* 1332 (*v.* **west**, **dík**; either with the OE masc. pers.n. *Wilheard* or with its ME surn. reflex *Willard*); *le Wrange* 12, *la Wrange* c.1200 (*v.* **wrang**; the OE adj. means 'crooked or twisted in shape', here evidently used as a sb. as 'the twisted one' to indicated a crooked piece of land).

East Langton

1. CHURCH LANGTON

Langetone 1086 DB, 1212 RBE (p), 1277 Hastings, *Langetona* Ric 1 ib (p), c.1245 AD, 1278 ChronPetr, *Langetun* 1189 (1332) Ch, *Langeton'* c.1130 LeicSurv, 1176 P (p) *et freq* to 1382 *Peake*, 1398 Fine *et passim* to 1465 *MktHPR*, 1472 *Peake*, *Langgeton'* p.1250 (1404) *Laz* (p), c.1291 Tax
Lagintone (sic) 1086 DB
Langtone 1086 DB, *Langtun* m.12 HCand, *Langtona* Hy 2 Dugd, *Langton* 1402, 1411 Cl, 1414 *Wyg* (p), 1439 *Peake et freq*
Lankton 1536 *Braye*, *Lancton* 1610 Speed, *Lanckton* 1724 LML

Affixes are added as:
Kirk(e) ~ 1305 Ipm, 1315 *Peake et passim* to 1327 Banco, 1462 Pat, *Kyrk(e)* ~ 1303 Ipm, 1315 *Peake et passim* to 1478 *ib*, 1523 *MktHPR*
Chirch(e) ~ 1316 FA, 1509 LP, *Church(e)* ~ 1518 Visit, 1535 VE *et passim* to 1610 Speed *et freq*

'The long village or estate', *v*. **lang**[1], **tūn**. Church Langton is styled *Church Towne* 1564 Nichols, 'the township with the church'. For the medieval and later affixes, *v*. **kirkja**, **chirche**, **churche**. A church may have existed here at least as early as the Norman period, since an effigy which is probably of this date is now located in the vestry passage of the present building, the earliest fabric of which is of the late 13th century. Church Langton may well have been the focus of the original Langton which stretched as far as East Langton, now a separate township a half mile to the south-east. Note *the township known as East Langton or Church Langton* 1846 White, *v*. East Langton *infra*.

CHURCH CAUSEWAY, *v*. **caucie**. THE RECTORY, 1877 White, *The Rectory House* 1821 *Terrier*, *v*. **rectory**; earlier is *the Mansion house* (*of the Rectory*) 1601, 1694, 1703, 1712, 1715, 1745 *ib*, *v*. **mansion-house**. ST ANN'S WELL, 1745 *Terrier*, *St Ans* ~ 1601 *ib*, *St Annes* ~ 1638 *ib*, *St*

Anns Well 1674, 1703, 1712, 1715 *ib*, *v*. **wella**; dedicated to St Anne, a patroness of wells who interceded for the childless. It is possible that Anne in the names of wells replaced a more ancient name of similar sound, alluding to a Celtic mother goddess such as Anu, a goddess of prosperity, *v*. J. Scherr, 'Names of springs and wells in Somerset', Nomina 10 (1986), 85–7, P. MacCana, *Celtic Mythology*, revised edn, London 1983, 132 and *The Place-Names of Roman Britain*, ed. A. L. F. Rivet and C. C. Smith, London 1979, 250 *s.n.* Anava. ST PETER'S CHURCH, *the Church*(*e*) 1601, 1674 *Terrier et passim* to 1745 *ib*, *Church (St Peter)* 1846, 1863, 1877 White, 1925 Kelly; it is earlier recorded as *ecclesie de Langeton* 1220 MHW, 1361 *Pat*, *ecclesie parochialis de Churche Langeton* 1554 *ib* (with MLat *parochialis* 'parochial'). Note also *the Church Yard* 1712, 1715, 1821 *Terrier*, *v*. **churchyerd**. STONTON RD, Stonton Wyville lying 2 miles to the north-east.

2. EAST LANGTON

For forms and interpretation of the place-name Langton, *v*. Church Langton *supra*.

Distinguishing affixes are added as:

Est ~ 1211 FF, 1243 Cur *et freq* to 1536 *Braye*, *East* ~ 1610 Speed *et freq*

Estere ~ p.1270 *Brai*

East Langton is recorded as *Est Towne* 1564 Nichols, 'the eastern township'. The affixes *Est* ~ and *Estere* ~ are from OE **ēast** 'east' and **ēastere** 'more easterly', so designated in contrast to West Langton *infra*, now a separate civil parish. By c.1130 LeicSurv, East Langton with Church Langton is distinguished from West Langton which is styled *alia Langeton'* (with MLat *alia* '(the) other').

BELL INN (lost), (*The*) *Bell* 1846, 1863 White, 1925 Kelly, *Bell Inn* 1877 White. BULL (P.H.) (lost), *Bull* 1846, ~ *Inn* 1863, 1877 White. DEAN COTTAGE, *Deene Cottage* 1925 Kelly. EAST LANGTON GRANGE, 1873, 1875 Sale, 1925 Kelly, *The Grange* 1863, 1877 White, *v*. **grange**. GRANGE FM. LANGTON BROOK. LODGE FM, 1877 White, *v*. West Langton Lodge *infra*. MELTON RD, Melton Mowbray lying 16 miles to the north. PARK FM (COTTAGE PARK 2½"), *v*. **park**. THORPE LANGTON RD, Thorpe Langton lying one mile to the east. WEST LANGTON LODGE,

1877 White, *v.* **loge**. WIDE BRIDGE, 1835 O; it is *White Bridge* 1843, 1872 Sale, 1861 *Surv*.

FIELD-NAMES

In (a), forms dated 1843, 1872 and 1875 are Sale; those dated 1861 are *Surv*. Forms throughout dated 1265 are Pat; those dated 1268 are Cur; p.1270 are *Braye*; 1315, 1439 and 1478 are *Peake*; 1324 are AD; 1601, 1625, 1638, 1674, 1694, 1703, 1712, 1715 and 1745 are *Terrier*.

(a) Crab Piece 1875 (*v.* **crabbe**, **pece**); Fludes Leys 1843, 1861, 1872 (*v.* **leys**; with the surn. *Flude*); The Home Cl 1875 (*v.* **home**); Horsey Cl 1843, 1861, 1872 (*v.* **hors**, **-ig**[3]); Redon Cl, Far Redon, ~ ~ Mdw 1843, 1872, Redow Cl, Far Redow, ~ ~ Mdw 1861 (*Red(d)owe* 1601, 1625, *Reddow* 1638, 1694, 1703, *Redow feild* 1601, 1638, *Redowe feilde* 1638, *Readow* ~ 1674, *Readon Feild* 1694, *Reddow field* 1703, 1712, 1715 (*v.* **feld**; one of the great open-fields of the Langtons, later called *Upper Field* 1745), *Redome* 1601, 1638, *Reedeholme* 1674, *Reedom* 1694, *Reed(h)am* 1712, 1715, 1745, ~ *Gap* 1715, 1745 (*v.* **gap**); the 19th-cent. forms *Redon* and *Redow* appear to be alternative styles for the same feature, both seemingly having developed either from an original 'headland with red soil' (*v.* **rēad**, **hōh**), or from a 'headland growing with reeds' (*v.* **hrēod**, **hōh**), with confusion in the earliest surviving spellings of the generic rather as **holmr** (> **hamm**) (suggesting the specific as the watery *hrēod* rather than *rēad*, although an open-field's name would sit more happily with the latter specific and its eventual name *Upper Field* would suggest a site away from water); the notion that two toponyms may have become confused here (i.e. a 'headland with red soil', *v.* **rēad**, **hōh** and a 'water-meadow growing with reeds', *v.* **hrēod**, **holmr**) is a tempting alternative; note *Redome gates* in adjacent Thorpe Langton f.ns. (b)); Top Cl 1875 (*v.* **top**).

(b) *Achre heads* 1601, ~ *hades* 1625, *Acre hades* 1674, 1703, 1715, 1745, *Acer hads* 1712 (*v.* **æcer**, **hēafod**); *Blackeleys* 1674 (*v.* **blæc**, **leys**; in eModE, *black* 'fertile' may be contrasted with *white* 'infertile'); *Bowdon* ~ 1601, 1674, *Bowden* ~ 1625, *Boudon Brooke* 1638, *Bowden brook* 1694, 1712, 1715, 1745 (*v.* **brōc**; forms part of the parish boundary with Great Bowden to the south); *Brinckes* 1601, *the brinkes* 1625, *Brinckes* 1638, *Brinks* 1674, 1694 *et passim* to 1745 (*v.* **brink**); *Tho. Buzzards hadland* 1694, 1703 (*v.* **hēafod-land**); *Carring* 1712, *Kirring gate* 1601, 1625, *Kerring* ~ 1638, *Caring* ~ 1674, *Carring* ~ 1694, 1712, 1715, *Carrying gate* 1745 (*v.* **gata**), *Over Carringate* 1703, 1712, 1715, *Over Carrying gate* 1745 (*v.* **ofer**[3]) (*v.* **cerring**; with Scand influence on the initial consonant); *Caudwell plank(e)* 1625, 1745, *Cawdell Plank* 1694, 1712, 1715 (*v.* **cald**, **wella**, **planke**); *the Churche Cloase* 1601, *the Church Close* 1694, *the Church clos(s)e side* 1625, 1703, 1715 (*v.* **sīde**), *the Far* ~ ~, *the Near Church Close* 1745 (*v.* **clos(e)**), (*the*) *Churchgate* 1625, 1638 (*v.* **gata**), (*one peece called*) *the Church florthe* 1601, (*a peece called*) *the churche floore*, (*one peece called*) *the churche floore* (*at the nether end of Clarnes leas*), (*one peece called*) *the church floore* (*in tybstaile*) 1625, *The Church Florth* 1638, (*a peice called*) *the Church Flore* 1694, *the Church Floor* 1715, *the Church* *floor* (*in Tipstell*) 1712, (*a Piece called*) *the Church Floor* (*in Tibstill*), (*a Piece called*) *the Church Floor* (*at the End of Clarnis Leys*) 1745 (*v. Clarnes Leaes* and *Tybstayle*, *infra*), *the Greate* ~ ~, *the Litle Church flower* 1674, *the Great* ~ ~, *the Little Church floowr* 1712, *the Little Church floor* 1715 (*v.* **flōr**; land endowed for the upkeep of the floor of the parish church; the 1601 record describes the ground as meadowland, so that reference seems to be to funds for the renewal of tiling or paving rather than for continual fresh rushes), (*the*) *Churchgate* 1625, 1638 (*v.* **gata**), *the Church Goale* 1674, *the Church Gole* 1745, *the Churche goale furlonge* 1601, (*the*) *Church Goale Furlong* 1694, 1703, 1712, 1715 (*v.* **furlang**) (*v.* **goule**), *the Churche heway* 1601, *the Church way* 1625, 1638 *et passim* to 1745 (*v.* **hēah-weg**, **weg**; prob. early allusions to Church Causeway *supra*), *the Churche Leaes* 1601, *the Church Leas* 1625, 1638, ~ ~ *lay*(*e*)*s* 1694, 1712, ~ ~ *leays* 1703, 1715, ~ ~ *Leys* 1745 (*v.* **leys**), *the Church Side* 1712 (*v.* **sīde**) (all with reference to St Peter's Church *supra*); *Tho. Clarkes hadley* 1712 (*v.* **headley**); *Clarnes Leaes* 1601, ~ *Leas* 1625, 1638, *Clarness Lays* 1694, ~ *Leays* 1712, *Clarniss leays* 1715, *Clarnis Leys* 1745 (partly uncertain, *v.* **leys**; rather than a surn. as the first word, perh. 'headland between two streams', *v.* **clā**, **nese**); *Clay Hill* 1601, 1625 *et passim* to 1745, *Cley Hill* 1674 (*v.* **clǣg**); *cockedoale* 1601, ~ *dole* 1625, (*the*) *Cockdole* 1638, 1694 *et passim* to 1745 (*v.* **cocc**[1], **dāl**); *the Colepit way* 1712, *the Coal pit way* 1715 (*v.* **col-pytt**; a place where charcoal was made); *Len Colmans hadley* 1712 (*v.* **headley**), *Leonard Colemans headland* 1715 (*v.* **hēafod-land**); *John Cooper*(*s*) *hadland* 1601, 1625 (*v.* **hēafod-land**); *Crossegate* 1601, 1625, 1638, *Crose gate* 1674, *Cros*(*s*)*gate* 1694, 1703, 1712, *Crossgates* 1703, 1712, 1715, 1745 (*v.* **cross**, **gata**); *Job Dexters hadley* 1694 (*v.* **headley**) (for the local occurrence of the surn. *Dexter*, note *Johannes le Dextere* as early as 1262 RFL (ME *dextere* 'a dyer')); *docke achre* 1601, 1625, *Dockacre* 1694, 1703, 1745 (*v.* **docce**, **æcer**); *Edward sycke* 1601, 1625, *Edwards Sick* 1638, *Edward Sick* 1694, 1703 *et passim* to 1745 (*v.* **sík**; with the surn. *Edward*(*s*)); *farrgates*, *farr*(*e*)*gatts* 1601, *Fargates* 1625, 1638, *Fargate* 1674, 1694, 1715, 1745, *Farget*(*t*) 1694, 1703, 1712, 1715, *Fargett hedge* 1712, 1715 (*v.* **hecg**), *farrgatts way* 1601, *Fargate* ~ 1625, 1674, *Farget*(*t*) *way* 1703, 1712, 1715 (*v.* **weg**) (*v.* **feor**, **gata**); *Foxton hedge* 1601, 1625 *et passim* to 1745 (*v.* **hecg**; the parish boundary hedge with Foxton which adjoins to the south-west); *Frenches headland* 1674, ~ *hadland* 1694, 1703 (*v.* **hēafod-land**; with the surn. *French*); *the Glibe Grass*, *the Glibe Gress hadley* 1712 (*v.* **græs**, **headley**), *the Glibe hadland* 1712, *the Glebe headland* 1715, ~ ~ *hadland* 1745 (*v.* **hēafod-land**) (*v.* **glebe**); *la Graue* 1268 (p), 1315 (p) (*v.* **grāf**); *greate ten hades* 1625 (*v.* **tēn**, **hēafod**); *Lawrence Greene his Backside* 1674 (*v.* **bak-side**); *Greeneham* 1638, 1712, *Over greenham* 1601, 1625, *Over Greeneholme* 1674, *Over Greenhome* 1694 (*v.* **uferra**), *Upper Greenham* 1715, 1745, *Greenham brydge* 1601, ~ *brigge* 1625, ~ *bridge* 1638, 1745, *Greenholme bridge* 1694, 1703 (*v.* **brycg**) (*v.* **grēne**[1], **hamm**; with later attraction to **holmr**); *Grescraft* 1712, 1715 (*v.* **græs**, **croft**); *Mr Hawfords hadley* 1601, *Mr Halfords hadlea* 1625 (*v.* **headley**); *Heyffer brydge* 1601, *Heffer bridge* 1625, 1638, *Heifor* ~ 1694, 1745, *Heiford Bridge* 1712, 1715 (*v.* **brycg**), *heyffers guttur* 1601, *Heffer Gutter* 1625, 1638, *Heifer* ~ 1694, *Heifers* ~ 1712, *Heifords* ~ 1715, *Heifers Gutter* 1745 (*v.* **goter**) (*v.* **hēahfore**); *Hen Acre* 1674 (*v.* **henn**, **æcer**); *the hoggs* ~ 1601, 1625, *Hoges* ~ 1674, *the Hog pasture* 1694, 1703, 1712, 1715, 1745, ~ ~ *paster* 1712 (*v.* **hogg**, **pasture**); *Jacomes house* 1601, *Jakims* ~ 1625, *Jacombs house* 1694 (cf. *William Jacome* 1601, ~ *Jakim* 1625; the surn. *Jacome*/*Jakim* is from *Jacun*/*Jakin*, diminutives of *Ja*(*c*)*k*); *Lanckhill* 1601, 1625, 1638, *Langhill* 1694, 1703, 1712, 1715, 1745 (*v*. **lang**[1], **hyll**); *atte Lane* 1265 (p) (*v*. **atte**, **lane**); *Leay hill* 1715 (*v*. **ley**); *Job Lesters hadleay* 1703 (*v*. **headley**), *Lestors Hadland* 1745 (*v*. **hēafod-land**) (the surn. is an early 17th-cent. form of *Leicester*); *Long hades* 1712, 1715, 1745 (*v*. **hēafod**); *the Long hadland* 1694, 1703, 1745 (*v*. **hēafod-land**); *Meare Heads* 1638 (*v*. **hēafod**), *the mear* 1712, 1715, *the Meer* 1745 (*v*. **(ge)mǣre**; of the great *Northe feilde*, *infra*); *Mickle* ~, *Myckle Medow*(*e*) 1601, 1625, *Mickle Meadow* 1638, 1694, 1715, 1745, *Mickel medow* 1712, *Mickel Meadowe Bridge* 1674 (*v*. **brycg**) (*v*. **micel**, **mikill**); *the Mills* 1745, (*the*) *Milne Feild* 1601, 1638, *the Millfeilde* 1625, *the Milfeild* 1674, *Mill Feild* 1694, ~ *Field* 1712, 1715, 1745 (*v*. **feld**; one of the great open-fields), *Milnegate* 1601, (*the*) *Millgate* 1601, 1625 *et passim* to 1745 (*v*. **gata**), *Mill Hole* 1601, 1625 *et passim* to 1745 (*v*. **hol**[1]), *Milne Moores* 1638 (*v*. **mōr**[1]), *Milne mount*(*e*) 1601, 1703, *Mill mount* 1625 (*v*. **mont**) (*v*. **myln**); (*the*) *Moore* 1601, 1625 *et passim* to 1745, *moouer* 1712, *Litle Moore* 1601, (*the*) *Little Moor*(*e*) 1625, 1674 *et passim* to 1745, *Litle More* 1638, *Litell more* 1712 (*v*. **lȳtel**), *the Over moore* 1674 (*v*. **uferra**), (*the*) *Moore gate* 1601, 1674, 1694, *Mor*(*e*)*gate* 1625, 1712, *Moorgate* 1638, 1703, 1715, 1745, *Litle murgate* 1712 (*v*. **gata**), *Moore leyes* 1674, *more lays*, *mour layes* 1712, *Moor leayes* 1715 (*v*. **leys**), *Moore Willowes* 1674 (*v*. **wilig**) (*v*. **mōr**[1]); *Mosewellehyl* 1324, *Mussill Hill* 1601, 1625, 1638, *Mussyll* ~ 1625, *Mussell* ~ 1694, 1715, *Muszill* ~ 1703, *Muzzell* ~ 1712, *Mustell Hill* 1745 (*v*. **hyll**), *Mussill Hole* 1601, 1625, 1638, *Musell* ~, *Mussel* ~ 1694, *Mu*(*s*)*zell* ~ 1703, 1712, *Muszill* ~ 1703, *Mussell* ~ 1715, *Mustel Hole* 1745 (*v*. **hol**[1]), *Muswell* ~ ~ 1674, *Mussell hole hedge* 1715 (*v*. **hecg**) (*v*. **mos**, **wella**); *the Nether field* 1712, 1715, 1745 (*v*. **neoðera**, **feld**; one of the great open-fields, earlier called *West feild*, *infra*); *Northe feild* 1601, 1625, (*the*) *Northfeild* 1638, 1674, *North field* 1712, 1715 (*v*. **norð**, **feld**; another of the great open-fields, from 1703 also called *Whorle Feild*, *infra*); (*the*) *North*(*e*) *hills* 1601, 1625 *et passim* to 1745 (*v*. **norð**, **hyll**); *Open Close* 1674 (*v*. **open**; an enclosure without a permanent gate, perh. closed off by hurdles as necessary); *Oxhed* 1439, *Oxeheads* 1601, *Oxe hades* 1625, *Oxheades* 1674, *Great Oxe heades* 1601, ~ *Oxeheads* 1638, 1694, ~ *Oxheads* 1703, 1712, 1712, 1745, *Little Oxheads* 1674, 1694 (*v*. **oxa**, **hēafod**); *Paddock well* 1674, 1745 (*v*. **padduc**, **wella**); *Sir Edward Pickering's hadland* 1745 (*v*. **hēafod-land**); *Presborow*(*e*) *Hill* 1601, 1638, *Presbro* ~ 1712, *Presborough* ~ 1715, *Presborrow Hill* 1745 (*v*. **prēost**, **berg**); *Prescott hill* 1625 (*v*. **prēost**, **cot**); *Prestcroft* 1674 (*v*. **prēost**, **croft**); *Prestwell'* 1315 (*v*. **prēost**, **wella**); *Pryckshoome* 1601, *Prycksome* 1625, *Pricksho*(*l*)*me* 1638, 1694, 1715, *Prickesholme* 1674, *Pricsholme* 1703, *Pricksome* 1712, 1745 (*v*. **holmr**; with the surn. *Pryke*, from ME *prike* 'a point, a pointed weapon', the surn. prob. metonymic for a maker of such weapons); *Saltingham lea*(*e*)*s* 1601, 1625, ~ *leyes* 1674, ~ *Layes* 1694, ~ *l*(*e*)*ays* 1703, 1712, 1715, ~ *Leys* 1745 (*v*. **leys**; no surn. or p.n. Saltingham is recorded elsewhere in England, so this appears to be a toponym pertaining to local salt production (note Salt Pitts in the area of the former *West Feild*, for convenience placed with West Langton f.ns. (a) *infra*); thus poss. 'the brine-pit meadow' or 'the salt-place meadow', *v*. **salt**[1], **-ing**[2], **hamm**); *Sandwell* 1601 (*v*. **sand**, **wella**); *Short Lays* 1712, ~ *Leayes* 1715, ~ *Leys* 1745 (*v*. **leys**); *Southell* 1601, 1638, 1712, *South hill* 1625, 1715, 1745, *Southill* 1674 (*v*. **sūð**, **hyll**); *Spryggs gate* 1601, *Sprigs gate* 1625 (*v*. **gata**; cf. *John Sprygge* 1601, ~ *Sprigg* 1625); *Steppings* 1745 (*v*. **stybbing**); *Stonnings* 1625, *Stonning* ~ 1601, 1625, 1638, *Stoneing hades* 1674 (*v*. **hēafod**) (*v*. **stān**, **-ing**[2]); *Stonton Brook*(*e*) 1601, 1625 *et* *passim* to 1715, *Stoneton Brook* 1745 (*v.* **brōc**; a brook forming boundaries of Stonton Wyville and the Langtons); *Mr Strelleyes longe hadland* 1601, *Mr Strellys long hadland* 1625 (*v.* **hēafod-land**; the Strelley family presum. originated from the village of this name, 34 miles to the north-west in Notts.); *Sumpters hadland* 1601, 1625, ~ *Headland* 1638 (*v.* **hēafod-land**), ~ *hadleae of grasse* 1601, ~ *hadlea* 1625 (*v.* **headley**) (with the surn. *Sumpter*, from OFr *som(m)etier* 'the driver of a pack-horse'); *Thrallhill* 1601, 1625 *et passim* to 1745, *Thralhill* 1694, 1703 (*v.* **hyll**; prob. with **þrǣl** but otherwise with its surn. reflex *Thrall*); *Tong* 1638 (*v.* **tunge**); *the townsend* 1601, 1625, 1694, 1703 (*v.* **ende**), *the Town Side* 1745 (*v.* **sīde**) (*v.* **tūn**); *Turlangton Meire* 1601, 1625, ~ *meer(e)* 1674, 1694, ~ *mear* 1703, *Tur Langton Meer* 1745 (*v.* **(ge)mǣre**; Tur Langton parish adjoins to the north); *Tybstayle* 1601, *tybstaile* 1625, *Tybstall* 1694, *Tipssell* 1715 (*v.* **tægl**; perh. with the surn. *Tibbs* (although alternatively, one is tempted to think of *Tibb* as a familiar name for a cat)); *Upper Field* 1745 (*v.* **feld**; one of the great open-fields, earlier called *Redow feild*, *supra*); (*the*) *West feild* 1601, 1625, 1638, 1694, ~ *field* 1703, 1712, 1715, 1745 (*v.* **west**, **feld**; one of the great open-fields, from 1712 also called *the Nether field*, *supra*); (*the*) *Whorle* 1601, 1625, 1638, *Whurle* 1674, *Whorl* 1694, 1712, *Wherl* 1712, *Whorle Feild* 1694, *Whorl field* 1703, 1712, 1745 (*v.* **feld**; one of the great open-fields, earlier called *Northe feild*, *supra*), *Whorl(e) sick(e)* 1601, 1625 *et passim* to 1745, *Whirlesick* 1638 (*v.* **sík**) (*v.* **hwerfel**); *Wildemore* 1478, *Wyld Moore* 1601, *Wildmo(o)re* 1625, 1638 *et passim* to 1745, *Wildmoore hadley* 1694, 1745 (*v.* **headley**), *Wildmore h(e)adland* 1712, 1715 (*v.* **hēafod-land**) (*v.* **wilde**, **mōr**[1]); *Woodgate* 1601, 1625 *et passim* to 1745 (*v.* **wudu**, **gata**); *Woolon Baulkes* 1625 (*v.* **balca**), *the Woolands* 1745 (*v.* **wald**, **land**).

Evington

Evington is now part of the Borough of Leicester.

EVINGTON

Avintone 1086 DB (×2), *Avinton'* 1075 × 1108 Nichols, 1207 ClR, *Auintona* c.1160 Dane
Euinton' c.1130 LeicSurv, 1248 *Rut* (p) *et passim* to c.1292 *LCDeeds* (p), l.13 *CRCart* (p), *Euintona* p.1250 (1404) *Laz*, *Evinton(e)* 1219 Cur, 1219 RHug, 1220 MHW *et passim* to 1318 Pat, 1325 Inqaqd, *Evintona* 1156 (1318) Ch, Hy 2 Dugd, 1190 × 1204 France, *Evintun* c.1225 GildR (p), *Hevintone* 1166 RBE
Euynton' c.1250 (1404) *Laz*, 1313 *LCDeeds* (p) *et passim* to 1413, 1435 *Comp*, *Evynton'* Hy 3 *Hazlerigg* (p), 1272 Ipm *et passim* to 1384 Pat, 1425 Coram
Eventon(e) c.1200 Hastings, 1268 Misc, 1276 Cl (p), 1308 GildR (p), 1338 Banco, *Euenton'* 1273 *LCDeeds* (p)
Euinctun c.1215 RegAnt (p), *Euincton'* Hy 3 *Crox* (p)
Evington 1250 Cur, 1254 Val *et passim* to 1580 LEpis, 1610 Speed *et freq*, *Evyngton* 1285 Banco, c.1291 Tax *et passim* to 1335 Ipm, 1338 GildR (p) *et freq* to 1539 MinAccts, 1547 Chap, *Euyngton'* 1343 *LCDeeds* (p), 1370 *Wyg* (p) *et passim* to 1451, 1456 *Comp*

'The village, estate associated with or called after a man named Eafa', *v.* **-ingtūn**. *Eafa* is an OE masc. pers.n. In Leics., place-names of the Evington type appear to belong to the 8th cent. and may indicate a developing manorial structure. They are present in particular in a group in the west of the county, an area which was exploited comparatively late, *v.* Barrie Cox, 'Aspects of place-name evidence for early medieval settlement in England', *Viator* 11 (1980), 35–50 at 44–5.

THE COMMON, *v.* **commun**. CROWN HILLS, 1809 *Valuation*, *(the) Crown Hill* 1627 *Map*, 1690, 1708 (18) *Terrier*, 1835 O; poss. a reduced form of *Crowdon* 1477 (e.16) *Charyte*, 'crow hill', *v.* **crāwe**, **dūn**, with the late addition of *hill*; but if not, *v.* **crowne**. ELMS FM, *v.* **elm**. EVINGTON

BROOK, *Evyngton broke* 1477 (e.16) *Charyte*, *v.* **brōc**. EVINGTON GRANGE, 1877 White, *v.* **grange**. EVINGTON HALL, 1846, 1868, 1877 White, *v.* **hall**. EVINGTON HO., *Evington House* 1846, 1863, 1877 White, 1925 Kelly. EVINGTON LANE. EVINGTON LODGE, 1835 O, 1846 White, *The Lodge* 1690 *Terrier*, *v.* **loge**. EVINGTON PARK, *le Park* 1335 *Deed*, *the Par(c)ke* 1600 *Ct*, 1690 *Terrier*, *The Park* 1708 (18) *ib*, 1846 White, *Evington Parks* 1863, 1877 ib, *v.* **park**. HIGH LEAS, 1925 Kelly, *v.* **hēah**[1], **leys**. HIGH ST. HORSE AND GROOM (P.H.) (lost), *Horse and Groom* 1863, 1877 White, 1925 Kelly. HORSE AND JOCKEY (P.H.) (lost), *Horse and Jockey* 1846 White. HORSTON HILL, *horston* l.13 *Wyg*, *Horse Stone Hill* c.1740 *Coleman*, *Horston(e) Hill* 1756 *ib*, 1761 *Sherrard*, 1809 *Valuation*, 1878 *PK*, 1907 *Surv*, *Harston Hill* 1757 *Coleman*, '(the hill of) the boundary stone', *v.* **hār**[2], **stān**. HYSSOP'S LANE, *Alsops Lane* 1761 *Sherrard*, *Easops* ~ 1809 *Valuation*, *Aesops Lane* 1878 *PK*, 1907 *Surv*, cf. *Nicholas Alsop* 1707 *Deed*. JUDGE MEADOW SPINNEY, *Judges Meadow* 1878 *PK*, cf. *William Judge* 1669 *Deed*, *v.* **spinney**. MAIN ST. MERE RD, an early boundary lane, *v.* **(ge)mǣre**. ST DENYS'S CHURCH, *the Church* 1708 (18) *Terrier*, *Church (St Denis)* 1846, 1863, 1877 White, *Church (St Denys)* 1925 Kelly; it is earlier recorded as *ecclesie de Evinton(e)* 1219 RHug, 1220 MHW, 1242 RGros, 1343 *Pat*, *ecclesia de Evinton* 1253 × 58 RTAL, *ecclesiarum de Evinton (et Humberstane)* 1318 *Pat*. SHADY LANE, *v.* **shady**. SPENCEFIELD LANE, 1907 *Surv*, 1925 Kelly; prob. an earlier *Spencers Field* 1809 *Valuation*, cf. *John Spencer* 1708 (18) *Terrier*. THE SPINNEYS, 1925 Kelly, *v.* **spinney**. SWAINS LODGE, *v.* **loge**; with the surn. *Swain*. THE VICARAGE, c.1740 *Surv*, 1809 *Valuation*, 1877 White, 1925 Kelly; it is *the Vicarage House* 1679, 1700, 1703, 1708 (18) *Terrier*, *the Vicariage house* 1690, 1698 *ib*, *v.* **vikerage**.

No early forms have been noted for the following Evington street-names: ALDGATE AVE, BLUNDELL RD, CORDERY RD, DOWNING DRIVE, ETHEL RD, GOODWOOD RD, HARWIN RD, HAWTHORN DRIVE, HEADLAND RD, HEXTALL RD, INGARSBY DRIVE, JUDITH DRIVE, LINDEN DRIVE, MICKLETON DRIVE, PILGRIM GARDENS, ST DENYS RD (*v.* St Denys's Church), SUSAN AVE, WHITEHALL RD.

FARMS, HOUSES AND COTTAGES

The following are cited in a 1708 (18) *Terrier*: *Beebys farme* (*v. Beeby's Close and Meadow* in f.ns. (b)), *Mr Bennington's Farme*, *Burley's Farme*, *Richard Cartwright's Farm*, *Jacombs Farme*, *William Johnson's*

Farme, Joseph Neal's Farme, Peter Plummer's Farme, Thomas Plummer's Farme, John Spencers Farme, James Thomson's Farm, Mr Townsends Ash-Field Farm (*v.* Ash Fd in f.ns. (a)), *Mr Van's Farm* (*v.* **ferme**); *Thomas Burley's house and Orchard, Thomas Fipps house and orchard, William Frostlin's House and Orchard, Widow Mawsons House and Backside* (*v.* **bak-side**); *John Astels Cottage, George Carricks Cottage and Close, Mr Collon's Ash-Field and his Cottage* (*v.* Ash Fd in f.ns. (a)), *Thomas Mawstons Cottage, Jane Noon's Cottage, William Smiths Cottage, Widow Spencers Cottage and Close, Joseph Whites Cottage and Close* (*v.* **cotage**).

FIELD-NAMES

In (a), forms dated 1756 and 1757 are *Coleman*; those dated 1761 are *Sherrard*; 1809 are *Valuation*; 1827 and 1907 are *Surv*; 1833 are *Deed*; 1850 are *TA*; 1878 are *PK*; 1913 are Sale. Forms throughout dated 1075 × 1108 are Nichols; those dated l.13 are *Wyg*; 1413, 1435, 1439, 1450, 1451 and 1456 are *Comp*; 1467 and 1492 are Hastings; 1477 (e.16) are *Charyte*; 1600 are *Ct*; 1607 and c.1740 are *Coleman*; c.1620 are MinAccts; 1627 are *Map*; 1637, 1674, 1690, 1698, 1700, 1703 and 1708 (18) are *Terrier*; 1733 are *Surv*.

(a) (The) Six Acres 1878, 1907, 1913, Seven ~, Ten ~, Eleven ~, Fourteen Acres 1850 (*v.* **æcer**); Amys Lodge 1809, 1827 (*v.* **loge**; with the surn. *Amys*); Ash Cl, ~ ~ Mdw 1761, Barn Ash Cl 1833, 1878, 1907 (*v.* **bern**), First ~ ~, Great Ash Cl 1809, Little Ash Cl 1761, 1833, Ash Close Hill 1761, 1833, Ash Fd, ~ ~ Mdw 1761, 1809, 1833, 1907, Nether Ash Fd 1809, 1833, 1878, 1907, Upper Ash Fd 1761, 1809 (*Mr Collon's Ash-Field* 1708 (18)), Ash Mdw 1809 (*v.* **æsc**); Back Orchard 1878, 1907 (*v.* **back**, **orceard**); Barn Cl 1761, 1809, 1878, 1907, Top Barn Mdw 1907, 1913 (*v.* **bern**); Barretts Cl (with the surn. *Barrett*); Bit 1850 (a small piece of land, *v.* **bit**); Bottom Mdw 1878, 1907, 1913; Broad Lane 1827 (*the Broad Lane* c.1740, *v.* **brād**, **lane**); Far ~ ~ 1878, 1907, Brook Cl 1756, 1757, 1761, 1809, 1878 (1708 (18), c. 1740, *v.* Evington Brook *supra*); Bull Leys 1809, 1827 (*the Bulleys* 1708 (18), *v.* **bula**, **leys**); Burnaby's Mdw, Burnaby's Piece (*v.* **pece**) 1878, 1907 (the *Burnaby* family were 19th-cent. landowners here); Butt Cl 1761, 1907, 1913 (c.1740), Butt Yard 1827 (*the But-yard* 1708 (18), *v.* **geard**) (*v.* **butte**; prob. land enclosed from open-field end pieces); Cavalry Cl 1756, Bottom ~ ~, Top Cavalry Cl 1878, 1907 (prob. a f.n. with some association with horses or horsemanship, *v.* **cavalry**; but poss. is a base with **cavel** 'a division or share of property made by lot, an allotment of land'); Church Cl 1761, 1907, ~ ~ Mdw 1761 (*Church close* 1674, 1708 (18)), Church Pingle 1756, 1761 (1708 (18), *v.* **pingel**) (*v.* St Denys's Church *supra*); Codham Nook 1761, 1809, 1827, Cobham Nook 1878, 1907, 1913 (*Codman Nook* 1627, 1708 (18), *v.* **nōk**; with the surn. *Codman*, an occupational name to be compared with eModE *codder*, a worker in leather or a saddler); Coopers Cl 1756, Bottom ~ ~, Top ~ ~ 1878, 1907 (*Coopers Close and Meadow* 1708 (18); with the surn. *Cooper*); The Coppice 1756, 1761, 1809 (1708 (18), *The Copy* 1674, *v.* **copis**; the spelling *copy* is due to the popular reconstruction of a 'singular' form); Far ~ ~, Middle ~ ~ 1907, Cottage Cl 1809, Cottage Fd 1756 (*v.* **cotage**); Cottagers Cl 1761, 1809 (c.1740, *v.* **cotager**); Cow Cl 1761, 1809, 1850, 1907 (1708 (18)), Little Cow Cl 1850, 1878, 1907, Big ~ ~ 1878, 1907, Far ~ ~, First Cow Cl 1878, 1907, Cow Hovel 1907 (*v.* **hovel**), Cow Pen Cl 1761, 1809 (*Cowpen Close* 1708 (18), c.1740, *v.* **penn**[2]), Cow Pen Close Mdw 1761 (*Cowpen Close Meadow* c.1740); Coxes Cl 1761, Cox Cl 1809, 1827 (*Cock Close* 1627, 1700, *Cox Close* 1674, *Cocks Close* 1690, 1698, 1708 (18), *Cocks Close Meadow* 1708 (18)), Cox Hill Cl 1761, 1809 (*Cock Close Hill* 1703, *Cocks Close Hill* 1708 (18)), Cox Hill Mdw 1761, 1809 (*Coxhill Meadow* c.1740) (prob. with the surn. *Cox*, but **cocc**[1] or **cocc**[2] is also poss.); Crown Hill Mdw 1809, 1833, 1850, 1878, 1907 (*v.* Crown Hills *supra*); Cub Mdw 1878, 1907 (*v.* **cubb**); Darkers Cl 1809, First ~ ~, Second Darker's Cl 1878, 1907 (*Darker Closes* 1708 (18); with the surn. *Darker*, cf. *John Darker* 1766); Debdale 1761, 1809, 1827, 1907 (*Deepdale*, *Meare Deepdales* 1627 (*v.* (**ge**)**mǣre**)), Horse Debdale 1761, 1809 (*v.* **hors**), Thirteen Acre Debdale 1878, 1907 (*v.* **æcer**), Debdale Hill, Debdale Mdw 1761 (*Deepdale Meadow* 1627) (*v.* **dēop**, **dalr**); Dents Mdw 1761 (with the surn. *Dent*); Dog Kennell Cl 1878, 1907, ~ ~ Mdw 1809, 1827 (*v.* **kenel**; such names sometimes refer to kennels in which hunting dogs were kept); Easops Lane Cl, ~ ~ Mdw 1809, Aesops Cl, ~ Mdw 1907 (*v.* Hyssop's Lane *supra*); Second ~ ~ 1907, English Cl 1756, 1761, 1809, 1878, 1907, Middle English Cl 1756, 1761, English Close Mdw 1756, 1761 (*English Close* 1627, 1674, *the English Closes* 1708 (18)) (with the surn. *English*; note *Robertus le Engleis* 12 Dane of Leics.); Evington Orchard 1878, 1907 (*v.* **orceard**); Far Fd 1809, Far Mdw 1761, 1878, 1907 (c.1740, 1757); Featherbed Lane 1878, 1907 (*v.* **feather-bed**; referring to peat-bog or spongy ground); Five Acre Mdw 1756, 1761, 1809 (c.1740, 1757, *v.* **æcer**); Five Shilling Mdw 1809, 1827 (1708 (18); land for use of which a rental was paid, *v.* **shilling** and Field 193); Flat Cl 1878, 1907 (*v.* **flatr**); Foalings 1878, 1907 (prob. land where foals were pastured or where foaling mares were kept, *v.* **fola**, **eng**, **foaling**); Four Acre Mdw 1756, 1757, 1761, 1809 (c.1740, *the Four Acres* 1708 (18), *v.* **æcer**); Four Ends 1761 (*the Forends* 1708 (18), *v.* **fore**, **ende**); Fourmens ~ 1761, Fourmans Fd 1809 (*Fourmens Field* c.1740), Fourmans Mdw 1809 (*Fourmens Meadow* c.1740; with the occupational surn. *Fourman* 'swineheard', from OE *fōr* 'pig' and *mann*); Fulsicks 1761, Fullsicks Cl 1809, First ~, Second ~, Third Fullvick 1878, 1907, Fouth Full Vick 1907 (*Full Sick* 1627, *the Fulsicks* 1708 (18), *v.* **fūl**, **sík**); Gallow Tree Cl (*v.* **galg-trēow**); George Mdw 1907, Georges ~ 1756, 1761, 1809, George Piece 1878, 1907 (*Georges Piece* c.1740, *v.* **pece**; with the surn. *George*); Gorse Cl 1761, 1809 (*v.* **gorst**); (the) Gorsey Cl 1809, 1827 (*Gossey Close* c.1740, *v.* **gorstig**); Great Cl 1761, 1809, Great Close Mdw 1761, 1833; Great Stone Bushes 1761, 1827, Great Stone Bush Cl 1761 (*v.* **grēat**, **stān**, **busc**; evidently an enclosure growing with bushes and located near a major boundary stone; note Horston Hill *supra* and the adjoining Humberstone parish (*Humberstane* c.1130, 'Hūnbeorht's stone', Lei **3** 133); Green Hedges 1761, 1827, 1878, 1907, 1913 (*v.* **grēne**[1]; either with **hecg** in its early sense 'a hedged enclosure' or with **edisc** or **etisc**); Bottom ~ ~, Top Hall Fd 1907, The Hall Yard 1756 (*the Hallyarde or Baylyffes Close* 1607 (*v.* **baillif**), *Hall Yard* 1627, c.1740, *the Hall yarde Coppice*

1607 (*v.* **copis**)), Hall Yard Cl 1878, 1907, 1913 (*v.* **hall**, **geard**; some f.ns. with reference to an earlier hall than Evington Hall *supra* which was built by Henry Coleman 1840–45); Harrols ~ 1761, Harrolds Cl 1907, First Harrolds Cl 1756, 1809, 1878, 1907 (*Herald* ~ 1627, *Har(r)olds Close* 1674, 1690, 1708 (18)), Harrol(d)s Close Mdw 1756, 1761 (*Harolds Close Meadow* 1690, 1708 (18)), Far ~ ~, Middle Harrolds Mdw 1878, 1907 (with the surn. *Har(r)old*); Harston Hill Cl 1757 (*v.* Horston Hill *supra*); Hay Gate 1761, Heygate 1809, 1827, High Gate 1878, 1907, 1913, Hay Gate ~ 1761, Heygate Mdw 1827 (*v.* **hēg**, **gata**); Middle ~ ~ 1761, Heath Cl 1827, 1878 (*the Heath Closes* 1708 (18), *v.* **hǣð**); Far ~ ~, Middle Heather Cl 1761 (*v.* **hǣddre**); Highway Cl 1761, 1809, 1907, Highway Fd 1761, 1878, 1913 (c.1740) (*v.* **hēah-weg**); Bottom ~, Top Hill 1850, Hill Cl 1833, 1850, 1878, 1907, Lower Hill Cl 1878, 1907 ((*the*) *Hill Close* 1627, 1674, 1690, 1708 (18)), (the) Hill Close Mdw 1756, 1761, 1809, Hill Mdw 1878 (1627) (*v.* **hyll**); Home Cl 1878, 1907 (c.1740, *v.* **home**); House Cl 1756, 1757, 1761, 1809 (c.1740), House Close Mdw 1756, 1757; Hovel Close Mdw 1833 (*v.* **hovel**); Humberstone Gate Cl 1878, 1907, 1913 (*v.* **gata**; Humberstone parish adjoins to the north); Hutchins Cl 1809, 1878, 1907 (with the surn. *Hutchins*); Judges Mdw 1907 (with the surn. *Judge*); Kiln Mdw 1850, Kilen Yard 1809, 1827 (*Kiln Yard* 1761, *v.* **geard**) (*v.* **cyln**); King's Orchard 1878, 1907, 1913 (with the surn. *King*); Nether ~, Langhill 1761, Bottom ~ ~, Top Long Hill 1878, 1907 (*Langhill* 1627, (*the*) *Langhill Close* 1708 (18), c. 1740), Langhill Mdw 1761 ((*the*) *Langhill Meadow* 1708 (18), c.1740) (*v.* **lang**[1], **hyll**); Large Mdw 1878, 1907; Lays Cl 1761 (*v.* **leys**); First ~ ~ ~, Second ~ ~ ~, Third Left Hand Cl 1878, 1907 (to the left of the main road to Leicester); Leicester Fd 1761 (c.1740; a field towards Leicester); Lime Kiln Mdw 1833, 1850, 1878, 1907 (*v.* **lim-kilne**); Little Cl 1761; Little Field Cl 1761; Little Mdw 1756, 1757; Long Mdw 1761, 1878, 1907; Lords Piece 1761, 1878, 1907, 1913 (*the Lords peice* 1708 (18), *v.* **pece**; property of the lord of the manor); The Meadow 1761, 1809, 1913; The Mear in Leicester Fd 1761 (*The Meer in Leicesterfield* c.1740; *v.* **mere**[1]); Middle Cl 1761 (*Midle Close* c.1740), Middle Close Mdw 1761 (c.1740), Middle Fd or Spencers 1761 (with the surn. *Spencer*), Middle Mdw 1757, 1878, 1907; Moat Cl 1809, 1827, Moat Mdw, Little Moat 1850 (*v.* **mote**; closes containing the earthwork remains of the manorial complex, of which the moat marks the site of the manor house and a large dam that of a watermill); Moor(e) Hill, ~ ~ Mdw 1761, 1809, 1878, 1907 (*Moorhill*, ~ *Meadow* c.1740), Moore Mdw 1761 (*Moor(e) Meadow* 1627, c.1740) (*v.* **mōr**[1]); Nether Cl 1761; New Mdw 1761, 1809; New Spinney (*v.* **spinney**); Orchard Cl 1850 (*v.* **orceard**); The Parks 1809, Bottom Park 1878, (the) Far Park 1756, 1761, (the) Highway Park 1756, 1757, 1761 (*v.* **hēah-weg**), Nether Park 1756, 1761, Far Park Cl 1757, Gimsons Park Cl 1756, 1757 (with the surn. *Gimson*), Phipps Park Cl 1756, 1757 (with the surn. *Phipps*), Top Park 1907, (the) Park Mdw 1756, 1809, (the) Far Park Mdw 1756, 1761, Middle Park Mdw 1756, 1761, Park End Cl 1756, 1757, 1809, Park End Close Mdw 1756, 1757 (*v.* **ende**), the Park House Cl 1756, (the) Park Leys 1756, 1761, 1809, Park Leys Cl 1756, 1757 (*Park Leys* 1708 (18), *v.* **leys**) (*v.* Evington Park *supra*); Pepper Hill Mdw 1850 (presum. with the surn. *Pepper*, but if an early name, then **pipere** 'a spring, a stream' may pertain); Pettifors ~ 1833, 1850, Pettifers Cl 1878, 1907 (with the surn. *Pettifor*); Pinkwell Cl 1761, 1809, 1827, 1878, 1907, 1913 ('minnow stream', *v.* **pinc**, **wella**); Poles Homestead 1809 (*v.* **hām-stede**, with the surn. *Pole*; note *Widow Poles Cottage* 1708 (18)); Pollards Cl 1809, 1827 (1708 (18); with the surn.

Pollard); Polton Hill 1878 (prob. with the surn. *Polton*, but earlier forms are needed); Road (land beside a highway); Bottom ~ ~, Middle ~ ~, Top Seddon's Cl 1878, 1907 (with the surn. *Seddon*); Old Seeds (*v.* **sǣd**; used of grasses sown for one year's mowing or grazing, as distinguished from permanent pasture); Slang 1878, 1907 (*v.* **slang**; a small narrow strip of land); Smith Hill 1761, 1809 (either with the surn. *Smith* or with **smið**); First ~ ~, Middle ~ ~, Upper Spencers Fd 1809, Bottom ~ ~, Top Spencers Fd 1878, 1907 (with the surn. *Spencer*); (the) Spinney Hill 1809, 1827, 1878 (1627, *Spinny Hill* 1733), Barn ~ ~, Middle Spinney Hill 1761 (c.1740, *v.* **bern**), Spinney Hill Mdw 1809, Spinney Moore 1809 (*v.* **mōr**[1]) (*v.* **spinney**); Springfield Mdw 1833, 1878, 1907 (*v.* **spring**[1]); Little Square Cl 1913, Square Mdw 1761, 1809, 1827 (1708 (18), c.1740, *v.* **squar(e)**); Stonebridge Mdw 1761, 1827 (1708 (18), *v.* **stān**, **brycg**); Stretton's Mdw 1878, 1907 (with the surn. *Stretton*); Swine Balk 1761, ~ Baulk 1809, 1827, Swines Balk 1878, 1907 (*v.* **swīn**, **balca**; a field boundary used as a pig-run); Tebble's Cl 1878, 1907, 1913 (with the surn. *Tebble*); Three Acre Mdw 1756, 1757 (*v.* **æcer**), Three Cornered Cl 1878, 1907 (*v.* **three-cornered**); Three Nooks 1761, 1827, 1907 (*v.* **nōk**); Top Mdw 1757 (*v.* **top**); Little ~ ~, Town Cl 1761, Town Fd alias Spencers 1761 (with the surn. *Spencer*), Town Piece 1761 (*Towns piece* 1627, *v.* **pece**) (*v.* **tūn**); Townsend ~ 1761, Townend Cl 1907 (*v.* **tūn**, **ende**); Two Cl 1809 (a double enclosure, two fields now united); Upper Close Mdw 1761 (*Upper Close* c.1740, *v.* **upper**); The Wad Cabin 1878, 1907 (land containing a shed in which woad leaves were fermented, *v.* **wād**, **cabane**); High Wanfield 1809, 1827 (*v.* **wand**); Wash Pit Mdw 1878, 1907 (*v.* **wæsce**, **pytt**); Wilcox Spinney 1809, ~ ~ Pingle 1827 (*v.* **pingel**) (*v.* **spinney**; with the surn. *Wilcox*); The Wong 1827, 1878 (c.1740, *v.* **vangr**); Worths Cl 1878, 1907, 1913 (cf. *Thomas Worth* 1809).

(b) *Abraham Woong* 1674, ~ *Wong* 1708 (18) (*v.* **vangr**; with the surn. *Abraham*, which was not confined to Jews); *Acre Dikes* 1627 (*v.* **æcer-dīc**; a common compound referring either to a ditch surrounding an arable plot or to a ditch marking the limit of ploughland; spellings with a final *k* are due to Scand influence); *Aldefeld* 1075 × 1108 (*v.* **ald**, **feld**); *Atkins Close* 1627 (with the surn. *Atkin*(*s*)); *Beeby's Close and Meadow* 1708 (18) (with the surn. *Beeby* of a family originally from the village of this name, 4 miles to the north-east); *broadfield* 1600 (*v.* **brād**, **feld**); *Cerssholme* 1413 (*v.* **cerse**, **holmr**); *Chambers Close* 1627 (with the surn. *Chambers*); *Chinkle Close* 1627 (*v.* **chingel**); *Copdale* 1627 (ostensibly **copp**, **dalr**; but this may conceal **copped**[1], **hyll**); *Corn-Close* 1708 (18) (*v.* **corn**[1]); *Cowpiece* 1627 (*v.* **cū**, **pece**); *Croudonsty*, *Crowdonsty ford* 1477 (e.16) (*v.* **stīg**, **ford** and Crown Hills *supra*); *the Cunnery* 1708 (18) (*v.* **coningre**); *Duck Meadow* 1627 (*v.* **dūce**); *Evington hole* c.1620 (*v.* **hol**[1]); *Evington thynge* 1492 (*v.* **thing**); *Gilleford* 1413 (*v.* **ford**; perh. with the ON masc. pers.n. *Gilli*, but a Scand pers.n. compounded with *ford* would be rare; **gylde**, alluding to local flora, is poss., but **gyll** 'a deep narrow valley' is otherwise found only in the south); *Gilmonlond* 1439, *Gylmynlond* 1450, *Gylmynland* 1451, *Gilmynland* 1456 (*v.* **land**; with the surn. *Gilman*, a reflex of the OFr masc. pers.n. *Guillemin*, a diminutive of *Guillaume*); *Hay Meadow* 1627 (*v.* **hēg**); *hilleshend'* 1413, *le hilend'* 1435, *hillesende* 1450, 1451 (*v.* **hyll**, **ende**); *horstonsikenethirhende* l.13 (*v.* **sík**, **neoðera**, **ende** and Horston Hill *supra*); *Jenkynnes pasture* 1477 (e.16) (*v.* **pasture**; with the surn. *Jenkyn*(*s*)); *John Jolly's Quarter of a Yard Land* 1708 (18) (*v.* **yerdland**); *Little Hill* 1627; *Longfield* 1600 (*v.* **lang**[1], **feld**); *Longlands* 1627 (*v.* **lang**[1], **land**); *the long lane* 1600 (*v.* **lang**[1], **lane**); *Meare Copp Meadow* 1627 (*v.*

copp), *Meare New Close* 1627, *Meare Park* 1627 (*v.* Evington Park *supra*) (*v.* **(ge)mǣre**); *le Nether heth* 1435, 1439, 1456 (*v.* **neoðera, hǣð**); *le Nethersty* 1477 (e.16) (*v.* **neoðera, stīg**); *Newsted*(*e*) 1439, 1450, 1451, 1456, *the Newstedes* 1708 (18) (two closes so called) (*v.* **nīwe, stede**); *Henry Palmers Spinay* 1627 (*v.* **spinney**); *the parke copice* 1600 (*v.* **copis** and Evington Park *supra*); *Portgate* 1467 (*v.* **port-gate**; the principal road to the market town of Leicester); *the Pylloke* 1708 (18) (*v.* **pyll, -uc**); *Siberdeslond* 1456 (*v.* **land**; with the surn. *Sibert*, a reflex of the common OE masc. pers.n. *Sigebeorht*); *Spinnaye Close* 1627 (*v.* **spinney**); *Starr Lane* 1627 (*v.* **stǫrr**[2], **lane**; note the later recorded extension of the lane in the Borough of Leicester, Lei **1** 65); *Stony Lands* 1627 (*v.* **stānig, land**); *Thorpewell* 1627 (*v.* **þorp, wella**); *Tommes Holme* 1607 (*v.* **holmr**; with the surn. *Tom* or *Tomes* or *Tommis*, all from the pet-form *Tom* of the pers.n. *Thomas*); *Wayne Way Close* 1627 (*v.* **wægn, weg**); *le Wendacre* 1075 × 1108 (*v.* **wende, æcer**); *Wild Willows* 1627 (*v.* **wilde, wilig**).

Fleckney

FLECKNEY

Flechenie 1086 DB (×2), *Flecheneia* c.1160 Dane (p), *Flec(c)henai* 1166 LN, *Flecheneya* 1246 × 49 BM
Flecneya c.1125 (c.1225) *Sloane*, c.1130 LeicSurv
Flekeneye c.1130 LeicSurv, 1249 Cur (p) *et passim* to 1306 *Peake et freq* to 1387 Banco, 1397 Cl, *Flekenai* 1166 RBE (p), *Flekeneia* 1192, 1230 P (p), *Flekeneie* 1230 ChancR, 1247 Hastings, *Flekeney* Hy 3 *Crox*, 1288 Banco *et freq* to 1537 CoPleas, 1539 MinAccts
Fleckenai 1166 LN (p), 1166 RBE, *Fleckeneya* 1230 P (p), *Fleckeneye* 1242 Fees, 1317 Cl, 1360 *Peake*, *Fleykeneye* p.1250 *ib*
Flekney 1220 MHW, 1239 Cur *et passim* to 1384 Coram, 1435 *Wyg et freq* to 1548 Fine, 1576 Saxton, *Flecney(e)* 1375 *Wyg*, 1489 Banco, 1540, 1548 Fine
Fleckney 1467 *Wyg*, 1540 MinAccts, 1544 Ipm, 1610 Speed *et freq*

Probably 'Flecca's piece of raised dry ground in surrounding wet land', *v*. **ēg**, cf. Flecknoe Wa 150. Fleckney lies in a shallow valley, the parish still retaining much standing water. The OE masc. pers.n. *Flecca* is unrecorded. Ekwall DEPN suggests that if the first el. is not a pers.n., it may be an unrecorded OE sb. **fleca** 'a hurdle', the source of *fleke*, a side-form of ME *flake* 'hurdle' (found from the 13th cent.), hence 'raised dry ground in surrounding wet land where wood for hurdles is obtained'.

ALBERT ST, with Victoria St *infra*, commemorating the marriage of Queen Victoria to Albert of Saxe-Coburg-Gotha in 1840. ARNESBY RD, Arnesby lying 2 miles to the south. BLEAK HO., prob. alluding to Charles Dickens' novel of this name, first published in instalments 1852–53. CROWN (P.H.), *Crown* 1846, 1863, 1877 White, *Old Crown Inn* 1925 Kelly. DUN COW (P.H.) (lost), *Dun Cow* 1846, 1863, 1877 White, *Dun Cow Inn* 1925 Kelly. ELIZABETH RD, commemorating the coronation of Queen Elizabeth II. THE ELMS. FLECKNEY LODGE, 1925 Kelly, *v*. **loge**.

GLADSTONE ST, named from William Gladstone, Liberal politician and Prime Minister between 1868 and 1894. GLEBE FM was *Fleckney Lodge* 1835 O, *Fleckney Lodge Farm* 1846 White, *v.* **loge**, **glebe**. HIGHFIELD ST. HIGH ST. KILBY RD, Kilby lying 2 miles to the north-west. LEICESTER RD, Leicester lying 8 miles to the north-west. LYNDON LODGE, *v.* **loge**. MAIN ST is *the Street* 1724 *Terrier*, *v.* **strǣt**. THE MEADOWS. ORCHARD ST. PARK ST. ST NICHOLAS'S CHURCH, *the Church* 1708 (18) *Terrier*, *Church (St Nicholas)* 1846, 1863, 1877 White, 1925 Kelly; earlier is recorded *capella de Flekeney* 1220 MHW (with MLat *capella* 'a chapel'). SCHOOL ST. SPINNEY HO., *v.* **spinney**. SPRINGS FM, *v.* **spring**[1]. THE VICARAGE, 1877 White, 1925 Kelly, *v.* **vikerage**. VICTORIA ST, *v.* Albert St *supra*. WHITE HOUSE FM, *le White house* 1636 Ipm, *v.* **hwīt**. THE WILLOWS. WOLSEY LANE, named from *Wolsey Ltd* 1925 Kelly, hosiery manufacturers, who established a steam factory for framework knitters. WOODBINE COTTAGE.

FIELD-NAMES

In (a), forms presented without dates are 1971 *Surv*; those dated 1769 are *EnclA*; 18 are *Map*; 1807 are *Valuation*; 1835 are O; 1881 are *Deed*. Forms throughout dated 1221 are Fine; those dated 1697, 1705, 1708 (18) and 1724 are *Terrier*.

(a) Four Acre, Five ~, Eleven ~, Twenty Acre (*v.* **æcer**); Allotment Fd (*v.* **allotment**); Askill's Mdw (with the surn. *Askill*, a reflex of the ON masc. pers.n. *Áskell* (a contracted form of *Ásketill*)); Banky Cl (*v.* **banke**, **-ig**[3]); Barn Cl (*v.* **bern**); Bartmore Hill 1807 (*Bratmer* ~ 1705, *Bratmore hill* 1708 (18), 1724), Lower ~ ~, Upper Bartmore Sytch 1807 (*v.* **sīc**), Bratmar 1971 (*v.* **brād**, **mōr**[1]); The Bogs 1807, Bog Cl 1971 (*v.* **bog**); Bottom Mdw (*v.* **bottom**); Brickyard, ~ Fd, ~ Mdw (*v.* **brike-yard**; brick-making was formerly an important industry in Fleckney); Bridge Cl 1807, 1971 (*v.* **brycg**); Further ~ ~ ~, Near ~ ~ ~, Burton Way Cl 1807 (*Burton way* 1705, 1724, ~ ~ *furlong* 1708 (18) (*v.* **furlang**); the road to Burton Overy which lies 4 miles to the north-west); Bottom ~ ~, Top ~ ~, Cow Cl; Dooms Day (a derogatory name for unproductive land); Feeding Cl (*v.* **feeding**; grazing ground, pasturage); Fleckney Gorse 1835 (*v.* **gorst**); Bottom ~ ~, Foal Pits (*v.* **fūl**, **pytt**); The Front, Front Fd (*v.* **front**); Further Mdw 1807 (*v.* **furðra**); Gamblers Cl (with the surn. *Gamble*, a reflex of the ON masc. pers.n. *Gamall* (ODan *Gamal*) 'old'); Gravel Hole 1971, Gravel Pits 18 (*v.* **gravel**, **hol**[1], **pytt**); Bottom ~, Top Greens (with the surn. *Green* in the possessive case); Bottom ~, Top Hallows (*v.* **halh**); Hamond (a close owned by the family *Hamond*, a surn. reflex of the OFr masc. pers.n. *Hamond*); Hobrook Fd 1769 (1708 (18), *Hobrook feild* 1705, *Howbrook Field* 1724 (*v.* **feld**; one of the great open-fields of the township), *hobrook* 1705, *Hobrook furlong* 1708 (18), *Howbrook furlong* 1724 (*v.* **furlang**) (*v.* **brōc**; prob. with **hol**[2] rather than with **hōh**);

Home Cl 1807, 1971, Home Fd (*v.* **home**); Hoppins (*v.* **hopping**); Horse Cl; House Cl; Jones Mdw (with the surn. *Jones*); Big ~, Little Kings (with the surn. *King* in the possessive case); Langdall 18, Longdale or Langle 1971 (*Langdale*, *Langdall* 1705, *Longdale lands ends* 1708 (18), *Langdale Lands ends* 1724 (*v.* **land**, **ende**), *v.* **lang**[1]; with **dalr** or **deill**); Lankersick 1881 (1708 (18), 1724, *Lankasick* 1705, *v.* **sík**; this maybe an early name, originally with **sīc** and an OE masc. pers.n. *Hlanc*(*a*) (cf. OE *hlanc* 'lanky, thin, lean'); but a reduced **lang**[1], **gāra** is also poss.); Long Guts (*v.* **langet**); His Lordship's Cl (with reference to the lord of the manor); Maines Cl (*Mains* ~ 1708 (18), *Manes Close* 1724; with the surn. *Main*(*e*)); Mans Horns (*Manshorn*(*e*) 1705, 1708 (18), 1724, *v.* (**ge**)**mǣnnes**, **þorn**); Mare Pit (*v.* (**ge**)**mǣre**, **pytt**); Marr Fd 1769 (1708 (18), 1724, *the marfeild* 1705 (*v.* **feld**; one of the great open-fields), *Marre* 1679, *v.* **marr**[1]); Middle Mdw 1807, 1971; Mill Hill 1971 (*v.* **myln**); Mill Stede 18, Minstead 1971 (*v.* **myln**, **stede**); Near Mdw 1807; The Nursery (*v.* **nursery**; a plantation of young trees); Oake Tree Fd (*v.* **āc**); Oxall 18, Oxler or Oxle 1971 (*v.* **oxa**, **halh**); Pen Cl (*v.* **penn**[2]); Pisamire (may allude to land with anthills, *v.* **pissemyre** 'an ant' (so called from the urinous smell of an anthill); but poss. also is a reference to land into which stables or cowsheds drained, with **pisse** and **mýrr**); Pony Cl (*v.* **pony**); Post Cl (*v.* **post**); Priest Mdw (1724, *Preist Medow* 1705, ~ *meadow* 1708 (18); prob. with **prēost** rather than with the surn. *Priest*); Quisick Fd 1769, Quissick One, ~ Two 1971 (*Quessock* 1697, *Quesick* 1705, *Quessick* 1708 (18), *the quesick* 1724, *Quesickfeild* 1705, *Quessick Field* 1708 (18), *Quesick* ~ 1724, *v.* **cwēad**, **sík**, **feld**; one of the great open-fields); Road Fd (land beside a roadway); Sand Hole (*v.* **hol**[1]), Sand Mdw (*v.* **sand**); Shellbard or Shulbard (*Shouldbrod* 1705, *Shoulbred* 1708 (18), *Shoulbard* 1724, *v.* **scofl-brǣdu**); Spinney Cl (*v.* **spinney**); Stainer 18, Staynor or Steiner 1971 (*Steno* 1705, 1724, *Stayno* 1708 (18); either 'stony spur of land', *v.* **stān**, **hōh**, or 'stony ground', *v.* **stǣner**, either with the influence of Scand **steinn** 'stone'); Top Fd, Top Mdw (*v.* **top**); Town Adley (*Town hadlay* 1705, *the Town Headley* 1708 (18), *The Towne hadley* 1724, *v.* **tūn**, **headley**); Tunnel Fds, Tunnel Mdw (land adjoining a tunnel built in 1796 on the Grand Union Canal); Top Warner's (with the surn. *Warner*); Well Wattering (*v.* **wella**, **wateryng**); West Mdw (*West medow* 1705, (*the*) *West Meadow*, ~ *Furlong* 1708 (18), 1724 (*v.* **furlang**)); Bottom Winnel, Top Winnel or Whin Hill (*v.* **hvin**, **hyll**); Wranglands (*v.* **wrang**, **land**).

(b) *Uper Cobles* 1705, *Upper Cobwells* 1708 (18), ~ *Cobbals* 1724 (*v.* **wella**; prob. with the OE masc. pers.n. *Cobba* rather than with **cobb**(**e**)); *the Common* (*v.* **commun**); *Cunegrey* 1705, *Conegray* 1708 (18), *Coneygray* 1724 (*v.* **coningre**); *Dunncroft* 1221 (*v.* **croft**; either with the OE masc. pers.n. *Dunna*, or with the surn. *Dunn* (from OE *dunn* 'dark, swarthy')); *Dribdall* 1705, *dribdale* 1724, *dribdall end* 1705, *Dribdale end* 1708 (18) (*v.* **ende**) (of uncertain meaning; the first el. may be **drib** in the sense 'something very small' (as in *dribs and drabs*), with **deill**); *Ferne hill* 1708 (18) (*v.* **fearn**); *Finsdole* 1708 (18), *Finsdale* 1724 (*v.* **dāl**; with the OE masc. pers.n. *Finn*); *Gorril* 1697, *gorill lays* 1705, *Gorrill Leys* 1708 (18), *Gorril Lays* 1724 (*v.* **leys**) (*v.* **gāra**, **hyll**); *Grene bank* 1705 (*v.* **grēne**[1], **banke**); *Gross*(*e*) 1708 (18), 1724, *Gros lays* 1705, *Gross Leys* 1708 (18), 1724 (*v.* **leys**) (*v.* **græs**); *Hatcham* 1708 (18), 1724 (*v.* **hæc**(**c**), **hamm**); *Robert Jacques's House and Yard* 1708 (18); *Kerkley* 1705, *Kickly* 1708 (18), *Kertly* 1724 (*v.* **kirkja**, **lēah**; the first el. was no doubt originally **cirice**); *Ladydole* 1705, 1708 (18), 1724 (*v.* **ladi**, **dāl**; such names generally indicate land dedicated to Our Lady, the Blessed Virgin, for the maintenance of a chapel or shrine; otherwise perh. the property of the lady of the manor); *Lemonsong* 1705, 1724, *Leamons wong* 1708 (18), *Uper Lemonsong* 1705, *Upper Leemans wong* 1708 (18) (*v.* **upper**) (*v.* **vangr**; with the surn. *Leamon*, a reflex of the OE masc. pers.n. *Lēofmann*, with reinforcement by ME *leman* 'lover, sweetheart', cf. *Willelmus Luveman* 1211 RFL); *Low way* 1705, 1708 (18), 1724 (*v.* **la(g)h**); *the mear* 1705, 1724, *the Meer* 1708 (18) (*v.* **(ge)mǣre**); *midle hill* 1705, *Middle hill furlong* 1708 (18), *midlehill furlong* 1724 (*v.* **furlang**) (*v.* **middel**); *the more medow* 1705, ~ ~ *meadow* 1724, *the Moor Meadow* 1708 (18) (*v.* **mōr**[1]); *Old Roods* 1705, 1708 (18), 1724 (*v.* **ald**, **rōd**[3]); *Pecks Close* 1708 (18), 1724 (with the surn. *Peck*); *Saddington Meer* 1724 (*v.* **(ge)mǣre**; Saddington parish adjoins to the south-east); *Sawbrook*(*e*) 1705, 1708 (18), 1724, *v.* **salh**, **brōc**); *Shorta Close* 1705, 1708 (18), 1724 (poss. with the surn. *Shorter*); *stone brige lane* 1705, *the Stone Bridge Lane* 1708 (18), 1724 (*v.* **stān**, **brycg**, **lane**); *the Town Furlong* 1705, 1708 (18), 1724 (*v.* **tūn**, **furlang**); *the Tyth*(*e*) *Barn*(*e*) 1705, 1708 (18) (*v.* **tēoða**, **bern**); *the Wall Slade* 1708 (18) (*v.* **slæd**; poss. with **wella**); *Walsick* 1705 (*v.* **sík**), *Walhill* 1725 (*v.* **hyll**) (*v.* **walu**); *waterthorows* 1705, *Waterfurrows* 1708 (18), 1724 (*v.* **wæter**, **furh** and *the water furrowes* in Billesdon f.ns. (b)); *West Brook* 1705, 1708 (18), 1724; *the Whitehouse lands* 1636 (*v.* **land** and White House Fm *supra*).

Foxton

FOXTON

Foxtone 1086 DB, Wm 2, e.12 Dugd, 1109 Nichols, *Foxtune* e.12 Dugd, 1109 Nichols, *Foxtunia* c.1147 BM, *Foxtun'* 1160 (p), 1180 P (p), *Foxton* 1109 Nichols, 1174 P *et freq*, *Foxon* 1674, 1679, c.1690 *Terrier*
Foxestone 1086 DB

Most probably 'the farmstead, village where foxes are frequently seen', *v*. **fox**, **tūn**. Note the tell-tale Foxborough in f.ns. (a) *infra*. The unique DB form *Foxestone* with its genitival construction hardly points to an unrecorded pers.n. *Fox* in the possessive case as the specific, although *Toue fox* (1154 × 89) of Saleby in Lincs. (with ODan *Tovi*, ON *Tófi*) indicates that *fox* was used as a by-name from at least the middle of the 12th cent.

BEAUCHAMP FM, on the parish boundary towards Kibworth Beauchamp which lies 3 miles to the north-west. BLACK HORSE (P.H.), *Black Horse* 1846, 1863, 1877 White, *Black Horse Inn* 1925 Kelly. BOWDEN INN FM was *Great Bowden Inn* 1835 O; on the parish boundary with Great Bowden which adjoins to the south-east. DEBDALE LANE, cf. *Debdale Meadow* 1968 *Surv*, *v*. **dēop**, **dalr**. The lane continues in Gumley. FOXTON LOCKS, 1835 O, 1846, 1863, 1877 White, 1925 Kelly, *v*. **lock**; a group of ten locks built in 1812, on the Grand Union Canal. FOXTON LODGE, 1863 White, *v*. **loge**. GALLOW FIELD RD, *the East feild alias Gallow feild* 1625 *Terrier*, *the Galloe filde* c.1685 *ib*, *the Gallofeald* 1690 *ib*, *the gallofeld* 1694 *ib*, *the Gallow Field* 1707 *ib*, 1707 (18) *ib*, *v*. **galla**, **hōh**, **feld**; one of the great open-fields of the township, *v*. *Galhou* in f.ns. (b) *infra*. GALLOW HILL, 1877 White; it is *Calowdon* 1328 Banco (*v*. **dūn**), *Calewehill* 1364 *Peake*, *Calewehille* 1364 Cl, *Caluhulle* 1386 Hastings, *Calwehull* 1419 Coram, *Calewhill(e)* 1426 Cl, 1433 *Peake*, 'the bare hill', *v*. **calu**, **hyll**; the early *dūn* in the toponym was replaced by *hyll* and the restyled name was later attracted to the unrelated Gallow Field *supra*. GRAND UNION CANAL, 1821 *Terrier*, 1835

O, 1846, 1877 White. THE GRANGE, 1925 Kelly, *v.* **grange**. GUMLEY RD, Gumley lying one mile to the west. HARBOROUGH RD, Market Harborough lying 2 miles to the south-east. LANGTON BROOK PLANTATION, *v.* **brōc**, **plantation**; the brook forms the parish boundary with West Langton. LANGTON RD, the route to East Langton which lies 2 miles to the north-west. MAIN ST. MANOR HO., *Manor House* 1846, 1863, 1877 White, 1925 Kelly, *v.* **maner**. MIDDLE ST. NORTH LANE, *v.* **norð**; the lane acts as a northern boundary to the village. ST ANDREW'S CHURCH, *the Church* 1707 *Terrier*, *Church (St Andrew)* 1846, 1863, 1877 White, 1925 Kelly; it is earlier recorded as *ecclesie de Foxton* 1220 MHW, 1241, 1250 RGros, 1558 *Pat*. Note also *the Churchyard* 1707 *Terrier*, *v.* **churchyerd**. SCHOFIELD FM, with the surn. *Schofield*. SHOULDER OF MUTTON (P.H.), *Shoulder of Mutton*, 1846, 1863 White, 1925 Kelly. SWINGBRIDGE ST, terminating at a swing-bridge over the Grand Union Canal. VICARAGE DRIVE, cf. *the Vicarage house* 1601 *Terrier*, *the Vicarage howsse* 1606 *ib*, *the vickrig hous* 1679 *ib*, *the Vickeridge house* c.1685 *ib*, *v.* **vikerage**.

FIELD-NAMES

In (a), forms presented without dates are 1968 *Surv*; those dated 1755 are *Deed*; 1781 are *Map*; 1835 are O; 1843 are Sale. Forms throughout dated 1343, 1463, 1494 and 1655 are *MktHPR*; those dated 1507 and 1523 are *Wyg*; 1601, 1606, 1625, 1679, c.1685, 1690, 1707 and 1707 (18) are *Terrier*.

(a) Two Acres, Four ~, Five ~ 1968, Six ~ 1843, Eight ~ 1968, Ten ~ 1843, 1968, Eighteen ~, Twenty-four ~ 1843, Thirty-one ~ 1968, Thirty-four Acres 1843 (*v.* **æcer**); Allotment Fd (*v.* **allotment**); The Big Fd; Blacklands 1755, Far Bleaklands 1781, First ~, Second Breaklands (sic) 1968 (*v.* **land**; with **blāc** or **blæc**); Bosworth Mdw (with the surn. *Bosworth* of a family prob. in origin from Husbands Bosworth, 5 miles to the south-west); Brook Cl (cf. *atte Brok* 1366 (p), 1368 Pat (p) (*v.* **atte**, **brōc**), *v.* Langton Brook Spinney *supra*); Burn Dale 1755, Burnt Dale 1968, ~ ~ Cl 1781 (*v.* **bryne**, **dalr**); (The) Canal Fd, Under Canal (*v.* Grand Union Canal *supra*); Charities Fd, Charity Cl (names indicating that the rent of these lands provided funds for charitable purposes); Chestnuts Paddock (*v.* **paddock**; a close with chestnut-trees); Church Cl formerly Church Hill Cl (*v.* St Andrew's Church *supra*); Corner Mdw (*v.* **corner**); Cottage Cl; Cricket Fd (for the game of cricket); The Dales 1781, The Dale 1968, (*betwene Dales* 1606 (*v.* **betwēonan**), *v.* **dalr**); Elbow Fd (*v.* **elbowe**; land with a sharp turn in its boundary); Far Fd; Fishers Fd (with the surn. *Fisher*); Five Acre Mdw (*v.* **æcer**); First ~ ~, Flat Mdw (*v.* **flatr**); Football Fd (for the game of football); Foxborough 1755, Foxborough Cl, ~ Mdw 1843, Foxborrow Cl 1968 (*Foxbarrow* 1601, 1606, 1625, *Foxburrow* 1679, *Foxboro* 1690, *Foxborro* 1694,

Foxborow 1707, 1707 (18); either 'hill frequented by foxes', *v.* **fox**, **berg**, or 'fox-earth', *v.* **fox**, **burgh**); Foxton Mill 1835 (*v.* **myln**; a windmill); Foxton Road Fd; Garborow 1755, Garbroad ~ 1781, Garboard Cl 1868 (*v.* **gorebrode**); Great Cl; Gutteridges (the surn. *Gutteridge* in the possessive case); Hall Cl 1968, Hall Leys 1755, 1781, First ~ ~, Second Hall Leys 1968 (*v.* **hall**, **leys**); Haynes Cl (with the surn. *Haynes*); the Headlands (*v.* **hēafod-land**); Hill Cl; Hills and Hollows (a close beside the manor house, which if on the site of the medieval hall, suggests early earthworks such as those for fish-ponds or banks concealing wall foundations, *v.* Field 44); Bottom ~, Middle Hogpit (*v.* **hogg**, **pytt**); Big Hollows (*v.* **holh**); Home Fd (*v.* **home**); Horse Cl; Horstead Cl, Horstead Sick 1781 (*v.* **sík**) ('the place where horses are kept', *v.* **hors**, **stede**); Hovel Fd, ~ Mdw (*v.* **hovel**); Hut Cl (*v.* **hut**); Langton Fd (adjoins East Langton parish); Leicester Road Cl; The Leys (*v.* **leys**); Little Fd; Lock Mdw (*v.* Foxton Locks *supra*); Long Mdw 1843, 1968; Lubenham Mdw (Lubenham parish adjoins to the south); The Meadow 1781, 1968; Middle Cl; Mill Cl 1781, Mill Furlong 1755 (*v.* **furlang**), Mill Pits Cl 1781, Mill Pits 1968 (*v.* **pytt**) (*v.* **myln**); Bottom Monks (with the surn. *Monk* in the possessive case; cf. *Joseph Monk* 1862 Census and *Reuben Monk* 1865 ib of Foxton), Kidmonks Cl (presum. belonging with the previous f.n.; *Kid* may be a voiced form by assimilation to *m* of *Kitt*, a pet-name for *Christopher*, since **kide** seems very unlikely); Mud Tip (beside an overflow of the Grand Union Canal; mud from the canal was tipped in this field); New Fd; New Hill; Nuts Cl (prob. with **hnutu**; cf. Chestnuts Paddock *supra*); Old Brick Yard (*v.* **brike-yard**); Old or Kate's Cl (with the surn. *Kates* (a reflex of the ON masc. pers.n. *Káti* or ODan *Kati*), cf. Kates Hill, Billesdon); The Orchard; Paddock; The Park (*v.* **park**); Perkins Cl (with the surn. *Perkins*); Plough Cl 1843 (*v.* **plōg**); Ravens Cl 1781 (cf. *John Raven* 1755); Reeves Cl (with the surn. *Reeves*); Road Cl, Road Fd (enclosures beside a highway); Rookery Nook (*v.* **rookery**, **nōk**); Rushy Mdw (*v.* **riscig**); The Seeds 1968, Far ~ ~, Near Seeds Cl 1843 (*v.* **sǣd**; used of grasses sown for one year's mowing or grazing, as distinguished from permanent pasture); Shoemakers Cl (with the surn. *Shoemaker*); Spoil Banks (adjoins an embankment of the Grand Union Canal); Stepbridge Fd (contains a footbridge over the canal); Swan Furlong (*v.* **swan**[1], **furlang**; beside the canal and thus poss. a site where swans nested regularly, but *furlong* may suggest use at an earlier date than that of the canal here (c.1792–1812)); Ten Acre Meadow 1843 (*v.* **æcer**); Great ~ ~, Little ~ ~, Top Cl (*v.* **top**); Big ~, Little Townsend (*v.* **tūn**, **ende**); Turnpike Cl (*v.* **turnepike**; beside the Market Harborough road); Washbrook Mdw 1781, *v.* **wæsce**, **brōc**); Watering Cl (*v.* **wateryng**; beside a canal dam and a site for watering cattle); Watery Baulk 1755 (*v.* **balca**), Watery Cl 1781, West Watery Cl 1968 (*v.* **wæterig**); Weetmans (the surn. *Weetman* in the possessive case); Westgate Cl (*v.* **west**, **gata**); West Mdw; Windmill Cl (the site of Foxton Mill *supra*, *v.* **wind-mylne**); Wranglings (*v.* **wrang**, **land**).

(b) *the North feild alias Burrowgh feild* 1625, *the borrofeeld* 1690, *the Borroe fild* c.1685, *the Borro feld* 1694, *the Burrough Field* 1707, 1707 (18) (*v.* **berg**, **feld**; one of the great open-fields of the township); *the Common* (*Cow*) *Pasture* 1601, 1606, 1625, 1707, 1707 (18) (*v.* **commun**, **cū**, **pasture**); *the East Fielde* 1601, *the East Feild* 1606, *the East feild alias Gallow feild* 1625 (*v.* **ēast**, **feld**; one of the great open-fields, *v.* Gallow Field Rd *supra*); *Galhou* 1343, *le Gallowe* 1463, *le Galowe* 1494, (*le*) *Galow* 1507, 1523, *Gallow*(*e*) 1601, 1606, 1625, 1655, 1679, 1707, *Gallo* 1690, 1694, *Gallow hades* 1606 (*v.* **hēafod**) ('the hill spur with spongy ground', *v.*

galla, **hōh**; this f.n. is unrelated in etymology to Gallow Hill *supra*); *Robert Goodrich's Land* 1707 (18) (*v*. **land**); *atte Grene* 1364 Pat (p) (*v*. **atte**, **grēne**[2]); *Longcraft* 1694 (*v*. **lang**[1], **croft**); *Lubnam mere* 1606 (*v*. **(ge)mǣre**; Lubenham parish adjoins to the south); *the West feild alias Mill feild* 1625, *the Milfild* c.1685, *the Mill feald* 1690, *the Mill fild* 1694, *the Mill Field* 1707, 1707 (18) (*v*. **myln**, **feld**; one of the great open-fields); *Nise* 1601, *Nyze* 1625, *Nies* 1679, *Niass* 1690, *Noys* 1694, *Noyes* 1707, 1707 (18) (*v*. **nese**); *the North Field* 1601, *~ ~ feilde* 1606 (*v*. **norð**, **feld**; one of the great open-fields, otherwise called *Burrowgh feild*, *supra*); *Rosehadland* 1707 (*v*. **hēafod-land**; earlier forms are needed for *Rose-*; the surn. *Rose* is poss. or the surn. *Rowe* in the possessive case (cf. *Alice Rowe* 1800 Census of Foxton), or a sb. **hors** (**hross**), cf. *Ross Leys* in Hallaton f.ns. (b)); *Smalltoaftes* 1601, *Smaltoftes* 1606, *Small toftes* 1625, *Smaltofts* 1679, *Smalltops* 1707, 1707 (18) (*v*. **smæl**, **toft**); *Stanipoll* 1601, *Stannye poole* 1606, *Stannie poole* 1625, *Stanipool* 1679, *Stannypool* 1690, *Stannepoole* 1694, *Stannipool(e)* 1707, 1707 (18), *v*. **stānig**, **pōl**[1]); *the stone meadow* 1625 (*v*. **stān**; either 'stony meadow' or a '*stoned* meadow', i.e. one having been cleared of stones, *v*. *the stone middow*, Lei **2** 19); *Taslye* 1601, *Tasley* 1606, 1625, 1679, 1707, *Tasle* 1690, *Tasele* 1694 (*v*. **tǣsel**, **lēah**); *the West Field* 1601, *the West feilde* 1606 (*v*. **west**, **feld**; one of the great open-fields, otherwise called *Mill feild*, *supra*); *Wilcroft* 1601, 1606, 1625, 1707, *Wilcraft* 1679, *Willcraft* 1690, 1694 (*v*. **croft**; either with the masc. pers.n. *Will*, a shortened form of *William*, or with its surn. reflex); *Wynnedoole* 1601, *Whynney dole* 1606, *Winnidole* 1679, *Whinnedoll* 1690 (*v*. **whinny**, **dāl**).

Frisby

FRISBY

Frisebi 1086 DB (×2), c.1130 LeicSurv, 1199, 1200 Cur, *Frisebie* 1086 DB, *Friseby* 1221 Fine, 1221 Ass *et passim* to 1355, 1403 Pat, (~ *iuxta Galby* 1306, 1313, 1328 Banco), *Frissebi* 1200 Cur (p), *Frisseby* 1338 AD, 1387 Pat (p)

Fryseby a.1250 *Peake*, 1255 AD *et passim* to 1332 SR (p), 1370 Ass (p), (~ *iuxta Gauby* 1255 AD, ~ *iuxta Galby* 1327, 1328 IpmR), *Frysseby* 1370 Ipm

Frysby 1385 AD, 1399 Pat *et passim* to 1528 Visit, 1535 VE, (~ *iuxta Galby* 1385 AD), *Frisby* 1550 AAS, 1610 Speed *et freq*, (~ *juxta Galby* 1611 LML)

Fresebi 1166 LN, *Freseby* 1166 RBE, *Fresseby* 1416 Nichols

'The farmstead of the Frisians', *v.* **Frīsa**, **Frēsa**, **bȳ**. The township is distinguished by the suffix ~ *iuxta Galby* (with MLat *iuxta* 'next to') from Frisby on the Wreake in East Goscote Hundred, *v.* Lei **2** 80. The site of a deserted medieval village, it is styled *Old Frisby* 1835 O. Galby lies a half-mile to its south-west.

FRISBY FM. FRISBY HOUSE FM, *Frisby House* 1846, 1863, 1877 White; the site of *Old Frisby* 1835 O. FRISBY LODGE, 1925 Kelly, *The Lodge* 1877 White, *v.* **loge**; the home of *Wm. Frisby, grazier* 1877 White and *Thomas Frisby, farmer* 1925 Kelly. FRISBY LODGE FM. GALBY LANE, GALBY RD, Galby lying a half mile to the south-west. HILL TAMBOROUGH, 1913 Sale, *Tamborow* 1625 *Terrier*, *Tamborough* 1638 *ib*, 1649 Nichols, 1662 *Clayton*, 1854 *Surv*, *Tamborough Hill* 1907 *ib*, *v.* **berg**; the specific *Tam* is of uncertain meaning, but may be a pre-English stream-name **Tamā*, as in the various English rivers called *Tame*, formed from an Indo-European root **tā* 'flow', the meaning of such names thus being 'water'. A stream runs south-west through the valley beneath the hill, eventually joining Billesdon Brook at Great Glen. For f.ns. arising, *v.* Tamborough in f.ns. (a) *infra*. HUBBARD'S SPINNEY, *v.* **spinney**; with the surn. *Hubbard*.

FIELD-NAMES

In (a), forms dated 1806 are Map; those dated 1854 and 1907 are *Surv*; 1878 are *PK*; 1913 are Sale. Forms throughout dated c.1250 and c.1280 are *Deed*; those dated 1625, 1638, 1679, 1690, 1703 and 1724 are *Terrier*; 1660 are *Conant*; 1662 and c.1700 are *Clayton*; 1727 are *Plan*.

(a) Seventeen Acres 1907, 1913 (*v*. **æcer**); The Bank 1913 (*v*. **banke**); Barn Cl 1907, 1913 (*v*. **bern**); Big Cl 1907, 1913; Billings Cl 1854, 1878, 1907 (with the surn. *Billing*, in the possessive case, of a family originally from the village of this name, 25 miles to the south in Northants.); Blank Mdw 1907 (*Blank(e)* 1625, *Blanck* 1638, *Blank Sike* 1625, *Blanck Sicke* 1638 (*v*. **sík**), *v*. **blank**); Bottom Mdw 1907, 1913 (*v*. **bottom**); Bottom ~, Top Broadsick 1878, 1907, 1913 (*Broad Sike* 1638, ~ *Sick* 1727, *v*. **brād**, **sík**); Bottom ~ ~, Top Cow Cl 1907, 1913; Crab Homestead 1907, 1913 (*v*. **hām-stede**; poss. with the surn. *Crabb*; otherwise alluding to land on which wild apple-trees grew, *v*. **crabbe**); Far Mdw 1907, 1913; First Mdw 1907, 1913; Fox Covert 1913 (*v*. **fox**, **cover(t)**); Frisby Gorse 1806 (*v*. **gorst**); Frisby Homestead 1907 (*v*. **hām-stede**); Little ~, Middle ~, Top Germany 1907, 1913 (either a name humorously indicating remoteness from a farmstead, or one alluding to a plant, such as German millet (*Sitoria germanica*) or German rice (*Hordeum zeocriton*); cf. Germany, Lei **2** 213 and Jarminy, Ru 261); Gravel Hole Cl 1854, 1907, 1913 (cf. *grauill pits* 1625, *Gravell pitts* 1638, *v*. **gravel**, **pytt**, **hol**[1]); Hardy's Leys 1907, 1913 (*Hardy leys* 1625, 1638, ~ *Leas* 1690, ~ *leaze* c.1700, *v*. **leys**; with the surn. *Hardy*); Hill Fd 1907, 1913; Bottom Hole Cl 1907, 1913 (*v*. **bottom**, **hol**[1]); Bottom ~, Great Holt 1907, 1913 (*v*. **holt**); House Cl 1907, 1913 (*v*. Frisby House Fm *supra*); Hull's Cl 1907, 1913 (with the surn. *Hull*, cf. *George Hull* 1835 Census and *Albert Hull* 1907, both of Frisby); Little Mdw 1907, 1913; Lodge Cl 1907, 1913 (cf. Frisby Lodge *supra*); Bottom ~, Top Marsdale 1907, 1913 (*the Marish* 1638, *Marishdale* 1662, *Marisdale* c.1700, *v*. **mersc**, **merisc**, **dalr**); Middle Mdw 1913; Bottom ~ ~, Top Nether Mdw 1907, 1913; The New Cl 1854, 1907, 1913; New Mdw 1907; Old Cl 1854, 1878, 1907 (*v*. **ald**); Great ~, Little Orids (sic) 1907, 1913 (poss. with **ord** 'a spit of land', or even a derogatory name for land difficult to cultivate, with *horrid* in an early sense 'rough, shaggy'); Palmer's Yard 1907, 1913 (*v*. **geard**; cf. *Palmers Cottage* c.1700, with the surn. *Palmer*); Old ~ ~ 1907, Plough Cl 1907, 1913, Plough Fd 1907 (*v*. **plōg**); Bottom ~, Great Roby 1854, 1907, 1913 (*Rouberue*, *Rouberuesike* (*v*. **sík**) c.1280, *Roborow(e)s* 1625, 1638, *Roborough* 1662, *Little Rowburroughs* 1727, *Robor(r)ough Close* 1660, 1692, *Rowborrow Close* c.1700, *Roborough Meadow* 1692, *v*. **rūh**, **berg**); Rough Cl 1907, 1913 (*v*. **rūh**); Sauntson's Cl 1907, 1913 (*Sandersons close* 1662, c.1700; with the surn. *Sanderson*); Scotches 1907, 1913 (poss. the surn. *Scott* in the possessive case; otherwise land originally subject to some kind of tax, *v*. **scot**); Seeds 1907, 1913 (*v*. **sǣd**; used of grasses sown for one year's mowing or grazing, as distinguished from permanent pasture); Small Cl, Small Piece 1878 (*v*. **pece**); Far ~, Near Stockwell 1913, Stockwell Cl 1854, 1878, 1907 (1662), Big ~ ~, Little Stockwell Mdw 1854, Little Stockwell 1878, 1907 ((*the*) *Stockwell* 1625, 1638, *v*. **stocc**, **wella**); First ~, Second ~, Third ~, Fourth ~, Fifth ~, Sixth Tamborough 1854, 1878, 1907, 1913, Flat Tamborough 1913 (*v*. **flatr**), Tamborough Mdw 1854, 1878, 1907, 1913 (*high* ~, *longe* ~, *low tamborow* 1625,

High ~, *Long Tamborough* 1638, *Tamborough Close* c.1700, *v.* Hill Tamborough *supra*); Top Homestead 1907 (*v.* **hām-stede**).

(b) *Barefoot Slade* 1638 (*v.* **berg**, **fōt**, **slæd**; cf. *Barfote* in Mowsley f.ns. (b) and *Barfoote* in Owston f.ns. (b)); *Bilsdon way* 1625 (*v.* **weg**; Billesdon lies one mile to the north-east); *boueton* c.1250 ('(the place) above the village', *v.* **bufan**, **tūn**); *brathorslade* c.1250 (*v.* **slæd**; earlier forms are needed to explain the specific, but poss. is the ODan pers.n. *Brōðir* or OE **brōðor**, ON **bróðir**. ON **breiðr** 'broad' may have influenced the initial vowel in the name); *Long* ~, *Short Breach* 1625, 1638 (*v.* **brēc**); *Butchers Close* c.1700 (with the surn. *Butcher*); *capellam de Friseby* 1220 MHW, *capelle de Friseb'* 1237 RGros (with MLat *capella* 'a chapel'; Frisby was a chapelry of the parish church of Galby); *Caudell* ~, *Caudill thornes* 1625, *Caudie* ~, *Caudy Thornes* 1638, *v.* **þorn**; prob. 'cold spring' (*v.* **cald**, **wella**) rather than 'cold hill'); *the Chappel Bank* 1690 (*v.* **chapel(e)**, **banke** and *capellam de Friseby*, *supra*); (*a piece of medowe called*) *the Checker* 1625 (*v.* **cheker**); *the Church Gate* 1625, 1638 (*v.* **churche**, **gata**; the road to St Peter's Church in Galby); *Colde foard* 1625, *Cole ford* 1638 (*v.* **cald**, **ford**); *Constables balke* 1638 (*v.* **conestable**, **balca**); *Cottiers bigger* ~, *Cottiers lesser close* 1662, *the Cottyers Close* c.1700 (*v.* **cottere**); *Crosons Close* 1724 (with a local form (in the possessive case) of the surn. *Croxton* of a family originally from South Croxton, 5 miles to the north; *v.* Lei **3** 72); *dedemor* c.1250, *Dedmore* 1625, *Deadmore* 1638 (*v.* **dēad**, **mōr**[1]; a common name for infertile wasteland); *Dene peice* 1625, *Deane Peece* 1638 (*v.* **pece**; either with **denu** or with the surn. *Dean*); *the East feild* 1625, *the East Feilde* 1638 (*v.* **ēast**, **feld**; one of the great open-fields); *elrenestub* c.1250 (*v.* **ellern**, **stubb**); *enedesike* c.1250 (*v.* **ened**, **sík**); *Eustace Gate* 1625, 1638 (*v.* **gata**), *Eustice meadow* 1638 (with the surn. *Eustace*); *Flax leys* 1625 (*v.* **leys**; poss. with a metathesized **flask** 'swampy grassland' rather than **fleax**, if *Flax* is not a memory of past arable use); *flaxlondes* c.1250, *Flaxland(s)* 1625, 1638 (*v.* **fleax**, **land**); (*the*) *Five Acres* 1679, 1690, 1724 (*v.* **æcer**); *Fox his closs* 1625, *Foxes Close* 1638 (*v.* **clos(e)**), *Fox his dole* 1625 (*v.* **dāl**) (with the surn. *Fox*); *Fox holes* 1703 (*v.* **fox-hol**); *Frisby Hall* c.1700 (*v.* **hall**; the site of the hall is presum. close to Frisby House Fm, where 16th-cent. masonry survives in outbuildings); *fulskyll* c.1250, *fuskhill* 1625 (*v.* **fūl**, **sík**, **hyll**); *Galby Meere* 1638 (*v.* **(ge)mǣre**; Galby adjoins to the south-west); *Goods Close* 1638 (with the surn. *Good*); *the greate closs hedge* 1625, *the Great Close hedge* 1638 (*v.* **grēat**, **clos(e)**, **hecg**); *grenesike* c.1250, *Green Sick* 1638 (*v.* **grēne**[1], **sík**); *the Gutter* 1638 (*v.* **goter**); *Haines hedland* 1638 (*v.* **hēafod-land**; with the surn. *Haines*, a reflex of the ODan masc. pers.n. *Haghni*); *Hall Hill* 1727 (*v.* **hall**; note *Frisby Hall*, *supra*); *hamelthoft* c.1250, *hameltoft* c.1280, *Hamble toft* 1625, 1638 (*v.* **toft**; with the ON masc. pers.n. *Hamall*); *the Hassocks* 1625, 1638 (*v.* **hassuc**); *hensike* 1625, *Hensick* 1638 (*v.* **henn**, **sík**); *High gate* 1625 (*v.* **gata**; with **hēg** or **hēah**[1]); *William Hills close* 1662, *Hills Cottage* c.1700; *homes gate* 1638 (*v.* **holmr**, **gata**); *hose wey* 1625 (*v.* **hōh** (**hōs** nom.pl.), **weg**); *Horwoods* c.1700 (the surn. *Horwood* in the possessive case); *Houtonemor* c.1250, *Houghton more* 1625, ~ *Moor* 1638 (*v.* **mōr**[1]), *Houghton Shrubbs* 1625 (*v.* **scrubb**) (Houghton on the Hill parish adjoins to the north-west); *Ilston Meer(e)* 1625, 1638 (*v.* **(ge)mǣre**; Illston on the Hill parish adjoins to the south); *lampittis* c.1250 (*v.* **lām-pytt**); *Langdike* 1625, *Longdike* 1638 (*v.* **lang**[1], **dík**); *langelond'* c.1250, c.1280, *Langlands* 1625, *Short* ~ 1638 (*v.* **lang**[1], **land**); *Great* ~, *Little Lowsden* 1679, 1690, 1703 (*v.* **hlōse**, **denu**); *Meersdale* 1625, 1638 (*v.* **(ge)mǣre**; with **dalr** or **deill**); *morrill sike hedge* 1638, *Moore Sick hedge* 1638 (*v.*

mōr[1], **hyll**, **sík**, **hecg**); *Narrow Pike* 1638 (*v.* **nearu**, **pīc**); *Neatshead* 1625, 1638 (*v.* **nēat**, **hēafod**); *old furlonge* 1625, 1638 (*v.* **ald**, **furlang**); *tholdforthegate* c.1250 (*v.* **þe**, **ald**, **ford**, **gata**); *the parsons gore* 1625, 1630 (*v.* **persone**, **gāra**); *peselond'* c.1250, *High ~*, *Low Peaselands* 1625, 1638 (*v.* **pise**, **land**); *radelond* c.1250, *redlande* 1625 (*v.* **rēad**, **land**); *rulond* c.1250 (*v.* **rūh**, **land**); *rushie medowe* 1625 (*v.* **riscig**, **mēd** (**mēdwe** obl.sg.)); *shortebuttis* c.1250 (*v.* **sc(e)ort**, **butte**); *shortland sike* 1625, *Shortland Sick* 1638 (*v.* **sc(e)ort**, **land**, **sík**); *Short*(*e*) *Tofts* 1625, 1638 (*v.* **sc(e)ort**, **toft**); *shouelebrodemedue* c.1250 (*v.* **scofl-brædu**, **mēd** (**mēdwe** obl.sg.)); *the Shrubs* 1638 (*v.* **scrubb**); *Six Acre* 1625, 1638 (*v.* **six**, **æcer**); *smalthornis* c.1250 (*v.* **smæl**, **þorn**); *smethemedwe* c.1250 (*v.* **smēðe**[1], **mēd** (**mēdwe** obl.sg.)); *the South Feild* 1625, 1638 (*v.* **sūð**, **feld**; one of the great open-fields); (*super*) *thachink* c.1250 ('place where thatching materials are got', *v.* **þæc**, **-ing**[2]); *Throwslade* 1625, *Thorowe Slade* 1638 (*v.* **slæd**; either with **þrūh** 'a conduit', figuratively also 'a deep valley' or with **þurh** 'through'); *threthornehul* c.1250 (*v.* **þrēo**, **þorn**, **hyll**); *Thurn*(*e*)*hill* 1625, 1638 (*v.* **þyrne**, **þyrnir**, **hyll**; poss. a later style for *threthornehul*); *Tofts Gate* 1625, 1638 (*v.* **toft**, **gata**); *Tongs gate* 1625 (*v.* **tunge**, **gata**); *the Twenty five Acres* 1679, *Five and twenty Acres* 1703 (*v.* **æcer**); (*on*) *Waterfall* 1625, 1638 (*v.* **wæter-(ge)fall**); *Waueremos* c.1280 ('the unstable boggy land', *v.* **wæfre**, **mos**); *Wheate more* 1625 (*v.* **wēt**, **mōr**[1]); *Willow Sike* 1625, 1638 (*v.* **wilig**, **sík**); *wodegatehul* c.1250, *Woodgate hill* 1625, 1638 (*v.* **wudu**, **gata**, **hyll**); *Wolda* c.1250, *þe Wold* c.1280, *The Woult* 1662, *The Woult meadow* 1662, *the Oult Meadow*, *the Oult Close* c.1700 (*v.* **þe**, **wald**).

Galby

GALBY (GAULBY 1")

Galbi 1086 DB (×2), 1206 Cur, 1206 P, 1306 Pap, *Galby* 1221 Fine, 1232 RHug *et freq*, *Galbya* 1286 BM, *Galbye* 1532 *Wyg*, 1549 Pat, 1604 SR

Gaubi 1190, 1191 P, l.13 (1404) *Laz*, *Gaubia* 1178 × 84 (1328) Ch, Hy 2 Dugd, John (1404) *Laz*, *Gauby* 1206 RFinib, 1220 RHug *et passim* to c.1292 *LCDeeds* (p), l.13 (1404) *Laz*

Galeby 1242 GildR (p), 1258 BM *et passim* to 1346 Pat, 1348 Cl, *Galleby* 1260 Cur, 1264 Cl, 1304, 1307 Pat, 1434 *Wyg*

Galdbye 1527 *Wyg*

Gaulby(*e*) 1576 Saxton, 1610 Speed, 1716 LML

Probably 'the farmstead, village on poor soil', *v*. **gall**, **bȳ**. Ekwall DEPN rightly observes that it is doubtful that the first el. is the ON masc. pers.n. *Galli* because of the absence of *e* between *l* and *b* in the earliest forms. He suggests the possibility, rather, that the specific is an unrecorded ON sb. *gald* 'sterile soil' (cf. OSwed *galder* 'sterile'). However, one would have expected by the time of DB *gald* > *galt* with the retention of *t*. More probably, the first el. is an unrecorded ON sb. **gall** 'a barren spot' related to OE *galla* 'a barren or wet spot in a field', LGerm *galle* 'a wet place', Du *gal*, Germ *galle* 'a barren spot in a field', Swed *gall* 'barren' and ModEdial. *gall* 'a barren spot in a field, spongy ground'. The township is surrounded by English settlements with names in *-tūn* — King's Norton, Little Stretton, Houghton, Illston, Rolleston and Burton Overy and would plainly have been settled on soils of inferior quality which earlier farmers had avoided. The soils here are chiefly of stiff clay and loam.

Spellings with *au* for *al* are due to AN influence.

BATH SPINNEY, 1913 Sale, 'clump of trees by a pool', *v*. **bæð**, **spinney**. 'In Bath Spinney there is a large spring which, by means of a water-ram, supplies water to part of Galby and King's Norton', *v*. VCHL **5** 97. CARRYGATE, 1640 LAS, 1907 *Surv*, 1913 Sale, *Carrigate* 1649 Nichols, *v*. **gata**; poss. with **calu**, cf. Carrywell in Illston f.ns. (a); but **kjarr** may pertain. CHAMBERLAIN'S NETHER CLOSE, 1913 Sale, *Chamberlains Close* 1695 *Terrier*; with the surn. *Chamberlain*. A Leonard Chamberlain was granted St John's Hospital lands here in 1542, *v*. VCHL **5** 98. GAULBY LODGE, *v*. **loge**. LIMES FM, *Limes Farm* c.1920 *Plan*, *v*. **lime**. MANOR HO., *Manor house* 1925 Kelly, *v*. **maner**. THE RECTORY, 1863, 1877 White, 1925 Kelly, *v*. **rectory**; it is *the Parsonage house* 1690, 1695 *Terrier*, *v*. **personage**. ST PETER'S CHURCH, *the* (*Parish*) *Church* 1625, 1638 *Terrier*, *the Church of Galbie* 1703 *ib*, *Church (St Peter)* 1846, 1863, 1877 White, 1925 Kelly; it is earlier recorded as *ecclesie de Gauby* 1220 MHW, 1236, 1237 RGros, ~ ~ *Galby* c.1250 *Deed*, 1347, 1353 *Pat*, *ecclesia de Galby* 1561 *ib*. Note also *the Churchyard* 1625, 1638 *Terrier*, *v*. **churchyerd**. TAMBOROUGH FM, named from Tamborough in adjacent Frisby.

FIELD-NAMES

In (a), forms dated 1806 are Map; those dated 1849 are *TA*; 1878 are *PK*; 1907 are *Surv*; 1913 are Sale. Forms throughout dated 1296 are *Wyg*; those dated 1337, 14, 1649 and 1732 are Nichols; 1429 are *AddCh*; 1625, 1635, 1638, 1679, 1690, 1695 and 1703 are *Terrier*.

(a) Barnett Cl 1878, 1907 (with the surn. *Barnett*); Barratt Cl 1913 (with the surn. *Barratt*); Beebys Cl 1907, 1913 (*Beebies Close* 1690, 1695, 1703; with the surn. *Beeby* of a family originally from the township of this name 5 miles to the north-west); Between Towns 1907, 1913 (*Tween Towns* 1649, *v*. **betwēonan**, **tūn**; land lying between two townships); Billing's Cl 1913 (with the surn. *Billing* of a family originally from the village of this name, 25 miles to the south in Northants.); Poll Bird's Mdw 1907, 1913 (land of a woman called *Polly Bird*; John Bird was a prosperous farmer in the 16th cent., but in 1851, John and Alfred Bird were agricultural labourers, *v*. VCHL **5** 99); Blacksmith's Cl 1907, 1913 (*v*. **blacksmith**); Bottom Cl 1907, 1913 (*v*. **bottom**); Bound Cl 1878 (*v*. **bounde**; a close on or near a boundary); Great ~, Little ~, Near Broadsacks 1907, ~, ~, ~ Broad-acks (sic) 1913 (*Broadsikes* 1649, *v*. **brād**, **sík**); Brook Ground 1907 (*v*. **brōc**, **grund**); Butt Cl 1907, 1913 (1649, *the But Close* 1690), Butt Close Mdw 1907, 1913 (*v*. **butte**; land enclosed from butt-pieces between furlongs); Carrygate Mdw, Little Carrygate Cl 1907, 1913 (*v*. Carrygate *supra*); Carter's Cl 1907, 1913 (with the surn. *Carter*); Lower ~, Upper Chamberlains Cl 1907, 1913, Far Chamberlains Cl 1907 (*v*. Chamberlain's Nether Close *supra*); Churchyard Cl 1878, 1907 (*v*. St Peter's Church *supra*); Clement's Cl 1907, 1913 (with the surn. *Clement*); Coulton's Gorse 1806 (*v*. **gorst**; with the surn. *Coulton*); Dams 1907, 1913 (*the Dams* 1649, *v*. **damme**); Decoy 1907, 1913 (*v*. **decoy**); Fishponds Spinney 1913 (*v*. **fisshe-ponde**, **spinney**); Flat Mdw 1907, 1913 (*v*. **flatr**); Flat Tamborough 1907 (*v*. Hill Tamborough in Frisby); Galby Cl 1907, 1913; Galby Wood Mdw 1907, 1913 (*Galbie* ~ 1625, *Galby wood* 1638, *v*. **wudu**); Goat Mdw 1907 (*v*. **gāt**); Goodman's Cl 1907, 1913 (*Goodmans*

Close 1649; with the surn. *Goodman*); Great Mdw 1907; First ~ ~, Second Hilly Mdw 1907, 1913 (*v.* **hyllig**); Bottom Holts 1907, 1913 (*v.* **holt** and Great Holt in adjacent Frisby f.ns. (a)); Bottom ~, Top Homestead 1913 (*the Homestead of Galbie* 1703, *v.* **hām-stede**); Bottom ~ ~, Top ~ ~, Hulls Homestead 1907 (*v.* **hām-stede**; cf. *George Hull* 1835 Census and *Albert Hull* 1847 ib of adjoining Frisby parish); Job's Cl, Job's Mdw 1907, 1913 (with the surn. *Job*; for an extended discussion of the various sources of this surn., *v.* Reaney *s.n.*); (The) Lake Mdw 1907, 1913 (*v.* **lake**); Land Cl 1907, 1913 (1649, *v.* **land**; prob. an enclosure consisting of selions of a former open-field); Little Mdw 1907, 1913; Lodge Cl 1913 (*v.* Gaulby Lodge *supra*); Long Mdw 1907, 1913; Middle Ground 1907 (*v.* **grund**); Middle Mdw; Mill Cl 1907, 1913 (*the Mill Close* 1649), Mill Mdw 1907, 1913 (*v.* **myln**); Near Mdw 1907; New Fd 1907, 1913; New Mdw 1913 (1649); Old Cl (*v.* **ald**); Old School 1878, 1907 (land near the old village school); Far Over Cl 1907, 1913 (*v.* **uferra**); Far ~ ~, Near Plough Cl 1907, 1913 (*v.* **plōg**); Far ~ ~, Middle ~ ~, Near Randall Walls, Randall Walls Mdw 1907, 1913 (*Randall Wall* 1625, 1638; poss. with *Randall*, a surn. especially common in nearby Billesdon, Tilton and Halstead (with **wella**); but the whole could be an original **rynel-wella* (> **rundle-well*) 'the spring source of the small stream'; but *v.* Wall Gates in nearby Little Stretton f.ns. (a)); Round Cl 1907 (*v.* **round**); Rowell's Cl 1878, 1907 (with the surn. *Rowell*); Spinney Cl 1907, First ~ ~, to Sixth Spinney Cl 1913, Great ~ ~, Little Spinney Mdw 1907, 1913 (*v.* Bath Spinney *supra*); Stocker Hill 1913 (*Scockrill* 1625, *v.* Stocker Hill in adjoining Houghton on the Hill f.ns. (a), Scockerhill in King's Norton f.ns. (a) and *Scockwell* in Little Stretton f.ns (b)); Top Cl 1907; Lower ~, Upper Townsend 1907, 1913 (*Townsend Close* 1649, *v.* **tūn**, **ende**); Triangle 1913 (a three-cornered enclosure); White's Yard 1907, 1913 (with the surn. *White*); Wood Mdw 1907, 1913 (1649, *v.* **wudu**).

(b) *Balland Sike* 1628, ~ *Sick* 1638 (*v.* **bēan**, **land**, **sík**); *Bull balk* 1638 (*v.* **bula**, **balca**; grazing for a bull); *the Brook(e)* 1625, 1638 (*v.* **brōc**); *Crakergate* 1337 ('road frequented by crows', *v.* **krákr** (**kráka** gen.pl.), **gata**); *the dalebeck gutter* 1625 (*v.* **dalr**, **bekkr**, **goter**); *Elliss Close* 1695 (with the surn. *Ellis(s)*); *the Gutter neare to Galbie Wood* 1625, 1638 (*v.* **goter**); *Houghton Brook Closes* 1649 (*v.* **brōc**; Houghton on the Hill adjoins to the north-west, the brook forming the parish boundary); *Huntsbecke* 1638, *Hunsbeck furlonge* 1625 (*v.* **furlang**) (*v.* **bekkr**; either with the ON masc. pers.n. *Hundr* or with the OE masc. pers.n. *Hund*; if the latter pers.n. pertains, **bekkr** may have replaced **brōc**; an ON sb. *hundr* or OE *hund* (both meaning 'hound') seem less likely; the stream name also appears in adjoining King's Norton); *Kestie* 1625, 1638 (*v.* **kjarr**, **stīg**); *longemur* 1296 (*v.* **lang**[1], **mōr**[1]); *Mealebecke* 1638, *Molebeck Gutter* 1638 (*v.* **goter**) (*v.* **mǫl**, **bekkr**); *Medburne sike* 1625, *Medborne* ~, *Medburne Sick* 1635, 1638 (*v.* **sík**; with the surn. *Medbourne* of a family originally from the township of this name, 8 miles to the south-east; note *Medburne hill* in adjacent King's Norton); *Milne Holme* 1429 (*v.* **myln**, **holmr**); *Norton Meere* 1625, 1638 (*v.* **(ge)mǣre**; King's Norton parish adjoins to the south-west); *the Parsonage Closs* 1625, ~ ~ *Close* 1679, 1703, *the Parsonage Home Close* 1732 (*v.* **home**) (*v.* **personage**); *Picks Close* 1679, 1703 (with the surn. *Pick*); *the Pond Close* 1649 (*v.* **ponde**); *the South Feild* 1625, 1638 (*v.* **sūð**, **feld**; prob. one of the settlement's great open-fields, but evidence for any others is lacking); *the Town street* 1690, 1703 (*v.* **tūn**, **strǣt**); *Westwelle* 14 (*v.* **west**, **wella**); *Whart gates* 1625 (*v.* **þverr** (**þvert** neut.), **gata**); *Willowes Croft* 1638 (*v.* **wilig**, **croft**).

Glooston

GLOOSTON

Glorstone 1086 DB, *Glorston* 1293 Pat
Gloreston c.1130 LeicSurv, 1163 P *et passim* to 1249 Cur *et freq* to 1384 Banco *et passim* to 1619, 1629 LML, *Glorestona* c.1160 Dane (p), 1209 × 19, 1227 RHug, *Glorestuna* 1209 × 19 ib, *Glorestone* 1222 ib, m.13 *Peake* (p), *Gloriston*' 1209 × 35 RHug, 1264 RGrav *et passim* to 1306 *Hazlerigg*, 1327 SR
Gloston 1269 Cur (p), c.1291 Tax *et passim* to 1465 Pat, 1517 DI
Gloueston 1344 GildR (p), 1368 IpmR *et passim* to 1475 × 85 ECP, 1510 Visit, *Glouston* 1535 VE, 1561 Fine, 1580 LEpis, 1637 Fine
Gloweston 1548 AAS, 1576 Saxton, 1610 Speed, *Glowston* 1481 ECP, 1510 LP, 1526 AAS, 1604 SR
Glooston 1798 Nichols, 1806 Map, 1824 O *et freq*

'Glōr's farmstead, village', *v.* **tūn**. The masc. pers.n. *Glōr* is OE.

ANDREW'S LANE, 1828 *EnclA*; with the surn. *Andrew*(*s*). It is *Leicester Lane* 1700, 1745 *Terrier*, the lane leading to Gartree Road, the route to Leicester. BLUE BELL (P.H.) (lost), *Bell* 1846 White, *Blue Bell* 1863, 1877 ib, 1925 Kelly. BROOKSIDE COTTAGE, cf. *the Brook*(*e*) 1628, 1634, 1700 *Terrier*, *the Town Brook* 1745 *ib* (*v.* **tūn**), *v.* **brōc**. BURROW HILL RD is *Burrow Road* 1828 *EnclA*; to the west of Crossburrow Hill *infra*. CRANOE RD, Cranoe lying one mile to the south-east. CROSSBURROW HILL, *Crosborowe* ~, *Crosbarowe hill* 1601 *Terrier*, *Crossborow* ~ 1628 *ib*, *Crasborrow Hill* 1634 *ib*, *Crosborough* ~ 1637 *Map*, *Crosborrow Hill* 1674 *Terrier*, *Crosbrowe* ~ 1638 *ib*, *Crose Borrowe* ~, *Cross Borroe* ~ 1690 *ib*, *Crossberry* ~ 1700 *ib*, *Crossbury* ~ 1745 *ib*, *Cross Barrow Hill* 1824 O, *Cross Burrow Hill* 1867 *Surv*; also called by the shortened form *Burrow Hill* 1601, 1634 *Terrier et passim* to 1745 *ib*; the extended name means 'the hill with a cross upon it', *v.* **cros**, **berg** (with pleonastic **hyll** added later). The hill overlooks Gartree Road. GLOOSTON LODGE, 1798 Map, *v.* **loge**. GLOOSTON WOOD, 1806 Map, 1925 Kelly, *The Wood* 1637 *Map*, *v.* **wudu**. THE HALL, *v.* **hall**. HARBOROUGH RD, Market

Harborough lying 5 miles to the south-west. HOME FM, *v.* **home**. THE RECTORY, 1925 Kelly, *v.* **rectory**; cf. *the Personage house* 1628 *Terrier*, *the Parsonage house* 1700, 1745, 1821 *ib*, *v.* **personage**. ST JOHN THE BAPTIST'S CHURCH, *Church (St John)* 1846, 1863, 1877 White, *Church (St John the Baptist)* 1925 Kelly; it is earlier recorded as *ecclesie de Gloriston* 1220 MHW and even earlier with the less exalted style as *capellam* de *Glorestona* a.1219 RHug (with MLat *capella* 'a chapel'). Note also *the Church Yard*(*e*) 1628, 1638 *Terrier et passim* to 1821 *ib*, *v.* **churchyerd**.

FIELD-NAMES

In (a), forms presented without dates are 1971 *Surv*; those dated 1828 are *EnclA*; 1867 are *Surv*. Forms throughout dated 1601, 1625, 1628, 1634, 1638, 1674, 1690, 1700, 1738 and 1745 are *Terrier*; those dated 1637 are *Map*.

(a) Five ~, Seven ~, Nineteen Acre (*v.* **æcer**); Aldwinkle's Mdw 1867 (with the surn. *Aldwinkle* of a family originally from the township of this name, 18 miles to the south-east in Northants.); Allotments (*v.* **allotment**); Bare Hill 1867 (1738, *Beare hill* 1628, 1634, 1638, 1690, *Beares hill* 1674, *Bears hill* 1700, 1745, *Beare hill leyes* 1638, *Bear hill*(*s*) *Leys* 1700, 1745 (*v.* **leys**), *v.* **bere**, **hyll**); Bean Cl 1828, 1971 (*v.* **bēan**); First ~, Second Blackwell (*Blakwell* 1601, *Blackwell* 1625, 1634 *et passim* to 1745, *Blakwell forlonge* 1601 (*v.* **furlang**), *Blackwell waye* 1625 (*v.* **weg**), 'the dark spring or stream', *v.* **blæc**, **wella**); Broad Furrows 1867, 1971 (1674, 1738, *brode thoroughs* 1628, *Broadfurrowes* 1634, *Broad Thurrows* 1700, 1745, *v.* **brād**, **furh**); Boney Corner 1828, 1971 (*v.* **boney**, **corner**; presum. alluding to skeletal remains found there); Church Fd (*v.* St John the Baptist's Church *supra*); Clarks Cl (with the surn. *Clark*); Colemans Fd (with the surn. *Coleman*); Cow Pen Cl 1828 (*v.* **penn**[2]); Cross Burrow Hill Cl, ~ ~ ~ Plantation 1867 (*v.* **plantation** and Crossburrow Hill *supra*); Dyers Cl, ~ Mdw 1828, 1971 (with the medieval occupational surn. *Dyer*); Elm Cl (*v.* **elm**); Flatt ~ 1867, Flat Cl 1971 (*v.* **flatr**); Gartree Road 1828 (the Roman *Via Devana*, later called Gartree Road, runs south-east through the parish from Leicester); Gorse Hill (*v.* **gorst**); Greens Mdw 1828 (with the surn. *Green*); Hill Brakes 1828, ~ Breaks 1971 (*v.* **bracu**), Hill Cl 1828, 1971, ~ Fd 1828, ~ Mdw 1828; Home Cl 1867, 1971, Homefield 1971 (*v.* **home**); Jessons (the surn. *Jesson* in the possessive case); Kibworth Road 1828 (Kibworth Harcourt lying 4 miles to the south-east); Little Fd 1828, 1867, Bottom ~ ~, Top Little Fd 1971 (*Littelfilde* 1601, (*the*) *Little feilde*(*e*) 1628, 1634 *et passim* to 1700, ~ ~ *Field* 1738, 1745 (*v.* **lȳtel**, **feld**); Lodge Mdw (1745, *v.* Glooston Lodge *supra*); Long Plantation (*v.* **plantation**); Bottom ~ ~, Mattin Cl 1828 ((*the*) *Matten close* 1634, 1690), Bottom Matins 1971 (*Easte mattins* 1601, *East* ~, *West Mattins* 1637, *Long mattins* 1601, 1738, *Shorte matten*(*s*) 1628, 1634, *Short Mattyn* 1674, ~ *Matten* 1690, ~ *Mattens* 1700, ~ *Mattins* 1738, 1745, *the Mattyns* 1674, *the Mattens* 1700, *Mattin Furlong* 1745 (*v.* **furlang**), *matten yate* 1628, *Matten gate* 1634, 1690, (*beneath*) *Mattin gate* 1638, 1745, *Mattyn gate* 1674 (*v.* **gata**) (of uncertain meaning; ME **matines** (eModE *mattyns*) 'morning' is possible, indicating some form of morning obligation or occupation (perh. cf. *morgen* 'morning' in Moundrell, Lei **2** 192 and maybe similarly *the shorte fridayes* in f.ns. (b) *infra*); the surn. *Mattin* is also poss., but this belongs to Derbys. and Notts. and evidence for its use in Leics. in the early 17th cent. is lacking); Millins Leys (*v.* **leys**; with the surn. *Millen*, a reflex of the OFr masc. pers.n. *Milon*); Mill Fd; Mill Mount 1867 (*Mill Mont* 1700 (*v.* **mont**), *the milne mote* 1601, *mill moote* 1628, 1634, 1638, *Mill moot* 1674, *Mill Mote* 1745, *v.* **myln**; with reference to a windmill and with **mote** in the sense 'an artificially raised mound', as in *the mill moote* in Cranoe *supra*); New Fd 1828, 1971; Back ~, Front Orchard; Bottom ~, Top Outwalks 1828, 1971 (*the Outwalks* 1637, *v.* **ūt**, **walk**; a range of pasture at the north parish boundary); Paradise 1867 (1738, *Parradice furlong* 1628, *Paradice Furlong* 1634, 1690, 1745, *~ furland* 1674 (*v.* **furlang**), *v.* **paradis**, early used of a garden or of an enclosed pleasure ground, but here perh. simply a complimentary name, cf. Lei **2** 360 and Lei **3** 344); Peace (*v.* **pece**); Piked Mdw 1867 (1738, *Picke medowe* 1601, *Pic(k) medow* 1625, 1634, *Pick(e) meadow(e)* 1628, 1638, 1674, 1700, *Peck Meadow* 1745, *v.* **pīc**, **piked**); The Plough Fd (*v.* **plōg**); Ramsbed Cl (1637, *v.* **hramsa**, **bedd**); Seed Fd (*v.* **sǣd**; used of grasses sown for one year's mowing or grazing, as distinguished from permanent pasture); 1st ~, 2nd Shepherd's Mdw 1867 (either with **scēp-hirde** or with the surn. *Shepherd* derived from it); Spinney Furlong, Spinney Gardens (*v.* **gardin**; land used for horticulture) (*v.* **spinney**); Stonton Foot Way 1828 (*v.* **fote-waye**), Stonton Road 1828 (is *Stanton lane* 1601, *v.* **lane**) (Stonton Wyville lies one mile to the south-west); Stone Pit 1828 (*v.* **stān-pytt**); Bit ~ (*v.* **bit**), Small ~, Hot ~ (*v.* **holt**), Thrawly (*Thrally* 1738, *v.* **þrǣl**, **lēah**); Timsons ~ 1828, Timson Cl 1971 (with the surn. *Timson*); Tiplers (the medieval occupational surn. *Tipler* (ME *tipeler* 'a seller of ale') in the possessive case); Village Mdw (*v.* **village**); Willow Sink Fd (sic) 1828 (*Willowe sicke* 1628, *Willow sick(e)* 1634, 1700, *Willowe sicke filde* 1601, *~ ~ feilde* 1628, *Willow sick ~* 1634, 1674, *Willow sike feild* 1637, 1700, *Willow Sick Field* 1738, 1745 (*v.* **feld**; one of the great open-fields of the township), *Willow sicke forlonge* 1601, *Willow Sick Furlong* 1738, 1745 (*v.* **furlang**), *Willow Sink Slade* (sic) 1738 (*v.* **slæd**), *v.* **wilig**, **sík**); Wood Cl 1828, 1971, ~ Mdw 1828, 1971 (*v.* Glooston Wood *supra*).

(b) *Ancle Close* 1738 (*v.* **angle**); *Banlandes* 1601, 1628, *Banlands* 1634, *Bandlands* 1674, 1700, *Bandland* 1745, *Banlandes browke* 1601, *Bandland ~* 1628, 1674, *Banlands brooke* 1638, *Bandlands brook & willows* 1700 (*v.* **brōc**, **wilig**), *Bandland Furlong* 1745 (*v.* **furlang**) (*v.* **bēan**, **land**); *Beggers ~* 1601, 1634, 1700, *Beggars Bush* 1738, *Beggars-Bush Furlong* 1745 (*v.* **beggere**, **busc**; literally 'scrubland haunt of beggars', a common f.n. which appears to denote poor, unproductive land); *Bonds Hadley* 1745 (*v.* **headley**; cf. *Jonathan Bond* 1745); *Brakey Close* 1637 (*v.* **braky**); *Breach*, *Breach Leys* 1738 (*v.* **leys**) (*v.* **brēc**); *Broad Meadow* 1738, 1745 (*v.* **brād**); *Brooke forlong* 1634, *Brook furland* (sic) 1674, ~ *Furlong* 1700, 1745 (*v.* **furlang**), *bruke hadland* 1601 (*v.* **hēafod-land**) (*v.* **brōc**); *the Lord Brudnells headland* 1700 (*v.* **hēafod-land**); *Burnet(t) corner* 1674, 1690, 1700, *Burnetts Corner* 1738 (*v.* **corner**), *Burnetts Slade* 1738 (*v.* **slæd**) (with the surn. *Burnett*); *Burrowefilde* 1601, *Burrow feild(e)* 1628, 1634, 1674, *Burrough or Crosborough Feild* 1637, *Burrow field* 1700, 1745 (*v.* **berg**, **feld**; one of the great open-fields, also called *Crossborow feild*, *infra*); *Bushy Meadow* 1738 (*v.* **busshi**);

Cattes aker 1601, *Cattes acre* 1628, *Catts Acre* 1638, 1738, 1745, *Cats Acre* 1700 (*v.* **æcer**; prob. with the surn. *Catt*, otherwise with **cat(t)**); *Chiscake dowle* 1601, ~ *dole* 1638 (*v.* **dāl**), *Cheeisecake meadow* 1628, *Chiskeke medow* 1634, *Chiscake meadowe* 1638, *Chees(e)cake meadow* 1674, 1700, 1745, *Cheescake piece* 1674, *Chiscake peece* 1690 (*v.* **pece**) (*v.* **chese-cake**); *the Church hadland* 1628, 1674, ~ ~ *headland(e)* 1638, 1700, 1745 (*v.* **hēafod-land**), (*the*) *Church leyes* 1634, 1638, (*the*) *Church Leys* 1674, 1700, 1745, *West* ~ ~, *Church Leys* 1738 (*v.* **leys**) (*v.* St John the Baptist's Church *supra*); *Clease leies* 1601, *Cleyes layes* 1634 (*v.* **leys**; with the surn. *Clay* or *Cley*); *Cockes glade forlonge* 1601 (*v.* **cocc**[2], **glade** 'an opening in a wood utilized for snaring birds', with **furlang**; the earliest entry in OED in this sense (*v.* OED glade sb.[2], 1b) is predated here by 16 years); *the Common Cowpasture* 1628 (*v.* **commun**), *the Cow Pasture* 1638, 1674 *et passim* to 1745 (*v.* **cū**, **pasture**); *Furlong Behind Coppy* 1738, *the Coppye Leys* 1628, *the Coppie leyes* 1634, *the Coppy leys* 1674, ~ ~ *Lees* 1700 (*v.* **leys**), *Coppee Furlong* 1745 (*v.* **furlang**) (*v.* **copis**; the spelling *Coppy* is due to the popular reconstruction of a 'singular' form); *Cranoe gleebe land* 1628, *Cranoe gleeb land* 1700, ~ *glebe land* 1745 (*v.* **glebe**; with reference to part of the benefice of the incumbent of St Michael's Church in adjacent Cranoe); *Crossborow* ~ 1628, *Crasborrow feild* 1634, *Crossborrow hill feild* 1674, *Crossberry field* 1700, *Crossbury Hill Field* 1745 (*v. Burrowefilde* and Crossburrow Hill, both *supra*); *Dickes* 1601, *Dikes* 1634, 1700 (*v.* **dík**); *John Frenches headland*, ~ ~ *headley* 1700 (*v.* **hēafod-land**, **headley**); *the shorte fridayes* 1601, *shorte frydaie furlonge* 1628, *Shortfridayes* 1634, *Short Frydays furlong* 1700, ~ *Fryday furlong* 1745 (*v.* **sc(e)ort**, **Frīgedæg**; because Friday was a day of fasting in the Middle Ages, it became used as a nickname for unproductive land, as perhaps here, but this instance may refer rather to land on which manorial service was performed on Fridays); *Mr Gold's headley* 1700 (*v.* **headley**), *Mr Gould's headland* 1700 (*v.* **hēafod-land**); *Goose Furlong* 1745 (*v.* **gōs**); *Greenegate* 1601, *Greengate* 1638, 1674, 1700, 1745, *greenegate balke* 1601, 1634, 1638, ~ *baulke* 1628, *Greengate balk* 1700, ~ *baulk* 1745 (*v.* **balca**) (*v.* **grēne**[1], **gata**); *Grimeslade* 1601, 1674, 1700, *grymeslad* 1628, *Grymeslade* 1700, *Grime Slade* 1745 (*v.* **slæd**; perh. with OE **grīma**[2] 'a goblin' or with an OE masc. pers.n. *Grīma*; *Grīm* too was used in OE as a by-name for the god Woden; it is less likely that a Scand masc. pers.n. ON *Grímr* (ODan *Grīm*) is present in Glooston, whose toponyms are so consistently English); *the Gutter* 1638, 1674, 1700, 1745 (*v.* **goter**); *the hall hadlond* 1628, ~ ~ *hadland* 1674 (*v.* **hēafod-land**), *Hall piece* 1738 (*v.* **pece**) (*v.* The Hall *supra*); *short hedge* 1628, *short heggende* 1601, *shorthedgend* 1634, *Short hedge end* 1674, 1700 (*v.* **ende**) (*v.* **sc(e)ort, hecg**); *the homested of Samuel Farmer* 1700 (*v.* **hām-stede**); *the hollow way* 1634, 1674, 1700 (*v.* **hol**[2], **weg**); *horsepul* 1601, *Hors(e)pool(e) me(a)dow* 1628, 1634, 1674, 1690, 1700 (*v.* **hors, pōl**[1]); *Mr Halfordes headlea* 1638 (*v.* **headley**); *Holt Piece* 1738 (*v.* **holt**, **pece**); *Hoo Baulk* 1738 (*v.* **hōh**, **balca**); *Hill Furlong* 1738; *Lady Close* 1738 (*v.* **ladi**); *Lambescoates* 1674, 1690, *Lambscoats* 1700, *Lamcotes Meadow* 1628, *lambcoats medowe* 1634 (*v.* **lamb**, **cot**); *North* ~, *West Langham* 1738 (*v.* **lang**[1], **hamm**); *Leicester Lane End* 1745 (*v.* **lane-ende** and Andrew's Lane *supra*); *The Leys* 1745 (*v.* **leys**); *Long(e) doles* 1634, 1674, 1700 (*v.* **dāl**); *longe gatte* 1601, *Longate* 1628, *Longgate* 1634, *Long Gate* 1738, *Longate* ~, *Long Gate Doles* 1738 (*v.* **dāl**), *Long-gate waye* 1625 (*v.* **weg**) (prob. **langet**; otherwise **lang**[1], **gata**); *the medowe* 1601, *the medowe close* 1628, 1634, *Meadowe closse* 1638, *Meadow close* 1674, 1700, 1745, (*the*) *medowe close forlong(e)* 1601,

1634, *Meadow Close Furlong* 1700, 1738, 1745 (*v.* **furlang**), *Top ~ ~*, *Long Meadow* 1738; *Melton gate* 1700 (*v.* **gata**; the road to Melton Mowbray, 14 miles to the north); *the Mill balke* 1700, *Mill Baulk* 1745 (*v.* **balca**), *Mill Door Furlong* 1738 (*v.* **myln**, **duru**, **furlang**); *Milneres hadlonge* (sic) 1601 (*v.* **hēafod-land**; prob. with the surn. *Milner* rather than referring to the local miller); *moares yeardes ende* 1601 (*v.* **geard**, **ende**), *Mores leyes* 1638, *Moors Leys* 1700, 1745 (*v.* **leys**) (with the surn. *Moor*); *New Close* 1637; *Nomans leys* 1634, *No Mans leys* 1638, 1700, 1738, 1745 (*v.* **nān mann**, **leys**); *the Parsons chiskeck* 1634 (*v.* **chese-cake**), *the Parsons tippit*(*t*) *dole* 1634, 1638, *~ ~ typpet ~* 1700, *the Parsons Tippet Dole* 1745 (*v.* **persone**), *the Tippitt Dole* 1674 (*v.* **typpett**, **dāl**; evidently with reference to the shape of the piece of ground, that of a tippet, a long narrow hanging part of a hood or sleeve, cf. The Tippets, Lei **1** 194); *Pinfolde leies* 1601, *Pinfould Leas* 1628, *Pinfold ley*(*e*)*s* 1634, 1738, 1745 (*v.* **pynd-fald**, **leys**); (*the top of*) *the Quagmire* 1638, 1700 (*v.* **quagmire**); *Redd furlonge* 1628, *Redland* 1738, *Red Lands* 1745 (*v.* **land**) (*v.* **rēad**); *Short Ridings* 1728 (*v.* **ryding**); *Round Hill piece* 1738 (*v.* **round**, **pece**); *Scutlows gate* 1628 (the first word may be a surn. in the possessive case (with **gata**), but such a surn. is unrecorded; if a toponym, then *v.* **hlāw**; ME **scut** 'a hare' may have had an OE predecessor cognate with ON *skutr* 'stern of a ship', cf. a rabbit's or hare's *scut*); *shorte furlong* 1628 (*v.* **sc(e)ort**, **furlang**); (*the*) *Slade* 1634, 1638 (*v.* **slæd**); *Slimeslade* 1601, 1628, 1634, *Slymeslade* 1638, 1674, 1700, *Slime Slade* 1690, 1745 (*v.* **slīm**, **slæd**); *stanmedowe* 1601 (*v.* **stān**; either 'stony meadow' or 'the stoned meadow', i.e. one having been cleared of stones, *v. the stone middow*, Lei **2** 19 and *the stone meadow* in Foxton f.ns. (b)); *Stanton ~* 1634, *Stonton Close* 1745, *Stonton Close hedge* 1634, *Stanton Clos*(*s*)*e hedge* 1638, 1700 (*v.* **hecg**), *Stonton gleeb close* 1700 (*v.* **glebe**), *Stanton heghe* 1601, *Stonton hedge* 1628, 1700, 1745 (*v.* **hecg**; a parish boundary hedge), *Stonton ~* 1634, 1745, *Staunton ~* 1674, *Stanton Meare* 1700 (*v.* **(ge)mǣre**), *Stonton Parsonage Close* 1745 (*v.* **personage**) (Stonton Wyville parish adjoins to the west); *Stonegate lane end* 1628 (*v.* **stān**, **gata**, **lane-ende**); *Stonhill* 1601, *Stonehill* 1628, 1634 *et passim* to 1745 (*v.* **stān**, **hyll**); *Stone Slade* 1738 (*v.* **stān**, **slæd**); *Swinglers hadley* 1694 (*v.* **headley**; with the surn. *Swingler*); *atte Syrwys* 1381 SR (p) (*v.* **atte**, **suer**); *Thorny medowe* 1634, *Thorny ~* 1674, 1700, *Thorney Meadow* 1738, 1745 (*v.* **þornig**); *Tomkins hadland* 1634 (*v.* **hēafod-land**; with the surn. *Tomkin*(*s*)); *the townes ende* 1601 (*v.* **tūn**, **ende**); *Triangle Meadow* 1738 (*v.* **triangle**; alluding to shape); *Wellam hedge* 1628 (*v.* **hecg**; a parish boundary hedge with Welham which at this date must have marched in part with Glooston); *West forlonge* 1601 (*v.* **west**, **furlang**); *Westland*(*e*)*s* 1634, 1638 (*v.* **west**, **land**); *Whetstone Meadowe* 1628 (with the surn. *Whetstone* of a family originally from the township of this name, 12 miles to the west); *the Whomestall of Robert Spence* 1628 (*v.* **hām-stall**); *Wilkinsons Close* 1738 (with the surn. *Wilkinson*); *Willowes* 1638 (*v.* **wilig**); *Windmill Furlong* (*v.* **furlang**), *Windmill Hill* 1738 (*v.* **wind-mylne**); *Wood Close Slade* 1738 (*v.* **wudu**, **slæd**).

Goadby

GOADBY

Govtebi 1086 DB, *Gouteby* 1156 (1318) Ch, 1259, 1267 Cur *et freq* to 1398, 1415 Banco *et passim* to 1509 CoPleas, 1517 Fine, (~ *iuxta Nousele* 1314 Banco), *Goutheby* 1276 RH, 1327 SR, *Goutby* 1275 Ipm

Gauteby 1232 Cur, 1445 Nichols

Goudeby 1415 Banco, 1419 *Peake et passim* to 1526 Ipm, (~ *iuxta Keythorpe* 1526 ib), *Gowdeby* 1415 *Deed*, 1429 *Peake*, 1441, 1465 BM (~ *iuxta Nowesle* 1415 *Deed*), *Goudby* 1381 SR, 1514 CoPleas

Gawdeby 1499 *Wyg*, 1518 Visit, *Gawdebe* 1527 LWills, *Gaudebe* 1527 ib, *Gawdby* 1540 *Hazlerigg*, 1575 LEpis

Godeby(*e*) 1509 CoPleas, 1576 Saxton, 1610 Speed, 1699 LML, *Goodby*(*e*) 1512 CoPleas, 1535 Ipm, *Goodeby* 1535 ib

Goadeby 1641 LML, *Goadby* 1798 Nichols, 1813 *Map et freq*

'Gauti's farmstead, village', *v.* **bȳ**. The ON pers.n. *Gauti* either represents a short form of names in *Gaut-* or is an original by-name meaning 'a man from Gautland'. The township's name is occasionally suffixed with reference to nearby Noseley or Keythorpe to distinguish it from Goadby Marwood in Framland Hundred (*v.* Lei **2** 125). Note MLat *iuxta* 'next to' used in the suffixes.

BASSETT'S HILL SPINNEY, *v.* **spinney**; with the surn. *Bassett*. GOADBY HILL. GOADBY HOME FM, *v.* **home**. GOWARD'S SPINNEY, *v.* **spinney**; with the surn. *Goward*, common in the late 19th cent. in nearby Market Harborough. GREEN ACRES, *v.* **æcer**. HILL FM. HORSE HILL, *v.* **hors**. KEYTHORPE WOOD, 1797 *Surv*, 1798 Map, 1824 O, *v.* **wudu**; Old Keythorpe lies a half mile to the north-east. MANOR FM (MANOR HO. 2½"), *Manor house* 1925 Kelly, *v.* **maner**. PALMER'S LANE, cf. *Wm. Palmer, farmer* 1863 White and *Arthur Palmer, grazier* 1925 Kelly. PEACE HILL, *v.* **pise**. ST JOHN'S CHURCH, *The Church* 1877 White, *Church (St John)* 1925 Kelly; earlier is recorded *capella*(*m*) *de Gouteby*

1220 MHW, 1477 (e.16) *Charyte* (with MLat *capella* 'a chapel'). TUGBY RD, Tugby lying 2 miles to the north-east.

FIELD-NAMES

In (a), forms presented without dates are 1847 *TA*; those dated 1797 are *Surv*; 18 and 1813 are *Map*. Forms throughout dated 1283 are Coram; those dated 1383 are SR; 1467 × 84 are *LTD*; 1527 are *Star*; 1601, 1625, 1690, 1694, 1703 and 1724 are *Terrier*; 1606 are Ipm; 1677 are *Deed*.

(a) Five Acres 18, 1847, First ~ ~ ~, Second Plowed Seven Acres 1797, First ~ ~ ~, Second Ploughed Seven Acres 1847 (*v.* **æcer**); Ash Spinney 1797, 1847 (*v.* **æsc**, **spinney**); Barn Cl 1797 (*v.* **bern**); Bassetts Cl, ~ Mdw 1797, 1847 (with the surn. *Bassett*, cf. Bassett's Hill Spinney *supra*); Bellamys Cl, ~ Mdw 1797, 1847 (with the surn. *Bellamy*); Lower ~ ~, Upper Black Hill (*v.* **blæc**); Blue Piece (*v.* **blár**, **pece**); Great Breakes, Far ~ ~, Near Breakes Mdw (*the Brakes* 1625, *v.* **bracu**); Captains Cl (*v.* **capitain** and Lei **2** 318 *s.v.*); Cloudhill (*v.* **clūd**); Great ~, Little ~, Long Coppice 1797, 1847 (*v.* **copis**); Dunmore's Hill 1797, 1847 (cf. *Sophia Dunmore* 1795 Census and *John Dunmore* 1819 ib, both of Goadby); Far Mdw 18; Flax Cl, ~ ~ Mdw 1797, 1847 (*v.* **fleax**); Herbert's Cl, ~ Mdw (with the surn. *Herbert*, a reflex of a masc. pers.n., either OFr *Herbert* (ContGerm *Her(e)bert*) or OE *Herebeorht*; Reaney *s.n.* believes that the pers.n. was a Norman introduction); Side of the Hill, Top of the Hill; Hill Ground 18, ~ ~ Cl 1847 (*v.* **grund**); Home Croft (*v.* **home**, **croft**); Honey Spot (*v.* **hunig**; presum. originally the more common 'Honey Pot', with **pot(t)** rather than **spot**); Hoppers Hill, ~ ~ Mdw 1797, 1847 (*Hopper hill* 1625, cf. *Hoppyngatfeld* 1467 × 84 (*v.* **gata**, **feld**), *v.* **hopping** and *Hopynges*, *Hoppers hill* in Billesdon f.ns. (b)); Keythorpe Leys 1797 (*v.* **leys**; Old Keythorpe lies a half mile to the north-east); Langdale 1847 (1467 × 84, 1625, *v.* **lang**[1], **dalr**); Marston' s Cl, ~ Mdw (with the surn. *Marston* of a family poss. originally from Marston Trussell, 9 miles to the south-west in Northants.); Middle Mdw 18, 1847; Mirey Hill (*v.* **myry**); Nether Furlong 18, 1847, ~ ~ Mdw 1847 (*v.* **neoðera**, **furlang**); Old Cl, Large ~ ~ ~, Little Old Close Mdw 1797, 1847 (*v.* **ald**); Nether ~ ~, Over ~ ~ (*v.* **uferra**), Old Fd 1847 (*the Old field* 1690, cf. *old feild close* 1527 (*v.* **clos(e)**), *the ould field hedge* 1625 (*v.* **hecg**), *the ouldfield layes*, *ouldfield leyes* 1625 (*v.* **leys**), *v.* **ald**, **feld**); Old Spinney 1847 (*v.* **ald**, **spinney**); Far Over Hill ('the far part of land across the hill', *v.* **ofer**[2]); Pinfold Cl (*v.* **pynd-fald**); Far Platt 1797, ~ Platts 1847 (*v.* **plat**[2]); Ramsbed 1847 (1601, 1625, *v.* **hramsa**, **bedd**); Redhouse Cl, ~ Mdw 1797, 1847 (with the surn. *Redhouse*, found occasionally in l.18th- and e.19th-cent. Leics.); Robinsons Cl 1813 (with the surn. *Robinson*); Smith's Cl 1797 (either with the surn. *Smith* or with **smið**); Top Mdw; Towns-end Cl 1797, Townsend's Cl 1847 (*v.* **tūn**, **ende**).

(b) *Banfurlong'* 1467 × 84 (*v.* **bēan**, **furlang**); *Barearse hill* 1625 (*v.* **bær**[1]; poss. a disparaging name for unproductive land, if the generic is **ears** 'an arse', but note the early *Barehers* in Drayton f.ns (b) and *Bareherse/Barearse* in Hallaton f.ns. (b) where **herse** 'a hill-top' may be present); *the brake hill* 1625 (*v.* **bracu** and Great

Breakes *supra*); *atte Brigg* 1383 (p) (*v.* **atte**, **brycg**); *Brokhols* 1467 × 84, *Brockhoales* 1625 (*v.* **brocc-hol**); *Bryngford* 1467 × 84 (*v.* **ford**; either with the OE masc. pers.n. *Brynca* or with **brink**); *le Burnt house yardeland* 1606 (*v.* **brend**, **hūs**, **yardland**); *Chaukdalsyke* 1467 × 84 (*v.* **calc**, **deill**, **sík**); *Church Close* 1690, *the Church lane* 1625 (*v.* **lane**), *the Churches glebe land* 1625 (*v.* **glebe**) (*v.* St John's Church *supra*); *the comon pasture* 1625 (*v.* **commun**, **pasture**); *Cuttisholme* 1456 × 84 (*v.* **holmr**; either with **cutte** or with the surn. *Cutt*, a pet-form of *Cuthbert*; later forms of the name appear in adjoining Hallaton f.ns. (b)); *the Eastfield towards Keythorpe* 1625, *East or Keythorpe Field* 1677 (*v.* **ēast**, **feld**; one of the great open-fields of the township, recorded earlier as *campus orientalis* 1467 × 84 (with MLat *campus* 'a field' and *orientalis* 'eastern'); Old Keythorpe lies a half mile to the north-east); *the Glebe Close* 1690 (*v.* **glebe**); *Godmanescroft* 1283 (*v.* **croft**; with the OE masc. pers.n. *Godmann*); *Greyfurlong'* 1467 × 84 (*v.* **furlang**; with either **grǣg**[1] or **grǣg**[2]); *Gryfe* 1467 × 84 (*v.* **gryfja**); *Keythorp furlong*, *~ hedge* 1625 (a furlong adjoining and a parish boundary hedge marching with Old Keythorpe); *the Mare Close* 1690 (*v.* **mare**); *the Meadows* 1690; *the Neather pasture* 1625 (*v.* **neoðera**, **pasture**); *the North field* 1625 (*v.* **norð**, **feld**; one of the great open-fields, earlier called *Salgatefelde* and later *Rolleston Field* (both *infra*)); *Nowesley broke* 1467 × 84, *~ brooke* 1625 (*v.* **brōc**; Noseley parish adjoins to the west); *the Old Inclosure* 1724 (*v.* **inclosure**); *the ould bridge* 1625 (*v.* **ald**, **brycg**); *penne close* 1527 (*v.* **penn**[2], **clos(e)**); *Peysland'* 1467 × 84 (*v.* **pise**, **land**); *Rainbysleyde* 1467 × 84 (*v.* **slæd**; *Rainby* appears to represent a lost early habitation site, hence perh. 'farmstead at the boundary', *v.* **rein**, **bȳ**, but earlier spellings are needed); *Redewong'* 1467 × 84 (*v.* **vangr**; with **hrēod** or **rēad** (if alluding to the colour of soil)); *Rolleston Field* 1677 (*v.* **feld**; one of the great open-fields, earlier called *Salgatefelde* and *the North field*), *Rowlston ~* 1625, *Rolston brook* 1694 (*v.* **brōc**) (Rolleston parish adjoins to the north-west); *Salgatefelde* 1467 × 84 (*v.* **feld**; one of the early great open-fields, later called *the North field* and *Rolleston Field*, *supra*), *Sawgate*, *~ hill* 1625 (*v.* **salh**, **gata**; there is no evidence that Goadby was on the route of a saltway/saltgate, thus **salh** is preferred to **salt**[1] as the specific here); *Brian Saterthwaite his myres* 1625 (*v.* **mýrr**); *Schorddall'* 1467 × 84 (*v.* **sc(e)ort**, **dalr**; with assimilation of *td* > *dd*; note Langdale *supra*); *Sowthfelde* 1467 × 84, *South or Nether Field* 1677 (*v.* **sūð**, **feld**; one of the early great fields, prob. to be identified with *the Westfield*); *Stonyforth* 1467 × 84 (*v.* **stānig**, **ford**); *Stronglond* 1467 × 84 (*v.* **strang**, **land**; referring to firm, compact soil); *the Water furrowes*, *Waterfurrowes furlong* 1625 (*v.* **wæter**, **furh** and *the water furrowes* in Billesdon f.ns. (b)); *Waterlandes* 1467 × 84 (*v.* **wæter**, **land**); *Wedefurlong'* 1467 × 84 (*v.* **wēod**, **furlang**); *Well sick* 1625 (*v.* **wella**, **sík**); *the Westfield towards Nowseley* 1625 (*v.* **west**, **feld**; one of the great open-fields, prob. to be identified with the earlier *Sowthfelde*, *supra*); *White leyes* 1625 (*v.* **hwīt**, **leys**; the name prob. denotes dry, open pasture, cf. *Whitleyes* in Billesdon f.ns. (b) and White Leys in Muston, Lei **2** 38); *Willyam Woodcockes yardes ende* 1625 (*v.* **geard**, **ende**); *Woodsick gutter* 1625 (*v.* **wudu**, **sík**, **goter**); *Wylowleyes* 1467 × 84, *Willow leyes* 1625 (*v.* **wilig**, **leys**); *Wylspole* 1467 × 84, *Willspoole* 1625 (either 'the water-beetle pool' (with **wifel**) or 'Wifel's pool' (with the OE masc. pers.n. *Wifel*), or 'Vífill's pool' (with the ON masc. pers.n. *Vífill*), *v.* **pōl**[1]).

Great Easton

GREAT EASTON

Estun 1041 × 57 (m.12), m.12 HCand, 1300 Ch, *Estone* 1086 DB, *Estona* 1125 × 28 LNPetr, a.1150 *Peake* (p), m.12 HCand, 1280, 1284 ChronPetr, *Eston'* 1146 Dugd, 1189 (1332), 1227 Ch *et freq* to 1583 LEpis, 1595 Ipm, *Heston'* l.13 *Peake*
Astuna m.12 HCand, *Aston'* 1327 *Peake* (p) *et passim* to 1346 *ib* (p)
Eyston 1481 Dugd, *Eystorn* 1609 LeicW
Easton 1576 Saxton, 1604 SR, 1610 Speed *et freq*

Affixes are variously added as:
~ *iuxta Rogingham Brigge* 1306 Ass (*v.* **brycg**), ~ *iuxta Rokyngham* 1305, 1343 Cl *et passim* with various spellings to 1435, 1459 Banco
~ *iuxta Brynghyrst* 1410, 1429 *Conant et passim* with various spellings to 1457 *ib*
~ *by Halyok* 1505 Banco
~ *super Weland* 1535 VE, ~ *by Willond* 1548 *Conant*, ~ *by Wolland* 1609 LeicW, ~ *juxta Willand* 1634 ib
~ *Magna* 1619 LML, 1628 SR
Great ~ 1717 LML

'The east farmstead', *v.* **ēast**, **tūn**. Probably the eastern farmstead in relation to the township of Medbourne, 3 miles to its west. There is a Weston which lies 1½ miles to the south-west of Medbourne, beyond the river Welland in Northants. The affixes refer to neighbouring Bringhurst, Holyoaks (in Stockerston) and Rockingham (across the river Welland in Northants.). It is uncertain why Easton was accorded the affixes ~ *Magna* and *Great* ~ from the 17th cent. onwards since no Little Easton or Easton Parva is recorded hereabouts.

Note in the affixes MLat *iuxta* 'next to', Lat *super* 'above, on' and *magna* 'great'.

BARNSDALE, *Barnesdale* 1505 (16) *SlCart*, *Barnesdale Soke* 1548 *Conant* (*v*. **sōcn**), *Barnsdale strete* (*infra villam de Eston*) 1547 *ib* (*v*. **strǣt**), *v*. **dæl**[1], **dalr**; with an OE masc. pers.n. such as *Beorn* or *Beornhard*. The valley of Barnsdale lies between Great Easton and Bringhurst. *Barnsdale strete* refers to the lost Roman road (Margary 571) which ran from *Via Devana* (Gartree Road) at a junction just south-east of Medbourne via Drayton, Great Easton, Caldecott in Rutland and King's Cliffe in Northants. to meet Ermine Street at *Durobrivae* (Water Newton). BROADGATE, cf. *Broadgate Close* 1879 *Plan*, *v*. **brād**, **gata**. BROADVIEW. BROOK LANE. CASTLE INN (lost), *Castle Inn* 1877 White, 1925 Kelly; it is *Railway Inn* 1863 White (located at the disused Rockingham Station), renamed from nearby Rockingham Castle. CROWN (P.H.) (lost), *Crown* 1863 White, *Crown Inn* 1877 ib. EYE BROOK, *v*. **ēa**; forms the boundary with Rutland here. For early spellings, *v*. Ru 1. GATEHOUSE LANE, cf. *Gate House Meadow* 1968 *Surv*, *v*. **gate-hous**; the lane once led directly to Rockingham Castle. GREAT EASTON LODGE is *Rhodes Lodge* 1824 O; most likely with the surn. *Rhodes*, cf. Rhodes Cl, ~ Orchard 1843 in West Langton f.ns. (a), but poss. with **rod**[1] ' a clearing', cf. *le Rode* in adjacent Nevill Holt (*Prestgrave*), *v*. **loge**. GREAT EASTON PARK is *Powers Park* 1486 Ipm (the property of *Johannes Powers* 1468 ib), *The Parke* 1535 VE, *Easton park*(*e*) 1602 LeicW, 1650 AAS, 1798 Nichols, c.1800 *Map*, *v*. **park**. GREAT MERRIBLE WOOD, 1840 *TA*, *Mirable Wood* 1798, 1815 Nichols, 1824 O. Earlier is recorded *capelle de Mirabel* 13 Nichols (with MLat *capella* 'a chapel'), *hermitagii de Mirabel* 1232 RHug, *Mirabel Hermitagium* 1262, 1270 RGrav (with MLat *hermitagium* 'a hermitage'). Merrible was originally the name of a hermitage with its own chapel, a medieval Christian foundation presumably sited close to the formerly pagan Anglo-Saxon Holyoaks in adjacent Stockerston as a counter to possible lingering heathen practices there. Nichols **2** ii 815 quotes Throsby as suggesting that the possible site of the hermitage was in Great Easton at a place called *Mirabel Hole*, but the site may rather have been in Holyoaks where is recorded *Holliock Merrybell* 1606 *ExchSpC*, *v*. **mirable**. HIGH ST. HOLT LANE, Nevill Holt lying 2 miles to the north-west. KING'S HEAD (P.H.) (lost), *King's Head* 1846, 1863, 1877 White. LONG LANE. MARQUIS OF GRANBY (P.H.) (lost), *Marquis of Granby* 1846, 1863, 1877 White; one of a series of hostelries so named from the title of John Manners, Marquis of Granby (1721 to 1770), a former heir of the Duke of Rutland, *v*. Lei **1** 132 and Cox[1] 25. PARK COTTAGES, ~ FM, *v*. Great Easton Park *supra*. RECTORY HO., *v*. **rectory**. ST ANDREW'S CHURCH, *Church (St Andrew)* 1846, 1863, 1877 White, 1925 Kelly;

earlier is *capella(m) de Eston* 1220 MHW, 1336 *Pat* (with MLat *capella* 'a chapel'). SHOULDER OF MUTTON (P.H.) (lost), *Shoulder of Mutton* 1846, 1863, 1877 White, 1925 Kelly. STOCKERSTON LANE, Stockerston lying 3 miles to the north. SUN (P.H.), *Sun* 1846 White, 1925 Kelly, *Sun Inn* 1863, 1877 White. THE VICARAGE, 1877 White, 1925 Kelly, *v.* **vikerage**.

FIELD-NAMES

In (a), forms presented without dates are 1968 *Surv*; those dated 1798 are Nichols; 1804 and 1810 are *EnclA*; 1806 and 1879 are *Plan*; 1824 are O. Forms throughout dated p.1250 and a.1290 are CN; those dated 13 are *Peake*; 13 (16) are *SlCart*; 1332 and 1381 are SR; 1410, 1414, 1450, 1457, 1463, 1496, 1543, 1544, 1560, 1581, 1582, 1587, 1595, 1596, 1599, 1621, 1630, 1638 and 1666 are *Conant*; 1486 are Ipm; 1535 are VE; e.17, 17 and 1712 are *Terrier*.

(a) Bottom ~ ~, Top Four Acre, Five Acres, The Six ~, East Nine ~, Eighteen Acre (*v.* **æcer**); America Park (*v.* **park**; a name prob. dating from the years of the War of American Independence, 1775–83, cf. Canada *infra*); Ashby's Piece (*v.* **pece**; with the surn. *Ashby*); Mrs Miller Bakewell's Paddock (*v.* **paddock**); Balls Cl (with the surn. *Ball*); Bank Fd (*v.* **banke**); Barn Cl (*v.* **bern**); Black Dyke Wood (*v.* **blæc**, **dík**); Bill Blount's Fd; Bosworth's Fd (with the surn. *Bosworth* of a family prob. originally from Husbands Bosworth, 14 miles to the south-west); Bottom Fd and Mdw; Bradley 1968, Bradley Wood 1798 (*v.* **brād**, **lēah**; poss. land given to Bradley Priory in neighbouring Nevill Holt by Willelmus de Ros in the 13th cent.); Brick Yard (*v.* **brike-yard**); Bridge Mdw; Great ~, Brimswell (*v.* **wella**; either with the OE masc. pers.n. *Brim* or with **brim** 'flood, water', cf. *Brimes dic* 683 (14) BCS 64 (S 232)); Browetts Cl (with the surn. *Browett*); Browns Mdw or Bullholmes (with the surn. *Brown*, *v.* **bula**, **holmr**); Burton's Cl (cf. *Edward Burtons hadlond* e.17 (*v.* **hēafod-land**)); Caldecott Fd (adjoins the boundary with Caldecott parish in Rutland); Canada (*v.* America Park *supra*); Christian Mdw (with the surn. *Christian*); Church Cl (*v.* St Andrew's Church *supra*); Clay Pit 1810 (*v.* **cley-pytt**); Fred Claypole's Paddock; Clint (*Clynt* 17, *v.* **klint**); Concrete Road Fd; Cottage Mdw; County Council First Fd, ~ ~ Second Fd, ~ ~ Third Fd; First ~ ~, Second ~ ~, Third Cow Fd, Cow Cl; Crapshill (perh. 'hill with outcrops or characteristic humps', *v.* **crop(p)**, **hyll**); Craythorn's Mdw, H. Craythorne's Paddock (*v.* **paddock**); Cricket Fd (for the game of cricket); Little Cunder, Cunder Hill (*v.* **cundite**); Darkins Headland (*v.* **hēafod-land**; with the surn. *Darkin*); Little ~, Deepdales (*v.* **dēop**, **dalr**); Doctors Cl (*v.* **doctour**); Drayton Road Fd (Drayton lies one mile to the south-west); East Fd 1804, 1810, 1968 (*the Est Field* e.17, *the East feild* 17, *East Field* 1712, *East Field dyke* e.17 (*v.* **dík**), *v.* **ēast**, **feld**; one of the great open-fields of the township); (Great) Easton Common 1798, 1824 (*v.* **commun**); Easton Mill 1824 (*v.* **myln**); Harry Elkins Little Fd; Far Cl 1879; Foots Mdw (with the surn. *Foot*, a reflex of the ON masc.

pers.n. *Fótr*); Bottom ~, Top Foxhole (*v.* **fox-hol**); Little ~ ~, Gravel Pit 1810, 1968 (*v.* **gravel**, **pytt**); Great Cl or Bullock Fd (*v.* **bulluc**); Green's First Fd, ~ Third Fd, ~ Top Fd, Green's Land (*v.* **land**) (with the surn. *Green*); Herbies Cl (presum. with the surn. *Herby*, more usual in Notts.; a poor form of the surn. *Herbit* is poss.); Home Cl 1879, 1968, Home Fd (*v.* **home**); Hovels Cl (*v.* **hovel**); Hut Cl (*v.* **hut**); Johnson's First Paddock (*v.* **paddock**); Harry Jones Mdw; Kirby's Mdw (with the surn. *Kirby*); Kitchen Quarter (prob. 'the small kitchen garden', *quarter* here being for 'a quarter acre'); Little Lawpon, Lawponsale (*v.* **sale**) (cf. *Loping lees* e.17 (*v.* **leys**), perh. 'the lopping place', *v.* **lopping**, either referring to trees which were regularly lopped or a place in the forest where the cut wood was stacked; but note *lawnd pound hollow*, *infra*, a toponym which may have influenced the development of these later forms); Longlands (*v.* **lang**[1], **land**); Malt Adland (*Malte hadland* e.17, *v.* **mealt**, **hēafod-land**); Tom Marchant's Little Fd; The Marshes (*le Mersch* 1410, *v.* **mersc**); Lower ~ ~, Meadow Dyke (*le Meduedik* a.1290, *v.* **mēd** (**mēdwe** obl.sg.), **dík**); Merrible Cl, ~ Fd, ~ Mdw, Furry Merrible (*v.* **fyrsig**) (*v.* Great Merrible Wood *supra*); Middle Fd 1879; Middle Mdw 1804 (*Middle medow* 1582, *the myddle medow* e.17, *the Midle meadowe* 17, *v.* **middel**, **mēd** (**mēdwe** obl.sg.)); Mill Fd (*v.* **myln**); Moors Cl (cf. (*le*) *Longemor* p.1250, a.1290 (*v.* **lang**[1]), *moreforlong* 13 (*v.* **furlang**) (*v.* **mōr**[1]); Morris's Land or The Seeds (*v.* **land**, **sǣd** and Big Seeds *infra*); Tom Mould's Top Fd (T. B. Mould owned land here in 1920–32); Nether Mdw 1804, 1806, 1810, 1968 (*Nether Medow* 1581, *Neather Meadow* 1621, *v.* **neoðera**, **mēd** (**mēdwe** obl.sg.)); Norris's Fd or Long Acre (*v.* **æcer**; with the surn. *Norris*); North Fd 1804, 1810, 1968 (1712, *the Northe Fielde* e.17, *the North Feilde* 17, *v.* **norð**, **feld**; one of the great open-fields); Oaksale (*v.* **āc**, **sale**); Old Allotments (*v.* **allotment**); Parks 1810 (cf. *Parke Leyes* 1638 (*v.* **leys**), *Parke Hill* 17, *Park hill* 1712, *v.* Great Easton Park *supra*); Bottom ~ ~, Top Parrot Hill (cf. *Paynottisbutes* p.1250 (*v.* **butte**); the modern f.n. contains a garbled version of the ME surn. *Paynot*, the ModE *Pannett*); Parson's Cl (*v.* **persone**); Peaches Cl (with the surn. *Peach*); Poors Cl (*v.* **pouer**(**e**); land dedicated to poor-law relief or charity); Pretty's Mdw (with the surn. *Pretty*); Rand's Paddock (*v.* **paddock**; with the surn. *Rand*); Redlands (*le Redelond* a.1290, *le Redelondes* 1463, *v.* **rēad**, **land**; referring to the soil colour of arable strips); Road Mdw (an enclosure beside a highway); Roberts Cl (with the surn. *Roberts*); Roman Well Fd (the so-called Roman well lies in a field about 150 yards north-east of Rectory House *supra*); Round Hill (*v.* **round**); First ~, Second ~, Third Rylands, Rylands Mdw (*v.* **ryge**, **land**); Sandpits or Sandholes (*Sand pytt furlong* e.17 (*v.* **furlang**), *Sandpitts* 17, *v.* **sand-pytt**, **sand-hol**); School Fd ('Thomas Collins, by will dated 1669, gave a yearly rent-charge of 40 shillings from 11 acres in Easton to the minister of Easton for the instruction of 4 poor children there', *v.* VCHL **5** 60); Big Seeds (*v.* **sǣd**; used of grasses sown for one year's mowing or grazing, as distinguished from permanent pasture); Station Fd, Station Road Little Fd (adjoin the disused Rockingham Station); Steppings 1968, Steppings Cls, Steppings Spinney 1810 (*v.* **spinney**) (*Stibbinges* 1581, *Stybbinges* 1621, *Stibbings* 1630, 1666, *v.* **stybbing**); Stocklands (*Stoklondes* 1410, *stoclondes* 1414, *Stocklandes* e.17, *v.* **stocc**, **land**); Stokes Paddock (with the surn. *Stoke*); Tennis Fd (presum. once containing tennis courts); Three Acre Mdw or Stangers Mdw (with the surn. *Stanger*); Top Cl, Top Paddock (*v.* **top**); Second ~ ~, Top Town, Top Turn (*v.* **top**, **tūn**; land at the upper end of the village); Two and Five Flood Acres (*v.* **flōd**, **æcer**; land subject to flooding); Upper Mdw 1804, 1810, 1968 (cf. *the over medow* e.17, *v.* **uferra**); Third

Waltons, Waltons Mdw (with the surn. *Walton*); Warners Mdw (with the surn. *Warner*); West Fd 1804, 1810, 1968 (1712, *the West Fielde* e.17, ~ ~ *feild* 17, *v.* **west, feld**; one of the great open-fields); Westbrook's Fd (*Westbrokys* p.1250, *Wesbrookes* 1595, *Westbro(o)kes* 1599, *West Brookes* e.17, 17, *West-brooks* 1712 (*v.* **west, brōc**); Little ~ ~, Second ~ ~, White Hills (*Wytehyl* p.1250, *v.* **hwīt, hyll**; prob. with reference to chalk, cf. *calcylsyche, infra*); Woodgate (e.17, 1712, *v.* **wudu, gata**); Wright's First Fd, Wright's Mdw (with the surn. *Wright*).

(b) *Aldeforthe* 1410 (*v.* **ald, ford**); *Aldeholm* p.1250, *Aldholm(e)* 1410 (×2) (*v.* **ald, holmr**); *Alynehegg'* 1410 (*v.* **hecg** (in its sense 'a hedged enclosure'); with the surn. *Alin*); *Ballondes* e.17 (*v.* **bēan, land**); *Barwells gate* 17 (*v.* **gata**; cf. *Wm. Barwell* 17, whose family presum. originally came from Barwell, 24 miles to the west); *Bayes hedge* e.17 (*v.* **hecg**; with the surn. *Bayes*); *Brachyard* 1496, 1596, *Bracheyard* 1543, 1560 (*v.* **geard**; **brache** 'hunting dog' is poss. as the specific, otherwise **brēc**); *Brokelesdale* p.1250 (with the OE masc. pers.n. *Brōcwulf*, cf. Broxtowe, Nt 140; it is uncertain whether an original **dæl**[1] was replaced by **dalr**); *Burmans Hill* 17 (*v.* **hyll**; with the surn. *Burman*); *calcylsyche* 13 (*v.* **calc, hyll, sīc**); *Caldecotegate* a.1290, *Calcott gate* e.17 (*v.* **gata**), *Caldecotehay* p.1250 (*v.* **(ge)hæg**), *Callcott leyes* e.17 (*v.* **leys**) (Caldecott parish in Rutland adjoins to the north-east); *Caldewellesike* p.1250 (*v.* **sík**), *Caldewelmore* 1410 (*v.* **mōr**[1]) (*v.* **cald, wella**); *Church hadeland* 17, ~ *headland* 1712 (*v.* **hēafod-land** and St Andrew's Church *supra*); *Cliftherne* p.1250, *Ouerclyftherne* a.1290 (*v.* **ofer**[3]) (*v.* **clif, þyrne**); *Richard Collyns hadland* e.17 (*v.* **hēafod-land**); *Coppemanheggate* p.1250, a.1290, *Coppenheggate* 1410 (*v.* **gata**), *Coppenheggeslade* 1410 (*v.* **slæd**) (*v.* **hecg** (in its sense 'a hedged enclosure'); with the surn. *Copeman*, a reflex of ON *kaupmaðr* 'a merchant'); *Coppydhyll* 1410, *Copnyll buske* e.17 (*v.* **buskr**), *Cocknyll gate* (sic) e.17 (*v.* **gata**) ('hill with a peak', *v.* **copped**[1], **hyll**); *the Crabtree Slade* e.17 (*v.* **crabtre, slæd**); *Crafts* 17, 1712 (*v.* **croft**); *Cratehaw* 13 (16) (*v.* **cræt, haga**[1]); *atte Crosse* 1381 (p) (*v.* **atte, cros**; recorded earlier as *ad crucem* p.1250 (p), with MLat *ad* 'at' and *crux* (*crucem* acc.sg.) 'a cross'); *the drawghtes* e.17 (poss. with **draught** in its eModE sense 'a cesspool, a sewer', OED *s.v.* draught, sb. XIII, 45; but also poss. here is its ME sense 'the action of dragging or pulling, esp. of a vehicle' (OED draught, sb. I, 1) transferred to a place where such dragging was necessary, as for adjoining Drayton); *Derneforde* 1582, *Deneford* 1596 (*v.* **derne, ford**); *Estbeyedyk* p.1250, *Estbedyk* a.1290 ('(a place) on the east side of the ditch', *v.* **bī, dík**; poss. originally with **ēastan** rather than with **ēast**); *Estmerishauedlond* p.1250 (*v.* **ēast, (ge)mǣre, hēafodland**); *East Wells* 17, 1712 (*v.* **ēast, wella**); *Field dyke* e.17 (*v.* **dík**); *Flascemore* 1410 (*v.* **flasshe, mōr**[1]); *Flaxdale* 1410, *Flax dales* e.17, 17 (*v.* **fleax**; with **dalr** or **deill**); *Flitlondis* p.1250, *Flytlondis* p.1250, a.1290, *Flyttlondes* 1410 (*v.* **(ge)flit, land**); *forewodes* 1414 (*v.* **fore, wudu**); *Froglane* 1496, *Frogg(e) Lane* 1543, 1560, 1596 (*v.* **frogga, lane**); *Gallakyrhil* p.1250, *Gallokerhyll*, *Gallokhyl* 1410 (*v.* **galla, æcer, hyll**); *Gallow hill* e.17 ('bare hill', *v.* **calu**); *the greatt hill* 17, *the Great-hill* 1712 (*v.* **grēat**); *othe grene* 1381 (p) (*v.* **grēne**[2]); *Hallyock gate* e.17 (*v.* **gata**), *Hallyock hedge* e.17 (*v.* **hecg**; a boundary hedge with Holyoaks); *Hernoldismor* p.1250 (*v.* **mōr**[1]; with the ContGerm masc. pers.n. *Ernald* (OFr *Hernaut*)); *hill leas dyke* e.17 (*v.* **hyll, leys, dík**); *Holte hedge* e.17 (*v.* **hecg**; the parish boundary hedge with Nevill Holt which adjoins to the noth-west); *hopyng* 1414 (*v.* **hopping**); *houdale* 1410, *howdale* 1410, 1414, *Houdalegate* p.1250, a.1290 (*v.* **gata**) (*v.* **hōh, dæl**[1], **dalr**); *Howse* 17, *House Lays* 1712 (*v.* **leys**) (prob. **hōh** (**hōs** nom.pl.)); *le hylles* 1410 (*v.* **hyll**); *Kyngisgate* a.1290, (*le*) *Kyngesgate* 1410, 1463, *Kinges gate* e.17 (*v.* **king, gata**; the principal highway); *landemeredale* 13 (*v.* **land-(ge)mǣre, dalr**); *lawnd pound hollow* e.17 (*v.* **launde, pund, holh**; but note Lawpon *supra*); *Henry Lowthes hadland* e.17 (*v.* **hēafod-land**); *Littly ford* 17 (*v.* **ford**; over Eye Brook, earlier called *Little Ey*, 'the little river', *v.* Ru 1 for early forms); *the Meadows* 17; *le medelfourlonge* 1450, 1457 (*v.* **middel, meðal, furlang**); *Merihegg* a.1290 (*v.* **hecg** (in its sense 'a hedged enclosure'); prob. with **myry**); *Midle gate* 17 (*v.* **middel, gata**); *Myckle dale* e.17, *Mykeldalehyl* 1410, *Myckle dale hill* e.17 (*v.* **hyll**) (*v.* **micel, mikill, dalr**); *by Neyton* p.1250, a.1290 (*v.* **bī, nēat, tūn**); *no mans butt* e.17 (*v.* **nān mann, butte**); *Northlangfurlong* 13 (16) (*v.* **norð, lang**[1], **furlang**); *Onhou* p.1250, *Onhouegate* p.1250 (*v.* **gata**) (*v.* **ān, hōh**); *Osewardiscroft* p.1250 (*v.* **croft**; either with the OE masc. pers.n. *Ōsweard*, or with its surn. reflex *Osward*); *Oswoldiscroft* a.1290 (*v.* **croft**; this may be a misunderstood later rendering of the previous p.n., otherwise either with the OE masc. pers.n. *Ōsweald* (or ON *Ásvaldr*), or with a surn. reflex of each, *Oswald*); *Our Ladyes Meadow* 1587 (*v.* **ladi, mēd** (**mēdwe** obl.sg.); land dedicated to Our Lady, the Virgin Mary, for the upkeep of a chapel or shrine); *the overthwart hill* e.17 (*v.* **ofer-þwart**); *Plottesgate* a.1290, 1410, *Plottesgatys* 1410 (*v.* **plot, gata**); *potteres hul* 13 (*v.* **pottere, hyll**; with reference to the usual hill-top site for medieval pottery kilns); *Powers Woode* 1486, 1535 (*v.* **wudu**; the property of *Johannes Powers* 1486, as was Great Easton Park *supra*); *Saxhegg'* 1410 (*v.* **hecg** (prob. in its sense 'a hedged enclosure'); with the surn. *Sax*, a reflex of the ON, ODan masc. pers.n. *Saxi*); *Sheepe Close* 1638 (*v.* **scēp, clos(e)**); *Sideholme furlonge* 1544 (*v.* **sīde, holmr, furlang**); *Smalthorn*(*es*) 1410 (×2) (*v.* **smæl, þorn**); *Spryngwelle* 1410 (*v.* **spring**[1], **wella**); *Sprynkelwell* 1410, *Sprinckle Well* e.17 (*v.* **sprynkil, wella**); *Stoniwelleslade* p.1250 (*v.* **stānig, wella, slæd**); *Stonlondis* p.1250, *longestonlondes* 1463 (*v.* **lang**[1]), *schortstonlondes* 1410 (*v.* **sc(e)ort**) (*v.* **stān, land**); *Sumebrygge* 1414 (*v.* **sumor, brycg**; a poor form, but presum. with reference to a stream crossing which could only be used in summer, which suggests an early name, with *brycg* in its old sense 'a causeway'); *Tommor* p.1250 (×2), *Tummore* e.17 (*v.* **mōr**[1]; poss. with **þūma** 'a thumb' used in some transferred sense such as 'a dwarf, a hobgoblin', recording a local superstition (cf. Tom Thumb and *v.* Tomley Hall (*Tomlowe* 1343 *LCh*), Cox[2] 106), or simply describing a small patch of wasteland); *the towne hadlond* e.17 (*v.* **tūn, hēafod-land**); *Wards-hill* 1712 (with the surn. *Ward*); *Warmwelle* 13, *Warmewell* e.17 (*v.* **wearm, wella**; cf. Warmwell, Do **1** 169); *atte Welle* 1332 (p) (*v.* **atte, wella**); *the water furroes* e.17, *the waterthorows* 17 (*v.* **wæter, furh**, and note comment on *the water furrowes* in Billesdon f.ns. (b)); *Wignall Field* 1638 (beneath Wignell Hill (*q.v.*) within Nevill Holt parish); *Wodesty* p.1250 (*v.* **wudu, stīg**); *in le Wro* p.1250 (p) (*v.* **vrá**); *Wyndmilnehyl*, *Wyndmylnehil* p.1250, *Wyndmylnhyll* 1410, *Wyndmyll hill* e.17 (*v.* **wind-mylne, hyll**).

Great Glen

GREAT GLEN

(*in loco qui nominatur*) *æt glenne* 849 (11) BCS 455 (S 1272), *Glenne* 1199 FF, 1268 RGrav, 1436 Fine, 1467 Nichols, 1549, 1550 Pat, *Glenn* l.13 CustRo, 1313 *Wyg* (p)
Glen 1086 DB, 1140 Reg *et freq*, *Glene* 1327 Pat, 1510 Visit, 1535 VE
Gleen 1308 *Wyg* (p), 1332 Misc, 1350 Pat, *Gleane* 1582 LEpis
Glynne 1535 VE

Affixes are variously added as:
Magna ~ 1238 RGros, 1247 Ass *et passim* to 1482 FA, 1519 EpCB
~ *Magna* 1274 Ass, 1329 Ipm *et freq* to 1576 LibCl, 1580 LEpis
Mikel ~ 1406, 1410 Pat
Much ~ 1568 LeicW, 1558 × 79 ECP
Great(*e*) ~ 1610 Speed *et freq*

Probably a place-name formed from an earlier name for the river Sence (which is an OE formation), a Brit **Glani̯ā* from **glano-* (PrW **glen*) 'clean, beautiful', hence 'the clean one' alluding to a clear stream, giving an early OE settlement-name '(the place which is called) At the Glen', cf. R. Glen, DLPN 50. Alternatively, because of early spellings with *-nn-*, a Brit **glennos* (Celtic **glĭn*, Gaelic *gleann*) 'a valley' may also be considered. However, although Great Glen lies in a pronounced valley of the river Sence at this particular location, Glen Parva which is situated some five miles to the west on the same stream, was established where a valley is much less noticeable. Hence, a Brit river-name seems likelier for the origin of both Great Glen and Glen Parva. The notion of the river as a Brit name meaning 'the clean one' is supported by its Anglo-Saxon name Sence (OE *senc* 'a draught, a drink') implying a copious supply of good drinking water.

If the origin of Great Glen and Glen Parva is indeed **glennos* 'a valley', it is possible that the name of the valley at Great Glen was extended to become a British district name, eventually applied to two settlements within its compass which were only coincidentally beside the river.

Eudo Martell held the manor of Great Glen c.1235 RHug, *Willelmus Martell* in 1247 Fine and *Rogerus Martel* in 1333 ib. Note MLat *magna* 'great' and *v.* **micel**, **mikill**, **much**, **grēat**.

AQUEDUCT SPINNEY, *Aquaduct* 1835 O, *v.* **aqueduct**; here, a raised section of the Grand Union Canal. CHURCH RD is (*the*) *Churchgate* 1601, 1698, 1708, 1712, 1715 *Terrier*, *v.* **churche**, **gata** and St Cuthbert's Church *infra*. CRANE'S LOCK, *v.* **lock**; on the Grand Union Canal. Note that *Crane* is an early Great Glen surname, cf. *Will'm Crane* and *Felicia Crane* 1332 SR, *Robertus Crane* 1381 ib. CRICK'S RETREAT, 1877 White, 1925 Kelly, cf. *Thomas Crick* 1863 White. Crick's Retreat was built in 1872 by Thomas Crick as 'an asylum for his relatives and poor persons of good character at an advanced age' 1877 White. CROWN (P.H.), *The Crown* 1695 *Deed*, *Crown* 1846, 1863 White, 1925 Kelly, *Crown Inn* 1877 White; continuity from the 17th to the 19th cent. is uncertain. FOX AND GOOSE (P.H.) (lost), *Fox and Goose* 1846, 1863, 1877 White. GLEN GORSE, 1806 Map, 1968 *Surv*, *v.* **gorst**. GLENN HO. is *Glen House* 1877 White, 1925 Kelly. GLENN VALLEY FM. GLEN OAKS, 1835 O, *v.* **āc**. GLEN WATER MILL, 1877 White, *Mill* 1835 O, *v.* **water-mylne** and Millerdale *infra*. GREAT GLEN HO., *Great Glen House* 1925 Kelly. GREAT GLEN MANOR, *Manor House* 1846 White, *The Manor* 1925 Kelly, *v.* **maner**. GREAT GLEN STATION, *Glen Station* 1835 O; on the *Leicester and Hitchin Railway* 1863 White, later the *Midland Railway* 1877 ib. GREYHOUND (P.H.), *Greyhound* 1846, 1863 White, 1925 Kelly, *Old Greyhound* 1877 White. THE HALL, 1925 Kelly, *Glen Hall* c.1850 *TA*, *Glenn Hall* 1863, 1877 White, *v.* **hall**. HIGH ST is *The Town Street* 1698 *Terrier*, *the Street of Great Glen* c.1850 *TA*, *v.* **tūn**. HILL TOP. LONDON RD is *Portwaye* 1601 *Terrier*, *Port Way* 1645, 1647 *ib et passim* to 1728 *ib*, *Pourtway* 1698 *ib*, *Poartway* 1708 *ib*, *v.* **port-wey**; so called because it was the road to the market town of Leicester, hence also *Leicester way* 1647 *Terrier*. MAIN ST. MARY'S MEADOW. No early forms are extant, but this was possibly land whose rents were dedicated to the maintenance of a chapel to the Blessed Virgin Mary in the parish church. MILLERDALE. Again no early forms, but sited at *Mill* 1835 O (*v.* Glen Water Mill *supra*) and beside a weir, *v.* **millere**; with **deill** or **dalr**. MOORBANK FM, *Moorbank Farm*, 1877 White, *v.* **mōr**[1], **banke** and Moor Head in f.ns. (a). THE MOUNT is *Mount Pleasant* 1846, 1863, 1877 White; a common complimentary name for a location, but one occasionally bestowed ironically. NEWTON LANE, Newton Harcourt lying one mile to the west. THE NOOK, 1925 Kelly, *v.* **nōk**. OAK COTTAGE, 1925 Kelly, *v.* **āc**. OAKS RD, leading to Glen Oaks *supra*. ORCHARD LANE, *v.* **orceard**. PEEP ROW (local), *v.* **rāw**; a line of houses with lattice windows (hence *peep*), built for framework knitters in the mid 19th cent. REDBANKS, *Redbank* 1925 Kelly, *v.* **banke**; prob. with **rēad**, beside the river Sence. ROYAL OAK (P.H.). RUPERT'S HO. is *Rupert's Rest* 1863 White, 1925 Kelly; local tradition has it that Prince Rupert spent the night here on the eve of the Battle of Naseby in 1645. ST CUTHBERT'S CHURCH, *Church (St Cuthbert)* 1846, 1863, 1877 White, 1925 Kelly, *the Church* 1601, 1645 *Terrier et passim* to 1712 *ib*; it is recorded earlier as *ecclesia de Glen* 1220 MHW, 1240 RGros, *ecclesie de Magna Glen* 1238 ib, 1341, 1361, 1413 *Pat*. Note also *the Church Yard* 1698, 1703, 1708 *Terrier*, *v.* **churchyerd**. SLUDGE HALL (GLENN MANOR FM 2½"); a humorous but derogatory name alluding to a muddy location, *v.* **sludge**. In the common minor name Frog Hall, *hall* is often a reflex of **halh** 'a hollow', but it is uncertain whether this pertains here. SPRINGFIELD LODGE, *v.* **spring**[1], **loge**. SQUARE SPINNEY, *v.* **squar(e)**, **spinney**; with reference to shape, although the spinney is now rectangular. STACKLEY HO., *Stackley house* 1925 Kelly; it is *Stackley Cottage* 1835 O (*v.* **cotage**), *Stackley Lodge* 1863 White (*v.* **loge**) and is located at *Stacklye* 1601 *Terrier*, *Stackley* 1645, 1647 *ib et passim* to 1728 *ib*, *Stackly* 1708, c.1715 *ib*, *v.* **staca**, **lēah**. Perhaps 'the wood where stakes are got', although *staca* was sometimes used of 'a boundary post' and possibly by extension 'a boundary'. Stackley lies at the northern limits of the parish, hence maybe rather 'the boundary wood'. STATION LANE, *v.* Great Glen Station *supra*. STRETTON HALL FM, near the parish boundary with Great Stretton, Stretton Hall lying immediately to its north. STRETTON RD is *Stretton gate* 1647 *Terrier*, *v.* **gata**; leading to Little Stretton which lies two miles to the north-east. THE VICARAGE, 1925 Kelly; it is *the vickeridg house* 1698 *Terrier*, *The Vicarage House* 1708, 1708 (18) *ib* and also *the mantione house* 1601 *ib* (*v.* **mansion-house**), *v.* **vikerage**. THE WOODLANDS, cf. *Woodland Spinney* 1862, *v.* **wudu**, **land**, **spinney**.

FIELD-NAMES

In (a), forms presented without dates are 1968 *Surv*; those dated 1759 are Nichols; 1806 are *Deed*; 1835 are O; c.1850 are *TA*; 1862 are *Surv*; 1918 are Sale. Forms throughout dated 1601, 1645, 1647, 1650, c.1650, 1674, 1679, 1690, 1698, 1703, 1708, 1708 (18), 1712, c.1715 and 1728 are *Terrier*; those dated 1695 are *Deed*.

(a) Seven Acre, Twelve ~, Thirteen ~, Fourteen Acre 1968, Forty-acre Cl 1862 (*v.* **æcer**); Aldergate 1968, ~ Cl, ~ Spinney 1862 (*v.* **spinney**) (*v.* **alor**, **gata**); Aquaduct Mdw 1862 (*v.* Aqueduct Spinney *supra*); Ball's Allotment c.1850 (*v.* **allotment**; with the surn. *Ball*); Bandy Lane Cl 1862 (also found in adjoining Little Stretton as Banny Lane 1771); Banland Spinney 1835 (*v.* **spinney**) (*Banlands* 1601, *Farre Bandlands* 1690, *Farbandlands* 1703, *Far Banlands* 1712, c.1715 (*v.* **feor**), *Further Bandlands* 1698, *Further Banlands* 1708 (*v.* **furðra**), *v.* **bēan**, **land**); The Barkhams (*Barkham* 1708, ~ *field* 1712, *v.* **berc**, **hamm**); Lower ~ ~, Upper ~ ~ 1862, Barn Cl 1862, 1968 (*v.* **bern**); Beadman's Bit 1862 (*v.* **bit**; with the surn. *Beadman*, from ME *bedeman* 'one who prays for the soul of a benefactor', cf. *Rebecca Beadman* 1810 Census, *John Beadman* 1812 and *Annie Beadman* 1873 ib of Great Glen); Black Hut Fd (*v.* **hut**); Boggy Cl 1862, ~ Fd 1968 (*v.* **boggy**); Bottom Bits (*v.* **bit**); Box Cl (a small, square enclosure); Brackley 1968, ~ Cl 1862 (*Brackley* 1645, 1647 *et passim* to 1703, *Braclye* 1601, *Brackle* 1679, *Brackly* 1690, c.1715, *v.* **bracu**, **lēah**); Brick Yard c.1850 (*v.* **brike-yard**); Bridge Cl, ~ Mdw 1862 (*v.* **brycg**); Far ~ ~, Near ~ ~, Brook Cl 1862 (*v.* **brōc**); Browns Cl (with the surn. *Brown*); Burton Lane c.1850 (Burton Overy lying one mile to the east); Cabbage Cl c.1850 (*v.* **cabache**); the Cake Mdw 1759 (poss. with eModE **cake** (OE *cac*) 'excrement'; otherwise an abbreviated form of **chese-cake**, alluding to shape); Calves Cl 1806 (*v.* **calf**); Chamberlain's Orchard 1862 (*v.* **orceard**; with the surn. *Chamberlain*); Chapel Cl (*v.* **chapel(e)**; with reference to the Methodist Chapel); Church Leys c.1850 (1703, *v.* **leys**), Church-yard Cl 1862 (*v.* **churchyerd**) (*v.* St Cuthbert's Church *supra*); Club Fd (prob. originally Cub Fd, with **cubb** 'a shed for cattle'); Cow Cl 1806; Darker's Cl (with the surn. *Darker*, from ME *darkere* 'a blackener, a darkener', a process in the tanning of leather); Colebreach 1759 (*v.* **cole**, **brēc**); The Croft 1862 (*v.* **croft**); Double Mdw (*v.* **duble**; a double enclosure, two fields now united, cf. *the Double Hedge* in King's Norton f.ns.(b)); East Fd c.1850 (*the Est Feilde* 1601, (*the*) *East feeld* 1679, *the East Feild or Nether end Feild* 1690 (*v.* **ende**), *East Feild* 1703, *the East Field* 1698 *et passim* to c.1715, *East Field Close* 1695, *the East feild(e) side* c.1650, 1690 (*v.* **sīde**), *v.* **ēast**, **feld**; an early large enclosure); Elsons (the surn. *Elston* in the possessive case, with typical Leics. loss of *t* in the group *-ston*; a family originally from Elston, 32 miles to the north in Notts.); Far Mdw 1862; Fish-pond Plantation 1862 (*v.* **fisshe-ponde**, **plantation**); Fold Yard c.1850 (*v.* **fald**); Frank's Cl (sic) 1862 (with the surn. *Franks*, cf. *John Franks* 1838 Census of Great Glen); Full Hill Mdw 1862 (*Neather* ~, *Fullhill* 1647, *Nether Fullhill* c.1650 (*v.* **neoðera**), *v.* **fūl**; poss. originally with **wella** rather than with **hyll**); Gimson's Cl 1862, 1968 (with the surn. *Gimson*); the Glebe Fd c.1850 (cf. *the Glebe land* c.1630, *the Old* ~ ~, *the New Glebe Close* 1708 (18), *v.* **glebe**); Gorse Mdw (*v.* **gorst**); Glen Hall Park 1968 (*v.* **park** and The Hall *supra*); Gravel-hole Cl 1862, The Gravel Holes 1968 (*v.* **gravel**, **hol**[1]); Graves (*v.* **græf**); Bottom ~ ~, Top ~ ~ 1862, Great Cl 1968; Hall Cl, ~ Fd 1862 (*v.* The Hall *supra*); Hardyman Mdw 1862 (cf. *George Hardyman* 1833 Census of Great Glen); Haymes Allotment c.1850 (*v.* **allotment**; cf. *Hames close* 1698 and *Rev. R. Haymes* c.1850); High Cl 1806, Highfields 1968 (*v.* **hēah**[1]); Hill Cl 1862, Hill Fd 1968; Far ~, Middle ~, The Near Holme 1862, Bottom ~, Middle Holmes 1968 (*v.* **holmr**); Homesteads c.1850, The Homestead 1968 (*v.* **hām-stede**); Horton's Cl (with the surn. *Horton*); Bottom ~, Top Hut (*v.* **hut**); Jobby Jack's Fd; Bottom ~, Middle ~ 1863, Top Lankley 1863, 1968 (*Lank(e)ley* 1645, 1647, 1728, *Lanckley* c.1650, *v.* **lang**[1], **lēah**); The Lawn 1863 (*v.* **launde**); Leicester Mdw 1862; Bottom ~, Top Lindock 1862, Lyndocks 1968, Lindock Spinney 1862 (*v.* **spinney**) (*Lindock* is perh. for *Linthwaite*, a small landowning family at the time of the Enclosure and earlier, cf. *William Linthwaite* 1647 and *Linthwaite hedge* in f.ns. (b)); Long Green 1968, Long Green Gutter 1759 (*v.* **goter**) (*v.* **lang**[1], **grēne**[2]); Long Mdw; Long Run (perh. a fanciful name; the field is very large, although a form of Long Green *supra* is poss.); Manor Park (*v.* **park** and Great Glen Manor *supra*); Lower ~, Middle ~, Upper Meadow (*the meadow* 1674, 1679); Meadow Cl 1806; Mickledale Cl 1806 (*Muckledale* 1601, 1654, 1728, *Muckhilldale* 1647, 1698, *Muckil(l)dale* 1674, 1679, c.1715, *Little Muckeldale* 1708, 1712, *Muckhilldale* ~ 1674, *Muckeldale hole* c.1650 (*v.* **hol**[1]) (*v.* **micel**, **mycel**, **mikill**, **dalr**); Middle Fd c.1850 (*the Myddle feilde* 1601, *the Middle field* 1645, 1647 *et passim* to 1728, *the midle feeld* 1674, (*the*) *Middle Field* 1690, 1708, 1712, *the Midle feild* c.1715, *v.* **middel**, **feld**; one of the great open-fields of the township); Middle Mdw 1862; Middle ~ ~, Top Mill Cl 1862, Mill Mdw 1862, 1968, Mill House c.1850 (*v.* **myln**); Lower ~ ~, Upper Far Moor 1862, Far Moor 1968, Lower ~ ~, Upper Middle Moor 1862, Lower ~ ~, Upper Near Moor 1862, Near Moor 1968 (*the Moore* 1601, c.1630 *et passim* to 1728, *the Moor* 1690, 1708 (18), 1712, *the More* 1708), Far ~ ~, Middle ~ ~, Near ~ ~, Upper Moor Head 1862, 1968, Nether Moorhead 1862 (*the more hed* 1601, (*the*) *Moore head* 1645, 1647, *the Moorhead* 1690, *the Moors Head* 1728, *v.* **hēafod**) (*v.* **mōr**[1]); Lower ~ ~, Upper Nether End 1862 (*v.* **ende**); North End Fds 1846, 1863, 1877 White (*the North end* 1708, 1712, *North end feild* 1690, *v.* **norð**, **ende**; fields at the northern end of the parish); Big Oaks (*v.* Glen Oaks *supra*); Oswins (the surn. *Oswin* in the possessive case; a reflex of the OE masc. pers.n. *Ōswine*); The Paddocks (*v.* **paddock**); The Park (*v.* **park**); the Patches 1759 (*v.* **patche**); Ploughed Cl 1862; Little ~ ~, Poor Cl 1862 (*v.* **pouer(e)**; land endowed for charity); Pudding Mdw 1759 (a fanciful name for soft, sticky ground); Road Fd c.1850 (a field beside a roadway); Round Cl 1862 (*v.* **round**; a field approximately circular in shape); Rowley's Big Fd (with the surn. *Rowley*); St Cuthbert's Fd 1918 (*v.* St Cuthbert's Church *supra*); Singers Fd 1918 (with the surn. *Singer*); Shotten Slade or Far Brook Cl 1862 (*Shortland slade* 1647, 1728, *v.* **sc(e)ort**, **land**, **slæd**); South End Fds 1846, 1863, 1877 White (*the South end* 1698, 1708, 1712, *v.* **sūð**, **ende**; fields at the southern end of the parish); Bottom ~, Top Stackley, Bottom ~ ~, Top Stackley Spinney 1862 (*v.* **spinney**), Stackley Fd c.1850 (1708, 1712, c.1715, *Stacklye Feilde* 1601, *Stackley Feild* 1647, 1690, ~ *Feeld* 1674, *Stackle Field* 1679; one of the great open-fields, also called *the Mill feild* 1645, 1650, *Gossells Feild* 1703 and *Burton field* 1728, *v.* **feld**), Stackley Mdw 1862 (*v.* Stackley Ho. *supra*); Stonehill (*v.* **stān**, **hyll**); Great ~ ~, Little Stoney Land 1862, Little ~, Stonylands 1968, Stonyland Spinny 1835 O (*v.* **spinney**) (*Stonylands* 1674, *v.* **stānig**, **land**); Bottom ~, Middle ~, Top Stygates (*v.* **sty-gate**); Swindley's Mdw (with the surn. *Swindley*); Little Tabbs (with the surn. *Tabb* in the possessive case; a reflex of the OE masc. pers.n. *Tæbba*); Three Cornered Mdw (*v.* **three-cornered**); Top Cl 1862; Top o' the Lane 1862 (*v.* **topp**); Top Townsend (*v.* **top**, **tūn**, **ende**); Lower ~ ~, Upper Townside Cl 1862 (*v.* **tūn**, **sīde**); Turnpike Spinney 1862 (*v.* **turnepike**, **spinney**); Upper Cl 1806; Wash-pit Ground 1862 (*v.* **grund**), Washpit Leys c.1850, 1968 (*v.* **leys**) (cf. *Washpit field* 1698, 1708, 1712, *v.* **wæsce**, **pytt**); Well Cl 1862 (*v.* **wella**); the West Brook c.1850; Windmill Cl (cf. *the Wynde myll feilde* 1601, (*the*) *Mill feild* 1645, 1650, 1698, *the Milne field* c.1650, *Mill Field* 1708, 1712, *v.* **wind-mylne**, **myln**; one of the great open-fields, also called Stackley

Fd *supra*); Wistow Fd c.1850 (*Wistow Church Feild* 1703; an enclosure next to the church of Wistow which lies adjacent to the south-western parish boundary of Great Glen), Wistow Leys 1862 (*v.* **leys**); Woodruffes (the surn. *Woodruff* in the possessive case).

(b) *the Acres* 1690, 1698, 1708, 1712, *the Aker furlong* c.1715 (*v.* **furlang**) (*v.* **æcer**); *Barry Bush* 1647, *Berries Bush* c.1650 (*v.* **busc**), *Thomas Berries Hadland* c.1650 (*v.* **hēafod-land**) (cf. *Thomas Barry* 1647, ~ *Berry* c.1650); *John Bates Headlea* 1647 (*v.* **headley**); *Boltons gate* 1647 (*v.* **gata**), *Boultons Hadland* c.1650 (*v.* **hēafod-land**) (with the surn. *Boulton*, at this date prob. that of a family originally from Boulton, 27 miles to the north-west in Derbyshire); *Bracklands* 1712 (*v.* **bracu**, **land**); *the Brook*(*e*) (*in Stretton Leys*) c.1650, 1674 *et passim* to c.1715, *Brooke Furlonge* 1601, *the Brook furlong* 1679, 1708, 1712, c.1715 (*v.* **furlang**) (*v.* **brōc**; no doubt referring to the river Sence); *John Bulls pen* c.1650, *Buls pen* 1674, *Bulls pen*(*n*) 1690, 1703, c.1715 (*v.* **penn**[2]), *Bulls Hadland* c.1650 (*v.* **hēafod-land**) (cf. *John Bull* c.1650, *Ralph Bull* 1690, *Samuel Bull* 1728); *Burton field* 1728 (a later name for Stackley Fd *supra*), *Burton mere* 1601, ~ *Meare* 1647, c.1650, ~ *Meer*(*e*) 1679, 1703 (*v.* **(ge)mǣre**), (*at*) *Burton mill* 1647, 1703, 1712, *Burton Mill Furlong* 1690 (Burton Overy parish adjoins to the east); *the Butts* c.1650 (*v.* **butte**); *above the Church* 1601, *near the Church* 1708, *Church Close* 1695, (*the*) *Church Furlong* 1647, 1674 *et passim* to 1728, ~ *forlong* 1698, *the Over Church furlong* 1674, 1690 (*v.* **uferra**), *Up*(*p*)*er Church Furlong* 1703, 1715 (*v.* **furlang**), *the Church corner* 1674 (*v.* **corner**), *the Church nook* c.1715 (*v.* **nōk**), *the Church side* 1679 (*v.* **sīde**) (*v.* St Cuthbert's Church *supra*); *at Colsons Hedge* c.1650 (*v.* **hecg**; either with the surn. *Colson* or with a typical Leics. reduction of the surn. *Colston* (*-ston* > *-son*) of a family originally from Colston Basset or Carcolston, 22 and 28 miles respectively to the north in Notts.); *the cowe pasture*, ~ ~ ~ *furlong* 1647 (*v.* **furlang**), *the Cowpaster* 1679, *the Cow pasture* 1703, *the Pasture* c.1650, 1708, 1712 (*v.* **cū**, **pasture**); *the Crosse Hedges* 1647, c.1650, *Croshedges* c.1715 (*v.* **cross**, **hecg**); *the Coggemire* 1690, *the Quogmire* c.1715 (*v.* **quagmire**); *Deadman* 1601, 1645 *et passim* to 1712, ~ *furlong* c.1715 (*v.* **dede-man**; more usually, such sites are called Deadman's Grave, poss. recording the discovery of pagan Anglo-Saxon burial sites, *v.* Lei **2** 325 and Lei **3** 301 *s.v.* **dede-man**); *Depdale* 1645, *Deepe Dale* 1647, *Debdale* 1650, 1679 *et passim* to 1712, *Nether* ~, *Upper Debdale* 1650, 1690 (*v.* **dēop**, **dalr**); *Duninge* 1601, *Dunninges end* 1647, *Dunells end* 1650, *Dunnings end* c.1650, 1690, 1708, *Dunins end* 1674, 1679, *Dunills End* 1703, *Dunings end* 1712, c.1715 (*v.* **ende**) ('the hill place', *v.* **dūn**, **-ing**[2]); *Edwardsdale* 1674, 1679, 1708, 1712 (*v.* **dalr**, **deill**; perh. with the surn. *Edward*(*s*), but if early, then with the OE masc. pers.n. *Ēadweard*); *the New* ~, *the Old Enclosure* 1708 (18) (*v.* **enclosure**); *the farre slade* c.1650 (*v.* **feor**, **slæd**); (*in*) *Flaxdale* 1601, 1645 *et passim* to 1712, *in Flaxedale* 1650 (*v.* **fleax**; with **dalr** or **deill**); *Mr Freemans Mill* 1708, 1708 (18); *Fulsick*(*e*) 1601, 1645 *et passim* to 1712, c.1715, *Fullsick* 1647, c.1650 *et passim* to 1703, *Fullseek* 1708 (*v.* **fūl**, **sík**); *Glaphole* 1645, c.1650 *et passim* to 1712, *Glephole* c.1715 (*v.* **glæppe**, **hol**[1]); *Goswell* 1601, *Gosells* 1645, *Gorssehills* 1647, *Gosils* 1674, *Gosil*(*l*)*s* 1708, 1712, *Great Goshills* 1679, ~ *Gossel*(*l*)*s* 1690, 1703, ~ *Goswils* c.1715, *Little Gossells* 1645, ~ *Gossills* c.1650, *Gossell greenes* 1645, *Gossil greenes* c.1650, *Gossell Grains* 1728 (*v.* **grein**), *Gossells Feild* 1703 (otherwise called Stackley Fd *supra*) (*v.* **gōs**, **wella**); *Greenesgate* 1647, *Greens gate* c.1650 (*v.* **gata**; cf. *Robert Greene* 1647); *Hartshorne* 1645 ('the stag's horn', *v.* **heort**, **horn**;

alluding to a hill supposedly resembling in shape a hart's or stag's horn, cf. Hartshorne, Db 637); *the Highwaye* 1601, 1645, *the Kings Highway* 1647 (*v.* **king**), *Hygh Waye feilde* 1601, *the Highway(e) feild* 1645, 1647 *et passim* to 1703, *the High Way feeld* 1674, 1679, (*the*) *Highway Field* 1708, 1712, 1728, *the north end highway field* 1698 (*v.* North-End Fds *supra*) (*v.* **feld**; one of the great open-fields) (*v.* **hēah-weg**); *Thomas Hobsons pen* 1708 (18) (*v.* **penn**[2]); *Kergate* 1647, 1649, *Kirgate* 1728, *Kergate end* 1645 (*v.* **ende**) (*v.* **kjarr**, **gata**); *Knaptoft* 1703, 1708, 1712, *Knaptaf* 1728, *Knaptofte Furlong* 1601, 1645, *Knaptoft Furlong* 1647, c.1650 *et passim* to c.1715, ~ *forlong* 1698, *Knaptoth furlong* 1674 (*v.* **furlang**) (*v.* **toft**; prob. with OE **cnapa** 'young man, servant', but the OE masc. pers.n. *Cnapa* or the ON masc. pers.n. *Knapi* may feature; cf. Knaptoft in Cox[2] 58 and SSNEM 214; such identical names with *toft* make the presence of a pers.n. less likely); *the lairing place* 1728 (*v.* **lairing**, **place**); *the Lammas Close* 1728 (*v.* **lammas**); *Langham me(e)re* 1645, c.1650 (*v.* **lang**[1], **hamm**; with **mere**[1] or **(ge)mǣre**); *Langton close* 1601 (*v.* **clos(e)**; cf. *Robert Langton* 1601); *Linthwaite hedge* 1647 (*v.* **hecg**; cf. *William Linthwaite* 1647); *Longdikes* 1645, 1647 (*v.* **lang**[1], **dík**); *Lytelyerd* 1342 Banco (*v.* **lȳtel**, **geard**); *the Middle Slade* 1645, 1650 (*v.* **slæd**); *the Milne* c.1650, *mylne hill* 1601, *Mill hill* 1650 (*v.* **myln**; with reference to a windmill); *myddle mere* 1601 (*v.* **middel**; with **mere**[1] or **(ge)mǣre**); *the Neather end feeld* 1674, *the Nether end feild* c.1715, 1690, *the Neither end Middle Feild* 1690 (*v.* **neoðera**, **ende** and East Fd *supra*); *Newton woollands* 1647 (*v.* **wald**, **land**), *Newton Me(e)re* c.1650, 1679 (*v.* **(ge)mǣre**) (Newton Harcourt parish adjoins to the south-west); *Normontoftes* 1601, *Normitoft* 1679 (*v.* **toft**; with OE **Norðman** 'a Scandinavian, especially a Norwegian' or with ME **Norman** 'a Norman of Normandy'); *Norton gate* 1645, 1647 (*v.* **gata**; King's Norton lies 2 miles to the north-east); *Oedbye mere* 1601, *Oadbye Meere* 1645, *Oadbie meare* 1647 (*v.* **(ge)mǣre**), *Olbie gate* 1650, 1728 (*v.* **gata**), *Olbiegate hedge* 1728 (*v.* **hecg**) (Oadby parish adjoins to the north-west); *the over end meer* 1679 (*v.* **uferra**, **ende**, **(ge)mǣre**); *the Pen Close* c.1650, *Edw. Staplefords Pen Close* c.1650 (*v.* **penn**[2]); *Piners gate* c.1650 (*v.* **gata**; cf. *Richard Piner* c.1650); *Widdow Plummer's land* 1728; *the pole* 1601 (*v.* **pōl**[1]); *Prat(t)s Furlong* 1690, 1703 (with the surn. *Pratt*); *Priors Round Hill* 1633 Ipm (*v.* **round**, **hyll**; with the surn. *Prior*); *Ravensaker* 1601, *Ravens Acre* 1647, c.1650, 1690, 1708, *Raines Acre* 1703, *Rauens aker* c.1715 (*v.* **æcer**; either with the OE masc. pers.n. *Hræfn* or the ON masc. pers.n. *Hrafn* or with **hræfn**); *Ridgwaye* 1601, 1650, *Rydgwaie* 1645, (*the*) *Ridg(e)way* 1647, c.1650 *et freq* to 1728, *Ridgeway hedge* c.1650 (*v.* **hecg**), *Ridgwaye sycke* 1601, *Rydgway Sicke* 1645, *Ridg(e)way Sick* c.1650, 1690 *et passim* to c.1715 (*v.* **sík**), *Ridgeway slade* c.1650 (*v.* **slæd**) (*v.* **hrycgweg**; the ridgeway runs on higher ground to the west of the township); *Sandelands* 1645, *Sandylands* c.1650, *Sanlands* 1674 (*v.* **sand**, **sandig**, **land**); *Silver hill* 1645, *Siluer hill* c.1650 (*v.* **seolfor**, **hyll**; poss. with *silver* as an elliptical form of an old plant-name such as *silver-thistle* or with reference to the richness of the ground or an allusion to rent paid or even to the presence of a source of pure water; note another Silver Hill in Theddingworth f.ns. (a)); *Sprats forlong* 1698, ~ *furlong* c.1715 (*v.* **furlang**), *Spratts Headland* 1708, *Sprats hadland* 1712 (*v.* **hēafod-land**) (with the surn. *Spratt*); *the Steeple end* c.1650 (*v.* **stēap**, **hyll**, **ende**); *Stenedale* 1601, *Stean(e)dale* 1647, c.1650 *et passim* to 1712, *Standale* 1650, *Steyndale* 1690, *Steendale* c.1715 (*v.* **steinn**; with **dalr** or **deill**); *Stonnydale* 1645 (*v.* **stānig**; with **dalr** or **deill**; poss. an alternative form of the previous f.n.); *Streton Closs* 1679 (*v.* **clos(e)**), *Stretton furlong* 1647 (*v.* **furlang**),

Stretton gutter 1647, c.1650, 1708, 1712, 1728 (*v.* **goter**), *Stretton hedge* 1645, 1647 *et passim* to 1712 (*v.* **hecg**; a parish boundary hedge), *Stretton lyes* 1601, ~ *leyes* 1645, 1650, 1690, ~ *Leys* 1703, c.1715, 1728 (*v.* **leys**), *Stretton meare* 1647 (*v.* **(ge)mǣre**) (both Great Stretton and Little Stretton parishes adjoin Great Glen to the north); *the Three Roods* 1690, 1698, 1708, *the 3 Roods* 1712, *the Three Rood furlong* c.1715 (*v.* **furlang**) (*v.* **rōd**[3]); *Mr Tompsons hadland* 1601 (*v.* **hēafod-land**); *the towne hadland* 1601, *the Town(e) syde* 1601, 1647, ~ ~ *side* 1640, 1650 (*v.* **sīde**) (*v.* **tūn**); *Tyltons close* 1635 Ipm (*v.* **clos(e)**; with the surn. *Tilton* of a family originally from Tilton on the Hill, 7 miles to the north-west); *the Waterthoroughs* 1728 (*v.* **wæter**, **furh** and *the water furrowes* in Billesdon f.ns. (b)); *Wayne way(e)* 1601, 1647, *Wane way* 1674, c.1715, *Wain way* 1679, *Weyneway* 1690, *Wayn Way side* 1645 (*v.* **sīde**) (*v.* **wægn**, **weg**); (*the*) *Willowes* 1645, 1647, 1650 (*v.* **wilig**); *the Wong* 1690, c.1715 (*v.* **vangr**).

Gumley

GUMLEY

Godmundeslaech 749 (12) BCS 178 (S 92), *Godmundesleah* 779 (8) BCS 230 (S 114), *Godmvndelai* 1086 DB, *Godmundele* 1254 Val

Gothemundele 1307 (p), 1308 *Wyg* (p) *et passim* to 1349 Ipm, 1350 Cl, *Gouthmundele* 1313 *Deed*, 1349 Ipm, *Gothemondele* 1360 Pat

Gommundele Wm 2, 13 Dugd, *Gomundeleg'* 1242 Fees, *Gomundele(y)* c.1253 Dugd (p), 1282 Ipm, c.1291 Tax, *Gomondele* 1266 Hastings

Gvtmvndeslea 1086 DB, *Gutmundelay* p.1150 Dugd, *Guttemundele* 1208 ChR (p), *Gutmundele(ye)* 1229 RHug, 1305 Ipm

Guthmundeley 1109 Nichols, c.1200, a.1250 Dugd, *Guthmundelay* e.12, 12 ib, *Guthmundelai* c.1147 BM, *Guthmundele* 1230 Cur (p), 1276 RH *et passim* to 1364 Pat, *Guthmondele(y)* 1332 SR, 1341 Pat, 1429 *ShR*, *Guthmoundele* 1349 *Wyg* (p), *Guthemundele(gh)* 1230 Cur, 1268 FineR (p), 1355 *MiD*, *Guthmundesleye* 1347 Pat

Gudmundel' 1200, 1226, 1230 Cur

Gumundel' 1199 MemR (p), 1237 RGros, 1249 RGrav, *Gumundeley* 1233 RHug

Gurmundeley(e) c.1250 Berkeley (p), 1253 × 58 RHug *et passim* to 1319 Hastings, *Gurmundeslay* 1321 (14) *BrCart* (p), *Gurmondele(y)* 1324 Ass (p), 1327 SR (p), 1338 (14) *BrCart*, *Gurmondlay*, *Gurmondle* 1338 (14) *ib*

Gormundeley 1312 *Peake* (p), 1317 Inqaqd, 1371 Banco (p), *Gormondelegh* 1317 Ipm, *Gormondeleye* 1375 Banco (p), *Gourmondle* 1375 *Wyg* (p)

Gromundesley 1356 RegAnt, 1426 BM, *Gromundley* 1402 Cl, *Grom(m)ondeley* 1411, 1421 ib

Gomondeley 1416 *Wyg*, 1428 FA, 1510 Visit, *Gomondley* 1428 FA

Gomeley 1517 DI, *Gomley* 1549 AAS, 1609 LML

Gummeley 1518 Visit, *Gumley* 1535 VE, 1576 Saxton, 1576 LibCl *et freq*

Gumbley 1606, 1617, 1630 LML

'Gōdmund's wood or woodland clearing', *v.* **lēah**. The OE masc. pers.n. *Gōdmund* which constitutes the first el. of Gumley appears from the later 11th cent. to have been influenced by the ON masc. pers.n. *Guðmundr* (ODan *Guthmund*). The late OE masc. pers.n. *Gūðmund*, with shortening in the first syllable, may also have played a part here.

William of Malmesbury in his *Gesta Regum Anglorum* (chapter 121) relates that King Alfred's opponent, the Danish king Guthrum, was called in English *Gurmundus*. The resemblance of *Gurmund* to *Gudmund* (< *Guðmund*/*Gūðmund*) could have given rise to the 13th- and 14th-cent. spellings in *Gurm-*. Note that Feilitzen (*s.n. Gūðmund*) treats the OE pers.n. *Gōdmund* as having a short vowel in the first syllable.

BELL (P.H.), *Bell* 1846, 1863 White, 1925 Kelly, *Bell Inn* 1877 White. DEBDALE LANE is *Debdayle gate* 1638 *Terrier*, *Debdaile gate* 1679 *ib*, *v.* **dēop**, **dalr**, **gata** and Debdale in f.ns. (a). DEBDALE WHARF, 1806 Map, 1835 O, *Depdale Wharf* 1846, 1863, 1877 White, *v.* **wharf**; the southern terminus of the Union Canal when construction was suspended in 1797. DEPDALE WHARF (P.H.) (lost), *Depdale Wharf* 1846, 1863 White; a canal-side inn at the above location. FOXTON RD, Foxton lying one mile to the east. GUMLEY COVERT is *Gumley Gorse* 1835 O, *v.* **gorst**, **cover(t)**. GUMLEY HALL (lost), *Gumley Hall* 1798 Nichols *et passim* to 1925 Kelly, *v.* **hall**; begun 1764 and demolished 1964. GUMLEY LODGE, *v.* **loge**. GUMLEY WOOD, 1635 Ipm, 1835 O, *The Wood* 1772 *EnclA*, (*The*) *Great Wood* 1638, 1679 *Terrier et passim* to 1824 *Deed*, *the Grate Wood* 1703 *Terrier*, *v.* **grēat**, **wudu**. HARTOPP ARMS (P.H.) (lost), (*the*) *Hartopp Arms* 1839 *Deed*, 1846, 1863, 1877 White; cf. *Sir Edmund Cradock-Hartopp, Bart.* 1846 ib, the lord of the manor and principal landowner. HOLLOWAY SPINNEY, *v.* **hol**[2], **weg**, **spinney** and *Holgate* in f.ns. (b). HOME FM, *v.* **home**. THE MOT, *v.* **mote**; at present the name attached to a Gumley Hall park water-feature by Capability Brown, but may have been transferred from what appears to be an early mill mound one hundred yards to its north-west, *v.* Mount Cl *infra*. OAK SPINNEY, *v.* **āc**, **spinney**. THE RECTORY, 1877 White, 1925 Kelly, *the Rectory House* 1707 (18) *Terrier*, *v.* **rectory**; note also *the Parsonage House* 1674, 1679, c.1690, 1707 *ib*, *v.* **personage**. ST HELEN'S CHURCH, *The Church* 1707 *Terrier*, *Church (St Helen)* 1863, 1877 White, 1925 Kelly; it is earlier recorded as *ecclesie de Gurmundel'* 1220 MHW, *ecclesiam* ~ ~, *ecclesie de Gumundel'* 1237, 1249 RGros. Note also *the Church Yard* 1707 *Terrier*, *v.* **churchyerd**. SPINNEY HILL, *v.* **spinney**. WHITE LION (P.H.) (lost), *the White Lyon* 1768 *Deed*, *The White Lion* 1769 *ib*.

FIELD-NAMES

In (a), forms presented without dates are 1821 *Deed*; those dated 1772 are *EnclA*; 1774, 1778, 1780, 1784, 1824 and 1828 are *Deed*; 1852 are *TA*. Forms throughout dated p.1270 are *Braye*; those dated 1601, 1638, 1674, 1679, c.1690, 1703, 1707 and 1707 (18) are *Terrier*; 1611 are *Deed*.

(a) Ashbed Cl (*v.* **æsc**, **bedd**); Badley's Cl (with the surn. *Badley*); Boare Plat(t) Cl 1821, 1828 (*Bors platt* 1601, *Bore platt* 1638, *Borsplat* 1674, *Boresplatt* 1674, 1679, *Boarplat* c.1690, *Boors platt* 1703, *Bors plat* 1707, *v.* **plat**[2]; with the surn. *Bore*, a reflex of OE *bār* 'a boar' used as a by-name); Brook Fd (1707, (*the*) *Brooke Feild*(*e*) 1601, 1674, 1679, c.1690, 1703, *v.* **brōc**, **feld**; one of the great open-fields of the township); Brown Slade Mdw 1821, 1828 (*Branslade* 1674, 1703, *Brantslade* 1679, *Braunt Slade* c.1690, *v.* **slæd**; with **brand** or **brant**); Burton's Mdw 1778 (with the surn. *Burton*); Bustans ~ 1824, Bustons Hill 1828 (*bustones hill* 1601, *bustandes* ~ 1638, *Bustorns* ~ 1674, c.1690, *Bustans Hill* 1707, *Cross bustandes hill* 1638, *Cross*(*e*) *Bustorns* ~ 1674, c.1690, *Cross Bustons* ~ 1679, *Cross Bustans Hill* 1707 (*v.* **cross**), *Short bustandes hill* 1638, *Long Bustans Hill* 1707, *v.* **hyll**; the surn. *Buston* in the possessive case seems unlikely here, since although common in Notts., it is rare in Leics.; perh. **burh-stall** may pertain (cf. Buxton's Hill in Hallaton f.ns. (a)), which would account for the recurring forms with *a*); Care 1772 (*car hill* 1601, *Care hill* 1674, 1679 *et passim* to 1707, *carr hill furlonge* 1601 (*v.* **furlang**), *v.* **kjarr**, **hyll**); Cat Grove 1821, Catgrove Cl 1772, 1824 (cf. *Catgrave Lawnde* 1611 (*v.* **launde**), *Catgraue Slade* 1674, 1679, 1703 (*v.* **slæd**), *v.* **cat(t)**, **grāf**); Clover Cl (*v.* **clāfre**; grown as a fodder crop); Cooper's Homestead 1778 (*v.* **hām-stede**; with the surn. *Cooper*); Cow Lawns (*v.* **cū**, **launde**); Long Croft Cl (*v.* **croft**); Crown Croft Homestead 1778 (*v.* **croft**, **hām-stede**; prob. with the surn. *Crown*); Debdale 1925 Kelly (*Debdale* 1601, 1674, c.1690, 1707, *Debdayle* 1638, *Debdaile* 1679, *Debdale Feild*(*e*) 1601, 1674, c.1690, 1703, *Debdayle feild* 1638, 1674, *Debdaile Feild* 1679, *Debdale Field* 1707 (*v.* **feld**; one of the great open-fields), *Debdale hadland* 1674 (*v.* **hēafod-land**), *the Homer side of Debdale* 1707 (*v.* **hamer**), *the Homeward side of Debdale* 1707 (18), *Debdale Lay*(*e*)*s* 1703, 1707, ~ *Leys* 1707 (18) (*v.* **leys**), *v.* **dēop**, **dalr**); Doak Cl 1821, 1828, Great ~ ~, Little Doak Cl 1824, 1828 (*v.* **doke** and OED *s.v.* doke and dolk 3); Dovecoat ~ 1772, 1821, Dovecot Cl 1824 (*v.* **dove-cot(e)** and the Fish Pond *infra*); The Dunstills 1821, Dunshill Cl 1772, 1824 (*Dunstall* 1674, *v.* **tūn-stall**); Fan Cl 1824 (this may be a later development of Fern Cl *infra*; if not, then presum. the reference was to shape); the Fellows Cl (with the surn. *Fellows*); the Fennyland Cl 1821, 1824, 1828 (*Ferneland* 1679, *fernieland hedge* 1601, *fernyland hedg* 1674, *Fennyland Hedg* c.1690, *ferneland* ~ 1707, *Fernland hedge* 1707 (18) (*v.* **hecg**), *v.* **fearnig**, **fearn**, **land**); Fern Cl 1772 (*v.* **fearn**); the Fish Pond or Dove Coat Cl (*v.* **fisshe-ponde** and Dovecoat Cl *supra*); Furry Cl (*v.* **fyrsig**); The Gore 1821, the Old Gores 1778 (*v.* **ald**) (*v.* **gāra**); Great Cl 1772, 1824; Great Wood Cls 1824 (1707, 1707 (18), cf. *the Great Wood grownd* 1638, *v.* **grund** and Gumley Wood *supra*); Gumley Groves 1804 Nichols (*v.* **grāf**); Hall Cl 1821, 1828 (*v.* Gumley Hall *supra*); Home Cl (*the Home Closes* 1674, *v.* **home**); Lawn Cl 1772, ~ Mdw 1772, 1821 (*The Lawnd* 1611, *Laune* ~ 1674, *Lawn*(*e*)

Corner 1679, 1707 (*v*. **corner**), *Laund lease* 1601, *Laune Lays* 1674, *Lawne leyes* 1679, *Laune Lay*(*e*)*s* 1703, *Lawn Lays* 1707, ~ *Leys* 1707 (18) (*v*. **leys**) (*v*. **launde**); Little Wood 1821, ~ ~ Cl 1772, 1824 (*the little wood* 1674, 1707, *v*. **wudu**); Matts Cl 1824 (with the surn. *Matt*(*s*), from *Mat*, a diminutive of *Matthew*, *v*. Purgatt Cl *infra*); (the) Mill Fd 1772, 1774, 1780, 1784 (*v*. **myln**); Mount Cl (*v*. **mont** and The Mot *supra*); Old Mill Cls 1778 (*v*. **ald**, **myln**); Pendock's Cl (with the surn. *Pendock*); Pinfold Cl 1774, 1821 (*v*. **pynd-fald**); (the) Purgatt Cl 1821, 1828, Purgate or Matts Cl 1824 (*Portgate* 1638, *Porgate* 1674, *Purgate* 1679, 1703, 1707, ~ *furland* 1674, ~ *furlong* 1679, c.1690 (*v*. **furlang**), ~ *h*(*e*)*adland* 1674, c.1690 (*v*. **hēafod-land**), 'the road to the market town', *v*. **port-gate**; the road joined the principal highway running between Leicester and Market Harborough and thus its name was doubly appropriate as the way to a market town); Ram Cl 1772, 1821, 1824 (*v*. **ramm**); Rectors Cls 1772 (*v*. **rectour**); Saxon Cl, ~ Mdw 1824 (with the surn. *Saxon*); Far ~ ~, Near Slade Mdw 1824, 1828 (*the Slade* 1679, c.1690, *v*. **slæd**); Three Corner Piece 1824, 1828 (*v*. **three-corner**, **pece**); Wood Barn Cl 1821 (*v*. **bern**), Wood Cl 1852, the Close under the Wood 1821 (*Gumley wood close* 1635, *v*. Gumley Wood *supra*).

(b) *Ales aker pitt* 1638, *Alis acres pitt* 1674, *Alices Acres pitt* 1679, *Ales acre pitt* c.1690, *Alice Acres pit* 1703, 1707, 1707 (18) (*v*. **æcer**, **pytt**; with the surn. *Alis*, a reflex of the OFr fem. pers.n. *Aliz* (modern *Alice*)); *arnet hill* 1601, *Arnett* ~ 1674, 1679, *Arnet* ~ c.1690, *Arnutt hill* 1703 (*v*. **eorðnutu**); *Ashby gate* 1601, 1674 *et passim* to 1703 (*v*. **gata**; the road to Ashby Magna which lies 7 miles to the west); *Astrope hill* 1601 (*v*. **hyll**), *Astrope slade* 1601 (*v*. **slæd**) (*v*. **ēast**; in view of the overwhelmingly early English nature of toponyms in this parish, the generic of the principal form may be an original **þrop** rather than a later metathesized **þorp**); *Bakon lays* 1707, *Baken Leys* 1707 (18) (*v*. **leys**; with the surn. *Bacon/Bakon*); *fatt banland* 1638 (*v*. **fætt**), *broad bawland* 1638 (*v*. **brād**), *Crosse banland* 1674, *Cross*(*e*) *Bawland* 1679, c.1690, *Cross Balland* 1707, 1707 (18) (*v*. **cross**), *Long banlond* 1674, *Long Bawland* 1679, c.1690, *Long balond* 1703, *Long Balland* 1707, *Watry Balland* 1707 (18) (*v*. **wæterig**), *banland doake* 1674, *Bawland Doke* c.1690 (*v*. **doke**), *Bawland doles* 1638, 1679 (*v*. **dāl**) (*v*. **bēan**, **land**); *blackferne* 1601, *black fearns* 1638, 1674, *Black fearne* c.1690, *Black Fern* 1707 (*v*. **blæc**, **fearn**); *blackpit* 1601, *Blackepitt* 1674, *Black pitt* 1679, *Blake pit* 1703, *Blackpit* 1707 (*v*. **blæc**, **pytt**); *the broke* 1601, *the Brooke* 1703, *brokleaes* 1601 (*v*. **leys**), *Brook Slade* 1707 (*v*. **slæd**) (*v*. **brōc**); *Brant hill* 1601, 1679, 1703, *Braunt hill* 1674, c.1690, *Brunt hill* 1707 (*v*. **brant**, **hyll**); *claridole* 1601, *Clarrie dole* 1638, *Clarre doles* 1679, *Claredols* 1703, *Clariddole* 1707 (*v*. **dāl**; with the surn. *Clare*, a reflex of the OFr fem. pers.n. *Claire* (Lat *Clara*), commonly used, poss. due to the popularity of St Clare of Assisi); *the Com*(*m*)*on* 1674, 1703, 1707 (*v*. **commun**); *the Common bolk* 1707, ~ ~ *Baulk* 1707 (18) (*v*. **balca**); *the Cow*(*e*) *pasture* 1638, 1674, 1679, *the paster* 1707, *the pasture* 1707 (18) (*v*. **cū**, **pasture**); *Crabtree* 1674, 1679, c.1690, 1707, *Crabtrey* 1703 (*v*. **crabtre**); *shortcroftes* 1601, *short crafts* 1638 (*v*. **sc**(**e**)**ort**, **croft**); *the cunstables bolk* 1707, *the Constables Balk* 1707 (18) (*v*. **conestable**, **balca**); *Deadman* 1601, 1674 *et passim* to 1707 (18), *dedman* 1707, *Deadman hadland* 1674, 1703, ~ *headland* c.1690, *Deadmans Hadland* 1679 (*v*. **hēafod-land**), *Deadman peece* 1679 (*v*. **pece**) (*v*. **dede-man**; poss. named from the discovery of a pagan Anglo-Saxon cemetery site); *farcome hill* 1601 (*v*. **feor**, **cumb**, **hyll**); *the Far hill* 1707 (18), *the fur hill* 1707 (*v*. **feor**); *folsike* 1601, *Foul*(*e*)*sicke* 1674, 1679,

Fowlesick(*e*) 1679, 1703, *Foulsick* 1707, *fulsick* 1707 (18), *great foule sicke* 1638, *Great foulsick* 1707, *folsike furlonge* 1601, *Foulsicke* ~ 1674, *Foulesick* ~ 1679, *Foulesike furlong* c.1690, *Foulesick headland* c.1690 (*v.* **hēafod-land**) (*v.* **fūl**, **sík**); *Foxon Mear*(*e*) 1674, 1679, c.1690, *Foxton Meare* 1679 (*v.* **(ge)mǣre**; the parish boundary with Foxton which adjoins to the east; some forms of the p.n. show typical 17th-cent. Leics. loss of *t* from the generic *tūn* when preceded by *s*); *Fredwell* 1674, 1679, c.1690, 1703, 1707 (*v.* **wella**; prob. with **freht** 'augury, divination', hence perh. indicating a wishing-well); *Freemans doake* 1703 (*v.* **doke**), *Freemans hadley* 1703 (*v.* **headley**) (with the surn. *Freeman*, a reflex of OE *frēomann* 'a freeborn man'); *garbrod* 1601, *Garbroad* 1674, *Garbrood* 1679, *Garbard* c.1690, *Garbred* 1703, *Garbord* 1707 (*v.* **gorebrode**); *gildhill* 1601, *Gayldhill* 1674, *Guild hill* 1679, c.1690, *Gaile hil* 1707, *Gails hill* 1707 (18) (*v.* **hyll**; with **gild**, which had the meanings 'sacrifice, worship, an idol, a god' and 'payment'; if one of the former group pertains, then a pagan religious site is indicated); *the Gleab Willows* 1679, *the Glibe Wilows* 1703 (*v.* **glebe**, **wilig**); *graines* 1601 (*v.* **grein**); *gutter lease* 1601 (*v.* **leys**), *the Gutter peece* 1679, *Guter Piece* 1703 (*v.* **pece**) (*v.* **goter**); *harbroue stong* 1601 (*v.* **hār**[2], **brū**, **stǫng**); *hanginge banke* 1601 ('steep bank', *v.* **hangende**, **banke**); *harlscross* 1601, *harles cross* 1638, *Halscrosse* c.1690, *Halscrose* 1703, *Harls Cross* 1707, *Longharlscros* 1679, *long halscrosse* c.1690, *Long halscrose* 1703, *Long*(*e*) *harls Cross* 1707, 1707 (18), *Short harlscross* 1674, *Short harlescros* 1679, *Short halscrose* 1703, *Short harls Cross* 1707, 1707 (18), *Harlscross hadland* 1674, *Hals cross Hadland* 1679 (*v.* **hēafod-land**) (*v.* **cros**; either with the surn. *Harle*, a reflex of OE *eorl* 'an earl', or with **eorl** itself); *heagate* 1601, *Hay gate* 1703, *Heaygate*, *Hay-gates* 1707, *Heygates* 1707 (18) (*v.* **hēg**, **gata**); *the Hedgrow* 1679 (*v.* **hegerǣw**); *long hillowe middow* (sic) 1638, *Hille Meaddow* 1674, *Hilly Meadow* 1679, c.1690, ~ *midow* 1703, *Hillie Meadow* 1707, *Cross hille Meadow* 1707 (18) (*v.* **cross**) (*v.* **hyllig**); *Holgate* 1601, 1679, *Houldgate* 1638, 1674, *Holegate* 1703, *Holgate Feild* 1601, *Houldgate* ~ 1674, *Holegate* ~ 1679, 1703, *Houlgate Feild* c.1690, *Holdgate feeld* 1707, ~ *Field* 1707 (18) (*v.* **feld**; one of the great open-fields), *holgate hyway* 1601 (*v.* **hēah-weg**) (*v.* **hol**[2], **gata**); *honypot* 1707, *the Honey Pot* 1707 (18) (*v.* **hunig**, **pot(t)**; used of 'sweet land', or of places where honey was found, or of locations with sticky soil); *Hunts halfe Acre* 1703 (*v.* **half-aker**; with the surn. *Hunt*); *kinges meddow* 1601, *Kings Meadow* 1679, 1707, ~ *medow* 1703, *long kinges middow* 1638, *Long Kings Meadow* 1707, *kinges medowe baulke* 1601 (*v.* **balca**), *kinges middow furlong* 1638, *Kings mead*(*d*)*ow furlonge* 1674, *Kings Meadow Furlong* 1679, c.1690; with the surn. *King*); *Lankthorne* 1601, *Long*(*e*) *thorne* 1638, 1674 *et passim* to 1707 ('the long patch of thorn-bushes', *v.* **lang**[1], **þorn**); *Langton Gate* 1601, c.1690, 1707 (*v.* **gata**; the road to Church Langton which lies 3 miles to the north-east); *Laughton Gate* 1674, 1679 (*v.* **gata**; the road to Laughton which lies one mile to the south-west), *Laughton Grounds* 1674, 1679 (*v.* **grund**); *the Lays* 1703, *the Leys* 1707 (18) (*v.* **leys**); *leasure* 1601 (*v.* **lǣs** (**lǣswe** obl.sg.)); *Litle* ~ 1601, 1638, 1703, *Little Hill* 1674, 1679, 1707; *merimedowe*, *merymedowe* 1601, *merrie middow* 1638, *Merry Mead*(*d*)*ow* 1674, 1679, *Merrie Meadow* c.1690, 1707, *Mer*(*r*)*y medow*, *Merrimidow* 1703 (*v.* **myry**); *midlecome hill* 1601 (*v.* **middel**, **cumb**); *Midle* ~ 1638, 1674, 1707, *Middle Hill* 1679, c.1690, 1707 (18), *langemiddelhull* p.1270 (*v.* **lang**[1]) (*v.* **middel**); *milngate* 1601, *Millgate* 1674, 1679 *et passim* to 1707 (18), *Mill gate Balke* 1703 (*v.* **balca**) (*v.* **myln**, **gata**); *moserne* 1601 ('the building beside boggy land', *v.* **mos**, **ærn**); *Moysland* 1674, c.1690, *Moiseland* 1679, *Moise Land Peice* 1703 (*v*. **pece**) (*v*. **land**; with the surn. *Moyse*, a reflex of the OFr masc. pers.n. *Moise*, from the masc. pers.n. *Moses* (from Hebrew via Greek)); *netle dole* 1601, 1638 (*v*. **dāl**), *Netels* 1703, *Neetl*(*e*)*s* 1707, 1707 (18) (*v*. **netel**(**e**)); *the Open Doke* 1707, 1707 (18) (*v*. **open**, **doke**); *the Parsons willowes* 1674 (*v*. **persone**, **wilig**); *Podocks Pit* 1703 (*v*. **padduc**, **pytt**); *rangland* 1601 (*v*. **wrang**, **land**); *reedland* 1601, *Redland* 1703 (*v*. **land**; prob. with **rēad** rather than **hrēod**); *rotcom* 1601, *Rottcum* 1674, *Rotcomb* 1679, *Rotcome* c.1690, *Rotcum* 1707 (*v*. **roð**, **cumb**); *Ruf sick* 1703 (*v*. **rūh**, **sík**); *Rushwell* 1674, 1679, c.1690 (*v*. **risc**, **wella**); *Saddington brooke furlong*(*e*) 1674, 1679 (*v*. **brōc**; the brook forms the boundary with Saddington parish for a short distance in the north-west); *Sandlands* 1707 (*v*. **sand**, **land**); (*the*) *Sandpits* 1601, 1703, 1707 (18), *Sande-pits* 1707, *Sandpitt hill* 1674, *Santpitt hill* 1679 (*v*. **sand-pytt**); *Sandylands* 1703, *Sandyland hadland* 1674, 1679, *Sandiland headland* c.1690 (*v*. **hēafod-land**) (*v*. **sandig**, **land**); *Shortlies* ~ 1707, *Shortleys hedge* 1707 (18) (*v*. **sc**(**e**)**ort**, **leys**, **hecg**); *shoulderbrod* 1601, *Shoulderbroade* 1674, *Showlder broad* 1679, *Shoulder Broad* c.1690, *Shoulder bone* (sic) 1703 (*v*. **scofl-brǣdu** 'a shovel's breadth', i.e. a very narrow strip of land; but clearly by the early 17th cent., a forgotten concept here); *skeveland* 1601, *Sce*(*a*)*ueland* 1674, 1707, *Sceaveland* 1707 (18), *Skeueland* ~ 1674, *Scaueland hadland* 1679 (*v*. **hēafod-land**) ('boundary land', *v*. **scēað**, **land**; with the specific influnced by ON **skeið** 'a boundary'); *Smeeton Hill* 1679, *Smeeton furhill* 1707 (*v*. **feor**), *Smeeton Stopers* 1703, *under Stopers* 1703 (*v*. **under**) (*v*. **stoppa**; Smeeton Westerby parish adjoins to the north); *standinge po*(*o*)*le* 1601 (*v*. **pōl**[1]; poss. an earlier variant of the following f.n. (with **Staning* 'the stony place', *v*. **stān**, **-ing**[2]), otherwise *v*. **standing** 'a place where cattle or horses may stand under shelter'); *Stanypoole*, *Stonypoole* 1674, *Stan*(*i*)*e Poole* 1679, 1703, *Stony Poole* c.1690, *Stannie pool* 1707 (*v*. **stānig**, **pōl**[1]); *stong* 1601 (*v*. **stǫng**); *Stonland* 1703 (*v*. **stān**, **land**); *stonpeices* 1601 (*v*. **stān**, **pece**); (*a furlong called*) *under the Sun* 1707 (*v*. **under**, **sunne**; alluding to ground which caught the best of the sun); *Thed*(*d*)*ingworth gate* 1674, 1679, c.1690, 1703, *Fedingworth Gate* 1707, *nether sid*(*e*) *of* ~ ~, *up*(*p*)*er sid*(*e*) *of fedingworth gate* 1601, 1707 (*v*. **gata**, **sīde**) (Theddingworth lies 3 miles to the south-west); *Thevdenes* 1601 (*v*. **þefa**, **denu**); *thornhill* 1601, *Thornehill* 1679, *Thorn Hill* 1707, (*the*) *backside Thornehill* 1674, 1679, c.1690 (*v*. **bak-side**), *Thornel* ~ 1601, *Thornhill hades* 1703 (*v*. **hēafod**), *Thornehill* ~ 1674, *Thornhill hadland* 1703, *Thornehill headland* c.1690 (*v*. **hēafod-land**) (*v*. **þorn**, **hyll**); *the townes end* 1638, *Against the Towns End* 1703 (*v*. **ageynst**), *Towns end Furlong* 1707 (*v*. **furlang**) (*v*. **tūn**, **ende**); *waterrey* 1601, *watterie* 1638, *Watree* 1707, *Short Watre* 1707, ~ *Watere* 1707 (18) ('the watery place', *v*. **wæterig**); *Wat*(*t*)*ering pitt furlong*(*e*) 1674, 1679, *watring pit furlong* c.1690 (*v*. **wateryng**, **pytt**); *Waxland* 1679, 1703, ~ *h*(*e*)*adland* c.1690, 1703 (*v*. **hēafod-land**) (*v*. **weax**, **land**); *welspringes* 1601, *Wellsprings* 1638, 1674 *et passim* to 1707, *longe welspringes* 1601, *Long wellsprings* 1674, 1679, c.1690, *short welspringes* 1601, *Short wellsprings* 1638, 1703 (*v*. **wella**, **spring**[1]); *weythey wonge* 1638, *Witheywong* 1674, *Withewong* 1679, *Withiwong* 1707, *Withywong* 1707 (18) (*v*. **wīðig**, **vangr**); *whitland* 1601, *Whiteland* 1674, *Short whit*(*e*)*land* 1601, 1674, 1679, 1703, *Long whitland* 1703, *Great Whitland* 1707, *Little Wheatland* 1707, *Whiteland Hadland* 1679, *Whitland headland* c.1690 (*v*. **hēafod-land**) (*v*. **hwīt**, **land**; in eModE, *white* 'infertile' is sometimes contrasted with *black* 'fertile'); *Williams Bush* 1674, c.1690, 1703, 1707, *Will'ms Bush* 1679 (*v*. **busc**; with the surn. *Williams*); *willowe meddowe*

1601 (*v.* **wilig**, **mēd** (**mēdwe** obl.sg.)); *wolfhill* 1601, *Woolefeild* 1674, *Wooll field* 1679, *Woollfeeld* 1703, *Woolfield* 1707, *Cross Woolfield* 1707 (*v.* **cross**), *Woolfeild Bushis* 1703 (*v.* **busc**), *Woolefeild hadlay* 1674, *Woolfield hadley* 1679 (*v.* **headley**) (*v.* **wulf**, **hyll**).

Hallaton

HALLATON

Alctone 1086 DB, *Halcton(e)* 1229 RHug, 1285 Ch
Halecton' 1167 ChancR, 1185 P, 1229 Pat, 1285 Ch, *Halectona* 1189 × 99 Hastings, *Halechton(e)* 1186 P, 1229 RHug
Halgeton' 1229, 1230 Cur, 1265 RGrav, *Halgheton* 1262 Cl, 1274 (1579) *LRoll*, *Halghton'* 1267 Cur, 1268 Abbr *et passim* to 1301, 1304 Ch *et freq* to 1380 Cl (p), 1387 *LCh*, *Halgton'* 1293 OSut, 1293 Cl, 1306 *Hazlerigg* (freq), *Halughton'* 1300 ChancW, 1306 Pat *et freq* to 1390 Hastings, 1397 Cl *et passim* to 1501 Banco, 1505 Pat, *Halugton'* 1289, 1298 *Peake et passim* to 1354, 1376 BM, *Haloghton'* 1402, 1415 *Wyg*, 1427 *Peake*, 1444 *ShR*, *Haloughton'* 1314, 1318 Banco *et passim* to 1374 Cl, 1384 Pat *et freq* to 1533 Fine, 1535 VE *et passim* to 1548 Pat, 1583 LEpis, *Halloughton'* 1465 *Wyg*, 1540 *Hazlerigg et passim* to 1604 SR *et freq* to 1619, 1630 LML
Haleton' 1167 P, 1220 MHW, *Halton(e)* 1203 Ass (p), 1205 P, 1224 RHug (p)
Halhton 1367 Cl
Haluton' 1225 GildR, 1264 *Hazlerigg et passim* to 1317 *Rut*, 1328 Banco, *Halutun'* 1260 *Rut*, *Halluton* 1284 Ch, *Haluthon'* l.13 *Peake*, *Haluetun* 1236 Fees, *Halueton* c.1291 Tax, *Haleuton'* 1242 GildR (p), a.1250 *Peake* (p), 1267 P, 1286 Coram, *Halouton'* 1276 (e.14) *BelCartA*, 1286 (e.15) *BelCartB et passim* to 1514, 1522 *Wyg*, *Haloutun'* 1286 (e.15) *BelCartB*
Alwetun c.1237 GildR (p), *Halwetone* m.13 *Peake* (p), *Haleweton'*, 1254 Val, 1259 Cur, 1290 Ipm, *Halighweton'* 1291 (1404) *Laz*, *Halugweton* 1350 Ipm
Halowton' 1426, 1446 *ShR*, 1489, 1508 Ipm, *Hallowton* 1618 LML
Hallaton 1576 Saxton, 1610 Speed *et freq*, *Hallaton called also Halloughton* 1622 Burton

'The farmstead, village in the nook of land', *v.* **halh**, **tūn**. The settlement lies in a narrow side-valley.

ALLEXTON RD, Allexton lying 3 miles to the north-east. CASTLE HILL, 1824 O, 1925 Kelly, *Hallaton Castle Hill* 1798 Nichols, 1846, 1863, 1877 White, *le castil* 1327 *Rut*, v. **castel(l)**; the earthworks remain of a Norman motte and bailey fortress. CHESTNUTS FM. CHURCH GATE, v. **gata** and St Michael's Church *infra*. COCK ABINGDON FM, *Cock Abington* 1928 Map. The farmstead is marked on the 1824 O.S. map, but is unnamed there. This is possibly an early site in **tūn**, the surn. *Abington* of a family once from the township of this name, 22 miles to the south in Northants. being less likely; *Cock* may have replaced an earlier *Clock*, with reference to a farm, v. Clock Cl in f.ns. (a). THE CROSS, 1925 Kelly, v. **cros**; a circular, solid little Butter Cross with a conical roof. EAST GATE, *Eastgate Street* 1783 *Deed*, v. **ēast**, **gata**. EAST NORTON RD, East Norton lying 2½ miles to the north. FEARN FM, ~ ~ COTTAGES, *Fearn(e)* 1601, 1718 *Terrier*, *Fern* 1707 *Surv*, *the Fearnes* 1771 *EnclA*, *Hallaton Ferns* c.1800, 1806 Map, 1824 O, *the Fearns* 1846, 1863, 1877 White, *against Fearn(e)* 1698, 1704, 1709, 1712 *Terrier*, *against Fern* 1745 *ib* (v. **ageynst**), *beyond Fearn* 1601 *ib* (v. **beyonde**), *Short Fearne* 1712 *ib* (v. **sc(e)ort**), *the Toppe of Fearne* 1606 *ib* (v. **topp**), *under Fearne* 1601, 1606, c.1700, 1705 *ib* (v. **under**), *Fern hedge* 1707 *Surv* (v. **hecg**), *Fearne hill* 1606 *Terrier*, *Fawn hill* 1707 *Surv*, *Fern side* 1601 *Terrier* (v. **sīde**), *Fern way* 1707 *Surv* (v. **weg**), v. **fearn** (used here as a collective for a ferny hill area) and Fern Brook in f.ns. (a). FOXHOLES, *Foxsholes* 1392 *FH*, *Foxholes* 1707 *Surv*, 1784 *Bewicke*, 1846, 1863, 1877 White, *Bewickes Fox Holes* (with the surn. *Bewicke*), *Big* ~ ~, *First Fox Holes* 1971 *Surv*, v. **fox-hol**. GOADBY RD, Goadby lying 2½ miles to the north-west. HALLATON GRANGE, 1925 Kelly, v. **grange**. HALLATON HALL, 1819 *Bewicke*, 1822 *Sale*, 1831 Curtis, 1865, 1872 *Bewicke*, *The Hall* 1707 *Surv*, 1863 White, v. **hall**. HALLATON MANOR, *Manor house* 1703 *Bewicke*, *Hallaton Manor House* 1846, 1863 White, v. **maner**. HALLATON WOOD is *Highwood* 1707 *Surv*, *Hallaton High Wood* 1806 Map, v. **hēah**[1], **wudu**. HARE PIE BANK, *hayre pye bank* 1698 *Terrier*, *Hare pye Bank* 1709, 1745 *ib*, *hair pye bank* 1712 *ib*, *Hearpye Banke*, *Hairepie bank* 1718 *ib*, *Hare Pie Bank* 1798 Nichols, 1824 O *et passim* to 1877 White, v. **hara**, **banke**; note that *the successive rectors should provide yearly 'two hare pies, a quantity of ale and two dozen of penny loaves, to be scrambled for on Easter Monday' at a place called Hare Pie Bank* 1846 White. HIGH ST, *the Highe strete* 1614 Ipm, v. **hēah**[1], **strǣt**. HOG LANE, perh. to be identified with *Hogsdrift*, ~ *Way* 1707 *Surv*, v. **hogg**, **drift**, **weg**. HORNINGHOLD RD is *Horninghold gate* 1707, v. **gata**; Horninghold lies a mile to the north-east. HORSECLOSE SPINNEY, *Horse Close* 1867 *Surv*, v. **hors**, **spinney**. HUNT'S LANE, *Huntes lane*

1601 *Terrier*, *Hunts lane* 1606 *ib*, cf. *Francis Hunte* 1601 *ib*, *v*. **lane** and *Hunts Laine End* in f.ns (b). MEDBOURNE RD, Medbourne lying 2 miles to the south-east. MOOR HILL, 1877 White, *v*. **mōr**[1]. MOOR HILL FM is *Moor Hill Lodge* 1824 O, *v*. **loge**. NORTH END, *v*. **norð**, **ende**. THE RECTORY, 1877 White, 1925 Kelly; earlier is *the Parsonage house* 1601, 1606, 1675, c.1700, 1705 *Terrier*, *v*. **personage**. ST MICHAEL'S CHURCH, *Church (St Michael)* 1846, 1863 White, 1925 Kelly; it is earlier recorded as *ecclesie de Haleton* 1220 MHW, ~ *de Halughton* 1338, 1368, 1370, 1387 *Pat*, ~ *de Halghton* 1347, 1367, 1370 *ib*, ~ *de Haluton* 1422 *ib*. Note *St Michaels Chappell* (sic) 1704 *Terrier*. ST MORRELL'S CHAPEL (lost), *St Morrills Chappell* 1601, 1606 *Terrier*, *the Chap(p)el* 1675, c.1700, 1705 *ib*; also *the Chapell yarde* 1601 *ib* (*v*. **geard**), *v*. **chapel(e)** and *Chapple furlonge*, *Chappill Hill* and *Chappel waye* in f.ns. (b) *infra*. It is unclear whether St Morrell's is an earlier dedication for the parish church of St Michael, whether there was a rationalization of *Morrel* > *Michael*, or whether St Morrell's represents a lost chapel of this name in the south of the township (*v*. *St Michaels Chappell* in the forms for St Michael's Church and (*at*) *St Morrels* in f.ns. (b)). St Morrell is unidentified. His probable association with the sacred *Stowe Welle* (*v*. f.ns. (b) *infra*) suggests an early Anglo-Saxon origin, with a pers.n. such as *Merewala*, *Merewald* or *Merewalh*. Symeon of Durham in *Historia Regum* (completed 1129) records an early St Merewald, while Merewala, who was brother of Wulfhere, king of Mercia, advised him to grant lands for the enrichment and glory of St Peter's Minster at *Medeshamstede*, now Peterborough (*v*. ASC E, *s.a.* 656). These lands included the very local Bringhurst, Great Easton, Church Langton and the lost *Prestgrave* (in Nevill Holt), as well as nearby Glaston, Tinwell and Ryhall in Rutland, a grant recorded in a charter of doubtful authenticity of 664 (BCS 22 (S 68)), so that even he may have become venerated. An alternative candidate is St Maurilius of Angers, a 5th-cent. bishop and disciple of St Martin of Tours. The families of the Norman lords of Hallaton originated in the Angers region, Maine-et-Loire, so that the transference to Hallaton of a cult of St Maurilius is possible — but unlikely of popular acceptance. The association of St Morrell with an OE **stōw** also makes this less likely and his sacred well here recalls that of the Anglo-Saxon St Tibba in Ryhall (Ru 164). STATION COTTAGES, beside a defunct railway branch line. TUGWELL LANE, *Tuppewell* 1601 *Terrier*, *Tup(p)well* 1606, 1705 *ib*, *Tupp well laine* 1698 *ib*, *Tupwell* ~ 1704, 1709, 1712, 1778 *ib*, *Tubwell Lane* 1718 *ib*, *v*. **tup**, **wella**, **lane**. VOWE'S GORSE, *v*. **gorst**; cf. *Thomas Vowe* 1846 White. Earlier in Hallaton are *Johannes Vowe* and *Willielmus Vowe* 1480 Ipm.

INN AND TAVERN NAMES

ANGEL (lost), *The Angell* 1614 Ipm. BEWICKE ARMS, 1846 White, 1861 *Sale*, 1863, 1877 White, 1925 Kelly; cf. *Calverley Bewicke, Esq., lord of Peverel's and Bardolf's Manors, Hallaton* 1846 White. FOX, 1846, 1863, 1877 White, 1925 Kelly. PARROT (lost), *Parrott* 1554 × 58 LAS. QUEEN'S HEAD (lost), *Queen's Head* 1846 White. ROYAL OAK (lost), *Royal Oak* 1846, 1863, 1877 White, 1925 Kelly, *Royal Oak Inn* 1867 *Surv*. SWAN (lost), *The Swann* 1705, 1711 *Bewicke*.

FARMS

Robert Arnolds Farme, *George Dodsons Farme*, *Edward Drake Senior his Farme* 1707 *Surv*, *Thomas Greens Farme*, *the Hall Farm(e)* 1703 *Bewicke*, 1707 *Surv*, 1714 *Bewicke* (*v*. Hallaton Hall *supra*), *Hallaton House Farm* 1856 *Sale*, *Barthol' Haycocks Farme*, *Peter James's Farme*, *Mr Daniel Judds Farme*, *John Scotts Farme* 1707 *Surv*, *Stafford's Farm* 1846, 1863, 1877 White, *Vowes farm* 1638 Ipm (*v*. **ferme**).

FIELD-NAMES

In (a), forms presented without dates are 1971 *Surv*; those dated 1771^1 are *EnclA*; 1771^2, 1774, 1784, 1812, 1813, 1820 and 1826 are *Bewicke*; 1783 are *Deed*; 1788 are *Terrier*; 1806 are Map; 1824 are O; 1867 are *Surv*. Forms throughout dated 1260, 1311, 1327, 1342, 1343 and 1352 are *Rut*; those dated 1300 are ChancW; 1318 are *LCh*; 1347 are *Peake*; 1361, 1631 and 1638 are Ipm; 1381 and 1639 are LAS; 1392 are *FH*; 1563 and 1713 are VCHL; 1573 are Fine; 1585 and 1588 are DKR; 1601, 1606, 1675, 1690^1, 1698, c.1700, 1704, 1705, 1709, 1712, 1718 and 1745 are *Terrier*; 1605 are *Conant*; 1690^2, 1695, 1703, 1711, 1714, 1724 and 1728 are *Bewicke*; 1707 are *Surv*.

(a) Five ~, Eight Acre 1971 (*Eight Acres* 1588), Fifteen ~, Twenty Acre 1971, Forty Acres 1867 (*v*. **æcer**); Back Cl (*v*. **back**); Bank Fd 1971, Banks 1867 (*v*. **banke**); Bannals, Johnsons Bannals (with the surn. *Johnson*), Bannals Bottom (*v*. **botm**) (*Banhil* 1318, *Banhill* 1601, 1606 *et passim* to 1718, *Middle ~*, *Nether ~*, *Bandhill* 1707, *v*. **bēan**, **hyll**); Far ~ ~, First ~ ~, Old Barley Hill (*Barlye hill* 1601, *Barlie ~* 1601, 1606, *Barly ~* 1675, 1698 *et passim* to 1718, *Barley hill* 1631, 1709, 1712, 1745, *Barlyhill Furlong* 1707 (*v*. **furlang**), *the Backside Barly hill* 1707 (*v*.

bak-side), *Barlye hill side* 1606 (*v.* **sīde**), *the Toppe of Barly hill* 1601, *the Topp of Barlie hill* 1606 (*v.* **topp**)), Barley Hill Fd 1771[1], 1771[2], 1784 (1639, 1695, *Barlie hill* ~ 1601, 1606, *Barly(e) hill Feild* 1601, 1675 *et passim* to 1718 (*v.* **feld**; one of the great open-fields of the township) (*v.* **bærlic**, **hyll**); Barn Cl (*v.* **bern**); Bassets Mdw (with the surn. *Basset* (OFr *basset* 'of low stature')); Baxters (the surn. *Baxter* in the possessive case); Berrys Cl, ~ Hill, ~ Mdw (with the surn. *Berry*); Big Fd; Billdyke (sic) (*Bulldike* 1601, 1698 *et passim* to 1745, *Buldike* 1606, 1707, 1709, *v.* **bula**, **dík** and *Bull-balk* in f.ns (b)); Blood Wood (1707, *Bloodwood Close* 1707, cf. *Bludbroke* 1573 (*v.* **brōc**), *v.* **blōd**; the water of the stream was evidently of reddish colour, prob. due to clayey soil in suspension; either with *brook* later altered to *wood* or with the specific *blood* compounded in the name of woodland in the region of the stream, cf. *Bludebec*, YN 113 and *Blodwelle*, Sa **1** 178); Bradders Hill 1971, Bradder's Home Cl 1867 (*v.* **home**) (with the surn. *Bradder*); Bradshaws (the surn. *Bradshaw* in the possessive case); Brasses Cl (with the surn. *Brass*); Old ~ ~, Brick Yard (*v.* **brike-yard**); Brikkle Cl (*v.* **brike-kiln**; beside Old Brick Yard *supra*); Bullock Cl (cf. *Stephensons Bullock Pen Close* 1703, 1714 (*v.* **penn**[2]; with the surn. *Stephenson*), *Bullock pasture* 1707 (*v.* **pasture**), *v.* **bulluc**); Bunch Bit (*Bunshpitt Close*, *Bunshpitt hades* (*v.* **hēafod**), *Bunshpitt hedge* (*v.* **hecg**) 1707, *v.* **bunche**, **pytt**; poss. referring to a place where bundles of reeds could be got, *v.* OED bunch sb.[1], 2); Buxtons Hill (*Burston hill* 1601, 1606, 1675, *Bruston* ~ 1601, 1698 *et passim* to 1712, *Burstall* ~ 1606, *Brustal* ~, *Brusthorne* ~ 1707, *Blustern* ~ 1707, 1745, *Briston* ~ 1709, 1712, *Brustons* ~, *Brustern* ~, *Burstons hill* 1718, *Buston hill more* 1675 (*v.* **mōr**[1]), *the Toppe of Burston hill* 1601, *the Topp of Burstall hill* 1606 (*v.* **topp**) (a wider variety of forms and earlier are needed, but prob. 'hill with the site of a (former) stronghold', *v.* **burh-stall**, **hyll**); *Tommy Butteriss* (with the familiar form of the pers.n. *Thomas* and the surn. *Butteriss* in the possessive case, from Les Bottereaux in Normandy); Calvert's Cl 1867 (with the surn. *Calvert*, from OE *calf-hirde* 'a calf-herdsman'); Cat Holes 1867, 1971 (*Catholehil* 1343 (*v.* **hyll**), *Catthole Furlong* 1707 (*v.* **furlang**) *v.* **cat(t)**, **hol**[1]); Clock Cl (cf. *Clock waye* 1601, *clock waie* 1606, *Clock way* 1675, 1707 *et passim* to 1745, *v.* **clok**, **weg** and cf. Clock Lane, Lei **2** 100; *clock* is of uncertain meaning in these instances, but poss. refers to dandelions (cf. ModE *dandelion clock*) or to some such flora; note the early instance of Clockwood (*Clocwode* 13), Nf **3** 134 and *v.* VEPN *s.v.* **clok**; the trackway here led towards Cock Abington *supra*); Clover Ground (*v.* **clāfre**, **grund**; clover was used as a fodder crop); Rest's Cole Cl 1867 (with the surn. *Rest*, a shortened reflex of the ContGerm masc. pers.n. *Restold*), Coles 1971 (*le Coulis* 1342, (*in*) *Cole* 1707, *Cole way* 1707 (*v.* **weg**), *v.* **cole**, **cūle**); Colemans Cl (with the surn. *Coleman*, prob. a reflex of the ContGerm masc. pers.n. *Col(e)man*); Bottom ~, Second Corblus, Top Corplus (prob. with the surn. *Corble/Corbell* in the possessive case); Cottage Cl (*v.* **cotage**); Cow Lair 1784, 1971 (1707, *v.* **cū**, **lair**); Cranes Cl (with the surn. *Crane*); Old Cricket Fd (for the game of cricket); Far ~ ~, First ~ ~, Middle Church Bridge 1867, Big ~ ~, Little Church Bridge, Garners (Second) Church Bridge (with the surn. *Garner*) 1971 (*the Further ~ ~ ~*, *the Nearer Church Bridge Close*, *Church Bridge Closes* 1707, *v.* **brycg** and St Michael's Church *supra*); Croft 1867 (*Croft Way* 1707, *v.* **croft**); Day's Cl (with the surn. *Day*); Dexters Castle Cl (with the surn. *Dexter*) ((*the*) *Castle Close* 1707, 1714, 1728, cf. *Castle Scike* (sic) 1707 (*v.* **sík**), *Castle Slade* 1707 (*v.* **slæd**), *v.* Castle Hill *supra*); Dockey Cl (*v.* **docce**, **-ig**[3]; cf. *Docks Acre* 1707, *v.* **docce**, **æcer**); Draycott's Cl 1867 (with the surn. *Draycott*); Drift, ~ Cl (*the Drifte* 1601, *the Drift*

1606, 1675 *et passim* to 1745, *the Common Drift* 1601, 1606 (*v.* **commun**), *the Drift way* 1707, 1745 (*v.* **weg**), *Cowdrift*, ~ *way* 1707 (*v.* **cū**), *v.* **drift**); Dry-hills 1788 (*v.* **drȳge**, **hyll**); the Close of Thomas Falkner 1788, Faulkner's Cl 1867 (once bordered by *Fauknеrs hedge* 1707, *v.* **hecg**); Fern Brook (*Fearn*(*e*) *Brook*(*e*) 1601, 1698 *et passim* to 1718, *Fern Brook* 1707, 1745, ~ ~ *peice* 1707 (*v.* **pece**), *v.* **brōc**), Fearn Fd 1784, Fern Field Cl 1812 (*Fearne Feild* 1601, 1606 *et passim* to 1718, *Fernefelde* 1631, (*the*) *Ferne feild* 1675, c.1700, 1705, *Fe*(*a*)*rn* ~ 1707, 1712, 1718, 1745, *Fearne Field* 1771[1] (*v.* **feld**; one of the great open-fields), Fearn Tongue 1971 (*Fern Tongue* 1707, *v.* **tunge** and Fearn Fm *supra*); Flat Cl (*v.* **flatr**); Old Football Cl (for the game of football); Great ~ ~, Small Footbridge Cl 1820, Foot Bridge 1971 (*v.* **fote-brydge**); Foul Syke (*Fulsic* 1260, *Foul*(*e*) *scike* 1707, *v.* **fūl**, **sík**); Bottom ~, Top ~, Fowlers (ostensibly with the surn. *Fowler* in the possessive case, but *v.* *Fullwell slade* in f.ns. (b)); Frisby's (the surn. *Frisby* in the possessive case; the family of this name may have come originally from Frisby (by Galby), 7 miles to the north-west); the Garden of Edward Ward 1788 (*v.* **gardin**); Garner's Cl 1871 (with the surn. *Garner*); Big ~, Bottom Goodmans, Goodmans Mdw (*Goodmans Closes* 1605; with the surn. *Goodman*); Gravel Pit 1867, ~ ~ Cl 1863, 1877 White (*v.* **gravel**, **pytt**); Great Close Mdw 1867; Little Green (cf. *othe grene* 1381 (p), *v.* **grēne**[2]); Top Greens (either with **grene**[2] or with the surn. *Green* in the possessive case); Hall Yard 1774 (*v.* **geard** and Hallaton Hall *supra*); Hare Crop Leys 1798 Nichols, 1846, 1863 White (*harcrofte*, *Harecraft* 1601, *harecroft* 1606, *Hair*(*e*) *Croft* 1718, *Hare-Crop* 1745, *Haire Craft* ~ 1698, *Harecraft* ~ a.1709, *Hair Croft Furlong* 1709, 1712 (*v.* **furlang**), *Harecrafte Leys* 1601, *Haire craft leas*(*e*) 1675, c.1700, *Hayre Craft Leayes* 1705, *Hare-crop Leys* 1707 (*v.* **leys**), *v.* **croft**; prob. with **hār**[2] rather than with **hara**, since the compound occurs also in Blaston and Smeeton Westerby f.ns. (a); note *harecroftgate* in adjoining Slawston f.ns. (b)); The Hermitage 1784, Armitage Cl 1813 (*the Hermitage* 1588, *le Hermitage close* 1631, *v.* **ermitage**); High Ash (*v.* **hēah**[1], **æsc**); Holland Mdw (poss. with the surn. *Holland*; otherwise *v.* **hol**[2], **land**); Hollows (*v.* **holh**); Home Cl (*the Home close* 1606), Home Fd (*v.* **home**); the Homestead of William Barnett (*v.* **hām-stede**); Honey Pots (1712, *Honey Pot* 1745, *v.* **hunig**, **pot**(**t**); used of 'sweet land', or of places where honey was found, or of locations with sticky soil); Hop Ground (*v.* **hoppe**, **grund**); Garners Horninghold Cl (with the surn. *Garner*; a close adjacent to the Horninghold parish boundary); House Cl; Hovel Cl 1867, Hovel Fd 1971 (*v.* **hovel**); Hut Cl (*v.* **hut**); Issets Side (*v.* **sīde**; a close adjacent to Isset's Lodge, Tugby and Keythorpe parish, Lei **3** 259); James Cl (with the surn. *James*); Knights Barn (a close so called; *v.* **bern**, with the surn. *Knight*); the Lady Cl 1813 (*v.* **ladi**); The Lair (*v.* **lair**); Lawn Bushes Cl 1783 (*Lawne bushes* 1707, *v.* **launde**, **busc**); Little ~ ~, Leicester Way (*Leicester Way Close* 1707; closes beside the old road to Leicester which lies some 14 miles to the north-west); Little Fd 1771[1], 1784 (1707); Long Fd (a long, narrow close); the Old Malt Kiln 1774 (*v.* **malte-kylne**); Manor House Great Cl 1867, Manor Big Fd 1971 (*v.* Hallaton Manor *supra*); First ~ ~, Second ~ ~, March Mdw 1867, Marshes 1971 ((*in*) *the March* 1601, 1606, 1675, c.1700, (*in*) *March* 1675, 1698 *et passim* to 1718, *the nether ende of March* 1606 (*v.* **ende**), *Nether* ~, *Upper March* 1745, *March*(*e*) *furlong* 1698, 1704 *et passim* to 1718, *March Nether Furlong* 1707 (*v.* **furlang**), *March Meddowe* 1601, ~ *meadowe* 1606, *March Way*(*e*) 1601, 1707 (*v.* **weg**), *v.* **mersc**); Margraves (*Margraues*, *Margraves* 1707; either 'fen ditches', *v.* **marr**[1], **græf**, or the surn. *Margrave* in the possessive case (cf. *Lizzie Margrave* 1866 Census of Newbold)); the Close of Mary Mason 1788; The Meadows; Mill Mount 1867, 1971 (*v.* **myln**, **mont**; a windmill site); Moor Hill Big Fd (cf. *Moorehill Close* 1707, *v.* Moor Hill *supra*); the Neats Pasture 1771[1] (*the Neates Pasture* 1585, *le Neats pasture* (*or Smallwood hill*) 1639, *v.* **nēat**, **pasture** and Smallwood Common *infra*); Norton Hill Barn (*v.* **bern**; adjacent to East Norton parish to the north); Top ~, Oaks, Oaks Mdw 1971, Oaks Common 1784 (*v.* **commun**) (*Oaks*, ~ *Cowpasture* (*v.* **cū**, **pasture**), ~ *hedge* 1707, *v.* **āc**); Othorpe Brook 1867, 1971 (*Oldthorpe* ~, *Owe Thorpe brook* 1707; forms the boundary with the deserted medieval village of Othorpe (Slawston parish), but earlier called *Ottebrook* 1707, *Otter Brook* 1745, *v.* **oter**, **brōc**); Owsley's (the surn. *Owsley* in the possessive case); Paradise 1867, 1971 (*v.* **paradis**; early used of a garden or of an enclosed pleasure ground, but here perh. simply a complimentary name, cf. Lei **2** 360 and Lei **3** 344); Parsons Leas (1709, *Parsons Leys* 1698, 1704, 1709, 1712, 1745, ~ *Layes*, ~ *Lees* 1718, *Parsonage Leys* 1601, *v.* **persone**, **personage**, **leys**); Bottom ~, Top Part (cf. *the Farme Part* 1707 (*v.* **ferme**), *v.* **part**); Pateman's Cl 1867 (with the surn. *Pateman*); Pecks Cl, Pecks High Cl (with the surn. *Peck*); Peppers Cl (with the surn. *Pepper*, in origin metonymic for a dealer in pepper and other spices); Old Ploughed Cl, ~ ~ Fd; Poles Cl 1813, Pole's Cl 1846, 1863, 1877 White (*Poles Close* 1707; with the surn. *Pole*); Potatoe Ground 1867 (*v.* **grund**), the Potatoe Piece 1867 (*v.* **pece**) (*v.* **potato**); Prettys (the surn. *Pretty* in the possessive case; a reflex of OE *prættig* 'astute, cunning'); Rales (poss. with **raile**; a surn. *Rale* in the possessive case is less likely); Ratley's Spinney 1824 (*v.* **spinney**), Rats Leas (sic) 1971 (with the surn. *Ratley*); Bottom ~, Top Ravens, Ravens Cl (with the surn. *Raven*); Robins Cl (with the surn. *Robins*); Roman Mdw (a site where Roman remains have been discovered); The Rookery 1867 (*v.* **rookery**); Round Hill (*v.* **round**); Bottom Sand Holes (*v.* **sand**, **hol**[1]); Sandy Brook (1707, *v.* **sandig**, **brōc**); Seeds (*v.* **sǣd**; used of grasses sown for one year's mowing or grazing, as distinguished from permanent pasture); Sedgleys (the surn. *Sedgley* in the possessive case); Shilcocks (the surn. *Shilcock* in the possessive case); Siddeboys (sic) (the surn. *Sideboy* in the possessive case); The Slade (*v.* **slæd**); Smallwood Common 1784 (*v.* **commun**) (*Smalewood* 1707, *Smallwood close*(*s*) 1639, 1703, 1714, *Smalewood Close* 1707, *Smallwood Feild* 1601, 1606 *et passim* to 1718, *Smalewood* ~ 1631, 1639, *Smallwood Field* 1712, 1745 (*v.* **feld**; one of the great open-fields), *Smallwood hill* 1639, ~ ~ *close* 1639, 1703, 1714, *v.* **smæl**, **wudu**); Smock Hedges ((*the*) *Smock hedg* 1601, c.1700, 1705, *Smock hedge* 1606, *Smock hedg furlong*, *Smock hedge way* (*v.* **weg**) 1707; the reference is to *smoke-silver*, a tax paid in lieu of tithewood to the incumbent of the parish, *v.* Smock Cl in Blaston f.ns. (a); either with **hecg** in its early sense 'a hedged enclosure' or with **edisc** or **etisc**); Bottom ~, Top Spinney (*v.* **spinney**); Station Cl (*v.* Station Cottages *supra*); Stafford's Cl 1867 (with the surn. *Stafford*); Stevens Cl (with the surn. *Stevens*); Stocking Cl (*le Stocking* 1327, *Stockyng*, *Stokking* 1342, *Stockin Close* 1707, 1728, *v.* **stoccing**); Stone Bridge (*Stonebridge furlong* 1707 (*v.* **stān**, **brycg**); Stone-pit Cl 1846, 1863, 1877 White, Stone Pit 1971 (*Stonpitt Furlong* 1707, *v.* **stān-pytt**); Stoney Furlong (*Stone furlonge* 1606, *stan furlong* 1705, *v.* **stān**, **stānig**); Store Cl 1867 (*v.* **stor**; either in the sense 'livestock' or with the complimentary meaning 'abundance, plenty', *v.* OED store sb. 2 and 4b); Stowe Cl 1788, 1971 (*Stow close* 1639, *v.* **stōw**; recording a former holy place, the site of *Stowe Welle*, presum. to be identified with *St Morrills well* in f.ns. (b), *v.* M. Gelling, 'Some meanings of *stōw*', *The Early Church in Western Britain and Ireland*, ed. S. M. Pearce, British

Archaelogical Reports 102 (Oxford 1982), 187–96); Suttons (the surn. *Sutton* in the possessive case); Swan Cl 1867 (may remember *The Swann* hostelry *supra*, but note *Swans Ricksted* of similar date in f.ns. (b) which suggests the surn. *Swan*); Swinny Mdw (*Swynhagh*, *Swynhawe* 1327, *Swinnow* 1601, 1606, *Swinnow Closes* 1703, 1711, *Middle* ~ ~, *Nether* ~ ~, *Upper Swinnow Close* 1707, *Swynnow Hills* 1585, *Swinnowe Hilles* 1605 (*v.* **hyll**), *Swynhawmedowe* 1392, *Swinnow meddow*, *Swinowe meddowe* 1601, *Swinnow(e) Meadow(e)* 1606, 1709 *et passim* to 1745, ~ *Medow* 1675, c.1700, ~ *Middow* 1698, *Swinow Meddow* 1704, *v.* **swīn**, **haga**[1]); Talbots Cl (with the surn. *Talbot*, a reflex of the OFr masc. pers.n. *Talebot*); (Kilby's) Tenter House 1867 (with the surn. *Kilby*), Top Tentus 1971 ((*the*) *Tenters* 1601, 1606 *et passim* to 1745, *Tentors* 1639, *Taintors* 1718, (*the*) *Tenters Close* 1707, 1714, *Tenters* ~ 1698, 1704, *Tentors furlong* 1709, 1712, *v.* **tentour**); Thammesen (*Tomasholme* 1605, (*in*) *Tomasin*, *Tomasin Close* 1707, *v.* **holmr**; with the surn. *Tomas*); Thorns 1788, Hallaton Thorns 1806, 1824, Bottom ~, Top Thorns 1971 (*le Thirne* 1347, *v.* **þyrne**, **þorn**); Thorny Cl 18677 (*v.* **þornig**); Bottom ~, Top Tomblins (with the surn. *Tomblin* in the possessive case); Top Cl 1867, ~ Fd 1971 (*v.* **top**); Towns End Cls 1826, ~ ~ Cl 1971 (*the Townsend* 1707, *v.* **tūn**, **ende**); Baker Wards, Wards Cl (cf. *Wardhill* 1707; with the surn. *Ward*); Bottom ~ ~, Top West Fd ((*the*) *West Field* 1707, *Westfield brook* 1707 (*v.* **brōc**), *West Field hedge* 1707 (*v.* **hecg**), *West Field way* 1707, *v.* **west**, **feld**); Wests Fd (with the surn. *West*); Whetstone ~ 1771[1], Wetstone Fd 1784, Whetstone Hill 1961, ~ ~ Mdw 1867 (*Whetston Cross* 1698, 1704, 1712, 1718, *Wetston cross* 1709 (perh. a wayside cross or a hill-top cross (*v.* **cros**), but a late use of **cross** for a cross-roads may pertain here, cf. *Limekiln cross* in f.ns. (b)), *Wistoue* ~, *Wistowe Hill* 1601, *Whiston hill* 1606, *Whetstone Hill* 1707, *Whiston waye* 1601, *Whetston way* 1675, c.1700, 1705, 1707, *v.* **wīc-stōw** (later confused with **hwet-stān**)); Willeys Cl (with the surn. *Willey*); Wilson Cl (with the surn. *Wilson*); The Wire (*v.* **weyour**); Top Wood 1971, (The) Wood Cl 1788, 1813, Wood Side 1971 (*v.* **sīde**) (*les Wood Closes* 1638, *Wood Close* 1703, 1707, 1711, *Wood Field* 1713, *v.* **wudu**); Wooden Hooks (*v.* **hōc**; with *wooden* in the sense 'belonging to the woods', *v.* OED wooden 1, 3); Workhouse Cl 1812 (*v.* **workhouse**; land which provided rental for the upkeep of a workhouse purchased in 1732 with money left by the Revd. Benjamin Bewicke).

(b) *Ash Close* 1728 (*v.* **æsc**); *Ashewell bridge* 1631, *Ashwell* ~ 1707, *Aswell Bridge* 1745 (*v.* **æsc**, **wella**, **brycg**); *Asshawe* 1367 (*v.* **æsc**, **haga**[1]); *Attons Close* 1707, 1714 (cf. *Richard Atton* 1707); *Bandlands*, *Bandland Furlong* 1707 (*v.* **bēan**, **land**); *Banforlong* 1300 (*v.* **bēan**, **furlang**); *Bareherse* 1606, *Barearse* 1606, 1675, c.1700, 1718, ~ *Peice* 1601 (*v.* **pece**), *Bararse* 1675, 1705, 1709, 1712, 1718 (*v.* **bær**[1]; either with **herse** 'a hill-top' or with **ears** 'arse', the latter perh. forming a disparaging name for unproductive land; cf. the early *Barehers* in Drayton f.ns. (b) and *Barearse hill* in Goadby f.ns. (b)); *Barly Hades* 1718 (*v.* **bærlic**, **hēafod**); *Barrsholme* 1631 (*v.* **holmr**; with the surn. *Barr*); *Bays land* 1690[2] (*v.* **land**; with the surn. *Bay*); *Beech Meadow* 1707 (*v.* **bēce**); *Beers Meadow* 1707 (with the surn. *Beer*); *Blastonbrok(e)* 1327, 1392, 1606, *Blaston brook(e)* 1601, 1606 *et passim* to 1718 (*v.* **brōc**), *Blaston gate* 1707 (*v.* **gata**), *Blaston Foot Bridge* 1707 (*v.* **fote-brydge**), *Blaston Footway* 1707 (*v.* **fote-waye**), *Blaston Spinney* 1707 (*v.* **spinney**) (Blaston parish adjoins to the south-east); *Blondes Lane* 1601 (*v.* **lane**; with the rare surn. *Blonde* of French origin); *Bolewyk* 1327 (*v.* **bula**, **wīc**); *Broadebaucke* 1601, *Broad balke* 1601, c.1700, 1705, *broadbawlke* 1606, *Brode baulke* 1675, *Broad*

Balk(*e*) 1704, 1709, 1712, 1718, 1745 (*v*. **brād**, **balca**); *Brook Field* 1713 (*v*. **brōc**); *Browns Leys* 1707 (*v*. **leys**; with the surn. *Brown*); *Bull-balk* 1709 (*v*. **balca**), *Bull Bush* 1707 (*v*. **busc**), *the Bull peice* 1707 (*v*. **pece**), (*the*) *Bull way* 1601, 1698 *et passim* to 1745 (*v*. **weg**) (*v*. **bula**; prob. alluding to plots with the right of pasture for one bull); *Bullymerysholme* 1392, *Bullimers* ~, *Bullimores holme* 1707 (*v*. **holmr**) (with the surn. *Bullimer*); *Burnebys* ~ 1704, 1709, 1745, *Burnbys Close* 1707, 1709, 1712 (cf. *Henry Burnbie* 1606); *Burnt Mill* 1707 (*v*. **brend**, **myln**; perh. to be identified with *le Brendemulne* in adjoining Medbourne f.ns. (b)); *Burton Close* 1712 (with the surn. *Burton*); *Caldewell* 1327, *Caudewell* 1601, 1606, c.1700, 1704, *Cawdwell* 1601, 1606, *Cardwell* 1698, *Cadwell* 1705, 1718, *Caudwell* 1707, 1709, 1712, 1745, *Cordwell* 1718, *Cawdwell Furlong* (*v*. **furlang**), *Caudwell way* 1707, *v*. **cald**, **wella**); *Castle Scyke* 1707 (*v*. **sík** and Castle Hill *supra*); *Catwell*, ~ *Close*, *Cattwell*(*s*) *Close* 1707 (*v*. **cat**(**t**), **wella**); *Chapple furlonge* 1606, (*the*) *Chap*(*p*)*ell furlong*(*e*) 1675, c.1700, 1705 (*v*. **furlang**), *Chappill Hill* 1601, 1606, *Chappel*(*l*) *way*(*e*) 1601, 1698 *et passim* to 1745, *Chapill way* 1718 (*v*. **weg**), *v*. **chapel**(**e**) and St Morrill's Chapel *supra*); *Cheescake peice* 1707 (*v*. **chese-cake**, **pece**); *Chethams Close* 1703, 1711 (with the surn. *Chetham*); *Cobtree*, *Coptree Furlong* 1707 (*v*. **furlang**) (*v*. **copped**[2], **trēow**); *the Common* c.1700, 1707 (*v*. **commun**); *Cooks peice* (*v*. **pece**), ~ *Ricksted* (*v*. **rickstead**) 1707 (with the surn. *Cook*); *The Copie* 1695, 1703 (*v*. **copis**; the spelling *copie* is due to the popular reconstruction of a 'singular' form); *le Cotes* 1311 (*v*. **cot**); *Coverlees* 1707 (*v*. **cover**(**t**), **leys**); *Cowdams* 1707 (*v*. **cū**, **damme**; for the watering of cattle); *le Cowel*, *le Cowelhegg'* (*v*. **hecg** (poss. in its early sense 'a hedged enclosure')) 1327 (*v*. **cū**, **wella**); *the Crossways* 1707 (*v*. **cross**, **weg**); *Cutts holme*, *Cuttholme* 1707 (*v*. **holmr** and *Cuttisholme* in adjoining Goadby f.ns. (b)); *Dalewaye* 1601, *Dale Way* 1606, 1698, 1712, 1745, *Daile Way* 1709 (*v*. **dalr**, **weg**); *Dalewonge* 1347 (*v*. **dalr**, **vangr**); *Deadmans grave* 1601, 1606 *et passim* to 1718 (*v*. **dede-man**, **græf**; a poss. reference to a lost pagan Anglo-Saxon inhumation burial site); *Dents land* 1690[2] (*v*. **land**; with the surn. *Dent*); *Dunmoors Mill* 1707 (*v*. **myln**; with the common Leics. surn. *Dunmore*); *Folkatmedowe* 1392 (*v*. **mēd** (**mēdwe** obl.sg.)), *foulkats* 1601, *foul*(*e*)*cattes* 1601, 1606, *foulcats* 1606, *Folecat*(*t*)*s* 1675, c.1700 *et passim* to 1718, *Folle catts* 1698, *Full catts* 1704, *Foldcat*(*t*)*s* 1707, *Folcats* 1718, *Fole-cats* 1745, *Vpper End Fole Catts* 1718 (*v*. **upper**, **ende**), *Foldcats Close*, ~ *Way* 1707 (ostensibly the name of a meadow belonging to a man called *Folkart* (from the ContGerm masc. pers.n. *Fulcard*), but the earlier forms *Folcotes* 1344, *Folcot'* 1357 in adjoining Medbourne and *folkotesyke* e.14 in adjoining Slawston point to 'shelters for foals', *v*. **fola**, **cot**); *the Flesh Shambles* 1588 (*v*. **flessh-shamel**); *Frewell* ~ 1707, *Free Well Close* 1714 (*v*. **wella**; if the specific is **frēo**, then the word would appear to be the sb. 'a woman, a lady' (usually found in poetic use) rather than the adj. **frēo** 'free (from customary obligation or charge)', (the implications of which when compounded with **wella** would be difficult to conceive), and so may indicate a spring thought to be associated with fertility; however, the specific may rather be a reduced **freht** 'augury, divination', hence perh. 'a wishing well'; cf. *Fredwell* in Gumley f.ns. b)); *Ful*(*l*)*well slade* 1601, 1606 *et passim* to 1718, *Fullwards* ~ 1675, *Fullers Slade* c.1700, 1705, 1707, 1745 (*v*. **fūl**, **wella**, **slæd** and Bottom ~, Top Fowlers in f.ns. (a)); *Gerardisvro* 1260 (*v*. **vrá**; with the ContGerm masc. pers.n. *Gerard* or its surn. reflex); *Grayes* ~ ~ 1675, c.1700, *Grays laine end* 1705 (*v*. **lane-ende**; with the surn. *Gray*); *the Hall Land* 1707 (*v*. **land**), *Hall Park* 1703 (*v*. **park**) (*v*. Hallaton Hall *supra*); *Hawsicke*

1631, *Hawscike*, ~ *peice* 1707 (*v.* **pece**) (*v.* **haga**[1], **sík**); *Barthol' Haycocks Great Close*, ~ ~ *Little Close* 1707, *Tho. Haycocks Hags* 1707 (*v.* **hǫgg**); *Hoctong'* 1392 (*v.* **hōc**, **tunge**); *Hoggs holme* 1698, *hog holm* 1709, *Hogs holme* 1712, *Hoggs holme drift* 1705 (*v.* **drift** and Hog Lane *supra*) (*v.* **hogg**, **holmr**); *Robert Arnolds* ~ ~, *Mr Daniel Judds* ~ ~, *John Scotts Homested Close* 1707 (*v.* **hām-stede**); *Hornyngwoldbryg'* 1392 (*v.* **brycg**), *Horningold Meere* 1601, 1698, ~ *Mear(e)* 1704, 1718, *Horninghold Mear(e)* 1709, 1712 (*v.* **(ge)mǣre**), ~ *Stile* 1707, 1745 (*v.* **stīg**) (Horninghold adjoins to the east); *the Horse Fair* 1707 (*v.* **hors**, **faire**); *Horsewood close* 1639, 1703, 1714, *Horss wood close* 1707 (*v.* **wudu**; if the specific is **hors** 'horse', it is difficult to be clear about the implications of the compound (cf. *the Horse Coppice*, Ch **4** 101), but the fruit of the horse-chestnut tree (*Castanea equina*) was early used as a cure for the ailments of horses); *le houe*, *Houewell* 1392 (*v.* **wella**) (*v.* **hōh**); *Hunts Laine End* 1698, ~ *Lane End* 1704, 1709, 1712, 1718, 1745 (*v.* **lane-ende** and Hunt's Lane *supra*; alluding to a piece of land); *att Immings House* 1707 (a furlong so called; with the surn. *Imming(s)*, cf. *Hugo Imayn* 1276 RH of Leics.); *Inggulberdhille* 1392, *Ingoldsby hole* 1707 (perh. with **hol**[1], but otherwise with a late reflex of **hyll**) (*v.* **hyll**; either with the ContGerm masc. pers.n. *Ingelberd* or with its surn. reflex); *Keythorp Closes* 1707 (adjoining Old Keythorpe which lies to the north-west); *le kyrkelane* 1352 (*v.* **kirkja**, **lane**; perh. the precursor of Church Gate *supra*); *Kirkwood*, ~ *Leys* 1601, *Kyrkwood Leayes* 1606 (*v.* **leys**) (*v.* **kirkja**, **wudu**); *Lamport Hill* 1675, 1707, 1745, *Lampert hill* c.1700, 1705 (*v.* **lām-pytt**, **hyll**); *Limekill* ~, *Limekiln cross* 1707 (*v.* **lim-kilne**), *Lime Pit(t) Cross* 1675, c.1700 *et passim* to 1745, *Limpi(t) Cross* 1695, 1709, *Limepit(t) Crose* 1718 (*v.* **lyme-pytt**) (presum. both at the same location, but a standing cross (*v.* **cros**) seems very unlikely at such a site, so a poss. explanation is an original confusion of long *r* and *l* in *closs* (for *close*) with subsequent repetition in a Glebe Terrier sequence); *Little dale* 1601, 1606 *et passim* to 1745, *Little(l) Dale* 1675, 1698, 1700, 1705, *Letteldale* 1718, *Little dale more* 1718 (*v.* **mōr**[1]) (*v.* **dalr**); *Little Land Meadow* 1707 (*v.* **land**; a small enclosure consolidating former open-field selions); *Longdale* 1601, 1606, 1707, *Londale meddow* 1606, *Longdale Meadow* 1707 (*v.* **lang**[1], **dalr**); *Longhill Meadow* 1707 (*v.* **lang**[1], **hyll**); *Longland* 1707 (*v.* **lang**[1], **land**); *the Mansion place* 1675, c.1700, 1705 (*v.* **mansion**, **place**; with reference to the site of *the Parsonage house*); *Marstons* ~ 1707, *Marsons Close* 1714 (with the surn. *Marston* of a family prob. originally from Marston Trussell, 9 miles to the south-west in Northants.; note the typical Leics. 17th-/e.18th-cent. loss of *t* from the group *-ston*); *Martyn Lane* 1588 (*v.* **lane**; with the surn. *Martin*); *Medburn meer furlong* 1601 (*v.* **furlang**), *(at) Medburne Meer* 1707 (*v.* **(ge)mǣre**; a short stretch of Medbourne's parish boundary adjoins to the south); *le Mermedewe* 1392 (*v.* **mēd** (**mēdwe** obl.sg.); with **mere**[1] or **(ge)mǣre**); *Middle Slade* 1707 (*v.* **slæd**); *Mill baulk* 1707 (*v.* **balca**), *Mill Feild* 1563 (*v.* **feld**), *Mill Furlong* 1707 (*v.* **myln**); *Norman scike* 1707 (*v.* **sík**; presum. with the surn. *Norman*, but coincidentally, a man called *Norman* held Hallaton from Goisfridus Alselin in 1086 DB); *the Parsonage Bush(e)* 1601, 1606, *Parsons bush* 1606 (*v.* **busc**), *the Parsonage whomsted* 1698, ~ ~ *Homestead* 1709, 1712 (*v.* **hām-stede**), *the Parsonage Sicke* 1601, *Parsons sicke* 1601, *(the) Parsons sick* 1606, 1675, c.1700, 1705, *Parsons Syke* 1745 (*v.* **sík**) (*v.* **personage**, **persone**); *Pastare Gapp* 1698, *Pasture Gap* 1709, 1718, 1745, *Paster gap* 1718 (*v.* **gap**), *Short pasture Leys* 1707 (*v.* **leys**) (*v.* **pasture**); *(in) Pecks Chambers* 1707 (*v.* **chambre**; with the surn. *Peck*; poss. a name for a group of small enclosures); *The Pikes* 1745 (*v.* **pīc**);

Pitt furlong(*e*) 1601, 1606 *et passim* to 1712, *Pit furlong*(*e*) 1601, 1606 *et passim* to 1745 (*v*. **pytt**); *Plumbetree Sicke* 1601, *Plumtree sick*(*e*) 1601, 1606, 1675, c.1700, 1705, ~ *Scyke* 1707 (*v*. **plūm-trēow**, **sík**; *Plumtree* is found as a surn. from at least the 14th cent. (perh. taken from Plumtree in Notts.), but is unlikely here); *Redgate* 1707 (*v*. **gata**; prob. with **rēad** rather than with **hrēod**); *Redlandes* 1601, *Redlands* 1606, 1675 *et passim* to 1712, *Red-Lands* 1745 (*v*. **rēad**, **land**); *Rodehill* 1392, *Roadhill* 1707 (*v*. **hyll**; with **rōd**[2] or **rod**[1]); *Ross Leys* 1707 (*v*. **hors**, **hross**, **leys**); *the Round Acre* 1707 (*v*. **round**, **æcer**); *Rowlands Furlong* 1707 (*v*. **rūh**, **land**); *Rushy Peice* 1707, ~ *Piece* 1745 (*v*. **riscig**, **pece**); (*at*) *St Morrels* 1601, *St Morrells*, *St Morrilles* 1606, *St Morells* 1705 (it is uncertain whether these forms simply represent the name of a lost chapel or name a furlong once adjacent to it, *v*. St Morrell's Chapel *supra*), *St Morills more* 1705 (*v*. **mōr**[1]), *St Morrills well* 1601, 1698, *St Morrel*(*l*)*s well* 1606, 1704, 1709, 1712, *St Morels well* 1675, *St Morills well* c.1700, *Morrells Well* 1707, 1718, *Morell's well* 1709, *Morrels-Well* 1745, *Morrell well furlong* 1707 (*v*. **furlang**) (*v*. **wella**; presum. to be equated with the sacred *Stowe Welle*, *infra*); *Sandlandes* 1392 (*v*. **sand**, **land**); (*the*) *Sandpitts* 1606, 1698 *et passim* to 1712, *Sandpites* 1718, *Sandpits* 1709, 1718 (*v*. **sand-pytt**); *Seavybroke* 1573, *Seavybrooke* 1631 ('the rushy brook', *v*. **sef**, **seavy**, **brōc**); *Sharpthorn*(*e*) 1707 (*v*. **scearp**, **þorn**); *Slauston feild side* 1675, c.1700, 1705 (*v*. **feld**, **sīde**), *Slawson brook* 1707 (*v*. **brōc**; with typical 17th-/e.18th-cent. Leics. loss of *t* from the group -*ston*) (Slawston parish adjoins to the south-west); *Smalehill* 1707 (*v*. **smæl**); *the Smythie* 1588 (*v*. **smiððe**); *Starholmes* 1707 (*v*. **stǫrr**[2], **holmr**); *Long*(*e*) ~, *Short*(*e*) *Stearn*(*e*) 1601, 1606, 1698, 1712, *Long* ~, *Short Stern*(*e*) 1601, 1606 *et passim* to 1745, *Stearne Furlonge* 1601 (*v*. **furlang**), *Sturnewood* 1631 (*v*. **wudu**) (*v*. **stǣner** 'stony ground'); *Stowe Welle* 1318, *Stowelle* 1392 (*v*. **stōw**, **wella**; a sacred spring or well, *v*. Stowe Cl and *St Morrills well*, *supra*); *Stump Cross* 1707 (*v*. **stump**, **cros**; the remains of a standing stone cross); *Swans Ricksted* 1707 (*v*. **rickstead**; prob. with the surn. *Swan*, cf. Swan Cl in f.ns. (a)); *Swansons baulk* 1675 (*v*. **balca**), ~ *Meadow* 1707, ~ *Willows* 1707, 1745 (*v*. **wilig**) (with the surn. *Swanson*); *Sword Croft*, *Swordcroft Furlong* 1707 (*v*. **furlang**) (*v*. **croft**; either with **sweord** used of 'a narrow strip, a headland' or with the surn. *Sword*, an occupational name once used of a sword-maker); *Swynemeadowe* 1631 (*v*. **swīn**); *Thornhill* 1707 (*v*. **þorn**, **hyll**); *Thumbe home* 1601, 1606, *Thum home* 1601, 1718, *Thumholm*(*e*) 1606, 1675 *et passim* to 1718, *Thumb-holm* 1745 (*v*. **þūma**, **holmr** and *Tommor* in Great Easton f.ns. (b)); *Tomlinson's Close* 1714 (with the surn. *Tomlinson*); *the Town hadland* 1707 (*v*. **tūn**, **hēafod-land**); *Tupwell Furlong* 1707, *Tupwell Leas* 1675, c.1700 (*v*. **leys**) (*v*. Tugwell Lane *supra*); *Mr Vows hadland*, ~ ~ *hadley* 1707 (*v*. **hēafod-land**, **headley**), *Mr Vowes windmill* 1601 (*v*. **wind-mylne**) (*v*. Vowe's Gorse *supra*); *Waterfalls*, *Waterfall furlong* 1707 (*v*. **furlang**) (*v*. **wæter-(ge)fall**); *Cow watering*, *New watering* 1707 (*v*. **wateryng**); *Wellholme* 1707, *Well-holm* 1745 (*v*. **wella**, **holmr**); *Wellwong* 1707 (*v*. **wella**, **vangr**); *Williams land* 1690[2] (*v*. **land**; with the surn. *Williams*); *High Willows*, *High Willow Bridge* 1707 (*v*. **hēah**[1], **wilig**); *Willow Scike*, ~ *Scyke* 1707 (*v*. **wilig**, **sík**).

Horninghold

HORNINGHOLD

Horniwale (sic) 1086 DB, *Horniuuald* Hy 2 (e.15) *BelCartB*, *Horniwold* 1316 FA
Horninuald Hy 1 (1333) Ch, Hy 2 (e.15) *BelCartB*, *Hornynwold'* 1328 (e.15) *ib*
Horningualt a.1155 (e.15) *BelCartB*, *Horningwald* 1174 × 82 *Rut*, 1221 (e.14) *BelCartA et passim* to 1322 *ib*, 1343 (e.15) *BelCartB*, *Hornyngwala* (sic) Hy 2 (e.15) *ib*, *Horningwaud* 1269 (e.14), 1276 (e.14) *BelCartA*, *Hornigwaud* 1249 RGros, 1277 *Rut*, 1333 Ch, *Hornigwald* 1254 Val, 1275 (e.15) *BelCartB et passim* to 1320 (e.15) *ib*
Horningwold(e) c.1151, 1135 × 54 *Rut et passim* to 1284 ChronPetr, 1305 *BelCartA*, 1576 LibCl, 1580 LEpis *et passim* to 1606 LML, *Hornyngwold(e)* 1233 (e.14) *BelCartA*, 1284 (e.15) *BelCartB et passim* to 1356, 1357 Pat *et freq* to 1439 *Peake*, 1465 *Wyg et passim* to 1553 Pat, 1590 Fine, *Horningswolde* 1578 LEpis
Horningewald 1163, 1167 P, *Hordingewalde* (sic) 1209 × 35 RHug, *Hordyngewald* (sic) 1325 *Rut*, *Hornigewald* 12 (e.15) *BelCartB*, *Hornigewalt* 1325 × 53 (e.15) *ib*
Hornyngold 1495 Ipm, 1535 VE, *Horningolde* 1578 LEpis
Hornynghold(e) 1475 × 85 ChancP, 1588 Fine, *Horninghold(e)* 1557, 1590 ib, 1610 Speed *et freq*

Horninghold is also found as a minor name in Skeffington parish, five miles to the north-west in East Goscote Hundred (*v.* Lei **3** 222), so it is possible that the whole of the higher land between the Skeffington and Horninghold townships was once called **Horningwald*. The generic of the name is **wald**, probably in its earlier sense 'woodland'. *Horning* can be interpreted in several ways. It may be thought of as a **horning** 'a horn-shaped hill', also 'a bend, a corner' (in formation, OE **horn** 'a horn' used topographically as 'a horn-shaped piece of land', with the noun suffix **-ing**[1], the whole acting as an appellative). Alternatively **horn** may here be suffixed by the place-name-forming **-ing**[2], giving an early place-name or hill-name **Horning*. A third possibility is that *Horning* is in origin a folk-name **Horningas*, either 'the people living at the horn-shaped piece of land' or 'the people of a man called Horn', although the OE masc. pers.n. *Horn* is rare, so the latter is less likely.

Ekwall DEPN opts for the folk-name in his interpretation; hence he considers the place-name as meaning 'the woodland of the *Horningas*'. He observes that the township 'is in a winding valley', and so believes that the *Horningas* may have been 'the dwellers in the horn or bend'. Ekwall's 'winding valley', however, is not immediately striking on the ground and the surrounding hill formations appear a likelier source of the place-name, with either an earlier hill-name **Horning* or the appellative use of **horning** (defining one of the curving hill-spurs above the village) constituting the specific. The most satisfying interpretation of the place-name Horninghold would appear to be 'the woodland on the horn-shaped hill', *v*. **horning**, **wald**; otherwise 'the woodland at or on *Horning*'. Such an interpretation as 'the woodland of the *Horningas*' is obviously possible (*v*. **horn**, **-inga-**, **wald**), but it should be noted that the spellings containing medial *-inge-*, which may be considered the reflex of *-inga-*, the gen.pl. of the folk-name-forming suffix *-ingas*, are sparse and apart from two consecutive instances from the Pipe Rolls, relatively late.

ALLEXTON LANE, Allexton lying 2 miles to the north-east. BELCHER'S HILL, BELCHER'S LODGE, *v*. **loge**; both with the surn. *Belcher*. BON HILLS SPINNEYS (2½"), cf. *Bone Hill Meadow* 1867 *Surv*, BURN HILL (2½"), *Burne Hill* 1681 *Terrier*, *Bunn Hill* 1840 *TA*, cf. *Burn Hill Close*, *Burn Hills Pasture* (*v*. **pasture**) 1742 *Map*, 'hill cleared by burning', *v*. **bryne**, **hyll**. DICK HILLS SPINNEY, *v*. **dík**, **hyll**, **spinney**. FRISBY'S SPINNEY, *v*. **spinney**; with the surn. *Frisby* of a family prob. in origin from the township of this name 6 miles to the north-west. GLOBE (P.H.) (lost), *Globe* 1846, 1877 White, *Globe Inn* 1863 ib. HEG SPINNEY, cf. *Hegesgate* 1269 (e.14) *BelCartA*, 1269 (e.15) *BelCartB* (*v*. **gata**), *Heg Field* 1730 EnclA (*v*. **feld**; one of the great open-fields of the township), *Heg Field Close*, *East ~ ~*, *West ~ ~*, *Little ~ ~*, *Heg Close* 1742 *Map*; with **hecg** in its early sense 'a hedged enclosure'. HOEBACK SPINNEY, *v*. **hōh**, **bæc**. HORNINGHOLD HALL (HORNINGHOLD HO. 2½"), *Horninghold House* 1925 Kelly. HORNINGHOLD WOOD, 1694 *Terrier*, *v*. **wudu**. KNOB HILL, ~ ~ FM, *Nob Hill* 1742 *Map*, cf. *Nab Hill Close* 1737 Nichols, 1743 *Will*, *v*. **knob**. MANOR HOUSE FM, *v*. **maner**. MUCKLEBOROUGH FM, ~ LODGE FM (~ LODGE 2½"), (*v*. **loge**), MUCKLEBOROUGH PLANTATION, (*v*. **plantation**), *Michelberwe* c.1270 (e.14) *BelCartA*, c.1270 (e.15) *BelCartB*, *Muckleborough* 1742 *Map*, *v*. **micel**, **mycel**,

berg. MUSHROOM FM. ST PETER'S CHURCH, *Church (St Peter)* 1846, 1863 White, 1925 Kelly; it is earlier recorded as *ecclesie de Horingwad'* 1220 MHW, ~ *de Horningwaud* 1249 RGros, *the Church* 1708 *Terrier*. Note also *the Church-Yard* 1708 (18) *ib*, *v*. **churchyerd**. THE SPINNEY. TOWN END COTTAGE (local), *v*. **tūn**, **ende**. THE VICARAGE, 1925 Kelly is *the Vicaridge House* 1606, e.18 *Terrier*, *the Vicarage-house* 1708 (18) *ib*, *v*. **vikerage**.

FIELD-NAMES

Forms in (a) dated 1797 and 1867 are *Surv*. Forms throughout dated 1269, 1305[1] and l.14 are *Rut*; those dated 1269 (e.14), 1270 (e.14) and 1305[2] are *BelCartA*; 1269 (e.15), c.1270 (e.15), 1284 (e.15), 1328 (e.15) and Hy 4 are *BelCartB*; 1332 are SR; 1408 are Coram; e.18 are *Terrier*; 1742 are *Map*.

(a) Andrews Cl 1797 (*Andrewes Close* m.17, with the surn. *Andrew*, *v*. *Mill feild*, *infra*); Borough Bridge 1797 (*Borough-brig Close* m. 17, *v*. **burh**, **brycg**); Brimstone Hill, ~ Mdw 1867 (with the surn. *Brimson* of a family originally from Briançun in Normandy, cf. Brimstone Hill in Little Wakering, Ess 204); Cow Cl 1797 (*le Cowe Close* 1620); Hill Mdw 1797; Hills Wood 1797 (1620, *Hills Wood Close* m.17, *v*. **hyll**, **wudu**); The Isle 1797 (poss. **hygel** 'a hillock', but more likely simply refers to an enclosure completely surrounded by other fields); the Meadow 1797 (*Great Meadow* m.17); Play Cl 1797 (*v*. **plega**; land used for recreation); Ramburrow Cl 1867 (*Ramsborowe* ~ 1620, *Ramsborough Close* m.17), Ramburrow Mdw 1867 (*Rammesberwe* c.1270 (e.14), 1284 (e.15), 1305[2], *Rammisberwe* c.1270 (e.15), l.14, *Ramesberwe* 1305[1], *v*. **berg**; with **hramsa** or **ramm**; later forms also appear in adjoining Stockerston); Wash-pit Piece 1846, 1863, 1877 White (*v*. **wæsce**, **pytt**, **pece**).

(b) *Alexton Hedge Close* 1742 (*v*. **hecg**; a parish boundary hedge), *Alexton Oate Close* 1742 (*v*. **āte**; at the Allexton boundary) (Allexton parish adjoins to the north-east); *Banbury Close*, ~ *Lane* 1742 (with the surn. *Banbury*); *Baron Brook Close* 1742 (*v*. **brōc**; additional forms are needed to explain the first word, but **bareyne** 'barren', alluding to the nature of the land through which the brook ran may pertain; although *Baron* could be a surn. alluding to the ownership of *Brook Close*, *v*. Barons Cl in West Langton f.ns. (a)); *Blaiston Gate Close* (*v*. **gata**; Blaston lies one mile to the south); *Bradegate* c.1270 (e.14), c.1270 (e.15), 1284 (e.15), 1305[1], 1305[2], l.14 (*v*. **brād**, **gata**); *Brocholegate* c.1270 (e.14), c.1270 (e.15) (*v*. **brocc-hol**, **gata**); *Breach pasture* 1742 (*v*. **brēc**, **pasture**); *Caldwell Close*, ~ *Pasture* 1742 (*v*. **cald**, **wella**); *Chapmans Leys* 1742 (*v*. **leys**; with the surn. *Chapman*); *Cockshoot Close* 1742 (*v*. **cocc-scēte**); *Colpit* c.1270 (e.14), c.1270 (e.15), l.14 (*v*. **col-pytt**; a place where charcoal was made); *Cow Pasture* 1730 (*v*. **cū**, **pasture**); *Crabtree Close* 1742 (*v*. **crabtre**); *Cream Pott Close* 1742 (a complimentary name for rich pasture, cf. Creampot Cl, Ru 154); *Dead Moor Close* 1742 (*v*. **dēad**, **mōr**[1]; a common name for infertile wasteland); *Dovecoate close* 1620, *Dove Court* ~ m.17, *Dove Cote Close* 1742 (*v*. **dove-cot(e)**); *Eaton Close* 1742 (with the surn. *Eaton* of a family originally from the township of this name 20 miles to the north); *Fletchers Leys* 1742 (*v*. **leys**; with the surn. *Fletcher*); *Fox's Close* 1742 (with the surn. *Fox*); *Green-seek Close* 1742 (*v*. **grēne**[1], **sík**); *Gudgers Close* 1742 (with the surn. *Gudger*); *Hall Hill Close*, *Hall Homestead* (*v*. **hām-stede**), *Hall Yard* (*v*. **geard**) 1742 (*v*. **hall** and Horninghold Hall *supra*); *Hectry Leys* 1742 (*v*. **leys**; earlier forms are needed to explain the first word); *Mr Roberts Home Close*, *Staffords Home Close* (with the surn. *Stafford*) 1742 (*v*. **home**); *on le Hull* 1332 (p), *del Hill* 1408 (p) (*v*. **hyll**); *Ladye grounde* 1620 (*v*. **grund**), *Ladyes Close* m.17 (*v*. **ladi**); *Little Field* 1730, ~ ~ *Close* 1742; *Little Meadow* m.17; *Long Moor Close* 1742 (*v*. **mōr**[1]); *Louths Close* 1742 (with the surn. *Louth*); *the Meadow close* 1620; *Middle Furlong Close* 1742 (*v*. **furlang**); *Mill feild or Andrewes Close* m.17 (*v*. **myln**, **feld**; originally the name of one of the great open-fields); *Moor Field* 1730 (*v*. **feld**; one of the early open-fields), *Moor Way Close* 1742 (*v*. **mōr**[1]); *Muckleborough Close* 1742 (*v*. Muckleborough Fm *supra*); *Narborough Hills* 1742 (poss. a topographical **norð**, **berg** rather than the surn. *Narborough* of a family from the township of this name, 17 miles to the west; earlier forms are needed); *Sharps New Close* 1742 (with the surn. *Sharp*); *le upper newe close* 1620 (*v*. **nīwe**); *New Pool Leys* 1742 (*v*. **pōl**[1], **leys**); (*le*) *Nortsyke* 1269, 1269 (e.15), *le northsike* 1269 (e.14) (*v*. **norð**, **sík**); *Old Meadow* 1742 (*v*. **ald**); *Palmers Close* 1620, m.17 (with the surn. *Palmer*); *Pond Close* 1742 (*v*. **ponde**); *Rose Lane* 1742 (*v*. **lane**; poss. with the surn. *Rose*, but **rose**, i.e. a wild rose such as the sweetbriar or dog-rose may also be thought of); *Schortecotes* Hy 4 (*v*. **cot**; the specific may be **scēot** 'a steep slope', but otherwise this may be another example of *Shirtecoat* in Great Bowden); *Sheep Dyke* 1742 (*v*. **scēp**, **dík**; prob. used as a sheep-dip); *Strutholegate* c.1270 (e.14), c.1270 (e.15), l.14 (*v*. **strūt**, **gata**; cartulary forms in which the second el. may have originally been **holmr** rather than **hol**[1], evidently alluding to disputed territory); *Suinsti* c.1270 (e.14), c.1270 (e.15), l.14 (*v*. **swīn**, **stig**); *Tomas' Close* 1742 (with the surn. *Tomas* (more commonly *Thomas*)); *Uppingham Poors Close* 1742 (*v*. **pouer(e)**; land endowed for the relief of the poor of nearby Uppingham in Rutland); *Vicaridge Close* 1742, *The Vicaridge Homestead* e.18 (*v*. **hām-stede**) (*v*. **vikerage**); *atte waterfal* 1328 (e.15) (p) (*v*. **atte**, **wæter-(ge)fall**).

Houghton on the Hill

HOUGHTON ON THE HILL

Hohtone 1086 DB, *Hohtona* l.12 Dane (p)
Hoctona 1130 P (p), *Hoctun'* a.1166 *Rut* (p), *Hocton'* 1209, 1210 Pat *et passim* to 1264 GildR (p), 1280 × 92 *Wyg*, *Hoctone* 1247 × 60 *ib*, *Hokton'* a.1250 *LCDeeds* (p)
Houcton(e) 1242 RGros, 1253 Cur *et passim* to 1280 × 92 *Wyg*, 1360 *Peake* (p), *Houchton* 1246 RGros
Hoghton(e) 1220 RHug, 1261 Cur (p) *et passim* to 1306 Pat, 1307 Banco (p) *et freq* to 1402 Pat *et passim* to 1437 Banco
Houton(e) 1253 × 58 RHug, 1273 *Wyg et passim* to 1349 Cl, 1370 Pat
Houghton 1247 (1579) *LRoll*, 1306 *Hazlerigg et freq*, (~ *on the Hill* 1628, 1708 LML), (~ *super Montem* 1723 ib, 1729 MiscAccts), *Howghton* 1535 VE, 1539 MinAccts, 1571 LEpis
Howten 1348 *Wyg*, *Howton* 1381 SR, 1386 Cl, *Howeton* 1403 AD
Hawton 1430 Fine, 1435, 1468 Cl, *Haughton* 1518 Visit, 1610 Speed

'The farmstead, village on the hill-spur', *v.* **hōh**, **tūn**. The 18th-cent. suffix ~ *super Montem*, with Lat *mons* (*montem* acc.sg.) 'a hill', is simply a clerical and learned version of the earlier popular ~ *on the Hill*.

BLACK HORSE (P.H.), *Black Horse* 1846, 1863, 1877 White, 1925 Kelly. BOOT (P.H.) (lost), *Boot* 1846 White, *Boot Inn* 1863 ib, *The Boot* 1877 ib; note that the innkeeper in 1846, Thomas Webster, was also a maker of footwear, hence perhaps the name of the hostelry. GALBY LANE is *Galbygate*, *Galbigate* 1477 (e.16) *Charyte*, *Galbygate* 1624 *Terrier*, *Gaulby* ~ 1709, 1710 *ib*, *Gallby* ~ 1713 *ib*, *Galby Gate* 1854 *Surv*, 1878 *PK*, 1907 *Surv*, 1913 Sale, 1941 *Surv*, *v.* **gata**; Galby lies 2 miles to the south-east. THE HALL, *Houghton Hall* 1636, 1677 *Terrier*, cf. *Ouerhall* 1467 × 84 *LTD*, 'the upper hall', *v.* **uferra**, **hall**. There were evidently two medieval halls in Houghton; for discussion of this frequent phenomenon, *v.* J. Turville-Petre, 'Overhall and Netherhall', JEPNS 31 (1998–9), 115–17. HOUGHTON LODGE, 1877 White, *v.* **loge**; it is

Houghton Hill Farm 1835 O. HOUGHTON TOLLBAR (lost), *Houghton tollbar* 1877 White, *v.* **toll-bar**. MAIN ST. MERE FM, *v.* **(ge)mǣre**; beside the ancient estate boundary called Old Mere, *v.* Newton Harcourt *s.n.* PALACE HILL, *the Pallace Hill* 1799 *Deed*, *Palace Hill* 1835 O, 1854 *Surv*, 1878 *PK*, 1907 *Surv*, 1913 Sale, *v.* **palis**. THE RECTORY, 1877 White; it is *The Rectory House* 1825 *Terrier*, *v.* **rectory**. Note earlier *the Parsonage House* 1690 *Terrier*, ~ ~ *howse* c.1700, 1707 (18) *ib*, *v.* **personage**. ROSE AND CROWN (P.H.), *Rose and Crown* 1846, 1863, 1877 White, 1925 Kelly. ST CATHERINE'S CHURCH, *Church (St Catherine)* 1846, 1863, 1877 White, *Church (St Catharine)* 1925 Kelly; it is earlier recorded as *ecclesie de Hocton* 1220 MHW, ~ *de Houcton* 1242 RGros, ~ *de Hoghton* 1339, 1349, 1351, 1356, 1402 *Pat*, ~ *de Houghton* 1346, 1349 *ib*, *the Church* 1707 *Terrier*, *Houghton Church* 1707 (18) *ib*. Note also *the churchyard* 1606 *Terrier*, *the Church-Yard* 1707, 1707 (18), 1825 *ib*, *v.* **churchyerd**. SCOTLAND, ~ LANE, *Scotland* 1941 *Surv*, cf. *Scotland Close* 1765 *EnclA*, *v.* **scot**, **land**; ground subject to the payment of some kind of tax or scot. STRETTON LANE is *Stretton Road* 1907 *Surv*, the road to Great Stretton which lies 2 miles to the south-west. SUNNY LEYS, 1854, 1907, 1941 *Surv*, 1878 *PK*, *v.* **sunni**, **leys**; on a south-facing hillside which catches the midday sunshine. UPPINGHAM RD, Uppingham in Rutland lying 12 miles to the east. WASH DYKE BRIDGE, *v.* **wæsce**, **dík**. WEIR LANE, cf. (*the*) *Wire Leys* 1799, 1801, 1826 *Deed* (*v.* **leys**), *v.* **weyour**; the lane leads to ponds. WOODLANDS.

FIELD-NAMES

In (a), forms dated 1752, 1758, 1760, 1775, 1799, 1801, 1814, 1818, 1826, 1828 and 1846 are *Deed*; those dated 1765 are *EnclA*; 1847, 1855, 1913 and 1928 are Sale; 1854, 1871, 1907 and 1941 are *Surv*; 1878 are *PK*. Forms throughout dated 1199 × 1216 are Berkeley; those dated 1309 are Banco; 1327 are SR; 1467 × 84 are *LTD*; 1477 (e.16) are *Charyte*; 1540 are Dugd; 1554 are Pat; 1574 and 1720 are VCHL; 1606, 1624, 1625[1], 1636, 1640, 1649, 1674, 1677, 1681, 1689, 1698, 1701, 1707, 1707 (18), 1709, 1710[1], 1710[2] and 1713 are *Terrier*; 1615 are Ipm; 1625[2], 1646, 1650, 1651, 1661, 1663, 1666, 1700, 1702, 1708, 1720, 1722, 1727, 1733, 1738 and 1749 are *Deed*; 1632 are *Potter*; 1717 are *Will*.

(a) 6 ~, 11 ~, 12 Acre 1941, The Sixteen Acres 1854, 1878, 1907, 1913 (*v.* **æcer**); Akerleys 1913 (*v.* **æcer**, **leys**); Banky Fd 1941 (*v.* **banke**, **-ig**[3]); Great Barn Cl 1847, Barn Fd 1941 (*v.* **bern**); Far Barrell 1907 (*v.* **bere**, **hyll**); The Beacon 1941 (*v.*

((ge)**bēacon**); Big Cl, ~ ~ Mdw 1871, 1941, Foster's ~ ~, Big Fd 1941 (with the surn. *Foster*); Great ~, Little Blackmire 1854, 1878, 1907, 1913, Big ~ ~, Little Black Mire 1941 (*Blackmyrs* 1636, *Blackmyres* 1677, 1681, *Blackmire* 1709, *Black Mires* 1710[1], *Blackmires* 1710[2], 1713, *v.* **blæc, mýrr**); Boggy Cl 1847, The Boggy Fd 1854, 1878, 1907, 1913 (*v.* **boggy**); Botany Bay 1941 (a transferred name for a piece of ground remote from the village, alluding to the former penal settlement in New South Wales; an association with hard labour may be implied); Bottom Fd 1854, 1907, ~ Mdw 1941 (*v.* **bottom**); Bradshaw's Cl 1871, Bradshaws ~ 1941 (with the surn. *Bradshaw*); Brides Piece 1941 (*v.* **pece**; with the surn. *Bride*); Broad Cl 1854, 1907 (*v.* **brād**); Brook Cl 1854, 1907, Beyond Brook Cl 1818, Brook Fd 1765 ((*the*) *Brooke Feild* 1625[1], 1636 *et freq* to 1717, *the Brook Feild* 1710[1], 1710[2], *v.* **feld**; one of the great open-fields of the township), Brook Mdw 1854, 1871 *et passim* to 1941 (*v.* **brōc**); The Broomhill 1846, Broom Hill 1941 (*Bromhyll* 1467 × 84, 1477 (e.16), *Bromehill* 1636, *Broom*(*e*) *hill* 1646, 1701, *v.* **brōm, hyll**); Brown's Cl (with the surn. *Brown*); Buckleys Ground 1941 (*v.* **grund**; with the surn. *Buckley*); Bull Piece 1855, 1941 (*v.* **bula, pece**); the Burnet Fd 1941 (despite the def.art., with the surn. *Burnet*, from OFr *burnete*/*brunette*, a diminutive of *brun* '(dark) brown', forming a by-name used of complexion; *burnete* was also used of a heavy, dark-brown wool-dyed cloth, so that the surn. could also have denoted a maker or seller of such); Bush Cl 1941 (*v.* **busc**); Bushby Cl 1941 (Bushby adjoins to the west); Butcher's Leys 1855 (*v.* **leys**; with the surn. *Butcher*); Far Chamberlains Cl 1878, 1913 (prob. with the surn. *Chamberlain*, but **chamberlain** is poss., especially since *baillif*, *heiward* and *pinder* may well appear in f.ns. (b)); Clement's Cl 1878, 1913 (with the surn. *Clement*); (the) Clover Cl 1799, 1847 (*v.* **clāfre**; grown as a fodder crop); the Common 1765 (*v.* **commun**); Corn Cl 1847 (*v.* **corn**[1]); (the) Cow Cl 1854, 1878, 1907, 1913, Far ~ ~, Near Cow Cl 1855, Cow Lair Cl 1818 (*v.* **lair**); The Cricket Fd 1941 (for the game of cricket); Debdale 1752 (1624, 1636, 1677, 1698, 1709, *Depdale* 1624, 1625[1], 1689, *Debdale hedge* 1701 (*v.* **hecg**), *Debdale knowle* 1624, 1698, 1709, 1713, ~ *knole* 1636, 1709, 1710[1], *Depdale knowle* 1625[1] (*v.* **cnoll**), *Debdale Slead* 1698 (*v.* **slæd**)), The Debdale Cl 1752 (*Debdale Close* 1709, 1710[1], 1713, ~ *Closse* 1710[2], *Debdall Close* 1713, 1717) (*v.* **dēop, dalr**); First ~ ~, Second Old Dikes 1854, First ~ ~, Second Old Dykes 1878, 1907 (*Houldykes* 1624, *Holdikes* 1625[1], *Holdickes* 1636, *Holdicks* 1677, *Old dikes* 1709, *Hold dikes* 1710[1], *Hold dicks* 1710[2], *Holedikes* 1713, *v.* **hol**[1], **dík**); Dollands 1941 (*v.* **dāl, land**); the Dovecote Cl 1752, 1758, 1828 (cf. *Dovecoat Land* 1709, *v.* **dove-cot**(**e**)); East Fd 1765 ((*the*) *East feild*(*e*) 1624, 1636 *et freq* to 1713, *v.* **ēast, feld**; one of the great open-fields); Far Cl 1847, 1878, 1907, Far Fd 1941, Far Mead 1855 (*v.* **mēd**); Ferny Lees 1847 (*v.* **fearnig, leys**); Frisby Leas 1941 (1710[2], *Frisby Ley*(*e*)*s* 1624, 1636 *et passim* to 1717, *Frysbie Leys* 1625[1], *v.* **leys**; Frisby adjoins to the south-east); Garden Cl 1941 (*v.* **gardin**; land used for horticulture); the Gorse Cls 1765 (*v.* **gorst**); Great Gossy Cl 1855 (*v.* **gorstig**); Gravel Hole Cl 1854, 1878, 1907, 1913, 1941, Gravel Holes 1941 (*v.* **gravel, hol**[1]); Gravel Pit 1847 (*gravell pitte* 1625[1], (*the*) *Gravell pitts* 1709, 1710[1], 1710[2], *Gravilpits* 1713), Gravel Pit Cl 1854, 1878, 1907, 1913 ((*the*) *Gravell pitt clos*(*s*)*e* 1709, 1710[1], 1717, *Gravell Pitt Closse* 1710[2], *Gravilpit Close* 1713, *v.* **gravel, pytt**); Graves Leys 1854, 1907 (*Grave Leys* 1709, 1710[1], 1713, *Graveleys* 1710[2], *v.* **leys**; with **græf** or **grāf**); Great Cl 1855; Great Mead 1855 (*v.* **mēd**), Great Mdw 1878, 1907, 1913; Middle Hags 1847, 1941 ((*the*) *Middle Haggs* 1625[1], 1640, 1709, 1710[1], 1713, *Midle Haggs* 1710[2], *v.* **hǫgg**); Hall Cl 1765, 1941 (1700), Hall

Close Lane 1765 (*v.* The Hall *supra*); Harp's Mead 1847 (*v.* **mēd**), Harps 1941 (*Harpes* 1636, 1677, 1709, 1710[1], 1710[2], *Harpess* 1701, (*the*) *Harps* 1709, 1713, *v.* **hearpe**; used topographically of harp-shaped pieces of ground); Haygate 1871, 1941 (*Heygate* 1624, 1636 *et freq* to 1717, *Haygate* 1681, 1709, 1710[1], 1710[2], 1713, *v.* **hēg**, **gata**); Hill Cl 1854, 1871, 1907, (The) Hills 1941; Bottom Holts 1913 (either with the surn. *Holt* of a family originally from Nevill Holt, 10 miles to the south-east or with **holt**); Home Cl 1854, 1878, 1907, 1913, Long ~ ~, Nether Home Cl 1855 (*v.* **home**); Hornleys Cl 1775 (1749, *Horne leys* 1709, 1710[1], 1710[2], *Shorthorn*(*e*) *leys* 1709, 1710[1] (*v.* **sc**(**e**)**ort**), *v.* **leys**; in the Mill Fd, *v.* *Hornell Leys* in f.ns. (b)), Horns Cl 1765 (*Hornes Closse* 1574, *v.* **clos**(**e**)) (all with the surn. *Horne*, cf. *Thomas Horne* 1760 of Houghton); Houghton Brook 1765 (1649, *the Broke* 1467 × 84, *Houhtonbrok*, *Howghtonbrok* 1477 (e.16), *v.* **brōc**); Big ~ ~, Middle Houghton Cl 1854, 1878, 1907; Big ~ ~, Little Houghton Fd 1878, 1907, 1913; Houghton Moor 1752, the Moor 1765, Upper ~ ~, Great Moor 1855 (*Houghton more*, *Howghtonmore* 1467 × 84, *Howtonmore* 1467 × 84, 1477 (e.16), *the Moore* 1624, 1625[1], *the Moores or Houghton Moores* 1632, *the moores* 1722, *v.* **mōr**[1]); House Cl 1854, 1871, 1878, 1907, 1941; Howhill Syck 1855 (*v.* **hōh**, **hyll**, **sík**); Bottom ~ ~, Top Hut(t) Cl 1854, 1878, 1907, 1913 (*v.* **hut**); Illifes Cl 1878 1907 (with the surn. *Iliffe*, a reflex of the ON masc. pers.n. *Eileifr*); Jelly's ~ 1854, 1878, 1907, Jelley's Cl 1913 (with the surn. *Jelly*, a late form of *Giles*); Job's Mdw 1913 (with the surn. *Job*); Johnson's Cl 1855, Johnsons Mdw 1941 (with the surn. *Johnson*); First ~ ~, Kesting Hill 1855, Keston Hills 1941 (*Kesten Hill* 1701, *Kesting hill* 1709; with the surn. *Kesten*, cf. *Hannah Kesten* 1854 Census of Houghton); Little ~, Keymoor 1855 (*v.* **cǣg**, **mōr**[1]; with *cǣg* prob. in its postulated sense 'stone, gravel'; note Keyham, Lei **3** 157 and *v.* VEPN *s.v.*); Kibble Hill 1871, 1941 (1709, 1713, *Kebble* ~ 1624, *Kible* ~ 1710[2], *Kibbil hill* 1738, *Kibble hill sick* 1709 (*v.* **sík**), cf. *Keabell gaytte* 1624 (*v.* **gata**); with the surn. *Keeble*/*Kibble*, either of a maker or seller of cudgels (ME *kibble*) or a by-name for someone heavy and stout like a cudgel; note *Thomas Kebell* 1500 of adjoining Stretton Magna and *Kybbles close* there); the Kiln Cl 1814 (*v.* **cyln**); (The) Lair 1846, 1941 (*v.* **lair**); the Lammas Ground 1765 (*v.* **lammas**, **grund**); the Layering place 1765 (*v.* **lairing**, **place**); The Linseed Fds 1941 (*v.* **linseed**); Little Mead 1855 (*v.* **mēd**), ~ Mdw 1854, 1878, 1907, 1913; Long Cl 1878, 1907, 1913; Long Hill 1854 (*Longhill* 1624, 1625[1] *et freq* to 1717, *Far*(*r*) ~ 1709, 1710[1], 1710[2], *Hither Longhill* 1701, *Longhill Sicke* 1624 (*v.* **sík**), *v.* **lang**[1], **hyll**); Long Mead 1847 (*v.* **mēd**), Middle ~ ~ 1878, 1913, Long Mdw 1871, 1941; Losebys Cl 1765, Looseby Cl 1855 (with the surn. *Loseby* of a family originally from Lowesby, 4 miles to the north-east; for spellings, *v.* Lei **3** 168); Middle Fd 1765, 1941; Milking Cl 1854, 1878, 1907, 1913, First ~ ~, Second ~ ~ 1941 (*v.* **milking**); Mill Fd 1765, 1941 ((*the*) *Mylne feilde* 1624, 1646, (*the*) *Milne Feild*(*e*) 1625[1], 1640 *et passim* to 1717, *the Millne feild* 1636, 1710[1], 1710[2], *the Mill Feild* 1689, 1698, 1701, 1709, *v.* **myln**, **feld**; one of the great open-fields); Moor Gate 1765 (*Mooregate* 1624, 1636 *et passim* to 1701, *Moregate* 1625[1], 1636, 1689, *v.* **gata**), the Moor Head Cl 1799 (*v.* **hēafod**), Moor Hill 1854, 1878, 1907, 1913, 1941 (*v.* Houghton Moor *supra*); New Cl 1878, 1907, 1913 (*the New Close* 1709, 1713, 1717, ~ ~ *Closse* 1710[1], 1710[2]); New Mdw 1847, 1854, 1878, 1907, 1913; North's Cl 1941 (with the surn. *North*); Oak Spinney 1855 (*v.* **āc**, **spinney**); Old Mdw 1854, 1878, 1907; The Old Yard 1854, 1878, 1907 (*the olde yard* 1554, *v.* **ald**, **geard**); The Paddock 1941; the Pallace Hill Cls 1799 (*v.* Palace Hill *supra*); Pen Cl 1907, 1941 (*the Penn* 1624, 1709, *the Penn Close* 1710[1],

1713, *the Closse called the Penn* 1710², *v.* **penn²**); Perrins Cl 1765 (with the surn. *Perrin*, an *-in* diminutive of *Perre* (*Peter*)); Phipsys 1941 (the surn. *Phipps* in the possessive case); Little Plough Cl 1871 (*v.* **plōg**); Ploughed Cl 1854, Far ~ ~, First Ploughed Cl 1878, 1907, 1941, Middle ~ ~ 1878; Pride Mead 1855 (*v.* **mēd**; poss. with the surn. *Pride*, although this would be unusual in 19th-cent. Leics.; otherwise with *pride*, indicating a valued piece of land); Rices Cl 1854, 1878, 1907, 1913 (with the surn. *Rice*); Road Cl 1854, 1871, Far ~ ~ 1878, 1907, 1913, 1941, 2nd Road Cl 1941 (land adjoining a roadway); Second Cl 1847, 1854, 1907, 1913; Bottom ~ ~, Top Sharpless Cl 1854, 1878, 1907, 1913, Bottom ~, Top Sharpils 1941 (with the surn. *Sharpless*); Sharps Lane 1764 (with the surn. *Sharp*); Far Shellshanks 1847, Shillshanks 1941 (*Schillesike* 1467 × 84, *Schulsyke* 1467 × 84, 1477 (e.16); if the specific is OE (Angl) **scille** 'noisy', then the generic would appear to be an original **sīc** 'a small stream' but modified by ON **sík**, hence 'the noisy (boundary) stream', but if **sík** is original, then the specific may rather be **scylfe**, hence 'the stream-side meadow on shelving ground'); The Slang 1941 (*v.* **slang**); Spinney Cl 1854, 1878, 1907, Spinney Fd 1941 (cf. *Spinnie hill* 1689, *v.* **spinney**); Spring Lane 1765 (*v.* **spring¹**); Steen Hill 1846, Stean Hills 1941 (*Steynhill* 1624, 1625¹, *Stenhill* 1677, *Steine hill* 1698, *Steenhill* 1698, *Steanhill* 1709, 1710¹, 1710², *Stenehill* 1709, 1710², *Stenell* 1710¹, 1713, *Steanehill* 1713, 1717, *Stenhillsicke* 1636, *Sten(e)hill Sick* 1677, 1689, 1709, *Steanhill sicke* 1709, *Stenell* ~ 1710¹, 1710², *Steanehill Sick* 1713 (*v.* **sík**)), Steen ~ ~ 1871, Stean Hill Mdw 1941 (*v.* **steinn**, **hyll**); Stock Leys 1878, 1913 (*v.* **leys**), Stock Mdw 1913 (cf. *Stokfeld* 1467 × 84 (*v.* **feld**), *Stocke* 1624, *Stock* 1710¹, *Stretton Meer(e) Stock* 1710², 1713 (*v.* **(ge)mǣre**), *v.* **stoc**; at the boundary with the Strettons, both adjoining to the south-west); Stocker Hill, ~ ~ Cl 1878, 1913 (*the Stockewell* 1624, *the Scockerill* 1709, *Stockerhill* ~ 1636, *Scockerhill* ~ 1636, 1677, *Stockrill bridge* 1677 (*v.* **brycg**)), Stockwell Cl 1799 (*v.* **wella**; either with **stoc** or **stocc**; **stocc-wella* is a common compound, but note the previous f.ns. in this same small area; *v.* also Scockerhill in adjoining King's Norton f.ns. (a) and *Scockwell* in Little Stretton f.ns. (b)); First ~ ~ ~, to Fourth Stretton Gorse Mdw 1854 (*v.* **gorst**), Stretton Hills 1941 (towards Great Stretton and Little Stretton), Stretton Road Cl 1878, 1907, 1913 (*v.* Stretton Lane *supra*); Great ~, Little Stripling 1871, Great ~, Little Striplings 1941 (*v.* **strīp**, **-ling**); Swing Gate 1941 (*v.* **swing-gate**); Tar Barrell 1854, 1878, 1907, 1913, Tarbarrels 1941 (*Tarbarrell* 1624, 1677, *Tarrbarrell* 1636, *Tarbarrells* 1709, *Tarbarls* 1710¹, 1710², *Tarbarleys* 1713, *v.* **tarbarelle**, used topographically of black, boggy ground; earliest literal citing c.1450 OED); the Ten Roods 1765, 1775 (*v.* **tēn**, **rōd³**); Thompson Cl 1855 (with the surn. *Thompson*); Thorney Leys 1854, 1878, 1907 (1709, 1710¹, *v.* **þornig**, **leys**); Top Cl 1941, Top Fd 1941, Top Town Cl 1941 (*v.* **tūn**) (*v.* **top**); Towsley Mdw 1941 (with the surn. *Towsley*); The Tree Fd 1941 (*v.* **trēow**); Turnpike Cl 1854, 1878, 1907, 1913, Turnpike Road 1765 (*v.* **turnepike**); the Upper Cl 1846; Wall Mdw 1941; Well Mead 1847 (*v.* **wella**, **mēd**; this may be an earlier form of the previous f.n.); the West Fd 1752 (*(the) West Feild(e)* 1624, 1636 *et freq* to 1717, *v.* **west**, **feld**; one of the great open-fields); Willow Cl 1907 (*v.* **wilig**); the Willow Sick 1799, 1818, Willow Syke 1941 (*(the) Willow sick(e)* 1624, 1625¹ *et passim* to 1710²), Willow Sick Cl 1907 (*the Willow Sick Closse* 1710¹, *Willosick* ~ 1713, *the Willowsick Close* 1717), Willow Sic Fm 1928 (*v.* **wilig**, **sík**); Willow Tree 1941; Winnidoles 1855 (*Whynedolis* 1467 × 84, *Whynedoles* 1477 (e.16), *v.* **whinny**, **dāl**).

(b) *Ach furlong* 1709, 1710[1], 1710[2], *Ash furlong* 1713 (*v.* **æsc**, **furlang**); *Appell tree hill* 1698 (*v.* **æppel-trēow**); *Thomas Bakers Ley* 1677 (*v.* **ley**); *Banehil* 1624, *Long Bandall* 1709, ~ *Bandalls* 1710[1], 1710 (*v.* **bēan**, **hyll**); *Banlandis* 1467 × 84, *Banlands*, *Banlandys* 1477 (e.16), *Banlands* 1625[1], *Longbanlond'* 1467 × 84, *Long Bandlands* 1713 (*v.* **lang**[1]), *Short Bandlands* 1709, 1710[1], 1710[2], 1713, 1717 (*v.* **bēan**, **land**); *le Bayly medowe* 1467 × 84, ~ ~ *Medewe* 1477 (e.16) (*v.* **mēd** (**mēdwe** obl.sg.), *the Bayleys Plott* 1467 × 84, *þe Balys plotte* 1477 (e.16) (*v.* **þe**, **plot**) (*v.* **baillif** and cf. *Robertus Bayly* 1477 (e.16)); *Blackmore* 1624 (*v.* **blæc**, **mōr**[1]); *Brackenhil* 1199 × 1216 (*v.* **braken**, **hyll**); *Breach* 1625[1], 1709, 1710[1], 1710[2], 1713, ~ *Furlong* 1717 (*v.* **furlang**), *Brech sicke* 1624, *Breach sick*(*e*) 1646, 1709, 1717 (*v.* **sík**) (*v.* **brēc**); (*the*) *Brick Close* 1720, 1727 (*v.* **brike**; a place for the manufacture of building bricks, cf. the Kiln Cl *supra*); *the Brigge* 1636 (*v.* **brycg**); *Brinkes* 1625[1], (*the*) *Brinks* 1689, 1738 (*v.* **brink**); *Bromhyll* 1467 × 84, 1477 (e.16) (*v.* **brōm**, **hyll**); *þe Broke toward Bylsdonfeld'* 1467 × 84 (*v.* **feld**) (*v.* **þe**, **brōc**, **tōweard**; Billesdon parish adjoins to the east); *Bullokesforth* 1467 × 84, 1477 (e.16), *Bullokysforth*(*e*) 1477 (e.16) (×2) (*v.* **bulluc**, **ford** and *Ouerforth*, *infra*); *Bushby meere* 1624, ~ *Mear*(*e*) 1689, 1717 (*v.* (**ge**)**mǣre**; Bushby adjoins to the west); *the Butts* 1709, 1710[1], 1710[2], 1713, *the Butt Close* 1717, ~ ~ ~ *balke* 1709 (*v.* **balca**) (*v.* **butte**); *Calvis croft* 1467 × 84, *Calvyscroft* 1477 (e.16), *Calverscraft* 1636, *Calverscroft* 1677 (*v.* **croft**), *Calves platt* 1624 (*v.* **plat**[2]) (*v.* **calf**); *Cart gate* 1640 (*v.* **gata**), *Cart*(*e*) *Gapp* 1709, 1710[1], 1710[2], 1713 (*v.* **gap**) (*v.* **carte**); *Catberwegate* 1477 (e.16), *Catchborrow gate* 1624 (*v.* **gata**), *Catchborough way* 1709, *Catburaway* 1710[1], *Catchburrough way* 1710[1], 1710[2], *Catchburrow* ~ 1710[2], *Cath*(*s*)*burrough* ~ 1713, *Catsborrow way* 1717 (*v.* **weg**) (*v.* **cat**(**t**), **berg**); *Cheiscake peece* 1681 (*v.* **chese-cake**, **pece**); *Christian hill* 1624 (with the surn. *Christian*); *Cockacre* 1636, 1677, *the Cockacres* 1709 (*v.* **æcer**, with either **cocc**[1] or **cocc**[2]); *Copthill* 1689, ~ *Sike* 1640 (*v.* **sík**) (*v.* **copped**[1], **hyll**); *the Crooked headland* 1624 (*v.* **croked**, **hēafod-land**); *Little Dale gate* 1624, 1625[1], 1640, 1709 (*v.* **gata**), *Littledale Sick* (*v.* **sík**) (*v.* **lȳtel**, **dalr**); *Dalehill* 1636, 1677 (*v.* **dalr**, **hyll**); *Docke acres* 1625[1] (*v.* **docce**, **æcer**); (*the*) *Dockholme* 1625[1], 1636, 1651, 1661, 1666, 1677, *Dockman hook*(*e*) (sic) 1709, 1710[1], 1710[2], 1713 (*v.* **hōc**) (*v.* **docce**, **holmr**); *Dogtree* 1636, 1709 (*v.* **dogge-tree**); *Drygwell furlong* 1681 (*v.* **drȳge**, **wella**, **furlang**); *Estdoles* 1467 × 84, 1477 (e.16) (*v.* **ēast**, **dāl**); *Farrhill* 1636, *Farr Hill* 1677 (*v.* **feor**); *le ferme place* 1540, ~ *Farme* ~ 1554 (*v.* **ferme**, **place**); *Flynty*(*e*) *Acre* 1624, 1646, *Flintiacres* 1636, *Flinty Acres* 1677, 1709, 1710[1], 1710[2], 1713, *Flinty Acre peice* 1717 (*v.* **pece**), *Flint Acre* 1709, 1710[2], 1713, ~ *Ackers* 1710[1] (*v.* **flinti**, **flint**, **æcer**); *Framptons yard*(*e*) 1615, 1650, *Frampton's yard* 1700 (*v.* **geard**; with the surn. *Frampton*); *Furlong Hill* 1708, 1713, 1717 (*v.* **furlang**); *Furrow Hill* 1708 (*v.* **furh**); *Galby Brooke* 1689 (*v.* **brōc**; this appears at this date to be an alternative name for the river Sence, *v.* Cox[2] 91), *Galbyforth* 1467 × 84, 1477 (e.16), *Galbeforth*(*e*) 1477 (e.16) (×2), *Galby ford Close* 1722 (*v.* **ford** and *le Netherforth*, *infra*), *Galbymere* 1467 × 84 (*v.* (**ge**)**mǣre**) (Galby lies 2 miles to the south-east, with a short stretch of a shared parish boundary); *Gambles Hadland* 1636, 1677 (*v.* **hēafod-land**; with the surn. *Gamble*, a reflex of the ON by-name *Gamall* 'old'); *Garbridge* 1624, 1713, *Garbidge* 1709, 1710[1], 1710[2] (*v.* **gorebrode**); *Goodmans sheepe coate* 1636, ~ *sheepcoat* 1677 (*v.* **scēp-cot**; with the surn. *Goodman*); *the Gore* 1467 × 84, *þe Gore* 1477 (e.16), *the Goare* 1698 (*v.* **gāra**); *Gosdale Sickes* 1625[1] (*v.* **gōs**, **dalr**, **sík**); *Greengate balk* 1625[1] (*v.* **grēne**[1], **gata**, **balca**); *Greenehill* 1624, *Grenehultunge* 1477 (e.16) (*v.* **tunge**) (*v.* **grēne**[1],

hyll); *Grindle* 1624, *Grindell* 1625[1], 1698, *Grindale* 1636, 1677, *Gryndall* 1646, *Grindhill* 1738, *Gryndall sick* 1646 (*v*. **sík**) (*v*. **grendel**); *Gunston* 1624, 1681, 1709, 1710[1], 1713, 1717, *Gunstone* 1709 (earlier forms are needed; poss. is the name of an early farmstead (*v*. **tūn**), with the ON masc. pers.n. *Gunni*, cf. Gunstone, St **1** 37; but *Gun* may be a pre-English hill-name (*v*. Gun, StH 288), perh. with a boundary-stone upon it (*v*. **stān**)); *the Hall baulke* 1689 (*v*. **balca**), *Halls dale sicke* 1624 (*v*. **dalr**, **sík** and The Hall *supra*); *Harcote* ~ 1640, *Harcotts more* 1689 (*v*. **mōr**[1]), *Harcourts peice* 1722 (*v*. **pece**) (*v*. **hār**[2], **cot**); *Hardhill* 1624, 1636 *et freq* to 1710[2], *Hardehill* 1713, *Herd Hill* 1717 (*v*. **heard**, **hyll**; alluding to land hard to till); *Harrow hole* 1689 (*v*. **hol**[1]; formally with **hærg** 'a heathen shrine', but earlier forms are needed); *Hassel(l)wood* ~ 1651, 1666, *Hasslewood leyes* 1661, *Hasselwood leys* 1663, *Hazlewood Leyes* 1677 (*v*. **leys**; with the surn. *Hazelwood*); *Heckston* 1624, 1636, 1677, *Hexton* 1624, *Greate Hecston furlong* 1681 (*v*. **furlang**), *Long Heckston* 1709, 1710[1], ~ *Heckstone* 1709, 1710[2], ~ *Hexton* 1713, 1717, *Short Heckston* 1709, ~ *Heckstone* 1710[1], 1710[2], ~ *Hexton* 1713, 1717, *the Hextons* 1717, *Long Heckston hedge* 1710[1], 1710[2], ~ *Hexton* ~ 1713 (*v*. **hecg**), *Hexton side* 1624 (*v*. **sīde**) (prob. the name of an early farmstead (*v*. **tūn**), with a masc. pers.n., either OE *Hēahstān* or ON *Heggr*; note *Long Hexton* in adjoining Bushby f.ns. (b) and cf. *Gunston*, *supra*; otherwise another boundary marker (*v*. **stān**); earlier forms are needed); *Hendoe* 1624 (*v*. **hōh**; either with **henn** or with **hēah**[1] (**hēan** wk.obl.), *d* being intrusive); *John Herick close*, *Herrick gate* 1624 (*v*. **gata**); *Hesdale sick* 1624 (*v*. **hǣs**, **dalr**, **sík**); *Hewdesmedowe* 1467 × 84, *Hewedesmedewe*, *Heydesmedow* 1477 (e.16) (*v*. **mēd** (**mēdwe** obl.sg.); prob. with **heiward** (cf. *le Bayly medowe*, *supra* and *Pindermedow*, *infra*), but otherwise with its surn. reflex *Heyward*); *Hilmarehaw*, *Hilmorehow* 1467 × 84, *Hylmarehaw* 1477 (e.16) (*v*. **hyll**, **(ge)mǣre**, **haga**[1]); *Holmesyke* 1467 × 84, 1477 (e.16), *Holme Sick* 1625[1] (*v*. **holmr**, **sík**); *the Homestall* (*of the Parsonage*) 1606 (*v*. **hām-stall** and The Rectory *supra*); *the Homested* 1606 (*v*. **hām-stede**); *the Hooke* 1666 (*v*. **hōc**); *Horkeleyes* 1309 (*v*. **hafoc**, **lǣs**); *Hornell Leys* 1636, 1677, *Hornold Leyes* 1646, *Horney Leys* 1709, 1710[1], 1710[2], *Horny leys*, *Horney leyes* 1713 (*v*. **hyll**, **leys**, with the surn. *Horne*; in the West Fd and not to be confused with Hornleys *supra* in Mill Fd); *Houghton cros* 1467 × 84 (*v*. **cros**); *Houghton hall peece* 1636, ~ ~ *peice* 1677 (*v*. **pece** and The Hall *supra*); *Ingarsbye Hedge* 1624, *Ingaersby* ~ 1625[1], *Ingersby hedge* 1709, 1710[1], 1710[2], 1713, 1717 (*v*. **hecg**; the boundary hedge with Ingarsby which adjoins to the north); *Kylne yarde* 1554 (*v*. **cyln**, **geard**); *Lamholes* 1624, 1636, 1677, *Lambe holes* 1640 (*v*. **lām**, **hol**[1]); *Leicester gate* 1624 (*v*. **gata**; the road to Leicester which lies 6 miles to the west); *Locyll*, *Losill*, *Losyll* 1624, *Loosehill* 1636, 1677, *Locill hill* (sic) 1640, *Losehill* 1681, 1709, 1710[1], 1710[2], 1713, 1717, *Lowsehill* 1701, *Locill gate* 1625[1] (*v*. **gata**) (*v*. **hlōse**, **hyll**); *Long thonge* 1624, 1636, 1677, *Longthong* 1701, 1709 *et passim* to 1713 (*v*. **lang**[1], **þwang**); *Lynfeild* 1624, *Linfeild* 1625[1] (*v*. **līn**, **feld**); *Middlehill* 1636, 1677, 1701, *Midle hill* 1689; *the Millne* 1710[1], *Mylne balke* 1624, *Mill* ~ 1709, *Millne Baulk* 1710[1], 1710[2], *the Milne Bauke* 1713 (*v*. **balca**), *the mylne gate* 1624 (*v*. **gata**), *Mylne hill* 1624, *Mille* ~ 1636, *Milne* ~ 1677, 1713, (*the*) *Mill* ~ 1701, 1709, *the Millne hill* 1710[1], 1710[2], *the old Mill Hill* 1717, *milne hill closse* 1625[1], *Milne Hill* ~ 1636, *Mill Hill Closes* 1640, *Mylne hill headland* 1624 (*v*. **hēafod-land**), *the Mylne Hole* 1624, *Mill hole* 1698 (*v*. **hol**[1]), *Mill sicke* 1624, *Milne Sick* 1677 (*v*. **sík**) (*v*. **myln**); *Moorecrosse* 1636, *Moore Crosse* 1677, *More crosse leys* 1625[1], *Moor Cross leyes* 1709 (*v*. **leys**) (*v*. **mōr**[1], **cros**); *le Netherforth vocat' Galbyforth* 1467 ×

84, 1477 (e.16) (*v.* **neoðera**, **ford** and *Galbyforth*, *supra*; with MLat *vocatus* 'called'); *Newdole* 1467 × 84, 1477 (e.16), *Newdall foard* 1624, *Newdale ford* 1636 (*v.* **ford**), *Newdale gate* 1640 (*v.* **gata**) (*v.* **nīwe**, **dāl**); *the old rood* 1709 (*v.* **ald**, **rōd**[3]); *Ouerforth* 1467 × 84, *le Ouerforth vocat' Bullokesforth* 1467 × 84, 1477 (e.16) (with MLat *vocatus* 'called'), *the Overforde* 1606 (*v.* **uferra**, **ford** and *Bullokesforth*, *supra*); *Ouerhall holm* 1467 × 84 (*v.* **holmr** and The Hall *supra*); *Palmers hadley* 1624 (*v.* **headley**; with the surn. *Palmer*); *the Parsonage ground* 1674 (*v.* **personage**, **grund** and The Rectory *supra*); *Pikes* 1624 (*v.* **pīc**); *Pindermedow* 1467 × 84, *Pyndermedow* 1477 (e.16) (*v.* **pinder**, **mēd** (**mēdwe** obl.sg.)); *the Pingle* 1708 (*v.* **pingel**); *Pissowe* 1625[1], *Pissoe* 1681, 1713, *Pissow* 1709, 1717, *Pisoe* 1709, 1710[1], 1710[2], *Pissoe furlong* 1681 (*v.* **furlang**) (*v.* **pise**, **hōh**); *Princehill* 1681 (*v.* **hyll**; with the surn. *Prince*); *the Quorton* 1646 (described as *a quartrone of parke land* 1646), *the Quartorne Land* 1733 (*v.* **quarterne**); *Rede holme* 1467 × 84, *Reedehome* 1606, *Reedam* 1707, 1707 (18) (*v.* **hrēod**, **holmr**); *Redland* 1624, *Red landes* 1625[1], *Redlands* 1701, *Redland(e) Hey* 1624, 1698 (*v.* **(ge)hæg**) (*v.* **rēad**, **land**); *Redesmore Sike* 1624, *Reddmore Sicke* 1636, *Redmore Sick* 1677 (*v.* **hrēod**, **mōr**[1], **sík**); *Rushbedds* 1624, 1625[1] (*v.* **risc**, **bedd**); *Rye furlong* 1624, 1640, 1677, 1701, 1709, *Rie* ~ 1636 (*v.* **ryge**, **furlang**); *Sampson yarde* 1554 (*v.* **geard**; with the surn. *Sampson*); *Sandhole* 1636, 1677 (*v.* **sand**, **hol**[1]); *the Sand Sick Close* 1708 (*v.* **sand**, **sík**); *Scraptoft Closse or Scraptoft Yard* 1625[2] (*v.* **clos(e)**, **geard**; Scraptoft closely borders Houghton to the north-west); *Seaven ley(e)s* 1624, 1661, *Seven leyes* 1677 (*v.* **seofon**, **leys**; when compounded with a numeral, *leys* represents grassland units of tenure corresponding to *lands* (i.e. selions or strips) similarly used of arable); *Sheepwash* 1709, *Shippwash* 1710[1], 1710[2], *Shipwash* 1713 (*v.* **scēp-wæsce**); *Shipcoates* 1624, *Sheepcotes*, *Sheepcoats* 1717 (*v.* **scēp-cot**); *Shoulbrede* 1624 (*v.* **scofl-brǣdu**); *Skegesmore* 1646, *Skegsmoore* 1681, 1701 (*v.* **mōr**[1]; most prob. with an ON masc. pers.n., *Skeggi* or *Skeggr*, original by-names from ON *skegg* 'a beard'); *Stany hill* 1624 (*v.* **stānig**); *Stavesacre* 1681, 1709, *Staves Acker* 1710[1], 1710[2], *Stauesacres* 1713 (*v.* **stæf**, **æcer**; in this case, the staves may have been used to mark off the land); *Stondoles* 1467 × 84 (*v.* **stān**, **dāl**); *Stonyforth* 1467 × 84 (*v.* **stānig**, **ford**); *Stotfold* 1467 × 84, *Stutfold* 1477 (e.16) (*v.* **stōd-fald**); *Stoten Closse* 1710[1], *Stoton close* 1713 (a field neighbouring Stoughton parish which adjoins to the south-west); *Stretton meere* 1624, ~ *Meare* 1636, ~ *Meer* 1677, 1709, 1710[1] (*v.* **(ge)mǣre**; Little Stretton parish adjoins to the south); *ageynst the Sunne* 1636 (*v.* **ageynst**), *next the Sonne* 1640 (*v.* **nexte**), *the Clos(s)e against the Sun* 1709, 1710[1], *the Close against the Sonn* 1713 (*v.* **sunne**); later called *the Sonn(e)y* ~, *the Sunney Close* 1717 (*v.* **sunni**), and presum. the location of Sunny Leys *supra*); *Edward Suttons Close* 1717; *Swans Crosse* 1636, 1646, 1677, (*at*) *Swanns Cross* 1698 (*v.* **cros**), *Swannestyle* 1624, *Swansstile* 1636, *Swanstill* 1677 (with **stīg** or **stigel**) (prob. both with the surn. *Swann*; otherwise with **swān**[2]); *Sykkedole* 1467 × 84, 1477 (e.16), *the Sickdoles* 1722 (*v.* **sík**, **dāl**); *Taylors* ~ 1625[1], *Tailors Bridge* 1709 (*v.* **brycg**; with the surn. *Taylor*); *Teneacres* 1467 × 84, *Teneacras* 1477 (e.16) (*v.* **tēn**, **æcer**); *Thistlyholm* 1467 × 84 (*v.* **thist(e)ly**, **holmr**); *Thornehill* 1709 (*v.* **þorn**, **hyll**); *Thorney baulke* 1681 (*v.* **þornig**, **balca**); *Thorniwong*, *Thornywong*, *Thorniwongforthe* 1477 (e.16) (*v.* **ford**) (*v.* **þornig**, **vangr**); *Toadhill* 1624, 1681, 1701 (*v.* **todd**, **hyll**); *the Towne furlong* 1624, 1625[1] (*v.* **furlang**), *the Town(e) ley* 1636, 1677 (*v.* **ley**[2]), *the Townesend* 1636, 1677 (*v.* **ende**) (*v.* **tūn**); *Waltons gate* 1636, 1677 (*v.* **gata**), *Waltons hedge* 1709, 1710[1], 1710[2] (*v.* **hecg**) (with the surn.

Walton of a family perh. originally from Walton on the Wolds, 11 miles to the north-west); (*the*) *Washpitt* 1646, 1698 *et freq* to 1717, *the Washpit* 1713 (*v*. **wæsce**, **pytt**); *Washpoole* 1636, 1677 (*v*. **wæsce**, **pōl**[1]); *Waterfurrowes* 1636, 1677, *Water Thorowes* 1698 (*v*. **wæter**, **furh** and *the water furrowes* in Billesdon f.ns. (b)); *Watmore* 1467 × 84, *Wetmore* 1477 (e.16), *Watter moor* 1624, *Watermore* 1689, *Watermore sick*(*e*) 1636, 1677 *et passim* to 1713 (*v*. **sík**), ~ *Slade* 1717 (*v*. **slæd**) (originally 'the wet moorland', *v*. **wēt**, **mōr**[1]; the specific later replaced by **wæter** 'water'); *Well hill* 1624 ('spring hill', *v*. **wella**, **hyll**); *Wellsicke* 1624, 1646, 1701, *Well Sick foard* 1698 (*v*. **ford**) (*v*. **wella**, **sík**); *Wether Close* 1709, *Weathers Closse* 1710[2], *Weather Close* 1713 (*v*. **weðer**); *Wharle* 1636, 1677, 1681, *Whorle hill* 1640, *Little* ~ 1646, *Long Whorle* 1689, *Hither* ~, *Wharle* 1701, *Under Wharle* 1709, ~ *Whall* 1710[1], 1713, ~ *Whale* 1710, *Whorle Sick* 1640 (*v*. **sík**) (*v*. **hwerfel**); *Stony wheathill* 1624, 1625[1], ~ *whatehill* 1636, *Stonywate hill* 1677, *Stoney Wheatehill* 1689, *Stony Wheathill* 1710[1], 1717 (*v*. **stānig**), *Stone Wheathill* 1709, 1710[1], 1710[2], 1713 (*v*. **stān**), *Wheat*(*e*)*hill sick* 1646, 1709 (*v*. **sík**) (*v*. **hwǣte**, **hyll**); *Whymmerhill* 1624, *Wimberill* 1709, *Whimberill* 1710[1], 1710[2], 1713, *Whimbrill* 1713, *Whimbrell* 1717 (*v*. **hyll**; poss. with the surn. *Wimmer*, a reflex of the OE pers.n. *Winemǣr*, cf. *Henricus Wymer* 1301 Cor of neighbouring Northants.; otherwise with a much reduced, smoothed and presum. forgotten **wind-mylne**); *Whynedolis* 1467 × 84, *Whynedoles* 1477 (e.16) (*v*. **whinny**, **dāl**); *Willow feild* 1640 (*v*. **wilig**); *the Wounge* 1624, 1625[1] (*v*. **vangr**); *in le Wro*(*o*) 1327 (p) (×2) (*v*. **vrá**); *Yesterdoles* 1636, 1677 (*v*. **eowestre**, **dāl**).

Husbands Bosworth

HUSBANDS BOSWORTH

Baresworde 1086 DB, l.12 *GarCart* (p), *Baresworda* a. 1108 (1317) Dugd, *Baresword'* 1205 Pap, 1214 × 21 Selby, *Bareswurd(a)* 1190 (p), 1191 P (p), 1204 Cur

Bareswerde 1086 DB (×2)

Basvrde 1086 DB

Barrehorde (sic) 1086 DB, *Barewrth* 1202 FF, *Barewurth'* 1220, 1228 Cur, *Barwrth'* 1230 MemR (p), *Bareworth(e)* 1283 IpmR, Edw 2 Dugd

Bareswrth(e) 1156 (1318) Ch, 1166 LN, 1200 Cur *et passim* to 1276 RH, *Bareswrð* 1210 P, *Baresworth(e)* 1166 RBE, 1151 × 73 Selby *et freq* to 1282 Cl, 1290 Banco, *Bareswurþe* l.12 Dane (×2), *Bareswurðe* 1208 (p), 1209 P (p), *Bareswurth'* 1230 Cur, 1243 RGros, 1243 Cur

Barsword l.Hy 3 BM, *Barsworth* 1238 RGros, Edw 2 Dugd, *Barswurth* 1238 RGros

Boresworth(e) 1189 Selby, 1243 Cur *et passim* to 1293 Ipm, 1301 Ch *et freq* to 1582 LEpis, 1585 LibCl *et passim* to 1629 LML, 1656 Fine, (*Husbond* ~ 1548 Pat, *Husbands* ~ 1553 ib, 1587 LeicW *et passim* to 1720 LML, *Husband* ~ 1601 LibCl), *Boresworðe* 1202 ChancR, *Boreswrð(e)* 1203 (p), 1204 P (p), *Boreswurth'* 1225, 1228 Cur *et passim* to 1305 GildR (p)

Borsewrthe 1306 *Peake* (p), *Borseworth* 1514 Ipm

Borsworth 1331 *Peake* (p), 1332 SR (p), 1378 AD, 1619, 1625 LML, (*Husbands* ~ 1619 ib)

Boresworth alias Bosworth 1544 Fine, *Bosseworth alias Boresworthe* 1551 Pat, *Boresworth alias Husbands Boseworth* 1555, 1574 Fine

Bosworth 1404 Pat, 1514 Ipm *et passim* to 1576 Saxton, 1577 LEpis *et freq*, (*Husband(s)* ~ 1605 LML, 1610 Speed *et freq*)

'Bār's enclosure', *v.* **worð**. The masc. pers.n. *Bār* is OE, prob. originally a by-name from *bār* 'a boar', cf. Barsham Nf and Sf. Seventy-five per cent of place-names with *worð* as the generic have a pers.n. as the specific and as spellings without genitival *s* are minimal, 'boar enclosure' is unlikely here. By the middle of the 16th cent., *Husband*(*s*) ~ was prefixed to the name to distinguish the township from Market Bosworth (*v.* Cox[2] 67) in Sparkenhoe Hundred, since by this time the forms of their names (although different in origin) had developed in such a way as to make them liable to confusion. The settlement was in a farming district, hence 'Husbandmen's ~', *v.* **husband**.

ALL SAINTS' CHURCH, *Church (All Saints)* 1846, 1863, 1877 White, 1925 Kelly; it is earlier recorded as *ecclesiam de Bareswortha* a.1219 RHug, ~ *de Barswurth* 1238 RGros, *ecclesie de Barisworth* 1220 MHW, ~ *de Boresworth* 1348, 1367, 1401 *Pat*, *ecclesiarum de Boresworthe alias Husbandes Boresworthe* (*et Lyndebye*) 1556 *ib*, *the Church* 1601 *Terrier*. Note also *the Churchyard* 1606, 1625, 1638, 1724 *ib*, *v.* **churchyerd**. BELL INN (P.H.), *Bell* 1846, 1863 White, *Bell Inn* 1877 ib, 1925 Kelly. BELL LANE, named from the Bell Inn *supra*. BOSWORTH GORSE, 1835 O, *v.* **gorst**. BOSWORTH GRANGE, 1925 Kelly, *Bosseworth Graunge* 1551 *Pat*, *le Graunge de Boresworthe* 1557 Nichols, *Boresworth Grange* 1619 Ipm, *grangia de Boresworth*(*e*) 1540 MinAccts, 1558 *Pat* (with MLat *grangia*), *v.* **grange**; in origin, an outlying property of nearby Sulby Abbey in Northants. BOSWORTH LODGE, *The Lodge* 1877 White, *v.* **loge**. BOSWORTH MILL, 1835 O; it is *The Water Mill* 1673 *Terrier*, *v.* **water-mylne**. BOSWORTH TUNNEL, carrying the Grand Union Canal. BRICKFIELD SPINNEY, *v.* **spinney** and Brickhill Clumps in f.ns. (a). BUTCHERS' ARMS (P.H.) (lost), *Butchers' Arms* 1846, 1863, 1877 White; in 1846, the tenant was Lucy Groocock, Francis Groocock being a butcher. BUTTS LANE, *Butts* 1726 *Terrier*, *v.* **butte**. CARLAND SPINNEY, *Carlon Spinny* 1835 O (*v.* **spinney**), *Careland* 1601 *Terrier*, *Carland* 1606, 1625 *ib et passim* to 1726, c.1800 *ib*, *Carrland* 1673 *ib*, *v.* **kjarr**, **land**; note later f.ns. with Carland in f.ns (a). CHERRY TREE (P.H.), *Cherry Tree* 1877 White, 1925 Kelly. CHURCH LANE, *v.* All Saints' Church *supra*. COLLIN'S HOLME, 1846, 1877 White, *Collins Holme* 1631 Nichols, *Collynholm* 1639 Ipm, *Collings holm* 1693 *Terrier*, *v.* **holmr**; with the surn. *Collin*(*s*). COTE HILL FM, *Coat hill* 1601, 1726, m.18 *Terrier*, *Cotehill* 1606, 1625, 1638, 1674 *ib*, *Coatehill* 1697, 1703, 1724 *ib*, 1803 *Surv*, *v.* **cot**, **hyll** and *Boresworthe Cootes* in f.ns. (b). THE COTTAGE, 1846 White, *v.* **cotage**. CROFT HOUSE FM, *v.* **croft**. EAST FIELD, 1802 *Deed*, 1846, 1863, 1877 White. ELKINGTON LODGE, 1925 Kelly, *v.* **loge**; possibly named from Elkington which lies 5 miles to the south in Northants., but *Elkington* is found as a surn. in 19th-cent. Leics. THE FIRS FM. GLEBE FM, *Glebe farm* 1877 White, 1925

Kelly, cf. *the Glebe land* m.18 *Terrier*, *v.* **glebe**. GRANGE FM, *Grange farm* 1877 White, *v.* Bosworth Grange *supra*. GRAVEL PIT SPINNEY, *gravel pittes* 1601 *Terrier*, *gravell pit(t)s* 1606, 1625, 1638, 1673, 1724 *ib*, (*the*) *Gravil(l) pitts* 1674, 1697, 1703, 1726 *ib*, cf. *the Gravell Pitts Flatt* 1673 (*v.* **flat**), *v.* **gravel**, **pytt**, **spinney**. GRAZIERS' ARMS (P.H.), *Graziers' Arms* 1877 White; nineteen graziers are listed for Husbands Bosworth in White's 1877 directory. THE HALL, 1601, 1638, 1673 *Terrier*, 1846, 1877 White, *Bosworth Hall* 1835 O, 1925 Kelly, *v.* **hall**. HIGHCROFT LODGE FM (HIGHCROFT FM 2½"), *highcroft* 1606, *highcraft* 1625, (*the*) *High Craft* 1638, 1697, 1724, 1726, m.18 *Terrier*, *heycraft* 1674 *ib*, *Highcrafte* 1693 *ib*, *Highcroft* ~ 1846, 1863 White, *Hycroft House* 1877 ib, *Highcroft Lodge* 1925 Kelly (*v.* **loge**), *v.* **hēah**[1], **croft**. HIGHFIELD HO. is *Highfield* 1925 Kelly. HIGH ST. HILL HO., *Hill House* 1925 Kelly. HONEY POT LANE, *Honey Pot(t)* 1724, 1726 *Terrier*, *Honey Pot otherwise Ox Close Furlong* m.18 *ib* (*v.* **furlang** and *Oxe close* in f.ns. (b)), *v.* **hunig**, **pot(t)**; used of 'sweet land', or of places where honey was found, or of locations with sticky soil. KILWORTH RD, North Kilworth lying 2 miles to the south-west. LAMMAS CLOSE, *the Hall Leys or Lammas Close* 1673 *Terrier* (*v.* Hall Leys in f.ns. (a)), *Wards Lammas Close* 1802 *Deed* (with the surn. *Ward*), *v.* **lammas**. LEICESTER RD, Leicester lying 13 miles to the north-west. LODGE FM. LODGE SPINNEY, *v.* **spinney**. LYNDENE LODGE, *v.* **loge**. MILL FM (BOSWORTH MILL FM 2½"), *v.* Bosworth Mill *supra*. MOWSLEY RD, Mowsley lying 3 miles to the north. NORTH KILWORTH WHARF, *v.* **wharf**; on the Grand Union Canal towards North Kilworth. THE RECTORY, 1877 White, 1925 Kelly, *v.* **rectory**; earlier is *the Parsonage House* 1606, 1625 *Terrier et passim* to 1724 *ib*, cf. *the Parsonage yard* 1601 *ib* (*v.* **geard**), *v.* **personage**. RED LION (P.H.) (lost), *Red Lion* 1846, 1863, 1877 White, *The Old Red Lion* 1925 Kelly. SCHOOL LANE. SIBBERTOFT RD is *Sib(b)ertoft(e) way* 1606, 1625, 1638 *Terrier*, *v.* **weg**; Sibbertoft lies 2 miles to the south-east in Northants. SOUTH FIELDS, *v.* South Fd in f.ns. (a). STATION RD, running westwards to the former Welford and Kilworth Station on the now dismantled *Rugby and Stamford Railway* 1863, 1877 White. THE STUD FM, *v.* **stōd**. SULBY RD is *Sulby gate* 1606, 1625 *Terrier et passim* to 1726 *ib*, *v.* **gata**; Sulby lies 2 miles to the south-east in Northants. THEDDINGWORTH RD, Theddingworth lying 2 miles to the north-east. UNION ANCHOR (P.H.) (lost), *Union Anchor Inn* 1835 O, *Union Anchor* 1846, 1863, 1877 White, 1925 Kelly; on the Grand Union Canal. WELFORD RD is *Welford way* 1606, 1625, 1638 *Terrier*, *v.* **weg**; Welford lies 3 miles to the south in Northants. WELFORD WHARF, *v.* **wharf**; on the Grand Union Canal towards Welford. WHARF HOUSE HOTEL, on the

Welford Branch of the Grand Union Canal; it is called *The George* 1846, 1863 White, *George Inn* 1925 Kelly. WHEAT SHEAF (P.H.) (lost), *Wheat Sheaf* 1846, 1863, 1877 White. WHELER LODGE, 1877 White, 1925 Kelly, *Wheeler Lodge* 1863 White, *v.* **loge**; with the surn. *Wheeler*. WHELER LODGE FM. WOODSIDE FM.

FIELD-NAMES

In (a), forms dated c.1780, 1782, 1792 and 1803 are *Surv*; those dated c.1800 and 1821 are *Terrier*; 1802 are *Deed*; 1918 are Sale. Forms throughout dated Hy 3 are *AddCh*; those dated 1467 × 84 are *LTD*; 1477 (e.16) are *Charyte*; 1489 and 1554 are *Pat*; 1515 × 29 are *Req*; c.1530 are *Depos*; 1601, 1606, 1625, 1638, 1673, 1674, 1679, 1693, 1697, 1703, 1708, 1724, 1726 and m.18 are *Terrier*; 1630 are Ipm; 1711 are LAS.

(a) Belgraves Willows 1803 (*Belgrave Willows* m.18, *v.* **wilig**; with the surn. *Belgrave* of a family originally from Belgrave, 14 miles to the north-west); Biggs Farm House c.1800 (with the surn. *Bigg*(*s*)); Black Miles 1803 (m.18, *black myles* 1601, *Blackmiles* 1638, 1697, 1724, *blackmills* 1726, *v.* **blæc**, **mylde**); Blakesley Cl c.1780 (with the surn. *Blakesley* of a family originally from Blakesley, 22 miles to the south in Northants.); Bosworth Gate 1835 O (a toll-gate); Bosworth Hill 1835 O; Breatch Cl 1803 (*Breche* 1477 (e.16), *Breach* 1601, 1693, cf. *Brechefurlong* 1467 × 84, *Brichefurlong* 1477 (e.16), *Breach furlong* 1606, 1625, 1638, 1724, m.18, ~ *forlong* 1726, *Long* ~ ~, *Short Breach Furlong* m.18 (*v.* **furlang**), *v.* **brēc**); Brickhill Clumps c.1800 (*v.* **clump**, here in the sense 'a cluster of trees or shrubs'), Brickiln Cl 1803 (*v.* **brike-kiln**); Broad Lane 1802 (cf. (*at*) *Broad lane end* 1606, 1625 *et passim* to 1726, m.18, *v.* **brād**, **lane**, **lane-ende**); Brook Fd 1782 (*v.* **brōc**); Browns Cl c.1800 (with the surn. *Brown*); Carland Cl 1803 (cf. *Carland forlong* 1726, *v.* **furlang**), Carland Hole Cl 1802 (*Carland hole* 1697, *v.* **hol**[1]), Carland New ~, Carland Old Mdw 1803 (*v.* Carland Spinney *supra*); The Causeway Land 1877 White (*v.* **caucie**, **land**; providing revenue for repairing the causeways); Back of Coate Hill 1803 (*v.* **back of**, Cote Hill Fm *supra* and *Boresworthe Cootes* in f.ns. (b)); Cowpasture 1782, c.1800 (*the Common Cow Pastur* 1673 (*v.* **commun**), *v.* **cū**, **pasture**); Dog Kennel(l) Cl c.1780, 1792, c.1800 (*v.* **kenel**; such names often relate to kennels for hunting dogs); Dove Cl 1782, 1792, Dovehouse Cl c.1780, c.1800 (these presum. represent the same close, the site of a dovecote, *v.* **dove-hous**); Dysons Cl c.1780, c.1800, Great ~, Little Dyson 1918 (cf. *Dysons Peece* 1726, *v.* **pece**; with the surn. *Dyson*); Far Cl 1803; Farm Cl 1792 (*v.* **ferme**); Next Fox Cover 1803 (*v.* **fox**, **cover(t)**; a close next to a fox covert); Foxhills 1918 (1708; this may be *Foxholes* 1703, 1726, *v.* **fox-hol**; otherwise, *v.* **fox**, **hyll**); Freemans Folly 1802 (*v.* **folie**, in f.ns., sometimes used of a small plantation; cf. *Freemans Farm* 1711, *Freeman's Gate* 1726 (*v.* **gata**), with the surn. *Freeman*); Glovers or Carland Fm 1803 (with the local surn. *Glover*; note f.ns. with Carland and Carland Spinney *supra*); Hall Cl 1782, 1792, c.1800 (*the Hall close* m.18), Hall Leys 1782, c.1800 (*the Hall lea*(*e*)*s* 1601, *the Hall Leys or Lammas Close* 1673, m.18 (*v.* Lammas Cl *supra*), *Hall-Leyes fourlong* 1726 (*v*. **furlang**), *v*. **leys** and The Hall *supra*); Hollow Mdw 1918 (*v*. **holh**); Holloway c.1800 (1697, 1703, 1724, m.18, *Hallowe waye* 1601, 1674, *neather* ~, *uper hollowell* 1606, *nether* ~, *midle* ~, *uper hallowell* 1625, *Neather* ~, *Middle* ~, *Upper Hollowell* 1638; in origin 'stream running in a deep hollow', *v*. **hol**[2], **wella**, but later transformed into a spurious road-name; note the early compounds *Holwellebroc* 1477 (e.16) (*v*. **brōc**) and *Holewelslade* 1467 × 84, 1477 (e.16) (*v*. **slæd**) which provide a clear etymology for Holloway; in the great open North Fd of the township); Homehall Cl c.1780, c.1800 (*v*. **home** and The Hall *supra*); House Ground 1803 (*v*. **grund**); Widow Knights Orchard c.1780 (*v*. **orceard**); Langhill, Little Langhill Mdw 1918 (*Longul* 1467 × 84, *Longhull* 1477 (e.16), *Westlonghul(l)* 1467 × 84, 1477 (e.16) (*v*. **west**), *Langhill* 1601, 1606 *et passim* to 1726, (*the*) *Backside Langhill* 1606, 1625 *et passim* to 1724 (*v*. **bak-side**), *v*. **lang**[1], **hyll**); (The) Lawn 1782, 1792, Lawn Cl c.1800 (*v*. **launde**); Long Cl 1803; Mill Slade 1803 (*the Millslade* 1674, *v*. **myln**, **slæd**; with reference to the watermill); (the) North Fd 1802, 1821 (1724, 1726, m.18, (*the*) *North feild* 1601, 1606 *et passim* to 1697, *the North feeld(e)* 1674, 1703, *v*. **norð**, **feld**; one of the great open-fields of the township); Pools House 1802 (*v*. **pōl**[1]); Side Mdw 1918 (*v*. **sīde**); South Fd 1821 (1726, m.18, (*the*) *South feild* 1601, 1606 *et passim* to 1724, *the South feeld* 1674, 1703, *v*. **sūð**, **feld**; one of the great open-fields); Sharfoot Mdw 1803 (*Sharfoot* m.18, *v*. **scearu**, **fōt**); Spinney Corner 1803 (*v*. **spinney**, **corner**; with reference to Carland Spinney *supra*); Stepnals 1918 (*Stepnill* 1606, 1625 *et passim* to 1724, *Stevnill* 1674, *Stepmill* 1697, 1726, *Stebnill* 1708, *Stepnell* m.18, *Steppmill more* 1726 (*v*. **mōr**[1]) ('(on the) steep hill', *v*. **stēap** (**stēapan** wk.obl.), **hyll**); Tafts Plowed, Old Tafts Grass 1803 (i.e. ploughed land and mowing grass) (*Toftes* 1601, *Tofts* 1606, 1625, 1638, *Tafts* 1674, 1697, 1724, 1726, ~ *forlong* 1726 (*v*. **furlang**), *v*. **toft**); Three Corner Cl 1803 (*v*. **three-corner**); Three Hedges 1803 (either with **hecg** in its early sense 'a hedged enclosure' or with **edisc** or **etisc**); Villers ~ c.1780, 1782, Villars Cl c.1800 (*Vylers Close* 1673), Villars Fd c.1800 (*Villers* 1601, 1697, 1726, *Villers land* 1630 (*v*. **land**), *Villers Furlong* m.18 (*v*. **furlang**); with the surn. *Villar(s)*/*Villers*); Walpoles Fm 1803 (with the surn. *Walpole*); Wards Cl c.1780, c.1800 (with the surn. *Ward*); Wash Pit 1803 (*Washpitt* 1703, 1726, m.18, ~ *forlong* 1726 (*v*. **furlang**), *v*. **wæsce**, **pytt**); Well Cl 1846, 1863, 1877 White (cf. *atte Welle* 1369 Cl (p), 1389 Pat (p) (*v*. **atte**), *v*. **wella**); (the) West Fd 1802 (1726, m.18, (*the*) *West feild* 1601, 1606 *et passim* to 1724, ~ *Feeld(e)* 1674, 1703, *v*. **west**, **feld**; one of the great open-fields).

(b) *Allings dich* 1674 (*v*. **dīc**; with the surn. *Al(l)ing*); *Andrews hedge* 1724 (*v*. **hecg**; with the surn. *Andrew(s)*); *Ouer Ashes* 1726 (*v*. **uferra**, **æsc**); *Ashlow* 1601, *middle* ~, *neather Ashlow(es)* 1606, *Midle Ashlowes*, *Nether* ~, *Upper Ashloes* 1625, *Middle Ashloes* 1638, *Middle* ~, *Nether Ashlows* 1726, *Middell Ashclose* 1703, *Middle Ash Close* 1724, *Middle* ~ ~, *Nether* ~ ~, *Upper Ash Close* m.18 (originally 'ash-tree hill', *v*. **æsc**, **hlāw**; the final el. was later confused with **clos(e)**); *Bandlands* 1606, 1625, 1638, 1724, m.18, *Banlands* 1674, 1697, *Over Banlans* 1703 (*v*. **uferra**) (*v*. **bēan**, **land**); *Barlihull*, *Barlichul* Hy 3 (*v*. **bærlic**, **hyll**); *betwene the sickes* 1601, *betweene the sicks* 1625, *between the sikes* 1638, *Between(e) Six* 1697, 1703, 1724, 1726 (('furlong lying) between the ditches', *v*. **betwēonan**, **sík**); *Betwext the Wayes* 1674, *Between(e) the way(e)s* 1703, 1724, 1726 (('furlong lying) between the tracks', *v*. **betwixt**, **betwēonan**, **weg**); *Betwixt Grain(e)s* 1625, 1638, 1674, 1724, *Between(e) Graines* 1697, 1703, *Between Grains* 1726 (('furlong lying) between forks of a stream', *v.* **grein**); *Blakebrok', Blachebroke* 1467 × 84, *Blak(e)broc, Blachebroc* 1477 (e.16), *Blackbroke* c.1530, *Netherblakebroke* 1467 × 84, *Nederblakebroc* 1477 (e.16) (*v.* **neoðera**), *Ouerblacbroke* 1467 × 84, (*the*) *Ouerblakbrok* 1477 (e.16) (*v.* **uferra**) (*v.* **blæc, brōc**); *Boresworthe Cootes, Bosseworthe Cootes* 1551 *Pat, Coates* 1601, *Cotes* 1606, 1625, 1638, *Coats* 1697, 1724, *Behind Cotes* 1625, 1628, ~ *Coats* 1724 (*v.* **behindan**), *the Backside Coat(e)s* 1674, 1697 (*v.* **bak-side**) (*v.* **cot**); *Brackill Layes, Breakill Lays* 1726 (*v.* **bracu, hyll, leys**); *Broad Hal(f)ford* 1726, m.18 (originally 'the ford in the bend of the stream', *v.* **halh, ford**; later with **brād** which may refer either to the ford or to the size of a furlong there); *the broad waye* 1601 (*v.* **brād, weg**; poss. an earlier name for Broad Lane *supra*); *Burtons lands alias Roundabout* 1630 (*v.* **land**; with the surn. *Burton*; and *v. Roundabout, infra*); *Bury* 1467 × 84, 1477 (e.16), *Berie* 1601, *Berrie* 1606, *Berry* 1625, 1638 *et passim* to m.18, *Berry Close* 1711, *Berry Hill(s)* 1697, 1724, 1726, *Berry holes* 1674, 1697, 1703 (*v.* **hol**[1]) (*v.* **burh** (**byrig** dat.sg.) and *Westbury, infra*); *Butcher(s) Field gate* 1673, 1697 (*v.* **geat**; with the surn. *Butcher*); *butlan* 1601 (*v.* **butte**; it is uncertain whether this is a poor early form for Butts Lane *supra*, but if not, then *v.* **land**); *Buttirhill* 1467 × 84, *Buterhil* 1477 (e.16), *Butter hill* 1601, *Long ~, Short Buttrill* 1638, *Long ~, Short Butterill* 1724, m.18 (*v.* **butere, hyll**; hillside pasture used in summer for the production of butter); *Carriers Thorn* m.18 (*v.* **þorn**), *Carriers Way(e)* 1693, 1726 (it is uncertain whether *carrier* here is a surn. or the occupational name which gave the surn. (*v.* **caryour**); *way* suggests a road for carters or carriers, but the compound with *thorn* indicates ownership and thus a surn.; however, *Carriers Thorn* may signify 'thorn-scrub beside *Carriers Way*'); *Catts furlong* 1601, 1638, 1697, *Cats forlong* 1606, 1724, m.18, *Cattsforlong, the backside Cattsforlong* 1726 (*v.* **bak-side**), *Cattsfurlong hill* 1697 (*v.* **furlang**; with either **cat(t)** or the surn. *Catt*); *Chambers londis* 1489 (*v.* **land**; with the surn. *Chambers*); *Chantry land* 1630 (*v.* **chanterie**; relating to All Saints' Church *supra*); *Chapman Hedge* (*v.* **hecg**; with the surn. *Chapman*); *Clenfurlond* (sic) 1467 × 84, *Clenfurlong* 1477 (e.16) (*v.* **clǣne, furlang**); (*on*) *Cobdale* 1601, 1625, 1638, *Cob(b)dill* 1674, 1726, *Long Cobdale* 1693, ~ *Cobdill* 1697, 1724, ~ *Cobdel* 1703, ~ *Cobbdill* 1726, *Long ~, Short Cobdill* m.18, *Cobdell Close* m.18 (poss. 'hill with a peak', *v.* **copped**[1], **hyll**); *Cockloe* 1673, 1697, *Cocklow* m.18, *Far ~, Hither Cocklow* 1638, *Far ~, Hither Cockloe* 1724, *the uper Cockland* (sic) 1673 (*v.* **upper**), *Over Coklow* (*v.* **uferra**), *Nether Cocklow* 1726 (*v.* **hlāw**; prob. with **cocc**[1], otherwise **cocc**[2]); *Cote furrs Peeces* 1673 (*v.* **pece**), *Coat furze, Coat(e) furs* 1726 (*v.* **fyrs**), *Cotemore* 1606, 1625, *Cotemoor(e)* 1638, 1693, m.18, *Coate Moore* 1703, *Coat(e)more* 1724, 1726 (*v.* **mōr**[1]) (*v.* **cot**); *Coxes howse* 1606 (*v.* **hūs**; with the surn. *Cox*); *Cranmer* 1606, 1625, 1638, 1697, 1724 (*v.* **cran, mere**[1]); *Cuthill* 1601, 1606, 1625, 1638, *Cuttill* 1697, 1703, *Cuttillhole* 1724 (*v.* **hol**[1]) (prob. **cutel**; otherwise *v.* **cutte, hyll**); *deadmore* 1601, 1606, *Deadmoor(e)* 1625, 1638 (*v.* **dēad, mōr**[1]; a common Leics. f.n., with reference to infertile wasteland); *deane hole* 1601, 1606, 1625, 1638, *Danehole* 1674, 1697, 1703, *Dean hole* 1724, ~ *forlong* 1726 (*v.* **furlang**) (*v.* **dene-hole**); *dodspole* 1606, 1673, *dodpole* 1625, *Dodspoole* 1638, 1697, 1724, m.18, *Dodspooll fourlong* 1726 (*v.* **furlang**) (*v.* **pōl**[1]; with the OE masc. pers.n. *Dodd* (cf. *Brictricus filius Doddi* 1086 DB); the common form of the pers.n. is *Dodda*); *the Doole* 1515 × 29, *the Dole* 1530 (*v.* **dāl**); *Drihtburhlawe* Hy 3 (*v.* **hlāw**; with an otherwise unrecorded OE fem. pers.n. *Dryhtburh*, comparative forms *Dryhthelm, Dryhtlāf, Dryhtmǣr, Dryhtnōð* and *Dryhtwald* all being masc. (*v.* Searle 169); a notional reduced **Dryhtnesburgeshlaw* 'the hill of the lord's stronghold' would suppose the unlikely loss of *n* as well as that of two gentival composition joints); *elder stub*(*b*) 1601, 1606, *Elder stub*(*e*)*s* 1625, 1674, 1703, 1724, *Elderstubbs* 1638, 1697, 1726 (*v*. **ellern**, **stubb**); *enland* 1601, *Inland* 1606, 1625, 1638, *England* 1674, *Long* ~, *Englands* 1693, 1703, 1724, *England Leys* 1697, m.18 (*v*. **leys**) (*v*. **eng**, **land**); *Flambuswong* 1477 (e.16), 1467 × 84 (*v*. **vangr**; either with the OFr masc. pers.n. *Flambard*/*Flambart* or with its surn. reflex); *Flaxwell sick*(*e*) 1625, 1638, 1697, *Flaxall sicke* 1674, 1703, *Flaxhall Sick forlong* 1726 (*v*. **furlang**), *Flaxensick* 1726, m.18 (*v*. **sík**) (*v*. **wella** and cf. *Flaxwell* in Stonesby (Lei **2** 258) for which a metathesized ODan *flask* 'swampy grassland' is tentatively suggested as first el.; but poss. in both names is OE **flaxe** 'a wooden vessel for liquids'; whether the word had some transferred topographical application, such as to a natural basin or hollow, or whether it indicated a spring enclosed by a tub set in the ground, or a well or spring supplied with a container for drawing water, is uncertain; cf. the common *Bidwell* or *Bedwell*, formed with OE *byden* 'a barrel, tub, vessel for liquids', *v*. VEPN *s.v.*; alternatively, the specific could indeed be **fleax**, and the stream was used for flax-retting); (*at*) *Fossells house* 1625, 1638 (*v*. **hūs**; land beside the home of the *Fossell* family (the usual form of the surn. is *Fussell*)); *fullpit* 1606, *fullpitt* 1625, 1638, *Fulpitt* 1724, *Nether Fulpit* m.18 (*v*. **fūl**, **pytt**); *Glouers Pitt forlong* 1726 (*v*. **pytt**, **furlang**; with the local surn. *Glover*, cf. Glovers Fm *supra*); *Godakers* 1673 (*v*. **gōd**, **æcer**); *godwell* 1625, 1638, *Short Goddill* 1697, 1724, m.18 (*v*. **gōd**, **wella**); *Goodriche Holme* 1554 (*v*. **holmr**; with the surn. *Goodrich*); *the Grange land* 1726 (*v*. **land** and Bosworth Grange *supra*); *guild*(*e*) *hall* 1606, 1625, 1638, (*on*) *guylde hall* 1674, *gild hall* 1703, (*on*) *Guild Hall* 1697, 1724, 1726, (*at*) *Guildhall* m.18 (*v*. **gild-hall**; land endowed for the upkeep of an unspecified guildhall, presum. one in Leicester, *v*. The Guildhall, St George's Guildhall and St Margaret's Guildhall, Lei **1** 105–7); *the Hall doole* 1601, *halldole* 1606, 1638, *Hall Dole* 1625, 1674 *et passim* to 1726, m.18 (*v*. **dāl**), *hallgate* 1606 (*v*. **gate**), *the Hall peice* 1638, 1724, m.18 (*v*. **pece**) (*v*. The Hall *supra*); *Hamrells* 1601, *Hemmerells* 1606, *Hembrils* 1625, *Hembrills* 1638, *neather* ~, *ouer hemberrills* 1674, *Ne*(*a*)*ther Hembrills* 1693, 1697, *Neather* ~, *Over hembrils* 1703, *Nether* ~, *Ouer Hembrills* 1724, 1726, *Nether* ~, *Over Hemberills* m.18 (*v*. **neoðera**, **uferra**) (*v*. **hyll**; prob. with **hamer** 'nearer home, nearer the village' (*v*. Lei **3** 314 *s.v.*)); *Hang-mans Rickstead* 1726, *Hangmans Rickstead Furlong* m.18 (*v*. **hangeman**, **rickstead**; cf. *Hangmans Hall* 1835 O in Sutton Cheney, Sparkenhoe Hundred (*v*. Cox[2] 46); a *Rogerus Hangeman* is recorded in Norfolk in 1310, but no such later surns. are extant; presum. the name here refers to the site of a gallows or a gibbet); *Harbarow Waye* 1674, *Harborrow*(*e*) *way*(*e*) 1697, 1703, *Harberrow way* 1724, *Harborough way*(*e*) 1726, ~ ~ *Furlong* m.18 (*v*. **furlang**) (*v*. **weg**; land beside the road to Market Harborough); *hardhill* 1601, 1606, 1625, 1638, *Hardill* 1674, 1703, 1724, *Hardell forlong* 1726, *Hardhill Furlong* m.18 (*v*. **furlang**) (*v*. **heard**, **hyll**; alluding to soil hard to till); *hareslade* 1601, 1606, 1625, 1638, *hearslade* 1693, *Nether Hareslad* 1726 ('the boundary valley', *v*. **hār**[2], **slæd**); *Hawards forlonge* 1625, *Howards furlong* 1638, *Howerds* ~ 1674, *Howards Forlong* 1697, *Huards* ~ 1703, *Howards Furlong* m.18 (*v*. **furlang**; prob. with **heiward** rather than with the surn. *Haward*/*Howard*/*Hayward*; cf. *hauards dole* in Burton Overy f.ns. (b)); *Hellholes* 1724, m.18 (*v*. **hell**, **hol**[1]; in f.ns., a frequent term of disparagement for uninviting ground, sometimes referring to damp hollows or to poor scrubland, *v*. Field 40); *the hey* 1601, (*the*) *Short*(*e*) *hey* 1606, 1625, 1638, 1697, 1724, *Shorte* *haye* 1703, *Long hey* 1693, *Short* ~, *Long Hay* 1726 (*v.* **(ge)hæg**); *Neather* ~, *Ouer highloes* 1638 (*v.* **neoðera**, **uferra**, **hēah**[1], **hlāw**); *Hills* 1693, 1726, *Nether Hills* 1726 (*v.* **neoðera**), *Hills Furlong* m.18 (*v.* **hyll**); *hoarestone* 1606, *hoareston* 1625, *Hoarston* 1638, 1673, *Hoorestone* 1697, *Hareston* 1703, *Hoarstone* 1724, *Horestone* m.18 ('the boundary stone', *v.* **hār**[2], **stān**); *Home Close* 1724 (*v.* **home**); *homesmeere* 1625, 1638, 1697, (*on*) *homes meare* 1674, *Homesmeer* 1724 (*v.* **holmr**, **(ge)mǣre**); *the House Closes* 1673 (enclosures adjacent to *the Mannor House* 1673 (*v.* **maner**)); *Howards Hole* m.18 (*v.* **hol**[1] and *Hawards forlonge*, *supra*); *the Ouer* ~ (*v.* **uferra**), *the Nether joints* 1726, *the Joints* (*on Tongue Hill*) m.18 (of uncertain meaning; poss. with a shortened form of *jointry* 'land held in jointure', implying a co-tenancy; *v. Tonghill*, *infra*); *Killworth Bridge forlong* 1726 (*v.* **brycg**, **furlang**), *Killworth brooke* 1606, 1697 (*v.* **brōc**), *Kilworth* ~ 1601, *Killworth hill* 1606, 1625, 1638, *Kilworth Hill Furlong* m.18, *Killworth way* 1697 (North Kilworth lies two miles to the south-west); *Knights house* 1674 (*v.* **hūs**; with the local surn. *Knight*, cf. Widow Knights Orchard *supra*); *langrass* 1601, *Langrasse* 1606, 1625, *Lang(g)eras* 1674, 1697, *Neather Langrass(e)* 1703, 1724 (*v.* **neoðera**), *Over Langrass* 1724 (*v.* **uferra**), *Nether* ~ ~, *Ouer-Land-grass* (sic) 1726, *Upper* ~, *Langrass* m.18 ('the long pasture or meadowland', *v.* **lang**[1], **græs**); *Laskrels* 1601, *Laskarills* 1697, 1726, *Lastrills* 1703, 1724, *Laskerills Furlong* m.18 (Professor R. Coates suggests that this may be a surn. *Lescureuil* or the like (from *écureuil* 'squirrel'), known in French); *Linch* 1601, 1674 *et passim* to 1726, *Lynch* 1606, 1638, *Ouer* ~, *Lynch* 1625, *Over Lynch* 1638 (*v.* **uferra**), *Linch Furlong* m.18 (*v.* **hlinc**); *Litlow* 1606, *litleloe* 1625, *Littleloe* 1638, 1724, *Long little low* 1726 (*v.* **lӯtel**, **hlāw**); *Long furlong(e)* 1601, 1606 *et passim* to m.18, *Long forlong* 1625, 1674, 1697, 1726, *Long furlong hadlea* m.18 (*v.* **headley**) (*v.* **lang**[1], **furlang**); *Lowson* 1601, *neather* ~, *uper Loosen* 1606, *nether* ~, *uper losen* 1625, *neather* ~, *upper looson* 1638 (*v.* **neoðera**, **upper**), *Luson* 1697, *Neather* ~, *Upper Loosen* 1724, *Lowsen forlong* 1726 (*v.* **furlang**), *Loosen Close* m.18 ('the pigsties', *v.* **hlōse** (**hlōsan** nom.pl.)); *Lovetts land* 1630 (*v.* **land**; with the surn. *Lovett*, cf. *Robertus Luvet* 1206 Cur of neighbouring Rutland); *Maydyn' well* 1467 × 84, *Maidenewell* 1477 (e.16) (*v.* **mægden**, **wella**; cf. *Maidewell'* in Nevill Holt f.ns. (b) and *Maydens well*, Lei **3** 141); *Meadow* ~ 1606, 1638, *medow breach* 1625 (*v.* **brēc**), *the Middowe Ford* 1674 (*v.* **ford**), (*the*) *Meadow* ~ 1693, 1697, 1726, *Middow* ~ 1703, *Midow side* 1724 (*v.* **sīde**), *Meadowside Furlong* m.18, *Meadow Close* m.18; *the mill dore* 1601, *the Mill Door* m.18, *watermill doore* 1606, *Water myll dore* 1625, (*at*) *Watermilldoor* 1638 (*v.* **myln**, **water-mylne**, **duru**; all forms refer to the same building complex); *the Mires* m.18 (*v.* **mýrr**); *Musehull* 1467 × 84, 1477 (e.16) (*v.* **mūs**, **hyll**); *Naill's Corner* 1726 (*v.* **corner**; with the surn. *Naill*, metonymic for ME *nayler* 'a maker of nails'); *Old Pen* m.18 (*v.* **ald**, **penn**[2]); *Oxe close* 1625, 1638, *Ox Close* 1725, *Honey Pot otherwise Ox close Furlong* m.18 (*v.* Honey Pot Lane *supra*) (*v.* **oxa**); *Palmers Leys* m.18 (*v.* **leys**; with the surn. *Palmer*); *Mr Pearce's hedge* m.18 (*v.* **hecg**); *Pessill* 1697 (*v.* **pise**, **hyll**); *Pinslade* 1467 × 84, 1477 (e.16), *Pinslad*, *Pynselade* 1477 (e.16), *Pynslade* c.1530 (*v.* **pynd**, **slæd**; cf. *Pynslade*, Lei **3** 242); *the Pond Close* 1673 (*v.* **ponde**); *Portgarth* 1477 (e.16) (this must allude to Market Harborough, 6 miles to the north-east, so rather than containing **garðr**, the form may well be a cartulary error for **port-gate** 'the road to the market (town)'); *Priest-home* 1726 (*v.* **prēost**, **holmr**); *Ranglands*, ~ *forlong* 1726, ~ *Furlong* m.18 (*v.* **furlang**) (*v.* **wrang**, **land**); *Redbrochforlang* Hy 3 (*v.* **furlang**), *Reed brook* 1601, 1638, 1724, *Reedbrooke* 1606, 1625, 1697, *Reedbroke*

1673 (*v.* **hrēod**, **brōc**); *Redgress* 1638, *Redgrese* 1674, *Redgrass*(*e*) 1697, 1726, *Redgrees* 1703, *Red Grase* 1724 (*v.* **hrēod**, **græs** and *Redegres*, Lei **3** 311); *Redloe* 1693 (*v.* **hrēod**, **hlāw**); *Kenelme Renoldes close* 1625; (*above*) *Rike place* 1673 (*v.* **hrēac**, **place**); *Ripepoole* 1601 (*v.* **rip(p)**, **pōl**[1]); *Roundabout* 1630 (*v.* **roundabout**; in f.ns., used of a piece of land with an isolated clump of trees within its limits or of land surrounded by trees, streams or roads); *Rowlotts* ~ 1726, *Rowletts Hedge*, ~ *Furlong* m.18 (*v.* **hecg**; with the surn. *Rowlett*); *Rushpittloe* 1625, 1638, *Russpitt Low* 1673, *Rispett Loe* 1674, *ruspittloe* 1697, *Ruspitt Loe* 1703, 1724, *Rushpitlow* m.18 (*v.* **hlāw**), *Ruspittlow forlong* 1726, *Rushpitlow Furlong* m.18 (*v.* **furlang**), *Ruspitt hole* 1697 (*v.* **hol**[1]) (*v.* **risc**, **pytt**); *rutpoole* 1625, *Ruttpoole* 1638, *Rutt Pool* 1693, *Rutepool or Honey Pot* 1724 (*v.* Honey Pot Lane *supra*) (*v.* **pōl**[1]; with as first el. an unrecorded OE **rūt** 'rough ground' (*v.* Löfvenberg 171)); *Sansoms ashe* 1625, *Santam's Ashe* 1726, *Sansom's Ash Furlong* m.18 (*v.* **æsc**; with the surn. *Sansom*); *Scherdyk* 1477 (e.16), *Sharedick* 1703, 1726 ('boundary ditch', *v.* **scearu**, **dík**); *Seaven acres* 1606, ~ *akers* 1674, *neather* ~ ~, *over seaven acres* 1625, 1638, *Neather* ~ ~, *Over Seaven akers* 1703, *Neather* ~ ~, *Over Seven Acres* 1724, 1726, (*v.* **neoðera**, **uferra**) (*v.* **seofon**, **æcer**); *Seyntmarecroft* 1477 (e.16), *Sancte Marie croft* 1467 × 84, 1477 (e.16) (*v.* **croft**), *Seynt Mary Acre* 1467 × 84 (*v.* **æcer**) (land endowed for the upkeep of a chapel dedicated to the Blessed Virgin Mary within the parish church); *Sedcop* 1606, 1625, *Sedcope* 1638, *Sidcock* 1724 (*v.* **set-copp**); *Sibbertoft hedge* m.18 (*v.* **hecg**; the parish boundary hedge with Sibbertoft which lies to the south-east in Northants.); (*on*) *Slide* 1606, 1625, 1638, 1697, 1724, ~ *forlong* 1726 (*v.* **furlang**) (*v.* **slide** 'a sliding, a slip', with reference to a place on a hillside where there had been a landslip); *smale meadow* 1601, *middle* ~ ~, *neather* ~ ~, *over* ~ ~, *small meadow*(*e*) 1606, 1638, *midle* ~, *nether* ~, *smalmedow* 1625, *Small Middow*(*e*) 1674, 1703, *Neather* ~ ~, *Small meadow* 1697, 1724 (*v.* **neoðera**, **uferra**, **smæl**); *Smiths Corner* m.18 (*v.* **corner**; with the surn. *Smith*); *sneald slade* 1601, *Snealslad*(*e*) 1606, 1638, 1697, 1724, *Snel*(*l*)*slade* 1674, 1703, *Sneal Slade* m.18, *Snealslad forlong* 1726 (*v.* **furlang**) (*v.* **snægl** (**snegl**), **slæd**); *spellow* 1601, *spello* 1606, *over* ~, *spellow*(*e*) 1625, 1638, *Neather* ~, *Over Spellow*(*e*) 1673, 1674, 1703, 1724, *Nether* ~, *Over Spellow*, 1726, m.18 (*v.* **uferra**) (*v.* **spell**, **hlāw**; a former moot site); *Stanslade* 1477 (e.16), *stonye slade* 1601, *Stonyslade* 1606, 1625, 1638, 1697, 1724, *Stoney slade* 1703, *Stonyslade hill* 1606, 1638, 1726, *Stonney slade hill* 1674 (*v.* **stān**, **stānig**, **slæd**); *Stodfold* Hy 3 (*v.* **stōd-fald**); *Stonehill hole* 1606, 1638 (*v.* **stān**, **hyll**, **hol**[1]); *Stonney holes* 1674 (*v.* **stānig**, **hol**[1]); *Ston*(*e*)*pits* 1606, 1625, *Stonepitts* 1638 (*v.* **stān-pytt**); *Sulbie* ~ 1601, *Sulby hedge* m.18 (*v.* **hecg**; a parish boundary hedge), *Sulby Corner* m.18 (*v.* **corner**) (Sulby in Northants. adjoins to the south-east); *Swartingslade* Hy 3 (*v.* **slæd**; with the ODan masc. pers.n. *Swærting* (ON *Svertingr*); *Swartslade* 1601 appears be a reduced late spelling of this f.n.); *the Tenters* 1697 (*v.* **tentour**); *Thedingworth hedge* m.18 (*v.* **hecg**; a parish boundary hedge with Theddingworth which adjoins to the north-east); *Tillies furres* 1606, *Tillys firs*, *Tillies* ~, *Tyllys furs* 1625, *Tillyes firrs*, *Tyllies furrs* 1638, *Tilleys Fores* 1674, ~ *fures* 1703, ~ *furze* 1724, *Tillis Furzes* 1697, *Tylly's* ~ 1726, *Tillys Furze* m.18 (*v.* **fyrs**; with the surn. *Till*(*e*)*y*; cf. *Thomas Tilly* m.18); *Tonghill* 1606, 1625 *et passim* to 1726, *Tumb hill* (sic) 1693, *Tongue Hill* 1726, m.18 (*v.* **tunge**, **hyll**); *the Towne Baulke* 1726 (*v.* **tūn**, **balca**); *Twynymill hill* 1606, *Twinymyll* ~ 1625, 1638, *Twinney Mill Hill* 1674, *Twinemillhill* 1697, *Twinymilhill* 1724, *Twyny Mill* ~ 1726, *Twynnymill hill* m.18 ('the hill with two windmills set apart upon it', *v.* **twyn(n)y**,

myln, **hyll**); *uper hedge* 1606, *Upper hedge* 1625, 1638, 1724 (*v.* **upper**, **hecg**); *walters hill* 1601, *woulters* ~ 1606, 1625, 1638, *Olster*(*s*) *hill* 1674, 1693, *Oltershill* 1697, 1724, *Oulters Hill* 1726, m.18 (*v.* **hyll**; either with the ContGerm masc. pers.n. *Walter* or with its surn. reflex *Walter*(*s*)); *Warclingesslade* 1477 (e.16) (*v.* **slæd**; with the AN masc. pers.n. *Walchelin* (here with AN dissimilation *l-l* > *r-l*)); *waterlag* 1601, *Waterlagg*(*e*) 1674, 1697, 1703, 1726, *ne*(*a*)*ther waterlagg*(*e*) 1606, 1625, *Neather Waterlag* 1724 (*v.* **neoðera**), *Waterlagghook* 1726 (*v.* **hōc**) (*v.* **wæter**, **lagge**); (*on*) *Waterfall* 1726, *Waterfall furlong* m.18 (*v.* **wæter-(ge)fall**); *Waterfurges* 1477 (e.16), 1467 × 84, *Water furrows* 1673 (*v.* **wæter**, **furh**; prob. 'furrows where water tends to lie', *v. the water furrowes* in Billesdon f.ns. (b)); *Wesbury* 1467 × 84, *Westbury* 1477 (e.16) (*v.* **west**, **burh** (**byrig** dat.sg.) and *Bury*, *supra*); *Whebrook*(*e*) 1601, 1625, 1638, 1697, *Wheybrook*(*e*) 1606, 1724, *Wheaye Brucke* 1674, *Wheabrooke* 1703, *Weybrookes* m.18, *Short Wheybrook* 1726 ('whey-coloured stream', *v.* **hwǣg**, **brōc**; alluding to the milky appearance of the water; recorded earlier in Theddingworth); *whinell dole* 1601, *whinnill* ~ 1606, *Whinill* ~ 1625, *Whinnyll dole* 1638, *Whinney* ~ 1674, *Whiny dole* 1697, *Whinidole* 1703, *W*(*h*)*inny Dole* 1724, 1726 ('the land-portion on Whinhill', *v.* **hvin**, **hyll**, **dāl**; the name later adapted with **whinny** 'growing with whin and gorse bushes'); *Willey* 1674, 1697, *Long Willy* 1693, *Furr* ~, *Short Willey* 1703 (*v.* **feor**), *Further* ~, *Long* ~, *Short Willy* 1726, *Long* ~, *Short Whilley* m.18, *willie hooke* 1601, 1606, *Willy*(*e*) *hooke* 1625, *willyhook* 1638, *Will*(*e*)*y Hook* 1724, m.18 (*v.* **hōc**) (*v.* **wilig**, **lēah**); *Willow*(*e*) *Pitt* 1673, 1674, 1697, 1703, 1724, *Willow Pit* m.18 (*v.* **wilig**, **pytt**); *Backside Wilsons Close* 1724 (*v.* **bak-side**; with the surn. *Wilson*); *Windloe* 1601, *Windlow*(*e*) 1606, 1625, 1638, *Windloes* 1697, *Windlose* 1703, *Windlows* m.18 (*v.* **wind**[1], **hlāw**); *Woodfords hedge* m.18 (*v.* **hecg**; with the surn. *Woodford*); *Woodway*(*e*) 1601, 1606 *et passim* to 1726, *v.* **wudu**, **weg**); *Woremill* 1674, *Wormhill* 1726, m.18 (*v.* **hyll**; the first el. could be an OE masc. pers.n. *Wyrm* or *Wyrma* (cf. Wormhill, Db 179) or OE **wyrm**, early used of 'a snake' but later also of a variety of creeping insects, larvae, ticks etc.); *Woostinsplat forlong* 1726, *Woostons Plott Furlong* m.18 (*v.* **plat**[2], **plot**, **furlang**; with the surn. *Woolston*).

Illston on the Hill

ILLSTON ON THE HILL

Elvestone 1086 DB (×2), *Eluestun* 1166 P, *Elueston'* 1176, 1185 ib
Nelvestone, *Neluestone* 1086 DB
Jelverston 1318 Pap
Ilueston' c.1130 LeicSurv, 1176 P (p) *et passim* to 1397 *Wyg*, 1402 *Hazlerigg*, *Iluestona* 1176 ChancR, *Iluestone* 1330 *Hazlerigg*, 1343 *Wyg*
Ylueston' 1181 P, a.1250 (1404) *Laz* (p), *Yluestona* a.1250 (1404) *ib*, *Ylvyston* 1220 MHW
Ilveston' 1203 FF (p), 1205 RotNorm *et freq* to 1438 Banco, 1443 *Wyg et passim* to 1549, 1572 Fine, *Ilvestona* 1190 × 1204 France
Iluiston' m.13 *Wyg*, Hy 3 *Crox et passim* to 1365, 1393 *Wyg*, *Iluyston'* 1393 *ib*
Illeston 1377 SR (p), 1381 LAS (p) *et passim* to 1426, 1435 Banco, *Yleston* 1507 Ipm, *Ileston* 1609 LML
Ilston 1410 *Wyg*, 1419 Banco *et passim* to 1604 SR, 1610 Speed, *Ylston* 1518 Visit, 1526 AAS, *Illston* 1625 *Terrier et freq*
Ylson 1537 MinAccts, 1545 SR, *Ilson* 1572 ib

In origin possibly 'Ælfhere's village, estate', *v.* **tūn**. The OE dithematic masc. pers.n. *Ælfhere* may have been shortened early, while the DB spellings *Elves-*/*Elues-* (and *Nelves-*/*Nelues-* with prosthetic *n*) perhaps show AN substitution of *e* for *æ* (*v.* Feilitzen 47), the unique *Jelverston* in the Papal Registers, which sometimes preserve early forms, echoing with its medial *-er-* the *-here* of the OE dithematic pers.n. A shortened *Ælfhere* may subsequently have become confused with, or even replaced by, the ON masc. pers.n. *Iólfr*. OScand *ió* was on occasion identified with OE *ēo*, giving *e* spellings in DB (*v.* Feilitzen 68), the form *Jelverston* perhaps indicating a sequence **Ælfheres-* > **Elveres-* > *Ielvers-* > *Ilves-*. If *Iólfr* replaced *Ælfhere* rather than having become confused with it, then the settlement may have been one appropriated by a Scandinavian from the Viking army which disbanded in 877. Note that Illston adjoins another township with a possible OE/Scand name, i.e. Rolleston.

The loss of *t* from the group *-ston* in 16th- and 17th-cent. Leics. place-name forms is typical — as *Ylson*, *Ilson*. For shortening of an OE dithematic pers.n., cf. Noseley and perhaps Rolleston, both *infra*. The suffix ~ *on the Hill* is modern.

ASHLANDS, *The Ashlands* 1877 White, 1925 Kelly, *v.* **æsc**, **land**. BARN CLOSE SPINNEY, *Barn Close* 1663 Nichols, 1848 *TA*, 1864 Sale, *v.* **bern**, **spinney**. BARN FM (SELBY'S LODGE 2½"), *Barn Farm* 1969 Sale; cf. *Henry and Thomas Selby, farmers* 1846 White. BLEAK HO., *Bleak House* 1877 White, 1925 Kelly; poss. named after Charles Dickens' *Bleak House*, published 1852–3. BURTON BROOK, *v.* Burton Overy *supra*. CARLTON CURLIEU MANOR HO. is *Illston Lodge* 1835 O, *v.* **loge**; Carlton Curlieu parish adjoins to the south-west. THE COTTAGE. FOURTEEN ACRE SPINNEY, 1848 *TA*, *v.* **æcer** and Fourteen Acres in f.ns. (a) *infra*. FOX AND GOOSE (P.H.), *Fox and Goose* 1863, 1877 White, 1925 Kelly. FOXHOLE SPINNEY, *v.* **fox-hol**, **spinney**. GALBY RD, Galby lying one mile to the north-west. THE HALL, 1877 White; cf. *atte halle* 1381 SR (p), *v.* **atte**, **hall**. ILLSTON GRANGE, 1891 Map, *v.* **grange**; it is *Ilston Lodge* 1750 LeicW, 1798 Nichols, *v.* **loge**. ILLSTON LANE. ILLSTON LODGE, 1846 White, *v.* **loge**. LIMEPIT FM, *lampittis* 1364 *Wyg*, *Lamb Pit* 1848 *TA*, *Lime Pits Farm* 1969 Sale, *v.* **lām-pytt**. LONG PLANTATION, 1835 O, *v.* **plantation**. MAIN ST. MANOR FM, *Manor House Farm* 1848 *TA*, *Manor farm* 1925 Kelly, MANOR HO., *Manor House* 1877 White, *v.* **maner**. NEW INN LANE, cf. *New Inn Farm* 1848 *TA*, 1969 Sale. NOSELEY RD, Noseley lying 2 miles to the south-east. ST MICHAEL'S CHURCH, *Church (St Michael)* 1925 Kelly; earlier is recorded *capellam de Ilveston* 1220 MHW (with MLat *capella* 'a chapel'). THISTLEY CLOSE COTTAGES, *Thistley Close* 1848 *TA*, 1874 Sale, *v.* **thist(e)ly**. THREE GATES, 1835 O, 1877 White, 1925 Kelly, THREE GATES FM, *Three Gates Farm* 1848 *TA*, 1969 Sale, *v.* **þrēo**, **gata**. TURNER'S BARN FM, with the surn. *Turner*. WADE LODGE, 1846 White, *v.* **loge**; cf. *Samuel Wade, farmer* 1863 ib. WASHPIT SPINNEY, *v.* **wæsce**, **pytt**.

FIELD-NAMES

In (a), forms presented without dates are 1848 *TA*; those dated 1806 are *Deed*; 1864 and 1878 are Sale. Forms throughout dated m.13, l.13, 1344, 1353, 1359, 1360, 1364, 1365, 1374, 1379, 1385, 1388, 1390, 1397, 1402 and 1410 are *Wyg*; those dated 1594 are ChancP; 1625 are *Terrier*; 1663 are Nichols.

(a) The Two Acres 1848, Four ~, The Six ~ 1864, The Seven ~, The Ten ~, Fourteen Acres 1848, 1864 (*v.* **æcer**); Ash Cl 1806 (*v.* **æsc**); Ash Furlong (*Ascheforlang* 1388, *v.* **æsc, furlang**); Backside Mdw (*v.* **bak-side**); Barn Mdw (*v.* **bern**); The Blank ('bare land', *v.* **blank**); Bottom Mdw (*v.* **bottom**); Great ~, Little Carrywell, Carrywell Mdw (*Calewell* 1344, *Kalwell* 1388, *Calewelletunge* 1344 (*v.* **tunge**), *v.* **calu, wella**); The Clay Pits (*v.* **cley-pytt**); Coleman's Cl, ~ Mdw (with the surn. *Coleman*); Cottage Holt (*v.* **cotage, holt** and The Cottage *supra*); Coxes Cl (with the surn. *Cox*); Croxton's Cl (with the surn. *Croxton* of a family prob. originally from South Croxton, 7 miles to the north); Dovecoat ~ 1806, Dovecote Cl 1848, 1864 (*Dove Cote Close* 1663), Dovecote Mdw 1848, 1864 (*v.* **dove-cot(e)**); Fallow Cl 1848, 1864 (*v.* **falh**); Far Cl 1874, Far Part 1848 (*v.* **part**); Far ~ ~, First Hill; The Flat Cl 1848, 1864, Bottom ~ ~, Top ~ ~, Flat Mdw (*v.* **flatr**); Footroad Cl 1848, 1864 (*v.* **foot-road**); Fox Hill 1848, 1874 (*v.* **fox**); Gravel Hole Hill (*v.* **gravel, hol**[1]); The Great Cl 1864; Great Mdw 1848 (1663, *v.* **grēat**); Great ~, Middle ~, Road Gulf (cf. *Gulf Meadow* 1663, 1723, *v.* **gulfe**); Hill Cl; Hilly Mdw (*v.* **hyllig**); Little ~, Lower ~, Upper Holt (*v.* **holt**); Home Cl (*v.* **home**); House Cl, ~ Mdw, ~ Pasture; Iacomb's Cl, ~ Mdw (with the surn. *Iacomb*, poss. a local form with prosthetic [j], of the p.n. Acomb (such as Acomb, YW **4** 228); Professor R. Coates wonders if it is rather a version of *Jacob*); Illston Spinny 1835 O (*v.* **spinney**); The Leys 1864, 1874, Leys Cl 1806 (*v.* **leys**); Lodge Cl (*v.* **loge**); Long Close Spinney (*v.* **spinney**); The Meadow 1848, 1864, Meadow Cl 1806; Middle Cl; Far ~ ~, Little ~ ~, Road Mill Fd (*v.* **myln**); The Mowwell (*Morewelle* m.13 (*v.* **mōr**[1], **wella**); Great ~ ~, Orchard Cl, Orchard Close Mdw (*Orchard Close* 1663, *v.* **orceard**); The Paddock (*v.* **paddock**); Pen Yard (cf. *the Pen Yard Close* 1663, *v.* **penn**[2], **geard**); Pinfold (*v.* **pynd-fald**); Plantation Cl (*v.* **plantation**); The Poor Cl (*v.* **pouer(e)**; land dedicated to poor relief or charity); Ram Mdw 1874 (*v.* **ramm**); Red Grass (*v.* **hrēod, græs**); Road Meadow Piece 1848, Road Piece 1864 (*v.* **pece**; closes beside a roadway); Same's Cl (poss. with the surn. *Sam(me)*, the reflex of a pet-form of *Sampson*; but note *Symshyl* in f.ns. (b) which, if related to the modern f.n., may indicate that the surn. is from *Simm*, a pet-form of *Simmond*, or *Sime* of *Simon*); Seed Cl (*v.* **sǣd**; used of grasses sown for one year's mowing or grazing, as distinguished from permanent pasture); Shear Hogs Cl (land on which young sheep were kept, *shear-hogs* being a term applied to sheep between the time when they were weaned until after their first shearing); Shoulder of Mutton (a common f.n. alluding to the shape of the close); Spring Hill 1848, 1864 (*v.* **spring**[2]); Bottom ~ ~, Middle ~ ~, Top Tomblin Cl, Tomblin Close Mdw (with the surn. *Tomblin*, a double diminutive with *-el* and *-in* of *Tom* (*Thomas*)); The Top Mdw (*v.* **top**); Town Cl (*v.* **tūn**); Wheat Cl 1848, 1864 (*v.* **hwǣte**); Bottom ~ ~, Top Willow Sick, Willow Sick Mdw 1848, 1874 (*Willow Seke* 1663, *v.* **wilig, sík**); Winnow Dale (*Wynydale* 1374, *Wynnydale* 1388, *v.* **whinny, dalr**).

(b) *Alby poyl* 1364 (*v.* **bȳ, pōl**[1]; with the ON masc. pers.n. *Áli*, and alluding to a lost farmstead); *Andlongbrodmerche* 1388, *Anlong Brodmersche* 1409 (*v.* **andlang, brād, mersc**); *barlilondys* 1364 (*v.* **bærlic, land**); *le ber'* 1360, *le byry* 1364 (*v.* **bȳre**); *Betuynegatis* 1364 (*v.* **betwēonan, gata**); *Blacmyldlond* 1388 (*v.* **blæc, mylde, land**); *Bikethorn* 1385 (*v.* **þorn**; perh. with the OE masc. pers.n. *Bica* or with the sb. **bica** 'a beak-like projection' used topographically, but note the following *bygthoryn* where this f.n. may belong); *bygthoryn, bygtoryn* 1364, *Nethere Bygthorne* 1402 (*v.* **neoðera**) (*v.* **byg, þorn**; the specific predates the earliest citation in OED in the sense 'of great extent' by some twenty years); *caryltonmer'* 1364 (*v.* **(ge)mǣre**; Carlton

Curlieu parish adjoins to the south); *Coldham* 1594, ~ *Close* 1663 (*v.* **cald**; with **hām** or **hamm**; poss. in origin, a lost early Anglo-Saxon settlement conforming to the pattern of such sites in close relationship to Roman roads, in this case *Via Devana* (Gartree Road), *v.* Barrie Cox, 'The significance of the distribution of English place-names in *-hām* in the Midlands and East Anglia', JEPNS 5 (1971–2), 15–73, reprinted in *Place-Name Evidence for the Anglo-Saxon Invasion and Scandinavian Settlements*, ed. Kenneth Cameron, Nottingham 1975, 55–98); *þe croftys* 1390 (*v.* **þe**, **croft**); *forwordheyl'* 1364, *Forwardhyl* 1388 (*v.* **foreweard**, **hyll**); *foxwellys* 1364, *Foxwelles* 1379 (*v.* **fox**, **wella**); *Fulwelhyl* 1388 (*v.* **hyll**), *fulwelseke* 1388 (*v.* **sík**) (*v.* **fūl**, **wella**); *gorebroyd* 1364 (*v.* **gorebrode**); *Greyston'* 1388 (*v.* **grǣg**[1], **stān**; prob. a boundary marker); *Hawerkil* 1388 (*v.* **hafoc**, **hyll**); *holdedam* 1364 (*v.* **ald**, **damme**); *Howgate* 1362, 1388 (*v.* **gata**; with **hōh** or **haugr**); *Hardyl* m.13 (*v.* **heard**, **hyll**; land hard to till); *Illston mill* 1625 (*v.* **myln**); *Kittuscrofte* 1410 (*v.* **croft**; with the surn. *Kitt*, from *Kytte*, a pet-form of both *Christopher* and *Catharine*); *Lammas Close* 1663 (*v.* **lammas**); *langlond* 1388, *Smalelongelond* l.13, *smalelangelond* 1388 (*v.* **smæl**) (*v.* **lang**[1], **land**); *Little Meadow* 1663, 1723; *le mersecroft* 1364 (*v.* **mersc**, **croft**); *mothoryn* 1364 (*v.* **mōt**, **þorn**; the site of a local assembly); *myddilyl* 1364, *mydylhyl* 1388, *stonymyddilyl* 1364 (*v.* **stānig**) (*v.* **middel**, **hyll**); *Nethirbanlont* 1344 (*v.* **neoðera**, **bēan**, **land**); *Nulane* 1365 (*v.* **nīwe**, **lane**); *Oldebolde* 1353, *Holdbolt* 1364 (*v.* **ald**, **bold**); *Pittiscroft* 1353 (*v.* **pytt**, **croft** and Limepit Fm *supra*); *Robalk* l.13, *Robalcsyke* 1379 (*v.* **sík**) (*v.* **rūh**, **balca**); *Rankey Close* 1663 (with the surn. *Rankey*); *le schortbrod* 1364 (*v.* **sc(e)ort**, **brode**); *Schythaysfurlonges* 1359 (*v.* **scite**, **(ge)hæg**, **furlang**); *Smethe Medewe* 1397 (*v.* **smēðe**[1], **mēd** (**mēdwe** obl.sg.)); *Stone Gate Close* 1663 (*v.* **stān**, **gata**); *atte stonyforthe* 1364 (*v.* **atte**, **stānig**, **ford**); *Symshyl* 1388, *Symesilsike* m.13, *Symmeshulsick* 1379 (*v.* **sík**) (*v.* **hyll**; with the surn. *Simm* or *Sime*; note Same's Cl *supra*); *underwytkotes* 1388 (*v.* **under**, **hwīt**, **cot**); *Watyrforouys* 1364, *Waterforoues* 1402 (*v.* **wæter**, **furh** and *the water furrowes* in Billesdon f.ns. (b)); *Wetelond* 1388 (*v.* **hwǣte**, **land**); *Weyrdic* 1364 (*v.* **weyour**, **dík**); *Wrong(e)lond* 1344, 1385 (*v.* **wrang**, **land**); *yolwell'* 1402, *Lyttelyolwell'* 1359 (*v.* **lȳtel**) (*v.* **wella**; with the OE masc. pers.n. *Iola*); *yommanyshorstede* 1364, *Yommaneshorsted* 1388 (*v.* **hors**, **stede**; either with **yoman** or its surn. reflex *Yeoman*).

Kibworth Beauchamp

KIBWORTH BEAUCHAMP

Chiburde 1086 DB, *Chiburd'* c.1130 LeicSurv, *Chibwrthe* 1166 LN
Chiborne (sic) 1086 DB
Chibeworth c.1150 Nichols (p), *Chibeword'* l.12 *GarCart* (p)
Kibwrd' c.1130 LeicSurv, *Kibwrth(e)* c.1130 ib, 1220 GildR *et passim* to 1293 OSut, 1298 ib (p), *Kibworth(e)* 1278 IpmR, 1308 Abbr, 1334 *Rut* (p) *et passim* to 1576 LibCl, 1604 SR *et freq*
Kibewrd(a) c.1160 Dane (p), 1209 × 35 RHug, *Kibewrth* 1265 Pat (p), 1276 RGrav (p), *Kibeworth* 1309 Cl
Kibbeworth(e) l.12 *Rut* (p), 1223 ClR *et freq* to 1342 Pat, 1344 *ShR* (p) *et passim* to 1386 Cl, 1405 PRep, *Kibbewrth'* 1263, 1275 RGrav *et passim* to 1290, 1291 OSut, *Kibbewurth'* 1233 Cur (p), 1290, 1294, 1296 OSut
Kybewrth 1220 RHug, *Kybeworth* c.1308, 1315 Ipm
Kybworth(e) 1239 RGros, 1242 Fees *et freq* to 1429 Pat, 1440 Pap *et passim* to 1511 Fine, 1535 VE, *Kybwrth(e)* 1254 Val, 1273 *Wyg*, 1278 Ipm
Kybbeworth(e) 1239 RGros, 1252 Fine *et freq* to 1405 PRep, 1443 *Wyg et passim* to 1510 Visit, 1513 LP, *Kybbewrth'* 1250 Cur, 1265 Misc, 1293 Ipm, *Kybbewurth'* 1291, 1294 OSut
Kybburth(e) 1311 *Wyg* (p), 1311 GildR (p)

Affixes are variously added as:
alia ~ c.1130 LeicSurv
~ *Beaucham* 1306 Pat, ~ *Be(a)uchamp(e)* 1315 ib, 1316 FA *et passim* to 1607 LML *et freq*
Nether ~ 1722 LML

'Cybba's enclosure', *v.* **worð**. The masc. pers.n. *Cybba* is OE. Some early spellings have AN orthographic *ch* for *c* [k] before *i*. The manor of Kibworth Beauchamp was held by *Walterus de Bello Campo* c.1130 LeicSurv, *Angareta de Bello Campo* 1239 RGros and remained with this family as late as *Ricardus de Bello Campo* 1407 Cl, while a *Thomas Beauchamp* is recorded associated with the manor in 1428 FA.

Note the prefixing of MLat *alia* 'the other (of two)'. The township adjoins Kibworth Harcourt *infra* but lies on slightly lower ground, hence *Nether ~*.

THE BANK, 1918 Sale, *v.* **banke**. BEAUCHAMP GRANGE, 1918 Sale, 1925 Kelly, *v.* **grange**. CHURCH HILL, 1694, 1700 *Terrier et passim* to 1771 *ib*, 1927 Sale, *v.* St Wilfred's Church *infra*. COACH AND HORSES (P.H.), *Coach and Horses* 1846, 1863 White, 1925 Kelly. ETTINGTON, 1925 Kelly; presum. a transferred name, *v.* Wa 253. FEATHERBED LANE, *v.* **feather-bed**, dial. for 'spongy ground, a quagmire'; cf. Feather Bed Lane, Ru 99 and 209. FLECKNEY RD, 1780 *EnclA*, Fleckney lying 3 miles to the west. HIGH ST, 1918 Sale; it is *the Street* 1708 (18) *Terrier*. KIBWORTH STATION, *The Railway Station* 1918 Sale; on the former *Leicester and Hitchin Railway* 1863 White. THE KNOLL, 1925 Kelly, *v.* **cnoll**. THE LOCK HO., *v.* **lock**; on the Grand Union Canal. MASON FM, cf. *John Mason, grazier* 1925 Kelly. MILL LANE, *v.* Mill Fd in f.ns. (a). MOSS FM, *Mosse* 1694 *Terrier*, *Mose* 1700 *ib*, *Moss* 1708, 1715, 1724 *ib*, *Nether ~*, *Over Mosse* 1694 *ib* (*v.* **uferra**), *Nether ~*, *Upper Mosse* l.17 *ib*, *Neather ~*, *Uper Moss(e)* 1700, c.1720 *ib*, *Lower ~*, *Up(p)er Moss* 1708, c. 1715, 1724, 1745 *ib*, *v.* **mos**. NEW TOWN, *Newtown* 1925 Kelly, *v.* **tūn**. OLD SWAN (P.H.), *Old Swan* 1846, 1863, 1877 White, *Old Swan Inn* 1925 Kelly. RAILWAY ARMS (P.H.), *Railway Arms* 1863, 1877 White, 1925 Kelly; it is *Railway Tavern* 1846 White, *v.* Kibworth Station *supra*. THE RECTORY, 1877 White, 1925 Kelly, *The Rectory House* 1821 *Terrier*, *v.* **rectory**; earlier is *The Parsonage House* 1708, c.1720, 1724, 1745, 1771 *ib*, *v.* **personage**. ROYAL OAK (P.H.) (lost), *Royal Oak* 1877 White, 1925 Kelly. ST WILFRED'S CHURCH, *the Church* 1708 *Terrier*, *Kibworth Church* 1708 (18) *ib*, *Church (St Wilfred)* 1846, 1863, 1877 White, 1925 Kelly; it is earlier recorded as *ecclesia de Kybewrth* 1220 MHW, *~ de Kibbeworth* 1294, 1371 *Pat*, *ecclesiam de Kybworth* 1239 RGros, *ecclesie parochialis de Kybworth* 1399, 1554 *Pat* (with MLat *parochialis* 'parochial, of the parish'). Note also *capelle libere de Kybbeworth* 1399 *ib* (with MLat *capella* 'a chapel' and *libera* 'free'). SMEETON RD, 1780 *EnclA*, Smeeton Westerby lying one mile to the south. STATION ST, *v.* Kibworth Station *supra*. TOP LOCK, *v.* The Lock Ho. *supra*. THE WARREN, 1925 Kelly, *v.* **wareine**. WEIR FM, WEIR HO., *Weir house* 1925 Kelly, WEIR RD, 1918 Sale, 1925 Kelly; *Wyer* 1708 (18) *Terrier*, *the Wire* 1724 *ib*, *v.* **weyour**. WHITE STACKS FM.

No early forms have been found for the following street-names: BULLER ST, COUNCIL ST, DOVER ST, GLADSTONE ST, HALFORD RD, HARCOURT RD, HILLCREST AVE, NEW RD, IMPERIAL RD, PROSPECT RD, WHITE ST.

FIELD-NAMES

In (a), forms dated 1771 and 1821 are *Terrier*; those dated 1780 are *EnclA*; 1918 and 1927 are Sale. Forms throughout dated 1394 are Banco; those dated 1609 are *Map*; 1694, l.17, 1700, 1708, 1708 (18), c.1715, c.1720, 1724 and 1745 are *Terrier*.

(a) The Allotment Fd 1918 (*v.* **allotment**); Ashpools 1771 (*Ashpoole* 1694, c.1715, c.1720, *~ furlong* l.17, 1700, *~ forlong* 1745 (*v.* **furlang**), *v.* **æsc**; surviving forms indicate **pōl**[1] as the generic, but this may well be one of a number of places where poles or stakes of ash-wood were got, *v.* **pāl** and cf. Ashpole Spinney in Nevill Holt *infra*, Ash Pole Spinney in Leesthorpe (Lei **2** 239) and in Cosby, Guthlaxton Hundred); Banwell 1780 (1609, *v.* **wella**; poss. with the OE masc. pers.n. *Bana*); Barn Cl 1821 (*v.* **bern**); Bearly furlong 1771 (c.1715, c.1720, *Barley furlong* 1694, l.17, 1708, 1708 (18), 1724, *~ forlong* 1745, *Barly furlong* 1700, *v.* **bærlic**); Berry's Fd 1927 (with the surn. *Berry*); Big Mdw 1918; Bottom Cl 1918 (*v.* **bottom**); Bray Furlong 1771 (1694, l.17, c.1715, c.1720, *~ forlong* 1745, *Brey furlong* 1700, *v.* **brēg**); Broad Green 1771 (*Broad Green*(*e*) 1694, l.17 *et passim* to 1745, *Brode Green* 1700, *Broad Green*(*e*) *Hole* 1694, l.17 (*v.* **hol**[1]), *v.* **brād**, **grēne**[2]); the Brook 1821 (*v.* **brōc**); Bush Furlong 1771 (*v.* **busc**); Long ~, Short ~, Cars 1771 (*Long ~*, *Short ~*, *Carres* 1694, l.17, 1745, *Long ~*, *Short ~*, *Cares* 1700, 1708, *Long ~*, *Short ~*, *Carrs* 1708 (18), c.1715, c.1720, 1724 (*v.* **kjarr**); Church Fd 1771 (*v.* **feld**; one of the great open-fields of the township, earlier called *Stubston Feild*, *infra*), Church Hill Cl 1821 (*v.* Church Hill *supra*), Church Well 1780 (*The Church Well* 1609, *v.* **wella**) (*v.* St Wilfred's Church *supra*); Coal Pit Lane 1771 (*Colepitt Lane* 1694, l.17, c.1715, *Colepit Lane* 1700, 1708 *et passim* to 1745, *Colepit lane end* c.1720 (*v.* **lane-ende**), *v.* **col-pytt**, **lane**; a place where charcoal was made); Colwell Cls 1821 (*v.* **cōl**[2], **wella**); Cricket Mdw 1918 (for the game of cricket); Cryndle Dyke 1918 (*v.* **crundel**, **dík**); The Dairy Cl 1918 (*v.* **deierie**); Dams Hadland 1771 (*v.* **hēafod-land**) ((*at*) *Damms* 1708, 1708 (18), c.1720, 1724 (*v.* **damme** and *Saddington Dammes*, *infra*); Dilcus Furlong 1771 (cf. *Delcross Meer* 1708, 1708 (18), 1724 (*v.* **(ge)mǣre**), *v.* **cros**; the first el. may be a reduced **delf** since *dell* appears to be restricted to southern and south-eastern counties); Drove Cl 1918 (*v.* **drāf**); Far Cl 1918; Garden Ground 1927 (*v.* **gardin**, **grund**; used for horticulture); Gas Cl 1918 (note *the Gas Works* 1918); Great Cl or Barn Cl 1821; Grick 1771 ((*upon*) *Gricke* 1700, (*on*) *Grick* 1708, 1708 (18), 1724, 1745, *the Grick* c.1715, *att Grick* c.1720, *Grick furlong* 1694, l.17, *Grick Meare* 1694, 1745 (*v.* **(ge)mǣre**); a pre-English hill-name, PrW **creig** 'hill', cf. Crick, Nth 68 and *Creak Hill* in Stonton Wyville f.ns. (b); it is uncertain whether the surviving initial consonant represents the voicing of *c* > *g* or is a 17th-cent. misreading of upper case *C* for *G*, followed by continual copying in a Glebe Terrier series); Hog Lane 1780 (*v.* **hogg**); Home Cl 1918 (*v.* **home**); Hovel Cl, ~ Mdw 1918 (*v.* **hovel**); King's Stone 1918 ((*on*) *Kingstone*, c.1715, c.1720, *v.* *Kingstocke Bridge furlong* in f.ns. (b)); Kilput Hole 1771 (*Kippex hole* 1708, 1708 (18), *Killpacks ~* c.1715, c.1720, *Kippecks hole* 1724, *v.* **hol**[1]), Kilput Leys 1771 (*Kilpex ~*, *Kippex Leas* 1708, *the Kilpex ~*, *Kippex Leys* 1708 (18), *~ Leyes* 1724, *Kilpot Layes* 1745, *v.* **leys**) (with the surn. *Kippax*); Knapp's Cl 1918 (with the surn. *Knapp*); Langton Gate 1771 (1700, *v.* **gata**; the road to West Langton which lies 2 miles to the south-east); High ~, Low Lickleys 1771 (*High* ~, *Low Licklisse* 1.17, ~, ~ *Licklyes* 1708, ~, ~ *Lickless* c.1715, c.1720, ~, ~ *Lyckleyes* 1724, *Low Lickless meere* c.1715, c.1720 (*v.* **(ge)mǣre**), 'pasture where wild garlic grows', *v.* **lēac**, **lǣs**); Little Cl 1821, 1918, 1927, ~ Mdw 1918, 1927); Long Yatts 1771 (*Long yeates* 1694, 1.17, 1708, ~ *yeats* 1745 1745 (*v.* **langet**); Lords Close 1771 (1694, 1.17 *et passim* to 1724, *v.* **lord**; note *Lord Hamiltons Close*, *infra*); Middle Cl 1918, ~ Fd 1927; Milestone 1918 (*v.* **mīl-stān**; a close so called *at the corner of the turnpike road* 1918); Mill Fd 1771 ((*the*) *Mill feild* 1694, 1700 *et passim* to 1745, *the Milfield* 1.17, *v.* **feld**; one of the great open-fields), Mill Furlong 1771 (1694, 1708, c.1715, c.1720, *v.* **furlang**), Mill Gutter 1771 (1694, 1700 *et passim* to 1745, *Millgutter furlong* 1694, *v.* **goter**) (*v.* **myln**); Moss Cl 1821, Moss Leys 1771 (*v.* **leys**) (*v.* Moss Fm *supra*); Muck Hill 1918 (*v.* **muk**); Nacher 1771 (*Natue furlong* 1694, 1.17, ~ *forlong* 1745, *Natu* 1700, c.1715, c.1720, *Nateyue* 1708, *Nate-you* 1724; earlier forms are needed, but 'the yew-tree under which cattle gather' may be thought of, *v.* **nēat**, **īw**); Nether Fd 1771 (*the Nether Feild* 1694, 1.17, 1708, *Neather feild* 1700, c.1715, c.1720, ~ *field* 1724, *v.* **neoðera**, **feld**; one of the great open-fields); Nutts Leys 1771 (*v.* **leys**; either with the surn. *Nutt*, an original by-name from ME *nutte* 'a nut', of a man with a round head or a brown complexion, or with **hnutu**, cf. *Nutts Nook* in Cranoe f.ns. (b)); Nichol's Cl 1918 (with the surn. *Nichol*); Pebberday's Mdw 1918 (with the surn. *Pebberday*; either a form of *Pepperday* or *Peberdy*); Port Hill 1771 (1694, 1.17, 1700, *Portle* c.1715, c.1720, 1724, *Portel* 1745; if an early market site, then *v.* **port**[2], **hyll**, but poss. is a reduced **port-wey**, **hyll**, the hill being that over which or beside which a road to Leicester ran, *v.* Cox[2] 81 for discussion of the common Port Hill); Priest Holm 1771 (*Prestholme* 1694, 1708, 1724, *Presthome* 1.17, 1700, *Priestholme* 1708 (18), 1724, *Preist holme* 1708 (18), 1745), Priest Holm Piece 1771 (*Prestholme piece* c.1715, *Prest holme peice* c.1720, *v.* **pece**) (*v.* **prēost**, **holmr**); Ranglands 1771 (1694, 1708 *et passim* to 1724, ~ *furlong* 1.17, *Wranglands forlong* 1745 (*v.* **furlang**), *v.* **wrang**, **land**); Red Hill 1771, Reddle Cl 1821 ((*on*) *Reddle* 1694, c.1715, c.1720, 1724, *Reddal* 1708, *Roddle* 1745, *Reddle furlong* 1.17, 1700, *Reddle meare* 1694, 1.17, c.1715, c.1720, *Roddle meare* 1745 (with **(ge)mǣre** or **mere**[1]), *v.* **hyll**; either with **rēad** or **hrēod**); Road Cl 1918 (beside a roadway); School Balk Cls 1821 (*v.* **balca**; alluding to *The Free Grammar School* 1846, 1863 White, (*the Schoole* 1745)); Six Cocks 1918 ((*the*) *Six Cocks* 1708 (18), *v.* **six**, **cocc**[1] and *Four Cocks*, *infra*); Smith Mdw 1771 (1694, 1700 *et passim* to 1724, *Smiths Meadow* 1708; with the surn. *Smith*); The Spinney 1821, Spinney Cl 1821, 1918 (*v.* **spinney**); Stoney Path 1771 (*Ston(e)ypath* 1694, 1700 *et passim* to 1724, ~ *furlong* 1.17, ~ *forlong* 1745, *v.* **stānig**, **pæð**); Suffurlong 1771 (*Suffir Long* 1694, (*the*) *Sufferlong* 1700, 1724, (*on*) *Suffer long* 1708, *Sufforlong* c.1715, *Sufferlong furlong* 1694, 1.17, 1708, 1724, *Sofferlong forlong* 1745; in origin 'the south furlong' of the great Nether Fd, *v.* **sūð**, **furlang**, but adapted popularly as 'Suffer Long', since the soil here may have been hard to till); Top Fd 1927 (*v.* **top**); Town End Lees 1918 (*v.* **tūn**, **ende**, **leys**); Upper Kibworth Mear 1771 (*v.* **(ge)mǣre**; the parish boundary of Kibworth Harcourt).

(b) *John Abbots hadland* 1.17 (*v.* **hēafod-land**); *acres gate* c.1715 (*v.* **æcer**, **gata**); *the Bailey-Hook* 1708 (18), *the Baily hook*(*e*) 1724, 1745 (*v.* **baillif**, **hōc**); *Beck furlong* 1708, 1708 (18), 1724 (*v.* **bekkr**, **furlang**); *Broad arse* 1708, 1708 (18), c.1715, c.1720, 1724 (perh. **brād**, **ears**, but may belong with the following f.n.); *Broadhurst* 1694, ~ *furlong* 1.17, ~ *forlong* 1745 (*v.* **brād**, **hyrst**); *Butlins* ~ 1708,

1708 (18), 1724, *Butlings Close* c.1720 (with the surn. *Butlin*); *Carres gate* 1694, l.17, 1745, *Cars* ~ l.17, *carrs gate* 1708, 1708 (18), c.1720, 1724 (*v*. **gata**), *Carrs Meer*(*e*)*s* 1708, 1708 (18) (poss. with **mere**[1] in its sense 'wetland'; cf. the following f.n.), *Carrs Mire* 1724 (*v*. **mýrr**), *Cars piece* l.17 (*v*. **pece**), *Carres well* 1694, 1745, *Cars Well* l.17, *Careswell* 1700, *Carrs Well* 1708, 1708 (18), c.1715, 1724 (*v*. **wella**) (*v*. Cars *supra*); (*the*) *Church Bridge* 1609, 1635 (*v*. **brycg**), *Church hadland* l.17 (*v*. **hēafod-land**), *The Church Leas* 1609 (*v*. **leys**), *the Church Swath*(*es*) 1609, 1635, 1708, ~ ~ *Swarth* 1708 (18) (*v*. **swathe**) (*v*. St Wilfred's Church *supra*); *Cuttings Close* c.1715 (*v*. **cutting**); *dale meare* 1694, (*the*) *Dale meere* 1700, c.1715, *Dale meeare* 1745, *dale meare furlong* l.17 (*v*. **dalr**; with **(ge)mǣre** or **mere**[1] 'wetland'); *Eastwoods Close* 1694, l.17, *Eastwoods* 1708 (18), ~ *Piece* 1724 (*v*. **pece**) (with the surn. *Eastwood*); *the Fielding Ground* 1708 (18), 1724 (*v*. **filden**, **felden**, **grund**); *Fintch foorde* 1609, *Finch Foord* c.1715, c.1720 (*v*. **finc**, **ford**); *Fleckney hedge* c.1720 (*v*. **hecg**; the parish boundary hedge of Fleckney which adjoins to the west); *the flitting meres* 1700 (*v*. **(ge)mǣre**; with **flytting** or **fliten**); *Four Cocks* 1708 (18) (*v*. **fēower**, **cocc**[1] and Six Cocks *supra*); *Foxton hedge* c.1715, c.1720 (*v*. **hecg**; a parish boundary hedge with Foxton which adjoins for a short stretch to the south-east); *Gallow meare* c.1715 (*v*. **calu**, **(ge)mǣre**); *the Gulfe* 1694, l.17, 1700, (*in*) *the Gulph* c.1715, c.1720, 1745, *Gulph furlong* 1708, 1708 (18), 1745 (*v*. **gulfe**); *the Haggs* 1708, 1708 (18) (*v*. **hǫgg**); *halfe acers* 1700, *halfe acre leys* c.1715 (*v*. **leys**) (*v*. **half-aker**); *Mr Halfords Hadland* l.17 (*v*. **hēafod-land**); *Haywards hill* 1694, c.1715, c.1720, *Hewards hill* l.17, 1708, 1708 (18), 1724, 1745, *huards hill* 1700, *Hewards nooke* l.17 (*v*. **nōk**) (prob. with **heiward**, but otherwise with its surn. reflex *Hayward*/*Heyward*, cf. *hauards dole* in Burton Overy f.ns. (b), *Hawards forlonge* in Husbands Bosworth f.ns. (b) and *Hewedesmedewe* in Houghton on the Hill f.ns. b)); *the Holme* 1708 (18), 1724, 1745, *Holm headley* 1708 (18), *Holme Hadley* 1745 (*v*. **headley**), *Holme Meadow* 1708 (18) (*v*. **holmr**); *Edward Iliffes Hadland* l.17, *Thomas Iliffs Hadland* 1708, ~ ~ *headland* 1708 (18) (*v*. **hēafod-land**), *Richard Iliffes headley* 1694, *Edward Iliffes Hadley* l.17 (*v*. **headley**), *Edw. Illiffes ley* l.17 (*v*. **ley**[2]); *Killpacks bush* c.1715, c.1720 (*v*. **busc**), *Kilpex head* 1708, 1708 (18), ~ *hade* 1724 (*v*. **hēafod**), *Kilpex hedge* 1708, 1708 (18), 1724, (*at*) *Killpacks hedge* c.1715, c.1720 (*v*. **hecg**) (*v*. Kilput Hole *supra*); *Kingstocke Bridge furlong* (sic) 1694, l.17, *Kingston bridge furlong* 1708, 1708 (18), 1724, ~ ~ *forlong* 1745 (*v*. **brycg**, **furlang**), *Kingston leys* c.1715, c.1720 (*v*. **leys**) (in origin perh. 'the king's place of assembly', *v*. **cyning**, **stoc** and note *the Stow Meadow*, *infra*; **stoc** may have been replaced in the compound by **stān** in the sense 'a standing stone' which could have been a marker for assemblies; note that Wistow adjoins to the north-west, traditionally the site of the murder of the Mercian prince Wigstan at a royal council meeting in 849; Kibworth Beauchamp with Wistow may well have been part of a large royal estate; but note also the earliest surviving form *Kingster* 1636 which is recorded for adjoining Smeeton Westerby, which may indicate **sterne** 'property, estate' as the generic); *the Kings way* 1694, *the Kings highway* l.17, 1700 *et passim* to 1745 (*v*. **king**, **hēah-weg**); *Langton hedge* c.1715, c.1720 (*v*. **hecg**; a parish boundary hedge, West Langton adjoining to the south-east); *High* ~ ~, *Low Littell hill* 1694, *High* ~ ~, *Low Little Hill* 1700, 1771; *Lord Hamiltons Close*, ~ ~ *hedge* (*v*. **hecg**) 1745; *the Lower feild* 1745 (*v*. **feld**; one of the great open-fields, usually called Nether Fd *supra*); *the Meadow* 1745; *the Mearis* 1694, *the Meares* l.17, 1700, c.1715, (*in*) *the Meeres* 1708, 1724 (with **mere**[1] or **(ge)mǣre**); *the old mill* c.1715, c.1720 (*v*. **ald**), *the Mill Balk* 1708, c.1720, ~ ~ *Baulk* 1708 (18), c.1715, 1724 (*v*. **balca**), *Millmeare* 1694, 1745, *Milmeare* l.17 (with **mere**[1] or **(ge)mǣre**) (*v*. **myln**); *Mony* ~ 1708, *Money hole* 1708 (18), 1724 (*v*. **moneye**, **hol**[1]; either naming land subject to a special money payment or alluding to the discovery of a buried hoard); *Moss hedge* c.1715, c. 1720 (*v*. **hecg** and Moss Fm *supra*); *Pepin Meare* 1694 (with **(ge)mǣre** or **mere**[1] (in the sense 'wetland'); with the surn. *Pep(p)in*, cf. *Reginaldus Peppin* 1205 Cur of Leics.); *Saddington Dammes* 1694, l.17, ~ *Dames* 1700, ~ *Dams* 1745 (*v*. **damme**; Saddington parish adjoins to the south-west); *the School(e) ground* 1708, 1724 (*v*. **grund**), *the School headland* 1694 (*v*. **hēafod-land**), *the School(e) Land* 1694, 1708, 1724, 1745 (*v*. **land**), *the School Swathes* 1694 (*v*. **swathe**) (with reference to the Free Grammar School); *Sliffurlong* c.1720 (*v*. **slif(u)**, **furlang**); *Smeeton Meare* 1694, ~ *meere* 1700, *Smeaton Meer* 1708, 1724 (*v*. **(ge)mǣre**; the boundary with Smeeton Westerby parish which adjoins to the south); *Mr Smith's Headland* c.1715, c.1720 (*v*. **hēafod-land**); *Speeds Dole* 1708 (18), 1724, 1745 (*v*. **dāl**; with the surn. *Speed*); *the Stow Meadow* 1708, 1708 (18) (*v*. **stōw** 'a place of assembly', cf. *Kingstocke*, *supra*); *Stubston* ~, *Stubston's Feild* 1694, *Stubtons* ~ l.17, 1708, *Stubsons* ~ 1700, *Stubbtons* ~ 1708, *Stub(b)ton's* ~ 1708 (18), *Stubstance* ~ c.1715, c.1720, *Stubbons* ~ 1724, *Stubstones Feild* 1745 (*v*. **feld**; one of the great open-fields, later called Church Fd *supra*), *Stubston's headland* 1694, *Stubtons* ~ l.17, *Stubsons hadland* 1700, *Stubstance headland* c.1715, c.1720, *Stubston's hadland* 1745 (*v*. **hēafod-land**); *Stubston's Well* 1694, *Stubtons* ~ l.17, *Stubsons* ~ 1700, *Stubbons* ~ 1708, 1724, *Stubstance* ~ c.1715, c.1720, *Stubston's Well* 1745 (*v*. **wella**) (an early settlement site, 'the farmstead among the tree-stumps', *v*. **stubb**, **tūn**); *the Swathes* 1694, l.17, 1700, *the Swaithes* 1745 (*v*. **swathe**); *Warwick baulk* c.1715, ~ *balk* c.1720 (*v*. **balca**; with the surn. *Warwick*); *the Watering att Moss* c.1715, c.1720 (*v*. **wateryng** and Moss Fm *supra*); *Welcotemor* 1394 (*v*. **wella**, **cot**, **mōr**[1]); *Wistow Enclosure* 1708, 1724 (*v*. **enclosure**), *Wisto(w) Close* c.1715, c.1720 (Wistow parish adjoins to the north-west); (*the*) *Wyer hedge* 1708, 1708 (18), *the Wire hedge* 1724 (*v*. **hecg** and Weir Fm *supra*).

Kibworth Harcourt

KIBWORTH HARCOURT

For forms and interpretation of the place-name Kibworth, *v.* Kibworth Beauchamp *supra*.

Affixes are variously added to the name of this township as:

Vuer ~ 1209 × 35 RHug, *Over* ~ 1705 LML, *Upper* ~ 1694, 1708 *et passim to* 1771 *Terrier*

~ *Harecurt* 1242 Fees, 1271 Fine, 1293 Ipm, 1303 Pat, ~ *Harecourt(e)* 1308 Abbr, 1315 Cl *et passim* to 1500 Banco, ~ *Harcourt(e)* 1500 ib, 1511 Fine *et freq*

The manor was held by *Iuo de Haruecurt* l.12 *GarCart*, by *Robertus de Harewecurt* 1202 Ass and remained with this family as late as *Johannes de Harecourt* 1326 Cl, *Nicholas Harecourt* 1327 SR. The settlement lies on ground higher than its immediate neighbour Kibworth Beauchamp, hence *Vuer* ~, *Over* ~ 'higher, upper', *v.* **uferra**.

ADMIRAL NELSON (P.H.) (lost), *Admiral Nelson* 1846, 1863, 1877 White, 1925 Kelly. ALBERT ST, formerly Hog Lane *infra*; no doubt renamed in honour of the marriage of Albert of Saxe-Coburg-Gotha to Queen Victoria in 1840. BRIDGE FM. CARLTON RD, Carlton Curlieu lying 2 miles to the north-east. THE CITY, an ironical name for a small group of houses, cf. The City in Empingham, Ru 140. FOX (P.H.) (lost), *The Fox* 1846, 1863 White; poss. to be identified with *Fox and Hounds* 1877 White, but in 1918 Sale, a messuage is described as being formerly *The Fox*. HALL CLOSE, 1798 Nichols, *v.* Kibworth Hall *infra*. HARBOROUGH RD, Market Harborough lying 5 miles to the south-east. KIBWORTH BRIDGE, 1825 *Terrier*, 1835 O. KIBWORTH COTTAGE (2½"), *The Cottage* 1925 Kelly. KIBWORTH HALL, 1846, 1863, 1877 White, 1925 Kelly. KIBWORTH HO. (2½"), *Kibworth House* 1877 White, 1925 Kelly. LEICESTER RD, Leicester lying 8 miles to the north-west. THE LODGE, 1918 Sale, *v.* **loge**. MAIN ST. MANOR HO., *The Manor House* 1863, 1877 White, 1925 Kelly, *v.* **maner**. MARSH DRIVE. THE MUNT (local), *v.*

mont, **munt(e)**. NAVIGATION (P.H.) (lost), *Navigation* 1846 White, *Navigation Inn* 1863 ib. NORTHFIELDS, 1925 Kelly, cf. *North feelde* 1609 *Map*, (*The*) *North Feild*(*e*) 1635 *ib*, 1694, 1700, c.1715, c.1720 *Terrier*, *v*. **norð**, **feld**; one of the great open-fields of the township. PYWELL'S LOCK, *v*. **lock**, with the surn. *Pywell*; on the Grand Union Canal. ROSE AND CROWN (P.H.), *Rose and Crown* 1846, 1863, 1877 White, 1918 Sale, *Rose and Crown Hotel* 1925 Kelly. SECOND LOCK, *v*. **lock**; as for Pywell's Lock *supra*. SPINNEY CLOSE (local), *Spinney Close* 1925 Kelly, *v*. **spinney**. TAYLOR'S TURNOVER LOCK, a lock on the Grand Union Canal at which the towpath changes sides and at which a horse could cross the waterway while still drawing a barge, without the need to unhitch the tow rope; with the surn. *Taylor*. THREE HORSESHOES (P.H.). TUR LANGTON RD, Tur Langton lying 2 miles to the east. WARWICK RD poss. remembers the surn. *Warwick* as in *Warwick baulk* c.1715 in adjacent Kibworth Beauchamp. WESTFIELD, 1925 Kelly, *West feelde* 1609 *Map*, *The Weste Feilde* 1635 *ib*, *West Feild* 1694, l.17, 1700 *Terrier*, *v*. **west**, **feld**; one of the great open-fields. WINDMILL FM, *the Windmill* 1821 *Terrier*; this windmill is *Mr Raies Mill* 1635 *Map*, *v*. **wind-mylne**. WISTOW RD is *Wistow Lane* 1918 Sale, Wistow lying 2½ miles to the north-west.

FIELD-NAMES

In (a), forms dated 1771 and 1821 are *Terrier*; those dated 1780 are *EnclA*. Forms throughout dated 1598, 1611 and 1626 are *Deed*; those dated 1609 and 1635 are *Map*; 1628 are Ipm; 1694, l.17, 1700, 1708, c.1715, c.1720, 1724 and 1745 are *Terrier*.

(a) Bremish 1771 (1708, 1745, *Bremartch Medow* 1609 ('broad marsh', *v*. **breiðr**, **mersc**; cf. Braymish in Little Bowden f.ns. (a), Bremish in Smeeton Westerby f.ns. (b)); Great Cl 1821; Hog Lane 1780 (*v*. **hogg**; a swine market was held here); Holme Cl 1821 (*v*. **holmr**); Langton Meer South Cl, ~ ~ Middle Cl or Gravel Pit Cl (*v*. **gravel**, **pytt**) 1821 (*v*. **(ge)mǣre**; Tur Langton parish adjoins to the east); Parson's Acre 1771 (*the Parsons Acre* 1694, l.17, 1708, 1724, 1745, *Parsons acer* 1700, *v*. **persone**, **æcer**); the Turnpicke Road 1821 (*v*. **turnepike**; the main road to Leicester); West Cl 1821.

(b) *Alldridge Home* 1609 (*v*. **holmr**; with the surn. *Aldridge*); *Mr Barnet's hedge* 1609 (*v*. **hecg**); *Beles Poole* 1609 (*v*. **pōl**[1]; with the surn. *Beel*, a reflex of OFr *bele* 'beautiful', used sometimes as a woman's name); *Nether* ~ ~, *Upper Broad Meadow* 1609 (*v*. **brād**); *Burges's hedge* 1745 (*v*. **hecg**; with the surn. *Burges*, cf. *Philippus Burgis* 1199 RFL of Leicester); *Burton Brigge* 1609 (*v*. **brycg**; at the parish boundary with Burton Overy to the north); *Carres* l.17, ~ *gate* 1694, *Cares gate* 1700 (*v*. **gata**),

Carr Meadow Leas 1609 (*v.* **leys**) (*v.* **kjarr**); *Colle Brigg foorde* 1609 (*v.* **cole**, **brycg**, **ford**); *Comes hedge* 1609 (*v.* **hecg**; with the surn. *Coom*); *Cowpaster* 1635 (*v.* **cū**, **pasture**); *Coxshoute* 1609 (*v.* **cocc-scēte**); *Cronsick* 1609 (*v.* **cron**, **sík**); *Debdale* 1609, 1635, ~ *hill* 1609 (*v.* **dēop**, **dalr**); *East*(*e*) *Feild*(*e*) 1609, 1635, 1694, l.17, 1700 (*v.* **ēast**, **feld**; one of the great open-fields); *Farnhill* 1609 (*v.* **fearn**); *Fishpoole close* 1628 (*v.* **fisc-pōl**; the site of medieval fish ponds); *Flax Medow* 1609 (poss. with a metathesized **flask** 'swampy grassland' rather than **fleax**, if *Flax* is not a memory of past arable use); *Green Martch* 1609 (*v.* **grēne**[1], **mersc**); *Hall Pasture* 1635 (*v.* **pasture**), *Hall stones* 1609 (*v.* **stān**; boundary markers) (*v.* Kibworth Hall *supra*); *Hobrinckes* 1609 (*v.* **hōh**, **brink**); *Lady poole Leas* 1609 (*v.* **ladi**, **pōl**[1], **leys**); *Littell Med*(*d*)*ow* 1609, 1700, *Little Meadow* 1694, l.17; *May Moore* 1609 (*v.* **mōr**[1]; either wasteland where May festivities were held or land growing with the hawthorn or may-tree); (*the*) *Mill Feild* c.1715, c.1720 (*v.* **myln**, **feld**); *Northsick* 1609 (*v.* **norð**, **sík**); *Oulde Medow* 1609 (*v.* **ald**); *Ould* ~ ~ 1609, *Owld Mill Hill* 1635 (*v.* **ald**, **myln**); *Parkers Headland* 1694, ~ *Hadland* l.17 (*v.* **hēafod-land**; with the surn. *Parker*); *Peascroft Meare* 1694, l.17 (*v.* **pise**, **croft**, **(ge)mǣre**); *Pelsick hadland* 1609 (*v.* **sík**, **hēafod-land**; with the surn. *Pell*, a reflex of a pet-form of *Peter*); *Piners Platt* 1609 (*v.* **plat**[2]; with the surn. *Pinner*); *Segges hedge* 1609 (*v.* **hecg**; with the surn. *Sedge*); *Upper Shittis acer* 1609 (*v.* **scite**, **æcer**); *Sindry Leas* 1609 (*v.* **leys**; with the surn. *Sindry*); *Slaf Medow* 1609 (*v.* **slæf**); *the Swathes* 1598, ~ *Swaithes* 1611, ~ *Swaythes* 1626 (*v.* **swathe**); *Thakines Bushe* 1609, *Thakens Bush* 1635 (*v.* **þæc**, **þak**, **-ing**[2], **busc**; a source of roofing materials, cf. *thachink* in Frisby f.ns. (b)); *Thorphill* 1609 (*v.* **þorp**, **hyll**); *Town Side* 1745 (*v.* **tūn**, **sīde**); *Wayne waye* 1609 (*v.* **wægn**, **weg**), *Wey Brigg Weir* 1609 (*v.* **weg**, **brycg**, **wer**); *Whistel Gate* 1609 (*v.* **gata**; with a metathesized **twisla**, *v.* Twizzle Cl in adjoining Tur Langton f.ns. (a)); *Whit Crose* 1609 (*v.* **hwīt**, **cros**; prob. a standing cross of limestone); *Wrangland meare* 1694, l.17 (*v.* **wrang**, **land**, **(ge)mǣre**).

King's Norton

KING'S NORTON

Nortone 1086 DB, 1235 RHug, *Norton* c.1130 LeicSurv, 1186, 1192 P *et passim* to 1271 Ipm, 1284 Ass *et freq*, *Nortona* Ric 1 (1253) Ch, *Nortun* 1237, 1238 RGros, 1368 *Wyg*
Northona 1190 × 1204 France, *Northon* 1221 Ass, 1262 RGrav, 1264 Cl

Affixes are variously added as:
Kynges ~ Ric 1 (1253) Ch, 1237 RGros, 1306 IpmR, *Kinges* ~ 1237 RGros, 1235 × 53 Dugd, *King's* ~ 1798 Nichols *et freq*
West ~ 1284, 1317 *Wyg et passim* to 1471 Cl, 1511 BM
~ *iuxta Galby*(*e*) 1284 Ass, 1288 Coram *et passim* to 1368 *Wyg* 1392 *RTemple et freq* to 1510 *Wyg*, 1524 *LCh et passim* to 1629, 1630 LML, ~ *iuxta Galleby* 1304, 1307 Pat, 1434 *Wyg*, ~ *iuxta Galbie* 1527 *ib*
~ *besydys Galbye* 1523 *Wyg*

'The north farmstead, village', *v.* **norð**, **tūn**. It is uncertain to which other settlement Norton originally related as 'the north farmstead'; possible is Burton Overy. In the Domesday Survey, Norton is described as a parcel of the royal demesne appendant to the manor of Great Bowden, hence *Kynges* ~, which style is certainly recorded from the 13th cent. and possibly from the reign of Richard I (1189–99). This affix appears to have fallen into disuse from early in the 14th until the late 18th cent., its reintroduction perhaps inspired by local antiquarians. The affix *West* ~ distinguished the township from East Norton (*v.* Lei **3** 177), but the common affix was ~ *iuxta Galby*, Galby lying one mile to Norton's north-east, *v.* **king**, **west**, **besyde**. Note also MLat *iuxta* 'near to'.

The substitution of *th* for *t* in some early forms is the result of AN orthographical interchange between the symbols *th* and *t* for etymological *t*.

ASH SPINNEY, *v.* **æsc**, **spinney**. BLACK SPINNEY, *v.* **blæc**. LARCH SPINNEY, *v.* **larch**. THE LODGE, *v.* **loge**. MANOR HOUSE FM, *Manor House* 1863, 1877 White, *v.* **maner**. NORTON GORSE, *v.* **gorst**. ST JOHN THE BAPTIST'S CHURCH, *Church (St John the Baptist)* 1846, 1863, 1877 White, 1925 Kelly; the present church was begun in 1760 and was completed in 1775, the earlier parish church being recorded as *ecclesie de Norton* 1220 MHW, 1238 RGros, 1344, 1556 *Pat*, *ecclesiam de Kingesnortun* 1237 RGros, ~ *de Westnorton* 1340, 1341 *Pat*, *ecclesie de Norton iuxta Galby* 1371 *ib*. Note also *the Churchyard*(*e*) 1601, 1605 *Terrier et passim* to 1709, *v.* **churchyerd**.

FIELD-NAMES

In (a), forms dated 1797 are *Surv*; those dated 1835 are O; 1847 are *TA*; 1907 are *Surv*. Forms throughout dated 1304 are Banco; those dated 1336 and 1410 are *Wyg*; 1381 are SR; 1601, 1605, 1625, 1635, 1638, 1679, 1694, 1697, 1703, 1704, 1709, c.1720, 1721 and 1725 are *Terrier*; 1622 are Ipm; 1627 are Farnham.

(a) One Acre, Five Acres 1847 (*v.* **æcer**); East ~, West Adwongs 1847 (*Adwong* 1622, cf. *Adwonge close* 1627, *v.* **ād**, **vangr** and Adwong in adjoining Little Stretton f.ns. (a); it is just poss. that this name is a late garbled form of the unexplained *Ablondes-* in f.ns. (b)); Akerleys 1847, 1907 (*v.* **æcer**, **leys**); Atkin's Cl 1797 (with the surn. *Atkin*(*s*)); Barn Cl 1907 (*v.* **bern**); Bridge Fd 1847, 1907 (*Brig Feild*, *Brig*(*g*) *fyeld* 1635, *v.* **brycg**, **feld**; one of the great open-fields of the township; also called *Carlton Gate Feild*, *infra*); Brood ~ 1847, Broad Mdw 1907 (*v.* **brād**); Broughton's Cl 1847 (with the surn. *Broughton*); Butchers Mdw 1847, 1907 (with the surn. *Butcher*); Cloysters 1847, Cloyster Fd, ~ Leys 1847, 1907 (*v.* **leys**), ~ Spinney 1907 (*v.* **spinney**) (*the Cloysters* 1625, 1638, 1697, *Cloyster*, ~ *furlong* (*v.* **furlang**), ~ *side* (*v.* **sīde**) 1635, *v.* **cloistre**; the implications of this name are uncertain, whether it is an oblique allusion to Owston Abbey, one of the largest medieval landowners in King's Norton, or whether it refers to a lost structure or simply retains an early sense 'enclosure'); Common Cl 1847 (*v.* **commun**); Old Corn Cl 1847, 1907 (*v.* **corn**[1]); Cow Cl 1797; Croxdale 1847 (cf. *Crosdale bush* 1635, *Crosdall bushes* c.1720 (*v.* **cross**, **deill**, **busc**); Darkers Cl 1847, 1907 (with the surn. *Darker*, from ME *darkere* 'a blackener, a darkener', a process in tanning leather); Dog Kennel Lane 1847, 1907 (*v.* **kenel**; prob. referring to kennels in which hunting dogs were housed); Fox Covert, ~ ~ Mdw, Old Fox Cover 1847 (*v.* **fox**, **cover**(**t**)); Furry Cl 1847, 1907 (*v.* **fyrsig**); Gravel Pit Cl 1797 (*v.* **gravel**, **pytt**); Great Cl 1797, Humphreys Great Cl 1847 (with the surn. *Humphrey*, a reflex of the OGerm masc. pers.n. *Humfrid*) (cf. *the great piece at the brooke* 1635, *v.* **grēat**); Great ~, Upper Greendale 1847, 1907 (*v.* **grēne**[1], **dalr**); Green Leys 1797 (*v.* **grēne**[1], **leys**); First ~ ~, Farthest ~ ~, Hack Moor (sic) 1847, 1907 (*Thackmore* 1625, 1635, 1638, *v.* **þak**, **mōr**[1]); Hedge Hog ~ 1847, Hedgehog Mdw 1907 (*v.* **heyghoge**); Twixt Hedges, ~

~ Mdw 1847, 1907 (*Between hedges* 1703, *v.* **betwēonan**, **betwixt**, **hecg**); Far ~, Middle ~, Near ~, Nether ~, Upper Holt, Iliffs Holt 1847 (with the surn. *Iliffe*, a reflex of the ON masc. pers.n. *Eileifr*), Lane Holt 1847 (*v.* **lane**) (*the Holt*, *the Olt* 1635, *Olt* 1638, *the Oult* 1697, *the Great* ~, *the Lit*(*t*)*le* ~, *the Far* ~, *the Mid*(*d*)*le Olt* 1721, 1725, *v.* **holt**); Hop Yard 1847 (*v.* **hop-yard**); Lambcot ~ 1847, Lambert Hill 1907 (*Lamcoate hill* 1635, cf. *Lamcote Closse* 1635, *v.* **lamb**, **cot**); Leaches Cl 1907 (with the surn. *Leach/Leech*, cf. Leeches Mdw in Carlton Curlieu); Leonard's Cl 1797 (with the surn. *Leonard*, a reflex of the ME pers.n. *Leonard*, from the ContGerm masc. pers.n. *Leonhard*); Long Mdw 1847, ~ ~ Spinney 1907 (*v.* **spinney**); Great Marr, ~ ~ Mdw, Nether ~, Upper Marr 1847, 1907, Top Marr 1907 ((*the*) *Marr* 1625, 1635, 1638, *Marrfeild* 1625, 1638 (*v.* **feld**; one of the great open-fields; also called *Scockerhill Feild* in f.ns (b)), *v.* **marr**[1]); Nether Cl 1847, 1907; Norton Nether ~, Norton Upper Fd, Norton Field East Mdw, ~ ~ West Mdw 1847; Norton Spinny 1835 (*v.* **spinney**); Nursery 1847, 1907 (*v.* **nursery**); Oat Cl 1797 (*v.* **āte**); New Orchard 1847, 1907 (*v.* **orceard**); Owsley's Lodge 1798 Map (*v.* **loge**; prob. with the surn. *Ousley*, but *Owsley* could be an error for *Mowsley*, the surn. of a family originally from the township of this name, 7 miles to the south-west); Rags Cl 1847 (*v.* **ragu**; the late spelling *rag* may represent OE **ragge*, a secondary form of *ragu* 'moss, lichen', evidenced from 1758, *v.* OED *s.v.*); Ram Mdw 1847, 1907 (*v.* **ramm**); Ramshead or Ramshill 1797 (*v.* **hēafod**, **hyll**; prob. with **ramm**, but **hramsa** is poss.); Rushy Cl 1847 (*v.* **riscig**); Great ~, Scockerhill 1847, Great ~ ~, Stocker Hill 1907 (*Scockerill* 1625, *Scockrill* 1625, 1635, 1638, *Scockrell* 1679, *Scockerill* 1694, *Far* ~, *He*(*a*)*ther Scock*(*e*)*rill* 1635 (*v.* **hider**), *Scockerhill Feild*, ~ *fyeld*, *Scockrill Feild*, ~ *fyeld* 1635 (*v.* **feld**; one of the great open-fields, also called *Marrfeild*, *supra*), *Scockrill hedges* 1625 (*v.* **hecg**)), Scockerhill ~ 1847, Stocker Hill Cl 1907 (*Scockrill Closse* 1635, *v.* **clos**(**e**)) (*v.* Stocker Hill in adjoining Houghton on the Hill f.ns. (a), Galby f.ns.(a) and *Scockwell* in Little Stretton f.ns. (b)); Smalleys Cl 1847, 1907 (with the surn. *Smalley*); Stone-pit Six Acres 1797 (*v.* **stān-pytt**, **æcer**); Top Mdw 1847; Townsend Cl 1797 ((*the*) *Townes end* 1625, 1635, 1638, *the Broad townes end*, (*the*) *Little Townesend* 1635, *v.* **tūn**, **ende**); Upper Cl 1847, 1907, ~ Mdw 1847; Wash Pit Cl 1847 (*Wash pitt* 1635, *v.* **wæsce**, **pytt**); Watts Mdw 1847, 1907 (with the surn. *Watt*(*s*), from a pet-form of *Walter*); Willow(s) Croft 1847, 1907 (*Willowes Croft* 1638, *v.* **wilig**, **croft**); Winney 1847 (*v.* **whinny**).

(b) *Ablondesaker* 1336 (*v.* **æcer**; earlier forms are needed to explain *Ablondes* which may contain a plural **land** with the OE masc. pers.n. *Abba* or even a reduced **abbaye**, since Owston Abbey was a major medieval landowner in King's Norton; perh. cf. Abbey Lands in Knossington f.ns. (a); no ME pers.n. or surn. in the possessive case springs to mind as an alternative); *Bannlands* 1635, *Balland Hill* 1625, 1638, ~ ~ *sike* 1625, ~ ~ *Sick* 1635, 1638 (*v.* **sík**), *v.* **bēan**, **land**); *Thomas Beaumonds Cottage*, *Beaumonds Farme* 1635, 1638 (*v.* **ferme**); (*uppon*) *Begger* 1625, 1635, (*on*) *Beggar*, *Great Beggar*, *Little-begger* 1635, *Beggar Hades* 1638 (*v.* **hēafod**), *v.* **beggere**; denotes poor or unproductive land); *Black Pit*(*t*)*s* 1625, 1635, 1638 (*v.* **blæc**, **pytt**); *Brimland*(*s*) 1625, 1635, 1638 (*v.* **brimme**, **land**); *Brink*(*e*)*s* 1635, 1638, *Brinkes dole* 1625 (*v.* **dāl**), *v.* **brink**); *Broadmore*(*s*) 1625, 1635, 1638, *Bradmores* 1635, *Broodmores* 1638 (*v.* **brād**, **mōr**[1]); *the Brook*(*e*) 1625, 1635, 1638 (*v.* **brōc**; forms part of the parish boundary with Galby); *Bullgores* 1625, 1638, *Bul*(*l*)*gore*, *Bulgoares* 1635, *the Backside of Bulgoares* 1635 (*v.* **bak-side**), *v.* **bula**, **gāra**); (*the furlong called*) *Burton street*(*e*) 1625, 1635, 1638 (*v.* **strǣt**; Burton Overy lies beyond the Roman Gartree Road which forms the parish boundary to the south-west); *Carlton gate* 1635, *Carlton Gate Feild* 1625, 1638 (*v.* **feld**; one of the great open-fields, also called Bridge Fd *supra*), *v.* **gata**; Carlton Curlieu lies 2 miles to the south-east); *Cattayle Closse* 1635 (rather than to shape, the reference most likely is to Timothy Grass (*Pheleum pratense*), an important fodder plant); *Caudill* 1625, *Caudell* 1625, 1638, *Cawdwell* 1635, *Cawdell* 1638, *Cawdwell Closse*, *Caudill close* 1635 (*v.* **cald**, **wella**); *the Comon pasture* 1638 (*v.* **commun**, **pasture**); *the Cow*(*e*) *Pasture* 1635; *the Double Hedge* 1635 (also in Lei **3** 140 and 219, *v.* **duble**; with either **hecg** in its early sense 'a hedged enclosure' or with **edisc** or **etisc**; cf. Double Mdw in Great Glen f.ns. (a)); *the dyke* 1635 (*v.* **dík**); (*a furlong called*) *Ouer East and West*, *Neather East and West* 1635 (*v.* **uferra**, **neoðera**); *Elderstubs* 1625, *Eldernstubs*, *Elnarstubs* 1635, *Elder Stubbs* 1638 (*v.* **ellern**, **stubb**); *Ender sike* 1625, *Endsick* 1635 (*v.* **ened**, **sík**); *Far ground* 1697 (*v.* **grund**); *Foxholes* 1635, *Foxennoles*, *Foxen-noles furlong* 1635 (*v.* **fox-hol**; these spellings appear to have been influenced by **fixen**, a form of *vixen* 'she-fox', current into the early 18th cent.); *Fulsick* 1635 (*v.* **fūl**, **sík**); *Galbie wood* 1625, *Galby wood* 1635, *Ga*(*u*)*lby wood hill*, *Ga*(*u*)*lby meare* 1635, ~ *meer*(*e*) 1635, 1638 (*v.* **(ge)mǣre**) (Galby parish adjoins to the east); *Gasling pits* 1635, *Gessling* ~, *Gossling Pitts* 1638 (*v.* **geslyng**, **pytt**); *the Gleab*(*e*), *the Gleabland* 1635 (*v.* **glebe**); *Glen gates* 1625, *Glengate* 1635, 1638, ~ *Meadow* 1638 (*v.* **gata**; Great Glen lies 2 miles to the south-west); *le gores* 1336 (*v.* **gāra**); *Green*(*e*)*gate*(*s*) 1625, 1635, *Green Gate* 1638 (*v.* **grēne**[1], **gata**); *the Gutter* 1635, 1638 (*v.* **goter**); *del Hall* 1410 (p), *Hall land* 1638, *the Hall lane end* 1625, 1635, 1638 (*v.* **lane-ende**) (*v.* **hall**); *the Hook*(*e*)*s* 1635 (*v.* **hōc**); *the Hospitall ley* 1635 (*v.* **ley**), *the Hospitall Land* c.1720, 1725 (*v.* **hospital**; the property of Wigston's Hospital in Leicester, *v.* Lei **1** 95); *Humphreys Norton Close* c.1720 (with the surn. *Humphrey*); *Hunsbeck* 1625, *Hunsback*, *Hunchback* 1635, *Huntsbecke* 1638, *Hunchback ford* 1635 (*v.* **ford**) (*v.* *Huntsbecke* in Galby f.ns. (b)); *Ilson dike*, *Ilston dyke*, ~ ~ *Closse* 1635 (*v.* **dík**; Illston on the Hill parish adjoins to the south-east); *the kinges high way* 1605, *the King's High way* 1697 (*v.* **king**, **hēah-weg**); *Kirks Yarde end* 1635 (*v.* **geard**, **ende**; with the surn. *Kirk*); *Leic'* (*high*)*way* 1635 (the road to Leicester which lies 6 miles to the north-west); *Little Hill*(*s*) 1625, 1635, 1638, ~ *Closse* 1635; *the Long close* 1635; *Long doles* 1625, 1635, 1638 (*v.* **dāl**); (*the*) *Long hadland*, ~ *hedland* 1635 (*v.* **hēafod-land**); *the longe leys* 1625, *the Long Leyes* 1635, 1638 (*v.* **leys**); *Long pitts*, *Longpit* 1635 (*v.* **pytt**); *Long Smale*, ~ *Smell* 1635 ('the long narrow one', *v.* **smæl**; here used as a sb.); *Medburne* ~ 1625, *Medbourne hill* 1638 (with the surn. *Medbourne* of a family originally from the township of this name, 8 miles to the south-east); *the Mid*(*d*)*le feild* 1625, 1635, 1638, ~ *fyeld* 1635 (*v.* **middel**, **feld**; one of the great open-fields); *Mid*(*d*)*lemore* 1625, 1635, 1638 (*v.* **mōr**[1]); *Midsomer bush* 1635 (*v.* **busc**; the allusion may be to the site of midsummer festivities or to seasonal exploitation in husbandry (*v.* Field 118 and *Midewinter stickes* in Stoughton f.ns. (b)), or otherwise *Midsomer* is a surn. here (*v.* Reaney *s.n.* Midsummer)); *the Milne* 1638, *Milne Balk*(*e*) 1625, 1638, *Milbalke*, *the Mill baulke* 1635 (*v.* **balca**), *Milne furlong*(*e*) 1625, 1638, *the Myll furlong* 1635 (*v.* **furlang**), *Mill Hill* 1635, *the Millhill leyes* 1635 (*v.* **leys**), *the Mill parte* 1635 (*v.* **part** 'a portion, an allotted share (of land)') (*v.* **myln**); (*the*) *Neatheards baulke* 1635 (*v.* **neetherd**, **balca**); (*the*) *New Close*, 1625, c.1720, *Newclose corner* 1635 (*v.* **corner**); *the New hedge* 1635 (*v.* **hecg**); *Norton lane* 1721, 1725; *Old furlonge* 1625 (*v.* **ald**, **furlang**); *the old pen* 1635 (*v.* **ald**, **penn**[2]); *the Old Yard* (*of William Whalley*) 1697,

1704, 1709 (*v.* **ald**, **geard**); *the Orchard of Mr Whalley* 1605 (*v.* **orceard**); *Peaselands* 1625, 1635, 1638 (*v.* **pise**, **land**); *the Pingle* 1635 (*v.* **pingel**); *Redbankes* 1625, 1635, *Redbanks* 1638 (*v.* **rēad**, **banke**; alluding to the clay soil); *the Rickstead* 1635 (*v.* **rickstead**); *Rassynhil* 1336, *Rossendale* 1625, *Rossondale* 1635, *Rosendale* 1638, *Rossendale baulke* 1635 (*v.* **balca**) (*v.* **ræsn**, **hyll**; perh. referring to a plank bridge or to planks laid across marshy ground, with early *hyll* replaced by **dalr**); *Rough Close* 1638 (*v.* **rūh**); *Sewall Close* 1638 (with the surn. *Sewall*, a reflex of the OE masc. pers.n. *Sǣweald*, cf. *Seuuale filius Fulgeri* Hy 2 Dane of Leics.); *del Shawe* 1381 (p) (*v.* **sceaga**); *Shouldbreads* 1625, 1638, *Shouldbredge*, *Shelbre*(*a*)*ds* 1635 (*v.* **scofl-brǣdu**); *the Sleites* 1635, *Sleights* 1638, *Middle Sleights* 1625, 1638, ~ *Slaight*(*e*)*s*, ~ *Sleites* 1635, *Neather Slaites*, ~ *Slaight*(*e*)*s* 1635 (*v.* **neoðera**) (*v.* **slæget**); *the Sling pits* 1625 (*v.* **sling**, **pytt**); *Smith Wong*(*e*) 1625, 1638 (*v.* **smēðe**[1], **vangr**); *South wonge* 1625 (*v.* **vangr**); (*upon*) *Stone* 1638 (*v.* **stān**); *Stonehill* 1635 (*v.* **stān**, **hyll**); *the Stone bridge* 1635 (this gave its name to Bridge Fd *supra*); *Stonepitts* 1635 (*v.* **stān**, **pytt**); *Stonie* 1625 (*v.* **stānig**; prob. to be identified with *Stone*, *supra*); *Stretton meere* 1625 (*v.* (**ge**)**mǣre**), *Stretton way* 1635 (Little Stretton parish adjoins to the west); *Swans poole* 1635 (*v.* **swan**[1], **pōl**[1]); *Tongue* 1635 (*v.* **tunge**); *Tyney hooke* 1635 (*v.* **tynie**, **hōc**); (*in*) *Undersike* 1638 (*v.* **under**, **sík**); *the Vicarage grounde* 1601 (*v.* **grund**), *the Vicar*(*r*)*age House* 1605, 1697, 1704, 1709, ~ *Vicaridge* ~ 1625 (*v.* **vikerage**); *Westewellesyk* 1304 (*v.* **west**, **wella**, **sík**); *Mr Whaley his closs* 1625 (*v.* **clos**(**e**)), *Mr Whalleys House* 1638; *the Wongs* (*v.* **vangr**).

Knossington and Cold Overton

1. KNOSSINGTON

Nossitone 1086 DB, *Closintone* (sic) 1086 ib
Knossinton' c.1130 LeicSurv, 1243 Fees, 1270 Pat, *Knossington* 1203 P, 1262 Fine *et passim* to c.1291 Tax, 1300 Ipm *et freq*, *Knossyngton* 1327 Banco, 1330 *Hazlerigg* (p) *et passim* to 1535 VE, 1537 MinAccts
Cnossintona a.1160, 1150 × 60 Dane, 1173 P (p), 1235 × 53 Dugd, *Cnossinton'* 1170, 1171 P (p) *et passim* to 1249 RGros, 1269 For, *Cnossington(e)* 1227, 1229 RHug *et passim* to 1324 Coram, 1367 Banco
Cnossenton(a) 1231, 1253 × 58 RegAnt, Hy 3 Dane
Knoston 1405 Fine, 1441 (1449) *WoCart et passim* to 1610 Speed, 1727 LML, *Knosson* 1572 SR, 1610 Speed, *Knawston* 1622 Burton, 1719 Nichols, 1721 LML

Ekwall DEPN suggests that the first element may be derived from an OE **cnoss* 'a hill' (related to ON *knauss* 'a knoll, a rounded hill', Swed dial. *knös* 'a rounded hill', Dan dial. *knøs* 'a sand-hill', MLG *knust* 'a knot', ModE *knot*), but an OE masc. pers.n. such as *Cnoss* or *Cnossa* may have developed from this stem (cf. OSwed *knös* 'a goblin, a terrible person', Norw and Dan *knøs* 'a proud, overbearing person'). Thus perhaps the place-name may be interpreted as 'the estate associated with or called after a man named Cnoss or Cnossa', *v.* **-ingtūn**, and be compared in construction with Loddington and Skeffington (Lei **3** 163 and 220) also in High Leicestershire, and Tur Langton *infra*.

Alternatively, OE *tūn* 'farmstead, village, estate' may have been added to an earlier OE place-name **æt Cnossing* '(the settlement) at the hill place', *v.* **æt**, **cnoss**, **-ing**[2], hence 'farmstead, village or estate at Cnossing', *v.* **tūn**. The present township crowns a prominent hill. It should be noted, however, that such formations suffixed by *tūn* are otherwise rare (as Penistone, YW **1** 336, where a compounded OE **Penning* may be a hill-name from PrW **penn* 'a head').

BLEAK HO., *Bleak House* 1863 White; prob. after Charles Dickens' novel of this name which was published 1852–3. It is *Knossington Lodge* 1824 O, *v.* **loge**. BRAUNSTON RD, Braunston lying 2 miles to the south-east. BRUCES LANE, cf. *Wm. Bruce, carrier* 1846 White, *William Bruce, farmer* 1863 ib. THE CARRIAGEWAY. CHESELDYNE SPINNEY, *v.* **spinney**; with the surn. *Cheseldyne*; it is TAMPION'S COPPICE (2½"), *Tampions ~* 1848 *TA*, *Tampion's Coppice* 1919 Sale, *v.* **copis**, and even earlier *Tampions Wood* c.1800, 1806 Plan; with the surn. *Tampion*. FOX AND HOUNDS (P.H.), *Fox and Hounds* 1863, 1877 White, 1925 Kelly. GREYHOUND (P.H.) (lost), *Greyhound* 1863, 1877 White, 1925 Kelly. KNOSSINGTON GRANGE, 1925 Kelly, *The Grange* 1877 White, 1919, 1949 Sale, *v.* **grange**. KNOSSINGTON LODGE FM, *v.* **loge**. LADY WOOD, ~ ~ FM, *Lady Woode* 1539 *Reeve*, *Lady Wood* 1602 DKR, 1745 *Terrier et passim* to 1848 *TA*, 1919 Sale, *v.* **ladi**, **wudu**; probably woodland whose rents were dedicated to the upkeep of a chapel to Our Lady, the Virgin Mary. LARCHWOOD RISE, *v.* **larch**, **rise**. LOCKWOOD COTTAGE, cf. *Walter Lockwood, builder* 1925 Kelly. MANOR FM, 1877 White, *Manor House Farm* 1916 Sale. MANOR HO., (*The*) *Manor House* 1745 *Terrier*, 1863 White, 1916 Sale, 1925 Kelly, *The Old Manor House* 1956 Sale, *v.* **maner**. OLD ~ ~, OAKHAM RD, Oakham in Rutland lying 3 miles to the east. OWSTON RD, Owston lying 2 miles to the south-west. PRESTON LODGE (PRESTON'S ~ 2½"), *Preston Lodge* 1925 Kelly, cf. *Peter Preston, farmer* 1846 White, *v.* **loge**. PRIORY FM. THE RECTORY, 1877 White, 1925 Kelly; earlier is *the Mansion howse* 1601, 1625 *Terrier* (*v.* **mansion-house**), *the Parsonage howse* 1606 *ib*, ~ ~ *House* 1638, 1697, 1718, 1745 *ib*, *v.* **personage**. RICKLEBURROW HILL, 1925 Kelly, *Rickelbarrow* 1601, 1601 (1638), 1638 *Terrier*, *Rickelboro* 1847 White, *v.* **berg**; either with the OE masc. pers.n. *Ricel* or, less likely, with the OE fem. pers.n. *Ricola*, *v.* Rickling, Ess 532. ST PETER'S CHURCH, *Church (St Peter)* 1846, 1863, 1877 White, 1925 Kelly; it is earlier recorded as *ecclesie ~ ~*, *ecclesiam de Cnossinton* 1220 MHW, 1249 RGros, *ecclesia de Knossinton* 1270 *Pat*. Note also *The Church Yard* 1708 (18), 1745 *Terrier*, *v.* **churchyerd**. SCONSBOROUGH HILL, *Skonsbor*(*r*)*ow* 1601, 1601 (1638), 1638 *Terrier*, *Sconborowe hill* 1628 Ipm, *Stansbury Hill* (sic) 1848 *TA*, *v.* **berg**; earlier forms are needed to explain the specific of the name of the hill, the site of a pagan Anglo-Saxon warrior inhumation. The medial *s* suggests an OE pers.n. in the possessive case, but no likely name is apparent, unless if what we have here is a modified OE masc. pers.n. *Stān* (> *Ston-* > *Skon-*). Alternatively, the eModEng *sconse/skance* 'a shelter' (of uncertain origin but cognate with MHG *schanze*, early Du *schantze* 'brushwood'), may have had an OE form with the same meaning, but otherwise unrecorded. SOMERBY RD, Somerby lying 2 miles to the north-west of Knossington. TAMPION'S COPPICE, *v.* Cheseldyne Spinney *supra*. WHALEBONES (local), (*The*) *Whalebones* 1877 White, 1919 Sale; the farm of this name formerly had a whale's jaw bone arching over its entrance gate. THE WILLOWS. WINDMILL LODGE, *v.* **wind-mylne**, **loge**.

FIELD-NAMES

In (a), forms presented without dates are 1848 *TA*; those dated 1824, 1835, 1860 and 1930 are *Deed*; 1916, 1948 and 1960 are Sale. Forms throughout dated 1269 are For; those dated m.13, Hy 3 and 1356 are Nichols; 1381 are SR; 1601, 1601 (1638), 1606, 1625, 1638, 1674, 1679, 1697, c.1708 (18), 1718 and 1745 are *Terrier*; 1628 are Ipm; 1723 and 1736 are *Deed*.

(a) Two Acres, Four ~, Five ~, Seven ~, Eight ~, Nine ~, Ten Acres (*v.* **æcer**); Abbey Lands (*v.* **abbaye**, **land**; with reference to the former Owston Abbey in adjacent Owston and Newbold parish); Alices Cl (either with the fem. pers.n. *Alice* or its surn. reflex *Alise* (various spellings)); Far ~, Ancliffs (the surn. *Ancliff* in the possessive case); Apple-Tree Cl (*v.* **æppel-trēow**); Barks Cl (with the surn. *Bark*, metonymic for ME *barkere* 'a tanner'); Barne Cl (*v.* **bern**); Far ~, Middle ~, Near Beetleboro', ~, ~, ~ Beetle Burrows (*Bettlebarrowes* 1601, *Beethelbarrows* 1601 (1638), 1638, *Beetle Barrows* 1745, *v.* **berg**; prob. with the OE masc. pers.n. *Byttel* or *Bitel*, cf. Bisbrooke, Ru 238 and Bittesby, Cox[2] 11; *bitela* 'beetle' is unlikely); Bog Holme (*v.* **bog**, **holmr**); Boro' Wong (*Burgwong* m.13, *v.* **burh**, **vangr**; poss. a field towards Burrough on the Hill); Bottom Mdw 1930 (*v.* **bottom**); The Brand, Brand Mdw 1835, Bottom ~, Middle ~, Top Brand 1848 (*the Brand* 1601, 1601 (1638), *Knoston Brand* 1610 Speed, (*the common pasture called*) *the Brand* 1638, *v.* **brand**); The Breach (1601, 1601 (1638), 1606, 1638, cf. *Breach Ground* 1601, 1601 (1638) (*v.* **grund**), *v.* **brēc**); Bucks Pasture (*v.* **pasture**; with the surn. *Buck*); Bushes (either the plural of **busc** or the surn. *Bush* in the possessive case); Nether ~, Upper Coppice, Coppice Mdw (*v.* **copis**); Cotchers Cl (*v.* **cottere**); Cottage Cl 1848, 1916 (*v.* **cotage**); Cow Cl; Cunnery (*v.* **coningre**); Nether ~, Upper Cutts Fd (cf. *Cuttefield Close* 1628, *v.* **cutte**); Far ~, Deepdale (cf. *dapdall hill* 1601, *dapedale ~* 1606, *Dapdale ~* 1638, *Depdale Hill furlong* 1601 (1638), 1638, *dapedale hill furlonge* 1606 (*v.* **furlang**), *v.* **dēop**, **dalr**); Deep Room (*v.* **dēop**, **rūm**[1]); Drews Cl 1848, 1916, ~ Mdw 1848 (with the surn. *Drew*); Dunmore's Mdw, ~ Plot (*v.* **plot**) (with the surn. *Dunmore*, common in the early 19th cent. in Leics. and Rutland); Far Mdw; Fir Hill 1848, 1916, ~ ~ Plantation 1848 (*v.* **plantation**) (*v.* **firr**); Lower ~ ~, Upper Forrest Cl (cf. *Short Forrest furlong* 1601 (1638) (*v.* **furlang**), *v.* **forest**; the land eventually became part of the great *Woode feilde*; and note Wild Harrey *infra*); The Gall 1916, Great ~, Gall 1848, 1916, Gall Hill 1848, 1916, ~ ~ Plantation 1848, Great ~ ~, Little Plough Gall 1848, 1916 (*v.* **plōg**), Gall Mdw 1848 (*the gall feild*

1638 (*v.* **feld**), *v.* **galla**); The Gath, Great ~, Little Gath (*long ~*, *short garth* 1601, 1601 (1638), 1606, 1638, *the west garth* 1601 (1638), 1638, *v.* **garðr**); Grass Yard (*v.* **græs**, **geard**); Gravel Pits (*gravell pittes* 1601, *~ pitts* 1601 (1638), 1638, *Gravel pitt close* 1628, *v.* **gravel**, **pytt**); Great Cl; Hawhead ((*the*) *hawhead* 1601, 1606, 1638, *hawhead furlong* 1601 (1638), 1638, *v.* **haga**[1], **hēafod**); Hewardines Cl 1848, 1916 (with the surn. *Hewardine*); High Cl; High Mdw 1835 (1601); Hill Cl; The Hives 1916, Hives Mdw 1848 (cf. *hives meadow leas* 1601 (1638) (*v.* **leys**), *v.* **hive**); Hollow Back 1848, ~ ~ Cl 1860, Bottom ~ ~, Top Hollow Back 1930 (*v.* **holh** (**holwe** dat.sg.), **bæc**) The Holme ((*on*) *Home* 1601, 1638), Holme Plantation (*v.* **holmr**); Far ~ ~, Home Cl 1848, 1916, Home Paddock 1916 (*v.* **paddock**) (*v.* **home**); Front ~, Homestead (*v.* **hām-stede**); Horse Cl 1846, 1916; House Cl; Hovel Cl (*v.* **hovel**); Kettles Cl 1930 (with the surn. *Kettle*, a reflex of the ON masc. pers.n. *Ketill*); Knawston Cl, ~ Mdw (retaining a 17th-cent. spelling of Knossington); Knoll Fm (*v.* **cnoll**); Knossington Holt 1960 (*v.* **holt**); Lady Wood Cl, ~ ~ Mdw (1745) (*v.* Lady Wood *supra*); Lammas Cl 1848, 1916 (*v.* **lammas**); Land Cl, ~ Mdw (enclosures formed from selions or 'lands' of a former great open-field); Little Dale (1606, *little dale hill* 1601, 1601 (1638), 1606, 1638, *~ ~ ~ hades* 1601 (1638), 1638 (*v.* **hēafod**), *v.* **dalr**); Little Mdw; Long Cl; Middle Cl; Mill Spot (*v.* **myln**, **spot**); Near Mdw; Nether Fd, Far ~ ~, Nether Ground (*v.* **grund**), Nether Marr (*v.* **marr**[1]); New Mdw; Nook (*v.* **nōk**); North Mdw; Ozier Bed (*v.* **oyser**, **bedd**); Peas Cl (*v.* **pise**); Peters Cl (prob. alluding to St Peter's Church *supra*); Pingle 1848, 1930 (*v.* **pingel**); Plough Cl (*v.* **plōg**); Sandy Leys (*v.* **sandig**, **leys**); Seed Cl (*v.* **sǣd**; used of grasses sown for one year's mowing or grazing, as distinguished from permanent pasture); South Cl; Spring Cl (*v.* **spring**[1]); Stearwong 1824 (*v.* **stēor**, **vangr**); Stevens Cl, ~ Mead (*v.* **mēd**) (with the surn. *Steven(s)*); Stowes Cl (with the surn. *Stowe*); Great Tampions Cl (*v.* Tampion's Coppice *supra*); Tiptafts Cl, ~ Mdw (with the surn. *Tiptaft/Tiptoft*); Top Mdw; Townsend Cl (*Tounesende close* 1628), Townsend Mdw (*v.* **tūn**, **ende**); Upper Cl; Wards Cl (with the surn. *Ward*); Well Cl (1628, *v.* **wella**); Wheat Cl (*v.* **hwǣte**); White Gate Cl (alluding to a white field-gate); Wiggintons Cl (cf. *William Wigginton* 1831 Census); First ~ ~, Wilcox Cl (with the surn. *Wilcox*; from *Wilcoc*, a pet-name for *William*); North ~ ~, South Wild Harrey (*Wildeharry* 1601, 1606, *Wildharrye* 1601 (1638), 1638, *Wildeharry hole* 1601, 1606, *Wildharrye hole* 1601 (1638), 1638 (*v.* **hol**[1]), *v.* **wilder** (**wild-dēor**), (**ge**)**hæg**, cf. *Wilderehey*, Ess 374; a portion of forest fenced off for hunting deer and other wild animals); Willow Cl (*v.* **wilig**); Wisp, ~ Plantation (*v.* **wisp** and The Wisp, Ru 74); Wood Corner (*v.* **corner**), Wood Mdw, Wood Nook (*v.* **nōk**).

(b) *barly croftes* 1601, *barlyechrafts* 1601 (1638), *Barlicroftes* 1606, *barlye crafts* 1638 (*v.* **bærlic**, **croft**); *baslandhill* 1601, *Basland hill* 1601 (1638), 1606, 1638 (*v.* **land**, **hyll**; the specific may be the OE masc. pers.n. *Basa* or **bæst** used of 'the lime-tree'); *blacklandes* 1601, *blacklands* 1601 (1638), 1638, *Blakelandes* 1606 (*v.* **blæc**, **land**); *boscum de Cnossinton'* 1269, Hy 3 (with MLat *boscus* 'a wood'); *Branson ~* 1601 (1638), 1638, *Brawnston hedge* 1606 (*v.* **hecg**; the parish (and county) boundary hedge with Braunston), *Branson ~* 1601 (1638), 1638, *Brawnston way* 1606 (Braunston in Rutland lies 2 miles to the south-east); *Brickman home* 1601, 1601 (1638), 1606, 1638 (*v.* **holmr**; with the surn. *Brickman*, since the survival of its source, the antecedent OE masc. pers.n. *Brihtman* (*Beorhtmann*), is very unlikely here); *the Brook* 1606, *the running brooke* (sic) 1638 (*v.* **runnyng**, perh. used to indicate a stream with a strong, continuous flow; otherwise a brook whose course was artificially channelled, *v.* **rennyng**); *the bull balke* 1601 (1638), 1638 (*v.* **balca**), *the bull peice* 1601 (1638), 1638 (*v.* **pece**) (*v.* **bula**; both grazing for a single bull); *caudwell furlong* 1601 (1638), 1638 (*v.* **cald**, **wella**, **furlang**); *Churchcrofte* 1606 (*v.* **croft**), *Church lane* 1601, 1606 (*v.* **lane**), *Church lane end* 1601 (1638), 1638, *v.* **lane-ende**) (*v.* St Peter's Church *supra*); *Cold Overton meere* 1601 (1638), 1638 (*v.* (**ge**)**mǣre**; the early parish boundary with Cold Overton *infra*); *the Com*(*m*)*on pasture* 1606, 1638 (*v.* **commun**, **pasture**); *the constables peece* 1601, 1606, ~ ~ *peice* 1601 (1638), 1638 (*v.* **conestable**, **pece**); *Costord* ~ 1601, *Costard hill* 1601 (1638), 1638 (*v.* **hyll**; either with the surn. *Costard* or with ME **costard** 'a ribbed apple of large size' from which the surn. was taken as a nickname for someone with a large, round head); *dunstall hill* 1601 (1638), 1606, 1638 (*v.* **tūn-stall**); *Elbowes* 1601, 1601 (1638), 1606, 1638 (*v.* **elbowe**); *Endri*(*e*)*s* 1601, 1638, *Endrees* 1601 (1638) (*v.* **ende**, **hrīs**, cf. *Endris Way*, Lei **3** 224); *eldern stubb* 1601, *elderstubbes* 1601 (1638), 1638 (*v.* **ellern**, **stubb**); *Ethwyn* 1601, 1638 (*v.* **ēðe**, **hvin**); (*the*) *Far Hill* 1601, 1601 (1638), 1606, 1638; *Flaxman more* 1601, 1601 (1638), 1638 (cf. *Sampson Flaxman* 1606, 1638); *Foxholes* 1601, 1601 (1638), 1606, 1628, 1638 (*v.* **fox-hol**); *the great Glebe* 1745 (*v.* **glebe**); *Greenehill* 1601, 1601 (1638), 1606, 1638, *Green*(*e*)*hill poole* 1601, 1601 (1638), 1606, 1638, *greenhilpoole* 1625, *Greenhill pool* 1674, 1679, 1718 (*v.* **pōl**[1]) (*v.* **grēne**[1], **hyll**); *green*(*e*) *seeke* 1601, 1601 (1638), 1638, *ou'whart*(*e*) ~ ~ 1601, 1601 (1638), *ouerwharte greene seeke* 1638 (*v.* **ofer-þwart**) (*v.* **grēne**[1], **sík**); *atte Hall* 1638 (p) (*v.* **atte**, **hall**; recording an early hall); *the hy medow* 1601, (*the*) *High Meadow* 1601 (1638), 1638, *the hy*(*e*) *meadow* 1606; *the hyther furlonge* 1601, 1606, *the hither furlong* 1638 (*v.* **hider**, **furlang**); *the Homestall* 1606, c.1708 (18) (*v.* **hām-stall**; belonging to *the Parsonage House*, *supra*); *the kings way* 1638, *the Kings Highway* 1674, 1679 (*v.* **king**, **hēah-weg**); *langlands* 1601 (1638), 1638, *langlandes*, *langlondes* 1606 (*v.* **lang**[1], **land**); *Little ash* 1601, 1638, ~ ~ *furlong* 1601 (1638), 1638 (*v.* **æsc**); *leathergraues* 1601, *leather* ~ 1601 (1638), 1638, *lether graves* 1606 (*v.* **lǣfer**, **græf**); *the Long Close* 1745; *maulpates* 1601, 1606, *maulpats* 1601 (1638), 1638 (*v.* **marle-pytt**); (*the*) *middle hill furlong*(*e*) 1601, 1601 (1638), 1606, 1638; *Mill Close* 1723, *the Mill hades* 1638 (*v.* **hēafod**) (*v.* **myln**); *the moores* 1601, 1601 (1638), 1606, 1638 (*v.* **mōr**[1]); *Mussell seeke* 1601 (1638), 1638 (*v.* **mos**, **wella**, **sík**, cf. Muswell, Bk 119); (*the*) *neather farme* 1601 (1638), 1638 (*v.* **neoðera**, **ferme**); *Nether feilde* 1601, 1606, *Nether fild* 1601 (1638), ~ *Feild* 1638 (*v.* **neoðera**, **feld**; one of the great open-fields of the township); *new crosse ford*(*e*) 1601, 1606, 1625, 1638, *nue crosford* 1601 (1638), 1638, *newcrosford* 1638, *Newcross ford* 1679, 1718, *New Cross Ford* c.1708 (18), *Newgosford or Newcross Ford* 1745, *Newcross ford close* 1674 (*v.* **nīwe**, **cros**, **ford**); (*on*) *Okes* 1601, (*on*) *Oakes* 1638 (*v.* **āc**); *Oulston* ~ 1606, *Owston hedge* 1638 (*v.* **hecg**; a parish boundary hedge), *Oulston* ~ 1601, *Owston meere* 1638 (*v.* (**ge**)**mǣre**) (Owston parish adjoins to the west); *the Overhouse* 1638 (*v.* **uferra**, **hūs**; poss. one of a pair of early upper and lower halls, *v. atte Hall*, *supra* and The Hall in Houghton on the Hill); *Parke wong*(*e*) 1601, 1606, 1638, *Parkwong* 1606, *Parke wong*(*e*) *furlong* 1601 (1638), 1638 (*v.* **park**, **vangr**); (*the*) *Parsonage wong*(*e*) 1601 (1638), 1606, *the Parsnage wong* 1638 (*v.* **personage**, **vangr** and The Rectory *supra*); *Anthonie Pecke his hadland* 1606 (*v.* **hēafod-land**); *Mr Peck's great Peter's Close*, *Mr Peck's Nether Field* 1745 (*v.* Peters Cl *supra*); *Prestrees* 1601, *Prestris* 1601 (1638), 1638 (*v.* **prēost**, **hrīs** and *Endrees*, *supra*); *the pryer wood* 1601 (1638), 1638 (*v.* **prior**; either with reference to the Prior of Launde Priory, 2½ miles to the south, or less likely, to the Prior of Owston Abbey, 1½ miles to the south-west); *Pullins Close* 1736 (with the surn. *Pullin*); *Ram close* 1601, 1606, ~ *closse* 1601 (1638), 1638 (*v.* **ramm**); *Redlandes* 1601, *Redlands* 1606, 1638 (*v.* **rēad**, **land**); *the Runlett (of the High Meadow)* 1638 (*v.* **runlet**; precedes the earliest OED entry *s.v.* runlet[2] by 117 years); *Shurly croftes* 1601 (1638), 1638 (*v.* **croft**; perh. with the surn. *Shirley*, but because of the plural form of the generic, the first word may rather be a p.n., *v.* **scīr**[2], **lēah**; but note *Shirtecoat* in Great Bowden, of which recurring p.n. type this may be a late-copied garbled instance); *Skonsborow feilde* 1601, *Skonsborrow Feild* 1601 (1638) (*v.* **feld**; one of the great open-fields, taking its name from Sconsborough Hill *supra*); *Sommerby meere* 1601 (1638), 1638 (*v.* **(ge)mǣre**; Somerby parish adjoins to the north-west); *(the) Southbrook* 1606, 1638, *Southbrook furlong* 1601 (1638), 1606, 1638 (*v.* **sūð**, **brōc**); *South hill* 1601, 1601 (1638), 1638; *high Stonehill furlong* 1601 (1638) (*v.* **stān**, **hyll**); *taftes* 1601, 1601 (1638), 1606, 1638 (*v.* **toft**); *tuthorne* 1601, 1601 (1638), 1638 (*v.* **tū**, **þorn**; cf. *threthorne* in Frisby f.ns. (b)); *the towne hadland* 1601 (1638), 1606, 1638 (*v.* **tūn**, **hēafod-land**); *Wadland* 1356 (*v.* **wād**, **land**); *wharthill* 1601 (1638), 1638, *wharthill hadland* 1606 (*v.* **þverr** (**þvert** neut.), **hyll**); *winpooles* 1601, 1601 (1638), 1638 (*v.* **hvin**, **pōl**[1]); *Withcockbalke* 1601 (*v.* **balca**), *Withcocke way* 1601 (1638), 1638 (Withcote in Framland Hundred (*v.* Lei **2** 282) lies 3 miles to the south); *the wong(e)* 1601, 1601 (1638), 1638 (*v.* **vangr**); *Woode feilde* 1601, *Woodfeild* 1601 (1638), 1638 (*v.* **feld**; one of the great open-fields), *Woodhome* 1601, 1601 (1638), 1638 (*v.* **holmr**) (*v.* **wudu** and *boscum de Cnossinton'*, *supra*).

2. COLD OVERTON

Cold Overton is a member of Framland Hundred.

(æt) Ofertune 1066–68 ASWills
Ovretone 1086 DB
Caleverton c.1130 LeicSurv
Ouerton' 1198, 1199, 1201 P, *Ouertun'* 1269 For, *Ouirton'* 1275 RGrav, *Overton(e)* 1201 Abbr, 1203 Cur *et freq*, (*Cald(e)* ~ 1201 Abbr, 1254 Val, *Kald* ~ 1203 Cur, *Cold(e)* ~ 1212 RBE, 1227 ClR *et freq*, *Caud* ~ 1220 MHW)
Oreton 1460 Pat, *Cold Orton* 1530 ib, 1576 Saxton

'The farmstead, village on the ridge', *v.* **ofer**[2], **tūn**. The prefix **cald** 'bleak, exposed' reflects the township's high, ridge-top location.

GODTORP (lost), *Godtorp* 1086 DB, *v.* **þorp**; with OE **gōd** or ON **góðr**, both meaning 'good'. The name of the vill is remodelled as *Gillethorp'* c.1130 LeicSurv, *v.* **þorp**; with the masc. pers.n. *Gilli*, presum. that of a new lord. Gilli, which appears to be a Scand formation, is a short form of Irish names in *Gilli-* and it may be that its bearer was of Celtic descent, cf. Gilroes, Lei **1** 221, *v.* Feilitzen 261 and SPNLY 100–1.

CLINT'S CREST, cf. *Great ~*, *Little Clint* 1838 *TA*, *v.* **klint**, **creyste**. COLD OVERTON GRANGE, *v.* **grange**. COLD OVERTON PARK WOOD, *Coldouerton parke* 1610 Speed, *Park* 1838 *TA*; it is earlier recorded as (*ad cornerium*) *parci de Ouerton* 1218 AAS (with MLat *cornerium* 'a corner'), *parci de Coldhauerton* 1227 ClR, *parcum de Ouertun'* 1269 For, *parcus de Cold Overton* 1340, 1348, 1405 *Pat* (with MLat *parcus* 'a park'), *Overton Wood* c.1800 Plan, 1815 Nichols, *v.* **park**. THE HALL, *Overton Hall* 1846, 1863, 1877 White, *Cold Overton Hall* 1925 Kelly; a mid 17th-cent. structure, but an earlier hall is recorded by *atte Hall* 1419 Fine (p) (*v.* **atte**), *v.* **hall**. THE LAKE, *v.* **lake**. MANOR FM, *v.* **maner**. NORTHFIELD FM, 1916, 1955 Sale, *North Field* 1838 *TA*, 1916 Sale; prob. the name of one of the former great open-fields (with Hill Fd and Mill Fd?). THE RECTORY, 1877 White, 1930 Sale, *v.* **rectory**; earlier is *the Parsonage House* 1707, 1709 *Terrier*, *v.* **personage**. ST JOHN'S CHURCH, *the Church* 1709 *Terrier*, *Church (St John)* 1846, 1863, 1877 White, *Church (St John the Baptist)* 1925 Kelly; it is earlier recorded as *ecclesie de Caudoverton* 1220 MHW, *~ de Overton* 1377, 1344 *Pat*, *~ de Cold*(*e*) *Overton* 1401, 1402 *ib*; note also *the Church Yard* 1709 *Terrier*, *v.* **churchyerd**. SOMERBY RD, Somerby lying 2 miles to the west. STONE HO., *Stone House Farm* 1949 Sale. Originally built as an orphanage for 20 girls: *Asylum for Female Orphans* 1846, 1863 White.

FIELD-NAMES

Forms in (a) presented without dates are 1838 *TA*; those dated 1780, 1801 and 1806 are Map; 1811 are Nichols; 1821 are *Terrier*; 1824 are O; 1877 are White; 1916 are Sale. Forms throughout dated 1227 are ClR; those dated 1327 and 1332 are SR; 1610 are Speed; 1694 are DKR; 1721 are LML.

(a) Seven Acres, Eight ~, Twelve ~, Twenty Acres (*v.* **æcer**); Barn Cl; Belt Plantation 1916 (*v.* **belt**, **plantation**); Brick Kiln Mdw (*v.* **brike-kiln**); Brighton Hill (prob. with the surn. *Brighton* (from Breighton, YE 239), *v.* Reaney *s.n.*); Broad Mdw; Bucks Mdw, ~ Pasture (*v.* **pasture**) (with the surn. *Buck*); Bushy Mdw (*v.* **busshi**); Butt Leys (*v.* **butte**, **leys**); Cord Leys, ~ Pasture (*Cord* is not recorded as a surn., so prob. from **cald**; *v.* **leys**, **pasture**); Corn Park (*v.* **corn**[1] and Cold Overton Park Wood *supra*); Cottage Pasture (*v.* **cotage**, **pasture**); Dockey Cl (*v.* **docce**, **-ig**[3]); The Face of the Hill 1811, Face o' the Hill 1838 (*v.* **face**); Falkners Cl (with the surn. *Falkner*; cf. *Ricardus facuner* 12 Dane of Leics.); Far Mdw; Furze Hill (*v.* **fyrs**);

Glebe Land (*v.* **glebe**); Far ~ ~, Near Great Cl, Great Ground (*v.* **grēat**, **grund**), Great Mdw; Hall Cl, Hall Yard (*v.* **geard**) (*v.* The Hall *supra*); Hartwell Cl (if not with a p.n. (*v.* **heort**, **wella**), then with the surn. *Hartwell* of a family originally from the settlement of this name, 38 miles to the south in Northants.); Hen Mdw (*v.* **henn**); Hewitts Park (either with the surn. *Hewitt* or with **hīewet** 'a place where trees are cut down', *v.* Cold Overton Park Wood *supra*); Highway Cl (*v.* **hēah-weg**); Hill Cl; Hill Fd (poss. the name of one of the original great open-fields); Hovel Cl (*v.* **hovel**); Land Mdw (*v.* **land**; an enclosure consolidating a group of selions or 'lands' of a former open-field); Little Cl 1838, Little Mdw 1838, 1916; Longdale Cls, ~ Mdw (*v.* **lang**[1], **dalr**); Middle Cl, ~ Mdw; Mill Cl; Mill Fd 1916 (*v.* **myln**; poss. originally the name of one of the former great open-fields); The Mires (*v.* **mýrr**); Nether ~ ~, Upper Moody Syke (*v.* **sík**; prob. with the surn. *Moody*, otherwise *v.* **muddig**); Near ~ ~, New Mdw; Oakham Gate Cl 1821 (1694, *v.* **gata**; Oakham in Rutland lies 3 miles to the south-east); Old Mdw 1838, 1916; Park Cl, ~ Mdw (*v.* Cold Overton Park Wood *supra*); Pickwell Hill Cl (Pickwell village lies a little to the north-west); Ploughed Cl 1838, Big ~ ~, Little Ploughed Cl 1916; Pocket Mdw (*v.* **poket**; usually alluding to a rounded field with a narrow entrance); Ranxborough, ~ Mdw (Ranksborough Hill bestrides the county boundary with Rutland; early forms are *Rankesberwe* 1227, *Rankesborowe* ~ 1610, *Rankesbro* ~ 1780, *Ranksborough Hill* 1801, *v.* **berg**; with the OE masc. pers.n. *Ranc*, a by-name from *ranc* 'proud'); Road Cl (an enclosure beside a roadway); Rocott Spinney 1916 (*v.* **spinney**) (*Rocote* 1801, *Rocart* 1806, 1824, *Rocott* 1877, 'cottage at the boundary', *v.* **rá**[2], **cot**; at the county boundary with Rutland, *v.* Ru 92); Rye Grass Cl (referring to common ryegrass (*Lolium perenne*), a valuable pasture grass, deliberately cultivated on sown meadows); Saracens Cl, ~ Mdw (with the surn. *Sarson*/*Saracen*, cf. *Oliverus Sarazin* 12 Dane of Leics.; from OFr *Sarrazin* 'a Saracen', used as a by-name for a man with a swarthy complexion); Senholme ('water-meadow subject to dispute', *v.* **senna**, **holmr**; cf. *Senholm* 1346, Ru 37); Shoulder of Mutton Piece (*v.* **pece**; a common f.n. referring to the shape of a close); Little ~ ~, Stock Hill (*v.* **stocc**); Stone Hill (*v.* **stān**); Stonepit Cl, ~ Mdw (*v.* **stān-pytt**); Townsend ~ 1838, Townend Cl 1916 (*v.* **tūn**, **ende**); Woolsdale ~ 1838, Wooldale Mdw 1916 (*v.* **wald**; with **dalr** or **deill**).

(b) *Coldoverton Moor* 1721 (*v.* **mōr**[1]); *ad crucem lapideam* (*q' stat super magnum cheminum extra Coldoverton' versus partem australem*) 1227 ('at the stone cross (which stands on/above the highway to the south outside Cold Overton)'), *atte Cros* 1327 (p), 1332 (p) (*v.* **atte**, **cros**); *atte Grene* 1327 (p) (*v.* **atte**, **grēne**[2]).

Laughton

LAUGHTON

Lachestone 1086 DB
Lacton' 1200, 1206 Cur *et passim* to 1254 Val, *Lactona* 1190 × 1204 France
Lectona c.1206 GildR (p), *Lectone* 1219 RHug, *Lehton'* 1207 FF, 1210 P (p), *Leicton* 1223 BM
Leitone p.1204, 1277 Hastings, *Leyton*(*e*) 1271 Ipm, 1277 Hastings
Lauchton(*e*) 1231, 1235 RGros *et passim* to c.1291 Tax, *Laucton* 1240 RGros, 1296, 1329 Ipm, *Lauhton* 1260 Misc
Laghton' 1273 Coram (p), 1315 Cl *et passim* to 1369 Ipm, 1391 Cl, *Laughton* c.1291 Tax, 1327 SR *et passim* to 1427 *Rut*, 1428 FA *et freq*, *Lawghton* 1516 Fine, 1601 LibCl, 1615 LML, *Lawton* 1549 Pat

'The leek or garlic enclosure', *v.* **lēac-tūn**.

BRIAN'S CLOSE (2½"), a house built in the 1930s; with the surn. *Brian*/*Bryan*, a Breton name introduced into England by the Normans. GUMLEY RD, Gumley lying one mile to the north-east. KICKLEWELL SPINNEY, *Kicklewell* 1968 *Surv*, cf. *Kickelwell hole* 1625 *Terrier* (*v.* **hol**[1]), *v.* **cetel**, **wella** and **spinney**. KILLOCK HO., *Killock House* 1710 *Deed*, 1925 Kelly; poss. with the surn. *Killick*. LAUGHTON HILLS, 1806 Map. THE LODGE, 1925 Kelly, *Laughton Lodge* 1812 *Deed*, 1835 O, *v.* **loge**. LODGE FM. MAIN ST is *the Street*(*e*) 1601, 1625, 1708, 1708 (18) *Terrier*. MANOR FM, *v.* **maner**. MILL HILL, cf. *Mill Hill Close* 1715, 1794, 1835 *Deed*, *v.* **myln**, **hyll**. OLD MILL BARN, *the Old Mill* 1601, 1625 *Terrier*, 1778 *Deed*, cf. *Old Mill Close* 1777, 1778 *ib*, *v.* **ald**, **myln**. THE RECTORY, 1877 White, 1925 Kelly, *v.* **rectory**; earlier is *the Parsonage House* 1708, 1708 (18), 1724, c.1725 *Terrier*, *v.* **personage**. ST LUKE'S CHURCH, *the Church* 1724 *Terrier*, *Church (St Luke)* 1846, 1863, 1877 White, 1925 Kelly; it is early recorded as *ecclesiam de Lectone* 1219 RHug, ~ *de Lauchton* 1235, 1248 RGros, ~ *de Laucton* 1240 ib, ~ *de Lauhthon* 1250 ib, *ecclesie de Lacton* 1220 MHW, ~ *de Laghton* 1322, 1349 *Pat*, ~ *de Leght'* 1343 *ib*.

FIELD-NAMES

In (a), forms presented without dates are 1968 *Surv*; those dated 1765, 1768, 1777, 1778, 1785, 1794, 1799, 1805, 1808, 1812, 1835, 1845, 1848, 1849, 1854, 1861, 1862, 1863, 1870, 1890 and 1903 are *Deed*; 1840 are *TA*; 1869 are Sale. Forms throughout dated 1200 are Cur; those dated 1327 are SR; 1477 (e.16) are *Charyte*; 1601, 1625, 1679, 1690, 1700, 1708, 1708 (18), 1724 and c.1725 are *Terrier*; 1648, 1663, 1682, 1723, 1730 and 1749 are *Deed*.

(a) Three Acre 1968, Four Acres 1840, (the) Six Acres 1777, 1840, Eight Acre 1968, (the) Ten Acres 1777, 1785, 10 Acre 1968, the Ten Acres Cl 1778, Twelve Acres 1785, 1968, Twelve Acre Cl 1778, 14 Acre 1968, the Sixteen Acres 1777, 16 Acre 1968, the Sixteen Acres Cl 1778 (*v.* **æcer**); Barley Furlong 1777, 1778, 1848, 1849, Perkins Barley Furlong 1778 (with the surn. *Perkins*), Barley Furlong Mdw 1778, 1968 (*Barley* ~ 1601, *Barlye Furlong* 1625, *v.* **bærlic**, **furlang**); Big Fd; Blackdole Cl 1799, 1808, 1848, 1849, First ~ ~ to Fourth Blackdole Cl 1854, 1890 (*Black Dole* 1708, *Shorte blackdole* 1601, *v.* **blæc**, **dāl**; either with reference to the colour of the soil or to its fertility); The Bog (*v.* **bog**); Bosworths Cl 1861, 1968 (with the surn. *Bosworth* of a family prob. originally from Husbands Bosworth, 3 miles to the south-west); the Bottom Cl 1861 (*v.* **bottom**); Brinspitt 1777, Brimspit 1968 (*Brinkspit*, *Over Brinkspitt* (*v.* **uferra**) 1625, *Brinspitt Close* 1724, *v.* **brink**, **pytt**); Browns Cl or Smiths Mdw 1777, Browns Cl 1778, 1968, the Brown Close Mdw 1777, Brown's Lane 1840 (all with the surn. *Brown*); Burden Wall 1777 (*Borden Well* 1601, *Berden well* 1625, 'the boundary valley stream', *v.* **bord**, **denu**, **wella**; cf. *bord dene* 956 (12) BCS 982 (S 619)); Burtons Mdw (1708, 1708 (18); with the surn. *Burton*); Butchers Cl, ~ Mdw 1840 (with the surn. *Butcher*); Buxton's Cl 1777 (with the surn. *Buxton*); Church hadland 1777, Far ~ ~, Near Church Headland 1840, Church hadland Cl 1768 (*Church hadland* 1682, *v.* **hēafod-land**), Far Church Mdw 1840 (*v.* St Luke's Church *supra*); Cooks Cl (with the surn. *Cook*); the Coome Fd 1890 (*Coomefyeld* 1601, *v.* **cumb**, **feld**; one of the great open-fields of the township); Coopers Cl 1778 (with the surn. *Cooper*); Old Cotes 1777 (*v.* **ald**, **cot**); the Cottager's Cl 1777, the Cottagers Cls 1778 ((*the*) *Cottagers Close* 1679, 1690, 1708, *v.* **cotager**); Daniels Cl 1777, 1861 (1682; with the surn. *Daniel*(*s*)); Dawson's Cl 1777 (with the surn. *Dawson*); Derne Slade 1777 (*dearne slades* 1601, 1625, *v.* **derne**, **slæd**); Dovecoat Cl 1778 (*v.* **dove-cot**(**e**)); Far Cl 1840; First or New Cl 1768, First Cl 1777, 1840, 1861 (*First Close* 1682); First Fd; Five Leys (*v.* **leys**; grassland units of tenure corresponding to *lands* similarly used of arable); Gravel Hill 1840, 1869 (*Gravell Hill* 1682, *v.* **gravel**); Great Cl 1840; the Great Ground 1785, Great Grounds 1968, Great Ground Cl 1778 (*v.* **grēat**, **grund**); (the) Hanging Mdw 1778, 1785, 1805, 1845, 1968 (*v.* **hangende**); Heyfords Far ~, Heyfords Near ~, Heyfords Home Cl (poss. with **holmr**), Heyfords Middle ~, Heyfords Top Cl, Bottom Heyfords 1840 (*v.* **hēg**, **ford**, cf. *Heiford way* in adjoining Theddingworth f.ns. (b)); Higgs Cl, ~ Mdw 1840 (with the surn. *Higgs*); First ~ ~, Second Hill Fd, Hill Side (*v.* **sīde**); (The) Hobgoblin 1777, 1869 ((*land known as*) *Hobgoblin*, *Hobgoblin Close* 1682, *v.* **hobgoblin**; another name for Robin Goodfellow, 'the drudging goblin', *v.* E. M. Wright, *Rustic Speech and Folk-Lore* (Oxford 1913), 201, B. Dickins,

'Yorkshire Hobs', *Transactions of the Yorkshire Dialect Society*, vii, 19–22 and Robin-a-Tiptoe Hill, Lei **3** 245); Far ~ ~, Near Home Cl 1840, 1968, Home Fd 1968 (*v.* **home**); the House Cl 1890; Hubbards Mdw (with the surn. *Hubbard*); (Smith's) Laughton Cl 1808, 1840, 1848, 1849, 1890; Laughton Gorse 1835 O (*v.* **gorst**); Laughton Mdw; Ley Cl 1840, the Far ~ ~, the Near Ley Cl 1777 (*v.* **ley**); Little or Lane Cl 1768, Little Cl 1777, 1840, 1861 (1682); Little Mdw 1840, 1863, 1870, 1968; Long Cl 1840, 1861 (1708, 1708 (18), Long Close Mdw 1840; First ~, Martins (the surn. *Martin* in the possessive case); the Meadow 1840, 1890; Meadow Plotts 1777 (*Medow plattes* 1601, *Long ~ ~*, *Short meddow plattes* 1625, *v.* **plat**[2], **plot**); Mercer's House or Derne Slade 1777 (with the surn. *Mercer*; *v.* Derne Slade *supra*); Middle Cl 1812, 1840, 1890, 1968; the Middlecombe 1778, 1785, Middlescomb 1903, Big ~, First Middlescomb 1968, Middlescome ~ 1777, Middlecombe ~ 1778, 1903, Middlescomb Mdw 1903, 1968, Middlescome Pasture 1777 (*v.* **pasture**) (cf. *Midelscome Hill* 1601, *v.* **middel**, **cumb**); Mill Barn Mdw 1968, Mill Cl 1840, 1863, 1870 (*v.* **myln**); Neale Cl, ~ Mdw 1840 (with the surn. *Neale*); (the) Old Cl 1778, 1785, 1805, 1845 (1679, 1690, 1708, 1708 (18), *v.* **ald**); Old Gauge (*v.* **gauge**; alluding to a measure of some kind, poss. Gunter's Chain used by early surveyors); Old Mill Cl 1778 (*v.* **ald**, **myln**); the Park(e) 1777, 1778, 1785, Parkleys 1848, 1849 (*Park Leys* 1708, 1708 (18), *v.* **leys**) (*v.* **park**); Paynes 1968, Paynes ~ 1785, Paines Leys 1805, 1845 (*v.* **leys**) (with the surn. *Payne*, from OFr *Paien* (in turn from MLat *paganus* 'heathen', earlier 'villager'), used in the 12th and 13th cents. as a Christian name and as a patronymic surn., cf. *Rotrotus Pagani* 1195 P of Leics.); Pen(n) Cl 1863, 1870 (*v.* **penn**[2]); the Nether ~ ~, the Upper Pessle Syke 1777 (*Peasefyeld seeke* 1601, *Peasald sicke* 1625 (*v.* **pise**, **feld**, **sík**); Pithill 1777 (*v.* **pytt**, **hyll**); the Nether ~ ~, the Over Ploughed Cl (*v.* **uferra**) 1812, 1890; Poor Mdw (*v.* **pouer(e)**; alluding to land dedicated to poor relief or charity); Primrose Mdw (*v.* **primerose**; land on which the primrose grows, *Primula vulgaris* being common in woodland and shady places); Red Furlong (*Red furlonge* 1601, *Red Furlong* 1625, 1679, 1690, 1708, 1708 (18), ~ ~ *Close* 1730, 1749, *v.* **rēad**, **furlang**; alluding to the colour of the soil); Road Cl 1840, ~ Mdw 1968 (fields bordering a roadway); Rush Cl 1799, 1854, 1890, 1968 (*v.* **risc**); Russells Mdw, ~ 2nd Mdw (*Russell* 1601, *russell hill* 1625, *v.* **risc**, **wella**); Sains Leys, formerly Old Mill Cl 1778, Saint Leys Mdw, ~ ~ Pasture 1777 (*Santelese* 1601, *Saunkles* 1625, *v.* **sand**, **lǣs** and Old Mill Cl *supra*); Sand Holes (*v.* **sand**, **hol**[1]); The Seeds (*v.* **sǣd**; used of grasses sown for one year's mowing or grazing, as distinguished from permanent pasture); Smiths Cl 1840, 1968 (prob. with the surn. *Smith*, cf. Smith's Laughton Cl *supra*); Smiths Mdw 1777 (*Smith meadow* 1601, *Smith med(d)ow hill* 1601, 1625; with either the surn. *Smith* or with **smið**); Thorn Bush Cl (*v.* **þorn**, **busc**); First ~, Second Thorncombe (*Thorn Coom(e)* 1679, 1690, *Thorncomb(e)* 1700, c.1725, *Thorn(e)come hill* 1601, 1625, *v.* **þorn**, **cumb**); Top Acre 1840 (*v.* **æcer**), Little ~ ~, Middle ~ ~, Near Top Cl 1840, the Top Cl 1861, Top Hole (*v.* **hol**[1]), Top Mdw 1968 (*v.* **top**); Great ~ ~, Little Townsend Cl 1840 (*Townes End Close* 1708, *Townsend Close* 1708 (18), *the South Townes end* 1601, *v.* **tūn**, **ende**); Town Syke Mdw, the Town Syke Pasture 1777 (*Towne seeke* 1601, ~ *Sick* 1708, *v.* **tūn**, **sík**); Turnip Cl (*v.* **turnepe**); Wadcombe 1840, Wadcom ~ 1765, 1785, Wadcomb Cl 1862, Wadcom ~ 1765, 1785, Wadcomb Mdw 1840, 1862 (*watcome* 1601, *Wat(t)coome* 1708, 1708 (18), *Watcome hill* 1601, 1625 (*v.* **cumb**; with **hwǣte** or **wād**); Walker's Cl 1777, 1778 (with the surn. *Walker*); Waples Cl 1777, Walpoles Far ~, Walpoles Near Cl 1840 (*Wapels Close* 1708, 1708 (18); with the surn. *Waple*;

cf. *Galfridus Waupol*, ~ *Wagpoll* 1271 RBL of Leicester); Warners Mdw 1840 (with the surn. *Warner*); Well Hill 1840, 1869 (*Welleshull'* 1200, *Wel(l) Hill* 1601, 1625), Well Hill Cl 1768, 1777, 1869 (1682) (*v.* **wella**, **hyll**); Well Mdw 1840 (cf. *atte Welle* 1327 (p), *v.* **atte**, **wella**); Wheatland Syke 1777 (*v.* **land**, **sík**; prob. with **hwǣte** but **wēt** is poss.).

(b) *Long ~, Short Ban(d)land* 1601, 1625 (*v.* **bēan**, **land**); *Beene* 1601, *longe Bene* 1625 (*v.* **bēn** 'boon, favour' and later, 'gift'; alluding to service in labour or in kind paid to a landlord by his tenent, cf. The Been, Brk **2** 419); *Beneath the low* 1601 (*v.* **hlāw**); *Berry doles* 1601 (*v.* **berige**, **dāl**); *Bondman leyes* 1601, ~ *leas* 1625 (*v.* **leys**; either with **bond-man** or with the surn. *Bondman*); *Bratlyse* 1601 (*v.* **brād**, **lǣs**); *longe bredseeke* 1601 (*v.* **brād**, **sík**); *Bridghooks* 1700 (*v.* **brycg**, **hōc**); *Brockholes* 1601 (*v.* **brocc-hol**); *the Burrow Meadow* 1723, *Burrow Meadow Closes* 1730, 1749 (with **burh** or **burgh**); *Burtons Close* 1708, 1708 (18) (with the surn. *Burton*); *Caudwell* 1625 (*v.* **cald**, **wella**); *Cogermans Iron(e)s* 1700, c.1725 (*v.* **hyrne**; with the surn. *Coggerman*, from ME *cogger*, 'a builder or sailor of a *cogge* (a small ship, a cog)'); *the Cottagers Pasture* 1724, c.1725 (*v.* **cotager**, **pasture**); *Deadman* 1601, ~ *leas* 1625 (*v.* **leys**) (*v.* **dede-man**; prob. named from the discovery of a pagan Anglo-Saxon burial site, since this appears to be a location at the parish boundary, *v. Mousley deadman, infra*); *the Gleabe Close* 1679, 1690, (*a close called*) *the Gleabe* 1700, c.1725 (*v.* **glebe**); *Gravell pittes* 1601, 1625 (*v.* **gravel**, **pytt**); *Gumley low* 1625 (*v.* **hlāw**; Gumley parish adjoins to the north-east); *þe halle* 1477 (e.16) (p), *the Hall Close* 1708, 1708 (18) (*v.* **þe**, **hall**); *Harborough Road* 1724 (Market Harborough lies 4 miles to the south-east); *Henchmans Land* 1648 (*v.* **land**; with the surn. *Henchman*, a reflex of OE *hengest* 'a horse' plus *mann*, hence 'a groom' and also 'a packhorse driver, a sumpter'); *the hills* 1601; *Iliffs Close* 1679, 1690 (with the surtn. *Iliff*, a reflex of the ON masc. pers.n. *Eileifr*); *Kett Johnsons Close* 1708; *Lambcome* 1601 (*v.* **lamb**, **cumb**); *litle hill* 1601 (*v.* **lȳtel**, **hyll**); *Lubnam gate* 1601, 1625 (*v.* **gata**), *Lubnam Meer* 1708, 1708 (18) (*v.* **(ge)mǣre**) (Lubenham parish adjoins to the south-east); *Marlepittes* 1601 (*v.* **marle-pytt**); *Marstall* 1601, *Mastill* 1625 (*v.* **mere-stall**); *Medow seeke* 1601 (*v.* **mēd** (**mēdwe** obl.sg.), **sík**); *Midlehill* 1601, *middle hill* 1625 (*v.* **middel**); *Millfyeld* 1601, *Mill feild* 1625 (*v.* **myln**, **feld**; one of the great open-fields); *Mousley deadman* 1601 (*v.* **dede-man**; prob. to be identified with the site of *Deadman*, *supra*; at the parish boundary with Mowsley which adjoins to the west); *Moyst Irons* 1601, *Moist irones* 1625 (*v.* **moyst**, **hyrne**); *the Nether Fyeld* 1601, *Nether Feild* 1625 (*v.* **neoðera**, **feld**; one of the great open-fields); *Nortens yard* 1601 (*v.* **geard**; with the surn. *Norton*); *Red hill* 1708, 1708 (18) (*v.* **rēad**; with reference to the colour of the soil); *Rickstides* 1625 (*v.* **rickstead**); *Ridlingtons close* 1625, *Thomas Ridlingtons two Home Closes* 1708, *William Ridlington's Land* 1708 (18) (the *Ridlington* family presum. came originally from the village of this name, 14 miles to the north-east in Rutland); *Longe ~, Shorte Ryland* 1601, *long ~, short Rieland* 1625 (*v.* **ryge**, **land**); *Sand(e)pittes* 1601, 1625 (*v.* **sand-pytt**); *Setcupp* 1601 (*v.* **set-copp**); *Stonehill* 1601, 1625 (*v.* **stān**, **hyll**); *South meddow* 1625; *Swarborrow* 1601 (*v. Swardboro* in Mowsley f.ns. (b)); *Thedingworth Leys* 1708 (18) (*v.* **leys**; Theddingworth parish adjoins to the south); *Tomlins Two Closures* 1708, 1708 (18) (*v.* **closure**; with the surn. *Tomlin*); *Towne Furlonge* 1601 (*v.* **furlang**), *the Towne hadland* 1601, 1625 (*v.* **hēafod-land**), *Town Sick* 1708 (18) (*v.* **sík**), *the towne side* 1625 (*v.* **sīde**) (*v.* **tūn**); *the Tythe Close alias Thorn Coom* 1679 (*v.* **tēoða** and Thorncombe *supra*); *Washpitt* 1625, *Washpytt hill*

1601 (*v.* **wæsce**, **pytt**); *Watermill Close* 1663, 1708, 1708 (18) (*v.* **water-mylne**); *Water thorowes* 1625 (*v.* **wæter**, **furh** and *the water furrowes* in Billesdon f.ns. (b)); *Wests Closures* 1708, 1708 (18) (*v.* **closure**; with the surn. *West*); *Long*(*e*) *white*(*s*) 1601, 1625 (*v.* **hwīt**; in eModE, *white* 'infertile' may be contrasted with *black* 'fertile'); *Wilsons four Upper Closes*, *Wilsons Lower Closes* 1708, 1708 (18) (cf. *Thomas Wilson* 1708 and *William Wilson* 1708 (18)); *Withy pittes* 1601 (*v.* **wīðig**, **pytt**); *Shorte wrangland* 1601 (*v.* **wrang**, **land**); *Wrong gates* 1601, 1625 (*v.* **wrang**, **gata**); *Wride willowes* 1625 (*v.* **wride**), *Wyndes willowes* 1601 (*v.* **(ge)wind**^{2}) (*v.* **wilig**); *the Wyer* 1708 (18), *Wyar Close* 1708, 1708 (18) (*v.* **weyour**).

Little Stretton

LITTLE STRETTON

For forms and interpretation of the place-name, *v.* Stretton Magna.

Affixes are variously added as:
~ *Parua* 1357, 1368, 1428 *Wyg*, 1518 Visit, ~ *Parva* 1303, 1314 Banco *et passim* to 1535 VE, 1537 MinAccts
Parua ~ 1327, 1357 *Wyg*, *Parva* ~ 1344 BM, 1344 *Pat*
Lyttle ~ 1601 *Terrier*, *Little* ~ 1610 Speed *et freq*

Little Stretton lies on the Roman Gartree Road (*Via Devana*) about one mile to the south-east of Stretton Magna. Note MLat *parva* 'small'.

ASH SPINNEY, 1907 *Surv*, 1913 Sale, *v.* **æsc**, **spinney**; it is *Ash Plantation* 1777 *Map*, *v.* **plantation**. COTTERILL SPINNEY, 1878 *PK*, 1913 Sale; with the surn. *Cotterill*, *v.* Cotterill Fm in adjoining Stretton Magna. CROW SPINNEY, 1907 *Surv*, 1913 Sale, *v.* **crāwe**. DOBB HALL (GLEBE FM 2½") (*v.* **glebe**), *v.* **daube**, **hall**; a humorously disparaging name for a poor site. THE LODGE, 1877 White, *v.* **loge**. THE MANOR, with fabric from c.1600 and presumably to be identified with *Little Stretton Hall* 1854 *Surv*; note the medieval *Halleplace* 1446 Banco (*v.* **place**) and earlier *atte Hall(e)* 1327 SR (p), 1332 ib (p) *et passim* to 1363 BPR (p), 1368 *Wyg* (p) (*v.* **atte**), *v.* **hall**. RED LION (P.H.) (lost), *Red Lion* 1846, 1877 White. ST JOHN THE BAPTIST'S CHURCH, *Church (St John the Baptist)* 1925 Kelly; earlier is recorded *capellam de Parva Stretton* 1344 *Pat* (with MLat *capella* 'a chapel'). TOP FM (HOME FM 2½", *v.* **home**).

FIELD-NAMES

In (a), forms dated 1751, 1766 and 1772 are *Deed*; those dated 1771 are *EnclA*; 1777 are *Map*; 1846, 1863 and 1877 are White; 1854 and 1907 are *Surv*; 1878 are *PK*; 1913 are Sale. Forms throughout dated 1601, 1605, 1625, 1674, 1697, 1704 and 1715 are *Terrier*; those dated 1654, 1663, 1671, 1682, 1716 and 1729 are *Deed*.

(a) The Half Acre 1777, The Two Acres 1907, Six Acres 1907, 1913, Little Forty Acre 1878, 1907, 1913 (*v.* **æcer**); Adwong 1766, 1771, 1772, West Adwong 1913 (*Under Adwong* 1715, *Adwong(e) Close* 1715, 1716, *v.* Adwongs in adjoining King's Norton f.ns. (a)); Mr Bates Allotment, Blount ~, Samuel Coleman ~, Mr William Coleman's ~, Cowdell ~, John Freer ~, Gilbert ~, Holbridge ~, Humfrey ~, Jeff ~, Kemp ~, Ludlam ~, Noble ~, Rowe ~, White ~, Sir George Robinson Allotment 1777 (*v.* **allotment**); Bandall Fd 1771 (1704, *Bannell field(e)* 1601, 1605, 1625, *Bandell feild* 1682, *Bandaile ~*, *The Bandal Field* 1697, *Banel-field* 1709, *the Bandale Feild* 1715 (*v.* **feld**; one of the great open-fields of the township), cf. *Bandale Ley(e)s* 1715 (*v.* **leys**)) (*v.* **bēan**, **deill**); Banny Lane 1771 (also found in adjoining Great Glen as Bandy Lane Cl 1862; most prob. with a reduced Bandall *supra*); Best Cl 1907, 1913 (*v.* **best**; a complimentary name for very fertile land); Boycroft 1766, 1772, The Boycroft Cl 1751 (*Boycroft* 1663, 1715, 1716, *v.* **croft**; either with the OE masc. pers.n. *Boia* or with **boia**); Brick Kiln Cl 1854, 1907, 1913 (*v.* **brike-kiln**); Brook Cl 1772, 1854, 1907, 1913 (*v.* **brōc**); Bulgar Leys, ~ ~ Cl 1771 (*v.* **leys**) (cf. *Ne(a)ther ~*, *Bulgore* 1715, *bullgoares sick* 1601, *bullgores sicke* 1605, 1625, *Bulgar ~* 1697, *Bulger ~* 1704, 1709, *Bulgore Sick* 1715 (*v.* **sík**) (*v.* **bula**, **gāra**); Buttleys, ~ Cl 1766 (*But Ley(e)s*, *Butt Leys* 1715, *v.* **leys**; with **but** or **butte**); Clarke's Cl 1878, 1907, 1913, ~ Mdw 1907, 1913 (with the surn. *Clarke*); Clover Cl, ~ ~ Mdw 1907, 1913 (*v.* **clāfre**; grown as a fodder crop); Coleman's Lane 1771 (cf. *Samuel Coleman* and *William Coleman* 1777); Little ~, Crawsdale 1771, Cross Dale 1878, 1907, 1913 (*Crosdale* 1601, 1605, 1625, 1697, 1704, 1715, *Great ~*, *Little Crosdale* 1709, 1715, *the Broad of Crosdale* 1715 (*v.* **brode**)), Crawsdale Cl 1771 (*Crawsdells Close* 1715) (*v.* **cross**, **deill**); Cross Leys 1777 (*v.* **cross**, **leys**); The Dovecoat Cl 1751 (*the Dovecoate Close* 1603), Dovecote Leys, ~ Mdw 1777 (*v.* **leys**) (*v.* **dove-cot(e)**); Far Mdw 1907, 1913; Freer's Cl 1854 (cf. *John Freer* 1777); Goldfinder 1878, 1907, 1913 (prob. a complimentary name for a very profitable field; but less likely, recording the chance find of a valuable (archaeological?) item); Glenn Lane Cl 1854, 1878, Glenn Sick Leys 1777 (*v.* **leys**), Glensick Cl 1771 (*Glen(n) Sick* 1715, *v.* **sík**; Great Glen parish adjoins to the south-west); Gravel Pit 1854, 1907, 1913 (*v.* **gravel**, **pytt**); Great Hill 1854, 1878, 1907, 1913 (*v.* **grēat**); Green Lane Cl 1907, 1913 (*v.* **grēne**[1]); Grubtoft Furlong 1771 (*v.* **furlang**) (*Grubtoft* 1715, *v.* **toft**; either with a reduced pa.part. *grubbed*, from **grubbe** 'to clear land of roots and stumps by digging up', or with the surn. *Grubb*, from ME *grubbe* 'a grub, a worm', used of a very short individual); Halfords Cl 1771, 1878, 1907, 1913 (cf. *Richard Halford* 1654 of Little Stretton); Hall Cl 1777 (*the Hall Closes* 1715), (the) Hall Leys 1715, 1854, 1878, 1907, 1913 (*the Hall Leyes* 1663, *v.* **leys**) (*v.* The Manor *supra*); First ~, Far ~, Middle Holt 1878, 1907, 1913 (*v.* **holt**); Home Cl 1854, 1907, 1913 (*v.* **home**); The Hooks 1751 (*the Hookes* 1663, 1715, *v.* **hōc**); Horseheads Furlong 1771 (*v.* **hors**, **furlang**; the second el. is prob. **stede**, but **hēafod** is poss.); Hospital Cl 1878, 1907, 1913 (*v.* **hospital**; the property of Wigston's Hospital in Leicester; note also *the Hospitall Land* in adjoining King's Norton); Hovel Cl 1907, 1913 (*v.* **hovel**); Intake 1854, 1907, 1913 (*v.* **inntak**); Kennys Lane 1771 (with the surn. *Kenny*); Kiln Fd 1777 (cf. *the Kiln Close* 1729, *v.* **cyln**); Leeches Cl 1913 (with the surn. *Leach/Leech*, from OE *lǣce* ' a physician'); Long Furlong 1777, 1854 (1715, *v.* **lang**[1], **furlang**; of the Ming Fd *infra*); Love Pit Leys 1854, 1907, 1913 (*v.* **pytt**, **leys**; presum. a place for secret dalliance); (the) Lower Fd 1771, 1772; Ludcroft Leys 1771 (1715, *v.* **leys**) (*Ludcroft*, *Lud-Croft* 1715, *v.* *Ludcroft* in Stretton Magna f.ns. (b));

Middle Cl, ~ Mdw 1907, 1913; Ming Fd 1771, 1846, 1863, 1877 (1697, 1704, 1715, *Mingled field*(*e*) 1605, 1625, *Mingfeild* 1671, *the Mingled feild* 1674, *Mingl'd feild* 1709, *v.* **myngled**; one of the great open-fields, otherwise called *the Stocke fielde*, *infra*; the great open-field shared with Stretton Magna, *v. Myngde Feilde* in Stretton Magna f.ns. (b)); Mire Cl 1777 (cf. *the Mires* 1715, *v.* **mýrr**); Moor Cl 1878 (*v.* **mōr**[1]); Nether Cl or Rundell 1777, 1907 (*v.* Rundell *infra*), Nether Cl 1913; The New Cl 1751, 1771, 1907, 1913 (*the New Close* 1663); Bottom ~ 1907, Church ~ 1854, Long Orchard 1878, 1907, 1913 (*v.* **orceard**); Ozier Bed 1907 (*v.* **oyser**, **bedd**); Pad Lands 1777, 1854, 1907, 1913 (*v.* **land**; prob. with dial. **pad** 'a path', otherwise with **padde**); Lower ~, Upper Plantation 1777 (*v.* **plantation**); Bottom ~ ~, Middle ~ ~, Top Ploughed Cl 1878, 1907, Ploughed Cl 1907, Great ~ ~, Little Ploughed Cl 1907, 1913); the Pool Cl 1751 (*v.* **pōl**[1]); the Rickyard 1766, 1772 (*the Ricke Yard* 1715, 1716, *v.* **rick-yard**); Rundell 1772, 1878, 1907 (1601, 1605, 1715, *Rundale* 1625, 1697, 1704, 1715, *Rundall* 1709, *Rundale ~*, *Rundell Head* 1715 (*v.* **hēafod**), *v.* **rynel**); Sherrards Bridge 1771 (*the Bridge* 1715, *v.* **brycg**), Sherrards Ford 1771 (*v.* **ford**) (poss. with the surn. *Sherrard*, but note the earlier surn. *Sherwood* in f.ns. (b) of which this may be a reduced form); Sink Hole Mdw 1878, 1907, 1913 (*v.* **sinke**, **hol**[1]); Slade Mdw 1878, 1907, 1913 (*v.* **slæd**); Springs Lane 1771 (*v.* **spring**[1]); Little ~ ~, Square Cl 1878 (*v.* **squar**(**e**)); First ~, Second Stackley 1854, 1878, 1907, 1913 (*Stackley*, *~ Ley*(*e*)*s* (*v.* **leys**) 1715, *v.* **staca**, **lēah** and Stackley House in adjoining Great Glen); Stear Hill 1878, 1907, 1913 (*v.* **stēor**); Stock Cl 1777 (*Stock Close*(*s*) 1715), Stock Leys 1771, 1854, 1878, 1907, 1913 (*Stockley*(*e*)*s* 1715, *v.* **leys**), Stock Mdw 1854, 1878, 1907, 1913 (*v.* **stoc**); Stone Green Lane 1771, ~ ~ Mdw 1854, 1878, 1907, 1913 (*Stongreen*, *Stone Green* 1715; *v.* Stone Green Mdw in Stretton Magna f.ns. (a)); Summer Fd 1777 (cf. *Summerfield Baulk* 1715 (*v.* **balca**), *v.* **sumor**; poor drainage limited the land's use to summer months only); Susans Headland 1771 (*Susanna Freyers headland*, *Widow Freers Head Land* 1715, *v.* **hēafod-land**); Tentery Cl 1771 (*v.* **tentour**; prob. with an eModE form **teyntree**); Three Cornered Mdw 1777 (*v.* **three-cornered**); Top Cl 1907, 1913; Town Croft 1777 (*v.* **croft**), Town Haggs 1854, 1878, 1907, 1913 (*the Haggs* 1715, *v.* **hǫgg**), the Town Homestead 1771 (*v.* **hām-stede**), Townlands 1777, Town Street 1771 (*v.* **strǣt**) (*v.* **tūn**); The Great Tythes 1777 (*v.* **tēoða**); Upper Cl 1913; Wall Gates 1854, 1878, 1907, 1913 (*Wall Gate* (×2), *Whale Gates* 1715 (of uncertain meaning; **hváll** or its cognate **hwæl** with **gata** may be thought of, but so may **wella**; and *v.* Randall Walls in nearby Galby f.ns. (a)); Well Cl 1766, 1772 ((*the*) *Well Close* 1715, 1716, *v.* **wella**); Wheat Cl 1907, 1913 (*v.* **hwǣte**); Whinney 1766, Winney 1913 (*Whinney Close* 1715, 1716, *v.* **whinny**).

(b) *the Backside Sherwoods*, *~ ~ Sheerwoods* 1715 (*v.* **bak-side**; with the surn. *Sherwood* in the possessive case); *Bateses Close*, *~ Peece* (*v.* **pece**) 1715 (with the surn. *Bates*); *Robert Brewins Headland* 1715 (*v.* **hēafod-land**); *Broad Land* 1715 (*v.* **brād**, **land**); *the Bush* 1715 (*v.* **busc**); *the Church close* 1682, *Church Leys* 1715 (*v.* **leys**) (*v.* St John the Baptist's Church *supra*); *Deadman* 1715 (*v.* **dede-man**; prob. the site of the discovery of an early burial); *Deep*(*e*)*dale* 1715 (*v.* **dēop**, **dalr**); *Fisel Baulke* 1715 (*v.* **þistel**, **balca**); *Five Ley*(*e*)*s* 1715 (*v.* **leys**; in compound with a numeral, *leys* represents grassland units of tenure corresponding to *lands* (i.e strips or selions) similarly used of arable); *Flaggy Hookes* 1715 (*v.* **flaggi**, **hōc**); *the Flatt* 1715 (*v.* **flat**); *Glenn Ditch* 1715 (*v.* **dīc**; presum. a boundary marker), *Glen*(*n*) *Hooke* 1715 (*v.* **hōc**) (Great Glen parish adjoins to the south-west); *Sir Richard Halfords*

Close 1715; *Hall Lane*, *Hall Lane End* 1714 (*v.* **lane-ende** and The Manor *supra*); *Home Ley*(*e*)*s* 1715 (*v.* **home**, **leys**); *Horsepool*(*e*) 1715 (*v.* **hors**, **pōl**[1]); *Houghton Meere* 1715 (*v.* **(ge)mǣre**; Houghton on the Hill parish adjoins to the north-east); *Huntsback*(*e*) 1601, 1605, 1625, 1709, *Hunch-Back* 1697, *Hunchback* 1704, 1715, *Hunch Backs* 1715, *Hunchback Gutter* 1715 (*v.* **goter**) (this is a topographical name alluding to a ridge of land, with the first el. being the surn. *Hunt* in the possessive case; if a large feature, then a name with **bæc**, but *back* here may be a late local reflex of **balca**; note that the earliest citation in OED for *hunchback* is dated 1712); *Hurrygurry*, *Hurrigurry* 1715 (of uncertain meaning; ostensibly a f.n. with a reduplicated extension of *hurry* (cf. *hurry-burry* and *hurly-burly*), perh. in its sense 'hasty motion, rush' (OED *s.v.* hurry sb. II 3), but if so, its application to toponomy or agriculture is unclear; in 1659, *hurry* is recorded with the meaning 'a small load of hay or corn' (OED *s.v.* hurry sb. 6a), while Lei dial. *hurr-burr* referred to the burdock (*Arctium lappa*), either of which, modified by a reduplication process, may pertain in some sort here); *Jaqueses Lane End* 1715 (*v.* **lane-ende**; cf. *Widdow Jaques* 1715); *Jeffs Leys* 1715 (*v.* **leys**; with the surn. *Jeff*, cf. Jeff Allotment in f.ns. (a)); *the Kiln Yard* 1714 (*v.* **cyln**, **geard**); *the Lammas Close* 1729 (*v.* **lammas**); *Longcroft*, ~ *Corner* 1715 (*v.* **corner**) (*v.* **lang**[1], **croft**); *Lyttle Stretton towne syde* 1601 (*v.* **tūn**, **sīde**); *Middle Hill* 1715; *Middle Sick* 1715 (*v.* **sík**); *Mus*(*s*)*dale* 1715 (*v.* **mūs**, **dalr**); *the Neather field*(*e*) 1601, 1605, 1625, ~ ~ *Feild* 1715, *the Nether* ~ 1697, *Neither Field* 1704 (*v.* **neoðera**, **feld**; one of the great open-fields of the township); *Neather Stock*, *Nether Stock Leys* 1715 (*v.* **leys**) (*v.* **neoðera**, **stoc**); (*John*) *Nobles Close* 1715; *Norton Closes*, *Norton Gate* (*v.* **gata**), *Norton Gate Ford* 1715 (*v.* **ford**) (King's Norton lies one mile to the east); *the olde brooke* 1601, *the old brooke* 1605, *the Old Brook* 1625, 1697, 1704, 1715 (*v.* **wald**, **brōc** and *atte Wolde*, *infra*); *Redmires* 1715 (*v.* **hrēod**, **mýrr**); *Sallow pitt* 1715 (*v.* **salh**, **pytt**); *Sand Holes* 1715 (*v.* **sand**, **hol**[1]); *Scamberdale*, ~ *green* 1715 (*v.* **grēne**[2]) (*v.* *Scamdale* in Stretton Magna f.ns. (b)); *Scockwell* 1601, 1605, 1625, *Scockeril*(*l*) 1697, 1704, *Skokerel* 1709, *Stockerhill*, ~ *Fo*(*a*)*rd*, *Stockerill Foard* 1715 (*v.* **ford**) (*v.* Stocker Hill in adjoining Houghton on the Hill f.ns. (a), Galby f.ns. (a) and Scockerhill in King's Norton f.ns. (a)); *The Seven Rood Peece* 1715 (*v.* **seofon**, **rōd**[3], **pece**); *Shelboards*, *Shelboardlands* 1715 (*v.* **land**) (*v.* **scofl-brǣdu**); *Slether Hill* 1715 (*v.* **slidor**); *the Stocke fielde or Mingled fielde* 1601, *Stockfield*(*e*) *or Mingled field*(*e*) 1605, 1625, *Stock Field or Ming Field* 1697, 1704, *Stock feild or Mingl'd feild* 1709 (*v.* **stoc**, **feld** and Ming Fd *supra*; the great open-field shared with Stretton Magna); *Stone Furlong* 1715 (*v.* **stān**, **furlang**); *Stretton Closes* 1715; *Stretton Hedge* 1715 (*v.* **hecg**; the boundary hedge with Stretton Magna); (*a place called*) *Thisseldale* 1601, *Thissledale* 1605, *Thistledale* 1625, 1709, *Thiseldale* 1704 (*v.* **þistel**, **dalr**); *the Town Headland* (*v.* **hēafod-land**), *the Town Ley* 1715 (*v.* **ley**[2]) (*v.* **tūn**); *Washpitt*(*e*) 1715 (*v.* **wæsce**, **pytt**); *Withey pool*(*e*) 1715 (*v.* **wīðig**, **pōl**[1]); *atte Wolde* 1327 (p) (*v.* **atte**), *the Oult* 1715 (*v.* **wald**).

Lubenham

LUBENHAM

Lobenho 1086 DB, Wm 2, p.1150 Dugd, 1270 RGrav, *Lobeho* c.1200 Dugd, *Lobehou* 1242 Fees, 13 *ShR*
Lubeho e.12 Dugd, 1109 Nichols, 1147 BM *et passim* to 1230 ChancR, *Lubehow* 1243 Fees, *Lubehou* 1253 × 58 RHug, *Lubehoo* 1364 BPR, *Lubbeho(u)* 1230 P, 1230 RGros (p), 1230 Cur (p), Hy 3 BM, *Lubbehow* 1243 RGros
Lubbenho 1109 Nichols, 1203 Ass, Hy 3 BM, *Lubenho* p.1150, 12 Dugd, 1203 Ass *et passim* to 1270 RGrav, 1276 RH, *Lubenhou* 1220 MHW
Lubeham 1086 DB
Lubanham 1086 DB, *Lubenham* 1260 Cur, c.1291 Tax *et freq* to 1481 Pat, 1497 *Deed et passim* to 1558 Will, 1613 LML *et freq*, *Lubbenham* 1261, 1317 Banco *et passim* to 1333 *Rut*, 1340 *Peake* (p) *et freq* to 1535 VE, 1540 MinAccts *et passim* to 1610 Speed, 1700 LeicW
Lobenham 1267 Cur, 1274 Coram *et freq* to 1430, 1451 *MktHPR et passim* to 1516 *Braye*, 1529 LinDoc, *Lobbenham* 1324 Pat (p), 1328 Banco *et passim* to 1420 Nichols, 1427 *Rut*, *Lobenam* 1347 *Peake* (p), *Lobnam* 1369, 1372 GildR (p)
Lubnam 1509, 1522, 1528, 1541 *MktHPR*, 1553 Pat

'(The settlement at) Luba's or Lubba's spur(s) of land', *v.* **hōh** (**hōe** dat.sg., **hōs** nom.pl., **hōm** dat.pl.). The OE masc. pers.ns. *Luba* (*Luban* gen.sg.) and *Lubba* (*Lubban* gen.sg.) are both attested independently.

The recorded place-name forms vary principally between *Lub(b)enho* and *Lub(b)enham*. The southern end of the hill-spur at Lubenham is forked, with the township situated on the eastern side of the western prong of the fork. The spur as a whole would have been the *hōh*, but the two minor prongs may have given rise to a plural *hōs* 'the spurs' (cf. Hose, Lei **2** 99). If the entire headland was called alternatively **Lub(b)anhōh* and **Lub(b)anhōs*, the early settlement name in the dat.sg. would have been *(*æt*) *Lub(b)anhōe* and in the dat.pl. *(*æt*)

Lub(*b*)*anhōm*, *v.* **æt**. A ME interchange between **Lub*(*b*)*enho* and **Lub*(*b*)*enhom* would have developed and in the latter form, the vowel of the final syllable could well have been shortened, hence *-hōm* > *-hom* > *-ham*, i.e. with subsequent confusion with the reflex of OE *hām*. Ekwall in Studies[3] points out the similarity of Lubenham to Bozenham (Nth 100) and to Cranham (Ess 124) where the same phenomenon appears to have occurred.

ALL SAINTS' CHURCH, *Church (All Saints')* 1846, 1863, 1877 White, 1925 Kelly; it is earlier recorded as *ecclesie de Lubenhou* 1220 MHW, ~ *de Lubbehow* 1243 RGros, ~ *de Lobenham* 1322, 1345, 1347, 1370, 1381 *Pat*, *ecclesiam de Wistowe et Lubenham* 1481 *ib*. BUNKERS HILL, 1925 Kelly; a transferred name which commemorated the battle of Bunker Hill in Massachusetts in 1775, at which the English defeated the colonial forces but suffered great losses. BUNKER'S HILL FM, *Bunkers Hill Farm* 1845 *TA*. CHURCH WALK, *v.* **walk** and All Saints' Church *supra*. COACH AND HORSES (P.H.), *Coach and Horses* 1816 *Map*, 1877 White, 1879 *Deed*, 1925 Kelly. THE COTTAGE, 1863 White, 1925 Kelly, *v.* **cotage**. DEACON'S MEADOW, 1846, 1863, 1877 White; with the surn. *Deacon*, a reflex of ME *deakne* 'a minor official of the Church'. FOXTON RD, Foxton lying 2 miles to the north. GORE LODGE, 1925 Kelly; the sometime residence of *John Benedict Gore* 1875 PR, *v.* **loge**. THE GREEN, *v.* **grēne**[2]. HILL COTTAGE. HOLME'S FM, *Holmes farm* 1925 Kelly, *Holmesham Farm* 1845 *TA*, cf. *Holmesome closes* l.17 *Terrier*, *v.* **hamm**; presum. with the surn. *Holmes*, since *holmr* with *hamm* would be pleonastic, but *v. Holmes Close* in f.ns. (b). LAUGHTON RD, Laughton lying 2½ miles to the north-west. THE LODGE. LOWER LODGE. LUBENHAM LODGE, 1877 White, 1925 Kelly, *Lubbenham Lodge* 1700 LeicW, *v.* **loge**. MAIN ST is *the High Street* 1671 *Deed*, *v.* **hēah**[1]. MANOR HO., *Manor house* 1877 White, 1925 Kelly, *v.* **maner**. MARSTON RD, Marston Trussell in Northants. lying one mile to the south-west. MILL HILL, *Milhill* 1602 *Deed*, *Mill Hill* 1694, 1697, l.17 *Terrier*, *v.* **myln**, **hyll**. OLD HALL, 1835 O, 1846, 1863 White, *v.* **ald**, **hall**. OLD HALL LANE. OLD ORCHARD, *The Old Orchard* 1734 *Deed*, 1846, 1863, 1877 White, *v.* **ald**, **orceard**. PAGET ARMS (P.H.) (lost), *Paget's Arms* 1877 White, *Paget Arms* 1925 Kelly (*Thomas Tertius Paget* is lord of the manor 1877 White); PAPILLON FM, PAPILLON HALL FM (PAPILLON HALL 2½"), *Papillon Hall* 1798 Nichols, 1835 O, 1846, 1863, 1877 White, 1925 Kelly; the local popular name is *Pamp's Hall* 1798 Nichols, *Pamps Hall Farm* 1845 *TA* (cf. *George Pampillion* 1666 SR); the earlier hall was built c.1620 by David Pampillion, a Huguenot fortifications engineer, the later hall by Sir Edward Lutyens (1902–4) and demolished in 1950. RED COW (P.H.) (lost) *Red Cow* 1820, 1835 *Deed*, 1846, 1863 White. RUSHES LANE, *v.* **risc**. SCHOOL LANE. SCOBOROUGH, ~ COTTAGE, *Scoborough* 1733 *Deed*, 1845 *TA*, *v.* **skógr**, **berg**. SHOULDER OF MUTTON (P.H.) (lost), *Shoulder of Mutton* 1835 *Deed*. THEDDINGWORTH RD, Theddingworth lying 3 miles to the south-west. THE VICARAGE, 1925 Kelly, *v.* **vikerage**. WASHPIT LANE, *the Wash Pitt* 18 *Surv*, *v.* **wæsce**, **pytt**. WESTGATE LANE, *v.* **west**, **gata**. WHITE SWAN (P.H.) (lost), *White Swan* 1846, 1863 White; it is *the Swan Inn* 1869 *Deed*.

FIELD-NAMES

Forms in (a) presented without dates are 1845 *TA*; those dated 1773 and 1869 are *Deed*; 1798 are Nichols; 18 are *Surv*; 1879 and 1924 are Sale. Forms throughout dated 1602, 1638, 1658, 1659, 1660, 1665, 1670, 1672, 1685, 1686, 1712, 1733 and 1734 are *Deed*; those dated 1694, 1697, l.17 and 17 are *Terrier*.

(a) Abbey's Great Cl, ~ Mdw 1924 (presum. with the surn. *Abbey*, cf. *Charles Abbey* 1856 Census of neighbouring Great Bowden. Although Sulby Abbey held the advowson of All Saints' Church in the 16th cent., this would not have pertained to land holdings in the parish; but note *the Abstrow Croft* and *Monks Close* in f.ns. (b)); Acre Dyke(s) 1845, 1879 (*Acredicke Close* 1686, *v.* **æcer-dīc**; a common compound alluding either to a ditch surrounding an arable plot or to a ditch marking the limit of ploughland; forms with a final *k* are due to Scand influence); Ashton's Mdw (with the surn. *Ashton*); Bawds (a memory of the local *Bawdesmanor* 1442 Fine, *v.* **maner** and cf. *Nicholas de Baud* 1240 RGros); Bottom Mdw (*v.* **bottom**); Bradleys Cls (with the surn. *Bradley*); Brickyard Cls (*v.* **brike-yard**); the Bridge Pasture 1869 (*v.* **brycg**, **pasture**); Brook Cl (*v.* **brōc** and *Bouden brooke*, *infra*); Bullsholme Cl, ~ Fould (*v.* **fald**), ~ Orchard (*v.* **orceard**) 18 (*v.* **bula**, **holmr**); Burnt Mills (*v.* **myln**; ostensibly with **brend** (cf. *Burnt Mill* in Hallaton f.ns. (b) and *le Brendemulne* in Medbourne f.ns. (b)); note the adjacent Burnmill Hill in Great Bowden to which this may relate); John Caves Close alias Dodmores 18 (*v.* Dodmore Cl *infra*); Chapmans Farm (with the surn. *Chapman*); Clarks Mdw (with the surn. *Clark*); Colemans Cl (with the surn. *Coleman*); the Cottiers Pasture 18 (*v.* **cottere**); Cow Cl 1879, ~ ~ Fm 1845; Cox's Nook (*v.* **nōk**; with the surn. *Cox*); Creswick 1845, 1879 (*v.* **cresse**, **wīc**); Cub Cl 1924 (*v.* **cubb**); Dodmore Cl 1845, Dodmores 18, 1845 (*Dodmore* l.17, *Dedmore Close* 1686, *v.* **dēad**, **mōr**[1]; originally, wasteland of poor quality); East Field Cls (*the est feild* 1694, *the East field* 1697, 1703, 18, *East or New Mill field* 17, *v.* **ēast**, **feld**; one of the great open-fields of the township); Fancourts Cls (with the surn. *Fancourt*); Fen Mdw 1924 (*v.* **fenn**); Fosters Farm (with the surn. *Foster*); Foxton Cl, ~ Great Cl 1924, ~ Road Cl 1845, Biggest ~ ~, Lesser Foxon Stiles (sic) 18 (*v.* **stīg**) (Foxton parish adjoins to the north); Gallow Cl, ~ Mdw (on the lower slopes of Gallow Hill which is presented in Foxton); Martha Gambles House Cl 18;

Great Cl 1845, 1879; Green Cl 18, 1845 (*v.* **grēne**[1]); Harboro' Cl, ~ Leys (*v.* **leys**), ~ Mdw (beside the boundary with Market Harborough to the east); Abigail Hartshornes Cl 18 (*Hartshorne Close* 1733, 1734); Highway Cl 18 (*v.* **hēah-weg**); Hill Cl 1845 (1734); the Hill Ground 18 (*v.* **grund**); Home Close Pasture 1869, Home Paddock 1845, 1879 (*v.* **paddock**) (*v.* **home**); Hopkin's Land (with the surn. *Hopkin*); Horse Cl (*v.* **hors**); Howes's Cl (with the surn. *Howes*); Miss Ingrams Farm; James's Mdw (with the surn. *James*); Judds Cl (with the surn. *Judd*); Lane Cl (*v.* **lane**); Little Cl; Little Mdw 18, 1869 (*Little Meadow in Scoborough* 1733, *v.* Scoborough Cottage *supra*); Little Paddock 1879 (*v.* **paddock**); Lodge Farm; the Long Cl, ~ ~ Mdw 18; Lubbenham Cl; the Meadow Pasture 1869; Midsummer Ground 18 (*v.* **grund**; alluding to seasonal use of pasture land that was flooded or very muddy for part of the year); Navigation Cl, ~ Mdw (beside Grand Union Canal); Nether Mdw 1869 (1712); Nine Acres Cl (*v.* **æcer**); Northfield Mdw (1733, 1734, *the North field* 1703, *Northfield* 1734, *v.* **norð**, **feld**; one of the township's great open-fields, previously called *the Old Mill feild*, *infra*); the Old Cl 1773, Old Close Farm 1845, the Old Close Mdw, ~ ~ ~ Pasture 1869 (*Old Close* 1670, *v.* **ald**); Over Cl 18 (*v.* **uferra**); Pasture Farm, ~ Mdw (*v.* **pasture**); Peter Stone Bridge 1798 (*v.* **peterstone**; Nichols writes: *fossils...vulgarly called Peter Stones...the place where they most abound is called Peter Stone Bridge, about a quarter of a mile from town on the road to Lutterworth*; cf. *le Peterstone Lane* in Belvoir, Lei **2** 9); Ploughed Cl 1845, Great ~ ~, Ploughed Cl 1879; Pontons Mdw (with the surn. *Ponton*); Queens Cl (presum. with the surn. *Queen*, since there is no record of land here endowed for Queen Anne's Bounty, the fund for the support of poor clergy, nor any record of an Oxford college holding); Ram Cl (*Ramme Close* 1734, *v.* **ramm**); Randalls Mdw (with the surn. *Randall*); Roundrick (if an early name, then poss. 'border strip of land', *v.* **rand**, **ric**); Sanderson(s) Mdw 1845, 1879 (with the surn. *Sanderson*); Simes Cl (with the surn. *Sime*, from a pet-form of *Simon*); Smarts Cl (with the surn. *Smart*); Spring Cl or Spinney Cl 1879 (*v.* **spring**[2], **spinney**); the Stake Mdw 18 (*v.* **staca**); Swinglers Paddock 1845, 1879 (cf. *Charles Swingler* 1840 Census); the Three Acre Cl 18 (*v.* **æcer**); Three Cornered Cl (*v.* **three-cornered**); Top Cl 1845, 1879, ~ Mdw 1845 (*v.* **top**); Bottom Town Cl (*v.* **tūn**); Turn Back 1924, Turnback Farm 1845 (*Turnebacke* 1658, 1659, 1660, *Tunback* 1694, 1697, l.17, 1703, *Turnbacke Close* 1686 (*v.* **þyrne**; either with **bæc** or with a late local reflex of **balca**); Turnpike Cls (*v.* **turnepike**); the Upper Mdw 1869 (1712); Walkers Farm (with the surn. *Walker*); Warren Cl 18, 1845 (*v.* **wareine**); Washpitt Cl 18 (*v.* **wæsce**, **pytt** and Washpit Lane *supra*); Waters Cl (with the surn. *Waters*, cf. *George Waters* 1822 Census of adjacent Market Harborough); Well Cl 1845, 1879 (*v.* **wella**); Workhouse Cl (*v.* **workhouse**; Lubenham had its own workhouse in 1763 *MiscAccts*); Wrights Farm (with the surn. *Wright*).

(b) *the Abstrow Croft* 1733 (*v.* **trog** 'a valley', **croft**; *Abs-* may be a shortened **abbaye** 'an abbey' in the possessive case (perh. with reference to Sulby Abbey, *v.* Abbey's Great Cl *supra* and *Monks Close*, *infra*) or the surn. *Abb* (also in the possessive), a reflex of OFr *abe* 'an abbot' (cf. *Galfridus le Abbe*, ~ *Labbe* Hy 2 Dane of Leics.)); *Apple Croft* 1734 (*v.* **æppel**, **croft**); *Blackbreche furlong* 1408 Pat (*v.* **blæc**, **brēc**, **furlang**); *Bouden Brooke* 1694, 1697, *Bowden brook(e)* l.17, 1703 (*v.* **brōc** and Great Bowden); *Bradgate holme* 1685 (*v.* **brād**, **gata**, **holmr**); *Bricksworth gate* 1602 (*v.* **gata**; Brixworth lies 10 miles to the south-east in Northants.); *Brittland* 1697 (*v.* **land**; most likely with the surn. *Britt*, a reflex of OE

Brit 'a Briton'; it is very doubtful that the sb. is present here); *Bulisick* 1694, 1697, *Bullisick* 1697, *Bulliseeke*, *Bullysick* l.17, *Bolysick* 1703 (*v.* **bula**, **boli**, **sík**); *Caldecotehil* 13 AD (*v.* **cald**, **cot**, **hyll**); *Calfes paster* 1694, *Calves pasture* 1697, l.17, 1703 (*v.* **calf**, **pasture**); *the Comon back* 1694 (*v.* **commun**, **balca**); *The Cony Gree* 1734 (*v.* **coningre**); *Cottons Close* 1733 (with the surn. *Cotton*, cf. *William Cotton* 1799 Census of Lubenham); *Farndon holme* 1685, 1697, l.17, ~ *home* 1694, 1703 (*v.* **holmr**; East Farndon in Northants. lies to the south-east beyond the river Welland which forms a short stretch of the parish boundary); *Foxon Moore* 1733 (*v.* **mōr**[1]; Foxton parish adjoins to the north); *the Great hill* 1703; *The Great Spinney* 1733 (*v.* **spinney**); *Guy Close* 1712 (with the surn. *Guy*); *the Hade* 1733 (*v.* **hēafod**); *Haddens pitts* 1602 (*v.* **pytt**; with the surn. *Hadden* of a family prob. originally from Haddon, 10 miles to the south-west in Northants.); *Harbrow* ~ 1694, *Harborough hill* 1697, l.17 (Market Harborough parish adjoins to the east); *Holmes Close*, *Inner Holmes* 1734, *the Little* ~ ~, *Inhomes Meadow* 1733 (*v.* **in**) (*v.* **holmr**); *Houseless Lane* 1665 (*v.* **housles**); (*on*) *Hundel*, *Hundle* 1703 (*v.* **hund**, **hyll**; recorded as *Hundhill* 1477 (e.16) in adjacent Theddingworth); *Lancesters gate* 1697 (*v.* **gata**; with the surn. *Lancaster*); *litleborow*, *litleburow* 1694, *littele barrow*, *Littel barow* 1697, *Littleburrow* l.17, 1703 (*v.* **lӯtel**, **berg**); *Short Madback* 1694, l.17, ~ *mad-back* 1703 (of uncertain meaning; *mad* may be the late reflex of **maða**, which was used esp. of the larva of the blow-fly, which causes disease in sheep, or represents (although formally presenting difficulty) an original **mægðe** 'may-weed'; the generic is either **bæc** or a late local reflex of **balca**, cf. *Stevenback*, *infra* and *Huntsback* in Little Stretton f.ns. (b)); *maedlin leas* 1694, *Maudlin*(*s*) *leys* 1697, 1703, *Maudlings Leyes* l.17 (*v.* **leys**; with the surn. *Maudling*); *the midel feild* 1694, *Middel field* 1697, *Middle Feild* l.17, 17, *the Middle-field* 1703 (*v.* **middel**, **feld**; one of the great open-fields); *Millgate* 1697, l.17, ~ *end* 1694, 1703 (*v.* **ende**; and cf. **lane-ende**) (*v.* **gata**), *the Mill peice* 1703 (*v.* **pece**) (*v.* **myln**); *Monks Close* 1733, 1734 (prob. with the surn. *Monk*, cf. *John Monk* 1807 Census of adjacent Foxton, but note Abbey's Great Cl and *the Abstrow Croft supra*); *Moor Close* 1670 (*v.* **mōr**[1]); *Nether Close* 1733; *Old hill* 1697, l.17, 1703, *ould hill closes* 1694 (*v.* **wald**); (*the*) *New Mill Feild* l.17, 17 (*v.* **nīwe**, **myln**, **feld**; otherwise East Fd *supra*, one of the great open-fields); *Nordrow* 1694, l.17, *Nodro* 1697, *Norderow* l.17, 1703 (*v.* **norð**, **rāw**); (*the*) *Old Mill Feild* l.17, 17 (*v.* **ald**, **myln**, **feld**; otherwise *the West feild*, *infra*, one of the great open-fields); The Old Orchard 1733 (*v.* **ald**, **orceard**); *Paines Close* 1733, 1734 (with the surn. *Paine*/*Payne*, *v.* Paynes in Laughton f.ns. (a)); *Pennythorn*(*e*) 1694, 1697, *Pennithorne* l.17 (*v.* **þorn**; either with the surn. *Penny* or with **peni**, indicating thorn-scrub on which a penny rent was once payable; a 15th-cent. spelling is recorded in adjoining Great Bowden f.ns. (b)); *Perwickes Close* 1672 (no such surn. is recorded, thus *v.* **pirige**, **wīc**); *the Great* ~ ~, *the Upper Scoborough Meadow* 1733 (*v.* Scoborough Cottage *supra*); *Seaven Wells* 1694, l.17 ('the seven springs', *v.* **seofon**, **wella**; perh. to be identified with *Seuenewell* listed in adjoining Great Bowden f.ns. (b) and the unlocated *Sevenewelles* n.d AD; a p.n. type which may belong to a tradition with origins in pre-Christian sacred springs, *v.* K. Briggs, 'Seven wells', JEPNS 39 (2007), 7–44); *Shil-board* 1703 (*v.* **scofl-brǣdu**); *The Spinney* 1734 (*v.* **spinney**); *Stevenback* 1694, 1697, 1703 (with the surn. *Steven*; either with **bæc** or with a late local reflex of **balca**); *Thed*(*d*)*ingworth gate* 1733, 1734 (*v.* **gata**; Theddingworth lies 2½ miles to the south-west); *Toftes* 1694, *Tofts* 1697, l.17, *Tofftes* 1703 (*v.* **toft**); *Upper Close* 1733; *Wateris* 1685 (*v.* **wæter**, **hrīs**); *Watterfall*

Close 1686 (*v.* **wæter-(ge)fall**); *the West feild* 1638, 1694, ~ ~ *field* 1697, *West or Old Mill feild* 17 (*v.* **west**, **feld**; one of the great open-fields, replaced by Northfield *supra*); *White Stone* 1694, l.17, 1703 (*v.* **hwīt**, **stān**; a boundary marker which is recorded in the 15th cent. in Great Bowden and another in Theddingworth).

Marefield

MAREFIELD

Merdefelde 1086 DB, *Merdefelda* c.1160 Dane (p), *Merdefeld* 1198 Fees, 1206 P *et passim* to 1333 IpmR, *Merdefeud'* 1250 Fees (p)
Merðefeld' 1169, 1177 P, *Mertefeld'* 1250 Fees
Mardefeud c.1130 LeicSurv, 1227 Fees *et passim* to 1276 RH, *Mardefeuda* Ric 1 (1253) Ch, *Mardefeld'* 1199 P, 1224 ClR *et passim* to 1285 OSut (p), l.13 *CRCart* (p) *et freq* to 1364, 1365 Fine *et passim* to 1402 FA, 1426 Pat, *Mardefeuld* 1287 Ipm, *Mardefild* 1287 ib, p.1290 *Wyg* (p)
Martefeuld 1233 Cur, *Marthefeld'* Edw 3 *Rental* (p)
Mardfeld 1310 Ipm, 1367 *AllS*
Marfeld 1405, 1426 Pat *et passim* to 1497 *AllS*, 1528 Visit, *Marfield* 1608 BM
Marefeld 1540 Ipm, *Marefeilde* c.1570 *Rental*, *Maresfeld* 1535 VE, 1541 MinAccts, *Marefield* 1824 O *et freq*
Merfeld 1443 *RTemple*, 1464 *Ct et passim* to 1478 *AllS*, 1502 *MinAccts*

Affixes are variously added as:
alia ~ 1086 DB, c.1130 LeicSurv
Altero ~ 1252 Fees
Sud ~ 1177 ChancR, 1177, 1199 P, *Suth* ~ 1276 RH, 1310 Fine *et passim* to 1327 ib, *South* ~ 1494 Pat, 1497 *AllS*, 1502 *MiscAccts et freq*, *Sowthe* ~ c.1570 *Rental*
~ *Sud* Edw 1 Nichols, ~ *Suth* 1276 RH, 1300 Ipm, ~ *South*(*e*) 1443 *RTemple*, 1464 *Ct*, 1502 *MiscAccts*, 1541 MinAccts

'Open country frequented by martens or weasels', *v.* **mearð**, **feld**. The settlement here was early called *alia Merdefelde* and *Altero Mardefeld'* (with MLat *alia* and *alter*, both meaning 'the other (of two)') to distinguish it from the lost *Old Marefield* which Nichols sites over the present parish boundary in Owston and Newbold parish. Subsequently **sūð** 'south' was usually affixed, but the more northerly township of the same name was styled *North*(*e*) ~ only infrequently, *v*. *Old Marefield* in Owston and Newbold parish.

BLACKSPINNEY LANE, *v*. **blæc**, **spinney**. DAWSON'S LANE, with the surn. *Dawson*. HILL TOP FM. MANOR FM, MANOR HOUSE FM, *v*. **maner**.

FIELD-NAMES

Names dated 1796 are *Surv*; those dated 1824 are O; 1847 are *TA*.

(a) Four Acres 1796 (*v*. **æcer**); First ~, Second Bowberry 1796 (*v*. **boga**, **berg**); Brackendale 1796, 1847 (*v*. **braken**, **dalr**); Bridge Leys 1796, 1847 (*v*. **brycg**, **leys**); Broad Mdw 1796 (*v*. **brād**); Far ~ ~ ~, Bushy High Leys 1796, 1847 (*v*. **busshi**, **hēah**[1], **leys**); Fishers House 1796 (with the surn. *Fisher*); Gang Would 1796, 1847 (*v*. **gang**, **wald**); Great Leys 1796 (*v*. **leys**); Hemp Hook 1796 (*v*. **hænep**, **hōc**); First ~ ~ ~, Second High Gate Cl 1796 (*v*. **hēah**[1], **gata**); First ~ ~ ~, Second Hill Gate Cl 1847 (a later refashioning of the previous f.ns.); Hillocky Cl, ~ Mdw 1796 (*v*. **hylloc**, **-ig**[3]); Hinks Gorse 1824 (*v*. **gorst**; with the surn. *Hinks*, a reflex of the OE masc. pers.n. *Hynca*); Home Cl 1796 (*v*. **home**); Hunt Moor Cl, ~ ~ Mdw 1796 (*v*. **mōr**[1]; either with **hunte** or with the surn. *Hunt*); Little Leys 1796, 1847 (*v*. **leys**); Martins House 1796 (with the surn. *Martin*); Near Croft 1796 (*v*. **croft**); Neds Piece 1796, 1847 (*v*. **pece**; with the pers.n. *Ned*, a pet-form of *Edward*); Nether Fd, ~ Mdw, ~ Yard (*v*. **geard**) 1796; Road Bit (*v*. **bit**), ~ Leys (*v*. **leys**) 1796, 1847 (fields beside a roadway); Rolston Yard 1796 (*v*. **geard**; with the surn. *Rolston* of a family originally from Rolleston, 5 miles to the south-west); Stone Furlong 1796, 1847 (*v*. **stān**, **furlang**); Swineherds Sitch 1796 (*v*. **swyneherd**, **sīc**); Town Street 1796 (*v*. **tūn**, **strǣt**); Under Wolds 1796, ~ Woulds 1847 (*v*. **wald**); Upper Fd 1796; Wash Bit 1796 (a small enclosure beside a meandering brook; either **wæsse**, **bit** or a restyled, more common **wæsce**, **pytt**).

(b) *Bolton thynge* 1502 *MiscAccts* (*v*. **thing**; with the surn. *Bolton*).

Market Harborough

1. MARKET HARBOROUGH

Haverbergam 1153 Reg, *Hauerberga* 1177, 1178 P *et freq* to 1197 ib
Hauerberg(*e*) 1197, 1198 P *et freq* to 1316 *Peake*, 1317 *Wyg*, *Hauerbergh*(*e*) 1227 Fees, 1314 *Peake et freq* to 1491, 1501 *MktHPR*, *Hauerbargh*' 1439 *ShR*, 1480 *MktHPR et freq* to 1504 *ib*, *Hauerbar*(*o*)*ugh*' 1465, 1471 *ib*, *Hauerboro*(*u*)*gh*' 1466 *ib et freq* to 1517 *ib*, *Hauerborgh*' 1498 *ib* (freq), *Hauerborowe* 1556 *Braye*, *Hauerburgh*' 1385 *Peake*, 1427 *MktHPR*, 1431 *Braye et freq* to 1550 *MktHPR*, *Hauerbrugh*(*e*) 1546 *ib*
Har(*e*)*berg*(*h*) a.1250 *MktHPR*, 1310 Cl *et freq* to 1350 *LCDeeds*, *Hareburgh*(*e*) 1347 Cl *et passim* to 1409 *Braye*, 1410 Fine *et freq* to 1520 *MktHPR*, 1522 *Wyg*
Har(*e*)*berowe* 1444 *MktHPR*, *Harborowe* 1459 *Wyg*, 1475, 1479 *MktHPR et freq* to 1521 *ib et passim* to 1553 Pat, *Harborough* 1613 Polyolbion, 1693 LML *et freq*
Herburgh 1424 Pat, 1425, 1450 Cl, *Herbourgh* 1453 Fine

'The hill where oats are grown', *v.* **hæfera**, **hafri**, **berg**. Market Harborough came into existence in the middle of the 12th cent., until then being only an outlying part of the fields of the manor of Great Bowden *infra*. It is sited at a point where the main Leicester to Northampton road crosses the river Welland. Being roughly a day's journey from either town, it became an ideal place for trade. Note *mercati de Haverberegh* 1219 ClR (with MLat *mercatum* 'market'), *Mercat Heburgh* 1312 BM and *Market*(*t*) *Harborow*(*e*) 1616, 1627 LML, *Markett Harborough* 1693 ib, *v.* **market**.

STREETS, ROADS AND LANES

ABBEY ST, 1925 Kelly. ADAM AND EVE ST, 1776 Map, 1846, 1863, 1877 White; cf. Adam and Eve in Inns and Taverns *infra*. ANGEL ST, 1877 White; cf. *Angel Row* 1846 ib (*v.* **rāw**) and Angel in Inns and Taverns *infra*. BATH ST, 1925 Kelly. BOWDEN LANE, 1863, 1877 White, *Gt. Bowden Lane* 1776 Map. CHURCH ST, 1846, 1863, 1877 White, *v*. Church of St Dionysius *infra* and note also *Churchgate* 1863, 1877 ib, *v*. **gata**. COVENTRY RD, 1877 White; it is *Coventry street* 1863 ib. CROSS ST, 1925 Kelly. FAIRFIELD RD, 1925 Kelly, cf. Horse Fair Cl in f.ns. (a). GARDINER ST, 1925 Kelly. GLADSTONE ST, 1925 Kelly. GOWARD ST, 1925 Kelly; with the surn. *Goward*, common in the area in the 19th cent. GRANVILLE ST, 1925 Kelly. GREAT BOWDEN RD, *Bowden road* 1863 White, *v*. Great Bowden *infra*. HEYGATE ST, 1925 Kelly, *v*. **hēg**, **gata**. HIGHFIELD ST, 1925 Kelly. HIGH ST, 1846, 1863, 1877 White, *le Highe Streete* 1515 *MktHPR*, *v*. **hēah**[1], **strǣt**; also called *the Great Street* 1776 Map. LATHKILL ST, 1925 Kelly. LEICESTER RD, 1846, 1863, 1877 White. LOGAN ST, 1925 Kelly. NELSON ST, 1925 Kelly; cf. Admiral Nelson in Inns and Taverns *infra*. NORTHAMPTON RD, 1846, 1863, 1877 White. PATRICK ST, 1925 Kelly; this may relate to *Patrick* in Great Bowden f.ns. (b). ST MARY'S RD, 1846, 1863, 1877 White, cf. *St Mary's Lane* 1776 Map, *v*. Church of St Mary in Arden, Great Bowden *infra*. SCHOOL LANE, cf. *Free Grammar School* 1846 White.

The following names either have not survived or cannot be related with certainty to modern thoroughfares or structures:

Bates' row 1846 White, *v*. **rāw**; with the surn. *Bates*.
The Butter market 1863 White, *v*. **butere**, **market**.
Chain Bridge 1721 VCHL, 1776 Map, 1780 *EnclA*, *v*. **cheyne**, **brycg**.
Cheapside 1846 White, *v*. **cēap**, **sīde** and Lei **1** 27 *s.n.*
Daglane 1463 *MktHPR*, *v*. **lane**; with **dag** 'to clog with dirt, to bemire'.
Le Fleyschamelis 1381 *MktHPR*, *le Fleschameles* 1406 *ib*, *Butchers Shambles* 1776 Map, *v*. **flessh-shamel**.
Little Street 1776 Map.
Lubbenham lane 1478, 1479, 1480 *MktHPR*, *Lubnamlayn* 1515 *ib*, *Lubenham lane* 1776 Map, 1786 *EnclA*, *v*. **lane**; Lubenham lies one mile to the west.
New street 1846 White.
Railway terrace 1877 White, *v*. **terrace**.
St Mary's Causeway 1776 Map, *v*. **caucie** and Church of St Mary in Arden *infra*.
Sheep market 1846, 1863, 1877 White, *v*. **scēp**, **market**.
Tripe Alley 1776 Map, *v*. **trype**, **aly**.
Le Westlane 1477 (e.16) *Charyte*, *v*. **west**, **lane**.

No early forms have been found for the following Market Harborough street-names:
ARDEN CL, ARDEN WAY (*v.* Church of St Mary in Arden, Great Bowden *infra*). ASTLEY CL, BIRCH'S CL, THE BROADWAY, BURNMILL RD (*v.* Burnmill Hill and Burnmill Lane, Great Bowden), CAXTON ST, CHARLES ST, CLARENCE ST, CLARKE ST, CLIPSTON ST, CONNAUGHT RD, CROMWELL CRESC, DODDRIDGE RD, EAST ST, FAIRFAX RD, FAIRWAY, HAMMOND WAY, THE HEADLANDS, HEARTH ST, HIGHCROSS ST, HILL RD, HILLCREST AVE, IRETON RD, KING'S RD, KNOLL ST, LENTHALL SQ, MILL RD, MORLEY ST, NASEBY CL, NEWCOMBE ST, NITHSDALE AVE, ORCHARD ST, THE OVAL, PARK DRIVE, THE RIDGEWAY, ROMAN WAY, ROWAN AVE, RUPERT RD, SKIPPON CL, SPRINGFIELD ST, STUART RD, VICTORIA AVE, VICTORIA RD, WALCOT RD, WARTNABY ST, WELLAND PARK RD, WESTERN AVE, YORK ST. (Charles, Cromwell, Fairfax, Ireton, Naseby, Rupert and Stuart, of course, are all names taken from the period of the English Civil War.)

INNS AND TAVERNS

ADAM AND EVE (lost), *Adam and Eve* 1624 *Rental*; in Adam and Eve St. ADMIRAL NELSON, 1925 Kelly; cf. Nelson St. ANCHOR (lost), *Anker* 1624 *Rental*. ANGEL, *Angel Inn* 1846, 1863, 1877 White. BEAR ON THE HOOP (lost), *le Bere super le Ho(o)pe* 1451, 1453 *MktHPR* (*v.* Cox[1] 11). BELL (lost), *le Bell(e)* 1515, 1546 *MktHPR*, *the Bell* 1522 *ib*, 1634 Ipm, *Bell* 1846, 1863 White, *Bell Inn* 1877 ib, 1925 Kelly; direct continuity is unlikely. BLACK SWAN (lost), *Black Swan* 1624 *Rental*. CHERRY TREE, 1846, 1863 White, *Cherry Tree Inn* 1925 Kelly. COACH AND HORSES (lost), *Coach and Horses* 1846, 1863, 1877 White. COCK (lost), *Cock* 1846, 1863 White, *Cock Inn* 1877 ib, 1925 Kelly. CROSS KEYS (lost), *the Cross Keyes* 1701 *Terrier*. DOLPHIN (lost), *Dolphin* 1846, 1863, 1877 White, 1925 Kelly. DUKE OF WELLINGTON (lost), *Duke of Wellington* 1846, 1863, 1877 White. FOX (lost), *Fox* 1846, 1863 White, *Fox Inn* 1877 ib. GEORGE (lost), *the George* 1776 Map, *George Inn* 1846, 1863 White, *George Hotel* 1877 ib. GREEN DRAGON (lost), *Green Dragon* 1846, 1877 White. HIND (lost), *Hind Inn* 1846, 1863 White, *Hind Hotel* 1877 ib. KATHARINE WHEEL INN (lost), *Katharine Wheel Inn* 1693 *Deed*. KING'S HEAD (lost), *King's Head* 1776 Map, *King's Head Inn* 1846 White. LION (lost), *the Lyon* 1577 Ipm. LION AND CASTLE (lost), *Lion and Castle* 1624 *Rental*. MERMAID (lost), *Mermaid* 1641 PR. NAG'S HEAD, 1846, 1863, 1877 White, 1925 Kelly. OLD CROWN (lost), *Old*

Crown 1846, 1877 White, *Crown* 1863 ib, *Old Crown Inn* 1925 Kelly. OLD GEORGE (lost), *le Olde George* 1517 *MktHPR*. PEACOCK, 1846, 1863, 1877 White, *Peacock Hotel* 1925 Kelly. RED COW, 1759 *MiscAccts*, 1846, 1863 White, 1925 Kelly; it is uncertain whether there is direct continuity here. ROSE AND CROWN (lost), *Rose and Crown* 1846, 1863, 1877 White. SUN (lost), *Sun* 1846, 1863 White, *Sun Inn* 1877 ib. TALBOT, 1846, 1863 White, *Talbot Inn* 1877 ib, 1925 Kelly. THREE CROWNS (lost), *Three Crowns* 1846 White. THREE SWANS, 1863, 1877 White, *Three Swans Inn* 1846 ib; it is *the Swanne* 1517 *MktHPR*, *Old Swanne* 1553 × 58 ECP. VINE (lost), *Vine* 1846 White, *Vine Inn* 1863 ib. WHEATSHEAF (lost), *Wheatsheaf* 1735 *MiscAccts*. WILLIAM IV (lost), *William IV* 1846, 1863 White, *King William* 1877 ib.

BOWLING GREEN, cf. *Bowlinggreen street* 1846 White, *v.* **bowling-green**. BURNMILL HO., *v.* Burnmill Hill in Great Bowden *infra*. CATTLE MARKET, 1925 Kelly, *v.* **catel**, **market**. CHURCH OF ST DIONYSIUS, *Church (St Dionysius)* 1846, *Church (St Denis or Dionysius the Areopagite)* 1863 White, 1925 Kelly. CHURCH SQUARE, 1846, 1863, 1877 White, *v.* Church of St Dionysius. CONGREGATIONAL CHURCH is *Independent Chapel* 1846 White. CORN EXCHANGE, 1863 White. FAIR LAWN (2½"), *v.* **faire**, **launde**. HIGHFIELD HO. (2½"). HILLCREST FM. LUBENHAM HILL, Lubenham lying one mile to the west. MARKET HARBOROUGH STATION, *Harboro' Station* 1854 O. MARKET PLACE, 1776 Map, 1863 White, *v.* **market**, **place**. MILL HILL, 1846, 1863, 1877 White, *v.* **myln**. MILL MOUND, *Mill Mount* 1786 *EnclA*, cf. *Harborough Mill* 1835 O, *Windmill* 1846, 1863, 1877 White, *v.* **myln**, **mont**, **wind-mylne**. THE MOUNT, ~ ~ COTTAGE, *v.* **mont**. STONE HO. UNION ROW, *v.* **rāw**, UNION WHARF is *Great Bowden Wharf* 1835 O, *v.* **wharf**; both with reference to the Union Canal. WELLAND PARK, *v.* **park**; beside the river Welland.

FIELDS, CLOSES AND YARDS

In (a), forms dated 1776 are Map; those dated 1786 are *EnclA*; 1798 are Nichols; 1863 and 1877 are White; 1925 are Kelly. Forms throughout dated 1388 are Misc; those dated 1439, 1486, 1489, 1497, 1498 and 1522 are *MktHPR*; 1721 are VCHL.

(a) the Bell or Commons Cl 1776 (*v.* Bell, Inns and Taverns *supra* and Commons Cl *infra*); the Chapel Yard 1776 (*v.* **chapel**(**e**)); Commons Cl 1776 (with the surn. *Common*); Cow Fair Leys 1798 (*v.* **cū**, **faire**, **leys**); Desborow Bogs 1798 (*v.* **bog**;

towards Desborough, 5 miles to the south-east in Northants.); Fox Yard 1877 (*v*. Fox, Inns and Taverns *supra*); George or Horse Fair Cl 1776 (*v*. George, Inns and Taverns *supra* and Horse Fair Cl *infra*); Horse Fair Cl, the Horse Fair Leys 1776 (*the leis within the willows in the horse faire* 1498 (*v*. **leys**, **wilig**) (*v*. **hors**, **faire**); Horsekeeper's Yard 1877 (*v*. **horskepere**); King's Head Cl 1776, 1786, 1863, 1877, King's Head Yard 1863 (*v*. King's Head, Inns and Taverns *supra*); Lady Well 1776 (*v*. **ladi**, **wella**; a sacred spring or well associated with Our Lady, the Virgin Mary); Quakers Yard 1877 (belonging to a former Quakers' meeting house); Sun Yard 1925 (*v*. Sun, Inns and Taverns *supra*).

(b) *the grene byneth the Bell* 1522 (*v*. **grēne**[2], **benethe** and Bell, Inns and Taverns *supra*); *le mylne howse* 1489, 1497 (*v*. **myln**, **hūs**); *Pensonland* 1388 (*v*. **land**; with the surn. *Penson*); *ponte de Hauerbergh* 1486 (with MLat *pons* (*pontis* gen.sg.) 'a bridge', *v*. *Large Bridge* in Great Bowden); *Smeton leyes* 1498 (*v*. **lǣs**; either recording a lost OE **Smeoðatūn* 'enclosure of the smiths', *v*. **smið** (**smeoða** gen.pl.), **tūn**, or less likely with the surn. *Sme*(*e*)*ton*); *Taylloursland* 1388 (*v*. **land**; with the surn. *Taylor*).

2. GREAT BOWDEN

Bugedone 1086 DB, *Bugedon'* 1180 × 1200 *MktHPR*, 1203 FF, 1205 ClR, 1224 RHug, *Bugedona* 1175 P, 1208 ChR, *Bugedun*(*e*) l. Hy 2 BM, 1199 FF, 1228 RHug

Buggedon' 1173, 1174 P *et passim* to 1227 Fees, *Buggedone* 1209 × 19, 1228 RHug, *Buggedona* 1209 × 19 ib, *Buggedun* 1210 GildR (p), *Bughedon'* 1220 Fees, 1229, 1234, 1237 Cl, 1247 Fees

Bugendon' 1188 P, 1200 Cur (p), *Buggendon* 1199 FF

Buggeden(*e*) 1174 ChancR, 1179 P *et freq* to 1214, 1215 ib, *Bugeden'* 1203, 1204 ib *et passim* to 1237 RGros

Buggenden' 1180 ChancR, 1180 (p), 1181 P (p), 1196 ChancR

Buedon(*e*) 1202 Ass, 1230 ChancR, 1242 ClR, *Buwedon'* 1230, 1242 P, 1247, 1249 RGros

Budon' 1234 Cl, 1247 Fine *et passim* to 1290, 1292 OSut, *Budun'* 1252, 1265 Pat

Boudon' 1220 MHW, a.1250 *MktHPR et passim* to 1343, 1344 *ib et freq* to 1514 *Wyg*, *Boudun* 1251 Cl, 1252 Lib

Bowedon' 1415, 1416 Pat *et passim* to 1471, 1481 *MktHPR*

Bowdon' 1416, 1425 *MktHPR et freq* to 1523, 1528 *Wyg et passim* to 1576 Saxton, 1577 LEpis

Bowden 1444 *MktHPR*, 1497 *Wyg et passim* to 1522, 1523 *Wyg et freq*

Affixes are variously added as:

Magna ~ 1180 × 1200 *MktHPR*, 1204 Cur *et freq*

~ *Magna* 1331, 1344 *MktHPR et passim* to 1479, 1480 *ib*
Mikell ~ 1467 × 72 ECP, *Mekell* ~ 1483 *MktHPR*
Much ~ 1486 × 1515 ECP, 1523 *Wyg*, *Meche* ~ 1500 *MktHPR*, *Mich* ~ 1508 *ib*, *Mych*(*e*) ~ 1516, 1518 *ib et passim* to 1530 *ib*, 1543 BM, *Moch*(*e*) ~ 1520, 1522 *MktHPR*
Gret(*t*) ~ 1515, 1520 *MktHPR et passim* to 1528 *ib*, *Great*(*e*) ~ 1522 *Wyg*, 1547 Chap, 1610 Speed *et freq*

Either 'Buga's hill' or 'Bucga's (Bugga's) hill', *v*. **dūn**. *Buga* (Redin 74) is an OE masc. pers.n., while *Bucga* (alternative form *Bugga*, Searle 119) is fem., in each case the *-en-* and *-un-* of some p.n. forms being survivals of a gen.sg. inflexion *-an*. Ekwall DEPN, *s.n.* Bowden, Great & Little, styles the OE masc. pers.n. as *Būga* and the fem. pers.n. as *Bucge*. A series of early spellings represents the generic as from OE **denu** 'a valley', presumably with reference to that of the river Welland which flows beside Bowden, while later spellings suggest a reforming of the name as if from OE **boga-dūn*, where **boga** is used in its topographically extended sense 'something curved', hence 'a curving hill or hill-side'.

For the affixes, *v*. **mikill**, **muche**, **grēat**. Note also MLat *magna* 'big, large'.

SHIRTECOAT (lost)

Scirdaykotys 1200 × 50 *MktHPR*, *Shirdaycotes* 1343 *ib*
Schirdecotes 1441 *MktHPR*, *Schirdecotys*, *Schyrdecotys* 1461 *ib*, *Schirdycotes*, *Shurdycotes* 1490 *ib*, *Shirdecotes* 1507 *Wyg*, *Sherdecotes* 1523 *ib*
Sherticotes 1635 *Terrier*, *Shirticoates* 1638, 1679 *ib*, *Shirtycotes* 1655 *MktHPR*, *Shirticoats* 1703 *Terrier*, *Shirtecoat* 1722, c.1730, 1744 *ib*

(Further examples of this name are *Schyrdaycotis* Edw 3 *Wyg* in Newton Harcourt *infra*, *Schirdiccotes* 1320 × 40 (1467 × 84) *LTD* in Thurmaston, Lei **3** 242, poss. *Schortecotes* Hy 4 in Horninghold *supra* and a late survivor *Shouldercoates* 1826 *Terrier*, *Shoulder Coat* 1969 *Surv* in Twyford, Lei **3** 263.)

The earliest forms all appear to present a name with three elements, the second of these being OE *dæg* 'a day'. If the second el. is indeed *dæg*, then the first would seem to be the OE adj. *scīr* 'bright, fair', so that the name (literally 'bright, fair day shelters') may be interpreted as 'fair-weather shelters', presum. alluding to summer shielings used in transhumance. An alternative explanation may be 'derelict cottages (or animal shelters)', with an unrecorded OE adj. *scirde* which may be compared with the OE adj. *sc(e)ard* 'broken'. The longevity of this name in the great north open-field of Great Bowden and its use elsewhere in the eastern hundreds of Leicestershire suggest a well-recognized adjunct of husbandry and hence the former interpretation may be preferable, *v.* **scīr**[2], **dæg**, **cot** (and **scirde**, (**-ig**[3]), **cot**).

INNS AND TAVERNS

BRITANNIA (lost), *Britannia* 1846 White. FREEMASONS' ARMS (lost), *Freemasons' Arms* 1846, 1863 White, 1925 Kelly, *Free Masons' Inn* 1877 White. GREAT BOWDEN INN (lost), *Great Bowden Inn* 1846, 1863 White. GREAT BOWDEN NEW INN (lost), *New Great Bowden Inn* 1846 White, *Bowden New Inn* 1863 ib. QUEEN (lost), *Queen* 1877 White; poss. the former Victoria *infra*. RAILWAY INN (lost), *Railway Inn* 1863, 1877 White, 1925 Kelly. RED LION, 1624 *Rental*, 1846, 1863, 1877 White, 1925 Kelly; direct continuity is unlikely. ROYAL OAK (lost), *Royal Oak* 1863, 1877 White, 1925 Kelly. SHOULDER OF MUTTON, 1735 *MiscAccts*, 1846, 1863, 1877 White, 1925 Kelly; direct continuity is uncertain. THREE HORSE SHOES (lost), *Three Horse Shoes* 1863, 1877 White. UNION (lost), *Union* 1846, 1863 White, *Union Inn* 1877 ib, 1925 Kelly; named from the Union Canal. VICTORIA (lost), *Victoria* 1846, 1863 White; poss. a renamed Queen *supra*.

BURNMILL HILL, 1925 Kelly, BURNMILL LANE, cf. *Burnemill holme* 1638 Ipm (*v.* **holmr**), *v.* **myln**; note Burnt Mills in adjacent Lubenham f.ns. (a) which presum. relates to the same feature. CHURCH OF ST PETER AND ST PAUL, *the Church* 1703, 1709 *Terrier*, *Church (St Peter)* 1846, 1863, 1877 White, *Church (SS. Peter and Paul)* 1925 Kelly; it is earlier recorded as *ecclesie de Boudon* 1220 MHW, 1275 *Pat*, ~ *de Bugeden* 1237 RGros, ~ *de Magna Boudon* 1322, 1323, 1333, 1472 *Pat*. Note also *the Churchyard* 1703, 1709 *Terrier*, *v.* **churchyerd**. CHURCH OF ST MARY IN ARDEN, 1846, 1863, 1877 White, 1925 Kelly, *St Maries Church* 1703 *Terrier*; it is earliest described as *capella sive ecclesia* 1220 RHug (i.e. 'chapel or church'). Note *the church yard off our Lady in Ardrone* 1526 *MktHPR*, *St Mary's Churchyard* 1776 Map, *v.* **churchyerd**. Arden is the name of a district of high ground to the west in Warwickshire. Whether the Forest of Arden was deemed in the early

16th cent. to stretch as far east as Market Harborough is uncertain, but Weston in Arden is located only 22 miles to its west. Arden is from Brit **ardu-* 'high, steep', plus the name-forming suffix *-enno-*, hence 'the high district', *v*. Wa 11. DINGLEY RD, Dingley in Northants. lying 2 miles to the south-east. GALLOW LODGE, *v*. **loge** and Gallow Hill in Foxton. THE GRANGE, 1863, 1877 White, 1925 Kelly, *v*. **grange**. GREAT BOWDEN HALL, *Bowden Hall* 1863 White, 1925 Kelly, *v*. **hall**. GREEN FORD, *v*. **ford**. GREEN LANE, cf. *Greenegate* 1638, 1703 *Terrier*, *Greengate* 1679 *ib*, *v*. **grēne**[1], **gata**. KNIGHT'S END, *v*. **ende**; with the surn. *Knight*. LEICESTER LANE, Leicester lying 14 miles to the north-west. MANOR RD, cf. *Manor House* 1846 White, *v*. **maner**. OLD RECTORY HO., *The Rectory or Parsonage house* 1703 *Terrier* (*v*. **personage**), *The Rectory* 1863 White, *Old Rectory House* 1925 Kelly, *v*. **rectory**. ST MARY'S BRIDGE, beside the Church of St Mary in Arden *supra*. TIN HOUSE FM. TOP YARD FM, *v*. **geard**. UPPER GREEN PLACE, *Upper Green* 1925 Kelly, *v*. **grēne**[2]. WELHAM RD, Welham lying 2 miles to the north-east. WHITE LODGE, 1925 Kelly, *v*. **loge**.

FIELD-NAMES

In (a), forms presented without dates are 1926 Sale; those dated 1751, 1772 and 1793 are MiscAccts; 1776 and 1798 are Nichols; 1786 are *EnclA*; 1836 are *Valuation*; 1842 and 1843 are Sale; 1846 and 1877 are White; 1925 are Kelly. Forms throughout dated 1203 are FF; those dated 1225 are ClR; 1200 × 50, p.1250, c.1300, 1325, 1343, 1344, 1374, 1383, 1385, 1392, 1396, 1431, 1435, 1439, 1441, 1446, 1458, 1461, 1463, 1466, 1471, 1477, 1478, 1479, 1483, 1484, 1485, 1488, 1490[1], 1494, 1495, 1497[1], 1498[1], 1501[1], 1508[1], 1520 and 1655 are *MktHPR*; 1327, 1332 and 1525 are SR; 1400, 1424, 1444, 1475, 1490[2], 1497[2], 1500, 1501[2], 1507, 1508[2], 1514, 1523 and 1524 are *Wyg*; 1403 and 1410 are *Rut*; 1486 × 1515, 1493 × 1500, 1529 × 32 and 1538 × 44 are ECP; 1492, 1498[2] and 1736 are *Deed*; 1624, 1625, 1634 and 1640 are Ipm; 1635, 1638, 1679, 1703, 1722, c.1730 and 1744 are *Terrier*; 1689 are *Will*; 1730 are MiscAccts.

(a) Balls Cl 1786 (with the surn. *Ball*); Barnscroft 1786 (*Barnecroft* 1625, *v*. **bern**, **croft**); Bassetts Cl (presum. with the surn. *Bassett* (from OFr *basset* 'of low stature'), but note Sutton Bassett in Northants. adjoining to the north-east); Bottom Ground (*v*. **grund**), Bottom Mdw (*v*. **bottom**); Buckby's Lane 1786 (with the surn. *Buckby*); Bush Cl (*v*. **busc**); Cheesecake Piece Furlong 1786 (*v*. **chese-cake**, **pece**, **furlang**); Clark's Cl 1786 (with the surn. *Clark*); Dexter Slade 1836 (*v*. **slæd**; with the surn. *Dexter*, an occupational surn. from OE *degestre* 'a dyer', cf. *Radulfus le Dextere* 1262 RFL); Dimigate 1842, Dimagate 1843, 1926, Dimi Gate Piece 1836 (*v.* **pece**) (*Demigard* 1638, 1679, 1703, *v.* **garðr**; poss. with **demming** 'a dam', but otherwise with **dimming** (*v.* Barrie Cox, 'Dimmingsdale', *A Commodity of Good Names: Essays in Honour of Margaret Gelling*, 2008, 350–1); the East Fd 1786 (*le Estfeld* 1463, *v.* **ēast**, **feld**; one of the great open-fields of the township, prob. to be identified with *Yngbarowefelde* in f.ns. (b); it is later recorded as (*in*) *campo orient'* 1523 (with MLat *campus* 'a field' and *orientalis* 'eastern'), and later still as *the Upper fyeld* 1635, *The Over field* 1703, *v.* f.ns. (b)); Far Cl 1836, 1843, 1926, Far Slade 1836, 1843, 1926 (*v.* **slæd**) (*v.* **feor**); The Five Acre Mdw (*v.* **æcer**); The Folly Pond 1798 (*v.* **ponde**), Folly Cl 1836, 1843, The Folly, Folly Seeds 1926 (*v.* **sǣd**; land on which grass or grain crops were grown for subsequent sowing; also used of grasses sown for one year's mowing or grazing) (*v.* **folie**); Foxes Lane 1786 (with the surn. *Fox*); Gallow Cl 1786 (*Gallow* 1635, 1722, c.1730, 1744, *Under gallow* 1635, 1703, 1722, c.1730), the Gallow Fd 1786 (1703, c.1730, 1744, *le gallowfeld* 1441, 1461, *Gallow fyeld* 1635, *the Gallowe Feild* 1638, *v.* **feld**; one of the great open-fields, also called *le Northfeld* 1463 in f.ns. (b), and otherwise recorded as (*in*) *campo borial'* 1523, with MLat *campus* 'a field' and *borialis* 'northern') (*v.* **galla**, **hōh** and Gallow Field Rd in Foxton); Nether Green 1925 (*v.* **grēne**[2]); Hassocks, ~ Piece (*v.* **pece**) (*v.* **hassuc**); Hay Mdw 1793 (c.1730, *the Hay Middow* 1722, ~ ~ *Meadow* 1744, *v.* **hēg**); Long Hollows 1836 (*le Halough* 1485, *the Hallow* 1524, *v.* **halh**); Horse Slade, ~ ~ Seeds (*v.* Folly Seeds *supra*) (*v.* **hors**, **slæd**); House Cl; Junction Cl (at the confluence of the river Welland and a tributary stream); Kestens Cl, ~ Mead 1836 (*v.* **mēd**), Keston's Cl, ~ Mdw 1843, Big ~, Little Kestins 1926 (cf. *Richard Kesten* 1679 of Great Bowden); Langton Town Land 1786 (*v.* **tūn**; the Langtons lie some 2 miles to the north-west); Leicester Land 1751, 1772, 1793 (1730, *v.* **land**; presum. the property of the Borough of Leicester); Little Mdw 1836; Meeting Pit Cl 1836 (*v.* **meeting**, **pytt**; the site of a pit for cock-fighting, a cock-pit); The Nine Acre Mdw (*v.* **æcer**); New ~, Old Seeds (*v.* **sǣd** and Folly Seeds *supra*); Potters Croft 1842, 1843, 1926, ~ ~ Piece 1836 (*v.* **pece**) (*Potterescrofft* 1507, *v.* **croft**; cf. *Pottersholme*, *Potersholme Este* 1497[1] (*v.* **ēast**) (*v.* **holmr**) (*v.* **pottere**); Saddingtons Cl 1786, 1836, 1843, Saddingtons 1926 (with the surn. *Saddington* of a family originally from the village of this name, 6 miles to the north-east); The Slip (*v.* **slipe**); Smith's Mdw 1836 (*Smethmedewe furlong* 1383 (*v.* **furlang**), *Smith Meadow* 1703, *v.* **smēðe**[1], **mēd** (**mēdwe** obl.sg.)); the South Fd 1786 (1703, c.1730, 1744, *le Southfeld* 1463, *South fyeld* 1635, *the South feild* 1722, *v.* **sūð**, **feld**; one of the great open-fields, prob. recorded earlier as *Efilde* 1477 (*v.* f.ns. (b)), and also as (*in*) *campo australi* 1523 (with MLat *campus* 'a field' and *australis* 'southern')); Stalland Leys 1786 (*v.* **leys**) (*Stalland* 1703, *v.* **land**; with **stall** or **stān**); Stanfurlong (*v.* **stān**, **furlang**); Sutton Bridge Cl, ~ ~ Mdw (Sutton Bassett lies 2 miles to the north-east in Northants.); Tipsall Cl 1926, Tipsholme Bridge 1786 (*Tipstone Bridge* 1703, *v.* **brycg**) (these three names presum. belong together; prob. is **holmr**, with the surn. *Tipp* or *Tibb*); Towcroft 1776, 1786, 1843, Big Tow Croft, Little Tow Croft Mdw 1926 (*Touecroft* 1203, *Toucroft* 1343, *Tocrofte* 1471, 1508[1], *Toecrafte* 1635, *Toecroft* 1638, 1655, *Toecraft* 1679, *Tocraft* 1703, 1722, *v.* **tōh**, **croft**; reflecting the nature of the clay soil); Way Post (perh. '(land by) a signpost', but this may be a late reflex of *Warpars* in f.ns. (b)); White Bridge 1786; Willowsgate 1836, 1843, ~ Cl 1846, 1877, Big ~, Little Willowsgate 1926 (*Wilardesgate* 1475, 1497[2], 1514,

Wylardisgate 1477, *Willersgate* 1497[2], 1638, *willowes gate* 1635, *Willowsgate* 1679, 1703, *willas gate* 1722, *Nethir Wylardisgate* 1477 (*v.* **neoðera**), *v.* **gata**; with the surn. *Willard*, a reflex of the OE masc. pers.n. *Wilheard*).

(b) *the Acres hades* 1635 (*v.* **æcer**, **hēafod**); *Adams yard* 1520 (*v.* **geard**; with the surn. *Adam(s)*); *Banham* 1500, 1501[2], 1507, 1635 *et passim* to 1744, *Shortebanham* 1494 (*v.* **sc(e)ort**) (*v.* **bēan**, **hamm**); *Banlond* 1508[1] (*v.* **bēan**, **land**); *Birdes lane* 1507, 1638, *Birds Lane* 1679, ~ *lane end* 1703 (*v.* **lane-ende**) (*v.* **lane**; either with **bridd** or with the surn. *Bird*); *Blakeland(e)s* 1203, 1492, 1638, *blacklands* 1635, *Blakelands* 1679, 1703, *blaklands* 1722 (*v.* **blæc**, **land**); *Bosworth mill way* 1635 (*v.* **myln**, **weg**; since Husbands Bosworth lies 7 miles to the south-west beyond Lubenham and Theddingworth, *Bosworth* here appears to be the surn. of a family originally from that township); *Bowghton* 1497[2] (rather than an erratic and unique spelling of *Bowdon*, this may be the name of a lost farmstead; if so, 'farmstead in the (river) bend', *v.* **boga**, **tūn**); *Branlands* 1635, 1722 (*v.* **land**; with **brant** or **brand**); *le Breche* 1471, 1508[1] (*v.* **brēc**); *le Brest(e)* 1343, 1410, 1463, 1507, 1523, *le Breeste* 1495, *Breestes* 1514, *Brest* 1635, 1655, *Breest* 1638, 1679 *et passim* to 1744, *le Weste breste* 1471, *le West Breyst* 1508[1] (*v.* **west**) (*v.* **brēost**); *broadbalke* 1635, *Broad(e) lake* 1638, 1679, 1703, 1744, *brode lake* 1722 (*v.* **brād**, **balca**; the generic seems to have become confused with **lacu** (*v. le Waterlakes*, *infra*), the positions of the forms in the Terriers confirming that they refer to the same feature); *Broddole* 1343 (*v.* **brād**, **dāl**); *Brownefurlonge* 1492, *Brownfurlong* 1523, *browne furlong* 1635, 1722, *Brown* ~ c.1730, 1744 (*v.* **brún**[2], **furlang**); *Buckwell* 1635, 1703, *Butwell* 1722, c.1730, 1744, *Bukwelmore* 1463, *Bukwellemore* 1507, 1523 (*v.* **mōr**[1]) (*v.* **bucca**, **wella**); *Cattes butts* 1635, *Catsbuttes* 1638, *Catts butts* 1679, 1703, *Cats buts* 1722, *Cats Butts* 1744 (*v.* **butte**; either with **cat(t)** or with the surn. *Catt*, cf. *Joh' le Cat* 1336 GildR of Leicester); *Cergates* 1635, *Cargats* 1722, *Car Gates* c.1730, *Cergatisholme* 1507, 1523 (*v.* **holmr**) (*v.* **kjarr**, **gata**); *Chapelenesthing* 1431(*v.* **thing**, here referring to a tenement; either with OFr **chapelain** or more likely with its surn. reflex *Chaplain*); *Clarkes goare* 1638, *Clarks* ~ 1679, *Clarkes gore* 1703 (*v.* **gāra**; with the surn. *Clark(e)*); *Cleypole* 1507, *Cleypoole* 1523 (*v.* **clǣg**, **pōl**[1]); *Colpitacur* 1507, *Colpittacr'* 1523, *Colepitt acre* 1635, *Colpit* ~ 1722, *Colepit Acre* c.1730, 1744 (*v.* **col-pytt**, **æcer**; a site for the manufacture of charcoal); *Colsis Quick* 1722, 1744 (*v.* **quyk** (here a short form of **quykset** 'a quickset hedge'); with the surn. *Coles*); *Comyn' Marlepyttes* 1471, 1508[1] (*v.* **commun**, **marle-pytt**); *John Cook(e)s furlong* 1638, 1679, 1703; *Coomes* 1638, 1703, *Cooms* 1679 (*v.* **cumb**); *Coops land* 1634 (*v.* **land**; with the surn. *Coope* (metonymic for ME *couper* 'a maker of wooden tubs and casks', cf. *Hugo le Coup* 1327 SR of Leics.); *Corts stile* 1722, *Cort's* ~ c.1730 (with **stīg** or **stigel**; cf. *James Cort* 1722); *le cowle* 1400, *Coule* 1424 (*v.* **cūle**); *the Cow pasture* 1638, 1679, 1703 (*v.* **cū**, **pasture**); *Cranesworth* 1439, *Craneworth* 1485, 1507, 1523 (*v.* **worð**; the specific could be **cran** 'a crane' (hence 'enclosure near which cranes are seen', cf. Cranworth, Nf), but it may be that the sb. is here used as a by-name for a man with long legs; as a surn., *Crane* is current from the 12th cent.); *Crowethorn(e)hyll* 1497[1], 1498[1] (*v.* **crāwe**, **þorn**, **hyll**); *iuxta Crucem* 1446 (MLat *iuxta* 'next to', *crux* (*crucem* acc.sg.) 'a cross'); *Dolecroft* 1703 (perh. 'the small enclosure held in common', *v.* **dāl**, **croft**); *Duehooke* 1703 (*v.* **dēaw**, **hōc**); *Dunningtons land* 1634 (*v.* **land**; with the surn. *Dunnington*); *Edwards his peece* 1703 (*v.* **pece**); *Efilde* 1477, *Efell'* 1494, *Effeald(e)* 1507, 1523, *Efeld* 1524 (*v.* **ēa**, **feld**; later the South Fd, *supra*, and presum. preserving its earlier name, perh. with reference to the river Welland, cf. *Hachey*, *infra*, also in this open-field); (*le*) *Estlonge* 1463, 1507, *Estlong* 1523, *Eastlong*(*e*) 1635, 1638, 1679, 1722, *East Long* 1703, 1744 (*v.* **ēast**, **lang**[2]); *Fargatys* 1471, 1508[1] (*v.* **feor**, **gata**); *Ferrars lane* 1501[1] (*v.* **lane**; with the surn. *Ferrar*, an occupational surn. from OFr *ferour* 'a smith, a worker in iron', cf. *Henricus le Ferrur* 1196 Cur of Leics.); *Fidelliswonge* 1344 (*v.* **vangr**; with the surn. *Fidel*, cf. *Willielmus Fidel* 1344; prob. a reflex of OE **Fitel* (cf. *Fitela*), an original by-name from the first element of OE *fitelfōta* 'white-footed', a name for the hare in ME); *Foxtonegate* 1343, *le Foxtongate* 1495, *Foxton gate* 1524 (*v.* **gata**), *Foxton Mor'* 1325, 1374, 1385, *Foxton* ~ 1638, 1679, *Foxon Moore* 1703 (*v.* **mōr**[1]) (Foxton lies 3 miles to the north-west); *fulforth* 1485 (*v.* **fūl**, **ford**); *Fullwell* 1635, 1638, 1703, 1744, *Fulwell* 1679, 1722, *fulwell banke* 1722, *Fullwell Bank* 1744 (*v.* **banke**) (*v.* **fūl**, **wella**); *Gasewell* 1343, *Gasylleseyke* 1392, *Gaswell Sicke* 1638, 1655, 1679, *Gazwell Sick* 1703, *Gasell Sick* 1722, *Gasel Sike* c.1730, 1744 (*v.* **sík**) (*v.* **gōs**, **wella**); *le gatemyll'* 1463, *le Gate Milne* 1507 (*v.* **gata**, **myln**); *the Gibb* 1703 (*v.* **gybbe**); *Gilbertes* ~ 1638, *Gilberts Slade* 1679, 1703 (*v.* **slæd**; with the surn. *Gilbert*, cf. *Henry Gilbert* 1689); *Goodinges oxe* 1638, *Goodwyns Ox* 1655, *Goodins Ox* 1679, 1703, *ubi Godwynesoxe moriebatur* 1343 ('(the place) where Godwine's ox died') (*v.* **oxa**; with the OE masc. pers.n. *Gōdwine*); *le Gore* 1492 (*v.* **gāra**); *Gosacur* 1507, *Gooseaker* 1638, *Goose acre* 1703, *ouergoseacur* 1507 (*v.* **ofer**[3]) (*v.* **gōs**, **æcer**); *le Gosse lands* 1640 (*v.* **gorst**, **land**); *Grannam Narrow*(*e*) 1638, 1703 (*v.* **grand**, **hamm**, **nearu**); *gravill pitts* 1635, *Gravelpittes* 1638, *Gravell Pitts* 1679, *Gravel pitts* 1703, *the gravell pits* 1722, (*the*) *Gravel Pits* c.1730, 1744 (*v.* **gravel**, **pytt**); *Grimesholme* 1638, 1679, 1703, *Grim*(*e*)*s home* 1722, c.1730 (*v.* **holmr**; with the ON masc. pers.n. *Grímr* (ODan *Grīm*), cf. *Grymyswong'*, *infra*); *le Grygges* 1495 (*v.* **grigg**(**e**) 'something of small size or below natural size', here perh. applied to short selions or small plots of land); *Grymyswong'* 1507, *Ouergrymeswong*(*e*) 1463, 1494, *ouergrimiswonge* 1507 (*v.* **ofer**[3]) (*v.* **vangr** and *Grimesholme*, *supra*); *Gunesbroke*, *le Gunnesbrok'* 1431 (*v.* **brōc**; *Gun* is poss. a hill-name of uncertain origin (cf. Gun Hill, Db 576, Gun Hills, Db 618 and Gun, StH 288), since the ON masc. pers.n. *Gunni* accorded a ME secondary genitive in *-es* would be unlikely compounded in a stream-name); *Hachey* 1638, 1679, 1703 (*v.* **hæc**(**c**), **ēa**); *les Hadys* 1441, 1461 (*v.* **hēafod**); *Harpers gate* (*v.* **gata**), *Myles Harpers hadland* 1635 (*v.* **hēafod-land**), *Harpers penn* 1635, *Harpers Pen* 1722, c.1730, 1744 (*v.* **penn**[2]) (with the surn. *Harper*, from OE *hearpere* 'a harper'); *Hauerberghemore* 1435, *Harborough* ~ 1638, *Harb*(*o*)*row Moore* 1679, 1703 (*v.* **mōr**[1]), *Hauerborgh Slade* 1507, *Hauerborugh slade* 1523 (*v.* **slæd**), *Harborough Pastures* 1538 × 44 (*v.* **pasture**), *Harborow hollow* 1635, *Harborough holow* 1722, ~ *Hollow* c.1730, 1744 (*v.* Long Hollows in f.ns. (a)), *Harborow Mere* 1703 (*v.* (**ge**)**mǣre**), *Harborough Town Land* c.1730, 1744 (*v.* **tūn**, **land**) (Market Harborough lies one mile to the south-west); *the Hay* 1635, 1638, 1703, *The Hey* 1679, *Hay feld* 1722, *Hay Field* c.1730, 1744 (*v.* (**ge**)**hæg**); *le Hayeleyis* 1439, (*le*) *Hayles* 1477, 1490[1], *le Hayley*(*e*)*s* 1485, 1490[1] (*v.* **hēg**, **lǣs**); *Helthirne* 1343, *Elderne* 1655, *longe helderne* 1490[2], *long eldurne* 1514, *Long Elderne* 1638, 1665, 1703 (*v.* **lang**[1]), *Short eldurne* 1497[2], *Short Elderne* 1655 (*v.* **sc**(**e**)**ort**) ('thorn-scrub slope', *v.* **helde**, **þyrne**); *Heyford* 1635 (*v.* **hēg**, **ford**); *High gates* 1638, 1679, 1703 (*v.* **gata**; with **hēg** or **hēah**[1]); *Longe* ~, *Short hilrene* 1343 (*v.* **lang**[1], **sc**(**e**)**ort**) (*v.* **hyll**, **rein**); *Hogges balk*(*e*) 1638, 1679, *the hoggs balke* 1703 (*v.* **balca**), *Hogges Foarde* 1638, *Hogges Foord* 1679, *Hoggs foord* 1703 (*v.* **ford**) (*v.* **hogg**); *Holebergh* 1343,

Holbarogh 1488, *ouerholborgh* 1507, *ouerholburgh* 1523 (*v.* **ofer**[3]) (perh. 'hill with animal burrows' or 'hill with a deep depression in it', *v.* **hol**[1], **berg**; the OE masc. pers.n. *Hōla* is also poss. as the specific); *hyllynges plott* 1507, *hillyngisplott* 1523 (*v.* **plot**; with the surn. *Hilling*, cf. *Ricardus Hilling* 1212 Cur of Leics.); *Hun(n)ies balke* 1638, 1679, 1703 (*v.* **balca**; either with the surn. *Honey* or **hunig**, alluding to a place where honey was found); (*in*) *the hyrne* 1332 (p), 1381 (p), 1424 (p), 1471 (p), (*en*) *le hyrne* 1439 (p), (*in*) *le hirne* 1463 (p), (*in*) *le Hyrne* 1493 × 1500 (p), 1486 × 1515 (p), *Hyrne lane* 1488 (*v.* **lane**) (*v.* **hyrne**); *Jonsty* 1507 (the surn. *John*, with **stig** or **stīg**); *kirk(e)gates* 1507, 1523 (*v.* **kirkja**, **gata**; poss. an early name for St Mary's Rd *supra*); *le kylnyerde* 1431 (*v.* **cyln**, **geard**); *kyngestirne*, *Kyngestyrne* 1343, *Kingsterne* 1655 (*v.* **þyrne**; with the surn. *King*); *Laconwell* 1655, *longelakynwell* 1475, *longelakenwell* 1497[2] (*v.* **lang**[1]) (*v.* **wella**; with the OE masc. pers.n. *Lāca* (*Lācan* gen.sg.)); *Lakefurlong* 1463 (*v.* **lacu**, **furlang**); *Lambersicke* 1703 (*v.* **lamb** (**lambra** gen.pl.), **sík**); *langtonbarowe* 1508[1], *Langton barrow hades* 1703 (*v.* **hēafod**), *langtonbarow sike* 1475, ~ *syke* 1514 (*v.* **sík**) (*v.* **berg**), *langton gate* 1524, *Langtongate foote* 1635 (*v.* **fōt**), *Ouerlangtongate* 1344 (*v.* **ofer**[3]) (*v.* **gata**) (Church Langton and East Langton lie respectively 2½ and 2 miles to the north-west); *Larchwell* 1638, 1679, 1703 (*v.* **læc(c)**, **wella**); *large bridg* 1635, *Large Bridge* 1703, c.1730, 1744, *Large brig* 1722; earlier recorded as *pontis magni* 1439 (with MLat *pons* (*pontis* gen.sg.) 'a bridge' and *magnus* 'great, large') (*v.* **large**, **brycg** and *ponte de Hauerbergh*, *supra*); *Larin hoks* 1722, ~ *Hooks* 1744 (*v.* **hōc**; the surn. *Larin* does occur, but it is not well evidenced in the Midlands); *le leywong* 1507, *le laywong* 1523 ('in-field with a pool', *v.* **ley**[1], **vangr**); *Leighfield* 1703 (prob. a later restyling of the previous f.n.); *Littlebarow* 1703 (*v.* **lȳtel**, **berg**); *Little slad* 1722, *Little Slade* c.1730, 1744 (*v.* **lȳtel**, **slæd**); *Lobenhambrok* 1343, *Lubbenham broke* 1477, *Lubenham brooke* 1703 (*v.* **brōc**; Lubenham lies 2½ miles to the south-west); *Long lane close* 1640 (*v.* **lang**[1], **lane**); *the Lords close* 1621, *le Lordes land* 1640 (*v.* **land**) (*v.* **lord**); *lygard* 1383, *Lyard* 1703 (*v.* **garðr**; poss. with **ley**[1] 'a pool', cf. *le leywong*, *supra*); *lyttylbergh* 1463, *lit(t)ilbergh* 1507, *Littlebarrow* 1635, *Littleborow* 1679, 1722, *Little borough* 1744 (*v.* **lȳtel**, **berg**); *Lyttylhill* 1463, *Litilhyll* 1507, *Little Hill* 1635, 1703, c.1730, 1744, *Littel hill* 1722 (*v.* **lȳtel**, **hyll**; this is not an alternative style for the previous f.n.); *Maynardesholm* c.1300, (*le*) *Maynersholme* 1403, 1507, 1523, *Manners holme* 1638, 1679, 1703, ~ *home* 1635, 1722, *Mannors* ~ c.1730, 1744, *Manor's Home* 1744 (*v.* **holmr**; either with the OFr masc. pers.n. *Mainard* or with its surn. reflex *Maynard*); *Midillfurlonge Weste* 1471, *Mydulfurlong West* 1508[1] (*v.* **middel**, **furlang**, **west**); *Mikelbergh* 1463, *mekelbarogh* 1494, *miculbergh* 1507, *miculbarow* 1507, 1514, *Mickilbergh* 1523, *Micklebar(r)ow* 1635, 1638, 1703, *mickelborow* 1722, *Mickleborough* 1744, *Mykelbarogh northe* 1494 (*v.* **norð**) (*v.* **micel**, **mikill**, **berg**); *Millholme* 1703 (*v.* **myln**, **holmr**); *at More* 1403 (p), 1444 (p), 1508[2] (p), *Morforlonge* 1494, *Morefurlong* 1507, 1523, *Moor(e) furlong* 1635, 1638, 1703 (*v.* **furlang**) (*v.* **mōr**[1]); *Musfurlong* 1463 (*v.* **mūs**, **furlang**); *Myllegat'* 1494 (*v.* **myln**, **gata**); *the neather fyeld* 1635, *the Nether field* 1703, *the neather feild* 1722, *the Neither Field* c.1730, 1744 (*v.* **neoðera**, **feld**; one of the great open-fields, earlier recorded as *West Felde* 1483 *infra*, and (*in*) *campo occidental'* 1523 (with MLat *campus* 'a field' and *occidentalis* 'western')); *Le Northfeld* 1463 (*v.* **norð**, **feld**; one of the great open-fields, later recorded as (*in*) *campo borial'* 1523 (with MLat *campus* 'a field' and *borialis* 'northern') and called also the Gallow Fd, *supra*); *Onowh* 1475, *Onow* 1497[2], *Onowgh* 1514, *Wannow(e)* 1635, 1638, 1679,

Wanah 1722, c.1730, 1744 (*v.* **ān**, **hōh**); *Ouergyfloke* 1485 (*v.* **ofer**[3], **gafeluc**); *Ouertoftys* 1494 (*v.* **uferra**, **toft**); *The Over field* 1703, *the Ouer feild* 1722 (*v.* **uferra**, **feld**; one of the great open-fields, earlier called *le Estfeld*, *supra* and *the Upper fyeld*, *infra*); *Packs myll* 1635, *Packes Mill furlong* 1703 (*v.* **myln**; with the surn. *Pack* (from OFr *Paque* 'Easter'), cf. *Rogerus Pake* 1195 P of Leics.); *Paddockes* ~ 1638, *Paddocks peece* 1679, 1703 (*v.* **pece**), *Paddockis Pyltche* 1485, *Paddockkys Pyltche* 1492 (*v.* **pilche** 'a garment made of skin dressed with the hair; a rug laid over a saddle' (*v.* OED pilch sb. 1 and 2a); perh. used figuratively of a small piece of rough ground; most prob. with ME **paddok** 'a frog' rather than with the surn. *Paddock* derived from it); *Pallmers land* 1624 (*v.* **land**; with the surn. *Palmer*); *parcis de Bugeden'* 1225 (with MLat *parcus* 'a park'); *Parkers Willows* 1703 (*v.* **wilig**; with the surn. *Parker*); *the Parsonage Land* 1722, c.1730, 1744 (*v.* **personage**, **land**); *the Pastor furlong* 1722, ~ *Pasture* ~ c.1730, 1744 (*v.* **pasture**); *le Patched close* 1640 (either with the ppl.adj. **patched**, perh. indicating a roughly repaired enclosure, or in original form, a *patchet* 'a very small piece of ground', from **patche** plus the diminutive suffix **-ette**); *Patrick* (sic) 1703 (*v.* **pat**(**t**)**e**, **ric**); *Paynesgore* 1463, 1494 (*v.* **gāra**; with the surn. *Payne*); *Penytherne* 1477 (*v.* **þyrne**; either with **peni**, alluding to a penny rent for the thorn-scrub, or with the surn. *Penny*, indicating ownership; cf. *Penymore* in Noseley f.ns. (b)); *Poles Slade* 1703 (*v.* **slæd**; either with the surn. *Pole* or with **pōl**[1]); *Portegate* 1514, *Portgate* 1655, *Porgate* 1722, *Por Gate* c.1730, *Longeport*(*e*)*gate* 1475, 1497[2], 1514 (*v.* **lang**[1]), *Nethirportgate* 1343 (*v.* **neoðera**) (*v.* **port-gate**; the road to Market Harborough); *Pyllokesholme* 1508[1] (*v.* **holmr**; poss. with the surn. *Pillock*, cf. *Johannes Pillokes* 1327 SR of Leics., but note *the Pylloke* in Evington f.ns. (b) and *Pyllok* in Medbourne f.ns. (b), *v.* **pyll**, **-uc**); *Pylwelfurlonge* 1495, *Pilwell furlong* 1638, 1679, 1703 (*v.* **wella**, **furlang**; prob. with **pyll** 'a small stream', but the OE masc. pers.n. *Pīla* is poss., since in names with *wella*, OE masc. pers.ns. freq. occur as the specific); *the far*(*r*) *quick*(*e*)*sett* 1635, 1638, 1679, 1703 (*v.* **quykset**); *Nethir* ~, *Ouer rademylde* 1343, *Nether* ~, *Over Redmyles* 1655 (*v.* **neoðera**, **uferra**) (*v.* **rēad**, **mylde**); *Rokhyll* 1490[1], 1494, 1507, *Rokhill* 1524, (*the*) *Rockhill* 1635, 1638, 1679, 1703, *Rockell* 1722, c.1730, *long Rokhyll* 1490[1], *Shortrokhyll* 1492 (*v.* **lang**[1], **sc**(**e**)**ort**) (*v.* **hrōc**, **hyll**); *round ford* (sic) 1635 (*v.* **ford**; a ford at *Round Hill*); *Round hill* 1703, ~ ~ *Close* 1736 (*v.* **round**, **hyll**); *Russhygore* 1494, *Rushey Goare* 1638, *Rushey* ~ 1679, *Rushie gore* 1703 (*v.* **riscig**, **gāra**); *against St Maries Church gate* (*v.* **gata**), *on the East* ~ ~ ~, *on the West side St Maries* 1703 (*v.* **sīde**) (furlongs so called, *v.* Church of St Mary in Arden *supra*); *Sand*(*e*)*furlong* 1463, 1507, 1638, 1679, 1703 (*v.* **sand**, **furlang**); *Sandpitts* 1703 (*v.* **sand-pytt**); *Sek*(*e*)*furlong* 1507, 1523 (*v.* **sík**, **furlang**); *Seuenewell* 1343 (*v.* **seofon**, **wella**; prob. to be identified with *Seaven Wells* in adjoining Lubenham f.ns. (b), *v.* K. Briggs, 'Seven wells', JEPNS 39 (2007), 7–44); *Sherwoodes land* 1529 × 32 (*v.* **land**; with the surn. *Sherwood*); *Shortwonge* 1477 (*v.* **sc**(**e**)**ort**, **vangr**); *Shuflebrode* 1494, *Shovelbrode* (×2), *Sholbrode* 1507 (*v.* **scofl-brædu**); *Sikegate* 1203 (*v.* **sík**, **gata**); *the slide* 1635 (*v.* **slide**); *Smalthornes* 1477 (*v.* **smæl**, **þorn**); *Snakesyke* 1463, *snakysseke* 1507, *Snakissike* 1523 (*v.* **snaca**, **sík**); *Snayllewelle* 1507 (*v.* **snægl**, **wella**); *Sowtorp'* p.1250 (*v.* **sūð**, **þorp**); *Stanhill* 1458, *Stonehill* 1638, 1655, 1703, *Stonhill* 1679, *Over Stonehill* 1703 (*v.* **uferra**) (*v.* **stān**, **hyll**); *Stanyhull* 1343 (*v.* **stānig**, **hyll**); *the Stepping Stones* 1703 (*v.* **stepping-stone**); *Stockefurlonge* 1477 (*v.* **stocc**, **furlang**); *Stonland* 1203 (*v.* **stān**, **land**); *Stretefurlonge* 1477 (*v.* **stræt**, **furlang**); *Nether* ~,

Over Sty 1703 (*v.* **neoðera**, **uferra**) (with **stīg** or **stig**); *Tagyllisdyke* 1492 (*v.* **dík**; because of the genitival composition joint, a surn. such as *Tagell* or *Tatchell* may be indicated, but otherwise a compounded toponym may be thought of, with **tagga** plus **hyll** or **wella**; additional forms are needed); *Targett holme* 1507, *Tergetholme* 1523 (*v.* **targett**, **holmr**; *targett* 'a light round shield' was poss. used with reference to the shape of the enclosure, since *target* in the sense 'a round mark for shooting at' is not recorded until 1757 OED); (*le*) *Thorpgate* 1492 (×2), *Thorpe gate* 1703 (*v.* **gata**; the road to Thorpe Langton which lies 2 miles to the north); *le Thwong* c.1300, *le Thonge* 1403, 1463, 1507, 1523 (*v.* **þwang**); *Tonghill* 1703 (*v.* **hyll**), *Tongstede* 1435 (*v.* **stede**) (*v.* **tunge**); *le Tudges land* 1495, 1498[2], *Tudges lande* 1484 (*v.* **land**; with the surn. *Tudge*, poss. a reflex of an OE masc. pers.n. *Tucca* or **Tucga*); *twardolys* 1507, *Twerdolys* 1523, *Whart doles* 1638, 1703, *Whardols* 1722, *Whardoals* c.1730, 1744, *neather wardoles* 1635 (*v.* **neoðera**) (*v.* **þverr** (**þvert** neut.), **dāl**); *Tymcrosse* 1507, *Timcross*(*e*) 1638, 1679, 1703 (*v.* **cros**; with the surn. *Tym*, a reflex of the OE masc. pers.n. *Tima*); *the Upper fyeld* 1635 (*v.* East Fd and *The Over Field*, *supra*); *Wakelopittes* 1507, 1523, *Waklins pittes* 1635, 1638, *Wakelins pitts* 1703, *Waklins pits* 1722, *Waklin Pits* c.1730, 1744 (*v.* **wacu**, **hlāw**, **pytt**); *Warpars* 1507, *Warpas* 1507, 1523, *Warpers bush*(*e*) 1635, 1638, 1679, 1703, *Warpors bush* 1722, c.1730, 1744 (*v.* **busc**) (*v.* **werpels**); *Wassford* 1494, *Waseforthe* 1524, *Washfoarde* 1638, *Washfoord* 1679, 1703, *Washford* 1722, c.1730, 1744, (*v.* **wæsce**, **ford**); *le Waterlakes*, *le Watyrlakes* 1383, *Waterlakys* 1477, *Waterlakes* 1484, 1638, 1679, 1703 (*v.* **wæter**, **lacu**; perh. signifying water-courses which never dried up); *Welles Close* 1703 (with the surn. *Wells*); *le West Ende* 1396 (*v.* **west**, **ende**); *West Felde* 1483 (*v.* **west**, **feld**; one of the great open-fields; also recorded as (*in*) *campo occidental'* 1523 (with MLat *campus* 'field' and *occidentalis* 'western') and later as *the Nether field*, *supra*); *Westwell* 1343 (*v.* **west**, **wella**); *Whildik'* 1523, *whield dykes* 1635, *Whold ditches* 1722, *Wold Ditches* c.1730, *Would Dikes* 1744 (*v.* **hwēol**, **dík**, **dīc**; the specific became confused with **wald**); *le Whiteston* 1485 (*v.* **hwīt**, **stān**; a boundary marker which is recorded later in Lubenham f.ns. (b)); *Whittersikk* 1523, *Whittersick*(*e*) 1638, 1679, 1703, *Wihitersick* 1722, *Whiter Sike* c.1730, 1744 (*v.* **sík**; with the surn. *Whitter*, originally occupational for 'a whitewasher' (from OE *hwītian* 'to make white')); *Wikmedow* 1507, 1523 (*v.* **wīc**, **mēd** (**mēdwe** obl.sg.)); *Windoles peece* 1635 (*v.* **hvin**, **dāl**, **pece**); *Wineworth* 1722, c.1730 (*v.* **worð**; with the OE masc. pers.n. *Wina*); *Wranglondis* 1439, *Wranglandes* 1492 (*v.* **wrang**, **land**); *Wyllerspyttis* 1494 (*v.* **pytt**; with a reduced form of the surn. *Willard*, a reflex of the OE masc. pers.n. *Wilheard*, cf. Willowsgate in f.ns. (a)); *Yngbarowefelde* 1466 (*v.* **ing**, **berg**, **feld**; one of the great open-fields of the township, prob. to be identified with the East Fd, *supra*).

3. LITTLE BOWDEN

For forms and interpretation, *v.* Great Bowden *supra*.

Affixes are variously added as:

Parva ~, *Parua* ~ 1220 Fees, 1247 RGros *et passim* to 1535 VE, 1541 *MktHPR*

~ *Parva*, ~ *Parua* 1346 *MktHPR*, 1398 *Braye et passim* to 1515 *MktHPR*, 1535 VE
The Lasse ~ 1450 × 53 ECP
Litell ~ 1464 Nichols, *Litull* ~ 1509 *MktHPR*, *Litill* ~ 1517 *ib*, *Lytyll* ~ 1528 *ib*, *Little* ~ 1610 Speed *et freq*

Little Bowden, lying south of the river Welland which formed the original county boundary in the south-east, was transferred from Northants. in 1888. For the affixes, *v*. **lȳtel**, **lasse** and note MLat *parva* 'small'.

BELLFIELDS LANE. BRAYBROOKE RD, Braybrooke lying one mile to the south-west in Northants. CLACK HILL, *v*. **clæcc**. GORES LANE, *v*. **gāra**. GREYHOUND (P.H.), *Greyhound* 1846, 1863, 1877 White, 1925 Kelly. KETTERING RD, Kettering lying 8 miles to the south-east in Northants. LITTLE BOWDEN LODGE FM (LITTLE BOWDEN FM 2½") is *Bowden Lodge* 1824 O, *v*. **loge**. OLD HALL, 1925 Kelly, *v*. **hall**. QUEEN ST. RECTORY LANE, *The Rectory* 1863 White, 1925 Kelly, *v*. **rectory**. ST NICHOLAS'S CHURCH, *Church (St Nicholas)* 1846, 1863, 1877 White. SCOTLAND END, *v*. **scot**, **land**, **ende**. WESTBROOKE HO. (2½"), *Westbroke house* 1925 Kelly, *v*. **west**, **brōc**.

FIELD-NAMES

Forms presented without dates are 1780 *EnclA*; those dated 1845 are *TA*; 1926 are *Sale*.

(a) The Five Acres, The Twelve ~, The Fourteen Acres 1926 (*v*. **æcer**); Ashley Hades Furlong (*v*. **hēafod**, **furlang**; either with the surn. *Ashley* or its source **æsc** plus **lēah**); Bastard Leys (*v*. **bastard**, **leys**; *bastard*, when applied to land, may be derogatory, used of fields of low yield or of abnormal shape, cf. Ru 224 and 262 *s.n.*); Bells Cl 1845 (either with the surn. *Bell* in the possessive case, or referring to endowed land for the provision and maintenance of church bells and their accoutrements, or for the payment of bellringers; perh. cf. Bellfields Lane *supra*); Bowling Leys (*v*. **bowling**, **leys**); Braymish ('broad marsh', *v*. **breiðr**, **mersc**; cf. *Bremish* in Smeeton Westerby f.ns. (b) and Bremish in Kibworth Harcourt f.ns. (a)); Breach Furlong (*v*. **brēc**); Long Brimley (*v*. **brēmel**, **lēah**); Brook Furlong (*v*. **brōc**); Catley Furlong, Long Catley (*v*. **cat(t)**, **lēah**); Chain Bridge Leys (*v*. **leys** and *Chain Bridge*, Market Harborough); Clack Hill Leys (*v*. **leys** and Clack Hill *supra*); Clarks Middle Cl 1845 (with the surn. *Clark*); Clay Pit Leys (*v*. **cley-pytt**, **leys**); Cow Pasture (*v*. **cū**, **pasture**); Crowthorn (*v*. **crāwe**, **þorn**); Middle ~ ~, Over Dale Acre (*v*. **uferra**) (*v*. **dalr**, **æcer**); Dodmoor (*v*. **dēad**, **mōr**[1]; the name also appears in adjoining Lubenham f.ns.); Dog Bank (*v*. **dogga**, **banke**); Dunslade, ~ Leys (*v*. **leys**) (*v.* **slæd**; with **dunn** or **dūn**); Elbow Leys (*v.* **elbowe**, **leys**); Above Farndon Way (*v.* **weg**; a furlong so called, East Farndon lying 2 miles to the south-west in Northants.); Fern Leys (*v.* **fearn**, **leys**); Flax Lands (*v.* **fleax**, **land**); The Gores (*v.* **gāra**); Great Cl 1926; Horse Cl 1845 (*v.* **hors**); High ~, Long ~, Short Howe (*v.* **hōh**); Large Bridge Furlong (*v. Large Bridge* in Great Bowden f.ns. (b)); Leys Across Braybrooke Way (*v.* **leys**, **weg**; Braybrooke lies one mile to the south-east in Northants.); Little Bowden Hill 1926; Little Hill Furlong (*v. Lyttylhill* in Great Bowden f.ns. (b)); Long Lands (*v.* **lang**[1], **land**); Meadow Hedge ~, Meadow Side Furlong (*v.* **furlang**) (*v.* **hecg**, **sīde**); Meer Furlong (*v.* (**ge**)**mǣre**); Peasland (*v.* **pise**, **land**); Great Quick, Mouses Quick (*v.* **mūs**) (*v.* **quyk**); Rookwell (this could be the earlier recorded *Rokhyl* of Great Bowden *supra*; otherwise *v.* **wella** and either with the OE masc. pers.n. *Hrōca* or with **hrōc**; cf. *Rokeswelle* in Drayton f.ns. (b)); Round Hill (*v.* **round**); Long ~, Short Ryelands (*v.* **ryge**, **land**); St Marys Hill (near the Church of St Mary in Arden *supra*); Shellands (*v.* **land**; poss. with **scelf** 'shelving terrain'); High ~, Long ~, Short Simborough, Simborough Slade (*v.* **slæd**) (*v.* **berg**; the first el. may be **sīma** 'a rope, a chain', perh. indicating the site of an early ropewalk or some kind of demarcation); South Sick (*v.* **sík**); Above ~ ~ ~, Below Stable Gate Way (furlongs so called; perh. 'roadway marked by posts', *v.* **stapol**, **gata**); Stinford Hill, ~ ~ Leys (*v.* **leys**) (*v.* **stint**, **ford**); Stockwell ('stream with a footbridge consisting of a tree-trunk', *v.* **stocc**, **wella**); Thornborough (*v.* **þorn**, **berg**); Water Furrows (*v.* **wæter**, **furh** and *the water furrowes* in Billesdon f.ns. (b)); Whitleather Furlong (*v.* **furlang**; with the surn. *Whitleather*); Wilsons Leys (*v.* **leys**; with the surn. *Wilson*); Wood Breach (*v.* **brēc**), Wood Gate (*v.* **gata**) (*v.* **wudu**).

Medbourne

MEDBOURNE

Medburne 1086 DB, 1203 Ass, e.13 *Peake et freq* to 1452, 1459 *ib et passim* to 1582 LEpis, 1620 LML, *Medburna* a.1150 *Peake*, 1165 P *et passim* to m.13 (e.15) *BelCartB*, 1284 ChronPetr, *Medburnia* 12 *Peake*, *Medburn'* 1171, 1172 P *et freq* to 1492, 1497 *Peake et passim* to 1545 MemR, 1557 Fine

Medborn(e) 1209 × 19 RHug, 1237 Cur *et passim* to 1615 Ipm, 1661 Fine, *Medbornia* 12 *Peake*

Medbourn' 1293 *Peake*, 1302 Pat *et passim* to 1371, 1378 ib, *Medbourne* 1322 Ipm, 1333 *Peake et passim* to 1421 *ib*, 1447 Fine *et freq*

Medeburn' 1243 Cur, 1253 Ch *et passim* to 1306, 1327 *Peake et freq* to 1388, 1389 *ib*, *Medeburna* 12 (e.15) *BelCartB*, *Medeburne* 12 (e.15) *ib*, 1280 ChronPetr *et passim* to 1394 *Peake*, 1401 (e.15) *BelCartB*, *Medeborne* 1344, 1389, 1417 *Peake*, 1426 *Conant*, *Medebourn(e)* 1291, 1316 *Peake et passim* to 1385 *ib*, 1413 Fine

Meddeburn(e) 1268 Pat, 1316 *Peake et passim* to 1389, 1424 *ib*, *Medd(e)borne* 1417 *Conant*

Meadborne 1551 *Peake*, *Meadbourn* 1700 LML

Metorne (sic) 1086 DB, *Metburna* Hy 1 (1333) Ch, Hy 2 (e.15) *BelCartB*, 1209 × 35 RHug, 1290 Ch, *Metburn(e)* m.13 (1404) *Laz* (p), p.1250 (1404) *ib*, 13, 1451 *Peake*, 1503 Ipm, 1518 Visit, 1519 *Peake*, c. 1545 Leland, *Metborne* 1566, 1567 AAS

Methburne m.13 (1404) *Laz* (p)

Most likely 'the meadow stream, the stream with meadows along its banks', *v.* **mēd**, **burna**. A broad stream divides the length of the township which is situated in rich meadowland. The few instances of spellings with *Met-* (10 out of some 600 before 1400 in the editor's collection) are presumably the result of the unvoicing of *d* to *t* before *b* through dissimilation. However, because forms with *Met-* are found as early as DB, **mægðe** 'maythe, may-weed' may perhaps also be thought of as the specific (note *Methburne* m.13 (1404)), though it should be observed that OE *æ* usually gives ME *a* in Leics. with only occasional *e* forms occurring.

Medbourne, beside the Roman *Via Devana* (later Gartree Road), is the site of a Romano-British settlement and villa.

ASHLEY RD, Ashley in Northants. lying 1½ miles to the south. BELVOIR LODGE, a modern allusion to the early lords of Belvoir who held land in Medbourne, *v.* **loge**. BROOKFIELD (local), 1925 Kelly. BURNSIDE, 1925 Kelly. CROWN (P.H.) (lost), *Crown* 1846, 1863, 1877 White, 1925 Kelly. DENT'S SPINNEY, *Dents Spinney* 1969 *Surv*, *v.* **spinney**; with the surn. *Dent*. THE HALL, 1697, 1703, 1724, 1762 *Terrier*, *Old Hall* 1925 Kelly, *v.* **hall**. HALLATON RD is *Halghtongate* 1310 *Peake*, *Haloughtongate* 1318 AD, 1402 *Peake*, *Haletongate* 1326 *ib*, *Haloutongate* 1350 *ib*, *Hallarton gate* 1601 *Terrier* (*v.* **gata**), *Hallarton Waye* 1601, *Halloughton way* 1647, 1690 *ib*, *Hallouton* ~ 1697 *ib*, *Hallowton* ~ 1697, 1700, 1703 *ib*, *Hallaton Way* 1724, c.1745 *ib et passim* to 1821 *ib* (*v.* **weg**); Hallaton lies 2 miles to the north-west. HOME FM, 1925 Kelly, *v.* **home**. HORSE AND TRUMPET (P.H.) (lost), *Horse and Trumpet* 1846, 1863, 1877 White, 1925 Kelly. MAIN ST. MANOR RD. MEDBOURNE BROOK, *le Brok*(*e*) 1318 AD, 1322 *Peake*, *the Brook*(*e*) 1601, 1697 *Terrier et passim* to 1969 *Surv*, cf. *by þe brok'* p.1250 *Peake* (p), *by the brok'* 1287 *ib* (p), *atte Brok* 1302 Fine (p) (*v.* **atte**), *del Brok* 1303 *Pat* (p), 1309 ib (p), *par le Brok* 1306 *Peake* (p) (with OFr *par* 'by'), *othe Brok* 1366 Ipm (p), *atte Brook* 1384 *Peake* (p), *v.* **brōc**. MEDBOURNE GRANGE, 1877 White, 1925 Kelly, *v.* **grange**. MEDBOURNE MANOR, *v.* **maner**. MILL FM. THE MOORS, 1844 *EnclA*, 1847 *TA*, 1969 *Surv*, *v.* **mōr**[1]. NEVILL ARMS (P.H.), *Nevill Arms* 1846, 1877 White, 1925 Kelly, *Neville Arms* 1863 White; *Charles Nevill* of Nevill Holt is lord of the manor in 1846 ib. NUT BUSH, 1969 *Surv*, *notebuske* l.13 *Peake*, *v.* **hnutu**, **busc**, **buskr**; recording an erstwhile patch of nut-bearing shrubs such as hazel. OLD HOLT RD is *Holt*(*e*)*gate* 1310, 1327, 1343, 1344 *Peake*, *v.* **gata**; Nevill Holt lies one mile to the north-east. PADGET'S FM, with the surn. *Padget*. PAYNE'S LANE, cf. *Joseph Payne* 1846 White (parish clerk), *John Payne* 1846 ib (farmer) and *Johnny Payne's* 1969 *Surv* (a field so called). QUEEN'S HEAD (P.H.) (lost), *Queen's Head* 1846, 1863, 1877 White. THE RECTORY, 1877 White, 1925 Kelly, *Old Rectory* 1969 *Surv*, *v.* **rectory**. RECTORY LANE. ST GILES'S CHURCH, *Church (St Giles)* 1846, 1863, 1877 White, 1925 Kelly; it is earlier recorded as *ecclesie de Medborne* a.1219 RHug, ~ *de Medburna* 1220 MHW, *ecclesia*(*m*) ~ ~, *ecclesie de Medburn* 1231 *Pat*, 1236 RGros *et passim* to 1377, 1400 *Pat*, *ecclesie de Med*(*e*)*burne* 1312, 1314, 1439 *ib*, ~ *de Medeburn* 1354,

1366 *ib*. SLAWSTON RD is *Slaustongate* l.13, 1310, 1343, 1344 *Peake*, 1352 (16), 1353 (16) *SlCart* (*v*. **gata**), *Slawson waye* 1601 *Terrier*, *Slasen way* 1697, 1700 *ib*, *Slawston(e) way* 1703, 1724 *ib et passim* to 1821 *ib* (*v*. **weg**); Slawston lies one mile to the north-west. UPPINGHAM RD, Uppingham in Rutland lying 6 miles to the north-east.

FIELD-NAMES

In (a), forms dated 1762, 1774, 1781 and 1821 are *Terrier*; those dated 1767, 1771 and 1787 are *Deed*; 1844 are *EnclA*; 1847 are *TA*; 1867 and 1969 are *Surv*; 1942 are Sale. Forms throughout dated 12, e.13, c.1230, 1244, m.13, p.1250, 1281, 1287, 1296, 1298, l.13, e.14, 1306, 1309, 1310, 1316, 1317, 1318, 1320, 1322, 1326, 1327, 1328, 1329, 1330, 1333, 1337, 1338, 1343, 1344, 1345, 1348, 1349, 1350, 1352, 1353, 1356, 1357, 1363, 1364, Edw 3, 1378, 1380, 1383, 1384, 1385, 1389, 1393, 1395, 1396, 1397, 1398, 1399, 1400, 1402, 1412, 1417, 1419, 1420, 1424, 1425, 1434, 1443, 1447, 1448, 1458 and 1478 are *Peake*; those dated l.13[2] are *CRCart*; 13 (16), 1303 (16), 1304 (16), 1337 (16), 1342 (16), 1348 (16), 1349 (16), 1351 (16), 1352 (16), 1353 (16) and 1417 (16) are *SlCart*; 1302, 1346 and 1615 are Ipm; 1318[2] are AD; 1400[2] are *Rut*; 1433 are *Conant*; 1446 are Cl; 1541 are LeicW; 1601, 1647, 1674, 1690, 1697, 1700, 1703, c.1710 and 1724 are *Terrier*; 1626, 1676, 1680, 1694, 1699 and 1736 are *Deed*.

(a) the Nine Acre, the Ten ~, the Eleven ~, Thirteen ~, the Sixteen Acre, Sixteen Acre or the Tree Fd, the Nineteen ~, Twenty-four ~, Forty Acre 1969 (*v*. **æcer**); Accommodation Piece 1867 (*v*. **pece**; representing an adjustment of land for mutual convenience); First ~ ~ ~, Second ~ ~ ~, Ash Hedge Cl 1844, 1847 (*v*. **æsc**, **hecg**); Ashley Bridge Mdw 1844, 1847, Ashley Road Cl, ~ ~ Piece 1844, 1847 (*v*. **pece**) (Ashley in Northants. lies 1½ miles to the south); the Avenue 1844, 1847 (*v*. **avenue**; a tree-lined approach); Back Fd 1969 (*v*. **back** and South Fd *infra*); Back of the Manor 1969 (*v*. **back of** and Medbourne Manor *supra*); Barearse 1762, 1774 *et passim* to 1821 (1601, 1690, 1703, c.1710, 1724, *bararse* 1697, *bareas* 1700; prob. a common derogatory name for unproductive land, in which case *v*. **bær**[1], **ears**, but the generic could rather be **herse** 'a hill-top'); Barn Cl 1847, ~ Fd 1969 (*v*. **bern**); Barry Cl 1969 (no doubt in error for *Berry*, *v*. Home Fd *infra*; George Berry of Blaston and Robert Berry of Ashley were major graziers here in the late 19th cent.); Basterd Layes 1762, Bastard Leys 1774, 1781, 1821, 1847 (*Bastard Leys* 1690, c.1710, *Basterd Layes* 1697, 1700, 1703, 1724, *Upper Bastard Leys* 1647), Ull Bastards 1969 (*v*. **hyll**) (*v*. **leys**; **bastard** was used of fields of abnormal shape or poor yield); Jane Bates's Headland 1762 (*Jane Batses headland* 1697, 1700, 1703, ~ *Bates* ~ c.1710, ~ *Bate's* ~ 1724, *v*. **hēafod-land**); the Batters 1969 (of uncertain meaning; the surn. *Batter(s)* in the possessive case is poss. or the reference may be to batterdock, otherwise called butterdock or butterbur (*Petasites vulgaris*), a plant whose soft large leaves were once used for the wrapping of butter); the Beare Way 1762, 1774 *et passim* to 1821 (1697, 1700, 1703, *Beare waye* 1601, *the Bear way* c.1710, 1724, *v.* **bere**, **weg**); The Big Fd, Big Mdw 1969; Blackmiles 1762, 1774 *et passim* to 1942 (*Blakemylde* 1320, *Blakmilde*, *Blakmulde* 1363, *Blacke Miles* 1601, *Blackmiles* 1674, 1679 *et passim* to 1724, *v.* **blæc**, **mylde**); Blackmoors or Back o' the Lodge 1969 (prob. with a late misformed Blackmiles *supra*; otherwise with the surn. *Blackmore* in the possessive case; with reference also to Belvoir Lodge *supra*, *v.* **back of**); Blacks ~ 1844, 1847, Black Cl 1969 (with the surn. *Black*); Bland's Mdw 1942, ~ ~ or Rusholme 1969 (with the surn. *Bland*; *v.* Rush Holme *infra*); Blaston Seek 1762, ~ Sike 1774, 1781, 1821, Nether ~ ~, Blaston Sink (sic) 1844, 1847, 1942, Blaston Sinks 1969 (*blastonsike* m.13, *Blastonesike* l.13, *Blastonsik* 1318, 1338, *Blastonsyk'* 1395, *Blason Sicke* 1601, *Blaston Seek(e)* 1647, 1703, c.1710, 1724, *Blason seeke* 1674, 1697, 1700, *v.* **sík**; Blaston parish adjoins to the north); Bottom Fd, ~ Mdw 1969 (*v.* **bottom**); Bottrell's 1969 (the surn. *Bottrell* in the possessive case); the Breach 1762, 1767 *et passim* to 1821, Breach Furlong 1844, 1847 (*the Breech* 1601, *the Breach* 1674, 1690 *et passim* to 1724, *v.* **brēc**); (the) Bridge Fd 1767, 1774, 1781, 1821 (*(the) Bridgfeild* 1601, 1697 *et passim* to 1724, *(the) Bridgfield* 1674, 1679, 1690, c.1710, *v.* **brycg**, **feld**; one of the great open-fields of the township); Bull Hook 1969 (*Bullhooke* 1699, *v.* **bula**, **hōc**); Calfers Leys 1774, 1781, 1821 (*Calvers leas* 1601, *~ leayes* 1647, *~ leys* 1690, *Calfers Leayes* 1697, 1700, *~ Lease* 1703, *Calfer Lay(e)s* c.1710, 1724, *v.* **calf** (**calfra** gen.pl.), **leys**; poss. attracted to the surn. *Calver* in the possessive case, from Calver (Db 54), otherwise a modern plural form); Cathill 1771 (*v.* **cat(t)**); Christian's 1969 (the surn. *Christian* in the possessive case); Church Fd 1969 (*v.* Town Mdw *infra*), Old Churchyard Cl 1844, 1847, Church Yard 1969 (*v.* **churchyerd**) (*v.* St Giles's Church *supra*); Corner Fd 1969 (*v.* **corner**); Coppses Acre 1762, 1774, 1781, 1821 (1703, 1724, *Copses Acre* 1690, *Coppeses acker* 1697, *Copes Acker* 1700, *v.* **æcer**; note also *Copsyesplace* 1446 (*v.* **place**); with the surn. *Copsey*, a reflex of the ON masc. pers.n. *Kupsi*); Council Fd 1969 (if recording an early name, then *v.* **counsayl**; but if modern, may simply relate to the local Council); Crowhill 1762, 1774 *et passim* to 1847, 1969 Far ~ ~, First Crowhill Way 1844, 1847 (*Crowhill'* 1425, *Croell* 1601, *Crowwell* 1674, *Crowhill* 1679, 1690, 1703, c.1710, 1762, *Crohill* 1697, 1700, *v.* **crāwe**, **hyll**); Dale Balk 1847 (*v.* **balca**), the Great Dale 1762, 1774, 1781, 1821, Big Dale or Oat Hill 1969 (*v.* Oat Hill *infra*) (*(the) Great Dale* 1601, 1647, 1697, 1703, c.1710, 1724, *the Grate dale* 1700, *the greate dale end* 1601 (*v.* **ende**); it was earlier called *Micledale*, *Mikeldale* e.13, *Mykyldale* 1396, *v.* **micel**, **mikill**, **grēat**), the Dale Fd 1762, 1771, 1774, 1781, 1787, 1821 (1674, 1679, 1690, c.1710, *Dale feilde* 1601, *the Dale Feild* 1697, 1700, 1703, 1724; earlier called *Micledalefeld*, *Mychyldalefeld*, *Mykel(e)dalefeld* m.13, *Mikyldalefeld* 1296, 1343, *Myckyldalefeld* 1296, l.13, *Mikildalefeld* 1320, *le Mikyldalfeld* 1393, *Mykyldal(e)feld* 1393, 1395, 1397, *Mykildalefelde* 1397, *v.* **feld**; one of the great open-fields), Little Dale 1762, 1774, 1781, 1821, 1969 (1690, c.1710, 1724, *litle dale* 1601, *the Littell Dale* 1697, 1700, 1703), Little Dale Hill 1762, 1774, 1821, Dale Hill 1847 (*litle dale hill* 1601, *Littelldale hill* 1697, 1700, *Little Dale Hill* 1703, 1724) (*v.* **dalr**); Deckers Cl 1867 (with the surn. *Decker*, a reflex of ME *dykere* 'a ditcher, one who digs ditches or dykes'); the Dip Fd 1969 (*v.* **dip** and Roe's Cl *infra*); Dodds Cl 1767, 1847 (prob. with the surn. *Dodd(s)*; note the following group of names to which this f.n. may relate); Dodsholme 1844, 1847, 1969, Dodd's Holme 1867, Far ~, First Dodsholme 1844, 1847, 1942, 1969, Dodsholme Cl, ~ Mdw 1844, 1847 (*v.* **holmr**; either with the OE masc. pers.n. *Dodd* or with the surn. *Dodd*(*s*)); Dorman's Cl 1969 (with the surn. *Dorman*, a reflex of the OE pers.n. *Dēormann*); Above ~, Beneath Drayton Way 1762, 1774, 1781, 1821 (1703, 1724; furlongs beside the road to Drayton which lies 2 miles south-east of Medbourne. The road is *Drayton Way* 1647, 1690, 1710, *draten way* 1697 (*v.* **weg**) and earlier *Draytongat*(*e*) p.1250, l.13, 1310, 1318, 1327, 1363, 1393, 1601, *Draitongate* 1320, *Draytonegate* 1397 (*v.* **gata**)); Far Cl 1844, 1847, 1969, Far Mdw 1844, 1847; Elliott's Mdw 1969 (with the surn. *Elliott*); Fillbarns 1844, 1847, 1969 (a complimentary name for very fertile land); First Cl, ~ Mdw 1844, 1847; the Flatt Haw(e)s 1762, 1774, 1821, Flathaws 1781, Great Flat Hawes 1847 (*flatte hawes* 1601, *Flathas* 1674, *Flathawes* 1697, 1700, *Flathaws* 1703, *the Flatthawes* 1724 (*v.* **flatr**, **haga**[1]); Folkecatts 1762, Foldcatts 1774, 1781, 1821, 1844, 1847, Folecatts 1787, Fold Cats 1867, Folcatts or Foggatts 1969, Foldcatts Spinney 1847 (*v.* **spinney**) (*Folcotes* 1344, *Folcot'* 1357, *Folcatts* 1647, 1674, *Folecats* 1679, *Fowlcotts* 1690, *Folkecat*(*e*)*s* 1697, 1700, 1703, *Folkecatts* 1724, 'shelters for foals', *v.* **fola**, **cot**; note *folkotesyke* in adjoining Slawston f.ns. (b) and *Folkatmedowe* in adjoining Hallaton f.ns. (b)); Genetts home 1762, Gennetts holm 1774, 1781 (*Gennitshome* 1647, *Gennettes* ~ 1697, *Genet*(*t*)*es home* 1700, 1703, *Gennets holm* c.1710, 1724, *v.* **holmr**; with the surn. *Jennett/Gennett*, a diminutive of the OFr masc. pers.n. *Jehan*); Mr Goodmans Headland 1762 (1697, 1700, 1703, c.1710, 1724), Mr Goodman Senior Headland 1762 (*Mr Goodmans Sener Headland* 1697, ~ ~ *Senior* ~ c.1710) (*v.* **hēafod-land**); Goose Acre 1942 (*v.* **gōs**, **æcer**); Gorse Cl 1969 (*v.* **gorst**); Great Cl 1844, 1847, Great Mdw 1847 (*Great Medowe* 1601); Mr Green (Senior) Headland 1774, 1781, 1821 (*v.* **hēafod-land**); Gumskull 1847, 1969 (*Gumscall* 1601, *Gomscoll* 1690), Gumscull ~ 1762, Gomscal Hole 1774, 1781, 1821 (*Gumscal hole* 1674, *Gomscole* ~ 1679, 1697, 1700, 1703, 1724, *Gomscoll* ~ 1697, *Gumscull hole* c.1710, *v.* **hol**[1]) (*v.* **skáli**; the specific is presum. a reduced masc. pers.n. such as ON *Guðmundr* (*v.* Gumley *supra*); poss. an early hall site); the Hall Ashgate Peice 1762 (1703, c.1710, 1724, ~ ~ ~ *peese* 1697, *v.* **pece**, The Hall *supra* and *Assegate* in f.ns. (b)); Hallaton Road Cl 1847, ~ ~ Strips 1969 (*v.* **strīp**) (*v.* Hallaton Rd *supra*); the Ham furlong 1847 (*v.* **furlang**), Ham's 1969 (*v.* **hamm**); Hater seek 1762, Hatter sike 1774, 1781, 1821 (*Haytersik*(*e*) l.13, 1310, *Hather sicke* 1601, *Haterseeke* 1679, 1697, 1700, 1703, *Haters seeke* 1710, *Hatter Seek* 1724, *v.* **sík**; with the surn. *Hayter*, from ME *heyt* 'height', i.e. *heytere* 'one who lives at the top of the hill'); Hawes, Hawe's Cl or Thirteen Acre 1969 (cf. *Henry Hawes* and *Thomas Hawes*, *graziers* 1863 White); Holt Hedge 1762, 1774, 1781, 1821 (1601, 1690 *et passim* to 1724, *v.* **hecg**; the parish boundary hedge with Nevill Holt), Holt Warren 1762, 1774, 1781, 1821 (1601, c.1710, 1724, *Holt waring* 1703, *v.* **wareine**) (Nevill Holt adjoins to the north-east); Home Cl 1847, 1969, ~ Fd 1969, Home Fd or Barry Cl 1969 (*v.* Barry Cl *supra*) (*v.* **home**); Honey Acre 1762, 1774, 1781, 1821 (*Huniakyr* 1310, *Huniakyr* 1318, *Huniakir*, *Hunniaker* 1320, *Hunyakyr* 1343, *hony acre* 1601, *Hunny Acre* 1679, *Hun*(*n*)*ey Acker* 1697, 1700, *Hunny Acer* 1703, *Honny Acre* c.1710, 1724, *v.* **hunig**, **æcer**; may allude to a place where honey was found or to 'sweet land' or to a spot with sticky soil); Hull's 1969 (this may be the surn. *Hull* in the possessive case, but it is likelier to be of the same late construction as Ham's *supra*, in which case, *v. le Hull* in f.ns. (b)); Mr Humphreys Headland 1774, 1781, 1821 (*v.* **hēafod-land**); Ingram's 1969 (the surn.

Ingram in the possessive case); Inner Cl 1844, 1847; Jackson's Paddock 1969 (*v.* **paddock**; with the surn. *Jackson*); Kendall's Fd 1969 (with the surn. *Kendall*); Klondike 1969 (a transferred name referring to land in a distant part of the parish; gold was discovered on the Klondike river in north-west Canada in 1896, leading to the gold-rush of 1897–8); Pains ~ ~, Lane Cl 1844, 1847 (*v.* Payne's Lane *supra*); Lane End 1969, ~ ~ Cl 1844, 1847 (*v.* **lane-ende**); The Lawn 1844 (*v.* **launde**; in late f.ns., alluding to grass ground); Leicester Way Cl 1844, 1847 (beside Gartree Road, the Roman *Via Devana*, the principal route to Leicester which lies 14 miles to the north-west); Lett's Cl 1969 (with the surn. *Letts*, a reflex of the fem. pers.n. *Lett*, a pet-form of *Lettice*; cf. *William Letts, grazier* 1863 White); The Leys 1847 (*v.* **leys**); Little Cl 1847, Holland's ~ ~ 1867 (with the surn. *Holland*); Little Fd 1844, 1847, 1867, 1969; Little Mere 1969 (poss. with **mere**[1], otherwise **(ge)mǣre**; note Big Mere *infra*); Little Mdw 1844, 1847 ((*the*) *Litle medowe* 1601, cf. *le Lytylmedowhoke* 1398 (*v.* **hōc**), *v.* **lȳtel**, **mēd** (**mēdwe** obl.sg)); Lodge Fd 1969 (*v.* Belvoir Lodge *supra*); Longcraft 1969 (*Langecroft* m.13, *Longcroft* 1399, *v.* **lang**[1], **croft**); Lower hall piece 1847 (*v.* **pece** and The Hall *supra*); Lower Mdw 1844, 1847; Malthouse yard 1847 (*v.* **mealt-hūs**, **geard**); Manor Fd 1969 (*v.* Medbourne Manor *supra*); Marsdale 1762, 1844, Maresdall 1744, 1821, Maresdale 1781 (*Mersedale* 1337, 1346, 1350, *Mershdal'* 1352, *Mersdale* 1363, *Marsdall* 1601, *Maresdale* 1674, 1697, 1700, 1703, 1724, *Mar*(*e*)*sdaile* 1679, 1690, *Marsdale* 1690, c.1710, *Marsdall end* 1601 (*v.* **ende**)), Marsdale Broad 1762, Maresdall ~ 1774, 1821, Maresdale Broad 1781 (*Mers*(*e*)*dalebrode* l.13, 1343, *Mersedale broad*(*e*) 1352 (16), 1353 (16), *Marsdall broade* 1601, *Maresdaile* ~ 1679, *Marsdell* ~ 1697, *Mearsdale Broade* 1700, *Maresdale* ~ 1703, 1724, *Marsdale Broad* c.1710, *v.* **brode**), First ~ ~ ~, Inner Marsdale Drain Cl 1844, 1847 (*v.* **drain**), Marsdale Fd 1762, Maresdall ~ 1774, 1821, Maresdale Fd 1781, 1787 (*Mersedalefeld* 1318[2], 1320, *Mershdalefeld* 1346, *Mersdal*(*e*)*feld* 1393, 1396, *Maresdaile* ~ 1679, *Maresdale feild* 1674, 1679, 1700, 1703, 1724, *Marsdale Field* c.1710, *v.* **feld**; one of the great open-fields) (*v.* **mersc**, **dalr**); Mayes Headland 1762, 1774, 1781, 1821 (1697, 1700, 1703, 1724, *Meas* ~ 1601, *Mays hadland* 1690, ~ *headland* c.1710, *v.* **hēafod-land**; with the surn. *Maye*(*s*)); the Meadow 1847, Medbourne Mdw 1942 (cf. *at Medu* 1326 (p), *atte Medew* 1343 (p), *atte Meduwe* 1344 (p), *othe Medewe* 1378 (p), *atte Medewe* 1350 (p), *v.* **atte**, **mēd** (**mēdwe** obl.sg.)); Between the Meadow Gates 1762 (c. 1710, *Between the Medowgates* 1674), Betwixt the Meadow Gates 1774, 1781, 1821 (1724, *v.* **betwixt**) (*the Medugate* 1344, *le Medugat'* 1393, *Medowgate* 1402, *Medowe gate* 1601, *the Meadow gates* 1690, 1700, 1703, *v.* **mēd** (**mēdwe** obl.sg.), **gata**); Medbourne Pasture 1806 Map, The Pasture 1847 (*Medbourne Pasture* 1541, *v.* **pasture**); the Meer(e) 1762, 1774, 1781, 1821, Big Mere 1969 (*le mare* 1320, 1331, 1333, 1363, *le mere* 1335, 1447, *the mare* 1601, (*Next*) *the Meer*(*e*) 1703, c.1710, 1724, *v.* **(ge)mǣre**); Middle Cl 1847; Mill Cl 1844, 1847, 1969; Mill Fd 1844, 1847, 1969 (*le mylnefeld* 1443, *Mill feilde* 1601, *v.* **feld**; prob. to be identified with Marsdale Fd *supra*), the Mill Home 1762, Mill Holm(e) 1774, 1781, 1844, 1847 (*millhome* 1601, (*the*) *Mill home* 1690, 1697, 1700, 1703, *Millholm*(*e*) c.1710, 1724, *v.* **holmr**), Mill Layes 1762, ~ Leys 1774, 1781, 1821 (*le milneleys* m.13, *milneleyes* 1330, *Mill leas*(*e*) 1601, 1679, ~ *leys* 1674, 1690, ~ *Lay*(*e*)*s* 1697, c.1710, 1724, *millayes* 1700, 1703, *v.* **lǣs**) (*v.* **myln**; these names appear to relate to a watermill); Mill Hill 1942 (a windmill site); Mutton Acre 1969 (*v.* **æcer**; poss. an abbreviated style for the common f.n. Shoulder of Mutton, i.e. relating to shape, but otherwise simply alluding to sheep pasture); the Neather ~ 1762, the Nether Mdw 1774, 1781, 1821 (*the Neather* ~ 1690, c.1710, 1724, *the Neither Meadow* 1697, 1700, 1703, *v.* **neoðera**); the Neather ~ 1762, (the) Nether Pasture 1781, 1847 (*the Neither Paster* 1697, 1700, 1703, *the Neather Pasture* c.1710, *v.* **pasture**); New Dike 1762, 1774, 1781 (1601, 1690, 1697, 1700, *New dicke* 1601, ~ *dik* 1703, ~ *Dycke* c.1710, *v.* **dík**); Oak Tree 1969 (*v.* **āc**; an enclosure named from a tree); Oat Hill 1762, 1774, 1781, 1821, 1969 (c.1710, *Oate Hill* 1679, 1697, 1703, 1724, *ote hill* 1700, *v.* **āte**); the Odd Willow 1762, 1774, 1781 (1690, 1697, c.1710, 1724, *the Od willow* 1700, 1703, *v.* **wilig**; presum. with **odde** 'single, odd', cf. *Le Hodde Willowe*, Lei **2** 73); Old Hall Paddock 1969 (*v.* **paddock** and The Hall *supra*); The Paddock 1847, 1969, First ~ 1844, 1847, Second Paddock 1847; William Paynes Headland 1762 (~ *Paines* ~ 1697, 1700, 1703, ~ *Payns* ~ c.1710, *Wm. Pains Headland* 1724, *v.* **hēafod-land**), Pains Cl 1969 (cf. *Robert Panes closse* 1601, *v.* **clos(e)**); the Parish Pound 1847 (*v.* **pund**; a parish enclosure for stray beasts); Parrs Layes 1762, ~ Leys 1774, 1781, 1821 Great ~, Little Parsleys 1969 (*Parrs leas* 1601, *Parsleys* 1647, 1690, *Pairsleys* 1674, *Pearsleys* 1679, *Pareslayes* 1697, 1700, *Parrs lay(e)s* 1703, c.1710, 1724, *v.* **leys**; with the surn. *Parr*); Mrs Peggs Pen 1774, 1781, 1821 (*v.* **penn**[2]); the Plot 1844, 1847, Plot adjoining Bridge 1844 (*v.* **plot** and Bridge Fd *supra*); Plowright's 1969 (the surn. *Plowright* in the possessive case, a reflex of ME *plowwryhte* 'a maker of ploughs'); the Quagmire 1762, 1774, 1781, 1821 (1697, 1703, c.1710, 1724, (*the*) *Quagmires* 1674, 1679, 1690, 1700, *v.* **quagmire**); Reading's Cl 1969 (with the surn. *Reading*, a reflex of OE *rydding* 'a clearing'); Red House Piece 1844, 1847, Reddus Piece 1969 (*v.* **pece**) (*the Red House* 1676, 1694, 1736); Roe's Cl 1942, Rose Cl or the Dip Fd 1969 (with the surn. *Roe*, *v.* the Dip Fd *supra*); Rush Holme, ~ ~ Mdw 1844, 1847, Rusholme 1969 (*le Russheholme* 1417, *v.* **risc**, **holmr**); Rowletts 1969 (the surn. *Rowlett* in the possessive case); the Rushes 1862, 1774, 1781 (1690, 1697, 1700, c.1710, 1724, *the Rushis* 1703, *v.* **risc**); Saddler's Cottage 1969 (with the surn. *Saddler*); Second Cl 1847; the Seed Fd, the Seeds 1969 (*v.* **sǣd**; used of grasses sown for one year's mowing or grazing, as distinguished from permanent pasture); The Seke 1969 (*v.* **sík**); the Sheep Pasture 1847 (*v.* **scēp**, **pasture**); Singleton's Mdw 1969 (with the surn. *Singleton*); Skeffington Pastures Gorse 1969 (*v.* **gorst**; with the surn. *Skeffington* of a family originally from the village of this name, 7 miles to the north-west); Skinner's Gap 1968 (*v.* **gap**; with the surn. *Skinner*, a reflex of ME *skinnere* 'a skinner'); Slawston Big ~, Slawston Little Fd 1969, Slawston Hill Foot Cl 1844, 1847, 1867, Slawston Meer 1774, 1781, 1821 (1724, *Slaustonmere* 1310, *Slawson meere* 1601, *Slawston Meere* 1690, 1703, 1762, *slosen meare* 1697, *Slawstone Meer* c.1710, *v.* **(ge)mǣre**), Slawston Road Cl 1844, 1847, 1942 (Slawston parish adjoins to the north-west); the Slip 1942, 1969 (*v.* **slipe**); Smith Mdw 1762 (*Smeeth Medowe* 1601, *Smith Meadow* 1647, 1690, 1700, c.1710; prob. with **smið** (but **smēðe**[1] is poss.) since the enclosure is identical with the following); Smithy Mdw 1774, 1781 (1697, 1724, *Smithey Meadow* 1703; prob. with **smiððe**, but the name may have arisen from a misunderstood **smēðe**[1]); South Fd or Back Fd 1969 (*v.* Back Fd *supra*); the Spinney 1969 (*v.* **spinney**); the Stable Fd 1969 (*v.* **stable**); Stone Pit 1844, 1847 (*v.* **stān-pytt**); Strips, ~ by the Brook 1969 (*v.* **strīp**); Tadder 1969 (the surn. *Tadder* is only very occasionally found; perh. a form of the surn. *Tadde*, from OE *tadde* 'a toad'); Three Streams 1969 (*v.* **strēam**); Top Mdw 1969; Town Mdw or Church Fd 1969 (*v.* Church Fd *supra*), Townsend Cl 1867 (*v.* **ende**) (*v.* **tūn**); the Tree Fd 1969 (*v.* **trēow** and Sixteen Acre *supra*); Mrs Tryons Headland 1774, 1781, 1821 (*v.*

hēafod-land); Turnip Fd 1844 (*v.* **turnepe**); Upper Langley Balk 1844, 1847 (*v.* **balca**; *Langley* in this area is likely to be a p.n. rather than a surn., although no early forms have survived, *v.* **lang**[1], **lēah**); Upper Cl 1969; the Upper Mdw 1762, 1774, 1781, 1821 ((*the*) *Upper Meadow* 1647, 1690, 1703, c.1710, 1724, ~ *Uper* ~ 1700); (the) Upper Pasture 1762, 1774 *et passim* to 1969 (*the Upper Pasture* c.1710, *the Uper Paster* 1697, 1700, 1703), Upper Pasture Piece 1867 (*v.* **pece**) (*v.* **pasture**); Mr Wades Headland 1774, 1781, 1821 (*v.* **hēafod-land**); Mrs Wadlands Headland 1762 (cf. *Mr Wadlands Headland* 1697, 1703, c.1710, 1724, *v.* **hēafod-land**), Wadlands 1969; Warner's 1969 (the surn. *Warner* in the possessive case, a reflex of the ONFr masc. pers.n. *Warnier*); the Washpitt 1762, the Washpit 1774, 1781, 1821 (*the Washpitt* 1690, 1697 *et passim* to 1724, *v.* **wæsce**, **pytt**); Watering Leys 1844, 1847, 1969 (*v.* **wateryng**, **leys**); Above ~ ~, Wellam Way 1762, Welham Way 1774, 1781, 1821, ~ Road 1969, (*Wollan Way* 1647, *Welham* ~ 1690, *Wellam* ~ 1697, 1700, 1703, c.1710, *Above* ~ ~, *Wellham Way* 1724), Wilham Way Cl 1844, 1847 (Welham lies 2 miles to the west); West Hades 1762, 1774, 1781, 1821, Westage 1969 (*le Westhauedes* 1309, *Westhavedis* 1443, *wast hades* 1697, 1700, *West Hades* 1724, *v.* **west**, **hēafod**); Wood Cl 1844, 1847, 1969, (the) Wood Fd 1762, 1774 *et passim* to 1942 (*le Wodefeld'* 1338, 1343, *þe Wodefeld* 1353, *le Wodfeld'* 1395, 1396, *Woode feilde* 1601, *the Woodfeild* 1690, 1697 *et passim* to 1724, *v.* **feld**; one of the early great open-fields of the township), Wood Leys 1844, 1847 (*v.* **leys**), the Wood Way 1762, 1774, 1781, 1821 ((*the*) *Wood Way* 1690, 1697 *et passim* to 1724 (*v.* **weg**); cf. *Ouerwodegate* 1329, *Netherwodegate* 1338, 1343, 1352, 1356, *nethirwodegate* 1389, *le Nederwodegate* 1396 (*v.* **uferra**, **neoðera**, **gata**) (*v.* **wudu**); Wootten 1969 (prob. the surn. *Wootten*); Worsted Balk 1847 (*v.* **balca**; with the surn. *Worsted*).

(b) *Mr Alsop(p)s pen* 1690, 1697, 1703, 1724, *Mr Alsops penn* c.1710 (*v.* **penn**[2]); *Assegate* 1296, 1310, *Has(s)egate* 13, *Asshgate* 1337, *Ayssegate* 1343, *Aschgate* 1363, *Ouer* ~ (*v.* **ofer**[3]), *Beneath* ~, *Ashgate* 1601 (*v.* **æsc**, **gata**); *le Banefurlong* 1303 (16) (*v.* **bēan**, **furlang**); *Bebroke* 1443 ('(land) by the brook', *v.* **bī**, **brōc**); *Belteslowe* 1310 (*v.* **hlāw**; poss. with the OE masc. pers.n. *Beald/Bald*, with AN *e* for *a*); *Berhull* 1330 (*v.* **bere**, **hyll**); *Berihull*, *Beryhull* 1322, *Beryhyll* 1399 (*v.* **berige**, **hyll**); *Bernardisplace* 1363 (*v.* **place**; with the surn. *Bernard*); *Bestonisacre* 1326, *Bestonesaker* 1349 (*v.* **æcer**; with the surn. *Beeston*); *Bilton'* 1402 (*v.* **tūn**; either with **bill** 'a ridge' or with the OE masc. pers.n. *Bila/Billa*); *Blakelanglondes* 1310, *le Blakelangelondes* 1330, *Blakelanglond'* 1396 (*v.* **blæc**, **lang**[1], **land**); *Bradley pathe* 1601 (*v.* **pæð**; the site of the defunct Bradley Priory lies 2 miles to the north-east of Medbourne); *Breachland* 1647 (*v.* **brēc**, **land**); *le Brendemulne* 1310 (*v.* **brend**, **myln**); *le Brokforlong* 1296, *le brocforlong* 1318, (*le*) *Brokfurlong* 1337, 1363, *Brookforlong* 1393 (*v.* **brōc**, **furlang**); (*le*) *Caluerbreche* m.13, l.13, 1363, 1398 (*v.* **brēc**), *Calvers Close* 1626 (*v.* **calf** (**calfra** gen.pl.)); *Cartersyerde* 1434 (*v.* **geard**; with the surn. *Carter*); *Canuilesorchard* 1328 (*v.* **orceard**), *Caunwilleyerd* 1326, *Caunuylesyeard* 1348, *Cawnelueherd* 1380 (*v.* **geard**) (with the surn. *Canville* of a family originally from the township of this name in Normandy); *Caundeleynysplace* 1364 (*v.* **place**; with the surn. *Candlin* (ME *Candelayn*, a variant of *Gandelayn*, from *Gamelin*, a diminutive of the ON masc. pers.n. *Gamall*)); *le Cokescroft* 1318, *le Cokyscroft* 1326 (*v.* **croft**; prob. with **cocc**[1] 'a hillock', less likely with **cocc**[2] 'a (wild) cock bird'); *the common grownde* 1601 (*v.* **commun**, **grund**); *Connynggarthe* 1445 (*v.* **coning-erth**); *Cressewell'* l.13[2] (*v.* **cresse**, **wella**); *Cretonesplace* 1383, 1384 (*v.* **place**; cf. *Henr' de Creton* 1384); *Crosgate* 1349 (16) (*v.* **gata**; with **cros** or **cross**);

atte Crosse 1342 (16) (p), 1351 (16) (p) (*v*. **atte**, **cros**); (*le*) *Dedemor* 1327, 1343, 1349 (*v*. **dēad**, **mōr**[1]; a common name for infertile wasteland); *le Dockaker* 1417 (16), *le Dockacre* 1420 (*v*. **docce**, **æcer**); *Dodemersdale* c.1230 (*v*. **dæl**[1]; poss. with the OE masc. pers.n. *Dodmǣr*, *v*. *Dodemerisdale* in Drayton f.ns. (b) and *Dodemeredale* in Nevill Holt f.ns. (b)); *Doodeslane* 1434 (*v*. **lane**; cf. *Joh' Dood* 1434); *Drayton meere* 1601 (*v*. (**ge**)**mǣre**; Drayton parish adjoins to the south-east); *Extonescroft* 1343 (*v*. **croft**; with the surn. *Exton* of a family originally from the township of this name, 14 miles to the north-east in Rutland); *le fallyngbrynk* 1399 (*v*. **felging**, **brink**); *Flaxlond*(*es*) 1363, 1402 (*v*. **fleax**, **land**); (*les*) *Foxholes* l.13, 1322 (*v*. **fox-hol**); *Gildmorysyerd* 1363, *Gyldemoreyerd* 1400[2] (*v*. **geard**; perh. with the surn. *Gilmore*, cf. the much later *Mary Gilmore* 1854 Census and *Agnes Gilmore* 1879 ib, both of Medbourne; note that Reaney *s.n.* Gilmore has no instances with medial *d*, which suggests here an alternative toponymic derivation of the surn. from **gylde*(*n*)-*mōr* 'wasteland, golden coloured with flowers'); *le Grene* 1309 (*v*. **grēne**[2]); *Hallebrechehafdys* 1353 (*v*. **brēc**, **hēafod**), *le Hallebuttes* 1327 (*v*. **butte**), *le hallegate* 1412 (*v*. **gata**), *le Hallelane* 1412 (*v*. **lane**), *le Hallestou* 1309 (*v*. **stōw**) (*v*. **hall**; the l.13th- or e.14th-cent. hall of the Chaworth family is contained within the structure of Medbourne Manor *supra*); *Haverberge* 1349 (16) (*v*. **hæfera**, **hafri**, **berg**); *le hill iuxta le mere* 1447 (*v*. **hyll**, (**ge**)**mǣre**; with MLat *iuxta* 'next to'); *Hokedsti* e.13, *le Hokedesty* 1330, *Hokedstye* 1419, *Hokydsty* 1443 (*v*. **hōcede**, **stīg**); *le Holdemulnehurst* 1310 (*v*. **ald**, **myln**, **hyrst**); *le holme* 1348 (16) (*v*. **holmr**); *Holt hades* 1697 (*v*. **hēafod**), *Holthyll* 1398 (*v*. **hyll**), *Holtmere*(*e*) 1330, 1397 (*v*. (**ge**)**mǣre**) (Nevill Holt adjoins to the north-east); *les Houbrinkes* 1298, *Houbringes* l.13[2] (*v*. **hōh**, **brink**); *le Hull* 13, 1327, 1329, 1330, 1345, *le hyl* 1318, *le Hulfeld* 1310, *le Hilfeld* 1326, *le hillefelde atteton hille* (sic) 1389 (*v*. **atte**, **tūn**, **hyll**) (*v*. **hyll**, **feld**; one of the early great open-fields); *Humberston place* 1458, 1478 (*v*. **place**), *Humberston thyng'* 1443 (*v*. **thing**) (with the surn. *Humberston* of a family originally from Humberstone, 13 miles to the north-west); *Hunrikismor* p.1250, *Hunrigesmor* l.13 (*v*. **mōr**[1]; with the OE masc. pers.n. *Hūnrīc*); *Langedole* Edw 3, *le Langedoledyke* 1309 (*v*. **dík**), *Northlangedole* l.13, *le Nortlangdol'* 1399 (*v*. **norð**), *Suthlangedole* e.13, (*le*) *Southlang*(*e*)*dole*(*s*) 1317, 1330, 1343, 1344, 1350, 1353, 1363 (*v*. **sūð**) (*v*. **lang**[1], **dāl**); *litledale* l.13 (*v*. **lȳtel**, **dalr**); (*le*) *longebreche* m.13, l.13 (×2), *the longbreche* 1393, *le longbrech* 1397, 1398 (*v*. **lang**[1], **brēc**); (*le*) *Mareleyus* 1380, 1398, *le mareleys* 1393, 1397 (*v*. (**ge**)**mǣre**, **lǣs**); *Dame Margarete thyng* 1424 (*v*. **thing**; poss. with reference to Margaret de Kirkby (d. 1324) who held a quarter of Kirkby's Manor in Medbourne); *le Medufeld* 1320, *le Medewfeld* 1343, *le Medowfeld* 1419, *le medowefeld subtus hokydsty* 1443 (with MLat *subtus* 'beneath'); *v*. *Hokedsti*, *supra*) (*v*. **feld**; one of the early great open-fields), *le medu hauedes* 1344 (*v*. **hēafod**) (*v*. **mēd** (**mēdwe** obl.sg.)); *le merefurlong* 1296, 1304 (16), *le merefurlonk* 1337 (16), *v*. (**ge**)**mǣre**, **furlang**); *Mersedale forlong* 1296, *mersedale furlong* 1353 (16) (*v*. **furlang**), *Mersedaleknoll* 1352, *Mersdaleknol* 1363 (*v*. **cnoll**), *Mersdalewell'* 1363 (*v*. **wella**) (*v*. Marsdale *supra*); *Netherstedeyerd'* 1400[2] (*v*. **neoðera**, **stede**, **geard**); *Oddestorp* 12 (×2) (*v*. **þorp**; with the ON masc. pers.n. *Oddr*); *Oldehall* 1400[2] (*v*. **ald**, **hall** and *le Hallestou*, *supra*); *the Old House* 1680 (*v*. **ald**); *Robert Panes Pen* 1601 (*v*. **penn**[2]), *Mr William Panes tonge* 1601 (*v*. **tunge**), *Paynes manor* 1615 (*v*. **maner**; a capital messuage owned by *John Payne* 1615 ib); *atte Park* 1349 (p) (*v*. **atte**, **park**); *Peyselondis* e.13, *Peyslondes* 1316, *Pease landes* 1601 (*v*. **pise**, **land**); *Potterisherþe* e.13 (*v*. **pottere**, **eorðe**); *Prikeputes* 1310 (*v*.

pric(c)a, **pytt**); *Pyllok* 1353 (*v*. **pyll**, **-uc**); *Reynoldespyt* 1318 (*v*. **pytt**; with the surn. *Reynold*, a reflex of the OFr masc. pers.n. *Reinald*); *Lady Roberts Wood* 1647; *la petite Rudde* 1244 (with OFr *petit* 'small'), *Rudde* 1281, e.14, *le Rudde* 1302 (*v*. **ryde**); *Schypmanhaluakyr* 1396 (*v*. **half-aker**; with the surn. *Shipman* (in this region, presum. from OE *scēp-mann* 'a shepherd')); *le Sidholm* 1309, (*le*) *Sydholm* 1330, 1344, *la Sydeholme* 1433 (*v*. **sīde**, **holmr**); *Siwardysakyr* l.13 (*v*. **æcer**; with the surn. *Siward*, a reflex of either the OE masc. pers.n. *Sigeweard* or the ODan masc. pers.n. *Sigvarðr*); *Standelfs* 1344 (*v*. **stān-(ge)delf**); *le Stocking* 1333 (*v*. **stoccing**); *Swanns Close* 1676 (with the surn. *Swann*); *Terbagyerde* 1400[2] (*v*. **geard**; *Terbag* is a lost surn., poss. a reflex of the OE fem. pers.n. *Theodburh* (*Teotberga*), but the surn. *Terbag* (prob. from the ContGerm fem. pers.n. *Theodberga* (Forssner 229)) is still found in Duitsland, Germany); *Teperwellesik* 1310, *Teperwelsek* 1350, *Teperwellesyke* 1352, *Teperwellsik* 1363 (*v*. **tæppere**, **wella**, **sík**; the first el. could be rather the ME occupational surn. *Tapper* (note *Ulfuine Teperesune* c.1095 of Bury St Edmunds), but this would be very unusual compounded late with *wella*); *Thorniholm* e.13, *Þorniholm* l.13 (*v*. **þornig**, **holmr**); *Thralholm* e.13 (*v*. **þrǣl**, **þræll**, **holmr**); *le Thwytelangelondes* 1345 (*v*. **lang**[1], **land**; the first el. is prob. ON **þveit** 'a clearing', but may be an example of disputed OE **þwīt** with the same meaning); *the towne baulke* 1601 (*v*. **tūn**, **balca**); *Ulketeleswod* 1244 (*v*. **wudu**; with the ON masc. pers.n. *Ulfketill*); *Vytharowe* 1363 (*v*. **wīðig**, **víðir**, **rāw**); *Waldrenysacr'* 1363 (*v*. **æcer**; with the surn. *Waldron*, a reflex of the ContGerm masc. pers.n. *Waleran*); *Mr Walldrones Pen* 1601 (*v*. **penn**[2] and the previous f.n.; the surn. lived on in the township); *Walewell* 1326 (*v*. **walu**, **wella**); *le wandoles* 1318 (*v*. **wandole**); *Wencelawedale* 1385 (*v*. **hlāw**, **dæl**[1], **dalr**; the first el. may be either **wince** or **wincel**); *Westfield* 1647; *Weston forde* 1601 (*v*. **ford**; Weston in Northants. lies 2 miles to the south-west, across the river Welland); *Wilgate* 13 (16) (*v*. **wilig**, **gata**); *Wrongedoles* 1310, *le Wrangedoles* 1330 (*v*. **wrang**, **dāl**); *le Wrongesik* 1310 (*v*. **wrang**, **sík**).

Mowsley

MOWSLEY

Mvselai 1086 DB (×2), *Museleia* 1166 RBE (p), *Muselea* 1166 LN (p), 1214 P (p), *Musele* Hy 2 Dugd, 1199 Cur *et passim* to 1255 Fine, 1270 Cur *et freq* to 1300 Ch, 1320 Banco *et passim* to 1358 GildR (p), *Muselei* 1202 FF, *Muselee* 1244 Fine, 1286 Banco, 1300 Pat, *Museleg'* 1247 Ass, 1247 Abbr, 1257 Fine, *Museleye* 1318 Pat

Muslai 1156 (1318) Ch, *Muslei* Hy 2 Dugd, *Muslegh* 1226 Fine, *Musle* 1242 Fees, Hy 3 *Crox*

Mousele 1277 Banco, 1292 Ipm *et passim* to 1318 Pat (p), 1325 Fine (p) *et freq* to 1348 Coram, 1355 *MiD*, *Mouseley* 1292 Cl, 1311 Banco *et passim* to 1540 MinAccts, 1551 Pat, *Mouselee* 1350 Cl, 1387 Banco

Mousle 1316, 1317 Ipm *et passim* to 1364 Pat, *Mouslegh* 1357 BPR, 1361 Cl, *Mousley(e)* 1358 Ipm, 1449 *WoCart*, 1535 VE, 1576 Saxton

Mowseley 1480 Hastings, 1510 Visit *et freq* to 1556, 1604 Fine, *Mowisley* 1502 *MiscAccts*, *Mowesley* 1524 Ipm, 1535 VE, 1604 SR

Mowsley 1605 LML, 1621 Fine *et freq*, *Mowslie* 1617, 1620 LML

'The wood or woodland clearing infested with mice', *v.* **mūs**, **lēah**.

DAG LANE, *v.* **dag**. LAUGHTON LANE is *Laughton gate* c.1690 *Terrier*, *v.* **gata**; Laughton lies one mile to the east. LEICESTER RD is *Leicester way* c.1690 *Terrier*; Leicester lies 10 miles to the north-west. LODGE FM. MAIN ST. MANOR FM, *v.* **maner**. MOWSLEY HILLS, *the Hills* c.1690 *Terrier*. MOWSLEY HILLS FM, 1919 Sale. MOWSLEY LODGE, 1835 O, *v.* **loge**. PEASHILL FM (~ LODGE 2½"), *Peyshyll* 1467 × 84 *LTD*, *Peshill* 1601 *Terrier*, *Pessell* 1638 *ib*, *Pescell* 1674 *ib*, *Peasehill* 1679, c.1690 *ib*, *Peasill* 1703 *ib*, *Pes(s)hill* 1745 *ib*, *v.* **pise**, **hyll**. THE RECTORY, 1877 White, 1925 Kelly, *v.* **rectory**; note *the Parsonage Dwelling House* 1748 *Terrier*, *v.* **personage**. SADDINGTON RD, Saddington lying 2 miles to the north-west. ST NICHOLAS'S CHURCH, *Church (St Nicholas)* 1846, 1863, 1877 White, 1925 Kelly. STAFF OF LIFE (P.H.), *Staff of Life Inn* 1846 White, *Staff of Life* 1863, 1877 White, 1925 Kelly. THEDDINGWORTH RD, Theddingworth lying 3 miles to the south-east.

FIELD-NAMES

In (a), forms presented without dates are 1968 *Surv*; those dated 1858 are also *Surv*; 1919 are Sale. Forms throughout dated 1269 are IpmR; those dated 1467 × 84 are *LTD*; 1477 (e.16) are *Charyte*; c.1530 are *Depos*; 1601, 1638, 1674, 1679, c.1690, 1703, 1712, 1745 and 1748 are *Terrier*; 1680 and 1736 are *Deed*.

(a) The Acre, Three Acre 1968, (The) Four ~ 1919, 1968, Five ~, Top ~ ~, Seven Acre, Eight ~, Nine ~, Ten ~, Eleven ~, Thirteen Acre 1968 (*v*. **æcer**); Arable Fd 1919, Bottom ~ ~, Middle ~ ~, Top Arable Fd 1968 (*v*. **arable**); Ash Cl (1680, *v*. **æsc**); The Bargles (prob. a late form with metathesis of *Bulgore* 1467 × 84, *v*. **bula**, **gāra**); Barn Cl 1858, 1919, 1968 (*v*. **bern**); Besicke (*Besyke*, *Bysyke* 1467 × 84, *Beesick* 1638, *Besekefelde* 1467 × 84, *Beesick(e) Feild* 1638, 1674, 1679, c.1690, 1712, ~ *Field(e)* 1703, 1745, 1748 (*v*. **feld**; one of the great open-fields of the township), *v*. **sík**; with **bēos** or **bēo**); Best Cl (*v*. **best**; a complimentary name for very fertile land); Blackbrook Cl 1919, Lower ~ ~, Middle Black Brook 1968 (*Blak(e)broc* 1477 (e.16) (×2), *Longblacbroke* 1467 × 84 (*v*. **lang**[1]), *v*. **blæc**, **brōc**); Bomb Cl (*v*. Troopers Mdw *infra*); Bottom Cl 1858, ~ Mdw 1919 (*v*. **bottom**); Brabazons (a close so called; poss. the site of the hall of Roger le Brabazon, principal manorial lord of Mowsley in the early 14th cent.); the Breach 1858 (*Breche* 1467 × 84, *Breach* c.1690, *v*. **brēc**); Brick Works 1835 O, Brick Yard 1968 (*v*. **brike-yard**); Brook Cl; Carpenters Cl (with the surn. *Carpenter*); The Clay (*v*. **clǣg**); Bottom Cover Fd 1919, 1968, Covert Fd 1919, 1968 (*v*. **cover(t)**); Cow Cl; Cricket Fd 1919, 1968 (for the game of cricket); Dairy Mdw (*v*. **deierie**); Dowell Mdw (*the Doole* c.1530, *v*. **dāl**); Farndon Cl (with the surn. *Farndon* of a family prob. originally from East Farndon, 5 miles to the south-east in Northants.); First Cl; Flat Mdw 1919, 1968 (*v*. **flatr**); Fludes Cl (with the surn. *Flude*); Foxon's Gravel (*the Gravell* 1638, c.1690, 1703, *the Gravill* 1745, *Grauil* 1748, *v*. **gravel**; with the surn. *Foxon* of a family originally from Foxton, 3½ miles to the east); Gravel Hill; Hardimans Hill 1919, ~ Cl 1968 (with the surn. *Hardiman*); Ho(e)brooks (*Holbrok* 1477 (e.16), *Ho(e)brooke* 1638, 1674, 1679, *Hoobrooke* 1703, *Hobrook* 1745, ~ *Leys* 1748 (*v*. **leys**) (*v*. **hol**[1], **brōc**); Holmans Big Fd, ~ Mdw (with the surn. *Holman*); First ~, Second Holt 1919, Big ~, First Holt 1968 (*v*. **holt**); Home Cl 1968, Home Fd 1919, 1968 (*v*. **home**); Hovel Mdw (*v*. **hovel**); Hut Cl (*v*. **hut**); Kenshill 1858 (*v*. **hyll**; with the surn. *Ken*, a reflex of AFr *ken* (OFr *chien*) 'dog'); Kingston, ~ Cl (with the surn. *Kingston*); Lamberts Cl (with the surn. *Lambert*); Long Hills 1919, 1968 (*Longhyl* 1467 × 84, *v*. **lang**[1], **hyll**); The Maltings (*v*. **malting**); Manor Cl (*v*. Manor Fm *supra*); Mawber Paddock (*v*. **paddock**; with the surn. *Marber*, a reflex of ME *marberer* (from OFr *marbrier*) 'a worker in marble'); The Meadow (c.1690); Middle

Mdw; Mill Cl, ~ ~ Mdw, Millands (*v.* **land**), Mill Leys (*v.* **leys**) (*v.* **myln**); Mowsley Gorse (*v.* **gorst**); Mowsley New Covert 1919, 1968 (*v.* **cover(t)**); Pit Cl (*v.* **pytt**); Podehill 1858 (*v.* **pode**, **wella** and Podell in adjoining Saddington f.ns. (a)); Polly Fox (a close in the ownership or tenure of a woman of this name); Ridgway (c.1690, *Rigeweye* 1467 × 84, *v.* **hrycgweg**; the trackway crosses the south of the parish, following the main ridge of the hills); Road Cl (a roadside enclosure); Saunts ~ 1919, Saunds Cl 1968 (*v.* **sand** and *Sandclyf*, *infra*); Seed Cl 1858, Seeds 1968 (*v.* **sǣd**; used of grasses sown for one year's mowing or grazing, as distinguished from permanent pasture); Thyon Leys (*v.* **leys**), ~ Mdw 1858 (*Thyrne* 1467 × 84, *Therne* 1477 (e.16), *Long Thyhorne* 1638, ~ *Thoyon* 1674, ~ *Thyorne* 1679, ~ *Thyon* 1703, *Longthiorn* 1745, *Longthyon* 1748, *Short Thyorne* c.1690, *v.* **þyrne**); Top Cl, ~ Fd (*v.* **top**); First ~, Second Townsend (*the Townesend* c.1690, *v.* **tūn**, **ende**); Troopers Mdw (First World War army huts were erected in the village, one being developed as the Village Hall in 1924); Windmill Fd (*v.* **wind-mylne**).

(b) *Amybalk* 1467 × 84 (*v.* **balca**; with the surn. *Amy*, either from OFr *ami* 'friend' or from the OFr masc. pers.n. *Amé* (from Lat *amatus* 'beloved') or its OFr fem. form *Amée* (from Lat *amata*)); *Aschefurlong* 1467 × 84 (*v.* **æsc**, **furlang**); *the Ashes* c.1690 (*v.* **æsc**); *Barfote*, *Barfotte* 1467 × 84, *Barfoote* 1638, c.1690, 1703, *Barefoote* 1679, *Bar(e)foot* 1745, 1748 (*v.* **berg**, **fōt**); *Bayardyshyll*, *Bayardshyll*, *Bayardhyll* 1467 × 84, *Byards hill* c.1690 (*v.* **hyll**; with the surn. *Bayard*, from OFr *baiard* 'bay-coloured' (of horses) and thus given to men with reddish hair but also applied to those with reckless dispositions; an occupational origin is also poss., from OFr *bayard* 'a barrow used for heavy loads', hence metonymic for OFr *baiardeur* 'a mason's labourer', ME *bayarder* 'a barrow-man working with heavy loads of stone'); *Blakmylland* 1467 × 84, *Blackmylands* c.1690 (*v.* **blæc**, **mylde**, **land**); *Bradway*, *Bradwey* 1467 × 84, *Broadway* c.1690 (*v.* **brād**, **weg**); *Bryggfurlong* c.1690 (*v.* **brycg**, **furlang**); *Caldwell* 1467 × 84, *Cawdel* 1638, *Chaudwell* 1674, c.1690, *Caudell* 1703, *Cawdle* 1745, *Caudwell* 1748 (*v.* **cald**, **wella**); *Clyfhadis* 1467 × 84 (*v.* **clif**, **hēafod**); *Colepitt hole* 1679, *Colepit hole* 1748, *Colepit(t) hole gate* 1703, 1745 (*v.* **gata**), *v.* **col-pytt**, **hol**[1]); *the Common* 1745, 1748 (*v.* **commun**); *Copedmore* 1467 × 84 (*v.* **copped**[1], **mōr**[1]); *the Cowpasture* 1748 (*v.* **pasture**); *Crose dyke* 1467 × 84 (*v.* **cross**, **dík**); *Dedechild* 1467 × 84 (*v.* **dēad**, **cild**; either the site of a child's death or that of the discovery of a pagan Anglo-Saxon inhumation grave); (*the*) *Deadman* 1638, 1674 *et passim* to 1748 (*v.* **dede-man**; prob. the location of the previous; appears also in adjoining Laughton as *Mousley deadman* 1601); *the Deyne* 1467 × 84 (*v.* **denu**); *Dobscroft* 1467 × 84 (*v.* **croft**; either with the surn. *Dobb*, a reflex of the pers.n. *Dobbe*, a pet-form of *Robert* or with *Dobbe* itself); *Eldurstobe* 1467 × 84 (*v.* **ellern**, **stubb**); *Field Close* 1680 (presum. a small enclosure beside one of the great open-fields of the township); *Flaxlandys* 1467 × 84, *Flaxlands* 1638, *Long Flaxlands* 1674, 1679 *et passim* to 1748, *Woldflaxlandis* 1467 × 84, *Old Flaxlands* 1638, 1674 *et passim* to 1748 (*v.* **wald**), *v.* **fleax**, **land**); *Fullebrook(e)* 1638, 1679, 1748, *Fullybrooke* 1674, 1703, *Fuley brook* 1745 (*v.* **fūl**, **brōc**); *Garbrode* 1467 × 84 (*v.* **gorebrode**); *Goswell* 1467 × 84 (*v.* **gōs**, **wella**); *Grenesyke* 1467 × 84, *Greensicke* 1638, *Greensick* 1703, 1745, 1748, *grene sicke furlonge* 1601 (*v.* **furlang**), *v.* **grēne**[1], **sík**); *Hardwykeslade* 1467 × 84 (*v.* **heorde-wīc**, **slæd**); *Hulcros*, (*crucem vocat'*) *Hulcrosse* 1467 × 84 (*v.* **hyll**, **cros**; also with MLat *crux* (*crucem* acc.sg.) 'a cross')); *Hymedowe* 1467 × 84 (*v.* **hēah**[1], **mēd** (**mēdwe** obl.sg.)); *Hywey*, *Heyweyforth* (*v.* **ford**) 1467 × 84, *v.* **hēah-weg**); *Jakson' sydling* 1467 × 84 (*v*. **sīdling**; with the surn. *Jackson*); *King's Close* 1736 (with the surn. *King*; *v*. *Kynkhadland*, *infra*); *Knaptoft hege*, ~ *heyge* 1467 × 84 (*v*. **hecg**; a parish boundary marker), *Knaptoft Stile* 1748 (*v*. **stīg**); Knaptoft parish in Guthlaxton Hundred adjoins to the west); *Kynkhadland* (*v*. **hēafod-land**), *Kynksty* (*v*. **stīg**) 1467 × 84; with the surn. *King*; note *King's Close*, *supra*); *Langesike* 1477 (e.16), *Longsyke* 1467 × 84, *Longesike ouerend* 1477 (e.16) (*v*. **uferra**, **ende**), *v*. **lang**[1], **sík**); *Lawton' broke* 1467 × 84, *Laughton brooke* c.1690 (*v*. **brōc**; the brook forms the parish boundary with Laughton to the east); *Long'*, *Longe* 1467 × 84, (*on*) *Long* c.1690 (*v*. **lang**[2]); *Longsyke* 1467 × 84 (*v*. **lang**[1], **sík**); *Lytulho* 1467 × 84 (*v*. **lȳtel**, **hōh**); *the Meyre* 1467 × 84, *the Meere* 1638 (because of the name's longevity, poss. **mere**[1] in its sense 'wetland' rather than **(ge)mǣre** 'boundary'); *Millnedykys* 1467 × 84 (*v*. **myln**, **dík**; this appears to refer to a watermill, *v*. *Water Mill Yard*, *infra*); *Milnefelde* 1467 × 84, *Milne feilde* 1601, *Millhill Feilde* 1638, 1674, 1679, c.1690, *Milhill fielde* 1703, *Millhill Field* 1745, 1748, *v*. **myln**, **feld**; one of the great open-fields, alluding to a windmill since located on *Millhill* 1638); *Mydulfurlong* 1467 × 84 (*v*. **middel**, **furlang**; of the *Milnefelde*); *Mydulhyl* 1467 × 84 (*v*. **middel**, **hyll**); *My Ladies hedge* 1679, c.1690 (*v*. **ladi**, **hecg**; bordering *Swarborrow Feild*, *infra*; but the identity of the lady is unknown); *Noston'* 1467 × 84 (×2), *Nosterne* c.1690 (*v*. **nōs(e)**, **tūn**; a lost farmstead on a promontory); *Oatelands* c.1690 (*v*. **āte**, **land**); *the Olt* c.1690 (*v*. **wald**); *Paynisich* (*v*. **sīc**), *Paynesyke*, *Paynisike* 1477 (e.16) (*v*. **sík**; either with the surn. *Payne*, or with its source, the OFr masc. pers.n. *Paien* (from Lat *paganus* 'villager'), cf. *Rotrotus Pagani* 1196 P of Leics.; note the local *ad fontem pagani* 1477 (e.16), i.e. 'at Paien's spring or well', with MLat *fons* (*fontem* acc.sg.)); *Pennesyke*, *Pensyke* 1477 (e.16) (*v*. **penn**[2], **sík**); *Pinslade*, *Pynslade* 1477 (e.16), *Pynsladdol(l)* 1467 × 84, *Pynslade dole* c.1530 (*v*. **dāl**), *Pinslade gate* c.1690 (*v*. **gata**), *Pinsladehadland* 1477 (e.16) (*v*. **hēafod-land**), *v*. **pynd**, **slæd**, cf. *Pinslade* in Husbands Bosworth f.ns. (b) and *Pynslade* Lei **3** 242); *Pynfold* 1467 × 84 (*v*. **pynd-fald**); *Redesdale* 1269 (*v*. **hrēod**, **dalr**); *Rowdikes* c.1690 (*v*. **rūh**, **dík**); *Rusyk* 1477 (e.16) (*v*. **rūh**, **sík**); *Rynkso*, *Ryncsoslade* (*v*. **slæd**) 1467 × 84 ('the warrior's headland', *v*. **rinc**, **hōh**; one is tempted to speculate about an individual pagan burial site); *Rysburgh* 1477 (e.16) (*v*. **hrīs**; prob. with **berg** rather than with **burh**, since no early earthworks are evident here, hence cf. *the Risborough*, Lei **3** 247); *Sadyngton meyre* 1467 × 84 (*v*. **(ge)mǣre**; Saddington adjoins to the north); *Sauntcliff* c.1690, *Sanclyf hyll* (*v*. **hyll**), *Sanclyfsyke* (*v*. **sík**), *Sandclyf fotte* (*v*. **fōt**) 1467 × 84 (*v*. **sand**, **clif**); *Scharphill*, *Charphylle* 1467 × 84 (*v*. **scearp**, **hyll**); *Sculbrode* 1467 × 84 (*v*. **scofl-brǣdu**); *Smalstret* 1467 × 84 (*v*. **smæl**, **strǣt**); *Stanwell* 1467 × 84 (*v*. **stān**, **wella**); *Sternedale* 1477 (e.16) (*v*. **dalr**; poss. with **stǣner**); *Stockeslade* 1601, *Stockslade* c.1690, 1703, 1745 (*v*. **slæd**; with **stoc** or **stocc**); *Stoney* 1467 × 84 ('the stony one', *v*. **stānig**); *Swardboro*, *Lytulswarboro* (*v*. **lȳtel**) 1467 × 84, *Long Swarborough* 1638, ~ *Swarborow* 1674, ~ *Sworborow* c.1690, *Longe Swarborrow* 1703, *Long Swarbrow* 1745, *Short Sworborow* c.1690, *Swarborofelde* 1467 × 84, *Swarbor(r)ow* ~ 1638, 1674, 1679, 1703, *Sworborow* ~ c.1690, *Swarborough Feild* 1710, *Swarbrow Field* 1745, 1748 (*v*. **feld**; one of the great open-fields), *Swarboro leyes* 1467 × 84 (*v*. **lǣs**), *v*. **sweart**, **berg**); *Swinsty* c.1690 (*v*. **swīn**, **stig**); *Thedyngworth mere* 1467 × 84 (*v*. **(ge)mǣre**; Theddingworth parish adjoins to the south-east); *Thornydale* 1467 × 84 (*v*. **þornig**, **dalr**); *atte Tonge* 1477 (e.16) (*v*. **atte**, **tunge**); *Totehille*, *Totyll'* 1467 × 84 (*v*. **tōt-hyll**); *Tykmanlow* 1467 × 84 (*v*. **hlāw**; the specific may be an unrecorded OE pers.n. or a sb. such as **ticc(n)a-mann* 'a goatherd'; the surn. *Tickman* was current in Kent in the 19th cent.); *Waterforos* 1467 × 84 (*v.* **wæter**, **furh** and *the water furrowes* in Billesdon f.ns. (b)); *the Watering* c.1690 (*v.* **wateryng**); *Water Mill Yard* 1638, 1679, 1748 (*v.* **water-mylne**, **geard**); *Whitecross* (*iuxta Sadington meyre*) 1467 × 84 (*v.* **hwīt**, **cros**; prob. an original boundary marker with Saddington which adjoins to the north); *Woollen hill* c.1690 (*v.* **wald**, **land**, **hyll**); *Wrangland'* 1467 × 84, *Ranglands* c.1690 (*v.* **wrang**, **land**); *Wyregate close* c.1690 (*v.* **weyour**, **gata**); *Yrland* 1467 × 84 (*v.* **gyr**, **land**).

Nevill Holt

NEVILL HOLT

Holt Hy 1 Dugd, a.1150 *Peake*, 1166 RBE, 12 *Peake* (freq) *et freq*, (~ *Abbotes* 1316 FA), (~ *iuxta Medburn'* 1425 *Peake*, ~ ~ *Meddeb'rn* 1443 *ib*, ~ ~ *Medborn'* 1444 *ib*)
Holte a.1250 *Peake*, 1299 *LCDeeds* (p), 1308 *Peake et freq* to1444, 1447 *ib et passim* to 1559 Pat, 1572 *Peake*, *Holtt* 1526, 1537 *ib*
Holth a.1250, 13 *Peake*
le Holt(*e*) 1302 Ipm, *the Holt*(*e*) 1537, 1542 *Peake*, c.1545 Leland, 1690 *Deed*
Hout' e.13 *Peake* (×2)

'The wood', *v*. **holt**. *Thomas Nevill'*, ~ *Nevyll* held the manor in 1498, 1502 *Peake*, *Johannes Nevell* in 1520 *ib* and another *Thomas Nevell* in 1537 *ib*. Earlier it was held by *abbas de Burgo Sancti Petri* 1316 FA (i.e. the Abbot of Peterborough), hence ~ *Abbotes* 1316 FA, *v*. **abbat**. The township lies one mile north-east of Medbourne. Note MLat *iuxta* 'next to, by' in the early suffix.

BRADLEY PRIORY

Bradel' l.12, 12 *Peake et passim* to l.13, 13 *ib* (freq), *Bradele* 12 *ib*, 1254 Val, 1264 RGrav, *Bradeleg*(*h*)' 1226 ClR, l.13 *Peake*, 1303 Cl, *Bradeley*(*e*) 1265 Pat, 1279 Cl *et freq* to 1365, 1375 *Peake et passim* to 1392 Pat, 1401 (e.15) *BelCartB*, *Bradeleia* Hy 2 (e.15), 12 (e.15) *ib*, 1234 RHug, 1275 (16), 13 (16) *SlCart*, *Bradeleya* a.1250 *Peake*, m.13 (e.15) *BelCartB*, 13 *Peake*
Bradleye 1278 (16) *SlCart*, 1317, 1327 SR (p), *Bradleya* e.14 *Peake*, *Bradleia* 1328 (e.15) *BelCartB*
Bradley 1274 (16) *SlCart*, c.1291 Tax *et passim* to 1425 *Peake*, 1427 *Rut et freq*

priorie Sancte Marie Bradeley(*e*) 1363, 1383, 1392 *Pat*, *priorat' de Bradley* 1535 VE

domus de Bradley 1481 *Pat*
Bradley Priory 1846, 1877 White

'The broad clearing or glade in woodland', *v.* **brād**, **lēah**. A priory for Augustinian Canons was founded here c.1200 by Robert Burneby. Note MLat *prioria* and *prioratus*, both meaning 'a priory', and MLat *domus* 'a religious house'.

PRESTGRAVE (lost)

Prestegraue c.1130 LeicSurv, a.1150 *Peake*, p.1150 *ib et passim* to l.12 *ib*, 12 *ib* (freq) *et freq* to 1365, 1368 *ib et passim* to 1427, 1428 *ib*, *Prestegrawe* e.13 (p), e.14 (p) *ib*
Prestesgraue 1173 ChancR (p), *Prestesgraua* 1174 P (p), 1175 ChancR (p)
Prestgraue a.1250 *Peake*, l.13 *ib* (freq), 1322 *ib et passim* to 1499, 1505 *ib*, *Prestgrave* 1416, 1419 Cl *et passim* to 1444, 1537 *Peake et freq*
Presgraue 1519 *Peake*, *Presgrave* 1525 *ib*

'Grove of the priests', *v.* **prēost** (**prēosta** gen.pl.), **grāf**. The Abbey of Peterborough held *Prestgrave* from the middle of the 11th cent. It formed part of the c.1041 × 57 grant to it by Earl Ralph of Hereford, kinsman of Edward the Confessor. Hugh Candidius, writing in the mid 12th cent., notes that *Raulfus comes propinquus Eduardi dedit Eston et Brinninghurst et Prestgrave et Dreitun et Glathestun*, i.e. the gift to the abbey of Great Easton with neighbouring Bringhurst, *Prestgrave* and Drayton in Leics., and Glaston in Rutland.

Historians have identified the unique *Abegrave* (*v.* **grāf**) of the Domesday Survey of 1086 with *Prestgrave*, but this identification presents problems. The specific of *Abegrave* appears to be the OE masc. pers.n. *Abba*. If *Abegrave* was renamed *Prestegrave*, a possible explanation is that Abba endowed the proceeds from this woodland to help support a community of priests serving a number of churches on his estates, cf. Prestwold, Lei **3** 180. However, the change of name may have occurred after *Prestgrave* became the property of the Abbey of Peterborough. Although it is most unlikely that the specific *Abe-* of *Abegrave* is a much reduced form of **abbaye** 'abbey', the *prēosta* of the later place-name could refer to the community of the abbey, especially if, as an early minster, the abbey provided priests for a wide area including a church in *Prestgrave*. A simple explanation of these difficulties is that *Abegrave* of 1086 was not the later *Prestgrave*. Either that or the name *Abegrave* was a local folk-memory at the time of the Domesday Survey and perhaps the subject of popular etymology in relating the name of the eventual township to the abbey.

Nichols **2** ii 523 notes, 'There are nearly 200 acres of this depopulated village in what is called at this time Holt lordship.' He observes that in his day there were foundations and earthworks visible and places the settlement south-east of Nevill Holt, north of Drayton and west of Great Easton. Presumably *Prestgrave* eventually became an outlying grange belonging to the Abbey of Peterborough.

AMERICA LODGE (~ FM 2½"), *v*. **loge**, AMERICA WOOD, 1919 Sale, 1968 *Surv*; together with Buffalo Lodge and New York Spinney *infra*, 'remoteness' names for sites towards the limits of the parish. THE AVENUE, a tree-lined approach to The Hall *infra*, *v*. **avenue**. BRADLEY LODGE, 1846 White, *v*. **loge** and Bradley Priory *supra*. BUFFALO LODGE, named from Buffalo in New York State, *v*. **loge** and America Wood *supra*. FISHPOND SPINNEY, 1919 Sale, *v*. **fisshe-ponde**, **spinney**. GRANGE COTTAGE, beside Medbourne Grange, *v*. Medbourne parish *s.n.* THE HALL, 1877 White, *Holt Hall* 1846, 1863 ib, 1925 Kelly, *v*. **hall**. HOLT SPA, 1824 O, 1925 Kelly, *The Spaw* 1968 *Surv*, *v*. **spa**; mineral springs were discovered here in 1728. HOLT WOOD, *Holtwode* 1377, 1425 *Peake*, *Holte wood* 1572 *ib*, *Holt Wood* c.1800 Map, 1824 O, 1919 Sale, *boscum de Holt* 1395 *Peake* (with MLat *boscus* 'a wood'), *v*. **wudu**. HOLY WELL, 1824 O; it is *Our Lady's Well* 1798 Nichols, 1831 Curtis, alluding to the Blessed Virgin Mary, *v*. **hālig**, **wella**. HOPYARD SPINNEY, *Hop Yard Spinney* 1846 *TA*, 1919 Sale, *Hopyards Spinney* 1968 *Surv*, *v*. **hop-yard**, **spinney**. LODGE FM, beside Southfield Lodge *infra*. NEVILL HOLT FM. NEVILL HOLT QUARRY. NEW YORK SPINNEY, 1846 *TA*; it is *New York Wood* 1919 Sale, *v*. **spinney**, Buffalo Lodge and America Wood *supra*. PASTURE FARM COTTAGE, adjacent to Pasture Fm in Blaston parish. PRIORY FM, beside the former Bradley Priory *supra*. ST MARY'S CHURCH, *Church (St Mary)* 1925 Kelly; early recorded as *capellam de Holt* 1220 MHW (with MLat *capella* 'a chapel'). SOUTHFIELD LODGE (*v*. **loge**), *Southe Feilde* 1595 *Conant*, *South Field* 1846 *TA*, *v*. **sūð**, **feld**; one of the early great open-fields of the township. STONE COTTAGE. WIGNELL HILL, *Wigenhoue* 13 *Peake*, *Wygynhow* 1335 *ib*, *Wiginhowe* 1373 *ib*, *Wygenhowe* 1395 *ib*, *Wignell* 1583 LAS, 1863, 1877 White, *v*. **hōh**, with the OE masc. pers.n. *Wiga* (*Wigan* gen.sg.); the name of a large hill-spur falling away to the east. WINGFIELD SPINNEY, 1846 *TA*, 1919 Sale, 1968 *Surv*, *v*. **spinney**; no early forms, but possibly with **vengi** 'a field' (cf. Wing, Ru 228) and the pleonastic *field* added late.

FIELD-NAMES

In (a), forms presented without dates are 1846 *TA*; those dated 1919 are Sale; 1968 are *Surv*. Forms throughout dated l.12, 12, e.13, p.1250, l.13, 13, e.14, 1306, 1319, 1320, 1333, 1334, 1335, 1336, 1340, 1345, 1351, 1360, 1365, 1371, 1372, 1373, 1375, 1377, 1394, 1395, 1421, 1422, 1425, 1427, 1466, 1526, 1569 and 1572 are *Peake* unless otherwise specified.

(a) Seventeen Acre 1846, 1968, Twenty-four ~, Forty Acre 1968 (*v*. **æcer**); Ashpole Spinney 1968 (*v*. **æsc**, **pāl**, **spinney**; a source of cut poles or stakes of ash-wood); Barn Cl 1968 (*v*. **bern**); Big Fd 1968; Bradley 1846, 1968, Great Bradley, Carr's Bradley (with the surn. *Carr*), Bradley Cl 1846, Bradley Wood 1798 Nichols, c.1800, 1806 Map, 1824 O, 1846 (*v*. Bradley Priory *supra*); Bradshaw's 1846, 1968 (the surn. *Bradshaw* in the possessive case); Buildings Fd 1968; Clarks Cl 1846, Clark's 1968 (cf. *John Clark* 1694 LML, *Thomas Clarke* 1730 Nichols, *Mary Clark* 1745 ib); Clifton's Cl (with the surn. *Clifton*); The Corner Fd 1968 (*v*. **corner**); Crow Spinney 1968 (*v*. **crāwe**, **spinney**); Danson Piece (*v*. **pece**; with the surn. *Danson*); Doctor's Cl (*v*. **doctour**); Down's Cl 1968 (with the surn. *Down*); Drayton Fd 1968, Drayton Wood c.1800 Map, 1846 (*Drayton Wode* 1395, 1427, *v*. **wudu**; Drayton parish adjoins to the south-west); Far Cl 1968; Fishpond Fd 1968 (*v*. Fishpond Spinney *supra*); The Flying Fd 1968 (used as an airfield during the First World War); The Front Fd 1968 (*v*. **front**); Fursey Cl 1968 (*v*. **fyrsig**); The Gallops 1968 (a site for racehorse training 1925–35); Gilford's Cl (cf. *Thomas Gilford* 1700 Nichols of adjoining Medbourne); Gorse Cl or Gosse Cl (*v*. **gorst** (dial. *gosse*)); Gravel Pit 1968 (*v*. **gravel**, **pytt**); Home ~, Middle ~, New Ground (*v*. **grund**); Hill Cl; Hinckley's Hobbs (*v*. **hobb(e)**; with the surn. *Hinckley* of a family originally from the township of this name, 24 miles to the west); Holt Cl, ~ ~ Mdw, Holt Hill Cl 1846, Holt Plantation 1919 (*v*. **plantation**); Home Cl 1846, 1968, Home Fd 1968 (*v*. **home**); Bottom ~ ~, Top Hop Yard 1968 (*v*. Hopyard Spinney *supra*); Horse Cl 1846, 1968; House Cl; King's Cl (with the surn. *King*); Lane Cl (×2) 1846, Lanes 1968 (*v*. **lane**); Little Cl; Lodge Fd 1968 (*v*. **loge**); Lucy's 1968 (with the surn. *Lucy* in the possessive case); Meadow Cl; First ~ ~, Second ~ ~, Third New Fd; Bottom ~, Top Paddock 1846, The Paddock 1968 (*v*. **paddock**); Great Park 1846, 1968, Squires Park (*v*. **squire**), The Park 1968 (1564 CoPleas, *v*. **park**); Bottom ~, Middle ~, Top ~, Great ~, Little ~, Green ~ (*v*. **grēne**[1]), King's ~, Osbourn's Pasture (with the surns. *King* and *Osbourn*) (*v*. **pasture**); Pole Cl 1968 (either with **pōl**[1] or **pāl**); Presgrave, ~ Cl 1846, Presgraves 1968 (*v*. *Prestgrave*, *supra*); Pudding Fd 1968 (a disparaging name for soft, sticky land); The (Rabbit) Warren 1846, The Warren 1968 (*v*. **rabet**, **wareine**); Ram Cl (*v*. **ramm**); Seven Oaks 1968 (*v*. **āc**; a close containing oak-trees); Brown Sheep Cl 1846, 1968 (poss. with the surn. *Brown*, but note *Brownefurlonge* in Great Bowden f.ns. (b)), Over ~ ~ (*v*. **uferra**), Sheep Cl 1846 (*le Shepe Close*

1572 (*v.* **scēp**, **clos(e)**); Skeffington's Cl, ~ Fd, ~ Mdw 1846, Skeffington's 1968 (with the surn. *Skeffington* of a family originally from the township of this name, 7 miles to the north-west); Smaller's Cl 1846, Smalley's 1968 (with the surn. *Smalley*); Snake Spinney 1968 (*v.* **snaca**, **spinney**); Spaw Cl (*v.* Holt Spa *supra*); Spinney Fd 1968; Stack Garth (*v.* **stakkr**, **garðr**); Terrill's ~, Tyrrel's Cl (cf. *Adam Tirrell* 1794 Nichols); Town End Cl (*v.* **tūn**, **ende**); Ward's 1968 (the surn. *Ward* in the possessive case); Washpit Cl (*v.* **wæsce**, **pytt**); Windmill Bank 1798 Nichols (*v.* **wind-mylne**, **banke**); Arthur Wignall's, Hill Wignall's 1846, Wignell's 1968 (cf. *William Wignall* 1729 Nichols and *Richard Wignall* 1777 ib of neighbouring Drayton); Wingfield Cl, ~ Wood (*v.* Wingfield Spinney *supra*); Great ~ ~, Little ~ ~, Wood Cl 1846, Wood Cl 1968.

(b) *Apiltregate* l.13, *Appultregate* 1422, 1466 (*v.* **æppel-trēow**, **gata**); *Barn close* 1564 CoPleas (*v.* **bern**, **clos(e)**); *Bellers Copie* 1526 (*v.* **copis**; the spelling *copie* is due to the popular reconstruction of a 'singular' form), *Bellereswode* 1533 Fine (*v.* **wudu**; with the surn. *Beller/Bellar*, either a ME occupational surn. from OE *belle* 'a bell', hence 'a bellringer' or 'a bell-founder' or a by-name from OFr *bélier* 'a ram'; note Kirby Bellars, Lei **3** 84); *Bernakestockyng* 1395 (*v.* **stoccing**; cf. *Hugo de Bernak* l.13); *Bernorcharde* 1372 (*v.* **bern**, **orceard**); *Bilingate* 1335, 1373, *Bylingate* 1373 (*v.* **billing**, **gata** and Billinge Hill, Ch **1** 138–9); *Blakemilde* p.1250, *Blakemylde* 1336, *le Blake Melde* 1373, *Blakemylde* 1427 (*v.* **blæc**, **mylde**); (*le*) *Blakewong* 1371, 1373, 1375 (*v.* **blæc**, **vangr**); *Broddole* 1372, *Holtbroddole* 1375 (*v.* **brād**, **dāl**); (*le*) *Brodegate* 1371, 1375 (*v.* **brād**, **gata**); *Catteholis* e.13, *Catholys* 1335, *Catholes*, *Catholis* 1373 (*v.* **cat(t)**, **hol**[1]); *Chalgate* 1279 Banco, ~ *sike* 1395 (*v.* **sík**) (*v.* **calc**, **gata**; palatalization of Angl [k] before *al* is unusual in this county, but perh. cf. *Chaluercroft*, *infra* and note *calcylsyche* in adjoining Great Easton parish); *Chelverscroft* 1279 Banco, *Chaluercroft* 1375 (*v.* **croft**; either with **calf** (**calfra** gen.pl.) or with the OE masc. pers.n. *Cēolfrið*; spellings with AN *e* for *a* appear as late as c.1300, *v.* *Chalgate*, *supra*); *Cocsitehil* e.13, *Kocsitehyl* l.13, *Cok(e)scetehul* 1306, 1360 (*v.* **cocc-scēte**, **hyll**); *Cotoneholme* 1335, *Cottenholm'* 1340 (*v.* **cote** (**cotan** nom.pl.), **holmr**); (*le*) *Crosgate* e.13, 1335 (*v.* **gata**; prob. with **cross**, otherwise **cros**); *atte Crosse* 1421 (p), *at Crosse* 1427 (p) (*v.* **atte**, **cros**); *Dodemeredale* 1334, 1335 (*v.* **dæl**[1]; recorded also as *Dodmerisdale* 1358 in adjoining Drayton and *Dodemersdale* in Medbourne); *Drake aker* 1335, *Drakeakir* 1395 (*v.* **æcer**; prob. with the surn. *Drake*, ME **drake** 'male of the duck' being less likely); *le Echel'* 13 (*v.* **ēcels**); *Eston brodedole* 1425 (*v.* **brād**, **dāl**; land towards Great Easton parish which adjoins to the east); *le Fordehurst* 13 (*v.* **ford**, **hyrst**); *Gaysacr'* 1345, 1371, *Gayesacre* 1375 (*v.* **æcer**; with the surn. *Gay*, an original by-name from ME *gai(e)* 'lighthearted, gay'); *Goldyngwong* 1335 (*v.* **vangr**; with the surn. *Golding*, a reflex of the late OE masc. pers.n. *Golding*); *Gongwode* 1335 (*v.* **gang**, **wudu**); *Gorewong* 1302 Ipm (*v.* **gāra**, **vangr**); *Haluetonegat* e.13, *Halutongate* 1372, *Halugthonegatewong* 1375 (*v.* **vangr**) (*v.* **gata**; the road to Hallaton which lies 2½ miles to the north-west); *Hassewell* l.12, *Aschewell'* 1395, *Hassewellegate* e.13 (*v.* **gata**), *Ayshewell' sydelondes* 1425 (*v.* **sīde**, **land**) (*v.* **æsc**, **wella**); *Haulsike* e.13, *Haussyke* 1279 Banco (*v.* **hals**, **sík**); *le Hawesnap* l.13 (*v.* **haga**[1]; with **snæp** or **snap**); *Holegate* 12 (*v.* **hol**[2], **gata**); *Holtmere* (*v.* **(ge)mǣre**), *Holtemilne* 1333 (*v.* **myln**) (in both names, *Holt* presum. refers to the township); *Holtewong* 13, *le Holt Wong* 1302 Ipm (*v.* **vangr**; with **holt** perh. here alluding to the wood from which the township took its name); *Houperyng* 1335, *Howpyng* (sic) 1371 (*v.* **eng**; either with **hōpere** 'a cooper' or its surn. reflex *Hooper*); (*le*) *Kirkehauedlond* 1336, 1395, *Kirke Hauedeland* 1395, *le kyrkehadelond* 1425 (*v.* **kirkja**, **hēafod-land**; alluding to St Mary's Church *supra*); *Kyrkstede* 1351 ('the church-site', *v.* **cirice-stede**; partly Scandinavianized, with the replacement of OE *cirice* by the cognate ON *kirkja*, and prob. referring to Bradley Priory *supra*); *Langlondfurlong* 13 (*v.* **lang**[1], **land**, **furlang**); *Larkhey* 1425 (*v.* **lāwerce**, **(ge)hæg**); *Le Leys* 13 (*v.* **lǣs**); *Litlemedwe* e.13 (*v.* **lȳtel**, **mēd** (**mēdwe** obl.sg.)); *the Lodge standing in the Warren* 1595 *Conant* (*v.* **loge**, **wareine**); *Maidewell'*, *Maydewelle siche* 13 (*v.* **sīc**), *maidewellewong* e.13 (*v.* **vangr**) (*v.* **mægd** (**mægda** gen.pl.), a shortened form of **mægden**, and **wella**; this is no doubt an early name of *Our Lady's Well*, once a sacred site associated with fertility (*v.* Holy Well *supra* and cf. *Maidenewell* in Husbands Bosworth f.ns. (b))); *Medburne mere* 13, *Medeburnemer'* 1335 (*v.* **(ge)mǣre**; the parish boundary with Medbourne which adjoins to the west); *Merehock* 1335 (*v.* **(ge)mǣre**, **hōc**); *le Milnefeld* 1395 (*v.* **feld**; one of the early great open-fields of the township), (*le*) *Milnegate* e.13, 1395, 1425, 1427 (*v.* **gata**), *le Mylnebalke* 1425 (*v.* **balca**) (*v.* **myln**); (*le*) *Morwelle* 1336, 1395, *Morewell'* 1427 (*v.* **mōr**[1], **wella**); *Mundeshowse* 1427 (*v.* **hūs**; with the surn. *Mund*(*e*), a reflex of the OE masc. pers.n. *Munda*); *le Netherorcherd* 1365, 1394, *le Nethyrorchard*, *neþerorchard* 1373 (*v.* **neoðera**, **orceard**); *le Newe close* 1469 *Rental* (*v.* **nīwe**, **clos(e)**); (*the*) *Northfeld* 1569 (*v.* **norð**, **feld**; one of the great open-fields); *Peselond* 13 (*v.* **pise**, **land**); *Redland'* 12, *Redlond'* 1336, *Longredlond'* 1336, *Long*(*e*)*redelond'* 1395, *Longe Redelondes* 1427 (*v.* **lang**[1]), *Schortheredelond'* 1395 (*v.* **sc(e)ort**) (*v.* **rēad**, **land**); *le Rightlondis* 1425 (*v.* **riht**[2], **land**); *Russewong* 1373 (*v.* **vangr**; either with **risc**, or with the surn. *Russ*(*e*), an original by-name from ME *rous*(*e*) 'red'); *Salteresgate* 13 (*v.* **saltere**, **gata**; referring either to the Roman Gartree Road which runs just to the south of the parish or to the lost Roman road (Margary 571) which branches from it at Medbourne via Drayton and Great Easton to reach *Durobrivae* (Water Newton) on Ermine Street); *Sandpytwong* 1375 (*v.* **sand-pytt**, **vangr**); *Sawpit* 1373, *Sawpitwong* 1371 (*v.* **vangr**) (*v.* **saw-pytt**; predating the earliest OED citation by 37 years); *Scottishalfaker* 1340 (*v.* **half-aker**; with the surn. *Scott*); *Sidelond*, *Sydlond* 13 (*v.* **sīde**, **land**); *Soken acr'* 1425 (*v.* **æcer**; poss. with **socen** 'wet, saturated', but note that Holt adjoins Great Easton and thus may have been part of the early *Barnsdale Soke*, hence **sōcn**); *Smalehauedys* 1335 (*v.* **smæl**, **hēafod**); *Staneibrigge* 12, *Stanibrighe* e.13, *Stanybryggesyk* 1319 (*v.* **sík**) (*v.* **stānig**, **brycg**); *le Stockyng'* 1373 (*v.* **stoccing**); *Stocwellelane* l.13 (*v.* **stocc**, **wella**, **lane**); *Stokenol* 13 (*v.* **stoc**, **cnoll**); *Sytforde* 13 (*v.* **scite**, **ford**); *Tarriwong* 1371, *Terrywong* 1375 (*v.* **vangr**; with the surn. *Tarry/Terry*, cf. *Radulphus Teri* 1199 RFL of Leicester, from the OFr masc. pers.n. *Thierri/Terri*); *Thirthyngys* 1351, *Thirthynges*, *Thirthynghauedis* (*v.* **hēafod**) 1422, 1466 (*v.* **þriðing**); *Thyrspyt* 1345 ('the demon's pit', *v.* **þyrs**, **pytt**; a name indicative of early popular superstition); *Toftis* p.1250, *le Toftes* 1425 (*v.* **toft**); *Umberbreche* 1375 (*v.* **umber**, **brēc**; alluding to newly broken-in ploughland in a wooded area); *Wambeley* 12, *Wambleye* l.13, *Wambeleye* 13 CN, 1302 Ipm (*v.* **lēah**; either with **wamb** or with the OE masc. pers.n. *Wamba*); *Warglondis* 13 (*v.* **land**; either with **vargr** 'a wolf' (cf. *Wolfhegys*, *infra*) or with **wærg** 'wretched', denoting soil of very poor quality); *Warinwell* 1395 (*v.* **wella**; poss. with the ContGerm/AN pers.n. *Warin*, otherwise with **wareine**); *the Warren* 1595 *Conant* (*v.* **wareine**); *le Watiri* 1373, *þe Wattery* 1395, *le Wattry* 1425 ('the wet ground', *v.* **wæterig**); *Wdegate* 12, *Wodegate* 13, e.14, 1395, 1425 (*v.* **gata**), *Wodesyke* 1314 Banco,

Wodesike 1371 (*v.* **sík**) (*v.* **wudu**); (*le*) *Wignell feild* 1583 (*v.* **feld**; one of the great open-fields, *v.* Wignell Hill *supra*); *Wlstaneshil* e.13, *Wlstanishull* 1279 Banco (*v.* **hyll**, with the OE masc. pers.n. *Wulfstān*); *the Wood close* 1564 CoPleas (*v.* **wudu**, **clos(e)**); *le Wrongbroke* 1422, 1466 (*v.* **wrang**, **brōc**); *Wygenhodale*, *Wyginhouedale* e.13, *Wygenhowedale* 1395 (*v.* **dalr**), *Wygonhohauedes* 1336, *Wygenhowehaued'* 1395 (*v.* **hēafod**) (*v.* Wignell Hill *supra*).

Names from early charters specific to the lost *Prestgrave* are:
Aldousdale e.13, *Aldusdale* p.1250, 13 (*v.* **dalr**), *Longhaldus* e.13 (*v.* **lang**[1]), *Sort Aldus* p.1250 (*v.* **sc(e)ort**) (*v.* **ald**, **hūs**); *Banelond* 13 (*v.* **bēan**, **land**); *Belund* l.12, *Beylund* 13, *Beylond'* l.13 (*v.* **beg**, **lundr**); *Bradheg* 12 (*v.* **brād**, **hecg** (in its sense 'a hedged enclosure')); *Brende* 13 (*v.* **brende**); *Crathawe* e.13 (*v.* **cræt**, **haga**[1] and *Cratehaw* 13 (16) in Great Easton which prob. refers to the same feature); *flaxyslond* 13 (*v.* **fleax**, **land**); *hauedlond aker* 12 (*v.* **hēafod-land**, **æcer**); *Heringhegis* 13 ('the enclosures at the stony place', *v.* **hær**, **-ing**[2], **hecg**); *horspol* 13 (*v.* **hors**, **pōl**[1]); *le Hungriaker* e.13 (*v.* **hungrig**, **æcer**); *landemeredale* e.13 (*v.* **land-(ge)mǣre**, **dalr**); *longecroft* l.12 (*v.* **lang**[1], **croft**); *Menegate*, *le Meneygate* l.13, *le Menigate* 13 CN, (*v.* **(ge)mǣne**, **gata**); *midelforlang* 12 (*v.* **middel**, **furlang**); *Midlondis* e.13 (*v.* **middel**, **land**); *Mikildal* 12, *Mikledale* 13 (*v.* **micel**, **mikill**, **dalr**); *Prestegrauegrene* 1334 (*v.* **grēne**[2]), *Prestegrauesthorte* e.13, *Prestgraue stort*(*e*) a.1290 CN (×2), *Prestegraue sorte* 13 (×2) (*v.* **storð**); *le Rode*, *le Rodishende* 13 (*v.* **ende**) (*v.* **rod**[1]); *settecuppe* 13, *Settecuppeforlang'* l.13 (*v.* **furlang**) (*v.* **set-copp**); *Sideholm* 12, e.13 (*v.* **sīde**, **holmr**); *Sutherhil* l.12, *Sowterhill* 13 (*v.* **sūðer**, **hyll**); *Stokkis* l.12 (*v.* **stocc**); *tirsinges* 12, *Tirsinggis* 13 (*v.* **þyrs**, **eng** and cf. *Thyrspyt*, *supra*); *Wolfhegys* 13 (*v.* **wulf**, **hecg**; with reference to hedged enclosures intended to keep out wolves, cf. *Wolfhegge*, Nth 123); *Wrangeland'* 12, *Wranglondes* l.13 (*v.* **wrang**, **land**).

Noseley

NOSELEY

Noveslei 1086 DB, *Noveslai* c.1131 Ord, *Novesleia* 1221 RHug, *Novesleya* 1228 ib, *Novesl'* 1254 Val
Nouesle 1229 Cl, 1230 Cur *et passim* to 1250, 1264 *Hazlerigg et freq* to 1330, 1338 *ib et passim* to 1402 *ib*, 1422 *Pat*, *Nouesley(e)* Hy 3 *Hazlerigg*, 1317 Ipm, 1387 Pat, *Noueslee* 1306, 1335 ib, *Nouisll'* c.1220 *Hazlerigg*, *Nouysle* 1276 RH
Nowesle Hy 3 *Hazlerigg*, c.1291 Tax *et passim* to 1415 *Deed*, *Nouwesle* 1292 OSut, *Noweselee* 1334, 1335 *Pat*, 1344 *Hazlerigg*, *Nowesley* 1378 Pat, 1389 *Win et passim* to 1535 VE, 1572 LEpis
Nousele Hy 3 *Hazlerigg*, 1274 (1579), 1307 (1579) *LRoll*, *Nousleye* 1374 *Deed*, 1374 Cl
Nows(e)ley 1471 *Hazlerigg*, 1478 *Peake*, 1516 Fine, 1535 VE
Nawseley 1430 *Ct*, 1540 *Hazlerigg*, *Nawisley* 1510 LP, 1540 *Hazlerigg*
Noseley 1509 *Hazlerigg*, 1510 LP *et passim* to 1529 *Wyg*, 1544 *Hazlerigg et freq*, *Nosley* 1510 Visit, c.1545 Leland, 1576 LibCl

'Nōðwulf's wood or woodland clearing', *v.* **lēah**; with early reduction of a dithematic OE masc. pers.n. *Nōðwulf*.

ABBEY WOOD, the Abbot of Leicester was holding a half carucate of land here in 1291. THE AVENUE, *v.* **avenue**. BEECH SPINNEY, *v.* **bēce**, **spinney**. BRADLEY. CAMBRIDGE SPINNEY. CONEY HILL PLANTATION, *Coney Hill* 1681 *Surv*, *v.* **coni**, **plantation**. CORONATION SPINNEY, *v.* Elizabeth Plantation and Philip Spinney *infra*. COTTON'S FIELD FM, 1924 Map, *Cottonfield farm* 1877 White, COTTON'S FIELD HO., COTTON'S FIELD PLANTATION, (*the*) *Cottons Feild* 1584 Ipm, 1592, 1698 *Hazlerigg*, *Cottons Further* ~, ~ *Nether* ~, ~ *Upper Field* 1681 *Surv*, *v.* **cote** (**cotan** nom.pl.), **feld**; one of the township's great open-fields); DOG KENNEL PLANTATION, *v.* **kenel**; such sites frequently refer to the sites of kennels for hunting dogs. ELIZABETH PLANTATION, with Coronation Spinney *supra* and Philip Spinney *infra*, alluding to the marriage of Princess Elizabeth and Philip Mountbatten and her subsequent coronation as Queen Elizabeth II. THE GARDEN HO., *v.* Garden Cl in f.ns. (a). GUNPOWDER SPINNEY, cf. *Gun Powder Close* 1968 *Surv*. HOME PLANTATION, *v.* **home**. ILLSTON RD, Illston on the Hill lying 2 miles to the west. JOINER'S CLOSE, 1968 *Surv*; with the surn. *Joiner*. LANE'S SPINNEY. MILKING PENS SPINNEY, *v.* **milking**, **penn**[2]. MILLFIELD CLUMP, 1968 *Surv*, *v.* **clump** and Millfield in f.ns. (a). NETHER COTTAGES. NEW INN (lost), *the New Inn* 1832, 1833 *Deed*. NEW PARK. NEW SOUTHFIELD SPINNEY, *v.* Southfield Spinney *infra*. NOSELEY HALL, 1804 Nichols, 1846 *Deed*, 1863, 1877 White, 1925 Kelly, *v.* **hall**. NOSELEY HOME FM, *v.* **home**. NOSELEY WOOD, 1806 Map, *Noseley Wooddes* 1544 *Hazlerigg*, *v.* **wudu**. OLD PARK, 1924 Map; it is *The Parke* 1544 *Hazlerigg*, *the Great Park* 1681 *Surv*, *v.* **park**. PHILIP SPINNEY, *v.* Elizabeth Plantation *supra*. POPLAR SPINNEY, *v.* **poplere**. ROLLESTON WOOD, 1824 O, *Rolson ~*, *Roulston Wood* 1681 *Surv*; on the parish boundary with Rolleston which adjoins to the north. ROSE COTTAGE. ROUND SPINNEY, alluding to shape. ST MARY'S CHURCH *Church (St Mary)* 1846, 1863, 1877 White, 1925 Kelly; the earlier church is recorded as *ecclesie de Nousel'* 1220 MHW, *ecclesiam de Nouesl'* 1240 RGros, *ecclesie de Nouesle*(*e*) 1306, 1335 *Pat*, *~ de Nouseleye* 1335 *ib*; replaced as the parish church by the free collegiate chapel at Noseley Hall, recorded as *capelle de Noweselee* 1334 *Pat*, *~ de Nousele* 1335, 1344 *ib*, *capelle Sancte Marie Nouesle* 1344, 1422 *ib*, *capelle de Nawesle* 1367 *ib*, *capelle Sancte Marie Nouesley* 1387 *ib*, *collegii vel capelle* (*libere*) *de No*(*o*)*seley* 1548, 1549 *ib*, *collegium vel capellam liberem de Noseley* 1549, 1550 *ib* (with MLat *capella* 'a chapel', *collegium* 'a brotherhood, a college of priests', *libera* 'free'), *ecclesia parochialis de Noseley* 1517 DI (with MLat *parochialis* 'parochial, of the parish'). SOUTHFIELD SPINNEY, *the Farther ~ ~*, *the Little ~ ~*, *the Middle South Field* 1681 *Surv*, *Little Southfield* 1698 *Hazlerigg*, *~ ~ Meadow* 1681 *Surv*, *Further ~*, *Hither Southfield* 1698 *Hazlerigg*, *Southfield* 1968 *Surv*, *~ Meadow* 1698 *Hazlerigg*, *v.* **sūð**, **feld**. THREE GATE RD. TOP LODGE, *v.* **loge**. WOOLPITS PLANTING (2½"), (*v.* **planting**), *Wolpits* 1467 × 84 *LTD*, *Woolpits* 1968 *Surv*, cf. *Wolpitt Close* 1544 *Hazlerigg*, *v.* **wulf**, **pytt**; alluding to early trapping of wolves, an animal which did not become extinct in England until the Tudor period.

FIELD-NAMES

In (a), forms presented without dates are 1968 *Surv*; those dated 1750 and 1751 are *Deed*; 1824 are O; 1924 are Map. Forms throughout dated c.1220, 1544 and 1698 are *Hazlerigg*; those dated 1467 × 84 are *LTD*; 1584 are Ipm; 1591 are *Farnham*; 1681 are *Surv*.

(a) The Ten Acres (*v*. **æcer**); Allen's Cl (with the surn. *Allen*); Big ~, Little Ashbeds (*v*. **æsc**, **bedd**); Barn Mdw (*v*. **bern**); Barrett's Cl (with the surn. *Barrett*); Little Best Mdw (*v*. **best**); Boundary Cl (*v*. **boundary**); Bridge Cl 1750, 1968, Brig(g) Cl 1751, 1968 (*v*. **brycg**); Brook Cl (*v*. **brōc**); Bottom ~, Middle ~, Top Cottage (*v*. **cotage**); Big Churchyard Cl, Little Churchyard (*the Church-Yard Close* 1681, *v*. **churchyerd**; the site of the original parish church); Cow Cl (*the Cow Close* 1681); Cradle Mdw (poss. alludes to the use of a *cradle*, a light frame of wood attached to a scythe, on which the corn was caught to lie more evenly in the swathe; otherwise topographical shape may be thought of); Far Side (*v*. **sīde**); Little ~ ~, Furrow Cl (*v*. **furh**); Garden Cl, ~ ~ Slang (*v*. **slang**) (*v*. **gardin**; land used for horticulture); Glovers Cl, ~ ~ Slang (*v*. **slang**) (with the surn. *Glover*); Granfer's Paddock (*v*. **paddock**; with *granfer*, a dial. form of *grandfather*); North High Fd (*v*. **hēah**[1]); Far ~, Near Homestead (*v*. **hām-stede**); Horse Pasture; Hortons Hill (with the surn. *Horton*); Humphreys Mdw (with the surn. *Humphrey*, a reflex of the ContGerm masc. pers.n. *Humfrid*); Lady's Mdw (*v*. **ladi**); Lodge Mdw (*v*. Top Lodge *supra*); Little ~, Millfield (*Mylnfelde* 1467 × 84, *the Myll Feild* 1544, *Mill Feild* 1584, *the Mill Field* 1681, *Hither ~*, *Further ~*, *Nether Milnefeild* 1698 (*v*. **myln**, **feld**; one of the great open-fields), Millfield Mdw (*the Milne Feild Meadow* 1698); Lower ~, Top Nether (sic), Netherfield (*Nether Feild* 1584, *the farther Nether Field* 1681, cf. *the Neather Field Meadow* 1681, *v*. **neoðera**, **feld**; one of the great open-fields); New Mdw; New Park 1924 (*v*. **park** and Old Park *supra*); Old Mdw; Overfield (*v*. **uferra**; cf. *the Upper Field Meadow* 1681); Peppers Mdw (with the surn. *Pepper*, from OE *pipor* and metonymic for 'a dealer in pepper, a spicer'); Old Plough Cl (*v*. **plōg**); Pond Cl and Slang (*v*. **slang**), East ~ ~, Lower Pond Cl ((*the*) *Pond Close* 1681, 1698), Pond Mdw ((*the*) *Pond Meadow* 1681, 1698) (*v*. **ponde**); Sand Cl (*v*. **sand**); Spade Bank (*v*. **banke**; land which has to be cultivated by means of the spade rather than the plough); Ward's Cl (with the surn. *Ward*); Wey Mdw (*v*. **weg**); Wheat Cl, ~ ~ Arable (*v*. **hwǣte**, **arable**); Willowbed (*v*. **wilig**, **bedd**); Wood Cl, ~ Mdw.

(b) *Algatewell'* 1467 × 84 (*v*. **ald**, **gata**, **wella**); *le Barnyard* 1467 × 84, *the Barne yard* 1681 (*v*. **barn-yard**; this instance predates the earliest citation in OED by some 50 years); *Blakheyrns* 1467 × 84 (*v*. **blæc**, **hyrne**); *Bottom feild* 1698 (*v*. **bottom**); *Brake*, *Brachewheye* (*v*. **weg**) 1467 × 84 (*v*. **bracu**); *Branthyll* 1467 × 84 (*v*. **brant**, **hyll**); *Brokfelde* 1467 × 84 (*v*. **brōc**, **feld**; one of the early great open-fields); (*super*) *Burro*, *Buruseyge* 1467 × 84 (*v*. **ecg**) (*v*. **berg**); *the Lords Busshefelde* 1544 (*v*. **busc**, **feld**; since c.1435, the lord of the manor has been a member of the Hazlerigg family); *the Butholde* 1544 (*v*. **butte**, **helde**); *Bynduls* 1467 × 84 (the first el. may be **binde**, a name given to some sort of climbing plant such as bindweed; with **wella**); *Cherlond* 1467 × 84 (*v*. **cerr**, **land**); *Clakshyll* 1467 × 84 (*v*. **hyll**; the ostensible genitival composition joint suggests either the surn. *Clack*, which may be a reflex of the ODan masc. pers.n. *Klak* or OE *Clacc*, or one of the pers.ns. itself as the first el.; Reaney *s.n.* indicates that this surn. could also be metonymic for *Clacker* (ME *clackere*), a poss. name for a miller, taken from the clack or clatter of his mill; also, as ME **clakke** denoted the clapper of a mill, the toponym may imply 'hill with a windmill upon it'; an additional complication is the poss. presence of the OE sb.

clæcc 'a hillock'; *v.* VEPN *s.v.*); *Coculs* 1467 × 84 (*v.* **cokel**, alluding to the fossilized remains of molluscs in the local stone, cf. *le Peterstone Lane*, Lei **2** 9 and Peter Stone Bridge in Lubenham f.ns. (a) *supra*; less likely with **coccel**); *the Colledge meadow* 1681 (*v.* **college** and *collegium vel capellam liberem de Noseley* (*v.* St Mary's Church *supra*)); *Coneyhill Meadow* 1681 (*v.* Coney Hill Plantation *supra*); *the Conyngree* 1544 (*v.* **coningre**); *the Cookes Close* 1681 (with the surn. *Cook*); *Cousell* 1467 × 84 (*v.* **cū**, **wella**); *Cowe pasture* 1591 (*v.* **cū**, **pasture**); *the Cundite* ~, *the Conduit Close* 1681 (*v.* **cundite**); *Etheherne* 1467 × 84 (*v.* **ēðe**, **hyrne**); *Flaxlandis* 1457 × 84 (*v.* **fleax**, **land**); *Freemans Meadow* 1681 (with the surn. *Freeman*); *Garmundis croft* 1467 × 84 (*v.* **croft**; with the OE masc. pers.n. *Gārmund*); *Gose acers* 1467 × 84 (*v.* **gōs**, **æcer**); *the Great Meadow* 1681; *Howndusdall'* 1467 × 84 (*v.* **dalr**, **deill**; with a masc. pers.n., either ON *Hundr* or OE *Hund*); *Hungurhill*, *Hungurhyll* 1467 × 84 (*v.* **hungor**, **hyll**); *Hopkin Wrytsmore* 1467 × 84 (*v.* **wrīð**, **mōr**[1]; with the surn. *Hopkin*); *the Hopyard* 1681 (*v.* **hop-yard**); *Langlond'*, *Longlond'*, *Longlondis* 1467 × 84 (*v.* **lang**[1], **land**); *the Little Meadow* 1681; *Longdales* 1467 × 84 (*v.* **lang**[1], **deill**); *Longhardell* 1467 × 84 (*v.* **lang**[1], **heard**; with **deill** or **hyll**, alluding to soil hard to till); *Long Meadow* 1681; *Longthakholme* 1467 × 84 (*v.* **lang**[1], **þak**, **holmr**); *Lytylwheyt* 1467 × 84 (*v.* **lȳtel**, **þveit**); *Midulhyll* 1467 × 84 (*v.* **middel**, **hyll**); *Mill home* 1681(*v.* **holmr**); *Milndam* 1467 × 84 (*v.* **myln**, **damme**; with reference to a watermill); *Mylnfurlong* 1467 × 84 (*v.* **myln**, **furlang**); *the Neather Ground* (*next Goadby*) 1681 (*v.* **neoðera**, **grund**; Goadby parish adjoins to the east); *Nethertoftes* 1467 × 84 (*v.* **neoðera**, **toft**); *Northwardehyll* 1467 × 84 (*v.* **norðweard**, **hyll**); *Northwell* c.1220 (*v.* **norð**, **wella**); *The Olde Felde* 1544 (*v.* **ald**, **feld**; a former great open-field); *Ordalys* 1467 × 84 (*v.* **ord**, **deill**); *Ouertoftes*, *Ouertoftis* 1467 × 84 (*v.* **uferra**, **toft**); *Penymore* 1467 × 84 (*v.* **mōr**[1]; as ME *peni* indicating a penny rent for waste moorland may seem unlikely, the first el. could be rather the surn. *Penny* (which was usually a nickname taken from the coin OE *pening*, ME *peni*), or if earlier, the OE masc. pers.n. *Pening* (also taken from the coin); cf. *Penytherne* in Great Bowden f.ns. (b)); *Peyslandis* 1467 × 84 (*v.* **pise**, **land**); *Pytfurlong* 1467 × 84 (*v.* **pytt**, **furlang**); *the Ram Close meadow* 1681 (*v.* **ramm**); *Rauenesthuett* c.1220 (*v.* **þveit**; either with a masc. pers.n., ON *Hrafn* or OE *Hræfn*, or with the bird-name ON **hrafn**, OE **hræfn** 'raven'); *Rawnseyth* 1467 × 84 (*v.* **ēðe**; with the first el. one of the possibilities as presented for the previous f.n., a pers.n. seeming likelier); *Robrechesyke* 1467 × 84 (*v.* **rūh**, **brēc**, **sík**); *Schortwellesyke* 1467 × 84 (*v.* **sc(e)ort**, **wella**, **sík**); *Scurvey* 1467 × 84 (poss. is 'the scummy stream', *v.* **sc(e)orf**, **scurf**, **ēa**, or 'a scaly, scurfy patch of land cut off by water', *v.* **ēg**, alluding to its surface appearance; in either case, with Scand influence on the opening syllable); *Sladlondis* 1467 × 84 (*v.* **slæd**, **land**); *Standall'* 1467 × 84 (*v.* **stān**, **dalr**, **deill**); *Stanmedow* 1467 × 84 (*v.* **stān**, **mēd** (**mēdwe** obl.sg.)); *Stevynsmore* 1467 × 84 (*v.* **mōr**[1]; with the surn. *Steven*(*s*), a reflex of the ME masc. pers.n. *Steffan/Stephen*, found in OE as *Stefhan* (also *Stephanus*)); *Stonhillis*, *Stonhyll'* 1467 × 84 (*v.* **stān**, **hyll**); *Styfurlong leys* 1467 × 84 (*v.* **stīg**, **furlang**, **lǣs**); *Thomysfurlong'* 1467 × 84 (*v.* **furlang**; either with the surn. *Thomas* or *Thom* or with their source, the pers.n. *Thomas*); *Thornfurlong'* 1467 × 84 (*v.* **þorn**, **furlang**); *Thurstanestok* c.1220 (*v.* **stoc**; with the ON masc. pers.n. *Þorsteinn* which has had its second el. *steinn* replaced by the cognate OE *stān*; cf. the treatment of this pers.n. in Thrussington, Lei **3** 231); *Thurstokys* 1467 × 84 (perh. a cartulary miscopied form of the previous f.n., but the generic in the plural suggests **stocc**, with the Anglo-

Scand masc. pers.n. *Þūr* (Feilitzen 390)); *Vndurcrosse* 1467 × 84 (*v.* **under**, **cros**); *Wrongfurlong* 1467 × 84 (*v.* **wrang**, **furlang**); *Wydfeld'* 1467 × 84 (*v.* **wudu**, **feld**; one of the early great open-fields).

Owston and Newbold

1. OWSTON

Osulvestone 1086 DB, Hy 2 Dugd, 1232, 1234 RHug, *Osulveston'* 1220 Cur, 1225 Cl *et freq* to 1369, 1383 Banco *et passim* to 1454 ib, 1527 AAS, *Osulvestun'* 1238, 1241 Cl

Osuluestun a.1160 BM, 1185 P, *Osulueston'* 1148 × 66 RegAnt, Hy 2 *AllS et passim* to 1239, 1241 RGros, *Osuluestona* 1148 × 1166 RegAnt

Osoluestona a.1160, 1150 × 60 Dane *et passim* to Hy 3 ib, *Osolueston(e)* 1153, 1154 BM *et freq* to 1331 (e.15), 1333 (e.15) *BelCartB et passim* to 1436, 1482 *Rut*, *Osoluestun'* Hy 2 Dane, 1241 (e.15) *BelCartB*

Osoluistona c.1130 LeicSurv, *Osoluiston'* m.13 (1404) *Laz*, 1258 RegAnt, *Osoluyston'* 1258 ib

Osolveston' Hy 2 Dugd, 1203 Fine *et freq* to 1481 Pat, 1486 AD *et passim* to 1523, 1530 AAS, *Osolvestone* 1219 RHug, *Osolvestun'* 1230 Cur, *Osolviston* 1252, 1289 OSut

Oselueston' 1202 Ass, 1233 (e.14) *BelCartA et passim* to 1497 *Rut*, 1518 Visit

Oselveston' 1208 FF, 1210 Cur *et passim* to 1528 Visit, 1535 VE, *Oselvestone* 1225 RHug

Oselweston' 1209 × 35, 1253 × 58 RHug *et passim* to 1493 *Rut*, 1541 MinAccts, *Osilweston* 1352 (16) *SlCart*, 1535 *Rut*, *Osolweston* 1401 Cl, 1535 VE, *Osulweston* 1510 LP

Oselston' 1276 RH, 1282 OSut, *Oseleston* c.1291 Tax, e.14 *BelCartA et passim* to 1353 Pat (p), 1428 FA, *Ossoliston'* 1296 *Peake*, *Osolston* 1300 Ipm, *Osilston'* 1339 *Rut*, *Oselton* 1377 ELiW, *Osulton'* 1378 *Rut*

Oulston 1537, 1541 MinAccts, *Ow(e)lston* 1549, 1560 Pat

Owestron (sic) 1502 *MinAccts*, *Oweston(e)* 1581 AAS, 1610 Speed, 1622 Burton, 1719 LML

Oueston 1576 Saxton, 1585 LibCl, *Ouston* 1621 Fine, 1629, 1728 LML, *Ouson* 1710 ib

Owston 1603 LibCl, 1604 SR, 1613 LML *et freq*

'Ōswulf's village, estate', *v.* **tūn**. The masc. pers.n. *Ōswulf* is OE. Note the typical 17th-cent. and earlier Leics. loss of *t* from the group *-ston* in the late form *Ouson*.

OWSTON ABBEY (OLVESTON ABBEY 2½")

abbatie de Oselveston 1220 MHW, 1401, 1421, 1467 *Pat*, *abbatia de Osolveston* 1268, 1328, 1349, 1355 *ib*
domus de Oselveston 1264 *Pat*
monasterii Sancti Andree Oselveston 1446 *Pat*, *monasterii Sancti Andree Apostoli* (*in*) *Osolveston* 1446, 1504 *ib*, *monasterii de Oselveston* 1467 *ib*, ~ *de Osolveston* 1481 *ib*, ~ *de Oselveston alias Owlston* 1549 *ib*
Owsen Abbay 1538 Leland, *the Abby* 1708 (18) *Terrier*

The abbey was founded for Augustinian Canons by Robert Grimbald, Justice of England, shortly before 1161 in the reign of Henry II. Fragments of the early building appear to survive in the present parish church, particularly in the nave and in the north aisle (*v.* St Andrew's Church *infra*). Note in the above MLat *abbatia* 'an abbey', MLat *domus* 'a religious house', MLat *monasterium* 'a monastery' and *v.* **abbaye**.

BRICKYARD FM, *v.* **brike-yard** and Brick Kiln Cl *infra*. CORN CLOSE FM, 1877 White, 1926 Sale, *v.* Corn Cl in f.ns. (a). COX'S LANE, with the surn. *Cox*. DEANE BANK FM, *v.* **banke**; prob. with **denu**, but poss. is a surn., note *Catherine Dain* 1833 Census of Owston. DOG AND GUN (P.H.) (lost), *Dog and Gun* 1846 White. FURZE HILL, 1795 Plan, 1806 Map, 1824 O, *v.* **fyrs** and Furze Hill Cl in f.ns. (a). FURZE HILL FM, 1926 Sale. GRANGE FM (OWSTON GRANGE 2½"), *The Grange* 1863 White, *Owston Grange* 1877 ib, 1926 Sale, *Owston Grange Farm* 1879 *Deed*, *v.* **grange**. GREEN LANE, *v.* **grēne**[1]. HILLCLOSE FM, *v.* Hill Cl in f.ns. (a). HILL TOP FM. KNOSSINGTON RD, Knossington lying 2 miles to the east. LONG LANE. MAIN ST is *the Street* 1708 (18) *Terrier*. MANOR FM is *Manor House* 1846, 1877 White, *v.* **maner**. NEWBOLD RD, *v.* Newbold *infra*. OUNDLE FM, named from Oundle, 20 miles to the south-east in Northants. OWSTON LODGE, 1926 Sale, *Ouston Lodge* 1824 O, 1877 White, *v.* **loge**. OWSTON WOODS (~ WOOD 2½"), *Osellweston wood* 1586 *Plan*, *Owston* ~ 1806 Map, *Ouston Wood* 1824 O, *Great* ~, *Little Wood* 1846 White, 1848 *Surv*, 1857 *Valuation*, 1863, 1877 White, *Owston Big* ~, *Owston Little Wood* 1926 Sale, *v.* **wudu**. PALMER'S ARMS (P.H.) (lost), *Palmer's Arms* 1863 White; *Frederick Palmer* of Withcote Hall was lord of the manor 1863 ib. THE PRIORY (local) was formerly *The Vicarage House* 1795 *Plan*, *The Vicarage* 1925 Kelly, *v.* **vikerage**. ST ANDREW'S CHURCH, *Church (St Andrew)* 1846, 1877 White, 1925 Kelly; the early parish church is recorded as *ecclesie de Oselveston* 1220 MHW, *ecclesie parochialis de Osolueston* 1236 RGros. Note also *the Church Yard* 1708 (18) *Terrier*, 1795 *Plan*, *v.* **churchyerd**. WASHDYKE RD, *v.* **wæsce**, **dík**. WHATBOROUGH RD, Whatborough lying one mile to the south. WHITE HOUSE FM.

FIELD-NAMES

In (a), forms dated 1786, 18 and 1848 are *Surv*; those dated 1795 are *Plan*; 1824 are O; 1877 are White; 1879 are *Deed*; 1926 are Sale. Forms throughout dated 1148 × 66 are RegAnt; those dated 1208 are FF; 1211 and 1328 are Nichols; 1536 and 1538 are *Rental*; 1539 are *Reeve*; 1704 and 1708 (18) are *Terrier*.

(a) Abbey Garden 1795 (*v.* **gardin**), Abbey Yard 1795, 1848 (*v.* **geard**) (*v.* Owston Abbey *supra*); Acre Cl 1848, Two Acre Cl 1795, 1848, Five ~, Seven ~, Ten Acres, Five Acre Mdw 1879 (*v.* **æcer**); Back Yard 1848 (*v.* **back**, **geard**); Ban Roods Cl 1848 (*v.* **bēan**, **rōd**[3]); Baileys Cl, ~ Mdw 1795, Bayleys Cl, ~ Mdw 1848 (either with the surn. *Bailey* or with **baillif** 'a bailiff, a steward', cf. the Bowbearers *infra*); Barwoods Cl 1795 (with the surn. *Barwood*); Beeby ~ 1795, Beebys Cl 1848 (with the surn. *Beeby* of a family originally from the township of this name, 7 miles to the west); Beggars Pad Cl 1795, 1848 (*v.* **beggere**, **pæð** (dial. **pad**)); Berrys Cl, ~ ~ Mdw 18 (with the surn. *Berry*, cf. Berry's Fd in Kibworth Beauchamp f.ns. (a)); Birstalls North ~, Birstalls South Cl 1848 (with the surn. *Birstall* of a family originally from the township of this name, 11 miles to the west); Great ~, Little ~, Green's Blackmoor (with the surn. *Green*), Blackmoor Stimsons (with the surn. *Stimson*) 1795, Great ~ ~, Little ~ ~, Greens Blackmoor Cl 1848, Blackmoor Hill 1824 (*v.* **blæc**, **mōr**[1]); the Bowbearers 1795, Bowbearers Cl 1795, 1848, ~ Mdw 1848 (*Bowbearers Close* 1704, 1708 (18), *v.* **bow-bearer**; an under-officer in a forest who looked after trespasses affecting vert and venison, the bowbearer may have been responsible for the abbey's woodland, surviving in part as Owston Woods *supra*); Brick Kiln Cl, ~ ~ Ground 1848 (*v.* **grund**) (*v.* **brike-kiln**; located at Brickyard Fm *supra*); Burbidges Homestead 1848 (*v.* **hām-stede**), Burbridges Cl (sic) 1879 (with the surn. *Burbidge* of a family originally from Burbage, 23 miles to the south-west); Bull Cl 1795 (*v.* **bula**; cf. Calves Cl and Cow Cls *infra*); Bushy ~ 1795, Bushey Cl 1848, Bushy Nook 1795, Bushey Nook Cl 1848 (*v.* **nōk**) (*v.* **busshi**); Great ~ ~, Little Butt Cl 1848 (*v.* **butte**); Calves Cl 1795 (*v.* **calf**); Chads Cl 1795, 1848 (with the surn. *Chad*, a reflex of the OE masc. pers.n. *Ceadd(a)*); Cheese Cake Cl 1848 (*v.* **chese-cake**); Cherry Tree Nook 1795, ~ ~ ~ Cl 1848 (*v.* **cheri-tre**, **nōk**); Cold Hill 1795, ~ ~ Cl 1848 (*v.* **cald** 'windswept, exposed'); Cooks Cl 1795, 1848 (with the surn. *Cook*); Corn Cl 1786, 1795, 18, Great ~ ~, Little Corn Cl 1848, Corn Close

Mdw 1786, 1795, 18, Great Corn Close Mdw 1848 (*v.* **corn**[1]); Cottage Cl 1795, 1848, Cottage Furlong Cl 1848 (*v.* **furlang**) (*v.* **cotage**); Cow Cls 1795, Great ~ ~, Little Cow Cl 1848, 1926, Cow Dam 1795, ~ ~ Cl 1848 (*v.* **damme**; a dam created for the watering of farm livestock), Cow Pasture 1795, ~ ~ Cl 1848 (*v.* **pasture**); Coxes Cl 1795, 1848 (with the surn. *Cox*, cf. Cox's Lane *supra*); Crow Orchard 1795, ~ ~ Cl 1848 (*v.* **orceard**; cf. *Benjamin Crow* 1850 Census of Owston); Cunnery Cl 1795, 1848, The Cunnery 1926 (*v.* **coningre**); Danseys Cl, ~ Mdw 1786, 18 (with the surn. *Dansey* of a Norman family originally from Anisy (Calvados) (*de Anesi* > *Danesi*)); Evitts ~, 1795, Evatts Cl 1848 (with the surn. *Evitt*, from *Evet*, a diminutive of *Eve*); Nether ~ ~, Upper End Cl 1795, 1848 (*v.* **ende**); Forty Cl 1795, 1848 (*v.* **forð-ēg** 'an island of higher ground standing out from surrounding marsh or low-lying land'); Freers Cl, ~ Mdw 1786, 18 (with the surn. *Freer*); Furlong Cl 1795 (*v.* **furlang**); Furze Hill Cl late Tiers Cl 1848 (*v.* Tiers Cl *infra*); East ~ ~ ~, South ~ ~ ~, Furze Hill Cl 1848 (*v.* Furze Hill *supra*); Far ~ ~, First Goose Green 1795, Far ~ ~ ~, Near Goose Green Cl 1848 (*v.* **gōs**, **grēne**[2]); Great Cl, ~ Mdw 1786, 18; Green Sink (sic) 1795, Green Sick Cl 1848 (*v.* **grēne**[1], **sík**); Greens Cl 1786, 1795, 18 (with the surn. *Green*); Harrolds ~ 1786, 18, 1848, Harrold's Cl 1926, Harrolds Mdw 1848 (with the surn. *Harrold*, a reflex of the ON masc. pers.n. *Haraldr* (ODan *Harald*)); Hill Cl 1786, 18, Great ~ ~, Little ~ ~, Upper Hill Cl 1848, The Hills 1879 (*v.* **hyll**); Hills Green Long Cl 1848, Hills Homestead 1795, 1848 (*v.* **hām-stede**) (with the surn. *Hill*); Hilly Mdw 1795 (*Hilly Medowe* 1539, *v.* **hyllig**, **mēd** (**mēdwe** obl.sg.)); Hinckleys Lane Cl, ~ Wood Cl 1795, 1848 (with the surn. *Hinckley* of a family originally from the township of this name, 23 miles to the south-west); Home Cl 1786, 1848 (*v.* **home**); Northward ~ ~, Southward Horse Cl 1786, 18, 1879, Top ~ ~ 1879, Horse Cl 18, 1879, Horse Close Mdw 1786, 1848 (*v.* **hors**); House Acre 18 (*v.* **æcer**), House Cl otherwise Stonepit Cl 1786 (*v.* Stone Pitts *infra*), House Cl 18, 1879, House Orchard 1848 (*v.* **orceard**) (*v.* **hūs**); Ingrams Cl 1848 (with the surn. *Ingram*, a reflex of the ContGerm masc. pers.n. *Ingelram* (OFr *Enguerran*)); Kemps Cl 1795, 1848 (with the surn. *Kemp*, a reflex of OE *cempa* 'a warrior'); Kiln Cls 1795 (*v.* Brick Kiln Cl *supra*); Ladies Ground, Ladies Far Ground 1795, Far ~ ~ ~, Great Lady Day Ground 1848 (*v.* **grund**; land whose rent fell due on 25 March, the Feast of the Annunciation, Lady Day being the first of the four traditional quarter days, dates for payment of quarterly rates and dues); First ~ ~, Upper Land Cl 1795, 1848 (*v.* **land**; closes formed from unspecified numbers of selions or 'lands' of former great open-fields); Leys Cl 1848, Leys End Cl 1795, 1848 (*v.* **ende**) (*v.* **leys**); Little Cl 1786, 1795, 18, 1879; Little Mdw 1786, 18, 1879; Long Cl 1795, 1848; Marefield Cl, ~ Mdw, Upper Marefield, ~ ~ Mdw 18 (*v.* Old Marefield *infra*); Great ~, Little Marsh 1795, Great ~ ~, Little Marsh Cl 1848 (*v.* **mersc**); Middle Cl 1795; Mill Cl 1795, Nether ~ ~, Upper Mill Cl 1848, Mill Hill Cls 1795 (*v.* **myln**; note the early *molendino de Osulueston'* 1148 × 66 (with MLat *molendinum* 'a mill')); Nether Mdw 1848; New Cl 1795, New Fd 1786, 18, New Field Cl 1848, Newfield Mdw 1786, 18, 1848, New Mdw 18, 1848; Old Mdw 18 (*v.* **ald**); the Orchard 1879 (*v.* **orceard**); The Pen Yard 1795 (*v.* **penn**[2], **geard**); the Pingle 1879 (*v.* **pingel**); Prestress Cl, ~ Mdw 1795, 1848 (*Prestres* 1211, *v.* **prēost**, **hrīs**; occurs also in adjacent Knossington f.ns. (b)); Ram Cl, ~ ~ Mdw 1786, 18, Ram Close Farm 1877 (*v.* **ramm**); Red Hound Cl 1795, 1848 (*Redehound* 1536; the generic appears to be much distorted, but 'reedy water-meadow' (**hrēod** with **hamm** or **holmr**) may pertain); Rileys 1795 (the surn. *Riley* in the possessive case); Road

Cl 1795, 1848 (beside a roadway); Robholme 1795, Robholm Cl 1848 (*v.* **holmr**; with the surn. *Robb*, from a pet-form of *Robert*); Rough Mdw 1786, 1795, 18, 1848 (*v.* **rūh**); Siddling 1795 (*v.* **sīdling**); Square Cl 1848 (*v.* **squar(e)**; alluding to shape); Smith Mdw 1795 (prob. with **smēðe**[1], otherwise **smið**); Steedholme Cl 1795, Stud Holme Cl, Steedholme Lane Cl 1848 (*v.* **stēda** (varying with **stōd**), **holmr**); Stevensons Cl, ~ Mdw 1795, 1848 (with the surn. *Stevenson*); Stimsons Cl 1795, 1848 (with the surn. *Stimson*); Stone Pitts 18, 1879, Stonepit Cl alias House Cl 18 (*v.* **stān-pytt**); Stontons Cl 1795, West ~ ~, Stantons Cl 1848 (with the surn. *Stanton*); Far ~ ~, Nether Swallow Thorn 1795, Far ~ ~ ~, Swallow Thorn Cl 1848 (*v.* **swalg**, **þorn**; prob. alluding to an old thorn-filled gravel pit or stone pit rather than to the bird **swalwa** 'a swallow'); Taylors Cl 1795, 1848 (with the surn. *Taylor*); Tiers Cl 1795 (cf. *John Tiers* 1795); Towns End Cl 1795 (*v.* **tūn**, **ende**); Turners Cl, ~ Nether Cl 1848, ~ Upper Cl 1795, 1848, ~ Homestead 1848 (*v.* **hām-stede**) (with the surn. *Turner*); Upper Cl, ~ Mdw 1795, 1848; Ugdens ~ 1795, Ogdens Cl 1848 (cf. *William Ogdin* 1612 RFL); Vicarstaff(s) Cl 1795, 1848 (with the surn. *Vickerstaff* of a family originally from Bickerstaffe, Lancs.); Wadd Leys 18, Northward ~ ~, Southward Woad Leys 1786, 18, 1848, Woad Leys Mdw 1786, 18 (*v.* **wād**, **leys**; land on which woad was processed); Water Furrows Cl 1795, 1848, 1926 (*v.* **wæter**, **furh** and *the water furrowes* in Billesdon f.ns. (b)); Wethers ~ 1795, Withers Cl 1848 (*v.* **weðer**); Wood Great Cl, ~ Little Cl 1795, Great Wood ~, Little Wood Cl 1848, the Wood Leys 1848 (*v.* **leys**) (*v.* Owston Woods *supra*).

(b) *Dedelane* 1208 (*v.* **dēad**, **lane**; may allude to a lane with a dead-end, or refer to a place where a violent death occurred, or to the discovery of human bones, *v.* Ru 104 and Lei **1** 30); *Estbreche* 1328 (*v.* **ēast**, **brēc**); *Estwoode* 1539 (*v.* **ēast**, **wudu** and Owston Woods *supra*); *the Fatt Close*, *Fat Close Meadow* 1708 (18) (*v.* **fætt**; alluding to rich land); *The Homestall* 1708 (18) (*v.* **hām-stall**); *New Close* 1538 (*v.* **nīwe**, **clos(e)**); *Wakoe* 1539 (*v.* **wacu**, **hōh**); *Westwoode* 1539 (*v.* **west**, **wudu** and Owston Woods *supra*); *Widow Dales Yard* 1708 (18) (*v.* **geard**).

2. NEWBOLD

Neubotel c.1130 LeicSurv, *Neubot* 1227 ClR

Neubold' c.1130 LeicSurv, a.1250 (1404) *Laz et passim* to 1327 SR, (~ *Sauce* 1327 ib)

Neoboldam e.Hy 2 Dane, (~ *iuxta Losebi* e.Hy 2 ib), *Neoboldie* Hy 2 ib

Neubolt Ric 1 (1253) Ch, 1243 Fees *et passim* to 1414 Pat, (~ *Saucy* 1414 ib), *Newbolt* 1349 AD, 1361 Nichols, (~ *iuxta Oseleston* 1349 AD)

Newbold 1308 Inqaqd, 1322 Pat *et passim* to 1604 SR, 1610 Speed *et freq*, (~ *Sauce* 1308 ib, 1416 Nichols, ~ *Saucy* 1414 Inqaqd, ~ *Sawcy* 1584 LeicW), *Newebold* 1309 Pat, (~ *Sauce* 1309 ib)

'The new building, the new dwelling', *v.* **nīwe**, **botl**, **bold**. The manor was held in 1243 Fees by *heres Roberti de la Sauce* (MLat *heres* 'an heir') and in 1252 AD by *Simon de la Saucey*. The family probably originally came from La Saussaye (Eure). Affixes refer also to Owston *supra* and to Lowesby in East Goscote Hundred (*v.* Lei **3** 168).

DAWSON'S LANE, with the surn. *Dawson*. MAREFIELD LODGE, *v.* **loge** and Old Marefield *infra*. NEWBOLD FM is *Newbold Lodge* 1877 White, *v.* **loge**. NEWBOLD GRANGE FM (THE GRANGE 2½"), *v.* **grange**. OWSTON LODGE is *Stimsons Lodge* 1825 O; with the surn. *Stimson*, *v.* **loge** and Stimsons Cl in Owston f.ns. (a). WHITE HOUSE FM.

FIELD-NAMES

Forms presented without dates are 1737 *Reeve*; those dated m.13 are Nichols.

(b) *Bobriggs Close* (*v.* **boga**, **brycg**, **bryggja**; cf. Bow Bridge (Cl), Lei **2** 122 and Lei **3** 229); *Borums* (the surn. *Borum* in the possessive case); *Burgwong* m.13 (*v.* **vangr**; lying towards Burrough on the Hill, *v.* Lei **2** 231), *Burrough Dyke* 1737 (*v.* **dík**; at this date the boundary ditch with Burrough on the Hill); *Busbrooke Close* (prob. with a stream-name, 'bush-lined brook', *v.* **busc**, **brōc**); *the Little ~ ~*, *Dam piece* (*v.* **damme**, **pece**); *Dry Hill Close* (*v.* **drȳge**, **hyll**); *the Far Close*; *Franethorp* m.13 (a lost farmstead, *v.* **þorp**; with a Scand masc. pers.n., either *Fræna* or **Frǽni* or **Fráni*, cf. Framland, Lei **2** 1); *Grococks Pasture* (*v.* **pasture**; that of *Matthew Grocock* 1737); *the Nether ~*, *the Upper Ground* (*v.* **grund**); *the Land Close*, *the Nine Lands* (*v.* **land**; enclosures comprising unspecified and specified numbers of selions or 'lands' of former open-fields); *the Six ~*, *the Ten Leys* (*v.* **leys**; grassland units of tenure corresponding to *lands* similarly used of arable); *Little Close*; *the Meadow Close*; *the Mires* (*v.* **mýrr**); *the Nether Close*; *the New Close*; *Owston Close* (located towards Owston *supra*); *the Pasture* (*v.* **pasture**); *the Sheep Wash Close* (*v.* **scēp-wæsce**); *Thurn Close* 1737, *Thyrnewong* m.13 (*v.* **vangr**) (*v.* **þyrne**, **þyrnir**); *Townsend Close* (*v.* **tūn**, **ende**); *ad vadum subtus Neubolt* 1227 ClR ('at the ford below Newbold'; marked but unnamed on O.S. maps at SK 764087).

OLD MAREFIELD (lost)

For forms and interpretation of the place-name, *v.* Marefield *supra*.

Affixes are variously added as:
~ *Luterel* 1227 Fees
North ~ 1252 Fees, 1276 RH, 1389, 1416 Nichols

~ *North(e)* 1276 RH, l.13 CustRo *et passim* to 1502 *Misc Accts*, 1541 MinAccts
Old ~ 1737 *Reeve*, 1798 Nichols

Andreas Lutrel held the manor for the king c.1240 Nichols. As to the location of this deserted township in Owston, Nichols writes: 'The Mardefield which is within the parish of Owston, anciently called North Mardefield and now Old Mardefield is wholly depopulated; but the site of the village is visible in a close between Owston and Twyford, about a mile and a half from each, about a mile from South Mardefield, and the same distance from Burrow, nearly in a direct line.' (*South Mardefield* here is Marefield *supra*, while *Burrow* is Burrough on the Hill in Framland Hundred (*v.* Lei **2** 231)). As late as 1940, the site of Old Marefield was still clearly marked by earthworks in a field a little to the west of the minor road from Marefield to Burrough on the Hill.

Rolleston

ROLLESTON

Rovestone 1086 DB
Rolvestone Hy 2 Dugd, *Rolvestona* 1156 (1318) Ch, *Rolveston'* 1198 Cur, 1199 Fine *et passim* to 1290 Ch, 1359 AD, *Rolvestun* 1183 × 95 *Rut* (p), 1227 GildR (p), *Rolvistun* 1242 ib
Rolueston' 1170 (p), 1171 P (p) *et passim* to c.1215 RegAnt (p), 1227 ClR, *Roluiston'* Hy 3 *Crox*, *Rolwiston* 1240 GildR (p)
Rolleston 1195 P, 1199 MemR *et passim* to 1282 Cl (p), 1292 (1449) *WoCart* (p) *et freq*, *Rolliston'* 1242 GildR (p), 1260 Cl *et passim* to 1286 *LCDeeds* (p), 1316 FA, *Roleston'* 1297 Pat, 1302 *RTemple*, 1332 SR (p), 1388 *Wyg*
Rolston' 1346 (p), 1348 (p), 1379 (p), 1385 *LCDeeds* (p), 1535 VE, 1605, 1615 LML, *Rolson* 1513 *MktHPR*
Rowleston 1539 MinAccts, *Rowlston* 1610 Speed, 1624 LML, *Roulston* 1619, 1620 ib

Either 'Hrōðwulf's village, estate' or 'Hrólfr's village, estate', *v.* **tūn**. The dithematic masc. pers.n. *Hrōðwulf* is OE and although uncommon, appears also in the place-name Rolleston in Staffs. (*Roðulfeston* 941 (14) BCS 771 (S 479), *Rolfestun* 1002 × 04 ASWills 46 (S 1536)). Early shortening of an OE dithematic pers.n. (as perhaps here) occurs in adjoining Noseley and possibly also in neighbouring Illston on the Hill.

Formally, the specific of Rolleston could also be the ON masc. pers.n. *Hrólfr* (ODan *Rolf*), in which case an original Anglo-Saxon settlement may have been appropriated and renamed from a Scandinavian of the Viking army which disbanded in the region in 877.

Note the very early example of typical 16th- and 17th-cent. Leics. loss of *t* from the group *-ston* in *Rolson* 1513.

BLENHEIM PLANTATION, *v.* **plantation**; commemorating the victory of the Duke of Marlborough at the Battle of Blenheim in 1704 during the War of the Spanish Succession. CRANHILL FM is *Cranhill House* 1925 Kelly, *v.* **cran**. CROW WOOD, *v.* **crāwe**. HOME FM, *v.* **home**. THE LODGE, *v.* **loge**. LONG PLANTATION. NEW INN (lost), *New Inn* 1806 Map. NEW ROLLESTON (2½"). OLD POND WOOD, *v.* **ponde**. POPE'S SPINNEY, *v.* **spinney**; with the surn. *Pope*. ROLLESTON HALL, 1831 Curtis, 1846, 1863, 1877 White, 1925 Kelly, *v.* **hall**. ROLLESTON LODGE FM, *Rolleston Lodge* 1877 White, *v.* **loge**. ROLLESTON WOOD. ST JOHN'S CHURCH, *Rolleston Church* 1846, 1863, 1877 White, *Church (St John)* 1925 Kelly; it is earlier recorded as *the Chappel of Rolloston* 1708 *Terrier*, *v.* **chapel(e)**. TOWNSEND CLOSE SPINNEY, *v.* **tūn**, **ende**. WHINNEY PIT SPINNEY, *v.* **whinny**, **pytt**, **spinney**.

FIELD-NAMES

In (a), forms presented without dates are 1968 *Surv*; those dated 1850 are *TA*. Forms in (b) dated 1477 (e.16) are *Charyte*.

(a) Five Acre, Nine Acre Bottom (*v.* **botm**), Ten Acre, Eleven ~, Twelve ~, Fifteen ~, Thirty Acre, Fifty Acres (*v.* **æcer**); Barn Fd (*v.* **bern**); Barnes Mdw (prob. with the surn. *Barnes*); Birds Mdw (with the surn. *Bird*); Black Hovel (*v.* **blæc**, **hovel**); Busshey Cl (*v.* **busshi**); Collins Cl (with the surn. *Collins*); The Dingles, Dingleside (*v.* **sīde**) (*v.* **dingle**); Doctors Cl (*v.* **doctour**); Flats (*v.* **flat**); Great Ground 1850 (*v.* **grēat**, **grund**); Harts Big Fd (with the surn. *Hart*); Hen Fd (*v.* **henn**); Top ~ ~, Bottom Little Fd; Long Fd; Long Mdw; Millfield (*v.* **myln**); Pond Cl (*v.* **ponde**); Redmire, ~ Mdw 1850 (*v.* **hrēod**, **mýrr**); Roadside Mdw; Skinners Mdw (with the surn. *Skinner*); Springfield (*v.* **spring**[1]); Tallowfat (sic) (either alluding to land likely to produce fat cattle, or, as tallow was obtained from the hard fat of ruminants, perh. a site for the local manufacture of soap and candles); Vale Mdw (*v.* **val**); Washpits (*v.* **wæsce**, **pytt**); Wood Hill; Wood Meadow Park (*v.* **park**).

(b) *Northefeld* 1477 (e.16) (*v.* **norð**, **feld**; one of the early great open-fields of the township); *Sowthefeld* 1477 (e.16) (*v.* **sūð**, **feld**; another of the open-fields).

Saddington

SADDINGTON

Sadintone 1086 DB, *Sadinton'* 1195 P, 1196 ChancR *et freq* to 1283 Cl (p), l.13 *RTemple et passim* to 1316 FA, c.1350 *Deed* (p), *Sadintun'* 1221, 1222 ClR, m.13 (1404) *Laz*
Setintone 1086 DB, *Seddinton* 1200 Fine
Satinton' 1176, 1177, 1181 P
Sadingtona l.12 *Rut*, *Sadington'* 1230, 1231 Cur *et passim* to 1248 *Rut* (p), c.1250 *Peake et freq* to 1549, 1554 Fine *et passim* to 1576, 1579 LEpis, (~ *Moeles* 1316 Ipm), *Sadingtone* 1231 RHug
Sadyngton' a.1250 (1404), m.13 (1404) *Laz et freq* to 1428 FA, 1437 Fine *et passim* to 1537 CoPleas, *Sadyngtone* 1324 (p), 1327 AD (p), *Sadynton'* 1322 *LCDeeds*, 1323 (1449) *WoCart et passim* to 1335 Pat (p), 1343 Fine (p)
Saddyngton 1536 *Braye*, *Saddington* 1576 LibCl, 1579 LEpis *et freq*

Saddington stands on high ground some nine miles south-east of Leicester and appears to belong to the group of OE place-names in *-ingtūn* to its east and south-east, including Evington, Loddington, Skeffington and perhaps Knossington. The pers.n. of the specific is uncertain. Ekwall (DEPN) suggests the masc. OE *Sǣgēat* (the reflex of which appears in DB as *Saiet*) but notes that one would perhaps have expected the *g* [j] to have left a trace, although Norman influence might be the reason for the monophthongization of *ai* to *a*. Mills (DBPN) as an alternative OE pers.n. suggests an unrecorded *Sǣhǣð*, while Watts (CDEPN) proposes an unrecorded OE monothematic masc. pers.n. *Sada*, noting in comparison the first el. of the Langobardic pers.n. *Sadipertus*. A further possibility, as suggested by the late Professor Bruce Dickins (personal communication), is an unrecorded OE by-name *Sæd*(*d*) from the adj. *sæd* 'sad, weary'. The other Leics. place-names with *-ingtūn* appear to contain monothematic rather than dithematic pers.ns., which would accord with their proposed 8th-cent. date (*v*. Barrie Cox, 'Aspects of place-name evidence for early medieval settlement in England', *Viator* 11 (1980), 35–60, at 44). Hence tentatively, one might think of

Saddington as 'the village, estate associated with or called after a man named Sæd(d) or Sada', *v.* **-ingtūn**.

Nicholaus de Moeles held the manor in 1316 Ipm and is the source of the uniquely recorded affix.

BARFORD HOUSE FM (BARFOOT LODGE 2½"), *Barfoote* 1601 *Terrier*, *Barefoote* 1638 *ib*, cf. *Barfoot Common* 1770 *EnclA* (*v.* **commun**), *Barfoot Bit* 1918 Sale (*v.* **bit**), *Top Barford Close* 1918 ib, *v.* **berg**, **fōt**. BREACH FM, *Breach* 1601, 1679, 1700, 1724, 1745 *Terrier*, cf. *Breach Close* m.17 *ib*, *Breach Feild* 1601, 1638 *ib* (*v.* **feld**; one of the great open-fields of the township, later called Mill Fd *infra*), *v.* **brēc**. CEDAR LODGE FM, 1953 Sale, *v.* **loge**. THE CEDARS. THE CHESTNUTS. FLECKNEY RD, Fleckney lying just over one mile to the north-west. FLECKNEY TUNNEL, popularly known as Saddington Tunnel, a half mile long and built c.1794 to carry the former Union Canal. THE GRANGE (local), *The Grange* 1925 Kelly, *v.* **grange**. KIBWORTH RD, Kibworth Beauchamp lying 2 miles to the north-east. MANOR FM, 1956 Sale, *Manor House* 1638 *Terrier*, 1925 Kelly, *v.* **maner**. MOWSLEY RD, Mowsley lying 2 miles to the south-west. OLD RECTORY, *The Rectory* 1925 Kelly, *v.* **rectory**; earlier is *The Parsonage House* 1638, 1724, 1822 *Terrier*, *v.* **personage**. QUEEN'S HEAD (P.H.), *Queen's Head* 1846, 1863, 1877 White, 1925 Kelly. SADDINGTON HALL, 1863 White, *The Hall* 1925 Kelly, *v.* **hall**. SADDINGTON LODGE, 1835 O, *v.* **loge**. SADDINGTON RESERVOIR (local), created in the 1790s to serve Union Canal, later the Grand Union Canal. ST HELEN'S CHURCH, *Church (St Helen)* 1846, 1863, 1877 White, 1925 Kelly; it is earlier recorded as *ecclesie de Sadington* 1220 MHW, 1246 RGros, ~ *de Sadyngton* 1322, 1354 *Pat*. WEIR RD, *v.* **weyour**. WHITE HO.

FIELD-NAMES

Forms in (a) presented without dates are 1973 *Surv*; those dated 1770 are *EnclA*; 1810 are Map; 1908 and 1918 are Sale. Forms throughout dated c.1230 are *Deed*; those dated 1601, 1638, m.17, 1679, 1700, 1724 and 1745 are *Terrier*.

(a) Four ~, Five ~, 8 Acres, Top Eight Acre 1973, the Ten ~ 1918, Eleven Acres 1918, 1973, 14 ~, 16 ~, 50 Acre 1973 (*v.* **æcer**); The Banks, Second Banks (*v.* **banke**); Bansland, Banslin, ~ Mdw (*Bandlands* 1601, 1679, 1700, 1724, 1745, *Bandlandes* 1638, *v.* **bēan**, **land**); Barn Cl 1918 (*v.* **bern**); Basin Mdw (a canal basin at the south-eastern end of the Fleckney Tunnel, for the turning, lading and unlading of barges); Barwell (cf. *Barnewell sicke* 1601, ~ *seeke* 1638, *v.* **sík**; if *Barnewell* is an early stream-name, then *v.* **wella**, with the OE masc. pers.n. *Beorna*, but otherwise it is the surn. *Barnwell* of a family originally from the township of this name, 24 miles to the east in Northants.); Big Cl; Big Fd; The Big Mdw; Blackmoor (1745, *Blakmore* 1601, *Blacke More* m.17, *Blakemore* 1724, *v.* **blæc**, **mōr**[1]); Bloxams (the surn. *Bloxam* in the possessive case, of a family originally from Bloxholm in Lincs.); Little ~, Top ~, Bontley, Big Buntley (*Bontley* 1601, 1638, 1724, *Bontlea* m.17, *Bontlay* 1678, *Bonthley* 1700, *Longebontley* 1601, *Long Bontley* 1638, 1724, ~ *Bonthley* 1700, ~ *Buntly* 1745, *v.* **beonet**, **lēah**); Bottom Mdw (*v.* **bottom**); Bridge Cl (*v.* **brycg**); Browns Allotments (*v.* **allotment**; with the surn. *Brown*); Bullheds (the surn. *Bulled/Bulleid* in the possessive case); Bumpipe Cl, ~ Mdw 1810, ~ Hill Cl 1973 (earlier forms are needed; perh. 'reedy water channel', *v.* **bune**, **pīpe**); Bush Cl 1918 (*v.* **busc**); Butchers Cl (with the surn. *Butcher*); Clump Cl (*v.* **clump**); The Conery (*v.* **coningre**); Cookes Cl, ~ Mdw 1918 (with the surn. *Cook*(*e*)); Cottage Piece 1918 (*v.* **cotage**, **pece**); Coxes Mdw (with the surn. *Cox*); Cow Cl; Cricket Fd (for the game of cricket); Dove Cote Fd 1918 (*v.* **dove-cot**(**e**)); Far Cl; Far Hill; First Mdw; Fishponds (*v.* **fisshe-ponde**); Five Fields (poss. alluding to an original five closes with the hedges grubbed out to make one large field, but poss. a misunderstood surn. *Fifield* in the possessive case, or even, if ancient, the toponymic source of the surn., i.e. OE **fīf-hīd* 'five hides of land'); The Little ~, The Long Flat (*the Flatt* m.17, *v.* **flat**); Flat Mdw (*v.* **flatr**); Fleckney Mdw (Fleckney parish adjoins to the north-west); Flints (the surn. *Flint* in the possessive case); Football Fd (for the game of football); Freemans Common (*v.* **commun**), Freemans Fd (with the surn. *Freeman*, a reflex of OE *frēomann* 'a free-born man'); Big ~, Little Gamble (poss. late altered forms of *Long Grindell* 1601, 1638, ~ *Grindle* 1679, 1724, 1745, *Short Grindell* 1601, 1638, m.17, ~ *Grindle* 1679, 1724, 1745, *v.* **grendel**; otherwise with the surn. *Gamble* (common in Leics.), a reflex of the ON masc. pers.n. *Gamall* (ODan *Gamal*)); Garden Cl (*v.* **gardin**; land used for horticulture); First ~, Second ~, Third Glebe (*v.* **glebe**); Bottom Gorse, Top Gorse Lane 1918, 1973 (*v.* **gorst**); The Grass Fd (*v.* **græs**; pasture or meadow land); Gravel Hill Cl 1810 (*Gravill Hill* m.17), Big Gravel Hole 1918 (*v.* **hol**[1]) (*v.* **gravel**); Great Cl; Green Lane (*v.* **grēne**[1]); The Grove (*v.* **grāf**); Handpost Mdw 1918 (*v.* **handpost**; land near a signpost); Harolds Cl (with the surn. *Har*(*r*)*old*); Hayfield (*v.* **hēg**); Hill Cl (cf. *agaynst the hyll* 1601, *against the hill* 1638, *v.* **hyll**); Lower Hilly Cl (*v.* **hyllig**); Home Fd 1918, 1973, Home Mdw 1973 (*v.* **home**); Far ~, Near Hook (*v.* **hōc**); Horse Cl; House Cl 1918, 1973; Hut Cl 1810, 1973, Double ~ ~ 1918 (*v.* **duble**), Little Hut Cl 1918 (*v.* **hut**); Island Mdw (*v.* **island**; used of land completely surrounded by other fields); Lammas Cl (1745, *v.* **lammas**); Big ~, Little ~, Top Limborough (*Linbarrow* 1601, 1638, *Lynbarrow* m.17, *Limboro* 1679, *Limbrow* 1700, *Limborow* 1724, *Limborough* 1745), Limborough Fd 1770 (*Linbarrow* ~, *Lynbarrow Feild* 1601, *Limbarrow* ~ 1638, *Lymbarrowe Feild* m.17, *Limboro* ~ 1679, *Limbro* ~ 1700, *Limborow* ~ 1724, *Limborough Field* 1745, *v.* **feld**; one of the great open-fields), Limborough Hill (*Linbarrowhyll* 1601, *Linbarrow hill* 1638, m.17, *v.* **hyll**) (*v.* **līn**, **berg**); Little Fd; Long Mdw 1918; Meadow Head 1918 (*v.* **hēafod**) (*the meddow* 1601, *the meadow* 1638, *the Meade close* 1638, *v.* **mēd** (**mēdwe** obl.sg.)); Middle Mdw; Mill Fd 1770, Milfield 1846, 1863, 1877 White (*Milne Feild* m.17, (*the*) *Mill Field* 1679, 1700, 1724, 1745, *v.* **feld**; one of the great open-fields, earlier called *Breach Feild*, *v.* Breach Fm *supra*), Mill Hill (*v.* **myln**); Northfield; The Old Plough Fd (*v.* **plōg**); the

Over Mdw 1770 ((*the*) *Ouer meadow* 1679, 1700, *the Upper meadow* 1724, *v.* **uferra**); Peashill 1908, 1973, Pessell 1973 (*Pessell* 1601, 1638, 1700, 1745, *Peassell* m.17, *Pessel* 1679, *Pessil* 1724, *Short Pessil* 1724, ~ *Pessel* 1745), Peasehill Fd 1770 (*Pessell* ~ 1601, 1638, *Peassell Feild* m.17, *Pessel* ~ 1679, 1745, *Pessell Field* 1700, 1724, *v.* **feld**; one of the great open-fields) (*v.* **pise**, **hyll**); Pen Cl 1973, ~ Mdw 1908 (*v.* **penn**[2]); Planks 1918 (*v.* **planke**); Podell, Podhill (*Podall* 1601, *Podel* 1679, *Podell* 1700, *Podwell* 1724, 1745, *Podwel layes* 1674 (*v.* **leys**), *v.* **pode**, **wella**; also recorded as Podehill in adjoining Mowsley f.ns. (a)); Pond Cl 1918 (*v.* **ponde**); Poor Cl (*v.* **pouer(e)**; land dedicated to poor relief or charity); Portland Mdw (*v.* **port**[2], **land**; presum. in some sort a former perquisite of Leicester Borough; otherwise, but less likely, a market site); Pump Fd (*v.* **pumpe**); Reservoir Mdw (*v.* Saddington Reservoir *supra*); Robinsons Cl 1918 (with the surn. *Robinson*); Lower ~, Riddlety Knob (a severely distorted modern form of *Littledale nob* 1679, 1700, *Litleton* ~ (sic) 1724, *Littleton nob* 1745, *v.* **lȳtel**, **dalr**, **knob** and *Little dale hill* in f.ns. (b)); Little ~, Lower ~, Top Ringshill 1908 (*Ringsow* 1638, *Ringshaw* m.17, *Rinso* 1679, 1700, *Ringsaw* 1724, 1745; either 'circular copse' (*v.* **hring**, **sceaga**) or 'Hring's hill-spur' (*v.* **hōh**; with the OE masc. pers.n. *Hring*)); Roly Mount (*v.* **mont**; either with the surn. *Rowley* or with a toponym, *v.* **rūh**, **lēah**); Roundhills (*v.* **round**, **hyll**); Row Acre, Rolliker (*Rowellcar* 1679, ~ *layes* 1700, *Rowelcar*(*e*) *Lays* 1724, ~ *Leys* 1745 (*v.* **leys**), *v.* **rūh**, **hyll**, **æcer**); Top Sandpit Mdw (*v.* **sand-pytt**); Far ~, First ~, Second ~, Third ~, Fourth Seeds (*v.* **sǣd**; used of grasses sown for one year's mowing or grazing, as distinguished from permanent pasture); The Slang, Bottom ~ ~, Slang Mdw (*v.* **slang**); Spinney Cl 1810, ~ Mdw 1973 (*v.* **spinney**); Strettons Cl, Little Stretton (with the surn. *Stretton*); Three-cornered Fd 1918, 1973 (*v.* **three-cornered**); Top Cl; Top Fd; Townsend Cl, Lower Townsend (*v.* **tūn**, **ende**); Tunnel Fd, Tunnel Mdw (*v.* Fleckney Tunnel *supra*); Tween ~, Twin Brooks (*Betweene the Brookes* 1601, 1638, *Betwene brookes* 1679, *Betwixt*(*e*) (*the*) *brookes* m.17, 1700, *Betwixt Brooks* 1724, 1745, *v.* **betwēonan**, **betwixt**, **brōc**); Underhill Cl (*v.* **under**, **hyll**); Warwick Hill, ~ Spinney (*v.* **spinney**) (with the surn. *Warwick*); Washpit Cl 1908, ~ Mdw 1973 (cf. *Washpit Bridge* 1745, *v.* **wæsce**, **pytt**); Waterman Hill (with the surn. *Waterman*, cf. *Wilke Waterman* 1196 RFL of Leics.); Weir ~, Wire Cl 1973, Bottom ~ ~, Top Wire Bit 1918 (*v.* **bit**) (*v.* Weir Rd *supra*); Well Cl (*v.* **wella**); Wilsons Cl (with the surn. *Wilson*); Bottom ~, Top Wrangland 1810 (*Wrangland*(*e*)*s* 1601, 1638, 1679, 1724, *Ranglandes* m.17, *Ranglands* 1700, 1724, 1745, *Wrangland way* 1601, 1638 (*v.* **weg**), *v.* **wrang**, **land**).

(b) *in Angulo* 1327 SR (p) (with MLat *angulus* 'a nook, a corner'; may relate to Far ~, Near Hook in f.ns. (a)); *Ash Close* 1679, 1724, 1745, ~ *Cloase* 1700, *Ashe* ~ 1601, *Ash furlong* 1638, 1679, 1700, 1724, 1745 (*v.* **furlang**) (*v.* **æsc**); *Assecroft* c.1230 (*v.* **æsc**, **croft** and *Hescroft*(*e*), *infra*); *Thomas Bakers Closse* m.17; *Barrett* ~ 1601, *Barrettes Leas* 1638 (*v.* **leys**; with the surn. *Barrett*); *Beamash* 1601, *Beamashe* 1638, m.17 (perh. alluding to an ash-tree from which stout timbers could be cut or even to a boundary-cross fixed to an ash-tree, *v.* **bēam**, **æsc**); *Blackett*(*e*)*s Close* 1601, 1638 (with the surn. *Blackett*); *the Brooke* 1601, 1745, *Brooke Leasure* 1601, 1679, *Brook Leasow* 1638, m.17, ~ *Leashure* 1724, ~ *Leisure* 1745 (*v.* **lǣs** (**lǣswe** gen.sg., dat.sg.)); *Callow hill* 1601, 1638 *et passim* to 1745, *behynd Callowhyll* 1601, *backside* (*of*) *Callow hill* 1679, 1700 (*v.* **bak-side**) (*v.* **calu**, **hyll**); *Catteswell* 1601 (*v.* **cat(t)**, **wella**); *Clarkwell Lays* 1724 (*v.* **clerk**, **wella**, **leys**); *Betweene the Closes* 1601, *Betwixt the Cloosen* 1724 (*v.* **betwēonan**, **betwixt**,

clos(**e**), **closing**; it is uncertain whether *cloosen* represents a local dial. pl. in -*en*, cf. *barlie haden*, *Crook haden* etc. in Burton Overy f.ns. (b)); *the Crooke* 1601, 1638, 1679, 1700, ~ *Crook* 1724 (*v*. **crōc**); *Crosse furlong* 1601, m.17 (*v*. **cross**, **furlang**; of *Breach Feild*); (*the*) *Dammes* 1601, 1638 (*v*. **damme**); *Debdale* m.17 (*v*. **dēop**, **dalr**); *Dodsicke* 1601, 1638, m.17, 1679, *Dodsick* 1700, 1724, 1745 (*v*. **sík**; either with **dodde**, or with the OE masc. pers.n. *Dodd*(*a*) or with its surn. reflex *Dod*(*d*)(*s*)); *Elrenstub'* c.1230, *Elderstubbes* 1601, *Elderstobes* 1638, *elder stubs* 1679, *Elder Stubes* 1700, *Elder Stubbs* 1745 (*v*. **ellern**, **stubb**); *Mr Facons hedge* 1638, *Facons hadland* 1724 (*v*. **hēafod-land**); *Flekeneydikes* c.1230 (*v*. **dík**), *Fleckney meare* 1601, m.17, *fleckny* ~ 1679, *Fleckney meere* 1700, ~ *Mear* 1724, ~ *Meer* 1745 (*v*. (**ge**)**mǣre**; Fleckney parish adjoins to the north-west); *Germundebrig* c.1230 (*v*. **brycg**, **bryggja**; formally either with the ContGerm masc. pers.n. *Germund* or with the ON masc. pers.n. *Geirmundr*, but note the 13th-cent. *Gurmund*- spellings for adjacent Gumley); *Gosclif* c.1230 (*v*. **gōs**, **clif**); *Gosseley hyll* 1601, *Gosley Hill* m.17, 1679, 1700, 1724, *Gostley hill* 1745, *Gosseley wea* 1601, *Gosley way* 1638 (*v*. **weg**) (most prob. a development of the previous f.n. *Gosclif*, in the sequence *Gosclif* > **Goslif* > *Gos*(*se*)*ley*, with **hyll** added; but if separate toponym, then *v*. **gorst** (dial. *gosse*), **lēah**); *Gumley ford* 1601, *Gumbley foard* 1724, ~ *Ford* 1745 (*v*. **ford**; Gumley parish adjoins to the south-east, the ford now lost beneath Saddington Reservoir); *Hamerill Hookes* m.17 (*v*. **hamer**, **hyll**, **hōc**; contrast with Far Hill *supra*); *Hendicke* m.17 (*v*. **henn**, **dík**); *Hescroft*(*e*) 1601, 1638, *Hease Craft* m.17, *Hares croft* 1724, *Long Hescroft*(*e*) 1601, 1638, ~ *harescraft* 1679, ~ *hearscrafte* 1724, *Short harescrafte* 1679, ~ *hears croft* 1724, ~ *Hares Croft* 1745 (poss. late reflexes of *Assecroft*, *supra*, but otherwise *v*. **hǣs**, **croft**; later confused with **hara**); *the hie medow* 1601, *the high meadow* 1638 (*v*. **hēah**[1]); *the hollow forowes* 1601, *hallow furrowes* 1638, 1679, 1700, *hollow thurrowes* m.17, ~ *furrows* 1724, 1745 (*v*. **holh**, **furh**); *The Homestall* 1723 (*v*. **hām-stall**); *Thomas Hortons headland* 1601 (*v*. **hēafod-land**), *Mr Ortons pen* 1679, *Bartholomew Hortons pen* 1700 (*v*. **penn**[2]); *John Johnsons headland*, ~ ~ *headley* 1601 (*v*. **headley**); *Kawelhul* c.1230 (*v*. **cawel**, **hyll**); *Kibworth brook*(*e*) 1601, 1638 *et passim* to 1745, *Kibworth hyll* 1601, ~ *hill* 1638, m.17 *et passim* to 1745 (Kibworth Beauchamp parish adjoins to the north-east); *Langelond* c.1230, *Longeland* 1601, *Longland* 1638 (*v*. **lang**[1], **land**); *Lawton Brook* 1745, *Lorton* ~ 1724, *Lawton Way* 1745 (*v*. **weg**) (Laughton lies 2 miles to the south); *Littell dale hill* 1601, *Littledale hill* 1638 (*v*. **lȳtel**, **dalr**, **hyll**; restyled *Littledale nob* by 1679, *v*. Riddlety Knob in f.ns. (a)); *Long hades* 1724, 1745 (*v*. **hēafod**); *Long furlong* 1601, 1638 (*v*. **furlang**); *Long roods* 1638 (*v*. **rōd**[3]); *William Manses Cloase* 1700 (*v*. **clos**(**e**)); *Michilburg* c.1230 (*v*. **micel**, **berg**); *Milnepol* c.1230 (*v*. **myln**, **pōl**[1]); *Moldhils* 1601 (*v*. **moldhille**); *the Mores* 1601, *the Moores* 1638, 1679, 1700, *the Moors* 1724, 1745, (*the*) *Upper Moors*, *Moors Close* 1724, 1745 (*v*. **mōr**[1]); *Mousle Meare* 1601, *Mowsley mere* 1638 (*v*. (**ge**)**mǣre**; Mowsley parish adjoins to the south-west); *Nether medow* 1679, *the Neather* ~ 1700, 1724, *the Nether Meadow* 1745; *Pagedole* 1601, 1638, 1745, *Padg dole* 1724 (*v*. **dāl**; with the surn. *Page*); *Quen furlong*(*e*) 1601, 1638, m.17, *Queenes furlong* 1679, *Quens furlonge* 1700 (*v*. **furlang**; in 1066, Saddington belonged to Queen Edith, wife of Edward the Confessor, and remained hers until her death in 1075 when it became the property of William I and this f.n. may be a memory of Queen Edith (*v*. **cwēn**); otherwise with the surn. *Queen*, since **cwene** 'a woman' is most unlikely as the specific); *Sauerland* 1601 (*v*. **sūr**, **land**); *Sawpittes* 1601, 1638, m.17, *Sawpits* 1679,

1724, 1745 (*v.* **saw-pytt**); *Severalland* 1638 (*v.* **severall, land**); *Seueshouhille* c.1230 (*v.* **hōh**, **hyll**; the first el. appears to be an OE masc. pers.n. in the possessive case, but nothing is obvious; perh. an ancient *Sceaf* may be thought of, while ON **sef** 'reed, sedge' with a second el. **haugr** is unlikely here); *Sheasbe meare* 1601, *Sheasby mear* 1700, 1724, *Shearsby meer* 1745 (*v.* **(ge)mǣre**; Shearsby parish adjoins to the west); *Smalethorne* 1601, *Small thorne* m.17, *Small Thorns* 1724, 1745 (*v.* **smæl, þorn**); *Smeeton hedge* 1679, 1700 (a parish boundary marker), *Smeeton sandpittes* 1601 (*v.* **sand-pytt**) (Smeeton Westerby parish adjoins to the east); *Snelistoft* c.1230 (*v.* **toft**; either with the OE masc. pers.n. *Snell* or with its surn. reflex *Snell*); *Stockewell* 1601, ~ *Leyes* m.17, *Stockwel* ~ 1679, *Stockwell layes* 1700, ~ *Leys* 1745 (*v.* **leys**) (*v.* **stocc**, **wella**); *next the Stone* 1638 (*v.* **stān**; a furlong beside a prob. boundary marker); *Thichethirne* c.1230 (*v.* **þicce**[2], **þyrne**); *the Three Lands furlong* 1724 (*v.* **þrēo**, **land**, **furlang**); *Towel(l)s* 1601, 1638 (*v.* **tū**, **wella**); *the towne land* 1601 (*v.* **tūn**); *Wakelow* 1601, *under Wakely* 1638, 1700, *Wakele* m.17, *Wakley* 1724 (*v.* **wacu**, **hlāw**); *Watermylhyll* 1601, *Watermill hill* 1638, m.17 *et passim* to 1745 (*v.* **water-mylne**); *Wellcoles* 1601, *Welcol(e)s* 1601, 1700, 1724, *Wellcolls* 1638, 1745, *Wel(l)coles* m.17, *Wellcoles* 1724 (*v.* **wella**, **cole**); *Whitland* m.17, *Witland* ~ 1601, *Whitland sicke* 1638 (*v.* **sík**) (*v.* **hwīt**, **land**; in eModE, *white* 'infertile' may be contrasted with *black* 'fertile').

Scraptoft

SCRAPTOFT

Scrapetoft 1043 (15) KCD 916 (S 1000), 1200 Cur (p), 1205 Fine *et freq* to 1332 Pat, 1348 *RTemple et passim* to 1371 (p), 1394 Pat (p)
Scraptofte 1043 (15) KCD 939 (S 1226), *Scraptoft* 1276 RH, 1278 Dugd *et passim* to 1497 *Deed*, 1510 *Rental et freq*
Scrapentot 1086 DB
Screpetoft 1191, 1192 P *et freq* to 1201, 1202 ib

Possibly 'Skrápi's homestead, curtilage', *v.* **toft**; with the ON masc. pers.n. *Skrápi*. However, also possible as the specific is ON **skrap** 'scraps, scrapings', perhaps referring to the produce of arid, barren soil (*v.* Lindkvist 122, 221). Lindkvist notes Norw dial. *skrapmark* 'land thinly covered by grass'. The settlement lies on a small area of sand and gravel overlying the predominant Boulder Clay.

ALL SAINTS' CHURCH, *Church (All Saints)* 1846, 1863, 1877 White, 1925 Kelly; it is earlier recorded as *ecclesie de Scrapetoft* 1220 MHW, 1237 RGros. Note also *the Church Yard* 1704, 1709, 1712 *Terrier*, *v.* **churchyerd**. BEEBY RD, Beeby lying 2 miles to the north-east. CHURCH HILL, with reference to All Saints' Church *supra*. COVERT LANE, *v.* **cover(t)**. HALL FM, formerly relating to Scraptoft Hall *infra*. HAMILTON LANE, Hamilton lying one mile to the north-west. KEYHAM LANE, 1830 *Surv*; Keyham lies 1½ miles to the north-east. LODGE FM. MAIN ST is *the Town Street* 1745 *Terrier*, *v.* **tūn**. THE MOUNT, 1835 O, 1850 *TA*, *v.* **mont**; the motte of an early castle. NETHER HALL, ~ ~ FM, *Nether Hall* 1830 Surv, 1835 O, 1846, 1877 White, 1925 Kelly, *v.* **neoðera**, **hall**. SCRAPTOFT BROOK. SCRAPTOFT GORSE, 1835 O, 1850 *TA*, *v.* **gorst**; the early Gorse lies a half mile to the north-west of its present site. SCRAPTOFT HALL, 1804 Nichols, 1863, 1877 White, 1925 Kelly; it is *Upper Hall* 1835 O, 1846 White, *v.* **upper**, **hall**. SCRAPTOFT HILL FM, 1835 O, cf. *The Hills* 1846 White. SCRAPTOFT LODGE, *v.* **loge**. SCRAPTOFT LONG SPINNEY, *The Long Spinney* 1835 O, *v.* **spinney**.

SCRAPTOFT RISE, *v.* **rise**. SNOW'S LODGE (2½"), *v.* **loge**, cf. *John Snow, farmer* 1863 White. SQUARE SPINNEY, 1850 *TA*, with **squar(e)** (of shape), but earlier designated *The Squires Spinny* 1835 O, *v.* **squire**, **spinney**. THORNE LODGE, 1925 Kelly; with the surn. *Thorne*. VICARAGE HO., *The Vicarage House* 1704, 1708, 1708 (18), 1712 *Terrier*, 1925 Kelly, *The Vicarage* 1877 White, *v.* **vikerage**. WIGLEY'S ARMS (P.H.) (lost), named from the Wigley family, formerly of Scraptoft Hall, as *Sir Edward Wigley* d.1710 and *James Wigley* d.1765, monuments in All Saints' Church *supra*.

No early forms have been found for the following street-names: ARCHWAY RD, BARRY RD, BOWHILL GROVE, BRIAR RD, BRIARFIELD DRIVE, BROOK RD, CARDINAL'S WALK, CRANBROOK RD, CRAYFORD WAY, CROSS KEYS GREEN, CROYLAND GREEN, THE DRIVE, EDDYSTONE RD, ELSTREE AVE, GREENBANK RD, HALL RD, HINCKS AVE, HOMESTONE GARDENS, IVYCHURCH CRESC, KEAYS WAY, KINSDALE DRIVE, KIRKWALL CRESC, LIMEHURST RD, LYMINGTON RD, LYNMOUTH RD, MAPLIN RD, MILNROY RD, MOORFIELDS, NEW ROMNEY CRESC, NURSERY RD, PARKSTONE RD, PORTCULLIS RD, PULFORD DRIVE, RAYLEIGH GREEN, RINGWOOD RD, ST AUSTELL RD, SELBY AVE, STATION RD, STOCKS RD, STORNAWAY RD, SUNBURY GREEN, THURNCOURT RD, WEAVER RD, WREFORD CRESC.

FIELD-NAMES

In (a), forms dated 1750 are Nichols; those dated 1781 are *Map*; 1825 are *Terrier*; 1830 are *Surv*; 1835 are O; 1850 are *TA*. Forms throughout dated 1332 and 1381 are SR; those dated 1348 are *RTemple*; 1607 are Ipm; 1623, 1658, 1708[1] and 1726 are *Deed*; 1704, 1708[2], 1708 (18), 1712, 1742 and 1745 are *Terrier*.

(a) Five ~ 1830, Nine ~ 1781, 1830, Ten Acres 1781 (*v.* **æcer**); Barn Cl 1830 (*v.* **bern**); Bartons Cl, ~ Mdw, Barton Hill, Barton Lane Piece 1850 (*v.* **pece**) (either with the surn. *Barton* or with **bere-tūn**); Bishops Cl 1830 (with the surn. *Bishop*); Blatchetts Cl 1850 (with the surn. *Blatchett*, cf. Blatchett's Cl in Shangton f.ns. (a)); Bleak Hill, ~ ~ Mdw 1830, 1850 (*Bleakhill* 1745, *v.* **bleikr**); Bottom Cl 1850 (*v.* **bottom**); Brickyard, ~ Cl 1850 (*v.* **brike-yard**); Brothertons Cl 1830 (with the surn. *Brotherton*); Bullstake Cl 1830 (*v.* **bula**, **staca**; records a field with a post to which bulls were once fastened for baiting, cf. Bulstake Bridge, Ox 35 and *Bulstake*, Wa 27); Bush(e)y Hill 1830, 1850, Bushy Hill Cl 1830, Bush(e)y Hill Mdw 1830, 1850, Nether Bushy Hill 1830, Over Bushey Hill 1850 (*v.* **uferra**), Middle Bushey Cl 1850 (*Gallow Hill or Bushy Close* 1708[1], *v.* **busshi** and *Gallow Hill*, *infra*); Bottom ~ ~,

Top ~ ~, Second ~ ~, Third Charity Cl 1850 (rents of this land provided funds for support of the village poor); Conery 1825, 1850, Cunnery 1830, Great Conery 1850, Phipps Coneries 1825 (with the surn. *Phipps*, from *Phip*, a pet-form of *Philip*) (*the Cunnery* 1708[2], 1708 (18), *the Cunery* 1712, *the Great* ~, *the Little Conerie* 1742, 1745, *Cunningree Close* 1607, *the Cunnery* ~ 1704, 1708 (18), *the Cunery Close* 1712, *v.* **coningre**); Cow Cl 1830, 1850 (1708[1]); Crabtree Cl 1830, 1850 (*v.* **crabtre**); Croxtons Cl 1781, ~ Great Cl, ~ Little Cl, ~ Mdw 1830, Crowsons Cl, ~ Mdw, ~ Big Mdw 1850 (with the surn. *Croxton* of a family no doubt originally from South Croxton, 4 miles to the north-east, *v.* Lei **3** 72); Davys Cl 1830 (with the surn. *Davy*); Depdale 1850, Nether ~, Over Depdale 1830 (*v.* **uferra**), Depdale Cl 1750, 1850, ~ Mdw 1830, 1850 (*v.* **dēop**, **dalr**); Dovecot or Orchard Cl 1830 (*v.* **dove-cot**(**e**) and Orchard Cl *infra*); Far Mdw, ~ ~ Top 1830 (*v.* **topp**); Fern Hill 1781, 1850, ~ ~ Mdw 1850 (*Fernehill Close* 1623, *v.* **fearn**); Foxcover 1830, 1850, ~ Cl 1850 (*v.* **fox**, **cover**(**t**)); Further Cl 1850 (cf. Nearer Cl *infra*); Glebe Land 1781 (*v.* **glebe**); Goose Acres 1850, ~ ~ Cl 1830 (*v.* **gōs**, **æcer**); Great ~ ~, Little Gorsey Cl 1830, 1850 (*v.* **gorstig**); Gravelpit Cl 1781, 1830 (*v.* **gravel**, **pytt**); (The) Great Meadow 1825, 1830 (1781); Greens Mdw 1830, 1850 (with the surn. *Green*); Hollands Cl 1830, 1850, Top Hollands Cl 1781, Great ~ ~, Little Hollands Cl 1850, Hollands Mdw 1830 (with the surn. *Holland*); Home Cl 1781, 1830, Lower ~ ~, Upper Home Cl 1825, Far Home Cl 1830 (*v.* **home**); Horse Cl 1781, 1850, Great Horse Cl 1781; Great ~ ~, Little House Cl 1830; Hovel Cl 1850 (*v.* **hovel**); Hursts Cl 1830, 1850 (with the surn. *Hurst*); Large Close Mdw 1830; Middle ~, Nether ~, Upper Leys 1830, Bottom ~, Top Leys 1850 (*Lower* ~, *Middle* ~, *Upper Leys* 1726, *v.* **leys**); Lime Kiln Mdw 1850 (*v.* **lim-kilne**); Little Mdw 1830; Long Mdw 1830, Long Cl, ~ ~ Mdw 1850; The Meadow, Meadow Cl 1830; Middle Cl 1781, Far ~ ~, Near Middle Cl 1830; Moat Cl, ~ Mdw 1850 (either with **mote** or **mōt**, *v.* Spell Cl *infra*); Mount Cl 1830, 1850 (*v.* The Mount *supra*); Muckhill Cl, ~ Mdw 1830, 1850, ~ Spinney 1850 (*v.* **spinney**) (*Mucklehill*, ~ *Meadow* 1623, *v.* **micel**, **mycel**, **mikill**, **hyll**; the late form is a reduction of the original, with replacement by **muk**); Nearer Cl 1850 (cf. Further Cl *supra*); Nether Cl, ~ ~ Mdw 1781, 1830; Nether Hall Cl 1830, ~ ~ Fd 1850 (*v.* Nether Hall *supra*); New Mdw 1830, 1850; New Piece 1830 (*v.* **pece**); Old Seeds 1830, 1850 (*v.* **sǣd**; used in modern f.ns. for areas of sown grass); Orchard Cl 1830 (*v.* **orceard** and Dovecot *supra*); Padgate Cl 1830, 1850 (earlier forms are needed; perh. 'the road infested with frogs', *v.* **padde**, **gata**); Pares Cl, ~ Great Cl, ~ Little Mdw, Pares Three Acres 1830, 1850 (*v.* **æcer**) (with the surn. *Pares*); Parsons Cl (*v.* **persone**); Pen Cl, ~ Corner 1850 (*v.* **corner**) (*v.* **penn**[2]); Picks Cl 1830, 1850, ~ Mdw 1850 (with the surn. *Pick*); Piggins Cl, Piggens Croft 1830 (*v.* **croft**) (either with the surn. *Pigeon* or with **pejon**, alluding to a pigeon-house); Pincham 1830, Bottom ~, Middle Pincham 1850 (*v.* **pinca**, **hamm**); Plowed Cl 1830, Bottom ~ ~, Top ~ ~, First ~ ~, Second ~ ~, Third ~ ~, Fourth Ploughed Cl 1850; Pool Cl 1830, 1850 (*v.* **pōl**[1]); Further ~ ~, Near Road Cl 1825, Miles Road Cl 1830 (with the surn. *Miles*), Bottom ~ ~, Middle ~ ~, Road Cl 1850 (*the Road Closes* 1742, 1745, earlier called *the Highway Closes* 1704, 1708[2], 1708 (18), 1712), Road Mdw 1850 (closes beside a highway); Scraptoft Cl, ~ Green 1850 (cf. *othe grene* 1381 (p), *v.* **grēne**[2]), Scraptoft Hill Cl, ~ Mdw; Best Sheep Cl, 1830, 1850 (*v.* **best**; a complimentary name for very fertile land), Hill ~ ~, Long ~ ~ 1830, Low Sheep Cl 1850 (*v.* **scēp**); Shoulder of Mutton Cl 1830, 1850 (a common f.n. referring to shape); Spell Cl 1830, Spells Cl 1830, 1850, ~ Mdw (perh. with the surn. *Spell*, but poss. is **spell** 'speech, discourse', signifying a meeting-place; note Moat Cl *supra*); New Spinney Cl 1830, Far ~ ~, Spinney End 1850 (*v.* **ende**), Spinney Hill 1830 (*v.* **spinney**); Stubble Cl 1830, 1850 (land upon which stubble was allowed to remain for an unusually long time); Sugar Hill 1781, 1830, 1850 (prob. a complimentary name for 'sweet' land (*v.* **sugere**), but poss. a reduced **Sugar Loaf Hill*, alluding to a hillock resembling a sugar loaf in shape); Tom Thumb 1781 (the reference may be to the nursery tale hero, Tom Thumb, the son of a ploughman who was only as tall as his father's thumb, hence describing a very small plot of land; otherwise the name may be *tom thumb*, that of a small wild flower, especially bird's foot trefoil (*Lotus corniculatus*)); Top Cl 1830, 1850; Top Mdw 1781; Townsend Cl 1850 (*v.* **tūn**, **ende**); Two Pool 1850 (*Two Pool Meadow* 1745, *v.* **tū**, **pōl**[1]); Washpit Mdw 1850 (*v.* **wæsce**, **pytt**); Watery Mdw 1830, 1850 (*v.* **wæterig**); Wigleys Yard 1830 (*v.* **geard** and Wigley's Arms *supra*); Wildman's Mdw 1850 (with the surn. *Wildman*); Willow Bed Cl 1830, 1850 (*v.* **wilig**, **bedd**); Worthingtons Cl 1830 (with the surn. *Worthington* of a family prob. from the township of this name, 18 miles to the north-west).

(b) *the Cottyers* ~ 1704, *the Cottiers Close* 1708[2], 1708 (18), 1712 (*v.* **cottere**); *Gallow Hill* 1708[1] (*v.* **calu**, **hyll** and Bushey Hill *supra*); *Hart Yard Close* 1607 (*v.* **geard**; *Hart* may be the name of a former hostelry); *the Keim Close* 1742, 1745 (an enclosure towards Keyham which lies 1½ miles to the north-east); *Lincroft Leys* 1726 (*v.* **līn**, **croft**, **leys**); *Seven Acres Meadow* 1708[1] (*v.* **æcer**); *Staveleys Close* 1658 (with the surn. *Staveley*); (*land called*) *Wingfeilds* 1745 (prob. the surn. *Wingfield* in the possessive case; otherwise, *v.* **vengi**); *Mr Woodcocks Lands* 1745; *in le Wro* 1332 (p) (*v.* **vrá**).

Shangton

1. SHANGTON

Sanctone 1086 DB (×2), *Sanctona* 1190 × 1204 France
Santone 1086 DB
Sanketon' l.12, e.13 *ShR et passim* to 1295, e.14 *ib*, *Sanketone* 13 *ib*
Scanketon' c.1130 LeicSurv, 1242 RGros *et passim* to l.13 *ShR*, 1299 Ipm, *Scanketona* l.12 *ShR*, *Scanketone* l.13 *ib*, *Scanketun* 13 *ib*, *Scancetona* l.12 *ib*
Schanketon' 1206 Cur, 1242 RGros *et passim* to 1310, 1315 *ShR et freq* to 1360, 1363 *ib et passim* to 1427, 1439 *ib*, *Schanketona* p.1250, 1274 *ib et passim* to 1363, 1378 *ib*, *Schankton'* 1403, 1452 *ib*, 1579 LEpis
Shanketon' 1206 RFinib, m.13 *ShR et passim* to 1330 FA, 1361 Cl
Shankton' 1344 *ShR*, 1352 Fine *et passim* to 1414 Pat, 1428 *ShR* (freq) *et freq* to 1483, 1484 *ib et passim* to 1622 Burton, 1688 LML, *Shancton'* 1410 *Ct*, 1414, 1454 *ShR*, *Shanckton* 1598, 1608, 1612 LML
Schangeton' 1274, 1295 *ShR et passim* to 1444, 1491 *ib*, *Schangton'* 1274 *ib*
Shangeton 1304, 1366 *ShR*, *Shangton* 1466 *ib*, 1535 VE, 1576 LibCl *et freq*, *Shangkton* 1623 ISLR
Saun(e)keton' 1295 *ShR*, *Scaunqeton* 1314, 1315 Cl

'The farmstead, village at the hill-spur', *v*. **scanca**, **tūn**. The township is situated in a valley below a narrow ridge which projects from high ground. OE *scanca* 'a shank, a leg' is here transferred to this configuration of land which bends at its southern end like a foot attached to a leg, *v*. Studies[2] 196. The eventual form of the name Shangton may have been influenced by the adjacent Langton

2. HARDWICK

Herdwic' 1200 Cur (p), 1285, 13, e.14 *ShR*, *Herdwich'* m.13 *ib* (p), *Herdwik'* m.13 (p), 1315 *ib* (p), *Herdwyk'* 1252 Cl, 1374 *ShR et freq* to 1344 *ib*, 1378 Pat, *Herdwyke* 1253 Cl

Herdewic' m.13 (p), 1320 *ShR* (p), 1329 Ipm, *Herdewich'* p.1250 *ShR* (p), 1326 Hastings, *Herdewik'* 1274, 1295 *ShR* (p) *et passim* to 1333 *ib*, 1378 Pat, *Herdewyk'* 1274, 1295 *ShR et passim* to 1392, 1404 Pat, *Herdewyke* 1327 SR (p), 1330 FA, 1361 Pat (p), *Herdeve(y)k* l.13 *ShR* (p), *Herdewek* 1295 (p), 13 *ib*, *Herdehuyc* 13 *ib*
Erdywyk 1426 *ShR*
Hardewyk 1428 *ShR* (freq), 1464 Pat
Hardwyke 1452 *ShR*, *Hardwick* 1659 *Deed*, 1732 LeicW *et freq*
Shangton Hardwick 1846, 1863, 1877 White

'The herd-farm', *v*. **heorde-wīc**. Hardwick is a deserted medieval village.

CONDUIT SPINNEY, 1835 O, 1842 *TA*, *v*. **cundite**, **spinney**. GARTREE ROAD, the Roman *Via Devana* (*v*. Gartree Hundred *supra*) is *Port(e)gate* 1601 *Terrier*, *Porgate* 1606, 1625 *ib*, *v*. **port**[2], **gata**; the highway to the market town of Leicester. HALL FM (THE HALL 2½") is on the site of *the mannor howse of Shankton* 1606 *Terrier*, *v*. **maner**. HARDWICK BRIDGE, 1637 *Bru*, 1835 O, 1846, 1863 White, *Hardwycke brigge* 1460 *Bru*, ~ *bridge* 1625 *Terrier*, *v*. **brycg**; cf. *ad pontem* m.13 *ShR* (p) 'at the bridge' (with MLat *pons* (*pontem* acc.sg)). The bridge carries Gartree Road over the former river *Lipping* at the parish boundary with Shangton. HARDWICK WOOD. HOLT FM, *v*. Shangton Holt *infra*. KATHERINE WHEEL (lost), *the Katherine Wheel Inn* 1693 *Deed*. LONG ACRE, *v*. **æcer**. MANOR COTTAGES, MANOR FM, *v*. Shangton Manor *infra*. ROUGH SPINNEY, *v*. **rūh**, **spinney**. ST NICHOLAS'S CHURCH, *Church (St Nicholas)* 1846, 1863, 1877 White, 1925 Kelly; it is earlier recorded as *ecclesie de Sanketon* 1220 MHW, *ecclesiam de Schanketon* 1242 RGros, ~ *de Sankethon* 1251 ib, *ecclesie de Shankton* 1380 *Pat*, *the Church* 1606 *Terrier*. SHANGTON GRANGE, *v*. **grange**; on the site of the former settlement of Hardwick. SHANGTON HOLT, *Shankton Holt* 1806 Map, 1835 O, *v*. **holt**. SHANGTON LODGE, *v*. **loge**. SHANGTON MANOR is *The Rectory* 1877 White, 1925 Kelly, *v*. **rectory**; earlier is *the parsonag howse* 1606 *Terrier*, *The Parsonage house* 1707 (18), 1745 *ib*, *v*. **personage**.

FIELD-NAMES

Forms in (a) presented without dates are 1969 *Surv*; those dated 1750, 1798, 1800 and 1848 are *Map*; 1835 are O; 1842 are *TA*. Forms throughout dated e.13, m.13, c.1270, 1285, 1295, 1296, l.13, 13, e.14, 1310, 1317, 1320, 1328 and 1452 are *ShR*; those dated 1464 are Pat; 1477 (e.16) are *Charyte*; 1601, 1606, 1625, 1700, 1703, 1708 (18) and 1745 are *Terrier*; 1723 are Nichols; 1732 are LeicW.

(a) Five Acre, Six ~, Eight ~, Nine ~, Ten ~, Eleven ~, Middle Twelve ~, Fourteen ~, Eighteen Acre (*v.* **æcer**); Ash Mdw 1750, 1842, 1969 (*v.* **æsc**); Left ~, Avenue (*v.* **avenue**; closes bordering a former avenue of elm-trees to the south of the village); Back Fd (*v.* **back**); Bakers Cl North, ~ ~ South 1848, Bakers Cl 1969 (with the surn. *Baker*); North Banky Cl, South ~ ~, Great ~ ~, Middle Banky Cl 1848, Bankers Cl 1969 (*v.* **banke**, **-ig**[3]); Barn Hill (*v.* **bern**); Lower ~ ~, Upper Beck Cl 1800, 1969, Beck Cl 1842, Beck Mdw 1800, 1842, 1969 (*v.* **bekkr** and *Becke feilde* in f.ns. (b)); Best Cl (*v.* **best**); Blatchett's Cl (with the surn. *Blatchett*, prob. a palatalized form of *Blackett*; perh. cf. *Robertus Blachet* 1208 Cur); Bryans Homestead 1842 (*v.* **hām-stede**; with the surn. *Bryan*); Church Cl 1800 (*v.* St Nicholas's Church *supra*); Little ~ ~ 1800, Conduit Cl 1842, 1969, Conduit Fd 1969, Great ~ ~, Little ~ ~ 1800, 1842, Conduit Mdw 1969, Little Conduit Mdw Spinney 1842 (*v.* Conduit Spinney *supra*); Cow Cl 1969, Cow Cl East, ~ ~ North, ~ ~ West, Cow Close Mdw 1800, 1842; Dove House ~ 1800, 1842, Duffers Cl (sic) 1969 (*v.* **dove-hous**); First Mdw; Front Fd (*v.* **front**); Furzy Cl 1750, Lower ~ 1800, Furzy Mdw 1800, 1842 (*v.* **fyrsig**); Gartree Bush 1798, 1969 (*v.* **busc**; the late name of the moot-site of the Gartree Hundred *q.v.*, which in the medieval period was called *Mathelou*, *infra*); Gartree Mdw 1800, 1969 (beside Gartree Road, *v. supra*); First ~, Middle ~, Top Glebe (cf. *The Glebe Close* 1700, 1703, *the Glebe Close and Meadow* 1745, *v.* **glebe**); Grazing New Piece (*v.* **grazing**, **pece**); Gravel Pit (*v.* **gravel**, **pytt**); Great Cl; Hall Cl 1800, 1842, First ~ ~, Second Hall Fd 1969 (*v.* The Hall *supra*); Hangings ('land on a steep slope', *v.* **hangende**); Nether ~, Upper Hardwick 1750, 1842 (*The Hardwicks* 1700, 1745, cf. *Hardewyk Clos* 1452, 1464 (*v.* **clos(e)**)), Hardwick Bottom 1835 (*v.* **botm**), Hardwick Lodge 1798 (1732, *v.* **loge**) (*v.* Hardwick *supra*); Nether ~, Upper Holt 1800, 1842, Little Upper Holt 1842, Long Holt 1969, Lower ~ ~, Middle ~ ~, Upper Long Holt 1800, 1842, 1848, Nether ~ ~, Upper Holt Mdw 1800, 1842 (*v.* Shangton Holt *supra*); Home Cl 1800, 1969, ~ Fd 1969 (*v.* **home**); House Cl; Lawn 1800 (*v.* **launde**); Little Cl 1848; Little Mdw 1750; Lodge Cl 1800, Lodge Ground 1750, 1842 (*v.* **grund**) (*v.* Hardwick Lodge *supra*); Lower ~ ~ 1800, Long Mdw 1750; Mair ~ 1750, Meer ~ 1842, 1848, Mare Pen 1969 (*the Mare Pens* 1723), Meer Pen Mdw 1842 (*v.* **(ge)mǣre**, **penn**[2]; at the parish boundary); Marriotts Mdw 1800, 1842 (with the surn. *Marriott*); Nether Ground 1800, 1842, 1969 (*v.* **grund**); Nether Mdw 1800, ~ ~ North, ~ ~ South 1848; New Mdw 1750; New Piece (*v.* **pece**); Over Close Mdw 1848 (*v.* **uferra**); Back Paddock (*v.* **back**), Church ~ (*v.* St Nicholas's Church *supra*), Little ~, Yard Paddock (*v.* **geard**) (*v.* **paddock**); Roadside Fd; Roundhill 1848 (*v.* **round**, **hyll**); Second Mdw; Seed Fd (*v.* **sǣd**; used of grasses sown for one year's mowing or grazing, as distinguished from permanent pasture); Spinney Cl 1848, 1969, Spinney Mdw 1800 (*v.* **spinney**); Three Corner Bit (*v.* **three-corner**, **bit**); Top Fd, ~ Mdw 1800, 1969; Town Fd 1842, 1969, ~ ~ North, ~ ~ South 1800, 1842, Little Town Fd 1800, 1969 (*v.* **tūn**); Bottom ~, Middle ~, Top Townsend 1969, Townsend Ground East, ~ ~ North, ~ ~ West 1800, 1842 (*v.* **tūn**, **ende**); Twofields Mdw, Southward Twofields

1800, 1842 (*v.* **tū** and South Wood Cl *infra*; presum. recording the merging of two separate fields); Upper Mdw 1800, 1969; Lower ~, Upper Washbrook 1800, ~ ~ Mdw 1842, Washbrooks 1969 (*v.* **wæsce**, **brōc**); Wood Cl, North ~ ~, South Wood Cl 1800, Northward Cl, Southward Cl 1842, 1848, Great ~ ~, Northward Fd 1800, 1842 (*v.* **wudu**; these forms appear to belong together, but if not, then *v.* **norðweard**, **sūðweard**).

(b) *Alwordissike* 13 (*v.* **sík**), *Aluuordiswong* 13, *Aylewordewong* 1320 (*v.* **vangr**) (either with an OE masc. pers.n., *Ælfweard* or *Æðelweard*, or with a surn. reflex of either of these, *Alward* or *Aylward*; the pers.ns. became confused in the 12th cent.); *Ash Close* 1723 (*v.* **æsc**); *Bactonishakis* 13 (*v.* **æcer**; with the surn. *Bacton*); *Banelond* 1285 (*v.* **bēan**, **land**); *Barlicrofht* l.13 (*v.* **bærlic**, **croft**); *the Becke feild*(*e*) 1601, 1625 (*v.* **bekkr**, **feld**; one of the great open-fields of the township, also called *the Nether feilde* 1601); *Blakemildehil* 13 (*v.* **blæc**, **mylde**, **hyll**); *le brakis* 13, *brakes furlonge* 1601 (*v.* **furlang**) (*v.* **bracu**); *Breches* e.13, *le Breche* l.13, 13, e.14 (*v.* **brēc**); *Brimbelbrinke*, *brimbilbring* l.13, *brimbilbrinc* 13 (*v.* **brēmel**, **brembel**, **brink**); *the carr* 13 (*v.* **kjarr**); *the East feilde* 1606 (*v.* **ēast**, **feld**; one of the great open-fields, also called *the Nether or Becke feilde* 1601); *Farmanneshill*, *Farmannishyl*, *Faremanneshil*, *Faremanishil* l.13, *faremannishil* 1295, *farmanishil* 13, *Farmanhil* e.14 (*v.* **hyll**; either with the ON masc. pers.n. *Farmann* or with its surn. reflex *Farman*); *le ferdgate* 13 ('the army road', *v.* **ferd**, **gata**; a prehistoric trackway which is also recorded as *le Ferdgate* in Harby (Lei **2** 97); the route ran south to cross the river Wreake at the ford at Melton Mowbray and thence via Burrough on the Hill, Tilton on the Hill, Skeffington and Illston on the Hill to cross Gartree Road in Shangton parish and continue through Kibworth Harcourt, Saddington and Mowsley); *Folewellehil* l.13 (*v.* **hyll**), *Folewellemor* l.13, 13, *Foleuellemor* l.13 (*v.* **mōr**[1]) (*v.* **fūl**, **wella**); *Garbrodelondis* l.13, *Garbidelond'*, *garbodelondes* 13 (*v.* **gorebrode**, **land**); *Grenesclade*, *Greneslade* l.13 (*v.* **grēne**[1], **slæd**); *the grove or spynye* 1601 (*v.* **grāf**, **spinney**); *Hatterwonge* 1601 (*v.* **vangr**; with the surn. *Hatter*, from ME *hattere* 'a maker or seller of hats'); *Harndale* e.13, 13 (*v.* **hæren**, with **dalr** or **deill**; presum. alluding to gravel or gravelly soil); *Heinouhull'* c.1270, *Heynowil* 13, *Heynowhill* 1317 (*v.* **hyll**), *Heynosike* 13 (*v.* **sík**) (*v.* **hægen**, **hōh**); *Heynewelle furlong'* 1317 (*v.* **furlang**), *Henwell* 1601, 1606, 1625, ~ *furlong*(*e*) 1601, 1625 (*v.* **wella**; with **hægen**, which was later replaced by **henn**); *Hengebek* 13 (*v.* **eng**, **bekkr**); *Kergate Furlonge* 1625 (*v.* **kjarr**, **gata**, **furlang**); *Kirkegate* 1285, *Kirkgate* 1601, 1606 (*v.* **kirkja**, **gata** and St Nicholas's Church); *toward Lipping* e.14 (*v.* **tōweard**; *Lipping* is an old Anglian river-name, poss. derived from the Germanic root **leib* 'to pour, to flow'; *v.* PN -ing 201 and Kristian Hald, 'Angles and Vandals', *Classica et Medievalia*, IV, Fasc. 1, Copenhagen 1941, 66–7); *le longewold'* c.1270 (*v.* **lang**[1], **wald**); *Lundhul* 13, *Lundhyl* e.14 (*v.* **lundr**, **hyll**); *via de Mathelou* (with MLat *via* 'a road'), *Mathelehougate*, *Melhougate* l.13 (×2), *Melogate* 13 (*v.* **gata**) ('the assembly or speech headland', *v.* **mæðel**, **hōh**; the moot-site of the Gartree Hunded, which was later known as Gartree Bush *supra*); *Medewelondis*, *Medewelond'*, *Meduelondes* l.13, *Medelond'* 1328, *medes landes*, *Meedlands*, ~ *furlonge* 1625 (*v.* **furlang**) (*v.* **mēd** (**mēdwe** obl.sg.), **land**); *the Midle feild*(*e*) 1601, 1625 (*v.* **middel**, **feld**; one of the great open-fields, also called *the West feild* 1606); *Millhill* 1601 (*v.* **myln**, **hyll**); *Muclecroft* e.14 (*v.* **micel**, **mycel**, **croft**); *the Nether feilde* 1601 (*v.* **neoðera**, **feld**; also called *the Becke feilde* 1601); *the newclose stile*, *at the stile* 1606 (*v.* **stigel**); *the Northe feilde* 1606 (*v.* **norð**, **feld**;

earlier called *the thirde feilde*); *Oxepol* 1296, l.13 (*v*. **oxa**, **pōl**[1]); *Peysehil* m.13, *Pesehil* l.13, *Peas(e)hill furlonge* 1601, 1606, *Peasewell furlong* 1625 (*v*. **furlang**), *Peseylmor* 13 (*v*. **mōr**[1]) (*v*. **pise**, **hyll**); *Portegate* ~ 1601, *Porgate furlonge* 1625 (*v*. **furlang** and Gartree Road *supra*); *Schort(e)furlongis*, *Sortefurlonges* l.13, *Scortfurulongis* 13 (*v*. **sc(e)ort**, **furlang**); *Sirichesike* l.13 (*v*. **sík**), *Sirichiswong* l.13 (*v*. **vangr**; with the OE masc. pers.n. *Sigerīc*); *þe smalesike* l.13 (*v*. **þe**, **smæl**, **sík**); *Smethemeduis* 1295 (*v*. **smēðe**[1], **mēd** (**mēdwe** obl.sg.)); *the Spyny(e)* ~ 1601, 1606, *the Spinney furlonge* 1625 (*v*. **spinney**, **furlang**); (*le*) *Stangate* m.13, l.13, 13, e.14, *Stanegate* 1295, *Stongate* 13 (*v*. **stān**, **gata**; referring to the Roman *Via Devana*, *v*. Gartree Road *supra*); *Stapillowil* 13, *Stapilhouhil'* 1320, *Staplehill* 1601, 1606, *Stablehill* 1625 (*v*. **stapol**, **hōh**, **hyll**; later with the medial *hōh* discontinued); *Stillepol* 13, *Stillepolholm* l.13 (*v*. **holmr**) (*v*. **stille**, **pōl**[1]); *under le sty* l.13 ((‘the land) beneath the path’, *v*. **under**, **stīg**); *the thirde feilde* 1601 (*v*. **thride**, **feld**; one of the great open-fields, later *the Northe feilde*; it is very doubtful whether *thirde* was anything but a late Terrier style); *Thogates*, *Tuogates* l.13 (*v*. **tū**, **gata**); *Tocharsike* 13 (*v*. **sík**; perh. with the Anglo-Scand masc. pers.n. *Tōka* or with ON *Tóki* (ODan *Toki*), but the medial *-ar-* may point rather to a poor form of ON *Þorgeirr* (ODan *Thorger* > *Turgar*) (*v*. Feilitzen 393) or influence from it. As a surn., *Tochar* is recorded in Scotland from 1821 to 1868 Census); *Townhill* 1601, 1606, *Towne hill* 1625 (*v*. **tūn**); *uestmedue* l.13 (*v*. **west**, **mēd** (**mēdwe** obl.sg.)); *le Wadsike* 13 (*v*. **wād**, **sík**); *le Waud* 13, *le Woylgate* e.14 (*v*. **gata**) (*v*. **wald**); *West brooke* 1625 (*v*. **brōk**); *Westcroftes* m.13 (*v*. **west**, **croft**); *the West feild* 1606 (*v*. **west**, **feld**; one of the great open-fields, also called *the Midle feilde*, *supra*); *Wetehil* 1285, 13, *Wethehul* 1310, *Wheatwell furlonge* 1601, 1606 (*v*. **furlang**) (*v*. **hwǣte**, **hyll** (later confused with **wella**)).

Slawston

1. SLAWSTON

Slagestone 1086 DB, *Slagestuna* 12 (e.15) *BelCartB*, *Slaghstuna* Hy 1 (1333) Ch, Hy 2 (e.14) *BelCartA*, Hy 2 (e.15) *BelCartB*, *Schlaghestunia* e.12 (e.15) *ib*

Slachestone 1086 DB

Slaueston' c.1130 LeicSurv, c.1250 (1404) *Laz* (p), 1308 Ipm, 1309 Cl

Slauston' c.1130 LeicSurv, e.13 *Peake*, 1220 MHW *et freq* to 1507 Ipm, 1510 Visit *et passim* to 1585 LEpis, 1610 Speed, *Slaustona* e.13 *Peake*, *Slaustone* 1274 (1579), 1276 (1579) *LRoll*

Slastone 1225 RHug, l.13 *Peake* (p), *Slaston'* 1226 Cur, 1395 (16) *SlCart*, 1447 *Peake*

Slaweston' 1238 RGros, 1242 Fees *et passim* to 1304 (16), 1306 (16) *SlCart et freq* to 1471 *Hazlerigg*, 1473 *Peake et passim* to 1514 CoPleas, 1528 Visit

Schlawestone 1232 RHug, *Sclawiston'* a.1250 (1404) *Laz* (p), *Sclauston'* 1359 *Wyg* (p), 1468, 1493 Pat

Slawston 1336, 1338 *Peake et passim* to 1501 *Wyg*, 1511 Ipm *et freq*

Slawson 1550, 1551 *Peake*, 1585 LEpis

Probably 'Slagr's village, estate', *v.* **tūn**. The ON masc. pers.n. *Slagr* appears to be an original early by-name, either from *slægr* 'sly, cunning' or, less likely, from *slagr* 'a blow, a stroke'. Slawston may well be a former Anglo-Saxon settlement appropriated by a Scandinavian from the Viking army which disbanded in the region in 877 rather than a later manorial creation. It is close to Blaston, a township probably with another such OE/Scand hybrid name which could represent similar appropriation.

Note the typical 16th- and 17th-cent. Leics. loss of *t* from the group *-ston* in the form *Slawson*.

2. OTHORPE

Actorp 1086 DB, 1223 Cur, 1243 Fees, 1289, 1300 *Peake*, *Acthorp* 1289 *ib*, 1316 FA

Achetorp 1163 P (p), *Accethorp* 1269 Cur

Aketorp' 1223, 1224 Cur *et passim* to 1287, 1295 *Peake*, *Akethorp'* 1250, 1269 Cur *et passim* to 1321 *Peake*, 1333 (16) *SlCart*

Octhorp 1199 *Deed* (p), 1331 (e.15) *BelCartB*, 1348 (16) *SlCart* (p), *Hocthorp(e)* 1243, 1269, 1270 *Deed* (p), *Hokthorp* 1303 Pat, 1327 SR

Outhorp(e) 1282, 1316 *LCDeeds* (p) *et passim* to 1391, 1392 Pat (p)

Hothorp(e) 1307, 1309 *Peake et passim* to 1499 *MiD*, *Huthorp* 1316 *Peake*, 1376 *Wyg*, *Huththorp* 1415 *ib*, *Houthorpe* 1353 (16) *SlCart*, *Hoothorpe* 1615 LeicW

Owethorp' 1417 *Peake*, *Owthorp(e)* 1535 VE, 1537 *MinAccts*, 1675 LML

Othorp(e) 1518 *Wyg*, 1524 Fine *et passim* to 1549 Ipm *et freq*, *Oatrope* 1969 *Surv*

Either 'the outlying farmstead at the oaks', *v*. **āc**, **þorp**, or 'Áki's outlying farmstead', *v*. **þorp**, cf. Oakthorpe in Repton and Gresley Hundred (*v*. Db 650).

The pers.n. *Áki* is OScand and would sit happily in an area comprising Slawston and Blaston, probably appropriated by Scandinavians following the disbanding of a Viking army hereabouts in 877. However, this once well-wooded area is known to have supported oak-trees (cf. Holyoaks in nearby Stockerston) and the several early spellings without medial *e* point to OE *āc* as the specific. The fact that a large percentage of place-names in *-þorp* are compounded with personal names speaks in favour of *Áki*, but *āc* 'an oak-tree' as the specific is supported by other place-names in *-þorp* that are compounded with the name of a tree-type, as Eastrip (W 94, with *æsc* 'an ash-tree'), Birthorpe (DLPN 15, with *birki* or *birce* 'a birch-tree'), Hollingthorpe (YW **2** 103, with *holegn* 'a holly'), Willingthorpe (L **1** 46, with *wilign* 'a willow'). Forms with medial *e* need not point to the gen.sg. *Áka* of *Áki*. Although *ācana* (757 × 75 (11) BCS 219 (S 142)) appears to be the only independently recorded gen.pl. form of *āc* (Campbell § 627), a more usual gen.pl. form *āca* no doubt also existed.

Othorpe is a deserted medieval village, now the site of Othorpe House *infra*.

ALL SAINTS' CHURCH, *Church (All Saints)* 1846, 1863, 1877 White; it is earlier recorded as *ecclesie de Slauston* 1220 MHW, *ecclesiam de Slaweston* 1238 RGros, *ecclesie de Slawston* 1549 *Pat*. THE BARRACKS, presumably **bere-wīc** in origin, but no early forms survive. BLACK HORSE (P.H.) (lost), *Black Horse* 1846, 1863, 1877 White, 1925 Kelly, *Black Horse Inn* 1944 Sale. BLASTON RD, Blaston lying 2 miles to the north-west. BLUE LION (P.H.) (lost), *Blue Lion* 1846, 1863, 1877 White. THE BOUNDARY KENNEL, at the parish boundary, *v*. **kenel**. COMMISSIONER'S LANE, an access road dating from the Enclosure of 1793, *v*. **commissioner**. GREEN LANE, *v*. **grēne**[1]. LANGTON RD, Thorpe Langton lying 2½ miles to the south-west. MEDBOURNE RD, Medbourne lying 1½ miles to the south-east. MILL FM, named from a windmill which once stood at the top of Slawston Hill, 400 yards to the farm's south-east, *v*. Mill Fd in f.ns. (a). OTHORPE HO., *Othorpe House* 1863, 1877 White; it is *Othorpe Lodge* 1720 LeicW, *Hoethorpe Lodge* 1806 Map, *v*. **loge** and Othorpe *supra*. PORT HILL, *Porthill* 1625, 1674 *Terrier et freq* to 1877 White, *Portehill* 1637 *Bru*. The hill carries the Roman *Via Devana* (Gartree Road) across its summit on its way to the market town of Leicester. The road is recorded as *le portgat'* 1318 *Peake*, *Portgate* 1352 (16) *SlCart* (*v*. **port-gate**) and *Le Porte Weye* 1322 *Peake* (*v*. **port-wey**). The several instances of Port Hill in the county appear to be shortenings of **Port-gate hill* and **Port-wey hill* rather than representing early hill-top market sites (**port**[2]), *v*. Cox[2] 81. SLAWSTON HILL, 1918 Sale; it is *le Bergh* 1331 (e.15) *BelCartB*, *Barrow Hill* 1637 *Bru*, *Slawston Barrow Hill* 1798 Nichols, *v*. **berg** and *Burrough hill Feild* in f.ns. (b). VALLEY FM. THE VICARAGE, 1877 White, 1925 Kelly; earlier is *the Vicaridge* 1625, 1703, 1712 *Terrier*, *the Vicarage House* 1707 (18) *ib* and *the Vicarage House* (*new built in 1735*) (sic) 1745 *ib*, *v*. **vikerage**. WELHAM RD, Welham lying 1½ miles to the south-west. WEST GATES, located south-east in the village.

FIELD-NAMES

Forms in (a) presented without dates are 1969 *Surv*; those dated 1762 are *Terrier*; 1867 are *Surv*; 1918 and 1926 are Sale. Forms throughout dated 1287, 1295, 1296, 1300, 1302, 1306, 1318, 1321 and 1322 are *Peake*; those dated e.14 are *BelCartA*; 1331 (e.15) are *BelCartB*; 1332 and 1381 are SR; 1333 are *Rut*; 1346 are AD; 1476, 1494, 1608, 1614 and 1637 are *Bru*; 1601, 1606, e.17, 1625, 1674, 1679, 1690, 1703, 1707 (18), 1709, 1712, 1724 and 1745 are *Terrier*.

(a) 48 Acre (*v.* **æcer**); Under the Bank 1762 (1724, 1745, *v.* **banke**); Big Fd, ~ Mdw; Bottom Mdw (*v.* **bottom**); Boundary Fd (cf. The Boundary Kennel *supra*); the Bullock Fd (*v.* **bulluc**); Bungalow Mdw; Butlees (*v.* **leys**; with either **but** or **butte**); Buxtons Cl 1918, 1926, 1969 (with the surn. *Buxton*); Chipel Cl (sic) (*v.* **chapel(e)**; alluding to a nonconformist chapel here which was demolished c.1955); Church Cl 1918, 1969, ~ Pasture 1918 (*v.* **pasture**) (*v.* All Saints' Church *supra*); the Cottage Fd (*v.* **cotage**); Covert Fd (*v.* **cover(t)**); Cow Cl 1918, 1926, 1969; Cross Gates (poss. **cross**, **gata**; but alternatively, note *ad Cruce'* 1321 (p) (with MLat *crux* (*crucem* acc.sg.) 'a cross'), *atte Cros* 1381 (p) and *Cranoe Cross* 1637 (at the parish boundary with Cranoe), *v.* **atte**, **cros**); East Long 1762 (1724, 1745, *Eastlonge* 1625, *v.* **ēast**, **lang**[2]); Flathaws 1762 (*flathawes* e.14, 1331 (e.15), *Flatt* ~ 1724, *Flat Hawes* 1745, *v.* **flatr**, **haga**[1], **hagi**); Gilbert's Hedge 1918 (*v.* **hecg**; with the surn. *Gilbert*); Gorse Fd (*v.* **gorst**); Lower ~ ~, Upper ~ ~ 1918, 1926, Bottom Great Cl 1969; Halford's Piece (*v.* **pece**; with the surn. *Halford*); Hanging Lands (*v.* **hangende**, **land**); Hawes Cl (*v.* Flathaws *supra*); Harts Slade 1762 (1707 (18), 1724, 1745, *v.* **slæd**), Hearts Mdw 1969 (with the surn. *Hart*); Higate 1762 (*Hygate* 1724, *Highgate* 1745, cf. *hyegate furlonge* 1625, *Highgate furland* (sic) 1674, ~ *Furlong* 1703, 1707 (18), 1712 (*v.* **furlang**), *hyegate syde* 1625, *Highgate side* 1674, 1703, 1707 (18), 1712 (*v.* **sīde**), *Hyegate waye furlonge* 1625, *Highgate way furland* (sic) 1674, ~ ~ *Furlong* 1703, 1707 (18), 1712 (*v.* **weg**), Higgit Garden 1969 (*v.* **gardin**; land used for horticulture) (*v.* **gata**; with **hēg** or **hēah**[1]; note *heygatepol* in f.ns. (b)); Against the Hill 1762 (1703, 1707 (18), 1712, 1724, 1745, *agaynst the Hill* (*towarde the towne*) 1625, *against the Hill* (*towards the Towne*) 1703 (*v.* **tūn**), *v.* **ageynst**), Top of the Hill 1762 (1745, *the Top of the Hill* 1705, 1724 (*v.* **topp**), also called *the browe of the hell* (sic) 1625, *the Brow of the Hill* 1703, 1707 (18), 1712 (*v.* **brū**); all with reference to Slawston Hill); Hill Cl, Far ~ ~, Middle ~ ~, Near Hill Fd; Edmund Hodgkins headley 1762 (*v.* **headley**; cf. (*Mr*) *Hodgskins Hadland* 1724, 1745, *v.* **hēafod-land**, *Richard Hodgkins Homestall* 1708 (18), *v.* **hām-stall**); Holliwell 1762, Holywell 1918, 1926, Hollywell 1969 (*Holywell* 1625, *Holleywell* 1703, *Hollywell* 1707 (18), 1712, 1724, *Holy-well* 1745), Holliwell Fd 1762 (*Hollywell Feilde* 1625, *Holywell* ~ e.17, *Hollywell* ~ 1674, 1707 (18), *Hollywel Feild* 1712, *Holleywell* ~ 1703, *Hollywell* ~ 1724, *Holly-Well Field* 1745, *v.* **feld**; one of the great open-fields of the township) (*v.* **hālig**, **wella** and *haliwelleforlong'* in f.ns. (b)); In the Hole 1762 ((*in*) *the Hole* 1724, 1745, *v.* **hol**[1]); Home Cl, ~ Fd 1969, ~ Paddock 1926 (*v.* **paddock**) (*v.* **home**); Jessons Cl (with the surn. *Jesson*); Kendals Mdw (with the surn. *Kendal*); Kings Cl 1969, King's Mdw 1918, 1926 (with the surn. *King*, cf. *Thomas Kings headlande* 1625, ~ ~ *hadland* 1712, *v.* **hēafod-land**); Ley Cl 1918 (perh. with ME **ley** 'a pool'); Little Fd, ~ Mdw; Long Dike (*longedyke* 1331 (e.15), *longdike* 1625, cf. *Longdike* ~ 1674, 1703, 1712, *Longdyke* ~ 1703, *Long Dike Way* 1707 (18) (*v.* **weg**), *v.* **lang**[1], **dík**); Longrom 1762, Longrames 1969 (*longe wonge* 1625, *Long wong(e)* 1674, 1703, 1707 (18), 1712, *Longwrong* 1724, *Longrom* 1745, *v.* **lang**[1], **vangr**); March ~, Marsh Side 1918 (*v.* **sīde**), The Marshes 1969 (*the Marsh(e)* 1625, 1637, *the March* 1703, 1707 (18), *v.* **mersc**); Marsdale 1762 (1745, *Mershdale* e.14, *Mersedale* 1321, *Mershdalle* 1331 (e.15), *Marshdale* (*by Meadburne feilde*) 1625 (bordering Medbourne to the south-east), *Marshdale* 1674 *et passim* to 1712, *Marshdall* 1703, *Maresdale* 1724, *Scortmersdale* 1295, *Schortmersedale* 1321 (*v.* **sc(e)ort**), cf. *Mersedaleforlong* 1321 (*v.* **furlang**), *Maresdale Cow Pasture* 1745 (*v.* **pasture**), *the Mares Meadow* 1637, *v.* **mersc**, **dalr**); the Meadow 1762 (1637, 1724,

1745, *the Common meadowe* 1625 (*v.* **commun**), *Slawston Meadow* 1709); Meadow Welham (meadowland bordering the Welham parish boundary to the south-west); Mere Furlong 1762 (*le mer(e)forlong* 1295, 1321, 1331 (e.15), *merefurlong* e.14, (*the*) *Meer furlong* 1724, 1745 (*v.* **furlang**), *the meares* 1601, 1606, 1625, *the Meers* 1709, (**ge**)**mǣre**); Middle Fd 1762 ((*the*) *Middle Feild*(*e*) e.17, 1625, 1674 *et passim* to 1745, *Midle Feilde* 1637, *v.* **middel**, **feld**; one of the great open-fields); Middle Ground (*v.* **grund**); Mill Fd 1762 (*Mill Feild*(*e*) 1679, 1724, 1745, *v.* **feld**; another of the great open-fields, earlier called *Burrough hill Feild*, *infra*), Mill Furrows 1762 (1703, 1724, 1745, *Milne furrowes* 1625, *Miln furrows* 1674, *Mill furrowes* 1679, ~ *forowes* 1690, *Miln furrow*(*e*)*s* 1707 (18), 1712, *v.* **furh**), the Mill Hill 1762 (1745, cf. *the Mill Hill ground* 1724 (*v.* **grund**), Mill Hill being another name for Slawston Hill *supra*) (*v.* **myln**); Mow Mdw (grass for mowing); Far ~ ~, Near New Cl 1867; Top Newlands (*v.* **nīwe**, **land**); Oatrope Hill (*v.* Othorpe *supra*); Old Cl 1918, 1926, 1969 (*v.* **ald**); Big ~, Little Parsons (*v.* **persone**); Pasture Hades 1762 (*the Pasture Hades* 1625, 1707 (18), 1712, 1724, 1745, ~ ~ *heads* 1703, *v.* **hēafod**), Pasture Mdw 1969 (cf. *Slawston cow pasture* 1625, *Cowpasture* 1637) (*v.* **pasture**); Plough Cl (*v.* **plōg**); Plowed Port Hill (a ploughed area of Port Hill *supra*); The Radleys, Big ~, Far ~, Near ~, Radley 1969, Radley's Cl 1918, 1926 (cf. *Radley gutter* 1625, 1637, 1707 (18), 1712, *Radeley* ~ 1703, *Raddley gutter* 1712 (*v.* **goter** and Cranoe f.ns. (b) *s.n.*), *v.* **rēad**, **lēah**; with reference to red soil); Reid's Cl (with the surn. *Reid*); Salter's Way 1918, 1926, 1969 (*v.* **saltere**, **weg**; the name of a field at the extreme west corner of the parish through which Gartree Road runs); (The) Seeds 1918, 1926, 1969 (*v.* **sǣd**; used of grasses sown for one year's mowing or grazing, as distinguished from permanent pasture); Seven Acres 1762 (1703, 1707 (18), 1712, 1724, 1745, *seueneacres* 1295, 1321, *Seuene accres* 1296, *le seuenacres* e.14, *Seaven acres* 1625, 1674, ~ *syde* 1625, *Seven acres side* 1674, 1702, 1707 (18), 1712 (*v.* **sīde**), *v.* **seofon**, **æcer**); Sewels Cl (with the surn. *Sewell*); Shrubs furlong 1762 (*v.* **furlang**), Shrubs 1969 (*at Shrub*(*b*)*s*, *next Shrubs* 1724, 1745, *v.* **scrubb**); Simmons Acre 1762 (*Semons acres* 1625, 1674, *Simons Acre* 1637, 1703, 1724, *Symons acres* 1674, *Sem*(*m*)*ons Acre*(*s*) 1707 (18), 1712, *Simmon*(*d*)*s Acre* 1745 (*v.* **æcer**; with the surn. *Simons*/*Semens*); Six Leys 1867, 1918 (*v.* **leys**; when compounded with a numeral, *leys* represents grassland units of tenure corresponding to *lands* (i.e. selions or strips) similarly used of arable); Little ~, Skeffingtons (with the surn. *Skeffington* of a family originally from the township of this name, 6 miles to the north-west); Slawston ~ 1918, Slawson Cl 1926, Slawston Leas 1762 (1745, *Slawston leyes* 1625, 1703, ~ *leys* 1674, 1707 (18), 1712, 1714, ~ *lease* 1679, *Slauston leeys* 1674, *v.* **leys**); The Slip (*v.* **slipe**); Smithers Green (*v.* **grēne**[2]; either with **smyther** 'a smith' or with the surn. *Smithers*); Spences (the surn. *Spence* in the possessive case; a reflex of ME *spence*/*spense* 'a man who worked at the buttery of a hall'); Spots (*v.* **spot**); Sutton's Cl 1918 (with the surn. *Sutton*); Thornpit Leas (*v.* **þorn**, **pytt**, **leys**); Big Top Cl; Top Mdw; Townsend 1762 (*the townes end* 1674, *Towne end* 1703, (*the*) *Towns End* 1707 (18), 1712, 1724, 1745, *v.* **tūn**, **ende**); Two Meadows 1969, Lower ~, Upper Mdw 1918, 1926; the Vicaridge piece 1762 (*the Vicars peece* 1625, ~ ~ *peice* 1674, 1703, *the Vicarage* ~ 1707 (18), *the Vicaridge piece* 1712, 1724, *v.* **vikere**, **vikerage**, **pece** and The Vicarage *supra*); Welham Cl (a field at the parish boundary with Welham to the south-west); Whartlands 1762, Waterlands 1969 (*le thwertelond*(*e*) e.14, 1331 (e.15), *thwertlondes* e.14, *Whartlandes* 1625, *Whartlands* 1674, 1707 (18), 1712, 1724, 1745), Great Whartlands 1918, 1926 (*Michelthwaertilondes* 1331 (e.15), 1333, *v.* **micel**; note also *Litelthwertlondes* 1331 (e.15), *v.* **lȳtel**) (*v.* **þverr** (**þvert** neut.), **land**); Windmill Hill (*v.* **wind-mylne**; presum. a local name for Slawston Hill *supra* upon which a windmill is sited on the 1st edn of the O.S. 1" map and upon which a mill is known to have stood since at least 1637).

(b) *the Akerys* 1287 (*v.* **æcer**); *Ashgate way*(*e*) 1625, 1674, 1703, 1707 (18), 1712 (*v.* **æsc**, **gata**, **weg**); *Attons hedge* 1745 (*v.* **hecg**; with the surn. *Atton*); *le baneforlong* 1302, *le banfurlong*, *banefurlonge* 1331 (e.15) (*v.* **bēan**, **furlang**); *Berehylfeld* 1476 ('barley hill field', *v.* **bere**, **hyll**, **feld**; one of the early great open-fields of the township, it may well be identified with *Burrough hill Feild*, *infra*); *bergh*(*e*)*fote* e.14, 1331 (e.15) (*v.* **berg**, **fōt**; presum. alluding to Slawston Hill *supra*); *blachill'* e.14, 1331 (e.15), *blakehull* e.14, *blackehil* 1331 (e.15), *Blakehill furlong*(*e*) 1625, 1712, *blackwell furland* (sic) 1674, *Blackwell furlong* 1703, 1707 (18) (*v.* **furlang**) (*v.* **blæc**, **hyll**); *Burrough hill Feild* e.17, *Borough hill Feilde* 1625, *Borough* ~ ~, *Borrow Hill feild* 1674, *Burrowgh Hill* ~ 1703, *Borough hill* ~ 1707 (18), *Borough* ~ ~, *Burrough Hill Field* 1712 (*v.* **hyll**, **feld**; one of the great open-fields, later called Mill Fd *supra*, the hill to be identified with Slawston Hill *supra*; this hill is earliest recorded as *le Bergh* 1331 (e.15) (*v.* **berg**) and the later *Burrough hill* appears formally to be its late reflex; but if *Berehylfeld*, *supra*, is an authentic and true earlier form for *Burrough hill*, then **bere** rather than **berg** must be the specific); *brooke furland* (sic) 1674 (*v.* **brōc**, **furlang**); *in campo occidentali* 1331 (e.15), 'west field', with MLat *campus* 'a field' and *occidentalis* 'west, western', also called *Hollywell Feilde*, *infra*, *de campo orientali* 1331 (e.15), 'east field', with MLat *orientalis* 'east, eastern', also called *Burrough hill Feild*, *supra*, *in medio campo* 1331 (e.15), 'middle field', with MLat *medius* 'middle', *v.* Middle Fd *supra*; *Wm. Cobleyes headlande* 1625, *William Cobleys Headland* 1712 (*v.* **hēafod-land**); *Dryelond* 1331 (e.15), 1333 (*v.* **drȳge**, **land**); *Esfeld* 1321, *asfeld* 1331 (e.15) (*v.* **æsc**, **feld**; one of the early great open-fields, prob. Middle Fd *supra*, cf. *Ashgate*, *supra*; the earlier form poss. influnced by ON **eski**); *Fallowe Close* 1637 (*v.* **falh**); *le fetheres* 1296, *le fitheres* 1321 ('the feathers', *v.* **feðer**, **fjǫðr**; poss. an allusion to a place frequented by flocks of birds); *folkotesyke* e.14, *folkitesike* 1331 (e.15) (*v.* **sík**; note *Folkatmedowe* in adjoining Hallaton f.ns. (b) and Folkecatts in adjoining Medbourne f.ns. (a)); *ad fontem* 1322 (p) (with MLat *fons* (*fontem* acc.sg.) 'a spring, a well'); *Against the Furlongs* 1724, 1745 (*v.* **furlang**; a plot of land so called); *Gooze* ~ 1625, *Goose acres* 1674, 1703, 1707 (18), 1712, *longegosacre* 1331 (e.15) (*v.* **lang**[1]) (*v.* **gōs**, **æcer**); *Hattslade* 1745 (*v.* **slæd**; either with **hæt(t)** 'a hat', used in some topographical allusion to a hill thought to resemble a hat, or with the surn. *Hatt*, metonymic for ME *hattere* 'a maker or seller of hats'); *Halloughton* ~ 1625, 1712, *Hallaton Gutter* 1703, 1707 (18), 1745 (*v.* **goter**; Hallaton parish adjoins to the north-east); *haliwelleforlong'* 1331 (e.15), *Haliwellforlong* 1333 (*v.* **furlang**), *Holliwell leyes* 1637 (*v.* **leys**), *Hollywell syde* 1625, *Hollywell* ~ 1674, *Holleywell* ~ 1703, *Hollywell side* 1707 (18), 1712 (*v.* **sīde**) (*v.* Holliwell *supra*); *harecroftgate* e.14, 1331 (e.15) (*v.* **gata** and Hare Crop Leys in adjoining Hallaton); *heygatepol* e.14 (*v.* **hēg**, **gata**, **pōl**[1]); *the hill syde* 1625 (*v.* **sīde**; with reference to Slawston Hill *supra*); *Holgate* e.14, 1321, 1331 (e.15) (*v.* **hol**[2], **gata**); *Inlond* 1333 (e.15) (*v.* **in**, **land**); *Ladyes land* 1494 (*v.* **ladi**, **land**; land whose rents were dedicated to the upkeep of a chapel to Our Lady, the Virgin Mary); *Below Liccister waye* 1637 (land adjoining the highway to Leicester); *longbergh'* e.14, 1331 (e.15) (*v.* **lang**[1], **berg**); *longehanefurlong*(*e*) e.14, 1331 (e.15) (*v.* **lang**[1], **hān**, **furlang**; land near a boundary stone); *Meadburne Meare* 1625, *Medburn Meer* 1703, *Medbourne Meare* 1707 (18), 1712 (*v.* **(ge)mǣre**; Medbourne parish adjoins to the south-east); *Othorpe little close* 1608, *Othorpe Close* 1614, *Othorp Great ~*, *Othorp Litle Feilde* 1637 (*v.* Othorpe *supra*); *pesehylle*, *peysehil* 1331 (e.15), *Peysehul* 1346 (*v.* **pise**, **hyll**); *peselondes* e.14, 1331 (e.15) (*v.* **pise**, **land**); *rademild* e.14, 1331 (e.15) (*v.* **rēad**, **mylde**); *le redehill'* 1331 (e.15) (*v.* **hyll**; with **rēad** or **hrēod**); *renyngdale* e.14, 1331 (e.15) (*v.* **rennyng** 'a watercourse, a channel', **dalr**); *the rope waie* 1625, *the Ropeway* 1674, 1703, 1707 (18), 1712 (presum. a local style for a rope-walk; otherwise, a rope-making site alongside a track); *Rushdale* 1637, *longerysshedale* 1332 (*v.* **lang**[1]) (*v.* **risc**, **dalr**); *schortefurlong* e.14, *shortefurlong'* 1331 (e.15) (*v.* **sc(e)ort**, **furlang**); *Edward Spencer's Headland* 1707 (18) (*v.* **hēafod-land**); *Mr Henry Stanfordes leyes* 1625, *Henry Stamfords Leys* 1703 (*v.* **leys**); *the Stint* 1745 (*v.* **stynt**; a boundary piece); *le tounfurlong* 1331 (e.15), 1333 (*v.* **furlang**), *the towne syde* 1625, *the Townside* 1674, 1703, 1707 (18), 1712 (*v.* **sīde**) (*v.* **tūn**); *waterrend*(*e*)*les*, *waterrenles* 1331 (e.15) (*v.* **wæter**, **rynel**); *Welham meare* 1625, *~ meere* 1674, *~ Mear* 1712, *Wellham Meer* 1703, *~ Meare* 1707 (18) (*v.* **(ge)mǣre**); *wilegate*, *wylgate* e.14, *Wilgate* e.14, 1333, *Wilgatte* 1331 (e.15), *Wilgate* 1625, 1703, *Willgate* 1674, 1707 (18), 1712 (*v.* **wīle** (presum. in its sense 'an engine, a mechanical contrivance'), **gata**; the allusion appears to be to a mill, cf. Croft (OE *crœft* 'a machine', there perh. used of a watermill, *v.* Cox[2] 28).

Smeeton Westerby

Originally two separate settlements, Smeeton of Anglo-Saxon origin and the later Westerby presumably an offshoot of Smeeton.

1. SMEETON

Smitetone 1086 DB (×2)
Esmeditone 1086 DB, *Esmedistona* 1190 × 1204 France
Smetheton' 1203 (p), 1204 P (p), 1252 Fine *et passim* to 1295, 1296 *ShR et freq* to 1343 *MktHPR* (p), 1345 *Peake* (p) *et passim* to 1369 Banco, 1414 *ShR*, *Smethetona* c.1250 *Rut*, *Smethton'* 1345 Pat (p), 1348 *Peake* (p), 1399 *Deed*
Smitheton' 1208 ChR, *Smytheton'* 1247 Abbr (p), 1361 Cl, *Smithton'* 1208 ChR, 1283 IpmR
Smitone 1086 DB, *Smiton* 1610 Speed
Smeton' 1311 *Wyg* (p), 1328 Banco, 1343 *MkyHPR* (p) *et passim* to 1392 Banco, 1394 *Deed et freq* to 1516 Fine, 1521 Ipm *et passim* to 1593 Moulton, 1606 Fine
Smeaton 1604 SR, *Smeeton* 1606, 1615 LML

'The enclosure or village of the smiths', *v.* **smið, tūn**. Forms with *Smeth*(*e*)- are in part due to the OE gen.pl. **smeoða** where *eo* developed from *i* through velar mutation. Note AN prosthetic *e* before *s* + cons. in two very early forms.

2. WESTERBY

Westerby c.1130 LeicSurv, 1204 FF *et passim* to 1527 LeicW, 1610 Speed, *Westerbi* 1206 Cur, *Westerbie* 1555 Pat, 1596 Ipm
Westrebi 1206 Cur
Westorby p. 1270 *Brai*, *Westyrby* 1399 *Deed*

'The western farmstead', *v.* **vestr, vestri, bȳ**. The settlement lay slightly to the west of Smeeton.

3. As SMEETON WESTERBY

Smetheton' Westerby 1279 Misc, 1327 SR
Smytheton Westerby 1316 FA
Smeton Westurby 1402 Cl, *Smeton Westorby* 1411, 1421 ib, *Smeton Westerby* 1593 Moulton, *Smeaton Westerbye* 1604 SR, *Smeeton Westerbie* 1606 LML, *Smeeton Westerby* 1615 ib *et freq*
Westerby Smeton 1559 Pat

It should be noted that *Smeeton* appears as a separate name as late as 1615 LML and *Westerby* 1610 Speed.

BROOK HO. (local), *Brook House* 1925 Kelly. BULL SPINNEY, *Bull Spinny* 1835 O, cf. *Bull Barn* 1835 ib (*v.* **bern**), *v.* **spinney**; prob. with the surn *Bull* rather than with **bula**, cf. Bulls Seeds in f.ns. (a). CHRIST CHURCH, 1925 Kelly, *Church (Christ)* 1863, 1877 White; the church was built 1848–9. Note also *Churchyard* 1850 *Map*, *v.* **churchyerd**. CRICKETERS' ARMS (P.H.) (lost), *Cricketers' Arms* 1877 White. CROWN AND SCEPTRE (P.H.) (lost), *Crown and Sceptre* 1846, 1863 White. DEBDALE FM, *Debdale Farm* 1943 Sale. DEBDALE LANE, leading to Debdale Wharf, *v.* Gumley *s.n.* GUMLEY RD, Gumley lying 2 miles to the south. HILL FM is *Hills Farm* 1943 Sale; on Smeeton Hill *infra*. HOME FM, *v.* **home**. KING'S HEAD (P.H.), *King's Head* 1846, 1863, 1877 White, 1925 Kelly. LODGE FM, *v.* **loge**. MILL LANE, leading to two former windmills on high ground to the north-west; these are marked on the 1st edn O.S. map of 1835. PIT HILL (local), *Pitts* 1745 *Terrier*, cf. *Pittfurlong* 1636 *ib*, *Pit Furlong* 1850 *Map* (*v.* **furlang**), *v.* **pytt**; alluding to gravel pits. THE RECTORY, 1925 Kelly, *v.* **rectory**. SADDINGTON RD, Saddington lying 1½ miles to the south-west. SMEETON GORSE, 1968 *Surv*, *v.* **gorst**. SMEETON HILL. SMEETON HO., *Smeeton House* 1846 White, 1925 Kelly. SPRINGFIELD FM, *Springfield* 1968 *Surv*, *v.* **spring**[1]. WESTERBY FM, *Westerby Farm* 1943 Sale. WESTERBY HO., *Westerby House* 1925 Kelly. WRENBURY FM.

FIELD-NAMES

In (a), forms presented without dates are 1968 *Surv*; those dated 1771 and 1821 are *Terrier*; 1779 are *EnclA*; 1781 are *Surv*; 1806 are *MiscAccts*; 1850 are *Map*; 1918 and 1946 are Sale. Forms throughout dated 1399, 1648, 1649, 1650, 1673, 1676, 1683, 1697 and 1744 are

Deed; those dated 1601, 1636, 1694, l.17, 1700, 1708, 1708 (18), c.1715, c.1720, 1724 and 1745 are *Terrier*.

(a) Three Acre, Five ~, Six ~, Eight ~, Ten ~, Thirteen Acre (*v.* **æcer**); Allens First ~, Allens Second Cl 1850 (with the surn. *Allen*); Allotments 1850, Brickyard Allotments 1968 (*v.* **allotment** and Brickyard *infra*); Arable, Little ~, Buntley Arable 1850 (*v.* **arable** and Buntley *infra*); Ash Cl 1850 (1683, *v.* **æsc**); Banburys First Cl 1850 (with the surn. *Banbury*, cf. *Elizabeth Banbury* 1811 Census and *Jonathan Banbury* 1835 ib of Smeeton); Barn Cl 1821, 1850 (named from Bull Barn *supra*); Barwells Cl 1850 (with the surn. *Barwell* of a family originally from the township of this name, 14 miles to the west); Bason 1850, Basin Cl 1968 (alluding to a canal basin on the Grand Union Canal); First ~, Second Basses (with the surn. *Bass*); The Bend (a close beside a pronounced bend in Grand Union Canal); Berrydale 1850 (of uncertain meaning; earlier forms are needed); Best Mdw (*v.* **best**; a complimentary name for very good land); Big Fd; Blackwells Cl 1850 (with the surn. *Blackwell*); Bottom Cl 1821, ~ Fd, ~ Mdw 1968 (*v.* **bottom**); Bowles' Cl 1918 (with the surn. *Bowles*); Brick Kiln Cl 1850, Brick Hill 1968 (*v.* **brike-kiln**); Bottom ~, Top Brickyard (*v.* **brike-yard**); Bridge Mdw 1850, 1968 (*v.* **brycg**); Broad Cl 1850 (*v.* **brād**); Brook Mdw, ~ Slade 1850 (*v.* **slæd**) (*the Brooke* 1601, 1636, *v.* **brōc**); Bulls Seeds (*v.* **sǣd**; used of grasses sown for one year's mowing or grazing, as distinguished from permanent pasture; prob. with the surn. *Bull*); Buntley 1850, 1968 (*Buncklye* 1636, *v.* **lēah**, prob. with **beonet**; a common toponym); Big ~, Little ~, Middle Burgess (with the surn. *Burgess*, cf. *Philippus Burgis* 1199 RFL); Burrows Cl 1850 (with the surn. *Burrows*, cf. *Sophia Burrows* 1825 Census and *Caroline Burrows* 1840 ib of Smeeton); Bush Cl (*v.* **busc**); Canal Mdw, ~ Piece 1850 (*v.* **pece**) (land beside the Grand Union Canal); the Chapel Yard 1781 (*v.* **chapel(e)**, **geard**; alluding to an early Baptist chapel); Church Cl 1850, ~ Fd 1968 (*v.* Christ Church *supra*); Clover Cl 1850 (*v.* **clāfre**; grown as a fodder crop); Cobleys Home Cl 1850 (*v.* **home**), Cobleys Lane 1968 (with the surn. *Cobley*, cf. *John Cobley* 1820 Census, *Elizabeth Cobley* 1829 ib and *James Cobley* 1833 ib, all of Smeeton); East ~, West Corkley 1850 (*Cawkeley*, *Cawkely lyes* 1636 (*v.* **leys**), *v.* **calc**, **lēah**); Cow Pasture 1850, Big Cow Pasture 1968 (*the Common Cowepasture* 1636, *v.* **cū**, **pasture**); Cranksland 1850 (*Cranck(e)sland* 1636, *v.* **land**; either with the surn. *Crank*, from ME *cranke* 'vigorous, lusty' or with **cranuc**); Creakely 1850, Crackley 1968 (*Cracley* 1636, *v.* **craca**, **lēah**); Cricket Cl 1850, ~ Fd 1968 (for the game of cricket); Crooks Acre 1850 (*croke acre* 1601, *v.* **æcer**; with **crōc** or **crocc**); Delkers 1850, 1968 (unexplained; poss. **dalr** with **kjarr** (ME **ker**)); Dileas 1771 (*v.* **dile**, **leys**); Drawstone 1850, 1968 (of uncertain meaning; earlier forms are needed); Elliots Cl 1850 (with the surn. *Elliot*); Far Cl 1850 (*v.* **feor**); Far ~, Small Feeder 1850, Feeder Cl 1968 (*v.* **feeder** 'a watercourse which supplies a canal by gravitation or natural flow'; here running from Saddington Reservoir into Grand Union Canal); Fleet Mdw 1850, 1968 (*v.* **flēot**, **fljót**); Flaxwell 1918 (*v.* **wella**; either with **flaxe**, or if the spring or stream was used for retting, then with **fleax**); Furze Cl 1821 (*v.* **fyrs**); Goodmans Barn Cl, ~ Seeds 1850 (*v.* **sǣd**; used of areas of sown grass) (with the surn. *Goodman*, cf. *Mary Goodman* 1818 Census and *John Goodman* 1820 ib of Smeeton); Gravel Hole 1968 (*v.* **hol**[1]), Gravel Pit Cl 1850 (*v.* **pytt**) (*v.* **gravel**); The Green 1850, 1918, 1946 ((*into*) *Greene* 1636, *v.* **grēne**[2]); Gutteridges Best Cl (*v.* **best**), ~ Mdw 1850, First ~, Second Gutteridges 1968 (with the surn. *Gutteridge*, a reflex of the OE masc. pers.n. *Cūðrīc*); Harcraft 1771 (1636, *v.* **hār**[2], **croft**); R. Haymes Homestead 1850 (*v.* **hām-stede**); Hen Fd (*v.* **henn**); Hill Cl 1821; Hills and Hollows (a common type of f.n. referring to the remains of former quarrying); Upper ~ ~, Hoe Furlong 1918, 1946 (*v.* **hōh**, **furlang**); Holmans Plough (*v.* **plōg**; with the surn. *Holman*); Home Cl 1850, 1918, 1946, 1968, ~ Fd 1968 (*v.* **home**); Hut Cl 1850, 1968, ~ Mdw 1968 (*v.* **hut**); Iron Gate (as a modern form, this may refer literally to a field with such a metal gate; but if a surviving early name, then *v.* **hyrne**, **gata**); Kingster 1850, King's Stone 1918, Kingstone 1946 (*Kingster furlong* 1636 (*v.* **furlang**); poss. 'the king's property, estate', *v.* **cyning**, **sterne**, King's Stone in Kibworth Beauchamp f.ns. (a) and *Kingstocke* in Kibworth Beauchamp f.ns. (b)); The Knoll (*v.* **cnoll**); Larkley, ~ Mdw 1850, 1968 (*Larkely* 1636, *v.* **lāwerce**, **lēah**); Laundons Cl 1850 (with the surn. *Laundon*); Leech' s Cl 1850 (with the surn. *Leech*, a reflex of OE *lǣce* 'a physician'); Little Cl 1918, ~ Mdw 1850, 1968; Long Hill, ~ ~ Mdw 1850, 1968 (*Longhill* 1636, *v.* **lang**[1], **hyll**); Long Mdw 1850, 1968; Masons Cl (with the surn. *Mason*); The Meadow 1821, 1968; Middle Fd 1779 (1636, 1673, *the Middell feild* 1601, *v.* **middel**, **feld**; one of the great open-fields of the township); Middle Piece 1850 (*v.* **pece**); Mill Cl 1968, (the) Mill Fd 1779, 1968 (1636, ~ *feild* 1700, c.1720, *v.* **myln**, **feld**; one of the great open-fields, also called *Rigges Feild*, *v.* f.ns. (b)); Mill Dam (*v.* **damme**), ~ Garden (*v.* **gardin**), ~ Yard 1850 (*v.* **geard**) (*v.* **myln**; alluding to a water-mill); Millers Acre 1850, 1968 (1745, *v.* **æcer**), ~ Cl 1850, ~ Maze 1968 (unexplained and nothing otherwise recorded) (*v.* **millere**); Muck Hill Grove 1850, 1918, 1946 (*Muckle groue* 1636, *v.* **micel**, **mycel**, **grāf**); Mud Tip (referring to a dredging site at Grand Union Canal); Narrow Croft 1850 (*v.* **nearu**, **croft**); Narrow Cl 1850; Neather ~ 1850, Nether Mdw 1968; the Nether Fd 1779 ((*the*) *Neather* ~ 1636, *the Nether* ~ 1694, *Neather feild* l.17, c.1720, *v.* **neoðera**, **feld**; one of the great open-fields, also called *the North Feild* 1708); Orchard; Far ~, First Overland 1850 (*v.* **uferra**, **land**); Over-Moore 1850, Overmoor 1968 (*v.* **uferra**, **mōr**[1]); Owls Moor, ~ ~ Mdw 1850 (*Owlesmore* 1636, *v.* **mōr**[1]; with **āwel** or **ǣwell**); Ozier Beds 1821 (*v.* **oyser**, **bedd**); The Park (*v.* **park**); The Paddock, Home ~ (*v.* **home**), Peggs Paddock (with the surn. *Pegg*, cf. *Sarah Pegg* 1861 Census of Smeeton) (*v.* **paddock**); Pear Tree (*v.* **pertre**); The Pen 1968, Pen Cl 1850, 1968 (*v.* **penn**[2]); Home ~, Top Plank 1968, Plank Cl 1850 (cf. *Planck* ~, *Planke Furlong* 1636 (*v.* **furlang**), *v.* **planke**); Ploughed ~ 1850, Plough Cl 1968 (*v.* **plōg**); Quartern Cl 1850, Quartern 1968 (*v.* **quarterne**); Rectory Fd (*v.* **rectory**; in 1850, the field was Saddington Rectory Fd); Red Bank (*v.* **rēad**, **banke**); Road Cl 1850 (a roadside enclosure); Robsholm 1850 (*Robsom* 1636, *v.* **holmr**; with the surn. *Robb*, from a pet-form of *Robert*); Ross's Cl 1850 (with the surn. *Ross*); Round Hill 1850, 1968 (*v.* **round**; a toponym common in Gartree Hunded); Rye Cl 1771 (*v.* **ryge**); Sand Hole (*v.* **hol**[1]); Seeds 1850, 1968 (*v.* **sǣd**; used of grasses sown for one year's mowing or grazing, as distinguished from permanent pasture); Sideling 1850, Sidings (sic) 1968 (*v.* **sīdling**); Six Cocks 1850, 1918, 1946 (*v.* **six**, **cocc**[1]); East ~, Slade 1850, Slades 1968 (*v.* **slæd**); Slang (*v.* **slang**); Smeeton Side (*v.* **sīde**); Spinney Cl 1821 (*v.* **spinney**); Spoil Banks 1850 (a close containing the residue of canal excavations, cf. Mud Tip *supra*); Stackyard (*v.* **stackyard**); Steward's Cl, Stewards Mdws 1850 (with the surn. *Steward*); Stinkley 1850 (*Stinkcliffe* 1601, *Stinkeley*, *Stinkely* 1636, *Stinkly* 1745, *v.* **clif**; with either **stynt** or **stint**); Stockwell 1850, 1968 (cf. *Stockwell hedge* 1636 (*v.* **hecg**), *v.* **stocc**, **wella**); Old Stonebridge 1850, 1968, Stonebridge 1968, ~ Cl 1918, 1946 (*Stonebridge* 1636), Stonebridge Way 1850

(*Stonebridge gate* 1694, l.17, 1700, *v.* **gata**) (*v.* **stān, brycg**); Stopars 1850, 1968 (*Stoupers* 1636; poss. is late ME **stolpe/stulpe** 'a post', indicating some sort of boundary marker); Stream 1850, Streams 1968 (cf. *Stockacre Streame* 1601 (*v.* **stocc, æcer**), *Stockwater streame* 1636 (this may belong with the previous form or be a variant of Stockwell *supra*), *v.* **strēam**); Streatfold 1850 (*Long Steadfold* 1630, *v.* **stōd-fald**; note also *Streete furlong* 1636 (*v.* **strǣt, furlang**) which may account for influence on the 1850 form; 'the Street' appears refer to the prehistoric trackway running south from the ford at Melton Mowbray via Burrough on the Hill, Tilton on the Hill, Illston on the Hill, Kibworth, Saddington and Mowsley, also called *le Ferdgate* 'the army road', *v.* Shangton f.ns. (b) *s.n.*); Tennis Fd (for the game of tennis); Thistles (*v.* **þistel**); Three Bushes 1850, 1968 (*v.* **þrēo, busc**); Three Corner (*v.* **three-corner**); Timms (the surn. *Timms* in the possessive case); Top Cl 1850, 1918, 1968, ~ Fd, ~ Mdw 1968, Top Part 1850 (*v.* **part**) (*v.* **top**); Topside 1850, 1968, ~ Mdw 1850 (*v.* **topp, sīde**); Upper ~, Tythe 1850 (*v.* **tēoða**); Watermill Cl 1779 (1649, 1676), Watermill Hill 1850 (1636) (*v.* **water-mylne**; the mill lay south-east of the village); Westerby Cl 1850, 1968; Whitelands 1850 (*Whiteland* 1636, *v.* **hwīt, land**; in eModE, *white* 'infertile' may be contrasted with *black* 'fertile'); Whittamers Cl 1850 (with the surn. *Whittamore*); Whitwells Cl 1850 (with the surn. *Whitwell*); Wiggley Mdw (with the surn. *Wigley*); Williams Cl 1850, Williams 1968 (with the surn. *Williams*); Workhouse 1850 (*the Old Workhouse* 1806, *v.* **workhouse**; Smeeton had a workhouse as early as 1776 Nichols).

(b) *Bremish* 1708 ('broad marsh', *v.* **breiðr, mersc**; cf. Braymish in Little Bowden f.ns. (a) and Bremish in Kibworth Harcourt f.ns. (a)); *Breachleys* 1673 (*v.* **brēc, leys**); *Brooks acre* 1745 (*v.* **brōc, æcer** and Brook Mdw *supra*); (*the*) *Church way* 1694, 1700 *et passim* to 1745; the road to St Wilfred's Church in Kibworth Beauchamp (Smeeton did not have its own parish church until 1849)); *Clarkes Barn* 1648, 1649 (with the surn. *Clark*(*e*)); *Cockash* 1694, l.17, 1724, 1745, *Coakash* 1700, (*the*) *Cockhash* 1708, 1708 (18) (*v.* **cocc**[1], **æsc**); *Cockland* 1636 (*v.* **cocc**[1], **land**); *the Dale* c.1720, (*the*) *Dale meare* 1636, c.1715 (*v.* **(ge)mǣre**) (*v.* **dalr**); *groufcloudys* 1399 (*v.* **grāf, clūd**); *Harborowe way* 1636 (*v.* **weg**; the road to Market Harborough which lies 5 miles to the south-east); *Haysicke* 1636 (*v.* **hēg, sík**); *heldyrstubb* 1399 (*v.* **ellern, stubb**); *Hespitte* 1636 (*v.* **hǣs, pytt**); *Hickes leyes* 1636 (*v.* **leys**; with the surn. *Hick/Hick*(*e*)*s*, from *Hick*, a pet-form of *Ricard*); *the Hills* 1636; *Lammas Close* 1673, ~ *Croft* 1636 (*v.* **croft**) (*v.* **lammas**); *Littell Hyll* 1601, *Little hill* 1636, 1745; *Andrew Markhams house* 1650; *the Midle meere* 1636 (*v.* **middel, (ge)mǣre**); *Millom hades* 1636 (*v.* **myln, holmr, hēafod**); *Moore furlong* 1636 (*v.* **mōr**[1], **furlang**); *Neather acre* 1636 (*v.* **neoðera, æcer**); *North croft* c.1715, c.1720 (*v.* **croft**); *the North feild* 1708, 1724, 1745 (also called the Nether Fd *supra*); *Pelsants land* 1697, 1745 (the property of *Wm. Pelsant* in 1697); *Rigges* ~ 1694, *Rigs* ~ l.17, *Riggs feild* 1708, 1724, 1745 (*v.* **hrycg, hryggr, feld**; one of the great open-fields, also called Mill Fd *supra*); *Sandland* ~, *Over Sandlands Furlong* 1636 (*v.* **furlang**), *Over Sandlands Meare* 1694 (*v.* **uferra**), *Upper Sandlands Meare* l.17, ~ ~ *meer*(*e*) 1700, 1708, 1724, ~ ~ *Meeare* 1745 (*v.* **(ge)mǣre**) (*v.* **sand, land**); *Tayle bush Furlonge* 1636 (*v.* **tægl, busc, furlang**); *the towne end* 1601, *the Townes end furlong* 1636 (*v.* **tūn, ende**); *the West feild* 1601 (*v.* **feld**; also called Mill Fd and *Rigges Feild*, both *supra*); *Wetland Furlonge* 1636 (*v.* **wēt, land, furlang**); *Woodwards furlong* 1636 (*v.* **furlang**; with the surn. *Woodward*).

Stockerston

1. STOCKERSTON

Stoctone (×2), *Stotone* 1086 DB
Stocfaston' c.1130 LeicSurv, 1220 MHW *et passim* to 1299 Ipm, 1305 (e.15) *BelCartB*, *Stokfaston'* 1285 Banco, c.1291 Tax *et passim* to 1330 FA, 1333 *Peake et freq* to 1428, 1437 Banco *et passim* to 1519 EpCB, 1576 Saxton
Stocfateston' 1167 P, *Stokfatestona* 1167 ChancR
Stokefaston' 1254 Val, 1304 Ch *et passim* to 1609 Ipm, 1618 Fine
Stokeuaston' 1284 (e.15) *BelCartB*, *Stokewaston* 13 (16) *SlCart*
Stokeston' c.1291 Tax, 1402 Banco, 1417 *BelCartB*, 1437 Banco
Stokerston 1526, 1530 AAS *et passim* to 1634 ISLR, 1697 LML, *Stockerston* 1567 AAS *et freq*
Stockerson 1572 SR, 1573 LEpis

This is a difficult name. The erratic DB forms indicate an original 'settlement with an attached dairy farm' (*v.* **stoc**, **tūn**), a direct parallel with Stoughton *infra*. However, the numerous forms from the earlier 12th cent. suggest rather 'the stronghold constructed of heavy timbers' (*v.* **stocc**, **fæsten**), a name perhaps recording an early forest border fortress facing an independent kingdom of Rutland, *v.* Ru xxxiii–xxxvii. Ekwall DEPN, presumably to account for the repeated *-ton* spellings, proposes that **tūn** may have been added to the original place-name form, hence a **Stocc-fæsten-tūn*. A further possibility is that Stockerston represents a **Stoc-fæsten* (*v.* **stoc**, **fæsten**), where the generic would indicate a secure and sheltered herding-place for a dairy farm's cattle which were nurtured in the local oak woodland-pasture. Such a site may once have related to Stoke Dry, one mile to the south-east in Rutland.

2. HOLYOAKS

Haliach 1086 DB, 1221 RHug, *Haliac*(*k*) 1163 P, 1201 OblR (p), m.13, 1330 *Peake*, *Hal*(*l*)*iak* l.13, 1318, 1330, 1338 *ib* (p),

Halyac(k) Hy 3 Blore (p), m.13 *Peake* (p), *Halihac* 12 *ib* (p), *Halihagh* 1239 Cur

Halioc e.13 *Peake*, 1275 (16) *SlCart*, l.13 *Peake*, 1327 SR, *Haliok* 1243 Cur, 1274 Banco *et passim* to 1375 *Peake*, 1386 Pat, *Halihoc* l.13, 13 *Peake* (freq), *Halihok* l.13 *ib* (p), 1296 SR (p)

Halyok(e) 1367 Pat, 1374 Cl *et passim* to 1537 MinAccts, 1560 LeicW, *Halleock* 1601 *Terrier*

Holiok 13 *Peake*, 13 (16) *SlCart*, *Holliock* 1606 *ExchSpC*, (*the Nether ~*, *the Upper ~* 1606 *ib*), 1652 *Deed*, (*Nether ~*, *Upper ~* 1652 *ib*), *Hollioakes* Chas 1 Nichols, (*Nether ~*, *Over ~* Chas 1 ib)

Holyoke 1537 AAS, *Holyoak* 1698 LeicW

Holyoakes 1722 LeicW, *Holyoaks* 1824 O

'The holy oak', *v.* **hālig**, **āc**. At the time of the Domesday Survey, *Haliach* was a substantial township with a valuable mill and its own woodland. Presumably it was originally a pagan Anglo-Saxon religious site associated with the god Thunor whose especial tree was the oak (note *þureslege*, probably 'the grove sacred to the god Thunor', in nearby Ayston parish in Rutland, *v.* Ru 174). It may be significant that the medieval hermitage of *Mirabel* with its chapel was located in close proximity to *Haliach*, perhaps to counter lingering local pre-Christian beliefs and practices among the peasantry here, *v.* Little Merrible Wood and The Hermitage *infra*.

Holyoaks Liberty, part of the manor of adjacent Stoke Dry in Rutland, was added to Stockerston by Local Government Order of 1885. With Stoke Dry, it was held by the Knights Hospitallers as early as 1206 Cur. It is perhaps described as a liberty on account of privileges once held by the Hospitallers. The last harvest at Holyoaks was gathered in 1496, after which Sir Robert Brudenell destroyed seven messuages and evicted thirty villagers to make way for sheep pastures.

ALLEXTON FIELD RD, Allexton lying 2 miles to the north-west. BOLT WOOD, 1609 Ipm, *Boutewod(e)* c.1270 (e.14) *BelCartA*, c.1270 (e.15) *BelCartB*, *v.* **bolt**, **wudu**. CHURCH LANE, *v.* St Peter's Church *infra*. FISHPOND SPINNEY, *v.* **fisc**, **ponde**, **spinney**; referring to stews of the early hall. GREAT SPINNEY. HARBOROUGH HILL RD, the hill on the road to Market Harborough which lies 9 miles to the south-west. THE HERMITAGE (2½"), possibly the site of *hermitagii de Mirabel* 1232 RHug, *Mirabell Hermitagium* 1262, 1270 RGrav, *Le Holliock Merrybell* 1606 *ExchSpC* (with MLat *hermitagium* 'a hermitage'), *v.* Great Merrible Wood in Great Easton and Little Merrible Wood *infra*.

HOLYOAKS LODGE, 1925 Kelly, *v.* **loge**; the site of the former township of Holyoaks. HOLYOAKS WOOD, 1824 O, *Halliock Wood* c.1800, 1806 Map. LITTLE MERRIBLE WOOD, *v.* The Hermitage *supra* and Great Merrible Wood in Great Easton. LODGE FM. MANOR FM, a building which dates from the 17th cent. PARK WOOD, 1824 O, 1840 *TA*, *v.* **park**; once part of the park of Stockerston Hall *infra*. ST PETER'S CHURCH, *Church (St Peter)* 1846, 1863, 1877 White, 1925 Kelly; it is earlier recorded as *ecclesie de Stocfaston* 1220 MHW, 1251 RGros, ~ *de Stokfaston* 1362 *Pat*, *the Church* 1601 *Terrier*. STOCKERSTON HALL, 1925 Kelly, *The Hall* 1863, 1877 White; the present building dates from the 17th cent., but an early hall is recorded as *in the Hall* 1396 Banco (p), *v.* **hall**. Note also *le manor house* 1609 Ipm, *v.* **maner** and Manor Fm *supra*; it is uncertain whether this record relates to the present hall site or to Manor Fm *supra*. UPPINGHAM RD, Uppingham in Rutland lying 2 miles to the north-east.

FIELD-NAMES

In (a), forms presented without dates are 1840 *TA*; those dated c.1800 and 1806 are Map; 1824 are O. Forms throughout dated c.1270 (e.15) and 1417 are *BelCartB*; those dated 1274 (16), 1275 (16), 1278 (16) and 13 (16) are *SlCart*; l.13 and 13 are *Peake*; 1377 are SR; 1501 are *Bru*; 1601, 1631, 1678, 1681, 1687, 1694, 1703 and c.1745 are *Terrier*; 1606 are *ExchSpC*; 1609 are Ipm; 1652 are *Deed*; Chas 1 are Nichols.

(a) Eight Acres, Fourteen ~, Thirty ~, Bottom ~ ~, Middle ~ ~, Top Forty Acres (*v.* **æcer**); The Bank (*v.* **banke**); Barn Cl (*v.* **bern**); Far Bottom Mdw, North Field Bottom Mdw (*v.* North Fd *infra*); Brown's Over Cl (*v.* **uferra**; with the surn. *Brown*); Cottage Cl (*v.* **cotage**); The Flats (*v.* **flat**); Ford Mdw (cf. *ford weye* l.13 (*v.* **weg**), *Stoke Forde* 1601, *v.* **ford**; Stoke Dry in Rutland lies one mile to the south-east); George's Cl (with the surn. *George*); Gibbins' Mdw (with the surn. *Gibbins*); Great Cl; Hall Cl (*v.* Stockerston Hall *supra*); Horse Cl; Lambs Cl (prob. with the surn. *Lamb*, otherwise with **lamb**); Lawn Fd (*le Lowndefeld* 1609, *v.* **launde**, **feld**; one of the great open-fields of the township, also called *Church feild*, *infra*); Far ~ ~, First ~ ~, Middle ~ ~, Lawrence's Lawn Mdw (with the surn. *Lawrence*) (*v.* **launde**); Far ~ ~, Middle Long Cl; Merrible Cl, Furry Merrible (*v.* **fyrsig**), Wards ~ ~ (with the surn. *Ward*), Merrible Mdw (*v.* Little Merrible Wood *supra*); Nether Cl; Far ~ ~, First North Fd (prob. in origin the name of one of the great open-fields, poss. to be identified with *Bridge Feilde*, *infra*; cf. South Fd *infra*); Old Cl, ~ Mdw (*v.* **ald**); Home ~ (*v.* **home**), Wood Park (*le Parke* 1609, *The Park* 1678, *v.* Park Wood *supra*); Parson's Cl, ~ Mdw (cf. *the parsons hooke* 1601 (*v.* **hōc**), *v.* **persone**); Peach's Cl (with the surn. *Peach*, cf. *Charles Peach* 1820 Census of Stockerston and *Hannah Peach* 1822 ib of Holyoaks); Ramsborough Mdw (cf. *Littell Ramsborrow* 1681, *v.*

berg; with **hramsa** or **ramm**; early forms appear in neighbouring Horninghold); Rawlings' Bottom ~, Rawlings' Top Mdw (with the surn. *Rawlings*); Shield's Cl, ~ Mdw (with the surn. *Shield*); Skeffington's First Lane, ~ Long Lane (prob. with **lane**, but **leyne** is poss.; with the surn. *Skeffington* of a family originally from the township of this name, 6 miles to the north-west); South Fd, ~ ~ Mdw, Nether ~ ~ ~, Kirby's South Field Mdw (with the surn. *Kirby*), Road or New South Field Mdw (beside a roadway) (*South Feilde* 1601, *le Southfeild* 1609, *v.* **sūð**, **feld**; one of the great open-fields); Steppings 1824, Halliock Stepings c.1800, 1806 (*v.* **stybbing** and Holyoaks Wood *supra*); Stockerston Woods c.1800; Top Mdw; Topley's Cl (with the surn. *Topley*); Waterfield's Mdw (with the surn. *Waterfield*).

(b) *Seven Acres* 1694, *Eight Acre Close* 1631 (*v.* **æcer**); *Blacmyld* 1275 (16), *Blacmilde* 13, *Blackmild* 13 (16) (*v.* **blæc**, **mylde**); *le Breaches* 1609, *Braaches ~*, *Breeches gate* 1601 (*v.* **gata**) (*v.* **brēc**); *Bridge Close* 1681, *Bridge Feilde* 1601 (*v.* **feld**; one of the great open-fields), *the bridge furlonge* 1601 (*v.* **furlang**) (*v.* **brycg**); *Broadgate Lane alias Stockerston Plaine* 1681 (*v.* **plain**) (*v.* **brād**, **gata**); *Brownes Lane* 1687 (with the surn. *Brown*, cf. Brown's Over Cl *supra*); *Bulhome ~*, *Bull home bush* 1601 (*v.* **busc**), *Bull home corner* 1601 (*v.* **corner**) (*v.* **bula**, **holmr**); *Butchers ~* 1609, *Buchers Close* 1681 (with the surn. *Butcher*); *Church feild alias le Lowndefeld* 1609 (*v.* **churche**, **feld**; one of the great open-fields, *v.* Lawn Fd *supra*); *Church sicke* 1601 (*v.* **sík** and St Peter's Church *supra*); *Crossegate* 1274 (e.16) (*v.* **gata**; prob. with **cross**, otherwise **cros**); *le Goris* 1278 (16) (*v.* **gāra**); *Great Feild* 1631 (*v.* **grēat**); *Gutteridge(s) Feild* 1681 (with the surn. *Gutteridge*, *v.* First Gutteridges in Smeeton Westerby f.ns. (a)); *the Hall close* 1609 (*v.* Stockerston Hall *supra*); *Hunger hill* 1601 (*v.* **hungor**); *le Kingsway* 1278 (16) (*v.* **king**, **weg** and Stockerston Road in Beaumont Chase, Ru 178); *Lampard sicke* 1601, *Great Lamberdike Close*, *Little Lamberdike Meadow* 1681 (*v.* **sík**; with the surn. *Lampard*); *the Lanes* 1703, c.1745 (poss. with **leyne**, cf. Skeffington's First Lane *supra*); *the Lands* 1687 (*v.* **land**; a close comprising an unspecified number of 'lands' of a former great open-field); *lokhawe* 1417, *Locco Wood* 1609, *Locker Wood* 1687 (*v.* **loc**, **haga**[1]); *the manor close* 1609 (*v.* **maner**; relating either to the 17th-cent. house on the site of Stockerston Hall *supra* or to the 17th-cent. Manor Fm *supra*); *Market sicke* 1601 (*v.* **sík**; a surn. as the specific would be expected and Reaney lists *Market(t)* as a surn., but it is rare and otherwise there is no evidence for its presence in the county; perh. a small local market site, *v.* **market**); *the Meadow* 1601, 1631; *Meribell Hill* 1601 (*v.* Little Merrible Wood *supra*); *Moone sicke* 1601 (*v.* **sík**; with the surn. *Moone*, a reflex of AFr *moun* 'a monk'); *the Parsonage Great Close* 1703, c.1745 (*v.* **personage**); *Rampins Meadow* 1681 (poss. with the plant name Rampion (*Campanula rapunculus*)); *Shepherds Copy* 1687 (*v.* **copis**; with the surn. *Shepherd* (*copy* arising from the popular reconstruction of a 'singular' form)); *Spoutehome* 1601 (*v.* **spoute**, **holmr**); *Stanhill hauedelond* 1275 (16) (*v.* **hēafod-land**), *Stonyhull* 1501 (*v.* **stān**, **stānig**, **hyll**); *of þe Ston* 1377 (p) (*v.* **þe**, **stān**); *Sweetehedge Feilde* 1601 (*v.* **swēte**, **feld**, with **etisc** or **edisc**; one of the great open-fields, the toponym appearing as Sweet Hedge in adjacent Allexton, *v.* Lei **3** 7); *Thacholme* 1275 (e.16) (*v.* **þak**, **holmr**); *the town side* 1601 (*v.* **tūn**, **sīde**); *atte Welle* 1377 (p) (*v.* **atte**, **wella**); *West Cliffe* Chas 1 (*v.* **clif**); *West Close* 1652.

Stonton Wyville

STONTON WYVILLE

Stantone 1086 DB (×2), *Stanton* c.1130 LeicSurv, l.12 *ShR*, 1220 MHW *et passim* to 1623, 1727 LML, *Estantona* 1190 × 1204 France

Staunton(*e*) 1230 RHug, 1232 Cur *et passim* to 1549, 1633 Ipm

Stonton 1306 *Hazlerigg*, e.14 *ShR et freq* to 1439 *Peake*, 1452 *ShR et passim* to 1609 *Bru*, 1639 ISLR *et freq*, *Stonton Wivill als. Stonton Brudenell* 1606 *Bru*, *Stonton Brudenell* 1637 *ib*

The usual affix is ~ *Wyvile* 1265 Misc, ~ *Wivell'* 1268 Cl *et freq*, with various spellings, but ~ *Brudenell* 1606, 1609, 1637 *Bru* also appears.

'The farmstead, village on stony ground', *v*. **stān**, **tūn**. *Robertus de Wivele* held the manor in 1230 RHug, with *Thomas de Wyvill* in 1240 RGros and so through to *Robert Wyvyll* in 1417 Fine. The tomb of *William Wyvile* (d. 1452) stands in the parish church, while the manor is recorded as being recently in the hands of *John Wyvell* in 1507 Ipm. The Brudenell family of Deene obtained the manor in 1533 and their family memorials are also to be found in the church: that of *Edmund Brudenell* (d. 1590), of *Thomas Brudenell* (d.1661) and of another *Thomas Brudenell* (d. 1707).

LANGTON CAUDLE, *Cawdwell* 1625, 1638 *Terrier*, *Caudwell* 1637 *Bru*, *Langton Cauldwell* 1806 Map, *Langton Caudwell* 1824 O, 'the cold stream', *v*. **cald**, **wella**. Langton Caudle is now the name of a major hill formation rising to some 500 ft at its northern end overlooking Stonton Wyville and forming a north/south ridge which bends to the south-east above Thorpe Langton and Welham. The watercourse which skirts its lower western and south-western reaches and flows south and south-eastwards into the river Welland was once known by the ancient Anglian name *Lipping* and is recorded as *Lyppyng* as late as c.1545 by the antiquary John Leland (earlier surviving forms are *Lippinge* 1218 *For*, *Lipping'* 1227 ClR, 1228 *For*, *Lipping* 1276 RH, e.14 *ShR*, *Lippinghe* 1284 Ass). Its name is also found in Angel in Jutland in the stream-name

Lipping Aa and is probably formed on the Germanic root **leib* 'to pour, to flow'. The gap in the historical record for the *Lipping* between c.1300 and c.1545 suggests that Leland's form is the result of his antiquarian searches rather than its being a living stream-name in his day, especially as the *Caldwell* is recorded contemporarily in 1545 in Welham. The forms which belong to Langton Caudle then continue from 1625 and point clearly to a stream **caldwella* rather than to a hill. The watercourse, obviously a very early eastern boundary marker for Tur Langton, Church ~ and East Langton and Thorpe Langton parishes, as well as a western boundary marker for Welham, has also given rise to the forms *Cauwell seeke* 1625 *Terrier* in Tur Langton, the name of a stream-side meadow, *Caudwell planke* 1625 *Terrier*, *Cawdwell Planke* 1694, 1712, 1715 *ib* in East Langton, alluding to a small bridge across the stream, *Caldwell* 1545 *Star* in Welham and Cawdell Farm in Thorpe Langton which retains in part the form of the generic *wella*.

**Caldwell* thus appears to be a medieval (alternative or replacement?) name for the *Lipping*, perhaps once referring to stream-side pasture on the lower slopes of Langton Caudle to the east of the stream and then transferred to the whole hill massif when confusion occurred because of the common e.17th-cent. interchange between *well* and *hill* in minor names arising from the shortening of such generics in compound. That Caudle is a **Caldhyll* 'cold, windswept hill' which, with a reduced generic, eventually gave its name to the stream as a mistaken **Caldwell* has no foundation in the surviving evidence.

FOX AND HOUNDS FM, *Fox and Hounds* 1846, 1863, 1877 White, 1925 Kelly; the farm was formerly an inn. KNAVE HILL (local), *The Neville* 1967 *Surv*, cf. *Navill close* 1601 *Terrier*, *Knavill ~*, *Knavehill closse* 1625, *v.* **cnafa, hyll**; the site of an early Anglo-Saxon settlement. MANOR HO., *v.* **maner**. MILL FM (WATER MILL HO. 2½"), *the Water mill* 1609 *Bru*, *the water milne* 1625 *Terrier*, *v.* **water-mylne**; also recorded as *Molendin' Aquat'* 1609 *Bru* (with Lat *molendinum* 'a mill' and *aquaticum* 'worked by water'). THE RECTORY, 1877 White, 1925 Kelly, *the Rectory House* 1831 *Terrier*, *v.* **rectory**; earlier is *the Parsonage* 1601 *ib*, 1606 *Bru*, *the Parsonage House* 1745 *Terrier*, *v.* **personage**. ST DENYS'S CHURCH, *the Church* 1745 *Terrier*, *Church (St Denis)* 1846, 1863, 1877 White, *Church (St Denys)* 1925 Kelly; it is earlier recorded as *ecclesiam ~ ~*, *ecclesie de Stanton* 1220 MHW, 1240 RGros, *ecclesiarum de Staunton* (*et Ayleston*) 1294 *Pat*. Note also *the Church Yard* 1625, 1698, 1831 *Terrier*, *v.* **churchyerd**. STONTON WOOD, 1609, 1637 *Bru*, *Stanton Wood* 1806 Map, *v.* **wudu**.

FIELD-NAMES

In (a), forms presented without dates are 1967 *Surv*; those dated 1824 are O. Forms throughout dated 1460, 1495, 1507, 1606, 1607, 1608, 1609 and 1639 are *Bru*; those dated 1601, 1625, 1637, 1638, 1679, 1690, 1694, 1698 and 1745 are *Terrier*; 1683 are Nichols.

(a) Seventeen Acre (*v.* **æcer**); Barn Mdw (*v.* **bern**); Bates (the surn. *Bates* in the possessive case); Big Fd, ~ Mdw; Buildings Fd; Burnt Ground (*v.* **brend**, **grund**); Bush Mdw (*v.* **busc**); Caudle Hill (*v.* Langton Caudle *supra*); Clover Cl (*v.* **clāfre**; grown as a fodder crop); First ~ ~, Second Cow Fd; Cowsic Cl (*Cowe sicke* 1601, *Cow Sicke*, *Cowsike* 1625, cf. *Cowsicke banke* 1625 (*v.* **banke**), *v.* **cū**, **sík**); Crow Trees (*v.* **crāwe**, **trēow**); Davis's (the surn. *Davis* in the possessive case); Far ~, Middle Gartree, Gartree Cl (fields beside Gartree Road which runs through the north of the parish); Bennetts ~ ~, Home Fd (*v.* **home**; with the surn. *Bennett*); Jessons, ~ Hill, Top Jessons, Jessons Cow Fd (with the surn. *Jesson*); Little Mdw; Long Mdw; Middle Fd; Over Cl (*v.* **uferra**); The Park (*The Parke* 1637, *v.* **park**); the Parson's Cl 1831 (*the Parsons Close* 1690), Parsons Piece 1967 (*v.* **pece**) (*v.* **persone**); Vendy's ~ ~, Old Plough (*v.* **plōg**; with the surn. *Vendy*, cf. *Wm. Vendy* 1877 Census of neighbouring Thorpe Langton); Berry's ~ ~, Round Fd (with the surn. *Berry*), Round Spinney (*v.* **spinney**) (*v.* **round**); Old ~, Seeds (*v.* **sǣd**; used of grasses sown for one year's mowing or grazing, as distinguished from permanent pasture); Spy and Cop (sic) (a hill named from the Battle of Spion Kop fought in 1900 some 20 miles south-west of Ladysmith in South Africa between British and Boer forces, resulting in a British defeat. The steep Spion Kop (Afrikaans *Spioenkop* 'look-out hill') was the largest hill in the region and an important military strong point); Staunton Gorse 1824 (*v.* **gorst**); Staunton Mill 1824 (*Stonton Mill* 1639; it is *the Windmill* 1609, *v.* **wind-mylne**); Stockings (*Stokings* 1637, cf. *the Grete Stoking* 1507, *v.* **grēat**, **stoccing**); Thistle Fd (*v.* **þistel**); Thorpe Fd (adjacent to Thorpe Langton); Vendy's (*v.* Vendy's Old Plough *supra*); Walker's (the surn. *Walker* in the possessive case); Watson's (the surn. *Watson* in the possessive case); Bottom ~ ~, Middle ~ ~, Top Wood Cl (*v.* Stonton Wood *supra*).

(b) *Bare Hill* 1601, 1625, 1638 (prob. with **bere** 'barley', cf. Bare Hill in Glooston f.ns. (a)); *Blackwell* 1679, 1690, 1694, 1698 (*v.* **blæc**, **wella**); *the Breches* 1638 (*v.* **brēc**); *Brenwode* 1507 (*v.* **brend**, **wudu**); *Brinks furlong* 1625 (*v.* **brink**, **furlang**); *the broke* 1601, *the Brooke* 1625, 1694, *Broke Feilde* 1601, *the Brooke nether feild* 1625 (*v.* **neoðera**), *Brooke Feilde* 1637, *Brook Feild* 1638 (*v.* **feld**; one of the great open-fields of the township), *Brooke furlong* (*v.* **furlang**), *Brooke syde* (*v.* **sīde**) 1625 (*v.* **brōc**); *Tho. Brudnels closse* (*v.* **clos(e)**), *Tho. Brudnells headlea* (*v.* **headley**) 1625, *Mr Brud(e)nells Orchard* 1679, 1690, 1698, 1745 (*v.* **orceard**); *Cawdwell gutter* 1625 (*v.* **goter** and Langton Caudle *supra*); *Clayes leas* 1625, *Cleys leyes* 1637, *Claies Leas side* 1625 (*v.* **sīde**) (*v.* **leys**; with the surn. *Clay*); *the church yard syde* 1625 (*v.* **sīde** and St Denys's Church *supra*); *the Common pasture* 1625, 1638, *the Comon Pasture of Hogates* 1625 (*v.* **commun**, **pasture** and *Howgate*, *infra*); *the Conigree* 1601, 1625, *the Conygree* 1606, 1608, *the Coneygree* 1638, *Conigree Hill* 1601, *Conigre(e) leas* 1625 (*v.* **leys**) (*v.* **coningre**); *Creak Hill* 1625 (a pre-English hill name, PrW **creig** 'hill', cf. Grick in Kibworth Beauchamp f.ns.

(a) and Crick, Nth 68); *deepdale* 1601, *depdale*, ~ *leas* 1625, *depthdale leas* (sic) 1638 (*v.* **leys**) (*v.* **dēop**, **dalr**); *dole holes* 1625 (*v.* **dāl**, **hol**[1]); *drouers close* 1601, *drovers closse* 1625, *Drovers Close* 1679, 1690, 1745, *drovers closse corner* (*v.* **corner**), ~ ~ *end* (*v.* **ende**) 1625 (either with ME **drovere** 'a drover' or its surn. reflex *Drover*); *Easte meddow closse* 1601, *East Meadow Close* 1606, 1607, 1609, 1637, *East medow closse*, ~ ~ ~ *hedge corner* 1625 (*v.* **hecg**, **corner**) (*v.* **ēast**, **mēd** (**mēdwe** obl.sg.), **clos(e)**); *Egill(s) farme* 1606, 1609 (*v.* **ferme**; at this date, the survival of the ON masc. pers.n. *Egill* is hardly to be expected, so this may rather represent the surn. *Edgell*, a reflex of the OE masc. pers.n. *Ecgel*, a diminutive of one of the various OE compound masc. pers.ns. with *Ecg-*); *the furr-leas of Edmond Smith* (*v.* **fyrs**, **leys**); *the Furres* ~, *the furs hill* 1625, *Furrs hill* 1638 (*v.* **fyrs**); *Glooston feild syde* 1625 (*v.* **sīde**; Glooston parish adjoins to the east); *the Gospell place* 1625 (a spot where a passage from the gospel was read when parish bounds were beaten, *v.* **godspel**, **place**); *the Greate Pasture* 1637 (*v.* **grēat**, **pasture**); *the Grete Clos* 1495, *Stonton Great Close* 1606, 1607, 1609, *Great closse hedge* (*v.* **hecg**), ~ ~ *yate* (*v.* **geat**) 1625 (*v.* **grēat**, **clos(e)**); *Gutteriges Close* 1637 (with the surn. *Gutteridge*); *the Hagges*, ~ *Hags* 1625 (*v.* **hǫgg**); *Harborow balke* 1625 (*v.* **balca**; butting on the road to Market Harborough); *Harborow waye* 1625 (*v.* **weg**; the road to Market Harborough which lies 5 miles to the south); *Hardwyke Brigge Clos* 1460 (*v.* **clos(e)** and Hardwick Bridge in Shangton); *Hardewicke Feilde* 1601 (*v.* **feld**; one of the great open-fields adjoining Hardwick in Shangton parish, also called *the Upper Feild* and *North Feild*, *infra*); *Hill Feild(e)* 1637, 1638 (*v.* **hyll**, **feld**; one of the great open-fields, earlier called *Wynde Myll Feilde* and *the Milne feild*, both *infra*); *agaynst the Hill*, *the Topp of the hill* (*v.* **topp**), *the Hill syde* (*v.* **sīde**) 1601, *the Hills* 1625 (at the boundary with Glooston parish); *Hogges home* 1601, *Hogs-home* 1625 (*v.* **hogg**, **holmr**); *Howgate* 1601, *Howgates*, *Hogates*, *Hogate furlong* (*v.* **furlang**), *Hogates grasse grownd* (*v.* **græs**, **grund**), *Hogates waye* 1625 (*v.* **gata**; with **haugr** or **hōh**); *Hutchins Fur-lea* (*v.* **ley**; with **feor** or **fyrs**), ~ *hagges* (*v.* **hǫgg**), ~ *Headland* (*v.* **hēafod-land**), ~ *headlea* (*v.* **headley**), ~ *leas* (*v.* **leys**) 1625 (cf. *Edmond Hutchins* 1625); *Jenkins closse* (*v.* **clos(e)**), *Tho. Jenkins meadow* 1625; *Lathyard*, ~ *furlong* 1625 (*v.* **hlaða**, **geard**); *the leas* 1625 (*v.* **leys**); (*the*) *Lit(t)le Feild* 1625, 1637, 1698, ~ *Field* 1679, 1690, 1745; (*the*) *Litle sicke* 1625 (*v.* **sík**); *the meddowe* 1601; *the mill* 1601 (*v.* **myln**; the windmill in *Wynde Myll Feilde*, *infra*); *the Miln(e) Lane* 1625, 1679, 1690, 1694, 1698, *The Mill Lane* 1745 (*v.* **myln**, **lane**; leading to the watermill, *v.* Mill Fm *supra*); *the Milne waye* 1625 (*v.* **myln**; leading to the windmill); *Monkes cheese-cake peece* (*v.* **chese-cake**, **pece**), ~ *lea* (*v.* **ley**[2]), ~ *lane end* (*v.* **lane-ende**) 1625 (with the surn. *Monk*); *Hen. Mores headland* (*v.* **hēafod-land**), *Henrie Mores leas* (*v.* **leys**) 1625; (*the*) *New Close* 1679, 1690, 1694, 1698, 1745; *the 9 foot doles* 1625 (*v.* **nigon**, **fōt**, **dāl**); *North Feild* 1637 (one of the great open-fields, earlier called *Hardewicke Feilde*, *supra*, otherwise *the Upper Feild*); *the Old Enclosure* 1698, 1745 (*v.* **enclosure**); *Parke peece* 1625 (*v.* **pece** and The Park *supra*); *Parsones sicke* 1601 (*v.* **persone**), (*the*) *Parsonage sicke* 1625 (*v.* **personage**) (*v.* **sík**); *the Pen yard* 1625 (*v.* **penn**[2], **geard**); *Poles* ~ 1606, *Pawles* ~ 1607, *Paules close* 1609, 1637 (with the surn. *Paul*); *the Round Hill* 1625 (*v.* **round**); *Shankton closse* 1638 (*v.* **clos(e)**), *Shankton hedge* 1625 (the parish boundary hedge with Shangton which adjoins to the north-west); *Shawes* ~ 1606, 1607, 1609, *Shaws Close* 1637 (with the surn. *Shaw*); *Short Lane end* 1625 (*v.* **sc(e)ort**, **lane**, **lane-ende**); *Smiths hade* 1625 (*v.* **hēafod**), *Henry Smiths Close* 1679, 1690, 1745; *Upper*

~ ~, *Sow Medow*, *Sow Medow leas* (v. **leys**) 1625 (v. **sūð**); *Stangate* ~, *Stongate furlong* (v. **furlang**), *Stongate lane* 1625 (v. **stān**, **gata**; the Roman Gartree Road which runs across the north of the parish); *Thorpe Hill* 1601 (at the southern end of the parish next to Thorpe Langton; presum. another name for Knave Hill *supra*); *Towne closes* 1606, *the Town end* 1694 (v. **ende**) (v. **tūn**); *the Upper Feild* 1625 (v. **upper**, **feld**; one of the great open-fields, also called *Hardewicke Feilde* and *North Feild*); *the Warren* 1609 (v. **wareine**); *the Water milne syde* 1625 (v. **sīde** and Mill Fm *supra*); *the woad-ground* 1683 (v. **wād**, **grund**); *Wynd Myll Feilde* 1601, *the Milne Feild* 1625 (v. **wind-mylne**, **myln**, **feld**; one of the great open-fields).

Stoughton

STOUGHTON

Stoctone 1086 DB, *Stoctona* 1156 (1318) Ch, 1174 BM, *Stocton'* 1202 FF, 1203 Cur (p) *et passim* to 1262 Fine, 1275 *RTemple* (p) *et freq* to 1374, 1376 *LCDeeds* (p) *et passim* to 1412 Pat (p), 1435 *Rut* (p), *Stoctun* c.1233 GildR (p), *Stocthon* 1220 × 50 *RTemple* (p)

Stokton' 1250, 1251 Cur (p) *et freq* to 1382 Cl, 1383 Hastings, *Stoktuna* Hy 2 Dugd

Stoketon' 1256 FineR (p), l.13 *RTemple* (p)

Stockton' 1277 Abbr, 1332 SR (p)

Stouton 1290, 1292 GildR (p), 1316 FA

Stoghton' 1320, 1322 GildR (p) *et passim* to 1352 *Wyg* (p), 1384 *LCDeeds* (p)

Stoughton 1349 *LCDeeds*, 1317 *Wyg* (p) *et passim* to 1526 AAS, 1535 VE *et freq*, *Stowghton* 1539 MinAccts

Staughton 1610 Speed, *Stawton* 1631 ISLR

'The settlement with an attached dairy-farm', *v.* **stoc**, **tūn**. For discussion of the element **stoc** and its combinations, *v.* Studies[2], 11–43.

BROOK SPINNEY, *v.* **brōc**, **spinney**. CHARITY FM, the rent of its land once providing funds for a Mountsorrel charity, *v.* Mountsorrel Land in Bushby f.ns. (a). CHURCH LANE, *v.* St Mary's Church *infra*. CLARKE'S BUSH, *Clarkes Bush* 1913 Sale, *Great* ~ ~, *Little Clark*(*e*)*'s Bush* 1848 *TA*, 1878, 1907 *PK*, 1906 *Surv*, 1913 Sale, *v.* **busc**; with the surn. *Clarke*. CORN CLOSE, 1845 *TA*, 1878 *PK*, 1906 *Surv*, 1907 *PK*, *v.* **corn**[1]. DAM'S SPINNEY, *Dams Spinney* 1906 *Surv*, *v.* **damme**, **spinney**. GARTREE ROAD, the Roman *Via Devana*, *v.* Gartree Hundred *supra*. GAULBY LANE, Galby lying 3 miles to the east. HOME FM, *v.* **home**. JONES'S SPINNEY, *Jones' Spinney* 1878 *PK*, *v.* **spinney**; with the surn. *Jones*. KETTLESBOROUGH (2½") is *Kesborough Hill* 1845 *TA*, 1878 *PK*, 1906 *Surv*, 1907 *PK*, *v.* **berg**; if the form on the 2½" O.S. map of 1951 represents an authentic tradition, then with the ON masc. pers.n. *Ketill*;

otherwise the first el. is obscure. LEICESTER EAST AERODROME. POLTON HILL, 1690, 1694 *Deed*, *Poltone Hill* 1690 *ib*, *Polton* ~, *Poulton Hill* 1878, 1907 *Surv*, *v.* Polton Hill in adjoining Thurnby f.ns. (a). RIDDLESTONE LODGE, *v.* **loge**; with the surn. *Riddlestone*. ST MARY'S CHURCH, *Church (St Mary)* 1925 Kelly; earlier is recorded *capellam Stocton* 1220 MHW (with MLat *capella* 'a chapel'). Note also *the Chappell yard at Stoughton* 1625 *Terrier* (a Thurnby document), *v.* **chapel(e)**. STOUGHTON GRANGE, 1835 O, 1846, 1863, 1877 White, 1925 Kelly, *v.* **grange**; demolished in 1926. STOUGHTON HALL, 1804 Nichols, *v.* **hall**. STOUGHTON LODGE, *v.* **loge**. THURNBY LANE is *Thurnby wey* 1477 (e.16), *v.* **weg**; Thurnby lies 2 miles to the north.

FIELD-NAMES

In (a), forms dated 1761 are Nichols; those dated 1845 are *TA*; 1878 and 1907 are *PK*; 1906 and 1968 are *Surv*; 1913 are Sale. Forms throughout dated 1276 and 1340 are Coram; those dated 1312 and 1554[1] are *Pat*; 1327 are SR; 1378 are Hastings; 1405 and 1729 are *Deed*; 1477 (e.16) are *Charyte*; 1467 × 84 are *LTD*; 1554[2] and 1559 are AILR.

(a) Three ~, Four Acres 1845, 1878, 1906, 1907, 1913, Five ~ 1845, 1878, Six ~ 1906, 1907, Seven ~ 1845, 1878, 1907, 1913, Eight ~ 1968, Twelve ~ 1907, 1913, 1968, Thirteen ~ 1968, Seventeen ~ 1845, 1878, 1907, 1913, Eighteen ~ 1968, Twenty ~ 1907, 1913, Far ~ ~, Middle ~ ~ 1845, 1878, 1907, 1913, Near Thirty Acres 1907, 1913, Thirty-three Acre 1968 (*v.* **æcer**); Aeroplane Fd 1968 (alluding to Leicester East Aerodrome *supra*); Ash Holt 1878, 1907, 1913 (*v.* **æsc**, **holt**); Barn Cl 1845, 1906, 1907, 1913, 1968, Big ~ ~, Little Barn Cl 1845, 1878, 1906, 1907 (*v.* **bern**); Bennett's ~ 1845, 1878, 1907, Bennet's Cl 1913 (cf. *William Bennett* 1822 Census of Stoughton); Blackberry Hill 1845, 1878, 1907, 1913 (*v.* **blæc**, **berg**); Bottom Mdw 1906, 1907 (*v.* **bottom**); Nether Breach 1878, 1907, Middle ~ ~, Upper Nether Breach 1878, 1907 (*v.* **neoðera**, **brēc**); Brook Fd 1906, 1907, 1913, ~ Mdw 1906, 1907 (*v.* **brōc**); Bushby Meer 1845 (*v.* **(ge)mǣre**; the boundary with Bushby which adjoins to the north-east); Butt Fd 1878, First ~ ~ 1878, 1906, 1907, Second Butt Fd 1906, 1907, Butt Field Mdw 1878, 1906, 1907 (cf. *Buttecloses alias Botecloses* 1554[1], *But closes* 1554[2], 1559, 1562, *v.* **butte**, **clos(e)**); Calves Mdw 1845, 1878, 1907 (*v.* **calf**); Clover Cl 1913 (*v.* **clāfre**; grown as a fodder crop); Cobblers Cl 1878, 1907 (with the surn. *Cobbler*, a reflex of ME *cobelere* 'a cobbler'); the Coney Greys 1761, Far ~, Great ~, Middle Conery 1878, 1906, 1907 (*v.* **coningre**); Corners Piece 1907, 1913 (*v.* **pece**; with the surn. *Corner*, cf. *Elizabeth Corner* 1825 Census, *Mary Corner* 1863 ib and *John Corner* 1865 ib, all of Stoughton); Cottam 1878, 1906, 1907 (*v.* **cot** (**cotum** dat.pl.)); Great ~, Little Covert 1845 (*v.* **cover(t)**); Cow Cl 1906, 1907, 1913, Little Cow Cl 1906, 1907, 1913; Croft 1906, Little Crofts 1878, 1906 (*v.* **croft**); Cricket Fd 1968 (for the game of cricket); Cross Leys 1968 (*v.* **leys**; poss. with **cros** (note *Thirneby Cros* in f.ns. (b) *infra*); otherwise **cross**); Dams

1906, Little ~ ~, Lower Damsford Cl 1878, 1907 (*v.* **ford**) (*v.* **damme** and Dam's Spinney *supra*); Fingerpost 1968 (*v.* **finger-post**); The Folly 1845 (*v.* **folie**); Fox Covert 1878 (*v.* **fox**, **cover(t)**); Lower ~ ~, Top Gallow Tree 1878, 1906, 1907, Galtree Spinney 1907 (*v.* **spinney**) (cf. *Galtre Close* 1554[1], 1554[2], 1559, 1562, *v.* **clos(e)**) (*v.* **galg-trēow**); Garden Cl 1906, 1907 (*v.* **gardin**; land used for horticulture); Gorman Cl 1845 (with the surn. *Gorman*); Gorse Cl 1845, 1878, 1906, 1907 (*v.* **gorst**); Gosby Thorn(e) 1845, 1878, 1907, 1913 (*Gosmerethorne* 1467 × 84, *v.* **gōs**, **mere**[1], **þorn**); Grants ~ 1878, 1906, 1907, Grant Leys 1907 (*v.* **leys**; with the surn. *Grant*); Gravel Hole 1968, ~ ~ Cl 1906, 1907 (*v.* **hol**[1]), Gravel Pit Piece 1878 (*v.* **pytt**, **pece**) (*v.* **gravel**); Great Cl 1913; Bottom ~ ~, Top Great Ground 1878, 1907 (*v.* **grund**); Gun Site 1968 (a f.n. from World War Two, relating to the defence of Leicester East Aerodrome *supra*); Hall Cl 1906, 1907 (*v.* Stoughton Hall *infra*); Bottom ~ ~ 1913, Handkerchief Mdw 1913, 1968 (fanciful names for small patches of land); Lower ~, Upper Hanging Lands 1845, 1878, 1906, 1907, 1913 (cf. *Hangynglondeshauedlond* 1467 × 84, *v.* **hēafod-land**) (*v.* **hangende**, **land**); Little Head Fd 1907, ~ ~ Mdw 1878 (*v.* **hēafod**); Hen Plot 1906, 1907 (*v.* **henn**, **plot**); Herricks Farm 1913 (with the surn. *Herrick*); Home Cl 1907, 1913, Little ~ ~, Home Fd 1878, Homefield 1907, 1968 (*v.* **home**); Great ~, Little Homestead 1906, 1907, 1913 (*v.* **hām-stede**); Hunts Fd 1845, 1878, 1907, 1913 (with the surn. *Hunt*, cf. *Frank Hunt* 1841 Census, *John Hunt* 1872 ib and *Amos Hunt* 1876 ib of Stoughton); Keeper's Cl 1878, 1906, 1907, ~ Cottage 1906 (referring to the Powys-Keck estate gamekeeper); Kesborough Hill Mdw 1845, 1878, 1906, 1907, ~ ~ Spinney 1845, 1878, Kesborough Spinney Cl 1845, 1878, 1906, 1907 (*v.* **spinney**) (*v.* Kettlesborough *supra*); Klondyke 1968 (a transferred name alluding to land distant from the village; gold was discovered in 1896 on the Klondike river in Yukon Territory in north-west Canada, leading to the gold rush of 1897–8); Long Mdw 1845, 1878, 1907, 1913, 1968; Long Walk 1878, 1906 (*v.* **walk**); Marl Cl 1878, 1906, 1907, ~ Piece 1845 (*v.* **pece**) (*v.* **marle**; marl consists of clay mixed with calcium carbonate and was spread on sandy soils to improve crop growth); Middle Fd 1845, 1878, 1907, 1913; First Bottom Mill Cl, Second ~ ~, Third Mill Cl, Great ~ ~ ~, Little Top Mill Cl, Mill Field Mdw 1878, 1906, 1907 (*v.* **myln**); Moore's Fd 1907 (with the surn. *Moore*); Mushroom Fd 1968 (land on which mushrooms could be gathered); New Cl 1913, ~ Fd 1906, 1907, ~ Mdw 1907; Noon's Cl 1845, 1878, 1906, 1907 (with the surn. *Noon*, cf. *Elizabeth Noon* 1833 Census and *Hannah Noon* 1841 ib, both of Stoughton); Over Cl 1845, 1907, 1913, Far ~ ~, Near Over Cl 1845, 1878, 1906, 1907, 1913 (*v.* **uferra**); Padlands 1968 (*v.* **land**; prob. with **padde**; otherwise with dial. **pad** 'a path'); Palmers Cl 1845, 1878, 1906, 1907, 1913, ~ Mdw 1845 (with the surn. *Palmer*); First ~ ~ ~, Second Pear Tree Mdw 1845, 1878, 1906, 1907 (cf. *atte Pertre* 1312 (p) (*v.* **atte**), *ad Pir'* 1327 (p) (with MLat *pirus* 'pear-tree'), *v.* **pertre**); Peberdy's Mdw 1913 (with the surn. *Peberdy*); Pig Hut 1968 (*v.* **pigga**, **hut**); Pine Yard 1878 (prob. a small enclosure containing pine trees; survival of ME **pine** 'labour, toil, effort' is very unlikely); Robinson's Cl 1906, 1907 (with the surn. *Robinson*); Seven Acre Mdw 1878 (*v.* **æcer**); Sinkhole 1968 (*v.* **sinke**, **hol**[1]); Great ~ ~, Little Acre Slade, Acre Slade Mdw 1845, 1878, 1906, 1907, 1913 (*v.* **æcer**, **slæd**); Smalley's Cl 1878, 1907 (with the surn. *Smalley*); Spinney Cl 1913, ~ Fd 1878, 1907 (*v.* **spinney**); Stackyard Cl 1878, 1906, 1907 (*v.* **stackyard**); Stretton Mdw 1845, 1878, 1906, 1907 (towards Great Stretton to the south-east); Swadborough Spinney, ~ ~ Cl 1845, 1878, 1906, 1907 (*v.* **berg**; an OE masc. pers.n.

such as *Sigeweard* is poss. as the specific, or a sb. **sweord**, used of narrow promontory); First ~ ~, Second ~ ~, Third Sykes Cl 1845, 1878, 1907, 1913 (*v.* **sík**); Great ~, Little Sybthorpe 1845, ~, ~ Sythorpe 1907, 1913 (*v.* **þorp**; poss. with the ODan masc. pers.n. *Sibbi* (a short form of *Sigbjǫrn*), but an earlier spelling *Sythorpes* is recorded in 1625 for adjoining Bushby which is in keeping with the early 20th-cent. forms and suggests that the medial *b* may be intrusive); Taddy Pond Fd 1968 (*taddy* is a common dial. form for *tadpole* 'the frog larva'); Three Cornered Cl 1906, 1909, ~ ~ Piece 1845, 1878 (*v.* **pece**) (*v.* **three-cornered**); Top Cl 1913, ~ Fd 1845, 1878, 1907, 1913, ~ Mdw 1906, 1907, ~ Park 1907 (*v.* **park**) (*v.* **top**); Townend 1907, 1913, ~ Cl 1845, 1878, First ~, Second Townsend 1845, 1878, 1907, 1913 (*v.* **tūn**, **ende**); Upper Cl 1845, 1878, 1906, 1907, 1913; Wakes Hill 1907, 1913, Wakeshill 1968 (*Wakerishul* 1477 (e.16), *le Wakerehull*, *le Wakereshyll* 1467 × 84, *v.* **hyll**; the specific may be the recorded OE masc. pers.n. *Wacer*, from the adj. *wacor*, *wæccer* 'watchful, vigilant' (cf. ON *vakr* 'watchful, alert'), but this hill located beside the major Gartree Road suggests that an adj. **wacor** in its name could have been used as a sb. meaning 'the watchful one, the watcher', or that surviving here is an otherwise unrecorded **wæccere** 'a watchman, a look-out' and that the hill was used as a look-out place); Walkers Farm 1913, Little Walkers 1968 (with the surn. *Walker*); Wilson Lovatt 1968 (the name of the field's owner); Witte Fd 1878 (with the surn. *Witte*, a form of *White*); Woodground 1878, ~ Mdw 1907 (*v.* **wudu**, **grund**).

(b) *Aboueþesti* 1467 × 84 (*v.* **aboven**, **þe**, **stīg**); *Ageythehull* 1467 × 84 (*v.* **ageynst**, **hyll**); *Astenhill* 1467 × 84 (*v.* **ēastan**, **hyll**); *le Blakpitt* 1467 × 84 (*v.* **blæc**, **pytt**); *Bradefurlong'* 1467 × 84 (*v.* **brād**, **furlang**); *le Breche* 1467 × 84 (*v.* **brēc**); *le Brok'* 1467 × 84, *Brocfurlong*, *le Brokfurlong* 1477 (e.16) (*v.* **furlang**) (*v.* **brōc**); *Brimelsyke*, *Brimilsike*, *Brymilsike* 1467 × 84, *Brymmilsyke* 1477 (e.16) (*v.* **brēmel**, **sík**); *Bussebybrokesende* 1467 × 84 (*v.* **brōc**, **ende**; Bushby parish adjoins to the north-east); *Caldewelslade* 1467 × 84 (*v.* **cald**, **wella**, **slæd**); *Campus versus Outheby*, *Campus versus Thurneby* 1467 × 84 (two of the early great open-fields, one in the direction Oadby to the south-west, the other in the direction of Thurnby to the north-east (with MLat *versus* 'towards')); *le Cornelandes* 1467 × 84 (*v.* **corn**[1], **land**); *Countasfurlong*' 1467 × 84 (*v.* **cuntesse**, **furlang**; presum. a memory of the manor's early possession by the Earls of Leicester (cf. *Cowntasbrygge* 1477 (e.16) in Leicester, *v.* Lei **1** 73)); *Derby wey* 1477 (e.16) (*v.* **weg**; the road to Derby which lies 28 miles to the north-west; into Leicester, this is Gartree Road); *le Dolemedowe* 1467 × 84 (*v.* **dāl**, **mēd** (**mēdwe** obl.sg.)); *Edrichisthwong* 1467 × 84 (*v.* **þwang**; with the OE masc. pers.n. *Ēadrīc*); *Edusmedwe* 1467 × 84 (*v.* **mēd** (**mēdwe** obl.sg.); the specific is either **ēde** 'a flock' or poss. the OE masc. pers.n. *Ēad* (cf. Eddisbury Ch **3** 213), but here this may be an abbreviated form of *Ēadrīc* of the previous f.n.); *Flakmydo* 1477 (e.16) (*v.* **flak**, **mēd** (**mēdwe** obl.sg.)); *atte Hagge* 1276 (p) (*v.* **hǫgg**); *atte Hall* 1378 (p) (*v.* **atte**, **hall**; a hall in this township is otherwise unrecorded until 1804, *v.* Stoughton Hall *supra*); *le Hardgore* 1467 × 84 (*v.* **heard**, **gāra**); *Hardmydo* 1477 (e.16) (*v.* **heard**, **mēd** (**mēdwe** obl.sg.)); *Helmpittis furlong* 1477 (e.16) (*v.* **helm**, **pytt**, **furlang**); *atte Hille* 1276 (p) (*v.* **atte**), *del Hulle* 1312 (p), 1340 (p) (*v.* **hyll**); *Houghtonmore* (*v.* **mōr**[1]), *Houghtonwellsike* (*v.* **wella**, **sík**) 1467 × 84 (Houghton on the Hill parish adjoins to the north-east); *le Hondfeld'*, *Houndfeld'* 1467 × 84 (*v.* **feld**; if this is a surviving name of a great open-field, then **hund** 'a hound' as the specific seems out of place; perh. **hūne** 'hoarhound' may pertain); *Intoþedikes*, *Intoþedikys* 1467 × 84 (*v.* **into**, **þe**, **dík**); *Kaspergate* 1477 (e.16) (*v.* **gata**; with the surn. *Kasper/Casper* (from a Persian word *kaspur* 'treasurer'), a name given by tradition to one of the three wise men who attended the birth of Christ; prob. introduced as a pers.n. by returning Crusaders in the 12th cent. and later developing into a surn.); *Knytonmore* 1477 (e.16) (*v.* **mōr**[1]; in its form as a separate township, Knighton once lay 9 miles to the west); *Longbygate* 1477 (e.16) (*v.* **lang**[2], **bī**, **gata**); *Longlond'* 1467 × 84 (*v.* **lang**[1], **land**); *le Longrodes* 1467 × 84, *les longas rodas* 1477 (e.16) (*v.* **lang**[1], **rōd**); *Longwong* 1405, 1477 (e.16) (*v.* **lang**[1], **vangr**); *Medewynterstykkes* 1477 (e.16), *Midewinter stickes* 1467 × 84 (*v.* **midwinter**, **stykke**; the name appears to identify woodland or shrub whose exploitation was restricted to the midwinter period, perh. cf. *Midsomer bush* in King's Norton f.ns. (b); the surn. *Midwinter* is unlikely); *le Mikel stikes* 1467 × 84 (*v.* **micel**, **mikill**, **stykke**); *le Morhauedes* 1467 × 84 (*v.* **mōr**[1], **hēafod** and *Knytonmore*, *supra*); (*the*) *New Close* 1477 (e.16), 1559, 1562, *the nether close alias le new close* 1554[1], *the Nether or New Close* 1554[2] (*v.* **neoðera**) (*v.* **nīwe**, **clos(e)**); *Nicolswong* 1477 (e.16), *Nicholeswong* 1467 × 84 (*v.* **vangr**; with the surn. *Nic*(*h*)*ol*); *Northemedo* 1477 (e.16), *le Northmedwe feldes* (*v.* **feld**), *Northmedewgate* (*v.* **gata**) 1467 × 84 (*v.* **norð**, **mēd** (**mēdwe** obl.sg.)); *Okley* 1477 (e.16) (*v.* **āc**, **lēah**); *le Peselandis* 1467 × 84 (*v.* **pise**, **land**); *le Portgate* 1467 × 84 (*v.* **port-gate**), *le Portwey* 1467 × 84, *the Port Way* 1729 (*v.* **port-wey**) (this is the Gartree Road to Leicester); *Sirestonsty* 1467 × 84 (*v.* **stīg**; the track to a lost 'Sigehere's farm', *v.* **tūn**; the masc. pers.n. *Sigehere* is OE, cf. Syerston, Nt 218); *Smalthorngate* 1477 (e.16) (*v.* **smæl**, **þorn**, **gata**); *Sowthefeld* 1477 (e.16) (*v.* **sūð**, **feld**; one of the early great open-fields); *le Stanyhill*, *le Stanyhull* 1467 × 84 (*v.* **stānig**, **hyll**); *Stoctonhilhadlond'* 1467 × 84 (*v.* **hyll**, **hēafod-land**; compounded with the township's name); *le Styh*, *le Sty versus Longlond'* 1467 × 84 (*v.* **stig** and *Longlond'*, *supra*; with MLat *versus* 'towards'); *le Sykedole* 1467 × 84 (*v.* **sík**, **dāl**); *Thirneby Cros* 1467 × 84 (*v.* **cros**; a cross on the parish boundary with Thurnby which lies to the north-east); *le Tunge* 1467 × 84 (*v.* **tunge**); *Thwertforowes* 1467 × 84 (*v.* **þverr** (**þvert** neut.), **furh**); *le Thwonge* 1467 × 84 (*v.* **þwang**); *le Toft'* 1467 × 84 (*v.* **toft**); *le Waterforow'* 1467 × 84 (*v.* **wæter**, **furh** and *the water furrowes* in Billesdon f.ns. (b)); *atte Welle* 1276 (p), 1312 (p) (*v.* **atte**, **wella**); *le Winyerd* 1467 × 84, *Wyndeyarde*, *þe Wyndyard* 1477 (e.16) (*v.* **vinyerd**); *Woldfurlong'* 1467 × 84, 1477 (e.16) (*v.* **wald**, **furlang**).

Stretton Magna

STRETTON MAGNA (GREAT STRETTON 2½")

Stratone 1086 DB, 1215 P, *Straton'* 1186 (p), 1190 ib (p) *et passim* to 1267 Pat, 1368 *Wyg*, *Stratona* 1202 ChancR
Strattun' 1155, 1156 P, *Stratton'* 1159, 1160 ib *et freq* to 1230, 1242 ib *et passim* to 1429 Fine, 1435 Cl, *Strattone* 1156, 1159 RBE, 1195 P, *Strattona* 1173, 1175, 1178 ib
Strettun' 1157 P, *Stretton* 1183, 1184 ib *et passim* to 1329 Ipm, 1330 *Wyg* (p) *et freq*, *Strettona* c.1250 *Rut*, *Strettone* 1306, 1357 *Wyg*

Affixes are variously added as:
~ *Magna* 1275 Coram, 1305 (1579) *LRoll et freq*
Magna ~ 1283 Dugd, 1301, 1302 Pat, 1314 Cl, 1344 Pat
Much ~ 1467 × 72 ECP
Great ~ 1610 Speed *et freq*

'The farmstead, village on the Roman road', *v.* **strǣt**, **tūn**; with the later affix ME **muche** (with loss of *-el* from OE **mycel**). Note also MLat *magna* 'great, large'. With neighbouring Little Stretton, located on the Roman *Via Devana* (Gartree Road) which extends south-eastwards from Leicester. Only the church remains standing amid a large area of medieval earthworks of the former village.

CHURCH CLOSE, 1878, 1907 *Surv*, *v.* St Giles's Church *infra*. COTTERILL FM, *Cotterill Farm* 1925 Kelly; with the surn. *Cotterill*, *v.* adjoining Cotterill Spinney in Little Stretton. FISH POND, *Fish-pond* 1862 *Surv*; a feature of Stretton Hall grounds. HIGHLAND CLOSE SPINNEY, *Island Close Spinney* 1849 *TA*, 1862 *Surv*, *v.* **island**, **spinney**. MERE RD is *the Meare lane* 1745 *Terrier*, *v.* (**ge**)**mǣre**; forms part of the boundary with Thurnby parish. POOR CLOSE SPINNEY, *Poor Close* 1862 *Surv*, *v.* **pouer**(**e**); land dedicated to poor-law relief or charity. ST GILES'S CHURCH, *The Church* 1708 *Terrier*, *Church (St Giles)* 1877 White, 1925 Kelly; earlier is recorded *capellam Stretton* 1220 MHW, *capellam Sancti Egidii Magna Stretton* 1344, 1403 *Pat* (with MLat *capella* 'a chapel';

Egidius is the MLat form of *Giles*). Note also *atte Kirke* 1335 *Pat* (p), *at the kyrke* 1467 × 84 *LTD* (p), *v.* **atte**, **kirkja**. STRETTON HALL (now The Glenfrith Hospital), *Stretton Hall* 1806 Map, 1835 O, 1862 *Surv*, 1925 Kelly, *Stretton Magna Hall* 1846, 1863 White, *v.* **hall**; cf. *attehall* (p), *at þe hall* (p) 1467 × 84 (*v.* **atte**, **þe**), relating to a former manor house of which the substantial moat remains. STRETTON LODGE (lost), 1877 White, *v.* **loge**; this was demolished in 1942. THE WILDERNESS, *v.* **wildernesse**; a feature of the grounds of Stretton Hall.

FIELD-NAMES

In (a), forms dated 1777 are *Map*; those dated 1849 are *TA*; 1862, 1878 and 1907 are *Surv*. Forms throughout dated 1332 are SR; those dated 1378 are Nichols; 1383 are Ass; 1467 × 84 are *LTD*; 1601, 1625, 1674, 1679, 1686, 1690, 1697, 1708, 1712, 1714 and 1745 are *Terrier*; 1695 are *Deed*.

(a) Six Acre Mdw 1849, 1862, The Ten Acre 1862, The Forty Acres 1849, 1862, Forty Acres Cl, The Forty Acres Spinney 1849 (*v.* **spinney**) (*v.* **æcer**); Barn Mdw 1849, 1878, 1907 (*v.* **bern**); Bottom Mdw 1862 (*v.* **bottom**); Brick Kiln Cl 1849, 1862 (*v.* **brike-kiln**); Brook Cl, ~ Mdw 1849, 1878, 1907 (*v.* **brōc**); First ~, Second ~, Third Cabin 1849 (*v.* **cabane**); Cart Hovel 1849 (*v.* **carte**, **hovel**); Church Mdw 1849, 1878, 1907 (*v.* St Giles's Church *supra*); Clover Cl 1849, 1878, 1907 (*v.* **clāfre**; grown as a fodder crop); Cross Leys 1777, 1849, Three Cornered Cross Leys 1878, 1907 (*v.* **three-cornered**) (*v.* **cross**, **leys**); Bottom ~ ~ ~, Top Dog Kennel Cl 1849, 1862 (*v.* **kenel**; such names often refer to kennels in which hunting dogs were kept); Far Mdw 1878, 1907; Garden Cl 1878, 1907 (*v.* **gardin**; land used for horticulture); First ~, Gorsey 1849, 1878, 1907, Gorsey East, ~ West 1878, 1907 (*v.* **gorstig**); Gravel Pit 1849, 1878, 1907 (*v.* **gravel**, **pytt**); Great Stretton Cl 1849, 1878, 1907; The Hills 1849, 1878, 1907; Horse Mdw 1849, 1878, 1907, ~ Pasture 1849 (*v.* **pasture**); Island Cl 1849, 1862 (*v.* Highland Close Spinney *supra*); Knight's Mdw 1849, 1878, 1907 (with the surn. *Knight*); Laphole Cl 1862 (*v.* **lappa**, **hol**[1]); The Lawn 1862 (in origin **launde**, but presum. alluding here to a formal lawn in the grounds of Stretton Hall); Long Mdw 1849, 1862, 1878, 1907, ~ ~ Spinney 1849, 1862 (*v.* **spinney**); Bottom ~ ~, Top Nether Fd 1849, 1907 (*Neather feild* 1674, *Nether feld* 1690, *v.* **neoðera**, **feld**; one of the open-fields of the township, earlier called *Kybbleclos feilde*, *infra*), Nether Field Mdw 1849, 1907; First ~, Bottom ~, Top Platt 1849, 1878, 1907, Platt Mdw 1878, 1907 (*v.* **plat**[2]); First ~, Second Quakers 1849 (either recording former quake-fen (*v.* **quake** and note *le Mersch* in f.ns. (b)) or alluding to Quaking Grass (*Brizia media*)); Road Cl 1907 (a close beside a roadway); Round Cl 1849, 1878 (*v.* **round**); Sir George's Mdw 1862 (with reference to Sir George Robinson, a former lord of the manor); the Slang 1849 (*v.* **slang**); Spinney Cl, ~ Mdw 1849, 1878, 1907 (*v.* **spinney**); Spring Cl, ~ Mdw 1849, 1878 (cf. *þe Welspryng'*, *Wellespring'* 1467 × 84 (*v.* **þe**, **wella**, **spring**[1]); Stock Cl

1777 (*Stok'* 1467 × 84, *v.* **stoc**); Stone Green Mdw 1878, 1907 (*at Stone* 1467 × 84, cf. *del Grene* 1383 (p), *v.* **stān**, **grēne**[2]; the nature of the stone is uncertain); Stretton Cl 1878, 1907; Stretton Gorse 1849, First ~ ~ ~, Second ~ ~ ~, Third ~ ~ ~, Fourth Stretton Gorse Mdw 1849, 1878, 1907 (*v.* **gorst**); Three Cornered Mdw 1777 (*v.* **three-cornered**); First ~ ~, Second ~ ~, Third ~ ~, Fourth Upper Fd 1849, 1878, 1907.

(b) *Addemermedwe*, *Haddemermedewe* 1378 Nichols (*v.* **adel**, **mere**[1], **mēd** (**mēdwe** obl.sg.)); *Albygate* 1467 × 84 (*v.* **gata**; a road to the lost *Alby*, some 2 miles to the east in Illston on the Hill parish); *Mr Andrews close*, *Mr Andrews Hedge* 1601; *Bannell* 1674, *Bandale* 1697 (*v.* **bēan**, **deill**); *Buxton*(*e*)*s close* 1679, 1690 (with the surn. *Buxton*); *Calverholm* 1378 (*v.* **calf** (**calfra** gen.pl.), **holmr**); *the Cowe pastor called Holdicke Leys* 1625 (*v.* **cū**, **pasture** and *Holdicke*, *infra*); *Depedale* 1467 × 84 (*v.* **dēop**, **dalr**); *Derby wey* 1467 × 84 (*v.* **weg**; the road to Derby which lies 28 miles to the north-west; as far as Leicester, this is a stretch of Gartree Road); *John Eytons bushes* 1625 (*v.* **busc**; the *Eyton* family prob. came originally from Eaton, 20 miles to the north-east, *v.* Lei **2** 118); *Furzy Close* 1686 (*v.* **fyrsig**); *the New ~*, *the Old Gleabe Close* 1708 (*v.* **glebe**); *Glenmere* 1467 × 84 (*v.* (**ge**)**mǣre**; the boundary with Great Glen which adjoins to the south), *Glen sicke* 1674 (*v.* **sík**; bordering Great Glen parish); *the Greate hill* 1625, 1674, *Grat hill* 1679, 1690 (*v.* **grēat**; also called *Mickle hill* 1625, *v.* **micel**, **mikill**); *Great Meadow* 1695; *Neather ~*, *Over Ground* 1695 (*v.* **neoðera**, **uferra**, **grund**); *Harewelsyke* 1378 (*v.* **sík**), *Harewelgreyne* 1467 × 84 (*v.* **grein**) ('boundary stream', *v.* **hār**[2], **wella**); *Helmesacre* 1467 × 84, *Hamesaker* 1625 (*v.* **æcer**; either with the OE masc. pers.n. *Helm* or its surn. reflex *Helm*); *the high meare*, *the high mears furlong* (*v.* **furlang**) 1625 (*v.* **hēah**[1], (**ge**)**mǣre**); *Holdale* 1467 × 84, *Holedale* 1601, *Lettell hodell* 1690 (*v.* **lȳtel**, **lítill**), *Holedale feilde* 1601, *Hoodalle Feillde* 1625, *the Hodell feild* 1686, *the Hodellfeld* 1690 (*v.* **feld**; one of the great open-fields of the township) (*v.* **hol**[2], **deill**); *Holdicke furlong* 1625 (*v.* **furlang**), *Holdicke Leys* 1625, *Hoddicklayes* 1690 (*v.* **leys**) (*v.* **hol**[2], **dík**); *le Holme* 1378, *the Holm at Stone* 1467 × 84 (*v.* **stān** and Stone Green Mdw *supra*) (*v.* **holmr**); *Home Leyes* 1674, *~ layes* 1690 (*v.* **holmr**, **leys**); *Hooton mere* 1601 (*v.* (**ge**)**mǣre**; Houghton on the Hill parish adjoins to the north-east); *of the hyrne* 1467 × 84 (p) (*v.* **hyrne**); *the New ~*, *the Old Inclosier* 1708, *the New ~*, *the Old Inclosure* 1712 (*v.* **inclosure**); *Joneswynesgore* 1378 (*v.* **swīn**, **gāra**; with the surn. *Jon*, from the OFr masc. pers.n. *Johan*); *the kinges high way* 1625 (*v.* **king**, **hēah-weg**); *Kybbles clos*(*s*)*e* 1601, *Kibbles Close* 1625, *Keeble Close* 1686, *Kybbleclos feild* 1601 (*v.* **feld** and *the Little Feild*, *infra*; one of the open-fields) (cf. *Thomas Kebell* 1500 Will of Great Stretton and *v.* Kibble Hill in adjoining Houghton on the Hill parish); *Langfurlong*' 1467 × 84, *the Long furlong* 1625, 1690, *~ forlong* 1679 (*v.* **lang**[1], **furlang**); *Little Meadow* 1695; *Lodecroft* 1378, 1467 × 84, *Ludecroft* 1467 × 84, *Ludcrafte* 1674, *Lodcraft hill* 1679, *Ludcraft layes* 1690 (*v.* **leys**) (*v.* **croft**; with an OE masc. pers.n. *Loda* or *Luda*); *the Little Feild to Kibbles Close* 1625 (otherwise *Kybbleclos feild*, *supra*); *the Little wong at the towns side*, *the Lyttle Wong* 1625 (*v.* **vangr**); *Meredale* 1378 (any compound of **mere**[1], (**ge**)**mǣre** and **dalr**, **deill** is poss.); *le Mersch* 1378, *le Mersh* 1467 × 84, *Marche* 1601, *March hadland* (*v.* **hēafod-land**), *~ Meadow* 1625 (*v.* **mersc**); *Middelsykende* 1378 (*v.* **middel**, **sík**, **ende**); *Midulhyll* 1467 × 84 (*v.* **middel**, **hyll**); *Milneholme* 1378 (*v.* **myln**, **holmr**; alluding to a water-mill); *le Mores* 1378, *bitwene the mores* 1467 × 84 (*v.* **betwēonan**) (*v.* **mōr**[1]); *Myngde Feilde* 1601, *the Myng feilde* 1625, *the Ming feld* 1679, 1690, *the*

Minge Feild 1686 (*v.* **feld**; one of the great open-fields, this shared with Little Stretton (there also recorded as *the Stockfielde or Mingled fielde*), hence **myngled** 'put together so as to make one, joined in company'); *Netherholmdale* 1467 × 84 (*v.* **neoðera**, **holmr**, **deill**); *Nortongate* 1467 × 84, 1601, 1674, 1679 (*v.* **gata**; the road to King's Norton which lies 2 miles to the east); *Outhebygore* 1467 × 84 (*v.* **gāra**; Oadby parish adjoins to the west); *Parsonage Close* 1712 (*v.* **personage**); *the Parsons Close* 1745 (*v.* **persone**; a later style for the previous f.n.); *the Parsons Platts* 1745 (*v.* **persone**, **plat**[2]); *Ryschfurlong'* 1467 × 84 (×2) (*v.* **risc**, **furlang**); *Scamdale* 1378 (×2), *Scamburdale* 1467 × 84, *Scamberdale* 1601, *Scammerdall baulke* 1625 (*v.* **balca**), *Scamberdell forlong* (*v.* **furlang**), ~ *hoke* 1690 (*v.* **hōc**) (*v.* **skammr**, **dalr**); *Scotosyke* 1601 (*v.* **sík**, with either **scot** or **Scot(t)**; whether the medial *o* represents **hōh** is uncertain); *Stoctonwolde* 1467 × 84 (*v.* **wald**), *Stoktonesyke* 1467 × 84, *Stoughton sicke* 1601 (*v.* **sík**) (Stoughton parish adjoins to the north-west); *Stodwoldhull* 1467 × 84 (*v.* **stōd**, **wald**, **hyll**); *the Thorn* 1467 × 84 (*v.* **þorn**); *the towne furlong* 1679 (*v.* **furlang**), *the towne syde* 1601 (*v.* **sīde**) (*v.* **tūn**); *Vppewelcroft*, *Vpwelcroft* 1467 × 84 (*v.* **up**, **wella**, **croft**); *att the welle* 1467 × 84 (p), (*ad fontem* 1332 (p), with MLat *fons* (*fontem* acc.sg.)), *v.* **atte**, **wella**); *the Wolde* 1467 × 84 (*v.* **wald**).

Theddingworth

1. THEDDINGWORTH

Tedingesworde 1086 DB
Tevlingorde 1086 DB (×2)
Tediworde, *Dedigworde* 1086 DB
Thaingewrtha c.1200 *Sloane*, *Teingeworth* 1200 Cur (p), *Teingewrthe* 1201 Pleas, 1201 Cur, *Tedingewrth*' 1206 ib (p), *Thedingewrth*' 1207 ib
Theingurda c.1140 BM, *Theingwrtha* 1154 × 58 (1340) Ch, Hy 2 Dugd, *Theingworth* 1156 (1318) Ch, 1220 MHW, 1272 Dugd, 1276 RH, *Theyngwrth* 1276 ib
Taingwurda 1140 Reg, Stephen (1340) Ch, *Tainguurda* c.1155 Dane, *Taingwrde* l.12 ib, *Taingwrth* Hy 2 Dugd
Teingwrth 1200 Cur, 1201 Abbr, 1202 FF, *Teingworth*(*e*) 1201 Nichols, c.1253 RHug, 1269 RGrav
Tedingwrth 1208 FF, 1209 Fine, *Tedingwurth* 1250 Cur, *Tedyngworth* 1330 FA, 1361 Cl,
Teddyngworth' 1524 *Braye*, *Tedingworth* 1535 VE, 1539 MinAccts
Thedingwrþe c.1130 LeicSurv, *Thedingworth*(*e*) 1242 Fees, 1247 Abbr *et passim* to 1299 Banco, 1302 Pat (p) *et freq* to 1373, 1385 Banco *et passim* to 1580 LEpis, 1607 LML, *Thedyngworth*(*e*) 1232, 1252 Fine *et passim* to 1313 Pat, 1323 Banco *et freq* to 1489, 1497 *Braye et passim* to 1538 Fine, 1556 *Braye*, *Thedyngwurth* 1250 Cur
Theddingworth 1340 *Peake*, 1610 Speed *et freq*, *Theddyngworth* 1346 Pat, 1540 MinAccts

Possibly 'the enclosure of Þēoda's or Tēoda's people', *v.* **-inga-**, **worð**. The OE masc. pers.n. *Þēoda* is unrecorded but appears to be a short form of dithematic pers.ns. in *Þēod-* such as *Þēodgār* and *Þēodwulf*. The form *Tēoda*, perhaps another shortened style of such pers.ns., does occur independently (as in 687 (12) BCS 89 (S 233) and 688 (12) BCS 72 (S 235)). However, the unique DB spelling *Tedingesworde* presents a genitive singular composition-joint which may well be significant, especially as a local *Thedyngesthorp* is recorded in 1327.

Watts CDEPN *s.n.* suggests as an alternative derivation for Theddingworth an earlier OE p.n. base **Thēoding* ('a place called after Theoda'), from the pers.n. *Þēoda* plus the p.n.-forming suffix -**ing**², hence the meaning of the whole being 'the enclosure of Theoding'. Whether he intends the enclosure to be **Thēoding* itself or at a location away from it is unclear. However, any proposed p.n. constructed of a pers.n. plus -**ing**² is open to serious doubt.

A more satisfactory explanation of Theddingworth is to take *Þēoding/ Tēoding* as an OE masc. pers.n. from *Þēoda/Tēoda* with an *-ing*³ suffix; -**ing**³ was commonly used in the formation of singular pers.ns. such as *Dēoring* (from *Dēor*), *Hemming* (from *Hemma*) and *Lulling* (from *Lulla*). Theddingworth would then mean 'Þēoding's or Tēoding's enclosure', *v.* **worð**, and *Thedyngesthorp* 'Þēoding's or Tēoding's outlying farmstead', *v.* **þrop**, **þorp**, where the generic may be the survival of a metathesized OE *þrop* rather than the common ON *þorp*, in an area of the Danelaw with only minimal Scandinavian influence.

ALL SAINTS' CHURCH, *Church (All Saints)* 1846, 1863, 1877 White; it is recorded earlier as *ecclesie de Theingworth* 1220 MHW, ~ *de Thedigworth* 1236 RGros, *ecclesia de Teingworth* 1253 × 58 RTAL, *ecclesie de Thed(d)yngworth* 1327, 1346, 1556 *Pat*. Note also *the Churchyard* 1703, 1706, 1821 *Terrier*, *v.* **churchyerd**. BOAT (P.H.) (lost), *Boat* 1846 White; on Grand Union Canal to serve the bargemen. BOSWORTH RD, Husbands Bosworth lying 2 miles to the south-east. CRICK'S LODGE, 1846 White, cf. *Thomas Crick* 1851 *TA*, 1863 White, *v.* **loge**. CROWN (P.H.), *Crown* 1846, 1863 White, *Crown Inn* 1877 ib. DAMSIDE SPINNEY, *v.* **damme**, **sīde**, **spinney**. HARE AND HOUNDS (P.H.) (lost), *Hare and Hounds* 1846 White. HOTHORPE RD, *v.* Hothorpe *infra*. IVY LODGE FM, *v.* **īfig**, **loge**. LODGE FM, at Theddingworth Lodge *infra*. MOWSLEY RD, Mowsley lying 3 miles to the north. THE PEAR TREE, *Pearetree* 1696 *Map*, *Pear Tree* 1835 O; note also *Pear Tree Ford* 1835 ib (*v.* **ford**), 400 yards to the south-west, *v.* **pertre**. PEBBLE HALL, 1925 Kelly, *v.* **hall**; named from its walls of flint pebbles (dial. *duckies*) with brick dressings (as with nearby Pebble Cottages (local) of the same construction, it was built c.1830). THEDDINGWORTH HOLLOW SPINNEY, *v.* **holh**, **spinney**. THEDDINGWORTH LODGE, 1835 O, *v.* **loge**. THEDDINGWORTH STATION, on the former *Rugby and Stamford Railway* 1854 O, 1863, 1877 White. THE VICARAGE, 1863, 1877 White, 1925 Kelly; note also *the Vicaridge yarde* 1601 *Terrier* (*v.* **geard**), *v.* **vikerage**.

FIELD-NAMES

In (a), forms presented without dates are c.1965 *Surv*; those dated 1821 are *Terrier*; 1830 are *Deed*; 1934 are Sale. Forms throughout dated Edw 2 are Dugd; those dated 1327 are Pat; 1398, 1409, 1518 and 1556 are *Braye*; 1477 (e.16) are *Charyte*; 1572 are Will; 1586, Eliz 1, 1601, 1674, 1679, 1690, 1703, 1706, 1706 (18) are *Terrier*; l.16, 1616 and 1714 are *Deed*; 1696 are *Map*.

(a) 2 Acre, Bottom 17 ~, 20 ~, 30 ~, 60 ~, 100 Acre (*v*. **æcer**); Barn Cl, ~ Hill 1934, c.1965 (*v*. **bern**); Birdwell 1934, c. 1965 (*v*. **brȳd**, **wella**; poss. denotes a spring formerly thought to promote fertility, though rather than the OE sb. meaning 'bride', the specific may be the postulated adj. with the same form meaning 'surging'); Black Brook, North ~, South Blackbrook (*Middle ~ ~*, *Neather ~ ~*, *Upper ~ ~*, *Black*(*e*) *Brook*(*e*) 1696, *v*. **blæc**, **brōc**); Blackmore Sick (1703, *Blackemo*(*o*)*re Sicke* 1601, *Blackmoor Sick* 1696, *Blackmoore sike furlong* 1674, 1679, *Blackmore Sick Furl'* 1706, *Blackmoor Sick Furlong* 1706 (18) (*v*. **furlang**), *v*. **blæc**, **mōr**[1], **sík**); Bottom Cl, ~ Mdw (*v*. **bottom**); Bradley (*v*. **brād**, **lēah**); Bridge Mdw (cf. *New Bridge Furlong* 1696, *v*. **brycg**); Little Brook Holme (*v*. **holmr**); Brook Mdw; Canal Fd, ~ Mdw c.1965, Canal Piece 1934, c.1965 (*v*. **pece**) (beside Grand Union Canal); Caves Cl (cf. *Edmund Cave* 1842 Census of Theddingworth); Cemetery Fd (land next to a cemetery); Charity Fd (rent of the land providing funds for a charitable purpose; once a year, money is still distributed to the elderly of the village); Chawntry (*Backside of Chauntry* 1696 (*v*. **bak-side**), *Chauntry Close*, *~ Leys* 1696 (*v*. **leys**), *the Chauntery feild* 1601, *v*. **chanterie** and The Nanalls *infra*; land formerly forming part of the endowment for a chantry, a chantry being a fund for the maintenance of a priest whose sole duty was to say mass daily for the souls of the founder and his family); Clover Cl (*v*. **clāfre**; grown as a fodder crop); Collins Mdw (with the surn. *Collins*); Corner Cl (*v*. **corner**); Cover Fd (*v*. **cover**(**t**)); Big ~, Little Cricks (*v*. Crick's Lodge *supra*); Big ~, Little Damside (*v*. Damside Spinney *supra*); Eight Acre Mdw (*Long ~ ~*, *Short Eight Acres*, *Eight Acre Furlong* 1696, *v*. **eahta**, **æcer**); Far Cl; Foxen Gate (*Foxen Gate Furlong* 1696 (*v*. **gata**, **furlang**), *Foxenway* 1696 (*v*. **weg**), *Middle ~ ~*, *Neather ~ ~*, *Upper Foxenway Leys* 1696 (*v*. **leys**); the road to Foxton which lies 4 miles to the north-east); Grazing Mdw (*v*. **gresyng**); North ~ ~, South ~ ~, Great Cl; Great Ground, ~ ~ Mdw 1934, c.1965 (*v*. **grund**); Green Dyke, ~ ~ Mdw (*Greenedyke* 1586, *Greene Dike* 1696, *v*. **grēne**[2], **dík**, note *Nether Greene* in f.ns. (b)); Green Lane, ~ ~ Mdw (*v*. **grēne**[1]); Guildhall Cl c.1965, East ~~, West Guildhall Mdw 1934, c.1965 (*Long ~ ~*, *Short Guild Hall*, *Guild Hall Leys* 1696 (*v*. **leys**), *v*. **gild-hall** and *guilde hall* in adjacent Husband Bosworth f.ns. (b)); Hanging Hill (cf. *Hanging Hill Leys* 1696 (*v*. **leys**), *v*. **hangende**); The Hassocks 1821 (*the Hassockes*, *~ Hassoxe* 1601, *~ Hassax* 1674, *Hasacks* 1690, *Hassocks ~* 1696, (*The*) *Hassock Leys* 1703, 1706 (*v*. **leys**) (*v*. **hassuc**); Hewitts Cl (with the surn. *Hewitt*); Home Cl 1934, c.1965 (1696, cf. (*against*) *Home Close stile* 1679 (*v*. **stigel**)), Little ~ ~, Home Fd (*v*. **home**); House Cl; Old House Fd; Left of ~, Right of Hovel (*v*. **hovel**); Hubbard's Orchard 1934, c.1965 (*v*. **orceard**; with the surn. *Hubbard*); Jennkins Cl (sic) (with the surn. *Jenkins*); Kendalls Cl 1934, c.1965 (with the surn. *Kendall*); Kicklewell (*Kickelwell*

Furlong, ~ *Leys* 1696 (*v.* **leys**), *v.* Kicklewell Spinney in adjacent Laughton parish); Kill Hill 1934, Great ~ ~ ~, Little Kill Hill Mdw c.1965 (*v.* **cyln**, **hyll**; prob. the site of a former pottery kiln); North ~ ~, South Kingston(e)'s Mdw, Kingston(e)'s Top Mdw 1934, c.1965 (*Kingsty Meadow* 1696; poss. with the surn. *King* and either **stig** or **stīg**); Knights Cl (with the surn. *Knight*); Bottom ~, Top Lees (*v.* **leys**); Little Cl 1934; Bottom ~ ~, Top Little Hill (*Lyttlilhull'* 1409, *Lyttle Hyll* 1586, *Backside Little Hill* 1696 (*v.* **bak-side**), *Little Hill Furlong*, ~ ~ *Slade* 1696 (*v.* **slæd**), *v.* **lȳtel**, **hyll**); Lost Mdw (a secluded piece of land, lost from view); Main Road Fd; Bottom ~, Top Marland c.1965, North ~, South Marland 1934, c.1965 (*Marlonde* 1601, *Long Morland* 1586, *Hadlands Long Marland* 1696 (*v.* **hēafod-land**), *Neather Long Marlands* 1696 (*v.* **neoðera**), *v.* **land**; **mōr**[1] has been influnced by or replaced by **marr**[1]); Middle Hill 1934, c.1965; Mill Cl 1830, Bottom ~ ~, Top Mill Cl c.1965 (*Mill Close* l.16, 1696, 1706, 1706 (18)), Mill Holme 1830 (*v.* **holmr**) (*v.* **myln**); Muson's Cl (with the surn. *Musson* of a family originally from the village of Muston, 34 miles to the north-east, *v.* Lei **2** 35); The Nanalls c.1965, East ~, West ~, Top Nanhill 1934, c.1965, Ireson's ~, Sim's Nanhill c.1965 (with the surns. *Ireson* (cf. *Job Ireson* 1881 Census of Theddingworth) and *Sim*) (*Knannels* 1586, *The Knallings* 1696, *Nanhills* 1706, *Knaunnells* ~ l.16, *Nanhills Close* 1706, 1706 (18), *Knannels fyelde* 1586, *Nanhylls* ~ Eliz 1, *Nanhills* ~ 1679, *Knanels Feild* 1690, *Knallings Field* 1703, 1706, 1706 (18) (*v.* **feld**; one of the great open-fields of the township, also called *the Chauntery feild* 1601 (*v.* Chawntry *supra*) and *Camsil* ~, *Campshill feild* 1674 (*v. Campshill*, *infra*), *Long Knalling Furlong* 1696 (*v.* **furlang**), *v.* **cnafa** (**cnafan** gen.sg., **cnafena** gen.pl.), **hyll**); New Cl 1934, c.1965; Newlands (*v.* **nīwe**, **land**); New Mdw; Norman's Nest 1934, c.1965 (*v.* **nest**; such names sometimes indicate the highest point in a district, while the surn. *Norman* occurs freq. in adjoining Lubenham in the 19th cent.; the gen.sg of **nān mann** is unlikely); North Mdw 1934; Old Cl (l.16, 1696, 1706, *Old Close Meadow* 1696, *v.* **ald**); Old Ridges Mdw (*v.* **hrycg**; alluding to former cultivation strips); Paddock Cl (*v.* **paddock**); Parson's Cl (*v.* **persone**); Payne's Cl c.1965, Payne's House Cl 1934 (cf. *Paynes Corner* 1696, *v.* **corner**), Payne's Leys 1934, c.1965 (*Paynes* ~ 1696, *Pains Leys* 1703, 1706 (18), *v.* **leys**) (with the surn. *Payne*); Plough Mdw (*v.* **plōg**); North ~ ~, South Ploughed Mdw; Pugh's Fd (with the surn. *Pugh*); Pump Fd (*v.* **pumpe**); Raikes Baulk (*v.* **balca**) (cf. *Upper Rakes* 1696, *v.* **rake**); Back of Railway (*v.* **back of**; land beside the former Rugby and Stamford Railway, now dismantled); Road Cl (land beside a roadway); Round Hill (*v.* **round**; a common hill-name in Gartree Hundred); Bottom ~, Top Rowell c.1965, North ~ ~, South Rowell Cl 1934, c.1965, North ~ ~, South Rowell Mdw c.1965 (cf. *Neather* ~ ~, *Upper Rowell Leys* 1696 (*v.* **leys**), *Rowell Furlong* 1696 (*v.* **furlang**), *v.* **rūh**; prob. with **hyll** rather than with **wella**); Saunt Cl, ~ Mdw 1934, c.1965 (*Santclose* 1674, 1679, *v.* **sand** and *Santleys Fyelde* in f.ns. (b)); Sheep Dip Mdw (*v.* **sheep-dip**); Sheep Pen Fd (*v.* **penn**[2]); Silver Hill (*v.* **seolfor**, **hyll** and *Silver Hill* in Great Glen f.ns. (b)); Harold Smith's Fd; South Mdw 1934; Station Fd (*v.* Theddingworth Station *supra*); Thistly Fd, ~ ~ Slang (*v.* **slang**) (*v.* **thist(e)ly**); Three Corner Fd (*v.* **three-corner**); Middle ~ ~, Tom's Cl, Tom's Close Mdw 1934, c.1965 (prob. with the pers.n. *Tom*, a pet-form of *Thomas*; the surn. *Tom/Thom* from the same source is infrequent in Leics.); Tower Fd (presum. alluding to a water tower); Wheat Cl 1934, c.1965 (*v.* **hwǣte**); Wright's Cl (with the surn. *Wright*).

(b) *Ashbys Hedge Furlong* 1696 (*v.* **hecg**, **furlang**; with the surn. *Ashby*); *Betwixt the Town*(*e*)*s* 1674, 1679, (*the Furlong*) *Betwixt Towns* 1703, 1706 (18), *Betweene the Townes* 1696, *Between Towns* 1706 (*v.* **betwixt**, **betwēonan**, **tūn**); *Blackpitt* 1696 (*v.* **blæc**, **pytt**); *the Bowlinge lease* 1601, *the Bowling leys* 1690 (*v.* **leys**), *Bowleing pitt furlong* 1674 (*v.* **pytt**) (*v.* **bowling**); *Brackleys* 1696 (*v.* **bracu**, **leys**); *Long* ~, *Short Breach* 1696 (*v.* **brēc**); *Broad Holme* 1586, *Broad Home*, ~ ~ *Leys* 1696 (*v.* **leys**) (*v.* **brād**, **holmr**); *Bullocks Pen Furlong* 1696 (*v.* **bulluc**, **penn**[2]); *Camsil*(*l*) 1601, *Campshill* 1679, 1703, 1706, *Campsell* 1690, *Short Campshill* 1696, *Camsil* ~, *Campshill feild* 1674 (*v.* **feld**; one of the great open-fields, also called *Knannels fyelde*, *supra*) (*v.* **camb**, **hyll**); *Church Hadland Furlong* 1696 (*v.* **hēafod-land** and All Saints' Church *supra*); *Cole Acres* 1696 (*v.* **cole**, **æcer**); *Curst Roods* 1696 (*v.* **cursed**, **curst**, **rōd**[3]; a derogatory name for very poor land); *Damfurlonge* 1586 (*v.* **damme**, **furlang**); *Dunwellefurlong* 1477 (e.16), *Dunwell Furlong alias Dunhill Furlong* 1556 (poss. 'the furlong below the spring or stream' (with **dūne**); otherwise 'the upland spring/stream furlong' (with **dūn**), *v.* **wella**, **furlang**); *Neather* ~ ~, *Middle* ~ ~, *Upper Farr Doles* 1696 (*v.* **feor**, **dāl**); *Flagdadmore* 1518, *Flagg Pagg Moor* (sic) 1696 (*v.* **flagge**, **dēad**, **mōr**[1]; 'Dead Moor' is a common name for infertile wasteland, cf. *St Leighs Dodmoor*, *infra*); *The Footes* 1696 (*v.* **fōt**); *The Goore* 1696 (*v.* **gāra**); *Gostill* ~ 1601, *Gostyll* ~ Eliz 1, *Gosthill feild* 1674, *Gausthill* ~ 1690, 1697, 1703, *Gaustill Field* 1706 (*v.* **feld**; one of the great open-fields, also called *Notbernehill feild* 1601, *v.* *Notebamhull*, *infra*), *Gosthill Furlong* 1696 (*v.* **furlang**), *Gausthill Head* 1696 (*v.* **hēafod**) (*v.* **gorst**, **hyll**); *Nether* ~ 1586, 1679, *Neather Greene* 1696 (*v.* **neoðera**), *Ouer Greene* 1601, *Over Green*(*e*) 1674, 1690, 1703, 1706, *Over Green Furlong* 1706, 1706 (18) (*v.* **uferra**), *Upper Greene* 1696 (*v.* **grēne**[2]); *Greens Hedge Furlong* 1696 (*v.* **hecg**, **furlang**; *Green* may be either a surn. in the possessive case or relate to *Nether Greene* and *Ouer Greene*, *supra*); *The Ham*(*m*)*e* 1601, *the Ham*(*m*) 1674, 1679, *The Hame* 1696, (*the*) *Ham Furlong* 1696, 1703, 1706 (18), *the Ham furl'* 1706, *Neather Ham Furlong* 1696 (*v.* **furlang**), *Upper Ham*, ~ ~ *Leys* 1696 (*v.* **leys**) (*v.* **hamm**); *Hasty way* 1696 (*v.* **stīg**, **weg**, **sty-way**; with **hǣs** or (**ge**)**hæg**); *Haverborowe waye* 1556, *Harborow Way* 1696 (*v.* **weg**; the road to Market Harborough which lies 4 miles to the east); *Heiford* ~, *Hayfords way* 1679, *Lower* ~ ~, *Upper Hayford Way* 1696, *Hefford way* 1703, 1706 (*v.* **hēg**, **ford**); *High hedge Furlong* 1696 (*v.* **hēah**[1], **hecg**); (*the*) *High Meadow* 1690, 1696, 1703, 1706; *Neather Hill Furlong* 1696 (*v.* **neoðera**, **hyll**, **furlang**); *the Homestead* 1703 (*v.* **hām-stede**); *the Homestall* 1706 (*v.* **hām-stall**); *Hopping Way* 1696 (*v.* **hopping**); *Horsepoole* 1586, 1696, *Horsepool Leys* 1696 (*v.* **leys**) (*v.* **hors**, **pōl**[1]); *Horswell'* 1518 (*v.* **hors**, **wella**); *Hundhill* 1477 (e.16), *Hundhill Pen Leys* 1696 (*v.* **penn**[2], **leys**) (*v.* **hund**, **hyll**); *Iliff hedge furlong* 1696 (*v.* **hecg**, **furlang**; with the surn. *Iliffe*); *Kylne close* 1572 (*v.* **cyln**, **clos**(**e**)); *Langdale* Edw 2 (*v.* **lang**[1], **dalr**); *Laughton way*(*e*) 1601, 1674, *Lawton* ~ 1696, *Lawghton way* 1703 (the road to Laughton which lies 2 miles to the north); *Lodge close* l.16, ~ *Ley*, ~ *Meadow* 1696 (with reference to Theddingworth Lodge *supra*); *Long Leys* 1696 (*v.* **leys**); *Longlubenhamhull'* 1518 (*v.* **lang**[1], **hyll**), *Lovenham Meer* 1696 (*v.* (**ge**)**mǣre**) (Lubenham parish adjoins to the north-east); *the meadow* 1601, *Meadow Close* 1696, 1706; *Mill Furlong* 1696 (*v.* **myln**); *New Farm* 1696; *Notebamhull* 1409, *Notbernehill* 1601, *Noburn Hill* 1696, *Notbernehill feild* 1601 (*v.* **feld**; one of the great open-fields, also called *Gostill feild*, *supra*) (*v.* **hnutbēam**, **hyll**); *Osterdame* 1601, *Osterdam* 1674, 1679, 1690, *Austerdam* 1696, 1703, 1706 (*v.* **ēastor**, **damme**; the OE specific has been influenced or replaced by ON **austr**); *Ouertwel* 1398 (of uncertain meaning; perh. 'land above the spring or stream' (*v*. **ofer**[3], **þe**, **wella**) or 'uncovered, laid-open spring' (*v*. **overte**, **wella**) may be thought of; but note *Upper Twills*, *infra*); *Pearetree Bridge* 1696 (by 1835, only a ford was available at this spot), *Peartree Haile* 1696 (*v*. **halh**), *Backside Pearetree* 1696 (*v*. **bak-side**) (*v*. The Pear Tree *supra*); *Hiderpeislond* 1409 (*v*. **hider**), *Peaseland Sycke* 1586, ~ *Sticks* (sic) 1696 (*v*. **sík**) (*v*. **pise**, **land**); *Pilchardescroft* (sic) n.d. Nichols, *v*. **croft**; prob. a f.n. of the 15th cent. with the surn. *Pilcher*, from the ME occupational name *pilchere* 'a maker or seller of leathern jerkins', here with excresent *d*); *the Pittes* 1601 (*v*. **pytt**); *Prestmedwe* 1409 (*v*. **prēost**, **mēd** (**mēdwe** obl.sg.)); *Pylland* 1518, *Over Pilland* 1586 (*v*. **uferra**), *Neather* ~, *Upper Pilland*, *Pilland Leys* 1696 (*v*. **leys**) (*v*. **land**; with **pyll** or **píll**); *Ranglands* 1696 (*v*. **wrang**, **land**); *Sandyhoke* 1696 (*v*. **sandig**, **hōc**); *St Leighs* 1696, *Sauntleys close* l.16, *St Leys Close* 1706, 1706 (18), *St Leighs Dodmoor* 1696 (*v*. **dēad**, **mōr**[1]), *Santleys Fyelde* 1601, *Sauntleys* ~ l.16, *Sontles* ~ 1601, *Santles* ~ Eliz 1, *Saintleys Feild* 1690, *St Leys Field* 1703, 1706 (*v*. **feld**; one of the great open-fields) (*v*. **sand**, **lǣs**); *Schortesmere* 1477 (e.16) (*v*. **sc(e)ort**; either with **(ge)mǣre** or with **mere**[1] in its sense 'a piece of boggy ground'; the medial *s* is intrusive); *the Sheire brooke* 1601 (*v*. **scīr**[1], **brōc**; this must refer to the river Welland, the county boundary here); *Stanley* ~ 1601, 1679, *Stanly way* 1674, 1696, 1703, 1706 (*v*. **weg**), *Stanly Bush Leys* 1686 (*v*. **busc**, **leys**) (*v*. **stān**, **lēah**); *Neather* ~, *Upper Stonidale* 1696 (*v*. **stānig**; **dalr**); *Stonymedow* 1477 (e.16) (*v*. **stānig**, **mēd** (**mēdwe** obl.sg.)); *Sturgis Close* 1616 (with the surn. *Sturges*, a reflex of the ON masc. pers.n. *Þorgils* (ODan *Thorgisl*)); *Tassel Sick* ~ ~ *Leys* (*v*. **leys**) 1696 (*v*. **tǣsel**, **sík**); *Tauftes* 1601, *Tofts* 1674, 1679, 1703, 1706, *Tafts* 1696 (*v*. **toft**); *Thedyngesthorp* 1327 (*v*. **þrop**, **þorp** and the discussion of the name Theddingworth *supra*); *Thorny Pytt* 1586, *Thurney Pitt Leys* 1686 (*v*. **leys**) (*v*. **þornig**, **þyrniht**, **pytt**); *Upper Twills* 1696 (unexplained; poss. a later form of *Ouertwel*, *supra*, or a poor form of the following f.n.); *Neather* ~, *Upper Twintill* 1696 (poss. 'the hill covered with shoots, saplings', *v*. **twigen**, **hyll**, with intrusive *t*; **twinn** 'double' as the specific seems unlikely); *Twodales* 1586, *Too Dales* 1696 (*v*. **tū**, **deill**); *Tythemedow* 1477 (e.16), *Tythe Meadow Corner* 1696 (*v*. **corner**) (*v*. **tēoða**, **mēd** (**mēdwe** obl.sg.)); *Water Furrows* 1696 (*v*. **wæter**, **furh** and *the water furrowes* in Billesdon f.ns. (b)); *Whaybrooke* 1586, *Whey Brooke* 1696 (*v*. **hwǣg**, **brōc**; also recorded in adjoining Husbands Bosworth); *Neather* ~, *Upper Whitlands* 1696 (*v*. **hwīt**, **land**; in eModE, *white* 'infertile' may be contrasted with *black* 'fertile'); *Whittley Furlong* 1696 (*v*. **hwīt**, **lēah**, **furlang**); *Whytestone* 1586, *Whitestone*, ~ *Leys* 1696 (*v*. **leys**) (*v*. **hwīt**, **stān**); *Widdows Hedge*, ~ ~ *Leys* 1696 (*v*. **hecg**; with the surn. *Widdows*, cf. *William Widders* 1576 RFL); *Wolfawell* Edw 2 (*v*. **wella**; prob. with the OE masc. pers.n. *Wulfa*, OE **wulf** (gen.pl. **wulfa**) being very unlikely in compound with a spring/stream name, in which pers.ns. are common).

2. HOTHORPE

Vdetorp 1086 DB, *Hudtorp* 1235 Fees

Huttorp c.1155 Dane, 1202 Ass (p), *Huttorph* c.1200 ib, *Hutthorpe*(*e*) e.13 BM, 1275 RH, *Hutorp* 1203 FF, *Huthorp* 1220 Fees

Huhthorp 1242 Fees, *Huchtorp'* 1247 *Ass*, *Hohttorp* 1302 Ipm, *Hokthorp* 1303 Pat, *Hucthorp* 1331 AD
Hothorp(*e*) 1247 *Ass*, 1284 FA, 1295 Cl *et passim* to 1706 *Terrier et freq*
Houthorp' 1261 *Ass*, *Howthorpe* 1576 Saxton, *Hoothorpe* 1601 *Terrier*, 1617 FF
Holthorp(*e*) 1674, 1679, 1690 *Terrier*

For this difficult name, Ekwall DEPN proposes the meaning 'Hūda's thorpe', with **þorp** 'a farmstead' and the OE masc. pers.n. *Hūda*. But this does not explain those forms with medial *h*, *ch*, *k* and *c*. Fellows-Jensen (SSNEM 111) suggests alternatively as the specific either an unrecorded OE **hūc** or an unrecorded Scand cognate **hūk**, both meaning 'a promontory', referring to the shape of the higher ground on which Hothorpe stands. A third possibility, which would suit the site admirably, is 'farmstead on the spur of land', with the specific as **hōh**, since the *d* of the 1086 and 1235 forms may be a result of the inability of Anglo-Norman scribes to deal with OE *h* and ME *gh*; but in this case the early *u* spellings are problematical (*v*. Nth 115–16).

Hothorpe was once part of the ancient parish of Theddingworth, even though lying in Northants. beyond the river Welland. Hothorpe Hall of c.1800 was the residence of the later lords of the manor of Theddingworth.

FIELD-NAMES

Forms dated 1601, 1674, 1679, 1690, 1703, 1706, 1706 (18) are *Terrier*.

(b) *Barrowe lease* 1601, *Barrow leyes* 1674, ~ *Leys* 1703, 1706 (*v*. **berg**, **leys**); *Broad thorrows* 1690 (*v*. **brād**, **furh**); *Burngrass* 1703, 1706, *Burne Grass* 1706 (18) (*v*. **græs**; with either **bryne** or **brún**[2]); *Butts furlong* 1703, 1706 (*v*. **butte**, **furlang**); *Flaxlands* 1674 (*v*. **fleax**, **land**); *Foxholes* 1679, *Foxall leases* 1601, *Foxhole* ~ 1674, *Foxhill leyes* 1690, ~ *Leys* 1703, 1706, 1706 (18) (*v*. **leys**) (*v*. **fox-hol**); *Harborough hill furlong* 1674 (*v*. **furlang**; a hill overlooking the road to Market Harborough which lies 4 miles to the north-east); *Under the Hill* 1703, 1706 (a furlong so called); *the Horsewell* 1679 (*v*. **hors**, **wella**); *Marston Cross furlong* 1703, 1706 (poss. alluding to a boundary cross (*v*. **cros**), otherwise *v*. **cross**), *Marston meere* 1674 (*v*. (**ge**)**mǣre**) (Marston Trussell parish adjoins to the east); *the Middle feild* 1601, 1674, 1679, 1703, *the Midle* ~ 1706, *the Middle Field* 1706 (18) (*v*. **middel**, **feld**; one of the great open-fields of the township); *the Neather* ~ 1601, 1674, *Nether Feild* 1679, *the Neather* ~ 1703, 1706, *the Nether Field* 1706 (18) (*v*. **neoðera**, **feld**; one of the great open-fields); *the Ouer* ~ 1601, *the Upper feild* 1703, ~ ~ *Field* 1706, 1706 (18) (*v*. **uferra**, **feld**; another of the great open-fields); *Rye furlong* 1674 (*v*. **furlang**), *Rye hil* 1601, *Ry hill* 1703, 1706, *Rye-hill* 1706 (18) (*v*. **ryge**); *the Shortbutts* 1690, *Shortbut Leys* 1674 (*v*. **leys**) (*v*. **sc(e)ort**, **butte**); *the Short meddow foote* 1601 (*v*. **sc(e)ort**, **mēd** (**mēdwe** obl.sg.), **fōt**); *Thornye Waye* 1601, *Thorney* ~, *Thorne way* 1674, *Thornway* 1690, 1703, 1706 (*v*. **þornig**, **þorn**, **weg**); *Thorpe furlonge* 1601 (*v*. **furlang** and Hothorpe *supra*); *the Town roodes* 1601 (*v*. **tūn**, **rōd**[3]).

Thorpe Langton

THORPE LANGTON

Torp 1086 DB (×3), c.1130 LeicSurv, 1156 (1318) Ch, 1220 MHW, 1243 Fees
Thorp c.1130 LeicSurv, 12 *Peake*, 1242 Fees *et passim* to 1309 Cl, 1316 *Wyg et freq* to 1519 EpCB, 1523 *MktHPR et passim* to 1548 Pat, 1576 Saxton
Thorpe 1267 Pat, 1333 (16) *SlCart et passim* to 1357, 1359 Pat *et freq*
Thorpp' 1359 *Wyg*, *Thorppe* 1427 *Peake*
Trop 1156 (1318) Ch, *Throp* 1475 *MktHPR*

Affixes are added as:
~ *iuxta Langeton'* c.1130 LeicSurv, 1278 Banco *et passim* to 1382, 1386 *Peake*
~ *Langeton'* 1327 SR, 1346 AD *et passim* to 1403 Fine, 1472 *Peake*, ~ *Langton* 1378 Pat, 1385 Fine *et passim* to 1439 *MktHPR*, 1450 *RTemple et freq*, ~ *Lan(c)kton* 1506 Ipm, 1536 *Braye*, 1610 Speed

'The outlying farmstead', *v.* **þorp**. This was a secondary settlement of Langton, *v.* East ~, Church Langton *supra* and note MLat *iuxta* 'next to'.

BAKERS' ARMS (P.H.), *Bakers' Arms* 1846, 1863, 1877 White, 1925 Kelly; Thomas Smith, mine host in 1846 through to at least 1863, was also a baker. BARLEY MOW (P.H.) (lost), *Barley Mow* 1846, 1863, 1877 White, 1925 Kelly. BOWDEN RD, Great Bowden lying 2 miles to the south. CAWDELL FM, *v.* **cald**, **wella** and Langton Caudle in Stonton Wyville *supra*. THE GRANGE, 1925 Kelly, *v.* **grange**. MANOR FM, *v.* **maner**; it is *Thorpe Langton Hall* 1787 VCHL, *v.* **hall**. MEADOW FM. PINFOLD HO., *v.* **pynd-fald**. ST LEONARD'S CHURCH, *Church (St Leonard)* 1925 Kelly; it is earlier recorded as *capellam de Langeton* 1220 MHW (with MLat *capella* 'a chapel') and much later *The Chapel* 1877 White, *v.* **chapel(e)**. Thorpe Langton was once a chapel within the parish of Church Langton *supra*. WELHAM RD, Welham lying one mile to the east; earlier called *East gate* 1588 Nichols, *v*. **ēast**, **gata**.

FIELD-NAMES

In (a), forms dated 1843, 1861 and 1872 are *Surv*. Forms in (b) dated 1385 are Ipm; those dated 1386 are *Peake*; 1529 and 1588 are Nichols; 1601, 1625, 1694, 1703, 1712, 1715 and 1745 are *Terrier*.

(a) Thorpe Field Cl, ~ ~ Mdw, Thorpe Langton Cl, ~ ~ Mdw 1843, 1861, 1872 (presumably alternative names for the same closes).

(b) *Brodedole* 1385 (*v*. **brād**, **dāl**); *Cawthorpe felde* 1529 (*v*. **feld**; recording a lost 'Kali's farmstead', *v*. **þorp**; with the ON masc. pers.n. *Kali*, cf. Cawthorpe, L **4** 6. One of two surviving names of the township's early great open-fields); *Cleyhill* 1529 (*v*. **clǣg**, **hyll**); *Debbedale* 1529 (*v*. **dēop**, **dalr**); *Dexters corner* 1601, 1624 *et passim* to 1745 (*v*. **corner**; with the surn. *Dexter*, a reflex of ME *dextere* 'a dyer', cf. *Radulphus le Dextere* 1262 RFL); *Fullwell meires* 1601, 1694, *Fullin meirs* 1625, *Fullwell myers* 1703, ~ *miers* 1712, ~ *mires* 1715, *The Fulling Mire* 1745, *v*. **fūl**, **wella**, **mýrr**; later poss. confused with fulling pits); *Goodins bridge* 1588 (*v*. **brycg**; cf. *Goodinges oxe* in adjoining Great Bowden f.ns.(b)); *Leverychewell* 1529 (*v*. **wella**; with the OE masc. pers.n. *Lēofric*; cf. *Willelmus filius Lefrich'* 1196 Cur of Leics.); *Muswell Hill* 1588 (*v*. **mos**, **wella**; earlier forms appear in East Langton f.ns. (b)); *the Mill furlong* 1712, 1715 (*v*. **furlang**), *the Mill way* 1712, 1715 (*v*. **myln**); *Paddock(e)well Stile* 1601, 1625, 1694, 1703 (*v*. **padduc**, **wella**, **stīg**); *the Persons hadland* 1601 (*v*. **persone**, **hēafod-land**); *Presborowe feld* 1529 (*v*. **prēost**, **berg**, **feld**; one of the great open-fields); *Redome* ~ 1601, 1625, *Redholmes gate* 1694, 1703, 1715, *Reedham Gate* 1712, 1745, *v*. **hrēod**, **holmr**, **gata**); *Mr Roberts neatespen* 1625 (*v*. **nēat**, **penn**[2]), *Mr Roberts orchard* 1715 (*v*. **orceard**); *Mr Streetes Neets pen* 1601, *Mr Streets neatspen* 1694, 1703 (*v*. **nēat**, **penn**[2]); *Mr Streets Pen* 1703, 1745 (*v*. **penn**[2]); *Town Lands* 1529 (*v*. **tūn**, **land**); *Water Nattocke* 1601 (*v*. **wæter**, **nattok**); *Wrangelondes* 1386 (*v*. **wrang**, **land**).

Thurnby

1. THURNBY

Turnebi 1156 (1318) Ch, l.12 Dane (p), *Turneby* Hy 2, 12 Dugd, 1220 MHW, 1227 Fees, 1231 Ch, c.1258 RHug
Sturnebi 1207 P, *Sturneby* 1207 RFinib
Thurneby 1208 FF, 1231 Cl *et passim* to 1585, 1589 Fine
Thorneby 1228 Ch, 1371 Ipm, 1535 VE, 1540 Dugd, 1558 *Pat*
Thirneby 1289 Ch, 1252 GildR *et freq* to 1420 Inqaqd, 1428 FA *et passim* to 1518 Visit, 1622 Burton
Thyrneby 1247 Fees, 1262 Fine *et passim* to 1449 *MiD*, 1526 AAS
Therneby 1255 Cl, c.1258 RHug *et passim* to 1352 Fine, 1361 Cl
Thurnby(e) 1386 Banco, 1477 (e.16) *Charyte et passim* to 1576 Saxton, 1624 Ipm *et freq*
Thornby 1371 Cl, 1507 Ipm, 1535 VE
Thirnby(e) 1535 VE, 1575 LEpis, 1633 ISLR, *Thirnbie* 1580 LEpis

'The farmstead where thorn-bushes grow' or 'the farmstead at the thorn-scrub' seems probable, *v.* **þyrne**, **þyrnir**, **þyrni**, **bȳ**. Formally, an OScand by-name *Þyrnir* (recorded as *Þirne* c. 1050 YCh 9) is also possible as the specific. However, when taken with adjoining Bushby *infra*, these names appear to record a former area of scrubland which had remained poorly exploited until the period of Scandinavian settlement. A few spellings indicate the occasional substitution of OE **þorn** 'a thorn-tree' as the specific. Note AN prosthetic *s* before *t* (for initial *þ*) in two early spellings.

THE COURT (lost), *Thurnby Court* 1877 White, *The Court* 1925 Kelly, *v.* **court**; demolished in 1916. FIRS FM is *The Firs* 1925 Kelly. GRANGE LANE, *v.* Thurnby Grange *infra*. THE HOLT, 1925 Kelly, *v.* **holt**. THE LODGE, 1877 White, 1925 Kelly, *v.* **loge**. LODGE FM, *Lodge farm* 1925 Kelly. MAIN ST is *the Towne Streete* 1625 *Terrier*, *v.* **tūn**, **strǣt**. MANOR HO., *Manor House* 1877 White, 1925 Kelly, *v.* **maner**. ROSE AND CROWN (P.H.), *Rose and Crown* 1846, 1863, 1877 White, 1913 Sale, 1925 Kelly, *Rose and Crown Inn* 1907 *Surv*. ST LUKE'S CHURCH,

Church (St Luke) 1846, 1863, 1877 White, 1925 Kelly; it is earlier recorded as *ecclesia de Turneby* 1220 MHW, 1253 × 58 RTAL, *ecclesie de Thurneb'* 1249 RGros, *ecclesiarum de Buckmynster Diseworth Thorneby et Humberston* 1558 *Pat*. Note also *the Churchyard* 1625, 18 *Terrier*, *v.* **churchyerd**. STATION FM, *Station farm* 1925 Kelly, STATION WHARF, 1925 Kelly, *v.* **wharf** and Thurnby and Scraptoft Station *infra*. THURNBY AND SCRAPTOFT STATION. THURNBY BROOK. THURNBY GRANGE, 1877 White, 1925 Kelly, *v.* **grange**. THURNBY HILL. THURNBY LODGE, 1877 White, *v.* **loge**. THURNBY NURSERIES, *v.* **nursery**. THE VICARAGE, 1877 White, 1925 Kelly; earlier is *The Vycaridge House* 1625 *Terrier*, *The Vicarage-House* 18 *ib*, *v.* **vikerage**.

No early forms have been noted for the following Thurnby street-names: ANTHONY DRIVE, CHARNWOOD DRIVE, COLTHURST WAY, COURT RD (*v.* The Court *supra*), DRUMCLIFF RD, FIONA DRIVE, FOREST RISE, HAVEN WALK, KINROSS AVE, ROBOROUGH GREEN, SEDGEFIELD DRIVE, SOMERBY RD, STATION RD, STOUGHTON RD.

FIELD-NAMES

In (a), forms dated 1776 are *Map*; those dated 1806 and 1810 are *Deed*; 1845 are *TA*; 1852 and 1907 are *Surv*; 1868 and 1913 are Sale; 1875 are *Plan*; 1878 are *PK*. Forms throughout dated 1332 are SR; those dated 1477 (e.16) are *Charyte*; 1622, 1640, 1641, 1642, 1652, 1666, 1678, 1685, 1690, 1694, 1698, 1709, 1713, 1721, 1725, 1729 and 1749 are *Deed*; 1625 are *Terrier*.

(a) Aesops Lane 1878, 1907 (a continuation of Hyssop's Lane in Evington; with the surn. *Aesop*, a later development of *Alsop*); Averys Mdw 1776 (with the surn. *Avery*); Bottom Cl 1878, 1907 (*v.* **bottom**); Brickyard Cl 1852, 1878, 1907 (*v.* **brike-yard**); Bottom ~ ~, Brook Cl 1852, 1878, 1907 (*Brook Close* 1749, *v.* **brōc** and Thurnby Brook *supra*); Top ~ ~, Cow Cl 1852, Cow Cl 1878, 1907 (cf. *the Cow Close Pasture* 1641, *v.* **pasture**); Daleacre, ~ Mdw 1845, 1868, 1878, 1907, 1913 (*v.* **dāl**, **æcer**; arable land held in common); Darkers Fd, ~ Mdw 1852, 1878, 1907 (with the surn. *Darker*); Dorkins Mdw 1878, 1907 (with the surn. *Dorkins*); Dudleys Cl 1875 (with the surn. *Dudley*); Evington Mdw 1878, 1907 (Evington parish adjoins to the west); Gilstead 1810, The Gilsteads 1907, 1913 (*Gilstead Close* 1640, 1685, *Guilsford Close* (sic) 1721, *v.* **stede**; earlier forms are needed to establish the nature of the first el., but **gylde** 'golden flower', as on gorse, may pertain; Gilstead is now the name of an old cottage on Main St); Gravel Pit Cl 1868, 1907 (*v.* **pytt**) (*v.* **gravel**); (The) Home Cl 1852, 1878, 1907, 1913 (*v.* **home**); Intake (×3) 1868 (*v.* **inntak**); Little Mdw 1776, 1907, 1913; North ~ ~, South Lower Cl 1845, 1868, 1907; Middle Cl 1776; Middle Fd 1852, 1878, 1907 (1622, *v.* **middel**, **feld**; the name of one of the great open-fields of the township); North ~ ~, South Lower Ground 1913, Far Side ~ ~, Middle Ground 1845, 1868, 1878, 1907, 1913, North Upper Ground 1845, 1878, 1907, 1913 (*v.* **grund**); Mirey Plantation 1878, 1907 (*v.* **plantation**), Mirey Spinney 1845, 1868, 1907 (*v.* **spinney**) (*v.* **myry**); New Mdw 1868, 1907 (*the New Meadow* 1725); Far Over Cl 1845, 1868, 1878, 1907, 1913 (*v.* **uferra**); Peas(e)y Cl 1845, 1868, 1878, 1907, 1913 (*v.* **pise**, **-ig**[3]); Peberdy(s) Mdw 1845, 1868, 1878, 1907 (with the surn. *Peberdy*); Far ~ ~, Near ~ ~, North ~ ~, East ~ ~, West ~ ~, Ploughed Cl 1845, Second ~ ~, Ploughed Cl 1878, 1907; Polton ~ 1845, Poulton Hill 1878, 1907, Great ~ ~, Little Poulton Hill 1845, 1878, 1907, 1913 (*Poultney ~*, *Pultney ~* 1652, *Poltone Hill* 1690, *Great ~ ~*, *Little Polton Hill* 1690, 1694; cf. *Poult(e)ney ~ ~* 1687, 1690, *Poultny Hill Close* 1687, 1690; with the surn. *Poultney* of a family originally from Poultney in Misterton parish, 14 miles to the south-west); Great ~, Little Roseley 1806 (cf. *Rosely Close* 1640, *v.* **hors**, **lēah**; the specific was presum. replaced by ON **hross** (**hrossa** gen.pl.), cf. Rosley, Cu 330); Top Round Cl 1878, 1907 (alluding to shape); Long Shrubbery 1913 (*v.* **shrubbery**; of shrubs in a mass); The Square Cl, Little Square Cl 1852, 1878, 1907 (*v.* **squar(e)**); Swans Mdw 1907, 1913 (with the surn. *Swa(i)n*, here prob. a reflex of the ON masc. pers.n. *Sveinn*; the Swain family was prominent in Thurnby, from *John Swain* 1840 Census to *William Swain* 1880 ib); Symons Mdw, Symons Nether ~, Symons Upper Cl 1776 (with the surn. *Symons*); Thurnby Green 1875 (*Thurnby grene* 1477 (e.16), *~ greene* 1641, *v.* **grēne**[2]); Thurnby Mdw 1875; Top Cl, 1878, 1907, ~ Fd 1852, 1878, 1907, ~ Mdw 1776 (*v.* **top**); Vicarage Mdw 1845 (*v.* The Vicarage *supra*).

(b) *Ash close* 1652 (*v.* **æsc**); *Banelondslade* n.d. AD, *v.* **bēan**, **land**, **slæd**); *Barnyarde* 1477 (e.16), *v.* **barn-yard**; the earliest citation for this compound in OED is dated 1513–75); *Bradsicke Close* 1642 (*v.* **brād**, **sík**); *the Britch furlong Close* 1640 (*v.* **furlang**; with **brēc** or **bryce**); *the Church causy close* 1652 (*v.* **caucie** and St Luke's Church *supra*); *Cow meadow brooke* 1640; *Doveland* 1652, 1698, 1725 (*v.* **land**; the specific may be OE **dūfe** or ON **dúfa** 'a dove, a pigeon'; but for Doveland (Lei **1** 221), a lost stream-name **Dove* (from Brit **dubo-* 'dark') is postulated and such may have been the ancient name of Bushby Brook which forms an early boundary here); *the Far(r)feild* 1709, 1713, *the Far pasture* 1652 (*v.* **pasture**) (*v.* **feor**); *the five acre close* 1640 (*v.* **æcer**); *Fosters Close* 1652, 1698, 1725 (with the surn. *Foster*); *Fouldikes Close* 1641 (*v.* **fūl**, **dík**); (*the*) *Greene meadow* 1640, 1642 (*v.* Thurnby Green *supra*); *Hardhill close* 1641 (*v.* **heard**, **hyll**; alluding to land hard to till); *Hassock* 1652, 1698, *Hassocks* 1725 (*v.* **hassuc**); *Haverell close* 1642 (*v.* **hæfera**, **hafri**, **hyll**); *the Homestall* 1625 (*v.* **hām-stall**); *the Homestead* 1652 (*v.* **hām-stede**); *Jarvis his Close* 1666, 1678, *Jervases Close* 1713 (with the surn. *Jarvis*/*Jervis*); *Knoles Laund Close* 1641 (*v.* **cnoll**, **launde**); *Leicester way* 1642 (Leicester lies 16 miles to the west); *Little Close* 1709, 1713; *the Meadow(e) Close* 1640, 1642; *the Neather ~* 1640, 1713, *Nether Croft* 1749 (*v.* **neoðera**, **croft**); *the New Close* 1652; *the North Close or the North Leys* 1725 (*v.* **leys**); *the North field* 1642, 1729 (*v.* **norð**, **feld**; one of the great open-fields); *the Penleies close* 1640 (*v.* **penn**[2], **leys**); *Plumers Close* 1640 (in the possession of *Peter Plumer* 1640); *the Sand Hill* (*v.* **sand**); *Sheepecoate leyes* 1678 (*v.* **scēp-cot**, **leys**); *the Southfeilde* 1640 (*v.* **sūð**, **feld**; one of the great open-fields); *South Leasow* 1749 (*v.* **lǣs** (**lǣswe** gen.sg., dat.sg.)); *the sow meadow close* 1642, *Sow meadow* 1713 (*v.* **sūð**); *Thurnebie Bridge* 1625 (cf. *ad pontem* 1332 (p), with MLat *pons* (*pontem* acc.sg.) 'a bridge'); *Thurnby Lane* 1725; *the Tythe barne yarde* 1625 (*v.* **tēoða** and

Barnyarde, *supra*); *the Upper Croft* 1713, 1749 (*v*. **croft**); *Wadland Close* 1640 (*v*. **wād**, **land**); *Wigston bushes Close* 1642 (*v*. **busc**; Wigston Magna lies 4 miles to the south-west beyond Stoughton and Oadby, so that *Wigston* here must either be the surn. of a family originally from that township or the property of Wigston's Hospital in Leicester (*v*. Lei **1** 95)).

2. BUSHBY

Bucebi 1175 (p), 1176 P (p), l.12 Dane (p), *Bucebia* e. Hy 3 Berkeley (p)

Buzcebi 1175 ChancR (p), *Buszebia* 1175 P (p), *Buzeby* 1209 × 35 RHug

Buscebi 1199 FF (p), 1209 GildR (p), 1210 P, 1225 GildR (p), *Buscebia* 1219 ib (p), *Busceby* 1237 Cur (p), 1240 GildR (p) *et passim* to 1298 *RTemple* (p), 1306 *LCDeeds* (p) *et freq* to 1323 *Wyg* (p), 1327 Inqaqd (p), *Bussceby* 1220 × 50 *RTemple* (p)

Boceby 1207 RFinib, *Bosceby* 1207 ClR, 1267 Cur (p), 1268 Abbr (p), l.13 CustRo (p), *Boisceby* 1267 Cur (p), *Bosseby* 1268 Abbr (p), *Bosby* 1399 Pat

Busseby 1249 GildR (p), 1255 Fine (p) *et freq* to 1398 Cl, 1420 Inqaqd

Bus(s)heby 1259 Cur, 1342, 1386 Banco, *Bushebye* 1604 SR

Buskeby 1331 *Deed* (p), 1477 (e.16) *Charyte*, *Buskby* 1410 ELiW, 1412 PRep, 1451 Pat

Busshby(e) 1507 Ipm, 1525 Fine, 1526 CoPleas, *Bushby* 1540 Ipm, 1610 Speed *et freq*

Ekwall DEPN takes the specific of this place-name to be an ON pers.n. *Butr*, hence 'Butr's farmstead, village', *v*. **bȳ**. An alternative Scand pers.n. which could formally be acceptable is *Butsi*, as in the Danish Busseby (DS 11.210) and Busserup (DS 2.6). Fellows-Jensen suggests that an original pers.n. as first element became confused with OE *busc* 'bush' or Scand *buskr* 'shrub', *buski* 'shrubland' (SSNEM 80). However, in view of the strong possibility that neighbouring Thurnby records a former area of thorn-scrub, it seems preferable to interpret Bushby as 'the farmstead at the scrubland', *v*. **busc**, **buskr**, **buski**, **bȳ**.

BEAUMONT HAMEL, 1925 Kelly; named from the village of Beaumont Hamel on the river Somme in northern France, the scene of fierce fighting in 1916 in the First World War and presum. reminiscent of its local topography, cf. the similar Vimy Ridge near Kinoulton, Notts.

BUSHBY BROOK, *Buskeby brook* 1477 (e.16) *Charyte*, *v*. **brōc** and *Doveland* in Thurnby f.ns. (b). BUSHBY HO. (2½"), *Bushby House* 1846, 1877 White. BUSHBY LODGE FM (~ LODGE 2½"), *Bushby Lodge* 1913 Sale, 1925 Kelly, *v*. **loge**. BUSHBY SPINNEY, 1913 Sale, cf. *atte Spyneye* 1327 SR (p) (*v*. **atte**), *de la Spine* 1477 (e.16) (p), *v*. **spinney**. HOME FM, *v*. **home**. NEWSTEAD. OLD HALL, 1925 Kelly, *v*. **hall**. RANDLES CLOSE, with the surn. *Randle*. RANGEMOOR, 1925 Kelly. SEALBY, 1925 Kelly; no doubt a recent fabrication based on the local surn. *Seal*, *v*. Seals Homestead in f.ns. (a) and cf. *Edward Seal* 1821 Census and *William Seal* 1824 ib of Bushby and *Harry Seal* and *William Seal* 1873 ib, both of Thurnby. SPRINGFIELD, 1925 Kelly, *v*. **spring**[1]. WINKADALE (WINKERDALE 2½"), *Winkendale* 1776 *Map*, 1845 *TA*, *Winkerdale* 1830 *Surv*, *Winkadale* 1925 Kelly, WINKADALE HILL, *Winkerdale Hill* 1835 O, *v*. **dæl**[1], **dalr**; with the OE masc. pers.n. *Wineca* (*Winecan* gen.sg.).

FIELD-NAMES

In (a), forms dated 1776 are *Map*; those dated 1830 and 1907 are *Surv*; 1845 are *TA*; 1868 and 1913 are Sale; 1878 are *PK*;. Forms throughout dated 1327, 1332 and 1377 are SR; those dated 1328 are Banco; 1477 (e.16) are *Charyte*; 1622, 1640, 1641, 1642, 1649, 1652, 1658, 1687, 1690, 1694, 1696, 1709, 1713, 1714 1729 and 1810 are *Deed*; 1625 are *Terrier*.

(a) Five ~ 1878, Eight Acres 1845, 1878, 1907, 1913 (*v*. **æcer**); Barn Cl 1878, 1907, 1913 (*v*. **bern**); Bennetts Homestead 1845 (*v*. **hām-stede**; with the surn. *Bennett*); Best Lands Hill 1845 (*v*. **best**, **land**; a complimentary name for very fertile ground); Bog Mdw 1845 (*v*. **bog**); Brook Furlong 1845, 1878 (*v*. **furlang** and Bushby Brook *supra*); Brunthill otherwise Padwell Leys 1810 (*v*. **leys**), Burnt Hill 1845 (cf. *Burnthill Close* 1658, *Brunthill Closes* 1658, 1694, 1696, *v*. **brend**, **hyll** and Padwell *infra*); Bushby Allottments 1878 (*v*. **allotment**); Bush Cl 1845 (*v*. **busc**); Bushby Glebe 1907 (*v*. **glebe**); Bushby Hill 1845; Bushey Cl 1878, 1907, 1913 (*v*. **busshi**); Charles Cl 1845 (with the surn. *Charles*); Clover Cl 1878, 1907, 1913 (*v*. **clāfre**; grown as a fodder crop); Coopers Hill 1845 (with the surn. *Cooper*); Mr Coopers Homestead 1776 (*v*. **hām-stede**); Devenports ~ 1776, Davenports Mdw 1830, 1845, Devenports ~ ~ 1776, Davenports Hill Cl 1830 (with the surn. *Davenport*); Dunslade 1845 (*Tunslade otherwise Towneslade* 1652, *Tunslade alias Townslade* 1687, 1690, *v*. **tūn**, **slæd**); Ford Mdw 1845 (*v*. **ford**); Gorsey Cl 1845, 1878, 1907, 1913 (*v*. **gorstig**); Top ~ ~, Grave Leys 1845, 1868, 1878, 1907, 1913 (*v*. **græf**, **leys**); Gravel Hole Cl 1845, Gravell Pitt ~ 1776, Gravel Pit Cl 1830, 1845, 1878, 1907, 1913 (*Gravell Pitt* 1687, (*the*) *Gravell Pitt* ~ 1652, 1690, *Gravile Pitt* ~ 1687, *the Gravaile pitt close* 1694, *v*. **gravel**, **pytt**); Great Cl 1878, 1907; North Upper Ground 1907 (*v*. **grund**); Bottom ~, Top Handkerchief Mdw 1845, 1907 (fanciful reference to small fields, though each of these is now just over 4 acres in area); Great Hill Cl 1776, 1830, Little Hill Cl 1776, 1830; Great ~, Little Homestead 1845, 1913 ((*the close called*) *the Homestead* 1694, *v.* **hām-stede**); Horse Pasture 1845 (*v.* **pasture**); House Cl 1878, 1907, 1913; Hut Cl 1845 (*v.* **hut**); Intake 1845, 1913 (*v.* **inntak**); Ladys ~ 1776, 1830, Ladies Mdw 1845 (*v.* **ladi**; perh. 'Our Lady's Meadow', indicating an endowment, although there is no record of this); Little Mead 1776, ~ Mdw 1830, 1878, 1907 (*v.* **mēd**); Lodge Cl 1845 (*v.* Bushby Lodge *supra*); Mawsons Mdw 1845, 1878 (with the surn. *Mawson*); Middle Mdw 1776, 1830, 1845; Moses Millers ~ 1776, Millers Homestead 1830 (*v.* **hām- stede**; with the surn. *Miller*); Mirry ~ 1776, Mirey Mdw 1830 (*v.* **myry**); Mountsorrel Land 1776, Mountsorrel Cl, Great ~ ~, Little Mountsorrel Mdw 1845, 1878 (in 1617, Richard Nedd gifted land in the parish of Thurnby and Bushby (with Stoughton) to provide funds for the poor of his birthplace, Mountsorrel; the land of Charity Fm in Stoughton also records this endowment); Nether Mdw 1776, 1830; New Cl 1907; New Mdw 1878, 1913; Nook(e) Cl 1845, 1878, 1907, 1913 (*v.* **nōk**); Bottom ~, Middle ~, Top ~, Padwell 1845, 1878, 1907, Padwell Leys 1810 (*v.* **leys**) (*v.* **padde**, **wella**); Pen Cl 1776, 1830, 1845 (*v.* **penn**[2]); Piece Cl 1845, 1878, 1907, 1913 (*v.* **pece**); Pingle 1845 (*v.* **pingel**); Great Pit Cl 1830 (*v.* **pytt**); Road Cl 1776, 1830, 1845, 1878 (an enclosure beside a roadway); Rush Cl 1845 (1729, *v.* **risc** and *Pastures Knowles* in f.ns. (b)); Rushy Cl 1845 (*Rushie Close* 1640, 1642, *the Rushy Clos* 1694, *v.* **riscig**); Seals Homestead 1868, 1878, 1907 (*v.* **hām-stede**), Seals Yard 1845, 1878 (*v.* **geard**) (with the surn. *Seal*, *v.* Sealby *supra*); Side Mdw 1776, 1830 (*v.* **sīde**); Spinney Cl 1878, 1907, 1913 (*the Spinney Close* 1709, 1713, *v.* Bushby Spinney *supra*); Town Cl 1845 (*v.* **tūn**); Winkendale Bottom ~, Winkendale Top Cl 1776, Winkerdale Bottom ~, Winkerdale Top Cl 1830, Bottom ~, Middle Winkendale, Winkendale Mdw 1845, 1878 (*v.* Winkadale *supra*).

(b) *at þe Ays* 1377 (p) (*v.* **þe**, **æsc**); *Breach furlong* 1642 (*v.* **brēc**, **furlang**); *the Brooke feild* 1714 (*v.* **brōc**, **feld** and Bushby Brook *supra*; one of the great open-fields of the township); *Bushby meer* 1714 (*v.* **(ge)mǣre**); *Bushebie Sythorpes* 1625 (*v.* Great ~, Little Sybthorpe in Stoughton f.ns. (a) which refer to the same lost farmstead); *Cockacres* 1714 (*v.* **æcer**; with **cocc**[1] or **cocc**[2]); *Cookes Close* 1649, 1729 (with the surn. *Cooke*); *Debdale* 1714 (*v.* **dēop**, **dalr**); *the East and West feild* 1714 (*v.* **feld**; one of the great open-fields); *Elbow leyes* 1714 (*v.* **elbowe**, **leys**); *Flax Leyes Close* 1729 (*v.* **fleax**, **leys**); *Frisby leys* 1714 (*v.* **leys**; with the surn. *Frisby* of a family prob. in origin from Frisby by Galby, 4 miles to the south-east); *Garbridge* 1714 (*v.* **gorebrode**); *hay gate* 1714 (*v.* **hēg**, **gata**); *Long Hexton* 1714 (presum. a lost farmstead, *v.* **tūn**; with a masc. pers.n. such as OE *Hēahstān* or ON *Heggr*, earlier forms appearing in adjoining Houghton on the Hill); *hird hill* 1714 (poss. with **hirde** 'a herdsman', but this may be a poor spelling for *Hardhill* in Thurnby f.ns. (b) *supra*); *Hollowslade* 1652, 1687, *Hallowslade* 1690 (*v.* **holh**, **slæd**); *Home Close* 1622, 1690 (*v.* **holmr**); *othe hyrne* 1377 (p) (*v.* **hyrne**); *Lammas Close* 1690 (*v.* **lammas**); *Long hill* 1714; *Lose hill* 1714 (*v.* **hlōse**); *the Mill feild* 1714 (*v.* **myln**, **feld**; one of the great open-fields, containing a windmill); *Neat(e)s Leys or Neates leys Close* 1641, 1709 (*v.* **nēat**, **leys**); *Pasture Knowles alias the Rush Close* 1729 (*v.* **pasture**, **cnoll** and Rush Cl *supra*); *at Mr Sherwoods gate* 1714 (*v.* **geat**; a furlong so called); *Staves acre* 1714 (*v.* **stæf**, **æcer**); *Stoughton balk* 1714 (*v.* **balca**; Stoughton adjoins to the south-west); *atte Thorn* 1332 (p) (*v.* **atte**, **þorn**); *Vnderbretlond* 1477 (e.16) (*v.* **under**, **breiðr**, **land**); *Upper Close* 1622, *Upper or*

Over Close 1641 (*v.* **uferra**); *atte Well(e)* 1327 (p), 1328 (p) (*v.* **atte**, **wella**); *Wharle*, *far Wharll* 1714 (*v.* **hwerfel**); *Willow Sick* 1714 (*v.* **wilig**, **sík**).

Tur Langton

TUR LANGTON

Terlintone 1086 DB, *Terlington'* 1205 Cur, *Terlinton'* 1206 RFinib, 1206 P

Cherlintone (rectius *Therlintone*) 1086 DB

Thurlington' c.1130 LeicSurv, *Thirlyngton'* 1288 *Wyg* (p)

Turlinton(e) 1156 (1318) Ch, Hy 2 Dugd, 1165, 1200, 1205 P, *Turlington* 1209 × 35 RHug, 1253 Cur, 1536 Ipm, 1546 AAS, 1617 LML, *Turlyngton* 1511 Ipm, 1515 CoPleas, 1556 Pat

Tirlinton' 1165 ChancR, 1166 P *et passim* to l.13 *ShR*, 1316 FA, *Tirlington'* 1288, 1299 Banco *et freq* to 1331 Inqaqd, 1333 GildR (p) *et passim* to 1349, 1352 *LCDeeds* (p), *Tirlyngton'* e.14 *ShR*, 1316 *Peake* (p) *et passim* to 1447 Fine, 1462 Pat

Tyrlington' 1261, 1265 Pat (p) *et passim* to 1510, 1518 Visit, *Tyrlinton* 1265 Misc, 1276 RH, *Tyrlyngton'* 1290 Ass, 1300 Banco *et passim* to 1534 Ipm, 1535 Fine

Tyrlangton 1504 Banco, 1526 LAS

Thurlangton 1576 Saxton, 1585 LibCl, 1617 LML, *Thurlanckton* 1722 ib

Turlangton 1555, 1559 Fine *et passim* to 1627, 1632 LML, *Turlanghton* 1604 SR, 1609 LML, *Turlancton* 1610 Speed

Tur Langton 1573 Fine, 1608, 1688 LML *et freq*

'The village or estate associated with or called after a man named Tyrhtel or Tyrli', *v.* **-ingtūn**. The OE pers.n. *Tyrhtel* is independently attested, though *Tyrli*, a presumed derivative of the OE pers.n. *Turla* (as in *Turlan homm* 940 (12) BCS 764 (S 467)), is unrecorded. Because of the township's proximity to Church ~, East ~ and West Langton, 16th-cent. and later spellings (with eventual metanalysis) have imitated Langton. The substitution of *th* for *t* in occasional early forms is the result of AN orthographical interchange between the symbols *th* and *t* for etymological *t*.

BULL'S HEAD (P.H.), *Bull's Head* 1846, 1863, 1877 White, 1925 Kelly. CHEQUERS (P.H.) (lost), *Chequers* 1863 White, ~ *Inn* 1877 ib. CRANOE RD, Cranoe lying 3 miles to the east. CROCK'S FM (local), CROXFIELD SPINNEY (*v.* **spinney**), cf. *Crocks way* 1601 *Terrier*, *Croxe way* 1653 *ib* (*v.* **weg**; the road east to Cranoe), *Croxie* 1625 *ib*, *Croxil* 1638, c.1650 *ib* (*v.* **hyll**), *Crox* 1708, 1745 *ib*, *upon Crox* 1708 (18) *ib*. Two possible explanations present themselves for these names: (i) either their base is **crocc** 'a crock, an earthenware pot', with reference to former pottery kilns which may have been sited at Croxfield, an ideal hill-top location for them to the east of the township, still served directly by roads from Tur Langton and Church Langton, or (ii) the base is the ON masc. pers.n. *Krókr*. However, Scand pers.ns. compounded with OE *weg* are very rare. Only *Ravenildesweye* (with the ON fem. pers.n. *Hrafnhildr*, *v.* Db 754) and the disputed Thoresway (with the ON masc. pers.n. *Þórir*, *v.* L **3** 150) have otherwise been identified. CROWN (P.H.), *Crown* 1846, 1863, 1877 White, 1925 Kelly. FARGATE FM, *fargatts* 1601 *Terrier*, *fargates* 1625 *ib*, *Fargate* 1638, 1708, 1745 *ib*, *v.* **feor**, **gata**. THE HALL, 1601 *Terrier*, *v.* **hall**. KIBWORTH RD, Kibworth Harcourt lying 2 miles to the west. KING CHARLES'S WELL, 1925 Kelly, *King Charles Well* 1798 Nichols; it is *Carles Trough* 1625, 1653, 1708 *Terrier*, *Charles Trough* 1708 (18) *ib*, *Carls Trofe* 1745 *ib*, *v.* **trog**. Popular tradition has it that in 1645, Charles I watered his horse at the chalybeate spring now so called during his flight from the battlefield of Naseby, but the name predates any such event. It may well be that the original specific was OE **ceorl**, replaced by ON **karl** (as in the name of adjoining Carlton Curlieu). MANOR HO., (*the*) *Manor House* 1872 Sale, 1877 White, 1925 Kelly, *v.* **maner**. MELTON RD, Melton Mowbray lying approximately 16 miles to the north; the road is *Northgate* 1625, *v.* **norð**, **gata**. ST ANDREW'S CHURCH, *Church (St Andrew)* 1925 Kelly, built 1865–6; the medieval church is recorded in *capellas Torp et Tirlington* 1220 MHW (with MLat *capella* 'a chapel'), *ecclesia de Turlington* 1559 *Pat* and *the Church* 1625 *Terrier*. Note also *the Church yard(e)* 1625, 1694, 1708, 1708 (18), 1745 *Terrier*, *v.* **churchyerd**. SHEEPTHORNS FM, *v.* Sheepthorns Spinney in adjoining Carlton Curlieu. TUR LANGTON LODGE, *v.* **loge**. THE WARREN, WARREN FM (local), *v.* **wareine**.

FIELD-NAMES

In (a), forms dated 1792 are EnclA; those dated 1798 are Nichols; 1843 and 1872 are Sale; 1861 are *Surv*. Forms throughout dated 1381 are SR;

those dated 1601, 1625, 1638, c.1650, 1653, 1694, 1708, 1708 (18) and 1745 are *Terrier*; 1641 are Ipm.

(a) Barn Cl 1843, 1861, 1872 (*v.* **bern**); Black Miles 1843, 1861, Black Mills 1872 (*blaakemyles* 1601, *blackemiles* 1625, *Blackmiles* c.1650, 1708, *Blakemiles* 1745, *v.* **blæc**, **mylde**); Branthill Cl 1843, 1861, 1872 (*Branthill* 1601, 1625, 1638, c.1650, 1745, *Brantil* 1694, *v.* **brant**, **hyll**); Broadham Cl 1843, 1861, 1872 (*Broadham* 1745, *v.* **brād**, **hamm**); Clark(e)'s Orchard 1861, 1872 (*v.* **orceard**); Close above Wood 1861, 1872; Dorothy's Cl 1843, 1861, 1872 (with the fem. pers.n. *Dorothy*); Home Cl 1861, ~ ~ Spinney 1872 (*v.* **spinney**) (*v.* **home**); Level Longs, ~ ~ Cl 1843, 1861, 1872 (*lavorlongs* 1601, *lauerlongs* 1625, *Laverlong* c.1650, *Leverlong* 1708, *Leaver Longs* 1745, *v.* **lǣfer**, **lang**[2]); Lords Cl 1791, 1843, 1872, ~ ~ Mdw 1843, 1861, 1872, ~ ~ Spinney 1861, 1872 (*v.* **spinney**) (*Lords closse* 1625, ~ *Close* c.1650, 1708, 1745; the township had a resident manorial lord in the medieval period and into the 18th cent., but *Lord* may be a surn. here); Muzzle Hole 1843, ~ ~ Mdw 1861, 1872 (*v.* **mos**, **wella**, **hol**[1]); Osbournes Mdw 1843, 1861, 1872 (*Osbernes Meddowe* 1601, *Osbornes* ~ c.1650, 1708, *Osborns Meadow* 1745; the property of *Thomas Osberne* 1601); Pepper Leys 1843, 1872, ~ ~ Cl 1861 (*v.* **leys**; with the surn. *Pepper*, metonymic for ME *pepperer* 'a dealer in pepper, a spicer'); Quartern Cl 1843, 1861 (*v.* **quarterne**); Rattens Cl, ~ Mdw 1843, 1862, 1871 (presum. with the surn. *Ratten* (from OFr *raton* 'a rat' (ME *ratoun*), either a nickname in origin or metonymic for a rat-catcher); *ratoun* itself is unlikely); Spinney Ho(l)me 1843, 1861 1872 (*v.* **spinney**, **holmr**); Turf Cl 1843, 1861, 1872 (*v.* **turf**; land containing or adjoining peat beds); Twizzle Cl 1843, 1861, 1872 (*Quissell* c.1650, 1708, *Quisill* 1745, *Quysle foote* 1601 (*v.* **fōt**), *Quysle furlonge* 1601 (*v.* **furlang**), *Quissell* ~ 1625, *Quisill gate* 1745 (*v.* **gata**), *v.* **twisla**); West Field Cl 1843, 1861, 1872 ((*the*) *Westfeild* 1601, c.1650, 1708, *v.* **west**, **feld**; one of the great open-fields of the township); Wildmoor 1843, 1861, Wildmore 1872 (*Wyld Moore* 1601, *Wildmore* 1625, c.1650, 1708, *Wildmoor* 1745, *v.* **wilde**, **mōr**[1]); Wind Mill Cl 1861, 1872 (*v.* **wind-mylne**); Wood Cl 1792, 1843, 1861, 1872 (*v.* **wudu**).

(b) *le Alder close* 1641 (*v.* **alor**); *Annis Leyes* 1653 (*v.* **leys**; with the surn. *Annis*, from OFr *Anés*, a popular form of *Agnes*); (*the*) *Becke* 1625, 1653, *Beck* c.1650, 1708, 1745, *Beckefurlonge* 1601 (*v.* **furlang**) (*v.* **bekkr**); *Bement Hill* 1708, 1709 (18) (with the surn. *Beament*); *Black* 1625, *Blake* 1638, 1745, *in Blacke half way throwth* 1708, *in Blacke half way through* 1708 (18), *Blaake furlonge* 1601 (*v.* **furlang**) (*v.* **blæc**; presum. alluding to the colour of the soil); *Brake sicke* 1625, 1708, *Brakesick* 1745 (*v.* **bracu**, **sík**); (*the*) *Breach* 1625, 1638, c.1650, 1708 (18), *Brech* 1708, *Breache furlonge* 1601 (*v.* **furlang**) (*v.* **brēc**); *Bryer* ~ 1601, 1708 (18), *Breyer* ~ 1625, 1708, *Bryar Hill* 1745 (*v.* **brēr**); *atte Brigg* 1381 (p) (*v.* **atte**, **brycg**); *broad marche* 1601, *Broadmarch* 1625, 1653, 1708, 1745 (*v.* **brād**, **mersc**); *Broadwong* 1625, c.1650, 1708 (*v.* **brād**, **vangr**); *the brooke* 1653, *the Broocke* 1708, *the Brook* 1708 (18) (*v.* **brōc**); *Bursted* 1601, *Bussted* 1625, *Busted* 1708, *Busteds* 1745 (*v.* **burh-stede**); *Carls Trough Hill* 1653 (*v.* King Charles's Well *supra*); *Carroll sycke* 1601, *Cauwell seeke* 1625, *Carle Sick*(*e*) 1708, 1745, *Carl Sick* 1708 (18) (*v.* **sík**; the first word appears to be the **caldwella* of Langton Caudle (*q.v.*), the stream which forms the eastern boundary of the parish, with late modification by attraction to *Carles Trough*, *v.* King Charles's Well *supra*); *Churchgate* 1638, c.1650 (alluding to the medieval church; *v.* **gata** and St Andrew's

Church *supra*); *cockle hill* 1601, 1625, *Cockel Hill* 1708, 1745 (*v*. **cokel**; less likely with **coccel**); *coombes hedge* 1601 (*v*. **hecg**; with the surn. *Coombes*); *Cowhill* 1745 (this may belong with *cauwell*, *supra*); *Crabtree Dole* 1638, 1708, 1745 (*v*. **crabtre**, **dāl**); *the daales* 1601, *dales* 1625, (*the*) *Doles* 1708, 1708 (18), *the Dales* 1745 (*v*. **dāl**); *Deadman* 1625, *Deadmans gate* 1601, c.1650, 1708, 1745 (*v*. **gata**) (*v*. **dedeman**); *the doales under Maulo hill* 1601, *the Doles under Mellow* 1745 (*v*. **dāl** and *Mallow*, *infra*); *East feild* 1601, c.1650, 1653, ~ *Field* 1708, *under estfeild ford* 1601 (*v*. **ford**) (*v*. **ēast**, **feld**; one of the great open-fields); *Flaxgate* 1601, 1625 *et passim* to 1745, *flaxgatts end* 1601, *Flaxgate end* 1708 (18), 1745 (*v*. **ende**) (*v*. **fleax**, **gata**); *the ford* 1601, *the fourd* 1708, *the Foord* 1708 (18) (*v*. **ford**); *the Greate close* 1641 (*v*. **grēat**); *the gutter in carrollsyckes* 1601 (*v*. **goter** and *carroll sycke*, *supra*); *the Hall Land* 1708 (*v*. The Hall *supra*); *Mr Hawfords cloase* 1601 (*v*. **clos(e)**); *Hogate* c.1650, 1708, *Howgate* 1745 (*v*. **hōh**, **gata**); *Hommes head* 1653 (*v*. **hamm**, **hēafod**); *the hye waye* 1601 (*v*. **hēah-weg**); *Joyning the Churchyard* 1694 (land adjoining the churchyard, *v*. **joynynge** and St Andrew's Church *supra*); *Langton meer(e)* 1601, 1708 (18), 1745, ~ *Meire* 1625, ~ *Meare* c.1650, 1708 (*v*. **(ge)mǣre**; alluding to the boundary with East Langton); *Litle hill* 1708, 1745, *Little Hill* 1708 (18), *litle hill ford* 1601, *Little Hill Fourd* c.1650, ~ ~ *Ford* 1745 (*v*. **ford**) (*v*. **lȳtel**); *Lords hedge* 1601 (*v*. **hecg** and Lords Cl *supra*); *the Lyes* 1601 (*v*. **leys**); *Mallow* 1708, 1708 (18), *Mellow* 1708, 1745, *Maalo* ~, *Maulo* ~ 1601, *Mallow Hill* c.1650, *Mellow hill* 1708, 1745, *Maalo cloase* 1601, *Mallow* ~ c.1650, *Mellow Close* 1708, 1745, *Mallow* ~ c.1650, *Mellow ford* 1708, 1745 (*v*. **ford**), *Melow lond* 1708 (either **mǣl**[2] (with **hōh**) or **malu** (**malwe** dat.sg.)); *le meadow* c.1650; *Meires* 1625, (*the*) *Mires* c.1650, 1708 (18), 1745, *Miers* 1708 (*v*. **mýrr**); *Millhole* 1601, 1625, 1638 *et passim* to 1745 (*v*. **myln**, **hol**[1]); *Mill wong* 1708 (*v*. **myln**, **vangr**); *the More* 1708, *the Moor(e)* 1708 (18), 1745, *the hether moore alias Easte moore* 1601 (*v*. **ēast**), *The Hither* ~, *Upper Moore* c.1650, (*the*) *Hither More* 1708, ~ ~ *Moor(e)* 1708 (18), 1745 (*v*. **hider**), *the Up(p)er Moor* 1708, 1708 (18), *the Over Moor* 1745 (*v*. **uferra**), (*the*) *Upper Mo(o)r(e) Side* c.1650, 1708, 1745 (*v*. **sīde**), *the moore furlonge* 1601 (*v*. **furlang**), (*the*) *Moor(e) Hill* c.1650, 1708, 1745, *Mooresyck(e) leaes* 1601 (*v*. **sík**, **leys**) (*v*. **mōr**[1]); *Mydlesycke* 1601 (*v*. **middel**, **sík**); (*the*) *New Close Side* c.1650, 1708, 1745 (*v*. **sīde**); *New Woods end* 1601 (*v*. **wudu**, **ende**); *No mans Bush* c.1650, 1708, 1745 (*v*. **busc**), *no mans forlonge* 1601 (*v*. **furlang**), *noe mans land* 1625 (*v*. **land**) (*v*. **nān mann**); *North feilde* 1601, ~ *Field* 1708 (*v*. **norð**, **feld**; one of the great open-fields); *the Parsonage Dole* c.1650, 1708, 1745 (*v*. **personage**, **dāl**); *the persons balke* (*v*. **balca**), *the persons cloase* (*v*. **clos(e)**), *persons cloase hedge* (*v*. **hecg**) 1601 (*v*. **persone**); *russhe farrgatts* 1601, *rush fargate* 1625 (*v*. **risc** and Fargate Fm *supra*); *salters peece* 1601, *Salters* ~ 1708, *Saltors piece* 1745 (*v*. **saltere**, **pece**; alluding to the saltway north to Melton Mowbray); *Shankton leas* 1625 (*v*. **leys**), *Shanckton Syckes* 1601, ~ *seekes* 1625, *Shankton Sicks* c.1650, 1708, *Shangton Sicks* 1745 (*v*. **sík**), *Shancton slaide* 1625, *Shan(c)kton* ~ c.1650, 1653, 1708, *Shangton Slade* 1745 (*v*. **slæd**), *Shan(c)kton* ~ c.1650, 1653, *Shangton Wood* 1708, 1745 (Shangton parish adjoins to the north); *Shovellbroades* 1625, c.1650, *Shoovel Broads* c.1650, *Shovel Bords* 1708, ~ *Boards* 1708 (18), *Shoovell Broades* 1745 (*v*. **scofl-brǣdu**); *Sowbarow* 1601, 1708, *Sow Barrow* 1625, c.1650, *Sowborow* 1745 (*v*. **sūð**, **berg**); *Stockwell Hill* 1601, c.1650, 1708, 1745 (*v*. **stocc**, **wella**); *Stonhill* 1601, 1625, c.1650, 1708, *Stonehill* 1653, 1745 (*v*. **stān**, **hyll**); *Stonton Brook(e)* c.1650, 1745 (*v*. **brōc**; Stonton Wyville parish adjoins to the north-east); *Suger leaes* 1601, ~ *leyes*

1653, *Sugar Leas* c.1650, ~ *Leayes* 1708, ~ *Leys* 1708 (18), 1745 (*v*. **sugere**, **leys**; a complimentary name for 'sweet' land); (*the*) *Tongs* 1601, c.1650, 1708, 1745, *Tongues* 1625, *Tonges* 1708 (*v*. **tunge**); *2 gattes leaes* 1601, *Towgatt leas* 1625, *Twogate Leys* 1694, 1708, 1745 (*v*. **tū**, **gata**, **leys**); *Upper Bushe furlonge* 1601 (*v*. **busc**); *the Vandies* 1708, 1708 (18), *the Vanties* 1708, *the Vandies*, *the Wandies* 1745 (prob. late plural forms for **wandale** (**wandole**) 'a share of the common arable land of the township'); *Watermill Hooke* c.1650, ~ *Hoke* 1708, 1745 (*v*. **water-mylne**, **hōc**); *Water furrowes* 1601, ~ *thorowes* 1625 (*v*. **wæter**, **furh** and *the water furrowes* in Billesdon f.ns. (b)); *Willar* ~ c.1650, *Willow Wong* 1745 (*v*. **wilig**, **vangr**); *Wisards Yards End* c.1650 (*v*. **geard**, **ende**; with the surn. *Wysard*, from the ONFr masc. pers.n. *Wisc*(*h*)*ard*); *Wiuells yeards ende* 1601, *Wivills yeard end* 1625 (*v*. **geard**, **ende**; with the surn. *Wyville*, as in the name of adjoining Stonton Wyville); *Wood Ende* 1601, (*the*) *Wood End* 1625, c.1650, 1708, 1745 (*v*. **wudu**, **ende**); *Wyment Layes End* 1708, ~ *Leys End* 1708 (18) (*v*. **leys**, **ende**; with the surn. *Whymant*, either from the OE masc. pers.n. *Wīgmund* or from the ON masc. pers.n. *Vigmundr* (ODan *Vimund*)); *Wyresleys Yard End* 1745 (*v*. **geard**, **ende**; with the surn. *Worsley*); *the Yate close* 1641 (*v*. **gata**).

Welham

WELHAM

Walendeha' 1086 DB
Waleha' 1086 DB
Weleha' 1086 DB, *Weleham* c.1130 LeicSurv, Hy 1 Dugd, l.12 *Rut* (p) *et passim* to 1328 *ShR* (p), 1331 (e.15) *BelCartB*
Welleham 12 *Peake*, 1221 Fine (p), e.13 *Peake* (p) *et passim* to 1315 GildR (p), 1362 *LCDeeds* (p)
Welham 1208 Fine (p), 1210 P (p), 1220 MHW *et passim* to 1247 RGros, 1254 Val *et freq*
Wellam c.1291 Tax, 1384 *Peake*, 1402 *Wyg*, 1540 *Conant*, 1550 *Peake*, *Welam* 13 *ShR*, 1427 *Peake*, 1439 *MktHPR*

Perhaps 'the village, estate by the stream', *v.* **wella**, **hām**; the watercourse in this case being the river Welland. Alternatively, the specific may be an unrecorded OE masc. pers.n. *Wēola*, a pet-form of names in *Wēoh-* (cf. OGer *Weila*), hence 'Wēola's village, estate'. The *Wal-* spellings in two of the DB forms are due to AN interchange of *a* and *e*, while *Walendeha'* of 1086 appears to show attraction to the river name.

BIRCH TREE FM, *v.* **birce**. BOWDEN LANE, Great Bowden lying 2½ miles to the south-west. HOME FM, *v.* **home**. MANOR HO., *v.* **maner**. THE OLD RECTORY, cf. *the Vicarage House* 1606, 1821 *Terrier*, *the Vicaridge house* 1709 *ib*, *v.* **vikerage**. OLD RED LION (P.H.), *Red Lion* 1846, 1863, 1877 White, *Old Red Lion* 1925 Kelly. ST ANDREW'S CHURCH, *the Parish Church of St Andrew* 1821 *Terrier*, *Church (St Andrew)* 1846, 1863, 1877 White; it is earlier recorded as *ecclesie de Welham* 1220 MHW, 1239, 1247 RGros, 1345 *Pat*. Note *the Church yard* 1709 *Terrier*, *v.* **churchyerd**. SLAWSTON RD, Slawston lying 1½ miles to the north-east. THORPE LANGTON RD, Thorpe Langton lying 1½ miles to the west. WELHAM LODGE, 1824 O, 1877 White, *v.* **loge**; also called *Nether Lodge* 1844 *TA* in relation to Serjeant's Folly (*v. infra*), formerly on higher ground to its west.

FIELD-NAMES

In (a), forms dated 1754 are *Deed*; those dated 1798 are Nichols; 1844 are *TA*; 1918 are Sale; 1968 are *Surv*. Forms throughout dated 1342 are Banco; those dated 1409, 1419 and 1608 are Ipm; 1545 are *Star*.

(a) The Four Acres, The Six ~ 1918, 1968, The Seven ~ 1918, (The) Eight ~ 1844, 1918, Bottom ~ ~, Top Eight Acres 1968, The Eleven ~ 1918, 1968, Twelve ~ 1844, 1918, The Fourteen ~ 1918, 1968, Twenty Acres 1844 (*the Twenty Acres* 1698, 1709, 1724), The Twenty-One Acres 1918, 1968 (*v*. **æcer**); Amen Corner 1918, 1968 (alluding to the Rogation-tide ceremony of beating the bounds of the parish, during which the procession would halt at specified places where prayers would be said); Baker's Cl 1844, 1968, ~ Mdw 1844 (with the surn. *Baker*); Barn Cl, ~ ~ Mdw 1844, 1918, 1968 (*v*. **bern**); First ~, Inner Blackwell 1844, Bottom ~, Top Blackwell 1968 (*Blackwell* 1601, 1606, *Great Blackewell* 1698, *the Great Blackwell* 1724, *the Ne*(*a*)*ther Blackwell* 1698, 1700, 1709, 1724, *the Upper* ~ 1698, 1709, 1724, *the Over Blackwell* 1700 (*v*. **uferra**), *Blackwell lay*(*e*)*s* 1606, 1625 (*v*. **leys**) (*v*. **blæc**, **wella**); Bowling Green 1844, ~ ~ Cl 1918 (*v*. **bowling-green**); Bryan's Mdw 1844, 1918, 1968 (cf. *Richard Bryan* 1803 Will of Welham); Cabin Cl 1844, 1913, 1968 (*v*. **cabin**); Caps Holme 1844, ~ ~ Cl 1968 (*v*. **holmr**; with the surn. *Capp*, metonymic for ME *cappere* 'a maker of caps'); Lower ~ ~, Upper Caudle Cl, Caudle Mdw 1844 (cf. *Nether* ~, *Over Caldwell* 1545 (*v*. **uferra**), *v*. Langton Caudle in Stonton Wyville which adjoins to the west); Church Cl, Church Paddock 1968 (*v*. **paddock**) (*v*. St Andrew's Church *supra*); Corner Cl 1968, ~ Piece 1844 (*v*. **pece**) (*v*. **corner**); Cottage Cl 1968, ~ Ground 1844 (*v*. **grund**) (*v*. **cotage**); Cranoe Field Mdw 1913, Cranoe Mdw 1968 (Cranoe parish adjoins to the north); East Mdw 1844; Elbow Mdw 1844 (*v*. **elbowe**); Old England 1844, 1918, England's, ~ Mdw 1969 (*v*. **eng**, **land**); Far Cl 1844, 1918, 1968; Farm Homestead 1844 (*v*. **ferme**, **hām-stede**); Featherstones 1968 (with the surn. *Featherstone* in the possessive case); Folly Orchard 1844 (*v*. **folie**, **orceard**; related to Serjeant's Folly *infra*); The Front Cl 1918, ~ Fd 1968 (*v*. **front**); Furze Hill 1844, 1918 (*the Furz hill* 1724, *v*. **fyrs**); Great Ground 1844, 1918, 1969, Middle Ground 1968 (*v*. **grund**); Hall Cl 1844, 1918, ~ Fd 1968 (cf. *the Hall home close* 1698 (*v*. **home**), *v*. **hall**; presum. with reference to the Manor House *supra*); *Hayes Cl* 1844, 1968 (prob. with the surn. *Hayes*, rather than with **hǣs** 'brushwood' from which the surn. derives); Hodgkin's Cl 1844 (with the surn. *Hodgkin*); Far ~ ~, Lower ~ ~, Upper Home Cl 1844, Home Cl 1918, 1968, Home Plot 1844 (*v*. **plot**) (*v*. **home**); Bottom ~ ~, Top Home Head 1844, 1918 (*v*. **holmr**, **hēafod**); Far ~ 1844, 1918, Hoppett 1918 (*v*. **hopet**); Hornsby's 1918 (the surn. *Hornsby* in the possessive case); Nanny King's Cl 1844 (*Nanny* is a pet-name for *Anne*), King's Cl 1968 (with the surn. *King*); Little Cl, ~ ~ Mdw 1844; Long Cl 1918, 1968; Long Spinney 1844 (*v*. **spinney**); Far ~ ~, Lower Cl 1844; First ~ ~, Second Lower Fd 1844; Far ~ ~, First ~ ~, Second Middle Fd 1844; Bottom ~, Top Moor 1918, 1968, Moor Fd, ~ ~ Mdw 1844, 1918, Great Moor Fds 1918, Moor Road Mdw 1844 (*v*. **mōr**[1]); Old Cl 1918 (*v*. **ald**); The Orchard 1918, 1968 (*v*. **orceard**); The Paddock 1918, 1968 (*v*. **paddock**); The Park 1918, 1968 (*v*. **park**); Pasture Cl, ~ ~ Spinney (*v*. **spinney**), Pasture Mdw 1844 (*the common pasture* 1601, 1606, 1625 (*v*. **commun**), *the Pasture* 1698, 1700, 1709, 1724, *v*. **pasture**); Payne's Cl 1844,

Payne's Mdw 1844, 1918, 1968 (with the surn. *Payne*); The Plot 1844 (*v.* **plot**); Great ~ ~, Little Ploughed Cl 1844; Ravens 1968 (with the surn. *Raven* in the possessive case); Road Cl 1918, ~ Mdw 1968 (roadside fields); Serjeant's Folly 1798 (*v.* **folie**; a former farmhouse built c.1750 by *William Serjeant* on the hill of Langton Caudle and called thus from its curious plan and isolated position); Sign Post Cl 1844 (alluding to a roadside finger-post); The Slang 1918, 1968 (*v.* **slang**); Spencer's Cl 1844, Spencers 1968 (with the surn. *Spencer*); Spinney Cl 1968 (*v.* **spinney**); Spring Cl 1918, ~ Mdw 1968 (*v.* **spring**[1]); Square Cl 1844 (*v.* **squar(e)**); Stanley's Cl 1844 (with the surn. *Stanley*); Stock Mdw 1968 (prob. alluding to livestock, *v.* **stock**; but **stocc** is poss.); Swanshouse 1754 (*v.* **hūs**; cf. *Thos. Swane* 1604 SR, the surn. being *Swain* (a reflex of the ON masc. pers.n. *Sveinn*) rather than *Swan*); Talbot's Cl 1844, 1968, ~ Hill 1968, ~ Mdw 1844 (with the surn. *Talbot*); Tarry Hill 1918, 1968 (with the surn. *Tarry*, a reflex of the OFr masc. pers.n. *Thierri*); Ting's Cl 1844 (this name is of the pattern of several of those of the parish Tithe Award, based on a surn. in the possessive case; but if the unusual *Ting* is not a surn., then poss. here is a memory of **þing** 'an assembly'); The Tofts 1844, Toffs (sic) 1968 (*the Great Tofts* 1698, *v.* **toft**); Bottom ~, Top Town Cl 1968, Town End Cl 1844, 1918 (*v.* **ende**) (*v.* **tūn**); Upper Cl 1918, ~ Mdw 1918, 1968; Walker's Cl 1844, 1968 (with the surn. *Walker*); Welham Gorse 1844 (*v.* **gorst**); West Cl 1844, ~ Fd 1918, 1968; Weston Mdw 1918 (a close adjacent to Weston by Welland parish which lies beyond the river Welland in Northants.); Wilkinson's Cl 1844, 1918 (with the surn. *Wilkinson*); Wood Cl 1968 (*v.* **wudu**).

(b) *Baneholm* 1342 (*v.* **bēan**, **holmr**); *Edward Bowfeilds ground* 1601 (*v.* **grund**); *the Bridge lane* 1698 (*v.* **brycg**, **lane**); *Broadmore* 1700, 1709 (*v.* **brād**, **mōr**[1]); *the Clay pit* 1698, ~ ~ *pits* 1700, 1709, 1724 (*v.* **clǣg**, **pytt**); *the Cow pasture* 1606 (*v.* **pasture**); *Foxholes* 1608 (*v.* **fox-hol**); *William Halford his ground* 1606 (*v.* **grund**); *le Holm* 1342 (*v.* **holmr**); *the Home close* 1700 (*v.* **home**); (*the*) *Home lays* 1698, 1700, 1709, *the Home leys* 1724 (*v.* **leys**) (with either **home** or **holmr**); *the Homestall* 1606 (*v.* **hām-stall**); *the House Close* 1709; (*a close called*) *the Idle or Ile* 1698 (unproductive land described in terms of the socially unacceptable, cf. Idle Fd, Brk **2** 328); *le Mares* 1409, 1419, 1608, *the Mares* 1698, 1700 (*v.* **marr**[1]); *Middle Furz close* 1724 (*v.* **fyrs**); *North field* 1724; *the Pasture lane* 1698 (*v.* **pasture**, **lane**); *Pellyng* ~, *Peydlyng Holm* 1545 (*v.* **holmr**; with the surn. *Pelling*, from spellings for Peatling Magna, 11 miles to the west (note *Willelmus de Pelling'* 1166 RBE, 1203 Cur, *Alanus de Pedling'* 1193 P and *Peytlyng Magna* 1517, 1558 AAS); *Slawson* ~ 1698, *Slawston meadow* 1700, 1724, *Slawston meare* 1606, 1625 (*v.* **(ge)mǣre**) (Slawston parish adjoins to the north-east); *the Smock close* 1698, 1700, 1709, 1724 (alluding to *smoke-silver*, a tax paid in lieu of tithewood to the incumbent of the parish).

West Langton

WEST LANGTON

A late civil parish. For forms and interpretation of the place-name Langton, *v.* East Langton parish *supra*.

Distinguishing affixes are added as:
alia ~ c.1130 LeicSurv
West ~ 1211 FF, 1243 Cur, 1278 Banco *et freq*
~ *West* 1316 FA, 1327 SR
Westere ~, *Westre* ~ p.1270 *Brai*

West Langton is recorded as *West Towne* 1564 Nichols, 'the western township'. The affixes *West* ~ and *Westere* ~ are from OE **west** 'west' and **westerra** 'more westerly', so designated in contrast to Church Langton with East Langton *supra*. Note MLat *alia* 'the other' to distinguish West Langton from Church Langton with East Langton *supra*.

EAST LANGTON STATION, on the former *Midland Railway (Leicester and Hitchin Branch)* 1854 O. THE HOLLIES. HOME FM, *v.* **home**. LANGTON HALL, 1831 Curtis, 1861 *Surv*, 1872 Sale, 1925 Kelly, *West Langton Hall* 1863 White, *The Hall* 1877 ib, *v.* **hall**. LANGTON HALL FM. THE NOOK, *v.* **nōk**. STATION COTTAGES, *v.* East Langton Station *supra*.

FIELD-NAMES

In (a), forms dated 1791 are Nichols; those dated 1843, 1872 and 1875 are Sale; 1856 are *Map*; 1861 are *Surv*. Forms throughout dated 1601, 1625, 1638, 1674, 1694, 1703, 1712, 1715 and 1745 are *Terrier*; those dated 1645 and c.1650 are Nichols; 1743 are VCHL; 1744 are *Surv*.

(a) Barons Cl 1843, 1861, 1872 (*Barons Close* c.1650; with the surn. *Baron*, cf. *Barons gate* c.1650, *v.* **gata**); Great ~ ~, Little Bells Cl 1791, 1843, 1861, 1872 (prob. with the surn. *Bell*; otherwise land endowed for the upkeep of the bells of the parish church in Church Langton); Bitchell Cl 1843, 1861, 1872 (with the surn. *Bitchell*); Carpenters Cl, ~ Mdw 1843, 1861 (with the surn. *Carpenter*); Coopers Meadow Platt 1843, 1861, 1872 (*v.* **plat**[2]; with the surn. *Cooper*); Cow Cl 1843, 1872 (1744), Cow Close Mdw 1843; Cow Home Cl 1843, 1861, ~ Holme ~ 1872, Cow Home Mdw 1843, 1861, ~ Holme ~ 1872 (*Cow holme* 1744, *v.* **holmr**); Cow Wong 1791 (*v.* **vangr**); Debdale 1843, 1861, 1872 (1601, 1638 et *passim* to 1745, *Depdaile* 1625), Debdale Cl, ~ Mdw 1843, 1861, 1872 (*v.* **dēop**, **dalr**); Doctor's Cl 1856 (*v.* **doctour**); Eighteen Acre Cl 1842, 1861, 1873 (*v.* **æcer**); Elm Spinney 1843, 1861, 1872 (*v.* **elm**, **spinney**); Far Cl 1843, 1861, 1872; Flax Cl 1791, Top ~ ~, Flax Cl 1843, 1861, 1872 (*Flax close* 1744, *v.* **fleax**); The Folly 1843, 1861, 1872 (*v.* **folie**); Hall Cl 1843, 1861, 1872, Hall Yard 1875 (*v.* **geard**) (*v.* Langton Hall *supra*); High Leys Cl 1843, 1861, 1872 (*v.* **hēah**[1], **leys**); Home Cl 1856, Upper ~ ~ 1843, 1861, 1872 (*the Home close* 1645, *v.* **home**); Hop Yard, ~ ~ Mdw, ~ ~ Orchard 1843, 1861, 1872 (*v.* **orceard**) (*v.* **hop-yard**); Great ~ ~, Little Hundred Cl 1843, 1861, 1872 (rarely are closes of one hundred acres in size; ironic application of the name to very small closes is common); Lamb Coat 1791, 1861, 1872, ~ ~ Mdw 1843, 1872, Lambcoat Mdw 1861 (*v.* **lamb**, **cot**); Marks Cl 1843, 1861, 1872 (with the surn. *Mark*(*s*)); Mill Hill Cl 1843, 1861, 1872 (*v.* **myln**); Nether Cl 1791, Nether Ground 1791, 1843, 1861, 1872 (*v.* **grund**), ~ ~ Plantation 1843, 1861, 1872 (*v.* **plantation**), Nether Mdw 1843, 1861, 1872; Nettle Cl 1843, 1861, 1872 (*v.* **netel(e)**); New Laid Down Cl 1843, 1861, 1872 (a close newly put under grass, converted from arable to pasture); Old Homestead 1861, 1872 (*v.* **hām-stede**); Old Orchard 1843, 1861 (*v.* **orceard**), ~ ~ Plantation 1872 (*v.* **plantation**); Old Spinney Mdw 1843, 1861, 1872 (*v.* **spinney**); Pinfold ~ 1843, 1861, Pinfold's Cl 1872 (*v.* **pynd-fald**); Plank Cl 1856 (cf. *the plank furlong* 1712, *Planck furlong* 1715 (*v.* **furlang**), *v.* **planke**; relates to *Caudwell planke* in adjoining East Langton f.ns. (b)); Ploughed Cl 1856; Far ~, Near Purgate 1843, 1861, 1872 (*Purgate* 1638, c.1650, 1674, 1694, 1703, 1712, ~ *Close* 1745, *v.* **gata**; either with **pyrige** 'a pear-tree' or with **pūr** 'a snipe, a bittern'); Rhodes Cl, ~ Orchard 1843, 1861, 1872 (*v.* **orceard**) (with the surn. *Rhodes*); Round Hill Cl 1791, 1843, 1861, 1872 (c.1650, *Round hill* 1744, *v.* **round**; a common toponym in Gartree Hundred); Salt Pitts 1791, Nether ~ ~, Over Salt Pits 1843, 1861, 1872 (*v.* **uferra**), Salt Pits Mdw 1843, 1861 (*v.* **salt**[1], **pytt**); Spiny 1856 (*the Spinaye* c.1650), Spinney Hill 1791, Spinney Leys 1791, 1843, 1861, 1872, ~ ~ Mdw 1843, 1861, 1872 (*v.* **leys**) (*v.* **spinney**); Spring Leys Cl 1843, 1861, 1872 (*v.* **spring**[1], **leys**); Stockhold Cl 1843, Stock-held ~ 1861, Stockheld ~ 1872 (*v.* **stock**; a close where a herd of cattle could be contained); Stone Hill, ~ ~ Cl 1843, 1861, 1872 (*Stonhill* 1601, 1694, 1703, 1715, *Stonehill* 1625, 1638 *et passim* to 1745, *Stonell hades* 1694, 1712, *Stonnill* ~ 1703, *Stonhill* ~ 1715, *Stonehill hades* 1745 (*v.* **hēafod**) (*v.* **stān**, **hyll**); Town End Cl 1843, 1861, 1872 (*v.* **tūn**, **ende**); Turf Cl, ~ Mdw 1843, 1861, 1872 (*v.* **turf**); West Town Orchard 1843, 1861, 1872 (*v.* **orceard**) (note *West Towne* 1564 Nichols *supra*); White Bridge Cl 1843, 1861, 1873, ~ ~ Spinney 1843, 1872 (*v.* Wide Bridge in East Langton *supra*); Windmill Cl 1872 (*v.* **wind-mylne** and Mill Hill Cl *supra*).

(b) *Bean Field* 1743 (*v.* **bēan**); *Crosour close* c.1650 (with the surn. *Croser*); *Fallow Field* 1745 (*v.* **falh**); *Little Hill* c.1650; *the Orchard Penne* 1645 (*v.* **orceard**, **penn**[2]); *Rundells* 1601, 1625, 1638, 1715, *Rundles* 1625, c.1650, 1674, 1694, 1703, 1712, 1745, *Short Rundles* 1745, *the West side Rundles* c.1650 (*v.* **sīde**) (*v.* **rynel**); *West Moor* c.1650 (*v.* **mōr**[1]); *Wheat Field* 1743 (*v.* **hwǣte**).

Wistow

1. WISTOW

Wistanestov 1086 DB, *Wistanestowe* 1199 ChR, *Wistanestou* 1236 Fees, *Wystanestowe* 1245 RGros, e.14 RydCart (p), *Wistanistoue* 1220 MHW, *Whistanestowe* 1244 Cur
Witenesto 1086 DB
Wikstanesthowa e.13 *Wyg*, *Wixstant*' 1208 MemR
Wistonestow(e) 1200 FF (p), 1208 P, *Wistenestou*' 1207 ib, *Wistenestow(e)* 1208 ChancR, 1242 Fees
Wistenstowe 1206 P, *Wistonstow(e)* 1208 ib, 1272 Pat, *Wystonstowe* 1292 Ipm, *Wistanstowe* c.1253 RHug, 1271 Pat *et passim* to 1313 Ipm, *Wystanstowe* 1254 Val, 1313 Ipm *et passim* to 1375 ib
Wystow(e) 1282 Pat, c.1291 Tax *et passim* to 1322 Fine, 1325 Banco *et freq* to 1436 Fine, 1467 *Wyg et passim* to 1572, 1582 LEpis
Wistou 1313 Pat, *Wistouwe* 1325 Ipm, *Wistowe* 1316 FA, 1327 SR *et passim* to 1572 LEpis, 1605 LML, *Wistow* 1514 EpCB, 1518 Visit, 1576 LEpis *et freq*

Most probably 'the holy place of (Saint) Wigstan', *v.* **stōw**. *Wīgstān* was a member of the Mercian royal family who was murdered during a royal council meeting in 849 at a place which the medieval *Life of St Wigstan* calls *Wistanstowe*. His body was taken for burial in the Mercian royal mausoleum at Repton where he was subsequently revered as a martyr. Wistow's parish church, which contains Norman fabric, is dedicated to St Wistan and is the traditional site of his death. The church stands on slightly raised ground away from the lower-lying village and this may indicate that the settlement on its less favourable site developed because the church became a place of pilgrimage. For *stōw*, 'a place associated with a saint' and 'a meeting place' are early senses.

COAL PIT LANE, cf. *Colepit Feild* 1631 *Surv*, 1632 *Map*, *Colepit hill* 1625 *Terrier*, *v.* **col-pytt**; a place where charcoal was made. FOX COVERT is *Coal-pit-lane Spinny* 1835 O, *v.* **spinney** and Coal Pit Lane *supra*. LONG WALK, *v.* **walk**. THE MOUNT, 1969 *Surv*, *v.* **mont**; the site of a former windmill. ST WISTAN'S CHURCH, *the Church* 1708 (18) *Terrier*, *Church (St Wistan)* 1846, 1863, 1877 White, 1925 Kelly; it is earlier recorded as *ecclesie de Wistanistoue* 1220 MHW, *ecclesiam de Wystannestowe* 1245 RGros, *ecclesie de Wistanstowe* 1271 *Pat*, ~ *de Wystowe* 1318, 1338, 1339, 1423 *ib*, ~ *de Wistowe* 1361 *ib*, *ecclesiarum de Wistowe et Lubenham* 1481 *ib*. Note also *the Church yard* 1631 *Surv*, 1708 (18) *Terrier*, *v*. **churchyerd**. WATERMAN'S SPINNEY, cf. *Near* ~, *Top Waterman* 1969, *v*. **spinney**; with the surn. *Waterman*, cf. *Wilke Waterman* 1196 RFL, from ME *waterman* 'a water-carrier, one who carts water for sale' and 'a boatman'. WISTOW GRANGE, 1925 Kelly, *v*. **grange**. WISTOW HALL, 1795 Nichols, 1846, 1863, 1877 White, 1925 Kelly, *v*. **hall**. WISTOW HOME FM, *v*. **home**. WISTOW LODGE, *v*. **loge**.

FIELD-NAMES

Forms in (a) presented without dates are 1969 *Surv*; those dated 1772 are EnclA. Forms throughout dated 1436 and 1631[1] are Ipm; those dated 1625 are *Terrier*; 1631[2] are *Surv*; 1632 are *Map*; 1638 are Farnham.

(a) Ten Acre (*v*. **æcer**); Barn Cl (*v*. **bern**); Big Hill Cl; Breach Mdw (*Breach meadow(e)* 1631[2], 1632, *v*. **brēc**); Breadons Mdw (with the surn. *Breedon* of a family prob. originally from Breedon on the Hill, 23 miles to the north-west); Carter's Cl (with the surn. *Carter*); Church Mdw (*v*. St Wistan's Church *supra*); Cotton Cl (earlier forms are needed; poss. with **cote** (**cotan** nom.pl.)); Far Side ~, Dams ((*The*) *Dames* 1625, 1632, *the Dammes* 1631[2], *the Dame Closse* 1631[2] (*v*. **clos(e)**), *v*. **damme**; relating to a watermill); Front Mdw (*v*. **front**); George's Mdw (with the surn. *George*); Guinea Cl (alluding to a former rent; the land was valued at one guinea per annum); Hall Fd, ~ Mdw (*v*. Wistow Hall *supra*); Holly Bush (*v*. **holegn**, **busc**); Home Cl (*v*. **home**); Horse Cl (*the Far* ~ ~, *the Middle* ~ ~, *the Near Horse Closse* 1631[2], *v*. **hors**, **clos(e)**); March Cl, ~ Leys (*v*. **leys**) (*v*. **mersc**); Middle Ground (*the midle grounde* 1631[2], *v*. **middel**, **grund**); Mill Cl (the site of a former windmill); The Nooks (*v*. **nōk**); Old Cl (*v*. **ald**); Old Fleckney Allotments (*v*. **allotment**; located towards Fleckney parish which adjoins to the south); Pitts Cl, ~ Slang (*v*. **slang**) (*v*. **pytt**); Long Plough, Bottom Plough Cl (*v*. **plōg**); Pond Side (*v*. **ponde**, **sīde**); Sand Pit Cl (*v*. **sand-pytt**); Seed Cl (*v*. **sǣd**; used of grasses sown for one year's mowing or grazing, as distinguished from permanent pasture); Shovels (*the Far* ~, *the Near Shovells* 1631[2], *v*. **scofl**; either alluding to land which could only be conveniently cultivated by digging with a shovel, or simply to a narrow strip of land (cf. **scofl-brǣdu**)); Spencer's Cl (with the surn. *Spencer*); Stallion Cl (*v*. **stallion**); Tebbs Cl (with the surn. *Tebb*, a pet-form of the ME masc. pers.n. *Tebbold* (OFr *Theobald*); cf. *Johannes Tebbe* 1316 FA of Leics.); Three Corner Cl (*v*. **three-corner**); Walnut Cl (a close containing or beside walnut trees; such trees were grown both for nuts and for timber); Wash Pit Cl (*v*. **wæsce**, **pytt**); Woad Cl (*v*. **wād**).

(b) *Amberdale* 1625 (*v.* **amer**, **dalr**); *Ash slade* 1625 (*v.* **slæd**), *the Asshe Closse* 1631[2] (*v.* **clos(e)**) (*v.* **æsc**); *Batches Doles* 1625 (*v.* **dāl**; with **bæce** or with the surn. *Batch* which developed from it); *Blackemiles* 1625 (*v.* **blæc**, **mylde**); *Hither* ~, *Old Bracklands* 1631[2] (*v.* **bracu**, **land**); *the Brooke Closse* 1631[2] (*v.* **brōc**); *East and West Bush* 1625 (*v.* **busc**); *Churchacres* 1625 (*v.* **churche**, **æcer** and St Wistan's Church *supra*); *the Coninger furlong* 1625 (*v.* **furlang**), *the Cony Gray* 1631[2] (*v.* **coningre**); *Cotebridge Meadowe* 1631[2] (*v.* **cot**, **brycg**); *Crosdoles* 1625 (*v.* **cross**, **dāl**); *the Dovecoate Closse* 1631[2] (*v.* **dove-cot(e)**); *the East Field* 1625 (*v.* **ēast**, **feld**; one of the great open-fields of the township); *de la Grene* 1327 SR (p) (*v.* **grēne**[2]); *the Far Grounde* 1631[2] (*v.* **feor**, **grund**); *Hall clos* 1436 (*v.* **clos(e)**), *le Halleyerde* (*v.* **geard**) 1436 (*v.* **hall**; these names refer to a medieval hall, prob. on the site of Wistow Hall *supra*); *Lankelie*, *Langhlie field* (*v.* **feld**; one of the great open-fields), *Lankelie slade* (*v.* **slæd**) 1625 (*v.* **lang**[1], **lēah**); *the Mill balke* 1625 (*v.* **balca**), *the Mill Field* 1625, 1632, ~ ~ *feild* 1631[2] (*v.* **feld**; one of the great open-fields) (*v.* **myln**; the site of a windmill); *Newton Meadow(e)* 1631[2], 1632 (land bordering Newton Harcourt *infra*); *the Parsons Closse* 1631[2] (*v.* **persone**, **clos(e)**); *Rushes* 1625 (*v.* **risc**); *Sandie* 1625 (*v.* **sandig**; a furlong so called); *le Thyrne* 1436 (*v.* **þyrne**); *The Town Feilde* 1631[2], ~ *Field* 1632 (*v.* **tūn**); *the Townesend ground* 1631[2], *Townsend Ground* 1632 (*v.* **tūn**, **ende**, **grund**); *the Vicarage* 1631[2] (*v.* **vikerage**); *Short* ~, *Waterthrowes* 1625 (*v.* **wæter**, **furh** and *the water furrowes* in Billesdon f.ns. (b)); *the Far* ~ ~, *the Hither Willow Bedes* 1631[2] (*v.* **wilig**, **bedd**).

2. NEWTON HARCOURT

Niuuetone 1086 DB, *Nieweton* 1202 Fine

Nevtone 1086 DB, *Neuton'* e.13 *Rut*, 1220 MHW *et passim* to 1243 Fine, 1247 *Wyg et freq* to 1393 *ib*, 1395 Banco *et passim* to 1446 ib, 1475 Pat, *Neutone* 1280 × 92, 1342, 1347 *Wyg*, *Neutona* c.1250 *Rut*, 1247 × 60 *Wyg* (p)

Neweton 1421, 1422 Fine, 1437 Pat, 1510 Visit

Newton 1393, 1417 *Wyg et passim* to 1604 SR, 1610 Speed *et freq*

The affix is added as:

~ *Harecurt* 1275 Banco, 1281, 1284 Pat, ~ *Harcurt* 1282 Banco, 1288 *Wyg*, ~ *Harecourt(e)* 1282 Pat, 1283 Banco *et passim* to 1475 Pat, 1559 Nichols, ~ *Harcourt* 1283, 1284 Banco *et passim* to 1524 Ipm, 1604 SR *et freq*

'The new settlement', *v.* **nīwe**, **tūn**. The manor was held by *Ricardus de Harcurt* in 1236 Fine and remained in this family through *Saerus de Harecurt* 1258 ib, *Alex' de Harecurt* 1273 *Wyg* to *Johannes de Harecourt* 1328 Banco; cf. Kibworth Harcourt *supra*.

THE COPPICE, 1925 Kelly, *v.* **copis**; a house built in 1898 beside a small plantation. FLAXMAN'S SPINNEY, *v.* **spinney**; possibly with the surn. *Flaxman*, from the ME occupational name *flaxman* 'a dresser or seller of flax', but note *Flaxlandes* in f.ns. (b), which *Flaxman's* may represent. GORSE SPINNEY, *v.* **gorst**. HIGH BRIDGE, *High Bridge* 1969 *Surv*; crosses Grand Union Canal. HIGH BRIDGE PLANTATION, *v.* **plantation**. THE ISLANDS, *v.* **ēa-land**. LOCKHOUSE SPINNEY, sited opposite *Lock-house* 1969 *Surv* at Newton Top Lock on the canal. MANOR HO., *Manor House* 1846, 1863, 1877 White, 1925 Kelly, *v.* **maner**. NEWTON BOTTOM LOCK, NEWTON TOP LOCK, *v.* **lock**; on the canal. NEWTON BRIDGE, carries a road to Wistow across the canal. OLD MERE, *v.* **ald**, **(ge)mǣre**; an ancient trackway and boundary forming part of the north-western limit of the parish. RECRUITING SERGEANT (P.H.) (lost), *Recruiting Sergeant* 1846, 1863 White. ST LUKE'S CHURCH, *Church (St Luke)* 1846, 1863, 1877 White, 1915 Kelly; it is earlier recorded as *capellam de Neuton* 1220 MHW (with MLat *capella* 'a chapel'), *the Chappel* 1708 (18) *Terrier*, *v.* **chapel(e)**. Newton Harcourt was a chapelry of Wistow. TURNOVER BRIDGE, a bridge which allowed a horse to cross a canal while still drawing a barge, without the need to unhitch the towrope. TYTHORN HILL, *Tythorn* 1969 *Surv*, 'boundary thorn', *v.* **tēo**, **þorn**; the hill, part of an ancient ridgeway, stands on the parish boundary. WAIN BRIDGE, *Wing Brig Meadow* (sic) 1969 *Surv*, *v.* **wægn**.

FIELD-NAMES

In (a), forms presented without dates are 1969 *Surv*; those dated 1772 are EnclA; 1794 are *Deed*; 1795 are Sale. Forms throughout dated Edw 3 are *Wyg*; those dated 1625, 1690 and c.1700 are *Terrier*.

(a) Five Acre, 6 ~, Top Seven ~, 7 ~, Ten ~, 12 ~, 14 ~, Top ~ ~, Fifteen Acre, 40 Acres (*v.* **æcer**); Alex Hedge (*v.* **hecg**; either with a shortened surn. or pers.n. *Alexander*); Allotments (*v.* **allotment**); Barley Hill 1969, ~ ~ Fd 1772 (*Barley Hill feild* 1625, ~ ~ *field* 1690, c.1700, *v.* **feld**; one of the great open-fields of the township) (*v.* **bærlic**, **hyll**); Barn Cl, ~ Fd (*v.* **bern**); Black Grounds (*v.* **blæc**, **grund**); Blands Hovel (*v.* **hovel**; with the surn. *Bland*, cf. *Elias Bland* 1837 Census and *William Bland* 1860 ib of Newton Harcourt); Bottom Mdw (*v.* **bottom**); Bridle Road (*v.* **brīdel**); Bottom ~, Top Brunskill (with the surn. *Brunskill*, cf. *Margaret Brunskill* 1868 Census and *Joseph Brunskill* 1874 ib of Newton Harcourt); Bull Cl (*v.* **bula**); Church Leys (*v.* **leys** and St Luke's Church *supra*); Bottom Clink Bank (*v.* **clinc**, **banke**); Bottom ~, Top Coopers (with the surn. *Cooper*); Top ~ ~, Cow Cl; Cow Moor (1690, *Cowmore* c.1700), Cowmoor Fd 1772 (1690, *v.* **feld**; one of the great open-fields, called *the North feild* 1625 and *Mill field* c.1700) (*v.* **cū**, **mōr**[1]);

Dick Follens (sic) (*Dicke forlonge* 1625, *Dick furlong* 1690, c.1700, *v.* **dík**, **furlang**); Far ~, West End, Top End Fd (*v.* **ende**); Gravel Follands (sic) (*v.* **gravel**, **furlang**); Glebe (*v.* **glebe**); Glen Workhouse (*v.* **workhouse**; land once providing rental for the workhouse which was established (1802–3) in neighbouring Great Glen for 14 persons); High Mdw (1690, *highe meddow* 1625, *v.* **hēah**[1], **mēd** (**mēdwe** obl.sg.)); Bottom ~, Middle ~, Top Hill (*v.* **hyll**); Home Cl (*v.* **home**); Top Hoskins (*v.* **top**; with the surn. *Hoskins*); Hovel Fd (*v.* **hovel**); Lammas Cl 1795 (*v.* **lammas**); Langor Slade Fd 1794 (*Langerslade feild* 1625, *Langarslade Field* 1690, c.1700, *v.* **feld**; one of the great open-fields), Langer Slade Mdw 1772 (*v.* **lang**[1], **gāra**, **slæd**); Laundons (with the surn. *Laundon* in the possessive case, cf. *Frederick Laundon* 1850 Census and *James Laundon* 1856 ib of adjoining Kilby); Bottom ~, Middle Light (*v.* **lēoht**; here prob. used as a sb. meaning 'a light place, a glade clearing'); Little Cl 1795; Little Inn Mdw 1772 (*Little in* 1690, c.1700, *v.* **lȳtel**, **lítill**, **eng**); Long Cl; Major's Mdw (with the surn. *Major*, a reflex of the OFr masc. pers.n. *Maugier*); Manor Fd, Manor House Fd, ~ ~ Mdw (*v.* Manor Ho. *supra*); the Meres (with **mere**[1] or **(ge)mǣre**); Middle Fd; Bottom ~ ~, Top Mill Bank (*v.* **myln**, **banke**); Mill Fd 1772 (c.1700, *v.* **myln**, **feld**; one of the great open-fields, earlier called *the North feild* and Cowmoor Fd); Mill Fd (containing a modern wind-pump); Nether Cl (*v.* **neoðera**); Manor House Paddock (*v.* Manor Ho. *supra*), The Oaks Paddock, The Poplars Paddock (*v.* **paddock**); First ~ ~, Second Ploud Fd (sic for *Ploughed*); Bottom ~, Middle ~, Top Plough (*v.* **plōg**); Pig Fd (*v.* **pigga**); Pinfold (*v.* **pynd-fald**); The Poor's Land 1772 (*v.* **pouer(e)**; it was allotted at the Enclosure in 1772 for charitable purposes and in 1837 consisted of 10 acres of land divided into small allotments); Rickyard (*v.* **reke-yard**); Rough Cl (*v.* **rūh**); Far Sandy Lands 1795 (*Sandelands* 1625, *Sandylands* 1690, c.1700, *v.* **sandig**, **land**); Signpost (a roadside field beside a finger-post); Silver Hill 1795, 1969, ~ ~ Cl 1795 (*v. Silver Hill* in Great Glen f.ns. (b)); The Slade Mdw (*v.* **slæd**); Bottom ~, Top Smeetons (with the surn. *Smeeton* of a family originally from Smeeton Westerby, 4 miles to the south-east); Spickers (the surn. *Spicker* in the possessive case); Target Fd (*v.* **targett**; cf. *Targett holme* in Great Bowden f.ns. (b)); Thistle Hill (*v.* **þistel**); Three Corner Fd (*v.* **three-corner**); Tip Bank (beside the canal and presum. a site for the dumping of dredged materials); Top Mdw; Bottom Tythorn (*v.* Tythorn Hill *supra*); Western ~ 1772, Weston Mdw 1795 (*Westin* 1625, *Westing* 1690, c.1700, *v.* **west**, **eng**); Wistow Mdw (land towards Wistow *supra*); Woolons (*v.* **wald**, **land**).

(b) *Beggars ~* 1690, *Beggers bush* c.1700 (*v.* **beggere**, **busc**; a common f.n. which appears to denote poor or unproductive land); *Brodelond* Edw 3 (*v.* **brād**, **land**); *the Calfes pasture* 1625 (*v.* **calf**, **pasture**); *Richard Chamberlaines farm* 1631 (*v.* **ferme**); *the Cheesecake piece* 1690, c.1700 (*v.* **chese-cake**, **pece**); *Davis meer* 1690, *~ meare* c.1700 (with **mere**[1] (in the sense 'wetland') or **(ge)mǣre** and the surn. *Davis*); *Flaxlandes* 1625 (*v.* **fleax**, **land**); *the Greines* 1625, *the Granes* 1690, c.1700 (*v.* **grein**); *Grenslade* 1690, c.1700 (*v.* **grēne**[1], **slæd**); *Haltree moore* 1625 (*v.* **mōr**[1]), *Haltry slade* 1690, c.1700 (*v.* **slæd**) (*v.* **trēow**; earlier forms are needed to identify the first el., which could be **hālig**, hence 'holy tree' (cf. Hallatrow in Somerset); otherwise **halh**); *Hey leys* 1625 (*v.* **leys**; with **hēg** or **hēah**[1]); *Hether dame* 1690, c.1700 (*v.* **hider**, **damme**); *the Leas* 1625 (*v.* **leys**); *the Marsh* 1690, c.1700 (*v.* **mersc**); *Mill field* c.1700 (*v.* **feld**; one of the great open-fields, earlier called *the North feild* and Cowmoor Fd), *Mill hedge* 1690, c.1700 (*v.* **hecg**), *Mill hill* 1625 (*v.* **myln**; alluding to a windmill); *More hooke* 1625 (*v.* **mōr**[1], **hōc**); *Niste hill* 1625 (poss. with **nest**, sometimes used to denote the highest point in a district); *the North feild* 1625 (*v.* **norð**, **feld**; one of the great open-fields, later called Cowmoor Fd and *Mill field*); *Schyrdaycotis* Edw 3, *v.* **cot** and *Shirtecoat* in Great Bowden *supra*); *Smitoft* 1690, *Smite off* (sic) c.1700 (*v.* **toft**; prob. with **smið**, otherwise with **smīte**); *the Sponges* 1625 (*v.* **spong**); *Whorle dikes* 1625 (*v.* **hwerfel**, **dík**); *Wigston corner* 1690, c.1700 (*v.* **corner**; towards Wigston Magna parish which adjoins to the north-west).

THE ELEMENTS, OTHER THAN PERSONAL NAMES, IN GARTREE HUNDRED'S PLACE-NAMES, FIELD-NAMES AND STREAM-NAMES

This list includes the elements in uncompounded and compounded place-names, field-names and stream-names. The names quoted in each entry are arranged in alphabetical order, with no distinction between uncompounded and compounded names. Names which survive on modern maps and also lost major names are listed first, followed by a summary of use of the elements in field-names and stream-names. Although a concise translation of each element is provided, for fuller discussion of its significance and use, reference should be made to *English Place-Name Elements* (EPNS, vols. 25 and 26, amended in JEPNS 1), *The Vocabulary of English Place-Names* (CENS, in progress), M. Gelling, *Place-Names in the Landscape*, 1984 and M. Gelling and A. Cole, *The Landscape of Place-Names*, 2000.

The elements are often given in an OE, ON or OFr form, but it should be remembered that many of these elements continued as common nouns in the English language and that many of the names in Leicestershire's Gartree Hundred are of more recent origin than the periods represented by the lexical head-forms used. Many terms are included which are not listed in the above-mentioned volumes, but it has not been felt necessary to distinguish these. Those elements marked * are not independently recorded in the head-forms cited or are hypothetical reconstructions from the place-name evidence.

A field-name which is common to a series of townships is sometimes quoted in a form which may have alternative spellings in those townships and which may appear for an individual township in either list (a) or list (b), depending on date. Where this occurs, the particular list in which the field-name features is not specified.

abbat OFr, ME, 'an abbot'. An affix for Nevill Holt.

abbaye ME, (OFr *abbaie*), 'an abbey'. Owston Abbey. Abbey Lands (f.n. Knossington), ?*Ablondesacre* (f.n. King's Norton).

aboven ME, **above** eModE, prep., 'above, over'. *Aboueþesti* (f.n. Stoughton), Above Town (f.n. Billesdon).

āc OE, 'an oak-tree'. Holyoaks, ?Othorpe; Glen Oaks, Oak Cottage. Oake Tree Fd (f.n. Fleckney), Oaks Cl (f.n. Burton Overy), Oaksale (f.n. Great Easton), Oaks Common (f.n. Hallaton), Oak Spinney (f.n. Houghton), Oak Tree (f.n. Medbourne), *Okley* (f.n. Stoughton), Seven Oaks (f.n. Nevill Holt). Recorded names with *āc* are limited to two areas, one in the south-east of the Hundred towards Rutland and the other in its north-west.

ād OE, 'a burning place, a site where fires are deliberately lit'. ?Adwong(s) (f.ns. King's Norton, Little Stretton).

adel OE, 'filth, foul liquid, a filthy place'. *Addemermedwe* (f.n. Stretton Magna).

ageynst ME, prep., 'facing, directly opposite'. *against Fearne* (f.n. Hallaton), *Against the Hill* (f.n. Cranoe), Against the Hill (f.n. Slawston), *Against the Towns End* (f.n. Gumley), *ageynst the Sunne* (f.n. Houghton), *Ageythehull* (f.n. Stoughton).

ald OE (Angl), adj., 'old, long-used; disused'. Common in f.ns.: esp. describing land units, e.g. *Aldefeld* (Evington), *Aldeholm* (Great Easton), Old Cl (Goadby, Welham), *old furlonge* (Frisby), Old Mdw (Houghton, Owston), *Old Roods* (Fleckney); or structures, e.g. *Oldebolde* (Illston), Old Cotes (Laughton), *Oldehall* (Billesdon, Medbourne), *the old mill* (Gumley, Kibworth Beauchamp, Laughton); or fords and bridges, e.g. *Aldeforthe* (Great Easton), *the oldforthegate* (Frisby), *the ould bridg* (Billesdon).

allotment ModE, 'a portion of land assigned to a particular individual', esp. in names recording the redistribution of land at Enclosure: as in Mr Bates Allotment (f.n. 1777, Little Stretton), Ball's Allotment, Haymes Allotment (f.ns. c.1850, Great Glen), Far Allotment (f.n. 1821, Billesdon); and later 'small portion of land let out to an individual (e.g. by a town council) for cultivation', e.g. (The) Allotment Fd (Foxton, Kibworth Beauchamp), Allotments (Glooston), Old Allotments (Burton Overy, Great Easton).

alor OE, 'an alder-tree'. *le Alder close* (f.n. Tur Langton), Aldergate (f.n. Great Glen).

aly eModE, 'a passage between buildings, a narrow street'. *Tripe Alley* (Market Harborough).

amer OE, a bird, prob. 'a bunting'. *Amberdale* (f.n. Wistow).

ān OE, num., adj., 'one, single'; in p.ns. presum. used sometimes with the sense 'alone, lone, isolated'. *Onowh* (f.n Great Bowden), *Onhou* (f.n. Great Easton).

andlang OE, prep., 'by the side of, along'. *Andlongbrodmerche* (f.n. Illston).

angle ME, 'an angle, a corner, a point of land'. *Ancle Close* (f.n. Glooston).

aqueduct ModE, 'a conduit, an artificial channel for the conveyance of water', esp. an elevated structure for this purpose. Aqueduct Spinney.

arable ModE, adj., 'being or capable of being ploughed; fit for tillage'. Arable Fd (f.n. Mowsley), Buntley Arable (f.n. Smeeton Westerby), Wheat Close Arable (f.n. Noseley).

āte OE, 'oats'. *Alexton Oate Close* (f.n. Horninghold), Oat Cl (f.n. King's Norton), *Oatelands* (f.n. Mowsley), Oat Hill (f.n. Medbourne).

atte ME, prep. with masc. or neut. def.art., 'at the'. Common in f.ns. and often used for ME toponymic surns. Examples in f.ns. are *atte stonyforthe* (Illston), *atte waterfal* (Horninghold), *atte Syrwys* (Glooston); toponymic surns. include *atte Chirche* (Billesdon), *atte Crosse* (Nevill Holt), *atte Grene* (Foxton), *atte Uphall* (Carlton Curlieu).

austr (**austarr** comp.) ON, adj., '(to the) east'. *Osterdame* (f.n. Theddingworth).

avenue ModE, 'a tree-lined approach'. Avenue (f.n. Shangton), The Avenue (f.n. Medbourne, Nevill Holt, Noseley).

āwel OE, 'a fork, a hook'. ?Owls-Moor (f.n. Smeeton Westerby).

æcer OE, 'a plot of cultivated land'; also 'an acre, a specified measure of ploughland', originally the unit which a yolk of oxen could plough in a day. The OE el. is generally indistinguishable from ON **akr** 'a plot of arable land'. Broad Acres, Fourteen Acre Spinney, Green Acres, Long Acre. Very freq. in f.ns.: as a simplex, e.g. *the Acres* (Great Glen); with a numeral indicating size, e.g. Nine ~, Seventeen ~, Nineteen Acres (Blaston), *Seaven acres* (Husbands Bosworth), Thirty-four Acres (Foxton); with an early pers.n. or its ME surn. reflex, e.g *banners aker* (Burton Overy), ?*cattes aker* (Glooston), *Gaysacr'* (Nevill Holt), ?*Ravensaker* (Great Glen), Watsons Acre (Blaston); with reference to location, e.g. *Colpitacur* (Great Bowden); to the nature of the soil, e.g. *Flynty Acre* (Houghton), *le Hungriaker* (Nevill Holt), Sand Acres (Billesdon), *Shittis acer* (Kibworth Harcourt); to flora, e.g. *Docke acres* (East Langton, Houghton), *Gorsacur* (Great Bowden); to fauna, e.g. *Goose acres* (Noseley, Slawston), *Hen Acre* (East Langton); to size or shape, e.g. Long Acre (Great Easton), *Mikelacr'* (Bringhurst), *the Round Acre* (Hallaton), *le Wendacre* (Evington).

æcer-dīc OE, perh. 'a ditch surrounding an arable plot' or 'a ditch marking the limit of ploughland'. Spellings with final *k* are due to Scandinavian influence. Acre Dikes (f.n. Evington, Lubenham).

æppel OE, 'an apple; an apple-tree'. *Apple Croft* (f.n. Lubenham).

æppel-trēow OE, 'an apple-tree'. *Apiltregate* (f.n. Nevill Holt), *Appell tree hill* (f.n. Houghton), Apple-Tree Cl (f.n. Knossington).

ærn OE, 'a building, a house'; in p.ns. chiefly in the sense 'a building used for a specific purpose'. *moserne* (f.n. Gumley).

æsc OE, 'an ash-tree'. Ashlands, Ash Spinney (Little Stretton, King's Norton). Freq. in f.ns. signifying (small) stands of ash-trees, e.g. Ashbed Cl (Gumley), Ashley (Carlton Curlieu, Little Bowden), Ashpole Spinney (Goadby, Nevill Holt), *Ouer Ashes* (Husbands Bosworth); boundary marks, e.g. *Sansoms ashe* (Husbands Bosworth); identifying individual closes, e.g. *Ash Close* (Carlton Curlieu, Evington, Hallaton), Ash Mdw (Carlton Curlieu), *Assecroft* (Saddington); hills marked by ash-trees, e.g. *Ashlow* (Husbands Bosworth), High Ash (Hallaton); streams, e.g. *Ashewell bridge* (Hallaton), *Aschewell* (Nevill Holt). *Esfeld* (Slawston) prob. shows the influence of ON **eski** 'a place growing with ash-trees', which suits the proposed interpretation of the township name. The distribution of ash-trees is widespread in the Hundred, but more densely represented in its west.

æt OE, prep. with dat., 'at'. ?Knossington.

ǣwell OE (Angl), 'a stream; the source of a stream'. ?Owls-Moor (f.n. Smeeton Westerby).

back ModE, adj., 'lying behind, hindmost'. Back Cl (f.n. Hallaton), Back Fd (f.n. Medbourne, Shangton), Back Paddock (f.n. Shangton), Back Orchard (f.n. Evington), Back Yard (f.n. Owston).

back of ModE, prep., 'behind'; elliptically 'that which lies at the back of, or behind, something'. Back of Coate Hill (f.n. Husbands Bosworth), Back o' the Lodge, Back of the Manor (f.ns. Medbourne), Back of Railway (f.n. Theddingworth).

***bagga** OE, prob. 'a badger'. Bagbeare Down (f.n. Billesdon).

baillif OFr, 'a bailiff, a steward'. ?Baileys Cl (f.n. Owston), *the Bailey-Hook* (f.n. Kibworth Beauchamp), *Baylyffes Close* (f.n. Evington), *le Bayly medowe* (f.n. Houghton).

bak-side ME, 'property behind a dwelling; the back, the rear'. Common in f.ns.: Backside Mdw (Illston), *the Backside Barly hill* (Hallaton), *the Backside of Bulgoares* (King's Norton), *backside Callow hill* (Saddington), *the backside Cattsforlong*, *the Backside Coates*, *Backside Langhill*, *Backside Wilsons Close* (Husbands Bosworth), *Backside of Chauntry*, *Backside Little Hill*, *Backside Pearetree* (Theddingworth), *the Backside Sherwoods* (Little Stretton), *the backside Thornehill* (Gumley), *Lawrence Greene his Backside* (East Langton), *Widow Mawsons House and Backside* (Evington).

balca OE, 'a ridge, a bank; a ridge of ploughland that marked the boundary between adjacent strips of a common field'. In late f.ns., may appear as *back* and thus confused with **bæc**. Freq. in f.ns: compounded with a surn. or with the title of a township functionary, e.g. *Constable balke* (Frisby, Gumley), *the Neatheards baulke* (King's Norton), *the persons balke* (Tur Langton), *Warwick baulk* (Kibworth Beauchamp); with reference to pasturage for farm animals, e.g. *Bull balk* (Galby, Hallaton), *Hogges balke* (Great Bowden), Swine Balk (Evington); to buildings, e.g. *the Mill balke* (Glooston, King's Norton, Nevill Holt), School Balk (Kibworth Beauchamp); to location, e.g. *greenegate balke*, *Hoo Baulk* (Glooston), *Mill gate Balke* (Gumley), *the Towne Baulke* (Husbands Bosworth); to size, e.g. *broadbalke* (Great Bowden, Hallaton); to flora, e.g. *Fisel Baulke* (Little Stretton).

***ball** OE (Angl), 'a ball'; topographically, 'a rounded hill; a mound of earth set up as a boundary marker'. *Balhul* (f.n. Billesdon).

banke ODan, **bank(e)** ME, 'a bank, a slope of a hill or ridge'. Deane Bank Fm, Hare Pie Bank, Moorbank Fm. Common in f.ns.: The Bank (Billesdon, Frisby, Kibworth Beauchamp, Stockerston); Bank Fd (Great Easton); Bankey Mdw (Carlton Curlieu), (The) Banks (Burton Overy, Hallaton, Saddington), Banky Cl (Fleckney, Saddington), Banky Fd (Houghton), Bottom Clink Bank (Newton Harcourt), Bushy Banks (Cranoe), *the Chappel Bank* (Frisby), Dog Bank (Little Bowden), *fulwell banke* (Great Bowden), *grene bank* (Fleckney), *hanginge banke* (Gumley), Hog Bank Cl (Burton Overy), Hollow Banks (Blaston), Home Bank (Burton Overy), Mill Bank (Newton Harcourt), Redbanks (Great Glen, King's Norton), Under the Bank (Slawston).

bareyne ME, adj., 'bare, barren, with little or no vegetation'. ?*Baron Brook Close* (f.n. Horninghold).

barn-yard ME, 'an enclosure around a barn, a farm-yard'. *le Barnyard* (f.n. Noseley), *Barnyarde* (f.n. Thurnby).

bastard OFr, adj., sb., '(a) bastard'; toponymically, used of fields of abnormal shape or poor yield and occasionally of selions of former great fields not completely swarded over. Bastard Leys (f.n. Little Bowden, Medbourne).

bay ME, 'an embankment to divert or dam a stream to form a pond for cattle or to serve a mill'. Bay Fd (f.n. Billesdon).

bæc OE, **bakke** ME, 'a back, a ridge'. Hoeback Spinney. Hollow Back (f.n. Knossington), ?*Huntsbacke* (f.n. Little Stretton), ?*Madback*, ?Turn Back (f.ns. Lubenham).

bæce OE, 'a stream, a valley stream'. *Batches Doles* (f.n. Wistow).

bær[1] OE, adj., 'bare, without vegetation'. Barearse (f.n. Medbourne), *Barearse hill* (f.n. Goadby), *Barehers(e)* (f.n. Drayton, Hallaton).

bærlic OE, 'barley'. Barley Cl (f.n. Billesdon), Barley Furlong (f.n. Laughton, Kibworth Beauchamp), Barley Hill Fd (f.n. Hallaton), *Barlicrofht* (f.n. Shangton), *barlie haden* (f.n. Burton Overy), *Barlihull* (f.n. Husbands Bosworth), *barlilondys* (f.n. Illston), *barly croftes* (f.n. Knossington), *Barly Hades* (f.n. Hallaton).

bæst OE, 'the fibrous inner bark of the lime-tree used for rope-making'. ?*baslandhill* (f.n. Knossington).

bæð OE, 'a bath; a pool, a pond'. Bath Spinney.

(ge)bēacon OE, 'a beacon, a signal fire'. The Beacon (f.n. Houghton), Beacon Hill (f.n. Billesdon).

bēam OE, 'a tree; a beam, a piece of timber; a cross'. *Beamash* (f.n. Saddington).

bēan OE, 'a bean'. Freq. in f.ns.: in the compound *bean-lands* (with various spellings in Billesdon, Burton Overy, Drayton, Glooston, Great Bowden, Great Easton, Gumley, Hallaton, Houghton, Husbands Bosworth, Illston, Nevill Holt, Saddington; *Balland Sike* (Galby), Banland Spinney (Great Glen)); *Banehil* (Houghton), *Baneholm* (Welham), *Banfurlong'* (Goadby, Hallaton), *Banham* (Great Bowden, Burton Overy), *Banslade* (Billesdon), Bean Cl (Billesdon, Glooston).

bearu OE, 'a grove, a small wood'. Bagbeare Down (f.n. Billesdon).

bēce OE, 'a beech-tree'. Beech Spinney. *Beech Meadow* (f.n. Hallaton).

bedd OE, 'a bed, a plot of land for growing plants'. Ashbed (f.n. Gumley, Noseley), Ozier Bed(s) (f.n. Knossington, Little Stretton, Smeeton Westerby), Ramsbed (f.n. Goadby, Glooston), *Rushbedds* (f.n. Houghton), Willow Bed (f.n. Burton Overy, Noseley, Scraptoft, Wistow).

beforan OE, prep., 'before, in front of, near'. *Biforbalhul*, *Biforesmereclif'*, *by fore the Scarth* (f.ns. Billesdon).

beg OE, 'a berry'. *Beylund* (f.n. Nevill Holt).

beggere ME, 'a beggar'; the common f.n. *Beggar's Bush* appears to denote poor or unproductive land (cf. EDD *beggar* 'to impoverish land, to exhaust soil of nutrients'). Beggars Pad (f.n. Owston), *Begger* (f.n. King's Norton), *Beggers bush* (f.n. Glooston, Newton Harcourt).

behindan OE, prep., 'behind, at the back of'. *Behind Cotes* (f.n. Husbands Bosworth).

bekkr ON, 'a stream'. *the Becke* (Tur Langton), Beck Cl, *Becke feilde* (f.ns. Shangton), *Beck furlong* (f.n. Kibworth Beauchamp), *the dalebeck gutter*, *Hunsbeck*, *Mealebecke* (Galby), *Hengebeck* (Shangton). The few surviving names with *bekkr* are limited to four townships to the north-west. In keeping with a region where Scandinavian influence on the toponymy appears minimal, OE **brōc** 'brook, stream' is dominant, *v.* Lei **2** 311 and Lei **3** 287.

belle OE, 'a bell'; topographically 'a knoll, a bell-shaped hill'. ?Bell Pool (f.n. Burton Overy).

belt ModE, 'a belt (of woodland), a screen of trees'. Belt Plantation (f.n. Cold Overton).

bēn OE, 'a favour, a request'; in ME, applied to gratuitous services, in kind or in labour, paid to a landlord by his tenent. *Beene* (f.n. Laughton).

benethe ME, prep., 'beneath, under, below'. *the grene byneth the Bell* (f.n. Market Harborough).

bēo OE, 'a bee'. ?*Besicke* (f.n. Mowsley).

beonet OE, 'bent grass'. Bontley (f.n. Saddington), Buntley (f.n. Smeeton Westerby).

***bēos** OE, 'bent grass, rough grass'. Bees Well Lane. ?*Besicke* (f.n. Mowsley).

berc OE (Angl), 'a birch-tree'. The Barkhams (f.n. Great Glen).

bere OE, 'barley'. Bare Hill (f.n. Glooston, Stonton Wyville), Barrell (f.n. Houghton), Beare Way (f.n. Medbourne), *Berehylfeld* (f.n. Slawston), *Berhull* (f.n. Medbourne), *Berrill* (f.n. Burton Overy).

bere-tūn OE, 'a barley enclosure, a barley farm'. ?Barton Hill (f.n. Scraptoft).

bere-wīc OE, 'a barley farm; a grange, an outlying or demesne farm'. The Barracks.

berg OE (Angl), 'a hill, a mound, a burial mound', **berg** ON, 'a hill'. Market Harborough; Barfoot Lodge, Crosburrow Hill, Hill Tamborough, Kettlesborough, Limborough, Muckleborough, Rickleburrow Hill, Scoborough, Sconsborough Hill. Common in f.ns.: compounded with an OE masc. pers.n., e.g. Beetleboro' (Knossington), Ranxborough (Cold Overton), ?Swadborough (Stoughton); with an el. indicating animals, e.g. *Catberwe* (Houghton), ?Foxborough (Foxton), ?Ramsborough (Horninghold, Stockerston); wild flora, e.g. ?Ramsborough (Horninghold, Stockerston), ?*Rysburgh* (Mowsley), Thornborough (Little Bowden); size, e.g. *Littlebarow* (Great Bowden, Lubenham), *Mikelbergh* (Great Bowden); aspect, e.g. Blackberry Hill (Stoughton), Swardboro (Mowsley). Often compounded as the specific, e.g. *Barrowe lease* (Hothorpe), *Borrough Hill* (Cranoe), *Burrowefilde* (Glooston, Foxton).

berige OE, 'a berry'. *Berihull* (f.n. Medbourne), *Berry doles* (f.n. Laughton), Berry Moor (f.n. Billesdon).

bern OE, 'a barn'. Barn Close Spinney. Barn Cl (f.n. Evington, Fleckney, Frisby, Goadby, Kibworth Beauchamp, Nevill Holt), Barn Ash Cl (f.n. Evington), Barn Fd (f.n. Burton Overy), Barnscroft (f.n. Great Bowden), Barn's Orchard (f.n. Billesdon), Barn Spinney Hill (f.n. Evington), *Bernorcharde* (f.n. Nevill Holt), *the Tythe Barne* (Fleckney), Wood Barn Cl (f.n. Gumley).

***berse** ME, '?a hedge made with stakes; ?an enclosed or fenced-in part of a forest'. *Bersaker* (f.n. Drayton).

best ModE, adj., 'best'. Best Cl (f.n. Burton Overy, Mowsley, Shangton), Best Mdw (f.n. Smeeton Westerby), Best Sheep Cl (f.n. Scraptoft), Little Best Mdw (f.n. Noseley).

besyde ME, prep., 'beside, next to, close by'. Affix for King's Norton.

betwēonan OE, prep., 'between, amongst', usually in compound p.ns. with the elliptical sense 'the place between'. *Betuynegatis* (f.n. Illston), *Between Graines*, *Between the wayes*, *betwene the sickes* (f.ns. Husbands Bosworth), *Between* *hedges* (f.n. King's Norton), Between Towns (f.n. Galby), *betwene Dales* (f.n. Foxton).

betwixt eModE, prep., 'between'; in p.ns., used as **betwēonan** *supra*. *Betwext the Wayes*, *Betwixt Graines* (f.ns. Husbands Bosworth), *Betwixte the brookes*, *Betwixt the Cloosen* (f.ns. Saddington), Twixt Hedges (f.n. King's Norton).

beyonde eModE, prep., 'on the farther side of'. *beyond Fearn* (f.n. Hallaton).

bī OE, prep., 'by, near'. *Bebroke* (f.n. Medbourne), *by Neyton*, *Estbedyk* (f.ns. Great Easton), *Longbygate* (f.n. Stoughton).

***bica** OE, of uncertain meaning, poss. 'a point; a beak-like projection'. ?*Bikethorn* (f.n. Illston).

bill OE, 'a sword', topographically 'a sharp ridge, a promontory'. ?Billesdon. ?*Bilton'* (f.n. Medbourne).

***billing** OE, 'a hill, a prominence, a ridge'. *Bilingate* (f.n. Nevill Holt).

binde OE, 'a climbing plant'. ?*Bynduls* (f.n. Noseley).

birce OE, 'a birch-tree'. Birch Tree Fm.

bit ModE, 'a bit'; topographically, 'a small piece of land'. Barfoot Bit (f.n. Saddington), Beadman's Bit (f.n. Great Glen), Bit (f.n. Evington), Bit Thrawly (f.n. Glooston), Bottom Bits (f.n. Great Glen), Road Bit (f.n. Marefield), Three Corner Bit (f.n. Shangton), ?Wash Bit (f.n. Marefield), Wire Bit (f.n. Saddington).

blāc OE, adj., 'pale, bleak'. ?Blacklands (f.n. Foxton).

blacksmith ModE, 'a blacksmith'. Blacksmith's Cl (f.n. Galby).

blank ME, adj., 'bare'. Blank Mdw (f.n. Frisby), The Blank (f.n. Illston).

blár ON, adj., 'dark, lead-coloured'; by extension as **blo** ME, adj., 'cheerless, cold, exposed'. Bluegate Cl (f.n. Bringhurst), Blue Piece (f.n. Goadby), Bluepott Cl (f.n. Burton Overy).

blæc OE, **blak(e)** ME, **black** ModE, adj., 'black, dark'; in eModE, also 'fertile' as against *white* 'infertile'. Black Dyke Wood, Black Spinney, Blackspinney Lane. Freq. in f.ns., principally with an el. signifying soil, e.g. *Blakelandes* (Great Bowden, Knossington), Blackmiles (Husbands Bosworth, Medbourne), *Blakemilde* (Billesdon, Nevill Holt), *Blacmyldlond* (Illston, Mowsley); or with an el. indicating a hill, e.g. Blackberry Hill (Stoughton), Black Hill (Goadby); or moorland, e.g. *Blackmore* (Houghton, Saddington); or a stream, e.g. *Blakebroc* (Husbands Bosworth), Blackwell (Glooston); or an enclosure, e.g. *Blaktoftes* (Burton Overy), *Blakewong* (Nevill Holt); or gloomy, overgrown pits, e.g. *Black Pitts* (Gumley, King's Norton).

blæc-þorn OE, 'a blackthorn, a sloe-tree'. *Blacthorne hole* (f.n. Billesdon).

bleikr ON, adj., 'pale'; perh. also 'bleak'. Bleak Hill (f.n. Scraptoft).

blōd OE, 'blood'; topographically may refer to the colour red. Blood Wood, *Bludebroke* (f.ns. Hallaton).

bog ME, 'a bog, a marsh'. The Bog (f.n. Laughton), Bog Holme (f.n. Knossington), Bog Mdw (f.n. Bushby), The Bogs (f.n. Fleckney), Desborow Bogs (f.n. Market Harborough), Franeys Far Close and Bog (f.n. Blaston).

boga OE, 'a bow; an arch or arched bridge; something curved or bent (as a curved valley or river bend)'. *Bobriggs Close* (f.n. Newbold), Bowberry (f.n. Marefield), ?*Bowdon londe* (f.n. Drayton), ?*Bowghton* (f.n. Great Bowden).

boggy ModE, adj., 'boggy'. Boggy Cl (f.n. Houghton), Boggy Fd (f.n. Great Glen).

***boia** OE, 'a boy, a servant'. Boycroft (f.n. Little Stretton).

bold OE, 'a dwelling, a house'. Newbold. *Oldebolde* (f.n. Illston).

bond-man ME, 'a husbandman, an unfree villager, a serf'. ?*Bondman leyes* (f.n. Laughton).

bolt OE, 'a bolt, an arrow'; topographically, prob. 'a headland, a ridge'. Bolt Wood.

boney ModE, adj., 'full of bones'. Boney Corner (f.n. Glooston).

bord OE, 'a boundary'. Burden Wall (f.n. Laughton).

bothe ME, 'a booth, a temporary shelter'. ?Boothys Mdw (f.n. Carlton Curlieu).

botm OE, 'a bottom'; in p.ns., esp. 'the floor of a valley'. Bannals Bottom (f.n. Hallaton), Berry Moor Bottom (f.n. Billesdon), Hardwick Bottom (f.n. Shangton), Kuffers Bottom (f.n. Billesdon).

bottom ModE, adj., 'bottom, lowermost' (by extension from **botm**). Bottom Cl (f.n. Billesdon, Burton Overy, Fleckney, Galby), Bottom Eleven Acre (f.n. Billesdon), Bottom Hole Cl, Bottom Mdw (f.ns. Frisby).

boundary ModE, 'a boundary, a border'. Boundary Cl (f.n. Noseley).

bounde ME, 'a boundary'. Bound Cl (f.n. Galby).

bow-bearer ModE, 'a forest official responsible for protecting deer and their habitat from trespassers'. The Bowbearers (f.n. Owston).

bowling eModE, vbl.sb, ppl.adj., 'the playing at bowls, the action of rolling a ball'. Bowling Leys (f.n. Little Bowden), *Bowleing pytt furlong*, *the Bowling Leys* (f.ns. Theddingworth).

bowling-green ModE, 'a smooth level lawn or green for playing bowls upon'. Bowling Green. Bowling Green Cl (f.n. Welham).

brache ME, 'a hunting dog'. ?*Brachyard* (f.n. Great Easton).

bracu OE, 'a thicket, a patch of brushwood'. *Brackill Layes* (f.n. Husbands Bosworth), *Bracklands*, Brackley (f.ns. Great Glen), *Brackleys* (f.n. Theddingworth), *Brake* (f.n. Noseley), *the brake hill*, Great Breaks (f.ns. Goadby), *Brake sicke* (f.n. Tur Langton), *le brakis* (f.n. Shangton), Hill Brakes (f.n. Glooston).

brād OE, adj., 'broad, spacious'. Bradley Priory; Broadgate. Common in f.ns.: e.g. *Bradelandes*, *Broddole*, *Broderodes* (Billesdon), *Bradgate* (Lubenham, Nevill Holt), *broadbalke* (Great Bowden, Hallaton), Broadholm (Blaston), Broad Lane (Evington, Husbands Bosworth), Broadsick (Frisby) etc.

braken ME, 'bracken, fern'. *Brackenhil* (f.n. Houghton), *Brakendale* (f.n. Billesdon, Marefield).

braky ModE, adj., 'overgrown with brushwood'. *Brakey Close* (f.n. Glooston).

brand OE, 'fire', used topographically of 'a place where burning has occurred'. The Brand (f.n. Knossington), ?*Branlands* (f.n. Great Bowden), ?Brown Slade Mdw (f.n. Gumley).

brant OE, adj., 'steep, steep-sided'. ?*Branlands* (f.n. Great Bowden), *Brant hill*, Brown Slade Mdw (f.ns. Gumley), *Branthyll* (f.n. Noseley, Tur Langton).

brēc OE (Angl), **breche** ME, 'land broken up for cultivation, newly broken-in ploughland'. The Breach, Breach Fm. Common if f.ns.: as a simplex, e.g. *le Breche* (Billesdon, Great Bowden, Tur Langton); or with a qualifier of location, e.g. (*le*) *Estbreche* (Billesdon, Owston) *le Suthbreche* (Billesdon), *Meadow breach* (Husbands Bosworth); or of ownership, e.g. *Osgotebreche* (Billesdon). Occasionally appears as a specific, e.g. *Breachleys* (Smeeton Westerby), *Brechewod* (Blaston). Note the unusual *Umberbreche* (Nevill Holt).

brēg OE (Angl), **breu** ME, 'an eyebrow'; prob. used topographically for 'the brow of a hill'. Bray Furlong (f.n. Kibworth Beauchamp).

breiðr ON, adj., 'broad'. Braymish (f.n. Little Bowden), Bremish (f.n. Kibworth Harcourt, Smeeton Westerby), *Brethornhil*, *Breycliue* (f.ns. Billesdon), *Vnderbretland* (f.n. Bushby).

brēmel, brembel OE, 'a bramble, a blackberry bush'; also used of other prickly plants, especially the dog-rose. *Brimbelbrinke* (f.n. Shangton), *Brimelsyke* (f.n. Stoughton), Long Brimley (f.n. Little Bowden).

brend OE, pa.part., 'burnt; cleared by burning, destroyed by fire'. *le Brendemulne* (f.n. Medbourne), *Brenwode*, Burnt Ground (f.ns. Stonton Wyville), Brunthill (f.n. Bushby), *le Burnt house yardeland* (f.n. Goadby), Burnt Cl (f.n. Billesdon), *Burnt Mill* (f.n. Hallaton), Burnt Mills (f.n. Lubenham).

***brende** OE, 'a burnt place, a place cleared or destroyed by burning'. *Brende* (f.n. Nevill Holt), *Brinynghurst Brende* (f.n. Bringhurst).

brēosa OE, 'a gadfly'. *Brosebrocfurlong* (f.n. Billesdon).

brēost OE, 'a breast'; prob. used topographically of 'a rounded slope or hill'. *le Breste* (f.n. Great Bowden).

brēr OE, 'a briar, a wild rose'. *Bryer hill* (f.n. Tur Langton).

bridd OE, 'a bird'. ?*Birdes lane* (f.n. Great Bowden).

brīdel OE, 'a bridle'; in compounds 'fit for the passage of horses but not vehicles'. Bridle Road (f.n. Newton Harcourt), Goadby Bridle Way, Slawston Bridle Way (f.ns. Cranoe).

brike ME, 'a brick'. Brick Cl (f.n. Carlton Curlieu, Houghton).

brike-kiln ME, 'a brick-kiln'. Brick Kiln Cl (f.n. Billesdon, Burton Overy, Husbands Bosworth, Owston, Smeeton Westerby, Stretton Magna), Brick Kiln Mdw (f.n. Cold Overton), Brikkle Cl (f.n. Hallaton).

brike-yard ME, 'a brick-works, a yard where bricks are made'. Brickyard Fm. (the) Brickyard (f.n. Burton Overy, Fleckney, Great Easton, Great Glen, Mowsley), Brickyard Cl (f.n. Lubenham, Scraptoft, Thurnby), Old Brick Yard (f.n. Foxton, Hallaton), Top Brickyard (f.n. Smeeton Westerby).

brim OE, 'flood, water'. ?Brimswell (f.n. Great Easton).

brimme OE, 'a bank, an edge, a shore'. *Brimlands* (f.n. King's Norton).

brink ME, 'a brink, an edge'. *Brimbelbrinke* (f.n. Shangton), *Brinckes* (f.n. East Langton, Houghton, King's Norton), *Brinks furlong* (f.n. Stonton Wyville), Brinspitt (f.n. Laughton), ?*Bryngford* (f.n. Goadby), *le fallyngbrynk*, *les Houbrinkes* (f.ns. Medbourne), *Hobrinckes* (f.n. Kibworth Harcourt), *le Prestisbring'*, *Stanbrynk'*, *Stokdolebring'* (f.ns. Billesdon).

brōc OE, 'a brook, a stream'. Billesdon Brook, Burton ~, Evington ~, Langton Brook, Langton Brook Plantation, Medbourne Brook, Washbrook Lane. Freq. in f.ns., esp. compounded with a township name and thus prob. identifying a more major stream, e.g. *Blastonbroke*, Othorpe Brook, *Slawson brook* (Hallaton), *Houghton Brook* (Galby), *Killworth brooke* (Husbands Bosworth), *Rolston brooke* (Billesdon); with flora, e.g. Fern Brook, *Seavybroke* (Hallaton), *lusthornebroc* (Drayton), *Sawbrooke* (Fleckney), Sea Brook (Burton Overy); with words describing aspect, e.g. *Blakebroc* (Husbands Bosworth, Theddingworth), *Bludbroke* (Hallaton), *Whebrooke* (Husbands Bosworth); rarely with wild fauna, e.g. *Otter Brook* (Hallaton). Freq. in the names of modern fields, e.g. Brook Cl (Foxton), Brook Fd (Burton Overy, Carlton Curlieu, Gumley, Husbands Bosworth), Brook Mdw (Billesdon, Carlton Curlieu).

brocc-hol OE, 'a badger-sett'. *Brockholes* (f.n. Goadby, Laughton), *Brocholegate* (f.n. Horninghold).

brode ME, 'a broad stretch of land'. *the Broad of Crosdale* (f.n. Little Stretton), Marsdale Broad (f.n. Medbourne), *le schortbrod* (f.n. Illston).

brōm OE, 'broom'. The Broomhill (f.n. Houghton).

brōðor OE, **bróðir** ON 'a brother'. ?*brathorslade* (f.n. Frisby).

brū OE, 'an eyebrow'; topographically 'a hill-brow, a steep slope'. *the Brow of the Hill* (f.n. Slawston), *Bruhawes* (f.n. Billesdon), *harbroue stong* (f.n. Gumley).

brún[2] ON, 'an edge, the brow of a hill'. *Brownefurlonge* (f.n. Great Bowden), ?*Burngrass* (f.n. Hothorpe).

brycg OE, 'a bridge, a causeway'; in the Danelaw, spellings of p.ns. with *brycg* may be influenced by ON **bryggja** 'a quay, a jetty'. Kibworth Bridge, Port Bridge. Sometimes compounded with a township name, e.g. Burton Bridge (Burton Overy, Kibworth Harcourt), *Hornyngwoldbryg'* (Hallaton), *Killworth Bridge* (Husbands Bosworth), *Rogingham Brigge* (Great Easton). Commonly compounded with OE *stān* ('stone') or *stānig* ('built of stone'), as Stone Bridge (Blaston, Evington, Fleckney), *Staneibrigge* (Nevill Holt). Note *Sumebrygge* (Great Easton) where a causeway may well be implied, since only viable in the summer months, and the unusual modern *Chain Bridge* (Market Harborough). *Germundebrig* (Saddington) is the only instance with a pers.n. in the Hundred.

brȳd OE, 'a bride, a wife; a young woman'; in compound with **wella** may denote a fertility spring. ?Birdwell (f.n. Theddingworth).

***brȳd** OE, adj., 'surging'. ?Birdwell (f.n. Theddingworth).

bryne OE, 'burning; a place cleared by burning'. Burn Hill. Burn Dale (f.n. Foxton), ?*Burngrass* (f.n.Hothorpe).

bucca OE, 'a buck, a male deer; a he-goat'. *Buckwell* (f.n. Great Bowden).

bufan OE, prep., 'above, over'. *boueton* (f.n. Frisby).

bula OE, **boli** ON, 'a bull'. Common in f.ns.: e.g. *Bull balk* (Galby, Hallaton, Knossington), *Bullgores* (King's Norton, Little Stretton), Bullholmes (Great Easton, Lubenham, Stockerston), *the Bull Peice* (Hallaton, Houghton, Knossington). Note Bullstake Cl (Scraptoft) and *Bolewyk* (Hallaton).

bulluc OE, 'a bullock'. Bullock Cl (f.n. Hallaton), Bullock Fd (f.n. Great Easton), *Bullocks Pen Furlong* (f.n. Theddingworth), *Bullokesforth* (f.n. Houghton).

bunche ME, 'a bundle (of reeds etc.)'. Bunch Bit (f.n. Hallaton).

bune OE, 'a reed'. ?Bumpipe Cl (f.n. Saddington).

burgh ME, 'an animal burrow'. ?*the Burrow Meadow* (f.n. Laughton), ?Foxborough (f.n. Foxton).

burh (**byrig** dat.sg.) OE, 'a fortified place'. Borough Bridge (f.n. Horninghold), Boro' Wong (f.n. Knossington), ?*the Burrow Meadow* (f.n. Laughton), *Bury*, *Westbury* (f.ns. Husbands Bosworth), ?*Rysburgh* (f.n. Mowsley).

burh-stall OE, 'the site of a stronghold'. ?Burstans Hill (f.n. Gumley), Buxtons Hill (f.n. Hallaton).

burh-stede OE, 'the site of a stronghold'. *Bursted* (f.n. Tur Langton).

burh-tūn OE, 'a fort enclosure; a farmstead with a palisade'. Burton Overy.

burna OE, 'a stream'. Medbourne.

busc OE, **bush** ME, 'a bush, a thicket, ground covered with shrubs'. ?Bushby; Clarke's Bush, Nut Bush, Holly Bush. Freq. in f.ns.: with surn. or el. signifying ownership, e.g. *Barry Bush* (Great Glen), *John Eytons bushes* (Stretton Magna),

Killpacks bush (Kibworth Beauchamp), *No mans Bush* (Tur Langton); prefixed by a locational el. or minor p.n., e.g. East and West Bush (Wistow), *Upper Bushe* (Tur Langton), Great Stone Bushes (Evington), Lawn Bushes (Hallaton), *Woolfeild Bushis* (Gumley); with a word defining the nature of the shrubs, e.g. *Thakines Bushe* (Kibworth Harcourt), Thorn Bush Cl (Laughton). May simply precede an enclosure el., e.g. Bushawe (Blaston), Bush Cl (Bushby, Great Bowden, Houghton, Saddington). Note the important Gartree Bush (Shangton) and *Midsomer bush* (King's Norton).

***buski** ON, 'shrubland, scrubland'. ?Bushby.

***buskr** ON, 'a bush, a thicket'. ?Bushby. *Copnyll buske* (f.n. Great Easton), *notebuske* (f.n. Medbourne), *Wythenbuske* (f.n. Billesdon).

busshi ME, adj., 'growing with bushes'. Bushey Cl (f.n. Burton Overy, Bushby, Carlton Curlieu, Owston, Rolleston), Bushey Hill (f.n. Scraptoft), *Bushy Banks* (f.n. Cranoe), Bushy High Leys (f.n. Marefield), Bushy Mdw (f.n. Cold Overton, Glooston).

but OFr, 'an archery butt'. ?Buttleys (f.n. Little Stretton, Slawston).

butere OE, 'butter'; often referring to rich pasture used in the production of butter. *Buterhil* (f.n. Husbands Bosworth), *The Butter market* (Market Harborough).

butte ME, 'a short strip of arable land'. Butts Lane. *the Butholde* (f.n. Noseley), *butlan* (f.n. Husbands Bosworth), Butt Cl (f.n. Galby), *les Buttes* (f.n. Billesdon, Burton Overy, Great Glen, Houghton), Butt Fd (f.n. Stoughton), ?Buttleys (f.n. Little Stretton, Slawston), *Butts furlong* (f.n. Hothorpe), Butt Yard (f.n. Evington), *Cattes butts* (f.n. Great Bowden), Great Butt Cl (f.n. Owston), *le Hallebuttes* (f.n. Medbourne), *no mans butt*, *Paynottisbutes* (f.ns. Great Easton), *shortebuttis* (f.n. Frisby, Hothorpe).

bȳ ODan, 'a farmstead, a village'. Bushby, Frisby, Galby, Goadby, Smeeton Westerby, Thurnby. *Alby poyl* (f.n. Illston), *Rainbyslade* (f.n. Goadby).

byg ME, adj., 'big, of great extent'. *bygthoryn* (f.n. Illston).

bȳre OE, 'a byre, a cowshed'. *le ber'* (f.n. Illston).

cabache ME, 'cabbage'. Cabbage Cl (f.n. Great Glen).

cabane ME, 'a temporary hut, a shed'. First Cabin (f.n. Stretton Magna), The Wad Cabin (f.n. Evington).

cake eModE, 'excrement'. ?the Cake Mdw (f.n. Great Glen).

calc OE, 'chalk, limestone'. *calcylsyche* (f.n. Great Easton), Chalgate (f.n. Nevill Holt), *Chaukdalsyke* (f.n. Goadby), Corkley (f.n. Smeeton Westerby).

cald OE (Angl), **cald**, **cold** ME, 'cold; exposed, wind-swept'. Cold Overton; Langton Caudle. *Caldecotehil* (f.n. Lubenham), *Caldewell* (f.n. Hallaton), *Caldewellesike*, *Caldewelmore* (f.ns. Great Easton), *Caldwell Close*, *~ Pasture* (f.ns. Horninghold), *Caudell thornes* (f.n. Frisby), *Caudwell* (f.n. East Langton), the Cawdell (f.n. Carlton Curlieu), *Coldham* (f.n. Illston), Cold Hill (f.n. Owston).

calf (**calfra** gen.pl.) OE, 'a calf'. Calf Cl (f.n. Blaston), Calfers Leys, *Calvers Close* (f.ns. Medbourne), *the Calfes pasture* (f.n. Lubenham, Nevill Holt), *Calverholm* (f.n. Stretton Magna), Calves Cl, ~ Pasture, ~ Plot (f.ns. Billesdon), Calves Cl (f.n. Owston), Calves Mdw (f.n. Stoughton), *Calvis croft*, *Calves platt* (f.ns. Houghton), ?*Chaluercroft* (f.n. Nevill Holt).

calu OE, adj., 'bare, lacking in vegetation'. ?Carrygate. *Callow hill* (f.n. Saddington), Carrywell (f.n. Illston), *Gallow hill* (f.n. Blaston, Foxton, Great

Easton, Scraptoft), *Gallow meare* (f.n. Kibworth Beauchamp).

camb OE, 'a comb, a crest'; used topographically to mean 'a hill-crest, a ridge'. *Camsill* (f.n. *Theddingworth*).

capitain ME, 'a military leader, the commander of a body of troops or of a fortress'; later, the military rank between major and lieutenant. Captains Cl (f.n. Goadby).

caryour ME, 'a carter, a carrier'. ?*Carriers Thorn*, ?*Carriers Waye* (f.ns. Husbands Bosworth).

carte ME, 'a cart'. *Carte Gappe*, *Cart gate* (f.ns. Houghton), Cart Hovel (f.n. Smeeton Westerby).

castel(l) ME, 'a castle'. Castle Hill.

catel ME, 'cattle, livestock'. Cattle Market.

cat(t) OE, 'a cat, a wild-cat'. *Catberwe* (f.n. Houghton), Cat Grove (f.n. Gumley), Cathill, *Catwell* (f.ns. Medbourne), Cat Holes (f.n. Hallaton, Nevill Holt), Catley (f.n. Little Bowden), ?*cattes aker* (f.n. Glooston), ?*Cattes butts* (f.n. Great Bowden), *Catteswell* (f.n. Saddington), ?*Catts furlong* (f.n. Husbands Bosworth), Catwell (f.n. Burton Overy).

caucie ONFr, **cauce**, **cause** ME, 'an embankment or dam; a raised way across marshy ground; a (raised) paved way'. Church Causeway. The Causeway Land (f.n. Husbands Bosworth), *the Church causy close* (f.n. Thurnby), *St Mary's Causeway* (Market Harborough).

cavalry ModE, 'horses; horsemen; horse-soldiers'. ?Cavalry Cl (f.n. Evington).

cavel ME, 'a division or share of property made by lot; an allotment of land'. ?Cavalry Cl (f.n. Evington).

cawel OE, 'cole, cabbage'. *Kawelhul* (f.n. Saddington).

***cǣg** OE, 'gravel, stone'. Keymoor (f.n. Houghton).

cēap OE, 'a market'. *Cheapside* (Market Harborough).

ceorl (**ceorlena** gen.pl.) OE, 'a (free) peasant, a churl'. Carlton Curlieu; ?King Charles's Well.

cerr OE (Angl), 'a turn, a bend'. *Cheredik* (f.n. Billesdon), *Cherlond* (f.n. Noseley).

cerring OE (Angl), 'a turn, a bend'. *Carring* (f.n. East Langton).

cerse OE, 'cress'. *Cerssholme* (f.n. Evington).

cetel OE, 'a kettle, a vessel for containing water'. Kicklewell Spinney.

chamberlain OFr, 'an officer who receives revenues on behalf of superiors; a servant'. ?Far Chamberlains (f.n. Houghton).

chambre OFr, 'a chamber'. *Pecks Chambers* (f.n. Hallaton).

chanterie OFr, **chaunterie** ME, 'a chantry'. Chawntry (f.n. Theddingworth), *Chantry land* (f.n. Husbands Bosworth).

chapelain OFr, 'a priest, a clergyman'. ?*Chapelenesthing* (Great Bowden).

chapel(e) OFr, ME, 'a chapel, an oratory'. St Morrell's Chapel; *The Chapel* (St Leonard's Church, Thorpe Langton), *the Chappel of Rolleston* (St John's Church, Rolleston). *the Chapel Close* (f.n. Blaston, Great Glen, Slawston), *the Chapel Yard* (f.n. Blaston, Market Harborough, Smeeton Westerby), *the Chappel Bank* (f.n. Frisby), *Chappell waye*, *Chappill Hill* (f.ns. Hallaton).

cheker ME, 'a chequer'; topographically usually alluding to land with a chequered appearance. *the Checker* (f.n. Frisby).

cheri-tre ME, 'a cherry-tree'. Cherry Tree Nook (f.n. Owston).

chese-cake ME, 'a cheesecake'; used topographically of a wedge-shaped field, alluding to a slice of the tart so called. Cheese Cake Cl (f.n. Owston), Cheesecake

Piece (f.n. Great Bowden, Hallaton, Houghton, Newton Harcourt, Stonton Wyville), *chiscake dowle*, *the Parsons chiskeck* (f.ns. Glooston), ?The Cake Mdw (f.n. Great Glen).

cheyne ME, 'a chain'. *Chain Bridge* (Market Harborough). Chain Bridge Leys (f.n. Little Bowden).

***chingel** ME, 'shingle, pebbles'. *Chinklle Close* (f.n. Evington).

chirche, **churche** ME, 'a church'. (Parish churches with their various dedications are not listed.). Church Langton. Freq. in f.ns.: e.g. *Churchacres* (Wistow), Church Cl (Evington, Church Langton, Foxton, Shangton), Church Fd (Blaston, Cranoe, Glooston, Stockerston), *the Church floore* (Church Langton), *the Church gate* (East Langton, Frisby, Great Glen), Church Hill Cl (Foxton, Kibworth Beauchamp), *the Church lane* (Cranoe), *Church leyes* (Glooston), the Church Walk (Carlton Curlieu), Church Well (Kibworth Beauchamp).

churchyerd ME, 'a churchyard'. Freq., some earlier instances being *the Churchyard* (belonging to the parish churches of Cranoe, Houghton, Husbands Bosworth 1606, Billesdon, Galby 1625); also Churchyard Cl (f.n. Great Glen, Hallaton, Noseley), *Joyning the Churchyard* (f.n. Tur Langton), Old Churchyard Cl (f.n. Medbourne).

cild OE, 'a child'. *Dedechild* (f.n. Mowsley).

cirice-stede OE, 'a church-site'. *Kyrkstede* (f.n. Nevill Holt).

***cis** OE, 'gravel'. Cheese Worms (f.n. Burton Overy).

clā OE, 'a claw'; used topographically of something claw-like or cloven, as a fork of a river or a tongue of land between two streams. ?*Clarness* (f.n. East Langton).

clāfre, OE, 'clover'. Clover Cl (f.n. Burton Overy, Gumley and 8 other parishes), Clover Ground (f.n. Hallaton), Clover Mdw (f.n. Little Stretton).

clakke ME, 'the clapper of a mill'. ?*Clakshyll* (f.n. Noseley).

***clæcc** OE, 'a hillock'. Clack Hill. ?*Clakshyll* (f.n. Noseley).

clǣg OE, 'clay'. The Clay (f.n. Mowsley), *Clay Hill* (f.n. East Langton), *Cleypole* (f.n. Great Bowden).

clǣne OE, adj., 'clean, clear of weeds etc.'. *Clenfurlong* (f.n. Husbands Bosworth).

clerk ME, 'a cleric, a (secular) churchman; a scribe, a scholar'. *Clarkwell* (f.n. Saddington).

cley-pytt ME, 'a clay-pit'. Clay Pit (f.n. Great Easton), The Clay Pits (f.n. Illston), Clay Pit Lane Cl (f.n. Burton Overy), Clay Pit Leys (f.n. Little Bowden).

clif OE, 'a cliff, a steep slope'. *Breycliue*, Home Cleaves, ?Ratcliffe Cl, *Smerclif'* (f.ns. Billesdon), ?Cliffs Cl (f.n. Blaston), *Cliftherne* (f.n. Great Easton), *Clyfhadis* (f.n. Mowsley), *Gosclif* (f.n. Saddington), Stinkley (f.n. Smeeton Westerby).

***clinc** OE, 'a cleft, a crevice'. Bottom Clink Bank (f.n. Newton Harcourt), *Clync* (f.n. Burton Overy).

***clodd** OE, 'a clod, a lump of earth'. Clod Leys (f.n. Billesdon).

cloistre OFr, ME, 'a cloister; an enclosure'. Cloysters (f.n. King's Norton).

clok ME, 'a clock'; in some modern f.ns. may allude to dandelion clocks.

clos(e) ME, 'an enclosure'. Very freq. in f.ns.: early examples are *Barn close* 1564, *le New close* 1469, *le Shepe Close* 1572, *the wood close* 1564 (all Nevill Holt), *New Close* 1538 (Owston), *penne close* 1527 (Goadby), *Thorney close* 1537 (Blaston).

closing ME, 'an enclosure'. ?*Betwixt the Cloosen* (f.n. Saddington).

closure ME, 'an enclosure'. *Tomlins Two Closures*, *West Closures* (f.ns. Laughton).

clūd OE, 'a mass of rock, a cliff, a hill'. Cloudhill. *groufcloudys* (f.n. Smeeton Westerby).

clump ModE, 'a cluster of trees'. Carlton Clump, Millfield Clump. The Brickhill Clumps (f.n. Husbands Bosworth), Clump Cl (f.n. Saddington).

cnafa (**cnafena** gen.pl.) OE, 'a boy, a youth; a servant'. Knave Hill. The Nanalls (f.n. Theddingworth).

cnapa OE, 'a boy, a youth; a servant'. ?*Knapcotes* (f.n. Billesdon), ?*Knaptoft* (f.n. Great Glen).

cnoll OE, 'a knoll, a hillock'. The Knoll. *Knoles Laund Close* (f.n. Thurnby), The Knoll (f.n. Smeeton Westerby), Knoll Fm (Knossington), *Mersedaleknoll* (f.n. Medbourne), *Pasture Knowles* (f.n. Bushby).

***cnoss** OE, 'a (rounded) hill'. ?Knossington.

***cobb(e)** OE, 'a round lump'. ?*Cobwells* (f.n. Fleckney).

cocc[1] OE, 'a heap; a hillock'; as a specific, difficult to distinguish from **cocc**[2]. ?*Cockacre* (f.n. Houghton), ?*Cockacres* (f.n. Bushby), *Cockash*, *Cockland*, Six Cocks (f.ns. Smeeton Westerby), *cockedoale* (f.n. East Langton), ?*Cockloe* (f.n. Husbands Bosworth), ?Coxes Cl (f.n. Evington), *Four Cocks*, Six Cocks (f.ns. Kibworth Beauchamp).

cocc[2] OE, 'a cock'. ?*Cockacre* (f.n. Houghton), ?*Cockacres* (f.n. Bushby), *cockes glade forlonge* (f.n. Glooston), ?*Cockloe* (f.n. Husbands Bosworth), ?Coxes Cl (f.n. Evington).

coccel OE, 'tares; cornfield weeds such as cockle and darnel'. ?*cockle hill* (f.n. Tur Langton).

***cocc-scēte** OE (Angl), 'a place where woodcocks dart', 'a glade across which nets are stretched to catch woodcocks'. *Cockshoot Close* (f.n. Horninghold), *Cockshote* (f.n. Blaston), *Cocsitehil* (f.n. Nevill Holt), *Coxshoute* (f.n. Kibworth Harcourt).

cokel ME, 'a cockle; the fossilized remains of a mollusc in the local stone'. ?*cockle hill* (f.n. Tur Langton), *Coculs* (f.n. Noseley).

cōl[2] OE, adj., 'cool'. Colwell Cls (f.n. Kibworth Beauchamp).

cole, ***cūle** OE, 'a hollow'. *Cole Acres* (f.n. Theddingworth), Colebreach (f.n. Great Glen), Coles (f.n. Hallaton), *Colle Brigg foorde* (f.n. Kibworth Harcourt), ?*Collecroft* (f.n. Billesdon), *Wellcoles* (f.n. Saddington).

college ME, 'a fraternity, a religious fellowship'. *the Colledge meadow* (f.n. Noseley).

col-pytt OE, 'a coalpit, i.e. a place where charcoal is made'. Coal Pit Lane. Coalpit Cl (f.n. Billesdon), Coal Pit Lane (f.n. Kibworth Beauchamp), *Colepitt'* (f.n. Burton Overy), *Colepitt hole* (f.n. Mowsley), *the Colepit way* (f.n. East Langton), *Colpit* (f.n. Horninghold), *Colpitacur* (f.n. Great Bowden).

colte ME, 'a young horse'. ?Colt's Plot (f.n. Billesdon).

commissioner ModE, 'a person appointed or deputed by commission to carry out some specified work'. Commissioner's Lane.

commun ME, used both as a sb. as 'common land' and as an adj. as 'shared by all, of a non-private nature'. The Common, Easton Common. Freq. in f.ns.: Barfoot Common, Freemans Common (Saddington), Beaconhill Common (Billesdon), *the Common* (Fleckney, Gumley, Hallaton), Cow Common (Blaston), Oaks Common, Smallwood Common (Hallaton); *the Common bolk* (Gumley), *the Common Cowpasture* (Foxton, Glooston, Husbands Bosworth), *the Common*

Drift (Hallaton), *the common pasture* (Goadby, Welham), *Comyn' Marlepyttes* (Great Bowden).

conestable ME, 'a constable'. *Constables balke* (f.n. Frisby), *the constables peece* (f.n. Knossington), *the cunstables bolk* (f.n. Gumley), *the Cunstables Hooks* (f.n. Burton Overy).

coni ME, 'a rabbit'. Coney Hill Plantation.

coning ME, 'a rabbit'. Coningsgrave Hill (f.n. Blaston).

coning-erth ME, 'a rabbit-warren'. ?Coningsgrave Hill (f.n. Blaston), *Connynggarthe* (f.n. Medbourne).

coningre, **coninger** ME, 'a rabbit-warren'. (The) Conery (f.n. Saddington, Scraptoft), *the Conyngree* (f.n. Fleckney, Lubenham, Noseley), *the Cunnery* (f.n. Evington, Knossington), Cunnery Cl (f.n. Owston), Great Conery (f.n. Blaston).

copis ME, 'a coppice'. Tampion's Coppice. *Bellers Copie* (f.n. Nevill Holt), *The Copie* (f.n. Hallaton), *the Coppye Leys*, *Furlong Behind Coppy* (f.ns. Glooston), Copy (f.n. Blaston), *the Hall yarde Coppice* (f.n. Evington), Long Coppice (f.n. Goadby), *Shepherds Copy* (f.n. Stockerston).

copp OE, 'a summit, a hill or ridge which has a narrow, crest-like top'. The Coplow. ?*Copdale*, *Meare Copp Meadow* (f.ns. Evington).

copped[1] ME, adj., 'having a peak'. *Cobdale* (f.n. Husbands Bosworth), *Copdale* (f.n. Evington), *Copedmore* (f.n. Mowsley), *Coppydhyll* (f.n. Great Easton), *Copthill* (f.n. Houghton).

copped[2] ME, pa.part., adj., 'pollarded, with the head removed'. *Coptree Furlong* (f.n. Hallaton).

***corf** OE, 'a gap'. Coverdale (f.n. Burton Overy).

corn[1] OE, 'corn, grain'. Corn Close. Corn Cl (f.n. Evington, Houghton, Owston), *le Cornelandes* (f.n. Stoughton), Corn Park (f.n. Cold Overton), Old Corn Cl (f.n. King's Norton).

corner ME, 'a corner, a nook'. Common in f.ns.: Boney Corner, *Burnetts Corner* (Glooston), *Bull home corner* (Stockerston), *Church corner* (Great Glen), Corner Fd (Billesdon, Medbourne, Nevill Holt), Corner Mdw (Foxton), *Laune Corner* (Gumley), *Longcroft Corner* (Little Stretton), Pen Corner (Scraptoft), *Smiths Corner*, Spinney Corner, *Sulby Corner* (Husbands Bosworth), *Wigston corner* (Nevill Holt), Wood Corner (Knossington).

costard ME, 'a kind of apple of large size'. ?*Costard hill* (f.n. Knossington).

cot neut. (**cote** dat.sg., **cotu** nom.pl.); **cote** fem. (**cotan** dat.sg., nom.pl.) (**cotum** dat.pl.) OE; **cotes** (nom.pl.) ME; **cotch** ModEdial., 'a cottage, a hut, a shelter'. *Shirtecoat*; Cote Hill Fm, Cotton's Field Ho. *Boresworthe Cootes* (f.n. Husbands Bosworth), *Caldecotehil* (f.n. Lubenham), *Cotebridge Meadowe* (f.n. Wistow), *le Cotes* (f.n. Hallaton), *Cotes peice furlong* (f.n. Drayton), Cottam (f.n. Stoughton), ?Draycotts Cl (f.n. Blaston), Folkecatts (f.n. Hallaton, Medbourne, Slawston), *Harcote* (f.n. Houghton), *Knapcotes* (f.n. Billesdon), Lamb Coat (f.n. West Langton), Lambcot Hill (f.n. King's Norton), *Lambescoates* (f.n. Glooston), Rocott Spinney (f.n. Cold Overton), *Schortecotes* (f.n. Horninghold), *Schyrdaycotis* (f.n. Newton Harcourt), *underwytkotes* (f.n. Illston), *Welcotemor* (f.n. Kibworth Beauchamp); *Cotoneholme* (f.n. Nevill Holt), Cotton Cl (f.n. Wistow); *Cochcraft* (f.n. Cranoe), *le Cotch Leys* (f.n. Drayton).

cotage ME, 'a cottage, a hut, a shelter'. Brookside Cottage, The Cottage (Husbands Bosworth, Illston, Lubenham), Dean Cottage, Fearn Farm Cottages, Grange

Cottage, Kibworth Cottage, Lockwood Cottage, Manor Cottages, The Mount Cottage, Nether Cottages, Pasture Farm Cottage, *Stackley Cottage* (Stackley Ho., Great Glen), Station Cottages (Hallaton, West Langton), Stone Cottage, Thistley Close Cottages, Town End Cottage. Cottage Cl (f.n. Evington, Foxton, Hallaton, Knossington, Owston), Cottage Fd (f.n. Evington, Slawston), Cottage Holt (f.n. Illston), Cottage Pasture (f.n. Cold Overton), Cottage Piece (f.n. Saddington), Top Cottage (f.n. Noseley). Note the range of early cottages listed for Evington.

cotager eModE, 'one who lives in a cottage', used esp. of the labouring population of rural districts. Cottagers Cl (f.n. Evington, Laughton), *the Cottagers Pasture* (f.n. Laughton).

cottere OE, 'a cottar, a cottager'. Cotchers Cl (f.n. Knossington), the Cottiers Pasture (f.n. Lubenham), *the Cottyers Close* (f.n. Frisby, Scraptoft).

counsayl ME, 'consultation, deliberation'. ?Council Fd (f.n. Medbourne).

court ME, 'a large house, a manor house'. The Court, Nether Court Fm.

cover(t) ME, 'a covert, a shelter for game'. Covert Lane, Fox Cover, Gumley Covert, *Sheephorne Fox Cover* (Sheepthorns Spinney). Botany Bay Fox Cover (f.n. Billesdon), Cover Fd (f.n. Mowsley, Theddingworth), *Coverlees* (f.n. Hallaton), Foxcover Cl (f.n. Scraptoft), Fox Covert (f.n. Frisby), Mowsley Fox Cover (f.n. Mowsley), Next Fox Cover (f.n. Husbands Bosworth).

crabbe ME, 'a crab-apple, a crab-apple-tree'. ?Crab Homestead (f.n. Frisby), Crab Piece (f.n. East Langton).

crabtre ME, 'a crab-apple-tree'. Crabtree (f.n. Drayton, Gumley), *Crabtree Close* (f.n. Horninghold, Scraptoft), *Crabtree Dole* (f.n. Tur Langton), *Crabtree Slade* (f.n. Great Easton).

***craca** OE, **kráka** ON, **crake** ME, 'a crow, a raven'. Crackley (f.n. Smeeton Westerby).

cran, **cron** OE, 'a crane, a heron'. Cranhill Fm. ?*Cranesworth* (f.n. Great Bowden), *Cranmer* (f.n. Husbands Bosworth), *Cronsick* (f.n. Kibworth Harcourt).

cranuc OE, 'a crane'. ?Cranksland (f.n. Smeeton Westerby).

crāwe (**crāwena** gen.pl.) OE, 'a crow'. Cranoe; ?Crown Hills, Crow Spinney, Crow Wood. *Crathornehull* (f.n. Billesdon), *Crowethornehyll* (f.n. Great Bowden), Crow Hill (f.n. Billesdon, Medbourne), Crow Spinney (f.n Nevill Holt), Crowthorn (f.n. Little Bowden), *Crowthornis* (f.n. Burton Overy), Crow Trees (f.n. Stonton Wyville).

cræt OE, **carte** ME, 'a cart, a waggon'. *Cratehaw* (f.n. Great Easton), *Crathawe* (f.n. Nevill Holt).

***creig** PrW, 'a cliff, a rock, a steep hill'. *Creak Hill* (f.n. Stonton Wyville), Grick (f.n. Kibworth Beauchamp).

cresse OE, 'cress'. Creswick (f.n. Lubenham).

creyste ME, 'the crest of a hill, an elevated ridge'. Clint's Crest (f.n. Cold Overton).

crōc OE, 'a crook'. *the Crooke* (f.n. Saddington), *Crook haden* (f.n. Burton Overy), ?Crooks Acre (f.n. Smeeton Westerby).

crocc OE, 'a crock, an earthenware pot'. ?Crock's Fm, ?Croxfield Spinney. ?Crooks Acre (f.n. Smeeton Westerby).

croft OE, 'a small enclosed field, a small enclosure near a house'. Croft House Fm, Hillcroft Holt. Very freq. in f.ns.: esp. with pers.ns. and surns., e.g. *Garmundis croft* (Noseley), *Godmanescroft* (Goadby), *Herewardescroft* (Drayton), *Oswoldiscroft* (Great Easton), *Bissopescroft* (Billesdon), *Extonescroft*

(Medbourne), *Howbyescroft* (Drayton); with crops, e.g. *Barlicroft* (Knossington, Shangton), *Grescraft* (East Langton), *Lincroft* (Scraptoft), *Peascroft* (Kibworth Harcourt), *Ryecroft* (Blaston); with fruit-trees, e.g. *Applecroft* (Lubenham), *Payretree Croft* (Carlton Curlieu); with livestock, e.g. *Calvis croft* (Houghton), *Pecocroft'* (Billesdon); with village structures, e.g. Barnscroft (Great Bowden), *Cochcraft* (Cranoe), *le Kyrkekroft* (Billesdon); with an adj. of size or shape, e.g. *longecroft* (Foxton, Gumley, Little Stretton, Medbourne, *Prestgrave*), *Muclecroft* (Shangton), *shortcroftes* (Gumley); with an indicator of location, e.g. *the Abstrow Croft* (Lubenham), Harcraft (Blaston, Slawston, Smeeton Westerby), *le mersecroft* (Illston), *Vppewelcroft* (Stretton Magna), *North croft* (Smeeton Westerby), *Westcroftes* (Shangton); on occasion appears as a simplex, e.g. *Crafts* (Carlton Curlieu, Great Easton, Hallaton). Note *Lammas Croft* (Smeeton Westerby) and *Seyntmarecroft* (Husbands Bosworth).

croked ME, adj., 'crooked, twisted'. *The Crooked headland* (f.n. Houghton).

crop(p) OE, 'a mound, a swelling'. ?Crapshill (f.n. Great Easton).

cros late OE, ME, 'a cross'; difficult to distinguish from **cross** *infra* when acting as a qualifier. The Cross, Crossburrow Hill. *atte Crosse* (p) (Cold Overton, Great Easton, Medbourne, Nevill Holt), *Carleton crose* (Burton Overy), *Cranoe Cross* (Cranoe), *Crossegate* (f.n. Nevill Holt, Stockerston), ?Cross Gates (f.n. Slawston), Cross Hill (f.n. Carlton Curlieu), Dilcus (f.n. Kibworth Beauchamp), *harlscross* (Gumley), *Houghton cros*, *Moorecrosse*, *Swans Crosse* (Houghton), *Hulcros*, *Whitecross* (Mowsley), ?*Limekiln cross*, ?*Lime Pitt Cross*, *Stump Cross*, ?*Whetston Cross* (Hallaton), *Marston Cross furlong* (f.n. Hothorpe), *new crosse forde* (f.n. Knossington), *Thirneby Cros* (Stoughton), *Tymcrosse* (Great Bowden), *Vndurcrosse* (f.n. Noseley), *Whit Crose* (Kibworth Harcourt).

cross ME, adj., 'athwart, lying across, crosswise'; in some modern minor names, used of cross-roads. *Crose dyke* (f.n. Mowsley), *Cross bustandes hill*, *Crosse banland*, *Cross hille Meadow*, *Cross Woolfield* (f.ns. Gumley), ?*Crossegate* (f.n. Nevill Holt, Stockerston), *Crossegates* (f.n. East Langton), ?Cross Gates (f.n. Slawston), *the Crosse Hedges* (f.n. Great Glen), *the Crossways*, ?*Whetston Cross* (f.ns. Hallaton).

cross-road(s) ModE, 'a place where two roads cross'. Stockerston Cross Roads. An earlier style in Gartree Hundred was *cross-gates*, *v*. **cross**, **gata**.

crowne eModE, 'a rounded summit'. ?Crown Hills.

crumb OE, adj., 'crooked, twisted'. *Croumbehalfrodes* (f.n. Billesdon).

crundel OE, 'a chalk-pit, a quarry'. Cryndle Dyke (f.n. Kibworth Beauchamp).

***crȳde** OE (Angl), 'weeds'; poss. used topographically as 'that which thrusts out, a headland'. ?Crowd Hayes (f.n. Burton Overy).

cū OE, **cou** ME, 'a cow'. Common in modern f.ns., esp. in Cow Cl (Billesdon, Burton Overy, Carlton Curlieu, Evington etc.) and (*the*) *Cow Pasture* (Burton Overy, Cranoe, Glooston, Great Bowden etc.); Cow Common (f.n. Blaston), *Cowdams* (f.n. Hallaton), Cow Lair (f.n. Billesdon), Cowmoor Fd (Newton Harcourt), Cow Pen Cl (f.n. Glooston), *Cowpiece* (f.n. Evington). Only *Cousell* 1467 x 84 (f.n. Noseley) is an early instance.

cubb ME, 'a stall, a pen, a shed for cattle'. ?Club Fd (f.n. Great Glen), Cub Cl (f.n. Lubenham), Cub Mdw (f.n. Evington).

cūle OE, 'a hollow, a hole'. *le cowle* (f.n. Great Bowden).

cumb OE, 'a hollow, a valley'. the Coombs (f.n. Carlton Curlieu), the Coome Fd, *Lambcome*, Thorncombe, Wadcombe (f.ns. Laughton), *Coomes* (f.n. Great Bowden), *farcome hill*, *midlecome hill*, *rotcom* (f.ns. Gumley).

cundite eModE, 'a conduit, an aqueduct'. Conduit Spinney. Cunder Hill, Little Cunder (f.ns. Great Easton), *the Cundite Close* (f.n. Noseley).

cuntesse OFr, ME, 'a countess'. *Countasfurlong'* (f.n. Stoughton).

cursed, **curst** ME, ppl.adj., 'accursed, detestable'. *Curst Roods* (f.n. Theddingworth).

cutel OE, ME, 'an artificial water-channel'. ?*Cuthill* (f.n. Husbands Bosworth).

cutte ME, 'a cut, a water-channel'. ?*Cuthill* (f.n. Husbands Bosworth), ?*Cuttisholme* (f.n. Goadby, Hallaton), Cutts Fd (f.n. Knossington).

cutting ME, 'a piece cut off'. *Cuttings Close* (f.n. Kibworth Beauchamp).

cwēad OE, 'dirt, mud'. Quisick Fd (f.n. Fleckney).

cwēn OE, 'a queen'. ?*Quen furlonge* (f.n. Saddington).

cwene OE, 'a woman'. ?*Quen furlonge* (f.n. Saddington).

cyln OE (Angl), 'a kiln'. Kill Hill, *Kylne close* (f.ns. Theddingworth), Kiln Fd (f.n. Little Stretton), Kiln Mdw (f.n. Evington), *le kylneyerde* (f.n. Great Bowden, Houghton, Little Stretton).

cyning OE, 'a king'. Kingster (f.n. Smeeton Westerby), *Kingstocke Bridge* (f.n. Kibworth Beauchamp), *v.* **king**.

dag ME, sb. 'dew, moisture', vb., 'to clog with dirt, to bemire'. Dag Lane. *Daglane* (Market Harborough).

dāl OE, **dole** ME, 'a share, a portion; a share in a common field'. Freq. in f.ns.: with a pers.n. or surn., e.g. *Finsdole* (Fleckney), *claridole* (Gumley), *Pagedole* (Saddington), *Speeds Dole* (Kibworth Beauchamp); with indicators of ownership other than the preceding, e.g. *Ladydole* (Fleckney), *the Hall doole* (Husbands Bosworth), *the Pasonage Dole* (Tur Langton), *the Parsons tippitt dole* (Glooston); with indicators of shape, size, e.g. *Broddole* (Billesdon, Great Bowden, Nevill Holt), *chiscake dowle* (Glooston), *Longe doles* (Billesdon, Glooston), *the 9 foot dole* (Stonton Wyville); with minor locational names prefixed, e.g. *cocke* doale (East Langton), *Dikedole* (Billesdon), *Pynsladdol* (Mowsley); with various flora, e.g. *Berry doles* (Laughton), *Crabtree Dole* (Tur Langton), *netle dole* (Gumley) and recurring names with *whin* 'whin, gorse', as *whinell dole*, *Windoles peece* (Husbands Bosworth), *Wynnedoole* (Foxton, Houghton).

dalr ON, 'a valley'; in later spellings, very difficult to distinguish from **deill** 'a share, a portion of land'. ?The Dales, Debdale Lane (Foxton, Gumley). Freq. in f.ns.: repeated are Debdale (Evington), *Depedale* (Drayton, Great Glen), *Flaxdale* (Great Easton, Great Glen), *Langdale* (Billesdon, Goadby, Hallaton), *Little dale* (Billesdon, Burton Overy, Hallaton), Marsdale (Frisby, Medbourne).

damme ME, 'a dam', usually created either for use at mills or for the watering of farm livestock. Damside Spinney, Dam's Spinney. *Cowdams* (f.n. Hallaton, Owston), Dams (f.n. Galby, Saddington, Stoughton, Wistow), *Damfurlonge*, *Osterdame* (f.ns. Theddingworth), *Dam piece* (f.n. Newbold), Dams Hadland, *Saddington Dammes* (f.ns. Kibworth Beauchamp), *holdeda'* (f.n. Illston), *Mill Dam* (f.n. Burton Overy, Noseley, Smeeton Westerby).

daube ME, 'clay or mud mixed with stubble or chaff, used with laths or wattle to form the walls of humble dwellings'. Dobb Hall.

dæg OE, 'a day'. ?*Shirtecoat*. ?*Schyrdaycotis* (f.n. Newton Harcourt), ?*Shortecotes* (f.n. Horninghold).

dæl[1] OE, 'a hollow, a valley'. ?Barnsdale, Winkadale. ?*Brokelesdale* (f.n. Great Easton), *Dodemeresdale* (f.n. Drayton, Medbourne, Nevill Holt), ?*Wencelawedale* (f.n. Medbourne).

dēad OE, adj., 'dead'; often used in p.ns. with reference to a site of violent death or to the discovery of human bones; but also may indicate infertile moorland. *Dedechild* (f.n. Mowsley), *Dedelane* (f.n. Owston), *Dedemor* (f.n. Blaston, Frisby, Horninghold, Husbands Bosworth, Medbourne), Dodmoor (f.n. Little Bowden, Lubenham), *St Leighs Dodmoor* (f.n. Theddingworth).

dēaw OE, 'dew'. *Duehooke* (f.n Great Bowden).

decoy ModE, 'a pond into which wild fowl are lured for capture'. Decoy (f.n. Galby).

dede-man ME, 'a dead man, a corpse'. *Deadman* (f.n. Great Glen, Gumley, Little Stretton, Laughton, Mowsley), Deadmans Cl (f.n. Carlton Curlieu), *Deadmans grave* (f.n. Hallaton), *Mousley deadman* (f.n. Laughton).

deierie ME, 'a dairy'. (The) Dairy Cl (f.n. Billesdon, Kibworth Beauchamp), Dairy Ground (f.n. Burton Overy), Dairy Mdw (f.n. Billesdon, Mowsley).

deill ON, 'a share, a portion of land'; in later spellings, very difficult to distinguish from **dalr** 'a valley', but pl. forms with *-dales* are sometimes indicators of *deill*. ?The Dales, ?Millerdale. *Bandale*, *Hoodalle*, *Netherholmdale* (f.ns. Stretton Magna), *Chaukdalsyke* (f.n. Goadby), ?Dale Fd (f.n. Carlton Curlieu), *dribdall*, Langdall (f.ns. Fleckney), *Edwardsdale*, ?*Flaxedale*, ?*Steyndale*, ?*Stonnydale* (f.ns. Great Glen), ?*Flaxdale(s)*, ?*Hodalegate* (f.ns. Great Easton), ?*Fouldale*, ?*Hwerluedale*, ?*Hyewulledale*, ?*Lituldalhull*, ?Long Dale (f.ns. Billesdon), ?*Lituldale*, ?*Ortondale*, ?*Oxdall'* (f.ns. Burton Overy).

delf OE, 'a digging, a pit, a quarry'. ?Dilcus furlong (f.n. Kibworth Beauchamp).

demming ME, 'a dam'. ?Dimigate (f.n. Great Bowden).

dene-hole ModE, 'a cylindrical shaft, sunk down to a chalk stratum and widening at the base'; a type early attributed to the Danes. *deane hole* (f.n. Husbands Bosworth).

denu OE, 'a valley'. Deane Bank Fm. Burden Wall (f.n. Laughton), ?*Dene peice*, *Lowsden* (f.ns. Frisby), *the Deyne* (f.n. Mowsley), *Thevdenes* (f.n. Gumley).

dēop OE, adj., 'deep'. Debdale Lane (Foxton, Gumley). Debdale (f.n. Evington), *Depdale* (f.n. Drayton, Great Glen).

derne OE, adj., 'hidden, obscure'. *Derneforde* (f.n. Great Easton), Derne Slade (f.n. Laughton).

dīc OE, 'a ditch'. *Allings dich* (f.n. Husbands Bosworth), Ditch End Cl (f.n. Burton Overy), *Whold ditches* (f.n. Great Bowden).

dík ON, 'a ditch'; the el. varies with OE **dīc** in some f.ns. *Billdyke* (f.n. Hallaton), Black Dyke Wood, *East Field dyke*, *Estbedyk*, *hill leas dyke*, Meadow Dyke (f.ns. Great Easton), *Cheredik*, *Dikedole*, *le Dikes*, Furzedike Cl, Long Dyke (f.ns. Billesdon), *dickes* (f.ns Glooston), *Dykus* (f.n. Burton Overy), *Hendicke* (f.n. Saddington), *Longdikes* (f.n. Great Glen), *Scherdyk* (f.n. Husbands Bosworth), *Sheep Dyke* (f.n. Horninghold), *Tagyllisdyke*, *Whildik* (f.ns. Great Bowden), *Weyrdic* (f.n. Illston), *Willardesdik'* (f.n. Drayton).

dile OE, 'dill'; ModEdial. **dill** 'vetch'. Dileas (f.n. Smeeton Westerby).

dimming ME, vbl.sb., 'the action of growing dim'. ?Dimigate (f.n. Great Bowden).

dingle ME, 'a deep hollow; a deep dell'. The Dingles (f.n. Rolleston).

dip ModE, 'a hollow or depression'. the Dip Fd (f.n. Medbourne).

docce OE, 'a dock'; poss. also 'a water-lily' when combined with words denoting water. *le Dockaker* (f.n. East Langton, Hallaton, Medbourne), Dock Cl (f.n. Blaston), Dockey Cl (f.n. Cold Overton, Hallaton), *Dokholm* (f.n. Drayton, Houghton).

doctour ME, 'a medical practitioner'. Doctors Cl (f.n. Great Easton, Nevill Holt, Rolleston, West Langton).

dodde ME, 'the rounded summit of a hill'. ?*Dodsicke* (f.n. Saddinton).

dogga late OE, **dogge** ME, 'a dog'. Dog Bank (f.n. Little Bowden).

dogge-tree eModE, 'the Common Dogwood or Wild Cornel'; sometimes applied to the Spindle-tree and the Elder. *Dogtree* (f.n. Houghton).

doke ModEdial., 'a hollow, a depression'. *banland doake*, Doak Cl, *Freemans doake*, *the Open Doke* (f.ns. Gumley).

dove-cot(e) ME, 'a dove-cote'. Dovecot or Orchard Cl (f.n. Scraptoft), Dovecote Cl (f.n. Gumley, Horninghold, Houghton, Illston, Laughton, Wistow), Dove Cote Fd (f.n. Saddington).

dove-hous ME, 'a dove-cote'. Dovehouse Cl (f.n. Husbands Bosworth, Shangton).

drāf OE, 'a herd, a drove; a drove-way'. Drove Cl (f.n. Kibworth Beauchamp).

drain ModE, 'a drain'. Marsdale Drain Cl (f.n. Medbourne).

drake ME, 'the male of the duck'. ?*Drake aker* (f.n. Nevill Holt).

draught ME, 'the action of dragging or pulling, esp. of a vehicle'. ?*the drawghtes* (f.n. Great Easton).

draught eModE, 'a cesspool, a sewer'. ?*the drawghtes* (f.n. Great Easton).

dræg OE (Angl), 'a drag, a portage'. Drayton. ?Draycotts Cl (f.n. Blaston).

drib ModE, 'a drop, a driblet; something very small'. ?*Dribdall* (f.n. Fleckney).

drift ModE, 'a track along which cattle are driven'. Hog Lane (earlier *Hogsdrift Way*). Drift Cl, *Hoggs holme drift* (f.ns. Hallaton), *the drift way* (f.n. Cranoe).

drovere ME, 'a man who drives herds of cattle or sheep, esp. to distant markets'. ?*Drovers Close* (f.n. Stonton Wyville).

drȳge OE, adj., 'dry, dried up; well-drained'. *Dryelond* (f.n. Slawston), *Drygwell* (f.n. Houghton), *Dry Hill Close* (f.n. Newbold), Dry-hills (f.n. Hallaton).

duble ME, adj., 'double'. *the Double Hedge* (f.n. King's Norton), Double Hut Cl (f.n. Saddington), Double Mdw (f.n. Great Glen).

dūce OE, 'a duck'. *Duck Meadow* (f.n. Evington).

dūfe OE, **dúfa** ON, 'a dove'; prob. also 'a pigeon'. ?*Doveland* (f.n. Thurnby).

dūn OE, 'a tract of hill country, an upland expanse; upland pasture'. Billesdon, Great ~, Little Bowden; Crown Hills (earlier *Crowdon*), Gallow Hill (earlier *Calowdon*). Bagbeare Down, Higher Down, Homes Down (f.ns. Billesdon), ?*Bowdon londe* (f.n. Drayton), *Duninge* (f.n. Great Glen), ?Dunslade (f.n. Little Bowden), ?*Dunwellefurlong* (f.n. Theddingworth).

dūne late OE, adv, 'down, below'. ?*Dunwellefurlong* (f.n. Theddingworth).

dunn OE, adj, 'dun, dull brown'. ?Dunslade (f.n. Little Bowden).

duru OE, 'a door, a gate; a gap'. *Mill Door Furlong* (f.n. Glooston), *the mill dore*, *watermill doore* (f.ns. Husband Bosworth).

dyncge OE, 'manured land'. Dungeon, Dungeon Plantation (f.ns. Blaston).

ēa OE, 'a river, a stream'. Eye Brook. *Efilde*, *Hachey* (f.ns. Great Bowden), ?*Scurvey* (f.n. Noseley).

eahta OE, num., 'eight'. Eight Acre Mdw (f.n. Theddingworth).
ēa-land OE, 'land by water or by a river'. The Islands.
***ēaren** OE, adj., 'gravelly'. *Arnaws* (f.n. Billesdon).
ears OE, 'an arse, a buttock', transferred topographically to 'a rounded hill'; difficult to distinguish from ***herse** 'a top, a hill-top'. ?Barearse (f.n. Drayton, Hallaton, Medbourne), ?*Barearse hill* (f.n. Goadby), ?*Broad arse* (f.n. Kibworth Beauchamp), ?*Wyndeshers* (f.n. Billesdon).
ēast OE, adj., 'eastern, east'. East Langton, Great Easton. Common in f.ns.: e.g. East Cl, *the East feild*, East Hill, *le Estbreche*, *Estbryge*, *Estwelle* (f.ns. Billesdon), *East Wells*, *Estmerishauedlond* (f.ns. Great Easton), *le Estlonge* (f.n. Great Bowden).
ēastan OE, adv., 'east, east of', used in p.ns. elliptically, '(place) east of'. *Astenhill* (f.n. Stoughton), ?*Estbedyk* (f.n. Great Easton).
***ēastor** OE, adj., 'eastern'. *Osterdame* (f.n. Theddingworth).
***ēcels** OE (Angl), 'an addition, land added to an estate'. *le Echel'* (f.n. Nevill Holt).
ecg OE, 'an edge; the edge of a hill, an escarpment'. *Buruseyge* (f.n. Noseley).
edisc OE, 'an enclosure, an enclosed park'; difficult to distinguish from ***etisc** 'a plot of pasture-land'. ?*the double hedge* (f.n. King's Norton), ?Green Hedges (f.n. Evington), ?Smock Hedges (f.n. Hallaton), ?*Sweetehedge Feilde* (f.n. Stockerston), ?Three Hedges (f.n. Husbands Bosworth).
ēg OE (Angl), 'an island, a piece of raised ground in wetlands, land partly surrounded by water'. Fleckney. ?*Scurvey* (f.n. Noseley), ?*Stoney* (f.n. Moseley).
elbowe ME, 'an elbow'; topographically 'a sharp bend'. *Elbowes* (f.n. Knossinton), Elbow Fd (f.n. Foxton), *Elbow leyes* (f.n. Bushby, Little Bowden), Elbow Mdw (f.n. Welham).
ellern OE, 'an elder-tree'. *eldern stubb* (f.n. Knossington), *Elderstubb* (f.n. Husbands Bosworth, King's Norton, Mowsley), *elrenestub* (f.n. Frisby, Saddington), *heldyrstubb* (f.n. Smeeton Westerby).
elm OE, 'an elm-tree'. Elms Fm. Elm Cl (f.n. Glooston), Elms Lane (f.n. Burton Overy), Elm Spinney (f.n. West Langton).
enclosure ModE, 'land surrounded by a fence or marked off by a boundary'. *the Old Enclosure* (f.n. Cranoe, Great Glen), *Wistow Enclosure* (f.n. Kibworth Beauchamp).
ende OE, 'the end of something', 'the end of an estate, a district or quarter of a township', *v.* **lane-ende**. Knight's End, North End, Scotland End, Town End Cottage. Freq. in f.ns.: e.g. *dribdall end* (Fleckney), *Dunningges end*, *Kergate end*, *the Steeple end* (Great Glen), *hillesend'*, *horstonsikenethirhende* (Evington), *moares yeardes ende*, *short heggende* (Glooston), *Nook End* (Cranoe), *le West Ende* (Great Bowden); recurring in the compound *town*(*s*)*end* (with various spellings in Cranoe, East Langton, Evington, Foxton, Galby, Goadby, Glooston, Great Glen, Gumley, Hallaton, Houghton, Kibworth Beauchamp, Laughton, Nevill Holt, Owston, West Langton).
ened OE, 'a duck'. *Ender sike* (f.n. King's Norton), *enedesike* (f.n. Frisby).
eng ON, 'a meadow, a pasture'. *enland* (f.n. Husbands Bosworth), ?Foalings (f.n. Evington), *Gosinges*, *Stainingges*, *Wronghenges* (f.ns. Billesdon), *Hengebek* (f.n. Shangton), *Houperyng*, *tirsinges* (f.ns. Nevill Holt), *Little Inn*, *Westing* (f.ns. Newton Harcourt), Old England (f.n. Welham).
eorl OE, 'a nobleman'. ?*harlscross* (f.n. Gumley).

eorð-burh OE, 'an earthwork, a fortification built of earth'. ?*the Arbour* (f.n. Burton Overy).

eorðe OE, 'earth, soil, ground; an animal's hole or lair in the earth'. Carlton Clump (?*Carlton Earth*). *Potterisherþe* (f.n. Medbourne).

eorð-hnutu OE, 'a pignut'. *arnet* hill (f.n. Gumley), *Erdenothull* (f.n. Billesdon).

eowestre OE, 'a sheep fold'. *Yesterdoles* (f.n. Houghton).

erber, **herber** OFr, ME, 'a grass-covered piece of ground; a garden'. ?*the Arbour* (f.n. Burton Overy).

ermitage OFr, ME, **hermitage** ME, 'a hermitage'. The Hermitage. The Hermitage (f.n. Hallaton).

erð OE, 'ploughed land'. Carlton Clump (?*Carlton Earth*).

eski ON, 'a place growing with ash-trees'. ?*Esfeld* (f.n. Slawston).

ēðe OE, 'waste land'. *Etheherne* (f.n. Noseley), *Ethwyn* (f.n. Knossington).

***etisc** OE, 'a plot of pasture land'; difficult to distinguish from **edisc** *supra*. ?*the double hedge* (f.n. King's Norton), ?Green Hedges (f.n. Evington), ?Smock Hedges (f.n. Hallaton), ?*Sweetehedge Feilde* (f.n. Stockerston), Three Hedges (f.n. Husbands Bosworth).

-ette OFr, diminutive suffix denoting 'little', added to p.ns. in ME. ?*le Patched close* (f.n. Great Bowden).

face ModE, 'a face'; used topographically of the front as opposed to the flanks of a hill. The Face of the Hill (f.n. Cold Overton)

faire ME, 'a periodical gathering of buyers and sellers at a place and time ordained by custom, a fair'. Fair Lawn. Cow Fair Leys (f.n. Market Harborough), *the Horse Fair* (f.n. Hallaton).

fald OE, 'a fold, a small enclosure for animals'. Bullsholme Fould (f.n. Lubenham), Fold Yard (f.n. Great Glen).

falh OE (Angl), 'land broken up for cultivation'; later 'fallow land'. Fallow Cl (f.n. Illston, Slawston), Fallow Fd (f.n. Cranoe, West Langton).

(ge)fall OE (Angl), 'a falling, a place where something falls; a fellingof trees'. *le Falshalfrodes* (f.n. Billesdon).

fæsten OE, 'a stronghold'. ?Stockerston.

fætt OE, adj., 'fat, rich'. *fatt banland* (f.n. Gumley), *the Fatt Close* (f.n. Owston).

fearn OE, 'ferns; a ferny place'. Fearn Fm. *blackferne* (f.n. Gumley), *Farnhill* (f.n. Fleckney, Kibworth Harcourt, Scraptoft), the Fennyland Cl, Fern Cl (f.ns. Gumley), Fern Leys (f.n. Little Bowden), *Long Fern* (f.n. Bringhurst).

fearnig OE, adj., 'ferny, growing with ferns'. the Fennyland Cl (f.n. Gumley), Ferny Lees (f.n. Houghton)

feather-bed ModE, sb., adj., 'a featherbed; a peat-bog or spongy ground; something soft and yielding'. Featherbed Lane. Featherbed Lane (f.n.Evington).

feeder ModE, 'a watercourse which supplies a canal or reservoir'. Feeder Cl (f.n. Smeeton Westerby).

feeding ModE, vbl.sb., ppl.adj.; for agriculture, 'feeding ground, pasturage'. Feeding Cl (f.n. Fleckney).

feld OE, 'open country', **feld(e)** ME, 'land for pasture or cultivation; a common or great open-field of a township', **field** ModE, 'an enclosed or fenced-in plot of land'. Marefield; Gallow Field, Northfields, Southfield Lodge, Westfield. Of Gartree Hundred's 62 townships, 42 have the names of their three great open-fields surviving in records and 4 have the names of two fields surviving. Only

Carlton Curlieu, Cold Overton, Illston, Little Bowden, Marefield, Owston, Newbold, Scraptoft, Welham and West Langton have no open-field names recorded. Billesdon, Burton Overy, Goadby, Husbands Bosworth, Kibworth Harcourt, Little Bowden, Shangton and Tur Langton had fields which were designated by combinations of the simple directional adjectives *north*, *south*, *east* and *west*. Blaston, Great Easton and Nevill Holt each had two great fields with names which were formed by such directional adjectives plus a topographically named third. There are 7 townships which had a Middle Fd; 18 had a Mill Fd. Otherwise the great open-fields were in general named from topographical features, as e.g. *Burrowefilde* (with various spellings in Cranoe, Foxton, Glooston), Besicke, *Swarboroough* (Mowsley), Coome (Laughton), Debdale (Gumley), Fearn, *Smallwood* (Hallaton), *Gosthill*, *Notbernehill*, *Santleys* (Theddingworth), Hobrook, Marr, Quisick (Fleckney). Changes in the names of a township's open-fields may or may not indicate the reorganization of the township's arable, but such changes of names or alternative names for great fields are evidenced in Burton Overy, East Langton, Foxton, Goadby, Great Bowden, Great Glen, Kibworth Beauchamp, King's Norton, Newton Harcourt, Shangton, Smeeton Westerby, Stockerston, Stonton Wyville, Stretton Magna and Theddingworth. *Aldefeld* (1075 x 1108, Evington) is prob. evidence for a very early open-field. Note also the *Myngde Feilde* (i.e. 'mingled'), shared by the townships of Little Stretton and Stretton Magna.

felging OE (Angl), 'a piece of ploughed or fallow land'. *Felinnges* (f.n. Billesdon), *le fallyngbrynk* (f.n. Medbourne)

fenn OE, 'a fen, a marsh, marshland'. Fen Mdw (f.n. Lubenham).

feor OE, **fur**(**re**) ME, **fur** ModEdial., **far** ModE, adj., 'far'. Fargate Fm. Common in f.ns.: e.g. Far Cl (Cranoe, Great Easton, Husbands Bosworth, Medbourne, Illston etc.), Far Mdw (Billesdon, Carlton Curlieu, Frisby, Medbourne etc.), *Far Cockloe*, *Furr Willey* (Husbands Bosworth), *farcome hill*, *Smeeton furhill* (Gumley), *fargatys* (Great Bowden), *Farre Bandlands*, *the farre slade* (Great Glen).

fēorðung, **fēorðing** OE, 'a fourth part, a quarter'; in later f.ns. it may denote either a measure of land or rental of a farthing. Farthings (f.n. Burton Overy).

fēower OE, num., 'four'. *Four Cocks* (f.n. Kibworth Beauchamp).

ferd OE (Angl), 'an army, a troop'; found on occasion in old-road names. *le ferdgate* (f.n. Shangton).

ferme OFr, ME, 'rent', eModE, 'land held on lease, an agricultural tenement, a farm'. Common in modern minor p.ns. In earlier instances, usually prefixed by a surn., e.g. *Beaumonds Farme* (King's Norton), *Richard Chamberlaines farm* (Newton Harcourt), *Freemans Farm* (Husbands Bosworth); *New Farm* (Theddingworth), *the neather farme* (Knossington). Note the range of farms dated 1708 (18) listed for Evington. F.ns. include Farm Cl (Husbands Bosworth), *the Farme Part* (Hallaton), *le ferme place* (Houghton).

feðer OE, **fjǫðr** ON, 'a feather'. *le fetheres* (f.n. Slawston).

fīf OE, num., 'five'. *Fyuerodesty* (f.n. Bringhurst).

***filden**, **felden** OE, adj., 'pertaining to open country'. *the Fielding Ground* (f.n. Kibworth Beauchamp).

finc OE, 'a finch'. *Finch Foord* (f.n. Kibworth Beauchamp).

finger-post ModE, 'a guide-post, a post with one or more arms, often terminating in the shape of a finger, set up at a road-junction to indicate direction, destination and distance'. Fingerpost (f.n. Stoughton).

fisc-pōl OE, 'a fish-pond'. *Fishpoole close* (f.n. Kibworth Harcourt).

fisshe-ponde ME, 'a fish-pond'. Fishpond Spinney. the Fish Pond (f.n. Gumley), Fish-pond Plantation (f.n. Great Glen), Fishponds (f.n. Burton Overy, Saddington), Fishponds Spinney (f.n. Galby).

fixene ME, **fixen** eModE, **vixen** ModE, 'a she-fox'. ?*Foxennoles* (f.n. King's Norton).

flagge ME, 'the flag-iris; a reed or rush; a place where reeds grow'. *Flagdadmore* (f.n. Theddingworth).

flaggi ME, adj., 'growing with reeds or rushes'. *Flaggy Hookes* (f.n. Little Stretton).

flak ME, 'a turf'. *Flakmydo* (f.n. Stoughton).

flask ODan, 'swampy grassland'. ?*Flax leys* (f.n. Frisby), ?*Flax Medow* (f.n. Kibworth Harcourt).

flasshe ME, 'flooded grassland; a sheet of shallow water'. *Flascemore* (f.n. Great Easton).

flat ON, 'a piece of level ground'. The Flats. *the Flatt* (f.n. Little Stretton), Flats (f.n. Rolleston), *the Gravell Pitts Flatt* (f.n. Husbands Bosworth), The Little Flat, The Long Flat (f.ns. Saddington)

flatr ON, **flat(te)** ME, adj., 'flat, level'. Flat Cl (f.n. Evington, Glooston, Hallaton, Illston), Flathaws (f.n. Medbourne, Slawston), Flat Mdw (f.n. Foxton, Galby, Illston, Mowsley, Saddington), Flat Tamborough (f.n. Frisby).

flaxe OE, 'a wooden vessel for liquids'. ?Flaxwell (f.n. Smeeton Westerby), ?*Flaxwell sicke* (f.n. Husbands Bosworth).

fleax OE, **flax** ME, 'flax'. Flax Cl (f.n. Goadby), *Flaxdale* (f.n. Great Easton, Great Glen), *Flaxgate* (f.n. Tur Langton), *Flaxlands* (f.n. Burton Overy, Frisby, Hothorpe, Little Bowden, Medbourne, Mowsley, Nevill Holt, Newton Harcourt, Noseley), *Flaxlandsyke* (f.n. Billesdon), ?*Flax leys* (f.n. Frisby), ?*Flax Medow* (f.n. Kibworth Harcourt), ?Flaxwell (f.n. Smeeton Westerby), ?*Flaxwell sicke* (f.n. Husbands Bosworth).

fleca OE, 'a hurdle'. ?Fleckney.

flēot OE, **fljót** ON, 'a small stream, a rivulet'. Fleet Mdw (f.n. Smeeton Westerby).

flessh-shamel ME, 'a butcher's shambles, a stall for the sale of meat'. *the Flesh Shambles* (Hallaton), *Le Fleyschamelis* (Market Harborough).

flint OE, 'flint'. *Flint Acre* (f.n. Houghton).

flinti ME, adj., 'flinty, full of flint-stones'. *Flynty Acre* (f.n. Houghton).

(ge)flit OE, 'strife, dispute', used in p.ns. of land in dispute. *Flitlond'* (f.n. Billesdon, Great Easton).

fliten OE, ppl.adj., 'disputed'. *Flitenewong* (f.n. Billesdon), ?*the Flitting meres* (f.n. Kibworth Beauchamp).

flōd OE, 'a flow of water'. Two and Five Flood Acres (f.n. Great Easton).

flōr OE, 'a floor, a pavement'; used in later f.ns. to allude to land dedicated to the upkeep of the parish church flooring. *the Church Flore* (f.n. East Langton).

flot[1] OE, 'deep flood water'. ?Float Mdw (f.n. Billesdon).

flǫt[2] ON, 'a piece of flat ground'. ?Float Mdw (f.n. Billesdon).

flytting ME, ppl.adj., 'shifting, unstable'. ?*the flitting meres* (f.n. Kibworth Harcourt).

foaling, ModE, vbl.sb., 'the bringing forth of a foal'. ?Foalings (f.n. Evington).

fola OE, 'a foal'. ?Foalings (f.n. Evington), *Folkatmedowe* (f.n. Hallaton), Folkecatts (f.n. Medbourne), *folkotesyke* (f.n. Slawston).

folie ME, 'a foolish enterprise; an extravagant or foolish building'; in f.ns. sometimes used of a small plantation. The Folly (f.n. Great Bowden, West Langton), Folly Cl, Folly Pond (f.ns. Great Bowden), Folly Orchard, Serjeant's Folly (f.ns. Welham), Freemans Folly (f.n. Husbands Bosworth).

foot-road ModE, 'a footpath'. Foot Road Cl (f.n. Burton Overy, Illston).

ford OE, 'a ford'. Green Ford. Freq. in f.ns.: common are locations, either minor local features, e.g. *Colle Brigg foorde* (Kibworth Harcourt), *Holoforth* (Burton Overy), *new cross forde* (Knossington) or neighbouring townships, e.g. *Galbyforth* (Houghton), *Neutoneforthe* (Billesdon); the appearance of the ford may feature, e.g. *Derneforde* (Great Easton), *fulforth* (Great Bowden), *Stonyforth* (Goadby, Houghton, Illston), *Sytford* (Nevill Holt); or an indication of the use of the ford by livestock, e.g. *Bullokesforth* (Houghton), *Hogges Foarde* (Great Bowden), *Nogges forde* (Burton Overy). Spellings in *-forth*(*e*) (arising from late ME *-rd* > *-rth* in unstressed syllables which occur only in the Danelaw and may be due to Scand influence) represent one third of surviving forms in Gartree Hundred.

fore OE, prep., 'in front of, before'; elliptically '(land, place, thing) in front of, lying or standing before something'. Fore of Life (f.n. Billesdon), *forewodes* (f.n. Great Easton), Four Ends (f.n. Evington).

forest OFr, ME, 'a large tract of woodland or of hunting country; a forest'. Forrest Cl (f.n. Knossington).

***forð-ēg** OE, 'an island in marshland'. Forty Cl (f.n. Owston).

fōt OE, 'a foot'; used esp. of land at the foot of a hill. Barfoot Lodge. *Barefoot Slade* (f.n. Frisby), *Barfoote* (f.n. Mowsley, Owston), *The Footes* (f.n. Theddingworth), *Langtongate foote* (f.n. Great Bowden), *Quysle foote* (f.n. Tur Langton), *Sandclyf fotte* (f.n. Mowsley), Sharfoot Mdw (f.n. Husbands Bosworth), *the Short meddow foote* (f.n. Hothorpe).

fote-brydge eMod E, 'a bridge for foot-passengers'. *Blaston Foot Bridge*, Small Footbridge Cl (f.ns. Hallaton), Gibbin's Footbridge Cl (f.n. Blaston).

fote-waye ModE, 'a footpath'. *Blaston Footway* (f.n. Hallaton), Hallaton Foot Way, Slawston Foot Way (f.ns. Cranoe), Stonton Foot Way (f.n. Glooston).

fox OE, 'a fox'. Foxton. Foxborough (f.n. Foxton), Fox Cover (f.n. Billesdon, Scraptoft), Fox Covert (f.n. Frisby), Fox Hill, *foxwellys* (f.ns. Illston), Foxhills, Next Fox Cover (f.ns. Husbands Bosworth).

fox-hol OE, 'a fox-hole, a fox's earth'. Foxholes, Foxhole Spinney. ?Foxhills (f.n. Husbands Bosworth), *Foxholes* (f.n. Burton Overy, Frisby, Great Easton, King's Norton, Knossington, Medbourne, Welham).

freht OE, 'augury, divination'. ?*Fredwell* (f.n. Gumley), ?*Frewell* (f.n. Hallaton).

frēo OE, sb., 'a woman, a lady'. ?*Frewell* (f.n. Hallaton).

frēo OE, adj., 'free'. ?*Frewell* (f.n. Hallaton).

Frīgedæg OE, 'Friday'. *the shorte fridayes* (f.n. Glooston).

Frīsa, **Frēsa** OE, 'a Frisian'. Frisby.

frogga OE, 'a frog'. *Froglane* (f.n. Great Easton).

front ME, 'the side of something which is seen first'. *Breyclyffront* (f.n. Billesdon), The Front (f.n. Fleckney).

front ME, adj., 'situated at the front'. Front Fd (f.n. Fleckney, Nevill Holt, Shangton, Welham), *le Frontgore*, Front Mdw (f.ns. Billesdon).

fūl OE, adj., 'foul, filthy, dirty'. *Fouldale* (f.ns. Billesdon), *fulforth* (f.n. Great Bowden), *Fullhill* (f.n. Great Glen), *fullpit* (f.n. Fleckney, Husbands Bosworth), *Fullwell* (f.n. Billesdon, Blaston, Burton Overy, Great Bowden, Hallaton), *Fulwelhyl* (f.n. Illston), *Fulsicke* (f.n. Evington, Great Glen, Gumley, Hallaton, King's Norton), *fulskyll* (f.n. Frisby).

furh OE, 'a furrow, a trench'; in ME, also used of 'a piece of arable land'. Broad Furrows (f.n. Glooston, Hothorpe), *Furrow Hill* (f.n. Houghton), *Holefurew* (f.n. Drayton), Mill Furrows (f.n. Slawston), *Thwertforowes* (f.n. Stoughton), *the Waterfurrowes* (f.n. with various spellings in Billesdon, Burton Overy, Fleckney, Great Easton, Great Glen, Houghton, Husbands Bosworth, Illston, Laughton, Little Bowden, Mowsley, Owston, Stoughton, Tur Langton).

furlang OE, 'the length of a furrow, a furlong, a piece of land the length of a furrow (esp. in a great open-field)'; in ME, 'a division of a great open-field cultivated as a unit'. Very freq. in f.ns., e.g. *Carland forlong*, *Catts furlong*, *Clenfurlong*, *Dean hole forlong*, *Dodspooll fourlong*, *Hawards forlonge*, *Redbrochforlang*, *Tafts forlong* etc. Husbands Bosworth), *little dale furlong*, *Hirnefulongis*, *Woldfurlonges*, *ynnefurlong* etc. (Billesdon). Many of the 'field-names' in ME sources are furlong-names.

furðra OE, adj., 'more distant'. *Further Bandlands* (f.n. Great Glen), Further Mdw (f.n. Fleckney).

fyrs OE, 'furze'. Furze Hill. *Cote furrs Peeces*, *Tillies furres* (f.ns. Husbands Bosworth), Forsell, *Furzedike Cl*, Spells Furze (f.ns. Billesdon), Furze Cl (f.n. Smeeton Westerby, Welham), Furze Hill (f.n. Cold Overton, Stonton Wyville, Welham).

***fyrsig** OE, adj., 'growing with furze'. Furry Cl (f.n. Gumley, King's Norton), Furry Merrible (f.n. Great Easton, Stockerston), Furzy Cl (f.n. Nevill Holt, Shangton, Stretton Magna).

gafeluc OE, 'a fork'; topographically, may be used of a stream-fork or of two selions joining at an angle. *Ouergyfloke* (f.n. Great Bowden).

gagel OE, **gaule** ME, 'gale, bog-mytle'. *Gaulond'* (f.n. Billesdon).

galg-trēow OE, **gálga-tré** ON, 'a gallows-tree, a gallows'. Gallow Tree (f.n. Stoughton), Gallow Tree Cl (f.n. Evington), *Galutresike* (f.n. Billesdon).

***gall** OScand, 'a barren spot; spongy ground'. Galby.

galla OE, 'a sore'; topographically, prob. 'a barren or wet spot in a field'. *Galhou* (f.n. Foxton), The Gall (f.n. Knossington), *Gallakyrhil* (f.n. Great Easton), *Gallow* (f.n. Great Bowden).

gandra OE, 'a gander, a male goose'. ?*Ghenderismore* (f.n. Billesdon).

gang OE, 'a way, a passage, a track'. Gang Would (f.n. Marefield), *Gongwode* (f.n. Nevill Holt).

gap ON, 'a gap, an opening', **gappe** ME, 'a breach or opening in a wall or fence'. *Carte Gapp* (f.n. Houghton), *Pastare Gapp* (f.n. Hallaton), *Reedam Gap* (f.n. East Langton), Skinner's Gap (f.n. Medbourne).

gāra OE, 'a point of land, a triangular plot of ground'. Gores Lane. ?The Bargles (f.n. Mowsley), *Bullgores* (f.n. King's Norton), *Clarkes goare*, *le Gore*, *Paynesgore*, *Russhygore* (f.ns. Great Bowden), *le Frontgore*, *Thornygore* (f.ns. Billesdon), *The Goore* (f.n. Theddingworth), The Gore, the Old Gores (f.ns.

Gumley), *the Gore* (f.n. Houghton), The Gores (f.n. Little Bowden), *Gorewong* (f.n. Nevill Holt), *Gorril* (f.n. Fleckney), *le Hardgore* (f.n. Stoughton), *Joneswynesgore*, *Outhebygore* (f.ns. Stretton Magna), *the parsons gore* (f.n. Frisby).

gardin ME, 'a garden, an enclosed plot used for the cultivation of fruit, vegetables etc.'. Abbey Garden (f.n. Owston), Garden Cl (f.n. Billesdon, Houghton, Noseley, Saddington, Stoughton, Stretton Magna), Garden Ground (f.n. Kibworth Beauchamp), Mill Garden (f.n. Smeeton Westerby), Spinney Gardens (f.n. Glooston).

garðr ON, 'an enclosure, a yard'. *Demigard*, *lygard* (f.ns. Great Bowden), *Gardisty*, *Selkisgerth* (f.ns. Billesdon), The Gath (f.n. Knossington), ?*Portgarth* (f.n. Husbands Bosworth), Stack Garth (f.n. Nevill Holt).

gāt OE, 'a goat'. Goat Mdw (f.n. Galby).

gata ON, 'a way, a road, a street'. Broad Gate, Carrygate, Church Gate, East Gate, Heygate St, Three Gates. In road-names, it is the dominant el.: it may be prefixed by a township name (as destination), e.g. *Caldecotegate* (Great Easton), *Horninghold gate* (Hallaton), *Laughton Gate* (Gumley), *Slawston Gate* (Blaston); compounded with an el. indicating topography, e.g. *Hamsgate* (Cranoe), *Houwisgate* (Drayton), *Kergate* (Shangton), *Tongsgate* (Frisby), *Wodegate* (Nevill Holt); or with a minor name defining a more precise location, e.g. *Balhulgate* (Billesdon), *Bilingate* (Nevill Holt), *Debdayle gate* (Gumley), *Strutholegate* (Horninghold). Local flora may be specified, e.g. Aldergate (Great Glen), *Apiltregate* (Nevill Holt), *Hawthorngate* (Burton Overy), *Wilughnegate* (Billesdon). Grassy tracks are freq. recorded, e.g. *Greengate* (with various spellings in Billesdon, Cranoe, Glooston, Great Glen); as are hard road surfaces, e.g. *Stone Gate* (Glooston, Illston). Township buildings appear as in *Church Gate* (Frisby, Great Glen), *hallgate* (Husbands Bosworth), *kirkgates* (Great Bowden), *Millgate* (with various spellings in Gumley, Great Bowden, Nevill Holt). Surnames may feature, e.g. *Eustace Gate* (Frisby), *Harpers gate* (Great Bowden), *Herrick gate* (Houghton), *Kaspergate* (Stoughton). *Portgate* recurs (as in Billesdon, Great Bowden, Gumley, Shangton), as does *Saltergate* (Cranoe, Drayton, Nevill Holt), with related *Salgate* (Billesdon). Note the important *le ferdgate* and *Mathelehougate* (Shangton). Many of these road-names have survived as furlong-names, even when not specifically designated as such.

gate-hous ME, 'a gate-house'. Gatehouse Lane.

gauge ME, 'a fixed or standard measure or scale of measurement'. Old Gauge (f.n. Laughton).

geard OE, 'an enclosure; a yard, a courtyard'. Freq. in f.ns., esp. with a surn., e.g. *Adams yard* (Great Bowden), *Cartersyerde*, *Caunuylesyeard*, *Gildmorysyerd*, *Terbagyerde* (Medbourne), *Framptons yarde*, *Sampson yarde* (Houghton); with reference to principal buildings, e.g. Abbey Yard (Owston), *the Chapell yarde* (Blaston, Hallaton), Hall Yard (Carlton Curlieu, Cranoe, Horninghold), *the Parsonage Yard* (Husbands Bosworth), *the Vicaridge yarde* (Theddingworth); or to village minor structures, e.g. *Kiln Yard* (Evington, Great Bowden, Houghton, Little Stretton), Malthouse Yard (Medbourne); or to small enclosures, e.g. Fold Yard (Great Glen), Pen Yard (Illston, Owston), Yard Paddock (Shangton).

geat OE, 'a gate'. *Butchers Field gate* (f.n. Husbands Bosworth).

geiri ON, 'a wedge-shaped piece of something'. ?Gartree Hundred.

geirr ON, 'a spear'. ?Gartree Hunded.
geslyng ME, 'a young goose, a gosling'. *Gasling pits* (f.n. King's Norton).
gil ON, ME, **gill** dial., 'a ravine with a stream'. ?*Gilleford* (f.n. Evington).
gild OE, 'sacrifice, worship; an idol, a god'; also 'payment '. *gildhill* (f.n. Gumley).
gild-hall ME, 'a guild-hall'. *guilde hall* (Husbands Bosworth), Guildhall Cl (f.n. Theddingworth).
glade eModE, 'a clear open space in a wood, an opening in a wood utilized for snaring birds'. *cockes glade forlonge* (f.n. Glooston).
glæppe OE, 'the buck-bean'. *Glaphole* (f.n. Great Glen).
glebe ME, 'glebe', i.e. land belonging to an ecclesiastical benefice. Glebe Fm. (Billesdon, Burton Overy, Husbands Bosworth, Fleckney). *the Churches glebe land*, *the Glebe Close* (f.ns. Goadby), *Cranoe gleebe land* (f.n. Glooston), *the Gleabland* (f.n. King's Norton), The Glebe (f.n. Carlton Curlieu), the Glebe Fd (f.n. Great Glen), *the Glebe headland* (f.n. East Langton), *the Glebe Land* (f.n. Burton Overy, Scraptoft), *the Gleab Willows* (f.n. Gumley), *Stonton gleeb close* (f.n. Glooston), Top Glebe (f.n. Blaston).
gnípa ON, 'a steep hill'. Nepwell Cl (f.n. Billesdon).
gōd OE, adj., 'good'. *Godtorp*. *Godakers*, *godwell* (f.ns. Husbands Bosworth).
godspel OE, 'the gospel'. *the Gospell place* (f.n. Stonton Wyville).
golde OE, 'a marigold, a marsh-marigold'. ?Gold Thorpe (f.n. Blaston).
gorebrode ME, 'a broad triangular strip of land'. *Garbrode* (f.n. Gumley, Illston, Mowsley), *Garbrodelondis* (Shangton), *les Garbrodrodes* (f.n. Billesdon), Garbroad Cl (f.n. Foxton); *Garbridge* (f.n. Bringhurst, Bushby, Houghton).
gorst OE, 'gorse, furze'; freq. in modern minor names and f.ns. in the sense 'a piece of ground covered with gorse, a fox-covert of gorse bushes'. Bosworth Gorse, Glen ~, Norton ~, Skeffington Pastures ~, Smeeton ~, Vowe's ~, Watson's Gorse. Freq. in f.ns. as in Bottom Gorse (Saddington), Coulton's Gorse (Galby), Fleckney Gorse (Fleckney), Frisby Gorse (Frisby), Gorse Cl (Nevill Holt), Gorse Hill (Glooston), Gorse Mdw (Great Glen), *Gosthill* (Theddingworth), *Gumley Gorse* (Gumley), Hinks Gorse (Marefield), Laughton Gorse (Laughton), Skeffington's Gorse (Blaston), Stretton Gorse (Stretton Magna), Under the Gorse (Billesdon), Welham Gorse (Welham). Note the dial. form *gosse* as in Gosse Cl (Nevill Holt), *le Gosse lands* (Great Bowden), *Gosseley* (Saddington), ?Goose Pits (Burton Overy).
***gorstig** OE, adj., 'overgrown with gorse'. Gorsey (f.n. Stretton Magna), Gorsey Cl (f.n. Bushby, Scraptoft). Great Gossy Cl (f.n. Houghton) records dial. *gossy* (cf. *gosse* in **gorst** *supra*).
gōs OE, **gás** ON, 'a goose'. *Gosacur* (f.n. Great Bowden, Medbourne), *Gose acers* (f.n. Noseley, Scraptoft, Slawston), Goose Green (f.n. Owston), ?Goose Pits (f.n. Burton Overy), Gosby Thorne (f.n. Stoughton), *Gosclif* (f.n. Saddington), *Gosdale Sickes* (f.n. Houghton), *Gosinges*, *Goswong* (f.ns. Billesdon), *Goswell* (f.n. Great Bowden, Great Glen, Mowsley).
goter ME, 'a gutter'. *Cawdwell gutter* (f.n. Stonton Wyville), *the Gutter* (f.n. Frisby, Galby, Glooston, King's Norton, Tur Langton), *gutter lease* (f.n. Gumley), *Hullaton Gutter* (f.n. Slawston), *Heffer Gutter* (f.n. East Langton), *Hunchback Gutter* (f.n. Little Stretton), Long Green Gutter, *Stretton gutter* (f.ns. Great Glen), Mill Gutter (f.n. Kibworth Beauchamp), *Radley gutter* (f.n. Cranoe, Slawston), *Woodsick gutter* (f.n. Goadby).

goule ME, 'a ditch, a stream, a channel'. *the Church Goale* (f.n. East Langton), ?Gold Thorpe (f.n. Blaston).

grāf OE, 'a grove, a copse'. *Prestgrave*. Cat Grove, Gumley Groves (f.ns. Gumley), *la Graue* (p) (East Langton), *Grauesyke* (f.n. Billesdon), Graves Leys (f.n. Houghton), *groufcloudys*, Muck Hill Grove (f.ns. Smeeton Westerby), The Grove (f.n. Saddington), Grove Fd, Grove Hill (f.ns. Bringhurst).

***grand** OE, 'gravel'. *Grannam Narrowe* (f.n. Great Bowden).

grange OFr, ME, 'a grange'; originally 'a granary, a barn', later 'a farm'; also 'an outlying farm belonging to a religious house or to a feudal lord, where crops were stored'; often used in modern p.ns., usually with an older p.n. prefixed, to convey a pretence of antiquity. Beauchamp Grange, Bosworth ~, Burton ~, Carlton ~, Cold Overton ~, East Langton ~, Evington Grange, The Grange (Cranoe, Foxton, Great Bowden, Saddington), Hallaton Grange, Illston ~, Knossington ~, Medbourne ~, Newbold ~, Owston ~, Shangton ~, Thurnby ~, Wistow Grange.

gravel ME, 'gravel'. Gravel Pit Spinney. Freq. in f.ns.: Gravel Hole(s) (Billesdon, Burton Overy, Fleckney, Great Glen), Gravel Hole Cl (Frisby), Gravel Hole Hill (Illston), *Gravelhyll* (Burton Overy), Gravel Pit(s) (Great Easton, Fleckney, Nevill Holt, Hallaton), Gravel Pit Cl (Billesdon, Carlton Curlieu, Scraptoft), *gravill pitts* (Great Bowden).

græf OE, 'a digging, a grave, a pit, a trench'. ?Coningsgrave Hill (f.n. Blaston), *Deadmans grave*, ?Margraves (f.ns. Hallaton), Grave Leys (f.n. Bushby), Graves (f.n. Great Glen), ?Graves Leys (f.n. Houghton), *leathergraues* (f.n. Knossington).

grǣg[1] OE, adj., 'grey'. *Greyston* (f.n. Illston), ?*Greyfurlong'* (f.n. Goadby).

***grǣg**[2] OE, 'a badger'. ?*Greyfurlong'*.

græs OE, 'grass, pasture'. *Burngrass* (f.n. Hothorpe), *the Glibe Grass*, *Grescraft* (f.ns. East Langton), The Grass Fd (f.n. Saddington), Grass Yard (f.n. Knossington), *Greyshill* (f.n. Burton Overy), *Gross*(*e*) (f.n. Fleckney), *langrass*, *Redgrass* (f.ns. Husbands Bosworth), Red Grass (f.n. Illston).

grēat OE adj., 'massive, bulky', **great** ME, 'big in size'. Great Bowden. Great Cl (f.n. Blaston, Burton Overy, Carlton Curlieu, Foxton, Great Glen), Great Dale (f.n. Medbourne), *great foule sicke*, *The Great Wood* (f.ns. Gumley), Great Mdw (f.n. Burton Overy, Illston), Great Stone Bushes (f.n. Evington), *the greatt hill* (f.n. Great Easton), *the Grete Close*, *the Grete Stoking* (f.ns. Stonton Wyville).

grein ON, 'a fork (of a stream)'. *Betwixt Graines* (f.n. Husbands Bosworth), *Gossells greenes* (f.n. Great Glen), *graines* (f.n. Gumley), *the Greines* (f.n. Newton Harcourt), *Harewelgreyne* (f.n. Stretton Magna).

***grendel** OE, 'a gravelly place or stream'. *Grandell* (f.n. Burton Overy), *Grindell* (f.n. Saddington), *Grindle* (f.n. Houghton).

grēne[1] OE, 'adj., 'green, grass-grown'. Green Hill, Green Lane (Billesdon, Great Bowden, Owston). *greene hades* (f.n. Blaston), *Greenehill* (f.n. Houghton), *Greengate* (f.n. with various spellings in Billesdon, Cranoe, Glooston, Houghton), ?Green Hedges (f.n. Evington), *Green Sick* (f.n. Frisby), *grene bank* (f.n. Fleckney), *Grenfurlong'* (f.n. Burton Overy).

grēne[2] OE, 'a grassy spot, a village green'. The Green, Upper Green Place. *atte Grene* (p) (Cold Overton, Foxton), Broad Green (f.n. Kibworth Beauchamp), Goose Green (f.n. Owston), Green Dyke, *Nether Greene* (f.ns. Theddingworth), ?Green Hedges (f.n. Evington), Little Green (f.n. Hallaton), Long Green (f.n.

Great Glen), *othe grene* (p) (Great Easton), *Prestgrauegrene* (f.n. *Prestgrave*), *Scamberdale green* (f.n. Little Stretton), Scraptoft Green (f.n. Scraptoft), Smithers Green (f.n. Slawston), *the grene byneth the Bell* (f.n. Market Harborough).

gresyng ME, vbl.sb., ppl.adj., 'pasturing'. Grazing Mdw (f.n. Theddingworth).

grigg(e) ME, 'something of small size or below natural size'. *le Grygges* (f.n. Great Bowden).

grīma[2] OE, 'a goblin'. ?*Grimeslade* (f.n. Glooston).

grubbe ME, vb., 'to clear land of stumps or roots by digging up'. ?Grubtoft (f.n. Little Stretton).

grund OE, 'ground; a stretch of land', **grund** ON, 'earth, a plain'; later also 'an outlying farm, outlying fields' and 'a piece of land enclosed for agricultural purposes'. Bottom Ground (f.n. Great Bowden), Burnt Ground (f.n. Billesdon), Clover Ground, Potatoe Ground (f.ns. Hallaton), Dairy Ground (f.n. Burton Overy), *Fielding Ground*, Garden Ground, *the Schoole ground* (f.ns. Kibworth Beauchamp), *the Great Wood grownd*, *Laughton Grounds* (f.ns. Gumley), Hill Ground (f.n. Goadby), House Ground (f.n. Husbands Bosworth), *Ladye grounde* (f.n. Horninghold), Midsummer Ground (f.n. Lubenham), *the Parsonage ground* (f.n. Cranoe), *the Upper Ground* (f.n. Blaston, Carlton Curlieu), *the Vicarage grounde* (f.n. King's Norton).

gryfja ON, 'a hole, a pit'. *Gryfe* (f.n. Goadby).

gulfe ME, 'a deep hollow'. Great Gulf (f.n. Illston), *the Gulfe* (f.n. Kibworth Beauchamp).

gybbe ME, ' a hump'. *the Gibb* (f.n. Great Bowden).

***gylde** OE, 'a golden flower'. ?*Gilleford* (f.n. Evington).

***gyll** OE, 'a deep narrow valley'. ?*Gilleford* (f.n. Evington).

gyr OE, 'mud, filth; a marsh'. *Yrland* (f.n. Mowsley).

hafoc OE, 'a hawk'. *Hawerkil* (f.n. Illston), *Horkeleyes* (f.n. Houghton).

haga[1] OE, 'a hedge, an enclosure', **hagi** ON, 'a grazing enclosure, a pasture'. *Arnaws*, *Bruhawes* (f.ns. Billesdon), Bushawe (f.n. Blaston), *Cratehaw* (f.n. Great Easton, *Prestgrave*), Flathaws (f.n. Medbourne, Slawston), *le Hawesnap* (f.n. Nevill Holt), Hawhead (f.n. Knossington), *Hawsicke*, *Swinhawe* (f.ns. Hallaton), *Hilmarehaw* (f.n. Houghton), *lokhawe* (f.n. Stockerston).

hagu-þorn OE, 'the hawthorn, the whitethorn'. *Hawthorngate* (f.n. Burton Overy).

half OE (Angl), adj., sb., 'half, a half part'. *Croumbehalfrodes*, *le Falshalfrodes* (f.ns. Billesdon).

half-aker ME, 'a half-acre'; in early f.ns., poss. 'a measure of land which a yoke of oxen could plough in half a day'. *halfe acers* (f.n. Kibworth Beauchamp), *Hunts halfe Acre* (f.n. Gumley), *le Redehalfacris* (f.n. Billesdon), *Schypmanhaluakyr* (f.n. Medbourne), *Scottishalfaker* (f.n. Nevill Holt).

halh OE (Angl), 'a nook, a corner of land; a water meadow; a tongue of land between two streams; a hollow, a secluded valley etc.'. Hallaton, ?Sludge Hall. Bottom ~, Top Hallows, Oxall (f.ns. Fleckney), *Broad Halford* (f.n. Husbands Bosworth), Long Hollows (f.n. Great Bowden), *Peartree Haile* (f.n. Theddingworth).

hālig OE, adj., 'holy, sacred'. Holyoaks, Holy Well. ?*Haltree moore* (f.n. Newton Harcourt), *Holiewellfurlong* (f.n. Cranoe), Holliwell (f.n. Slawston), *holy roode leyes* (f.n. Burton Overy).

hall OE (Angl), 'a hall, a manor house'. Blaston Hall, Carlton Curlieu ~, Evington ~, *Frisby* ~, Great Bowden ~, Gumley Hall, The Hall (Cold Overton, Great Glen, Glooston, Houghton, Husbands Bosworth, Illston, Medbourne, Nevill Holt, Tur Langton), Hallaton Hall, Kibworth ~, Langton ~, Nether ~, Noseley ~, Old ~, Pebble ~, Rolleston ~, Saddington ~, Scraptoft ~, Stockerston ~, Stoughton ~, White Hall. *atte Hall* (p) (Knossington), *Hall close* (f.n. Blaston, Bringhurst, Foxton), *le Hallemedowe* (f.n. Billesdon), *le halle thing* (f.n. Drayton), *Hall Hill* (f.n. Frisby), *Hall land* (f.n. King's Norton), *the Hall yard* (f.n. Cranoe).

hals OE (Angl), ON, 'a neck', **halse** ME 'a narrow neck of land'. *Haulsike* (f.n. Nevill Holt).

hām OE, 'a village, an estate; a homestead'. Welham. ?*Coldham* (f.n. Illston).

hamer ME, adj., comp., 'nearer home, nearer the village'. *Hamerill Hookes* (f.n. Saddington), *Hamrells* (f.n. Husbands Bosworth), *the Homer side* (*of Debdale*) (f.n. Gumley).

hamm OE, 'a water-meadow, land hemmed in by water or marsh, wet land hemmed in by higher ground'. *Banham*, *Grannam Narrowe* (f.ns. Great Bowden), Banham Mdw (f.n. Burton Overy), The Barkhams (f.n. Great Glen), Broadham Cl, *Hommes head* (f.ns. Tur Langton), ?*Coldham* (f.n. Illston), *Greeneham*, *Saltingham leaes* (f.ns. East Langton), Great ~, Higher ~, Lower ~, Rushy Ham (f.ns. Billesdon), *the Ham furlong* (f.n. Medbourne), *The Hamme* (f.n. Theddingworth), *Hamsgate*, *Langham leas* (f.ns. Cranoe), *Hatcham* (f.n. Fleckney), *Holmesham* (f.n. Lubenham), *Langham* (f.n. Glooston, Great Glen), Pincham (f.n. Scraptoft), ?Red Hound Cl (f.n. Owston).

hām-stall OE (Angl), '(the enclosure of) a homestead'; surviving as **homestall** ModEdial., 'a farm-yard'. *the Homestall* (f.n. Burton Overy, Houghton, Knossington, Owston, Theddingworth), *the Whomestall of Robert Spence* (f.n. Glooston).

hām-stede OE, 'a homestead, the site of a dwelling', **homestead** ModE, 'the home buildings'. Common in f.ns.: Bryans Homestead (Shangton), Burbages ~, Hills ~, Turners Homestead (Owston), Cooper's ~, Crown Croft Homestead (Gumley), Crab Homestead (Frisby), Front Homestead (Knossington), Great Homestead (Stoughton), *Hall Homestead* (Horninghold), Homestead (Burton Overy, Glooston, Hallaton, Houghton, Theddingworth), Homesteads (Great Glen), Maydwells ~, Muggletons Homestead (Blaston), Near Homestead (Noseley), Old Homestead (West Langton), *the Parsonage whomsted* (Hallaton), Poles Homestead (Evington), Top Homestead (Galby), *The Vicaridge Homestead* (Horninghold).

hān OE, 'a hone; a stone, a boundary stone'. *longehanefurlonge* (f.n. Slawston).

handpost ModE, 'a guide-post', i.e. one with hands terminating the direction boards, cf. **finger-post**, *supra*. Handpost Mdw (f.n. Saddington).

hangeman ME, 'a hangman'. *Hang-mans Rickstead* (f.n. Husbands Bosworth).

hangende OE, **hengjandi** ON, pres.part., ppl.adj., 'hanging'; used in p.ns. of places on a steep slope or hillside. *hanginge banke* (f.n. Gumley), Hanging Hill (f.n. Theddingworth), Hanging Mdw (f.n. Laughton), Hanging Lands (f.n. Slawston, Stoughton), Hangings (f.n. Shangton).

hār[2] OE, adj., 'hoar, grey', especially 'grey through being overgrown with lichen'; prob. came to mean 'boundary' because of its freq. use with features forming boundary marks or lying on boundaries. Horston Hill. *harbroue stong* (f.n.

Gumley), *Harcote* (f.n. Houghton), Harcraft (f.n. Smeeton Westerby), Hare Croft (f.n. Blaston), *harecroftgate* (f.n. Slawston), ?Hare Crop Leys (f.n. Hallaton), *hareslade*, *hoarestone* (f.ns. Husbands Bosworth), *Harewelsyke* (f.n. Stretton Magna).

hara OE, 'a hare'. Hare Pie Bank. ?Hare Crop Leys (f.n. Hallaton).

hassuc OE, 'a clump of coarse grass'. *Hassacks* (f.n. Burton Overy), *Hassock* (f.n. Thurnby), *the Hassocks* (f.n. Frisby), Hassocks (f.n. Great Bowden, Theddingworth).

haugr ON, 'a hill, a hill-top; a burial mound'; sometimes difficult to distinguish from OE *hō*(*e*), dat.sg. of **hōh**. ?*Howgate* (f.n. Stonton Wyville).

hæc(c) OE (Angl), 'a hatch; a sluice, a flood-gate'. *Hachey* (f.n. Great Bowden), *Hatcham* (f.n. Fleckney).

hǣddre OE, 'heather'. Heather Cl (f.n. Evington).

***hæfera** OE, **hafri** ON, 'oats'. Market Harborough. *Haverberge* (f.n. Medbourne), *Haverell close* (f.n. Thurnby).

(ge)hæg OE, **hay** ME, 'a fence, an enclosure'. *Caldecotehay* (f.n. Great Easton), Crowd Hayes (f.n. Burton Overy), ?*Hastyway* (f.n. Theddingworth), *the Hay* (f.n. Great Bowden), Hayse, Mowhay (f.ns. Billesdon), *the hey* (f.n. Husbands Bosworth), *Larkhey* (f.n. Nevill Holt), *Redland Hey* (f.n. Houghton), *Schythaysfurlonges* (f.n. Illston), Wild Harrey (f.n. Knossington).

***hægen** OE, 'an enclosure'. *Heinouhull'*, *Heynewelle* (f.ns. Shangton).

hænep OE, 'hemp'. Hemp Hook (f.n. Marefield).

***hær** OE, 'a heap of stones'. *heringhegis* (f.n. *Prestgrave*).

***hæren** OE, adj., 'stony'. *harndale* (f.n. Shangton).

hærg OE (Angl), 'a heathen temple'. ?*Harrow hole* (f.n. Houghton).

***hǣs** OE (Angl), 'brushwood'. ?*Hasty way* (f.n. Theddingworth), Hayes Cl (f.n. Welham), ?*Hescrofte* (f.n. Saddington), *Hesdalesick* (f.n. Houghton), *Hespitte* (f.n. Smeeton Westerby).

hǣð OE (Angl), 'a heath, heather'. Heath Cl, *le Nether heth* (f.ns. Evington).

headley ModEdial., '?a swarded-over or 'grass' headland; ?an end unit of grassland'. *John Bates Headlea* (f.n. Great Glen), *Bonds hadley*, *John Frenches headley*, *Mr Gold's headley*, *Mr Halfordes headlea*, *Swinglers hadley* (f.ns. Glooston), *Tho. Clarkes* ~, *Len Colmans* ~, *the Glibe Gress hadley* (f.ns. East Langton), *Freemans* ~, *Woolfeild hadley* (f.ns. Gumley), *Holm headley*, *Edward Iliffes Hadley* (f.ns. Kibworth Beauchamp), *Palmers hadley* (f.n. Houghton), Town Adley (f.n. Fleckney), *Mr Vows hadley* (f.n. Hallaton).

hēafod OE, 'a head; the (top) end of something, a headland, unploughed land at the end of the arable where the plough turns', cf. **hēafod-land**. Freq. in f.ns., and very often in the pl. referring to headlands at the end of the arable, e.g. *Barley Hades* (Hallaton), *barlie haden*, *Crook* ~, *ould meadow* ~, *Watho* ~, *Whatston* ~, *Wranghaden* (Burton Overy), *Gallow hades* (Foxton), *greene hades* (Blaston), *Smalehauedys* (Nevill Holt), *the West hades* (Bringhurst). Sometimes in the sg., alluding to a larger physical feature, e.g. *Gausthill Head* (Theddingworth), *Hommes head* (Tur Langton), *Kilpex head* (Kibworth Beauchamp), Moor Head (Great Glen, Houghton), *Neatshead* (Frisby), *Oxhead* (East Langton), Ramshead (King's Norton).

hēafod-land OE, 'a strip of land at the head of a furlong left for turning the plough'. Freq. appears in f.ns., usually with a villager's name prefixed, e.g. *Thomas Berries* ~, *Boultons* ~, *Bulls Hadland*, *Spratts Headland*, *Mr Tompsons hadland*

(Great Glen), *Edward Burtons ~*, *Richard Collyns ~*, *Henry Lowthes hadland* (Great Easton). The parish church is occasionally specified, e.g. (*the*) *Church had*(*e*)*land* (Glooston, Great Easton), *le Kirkehauedlond* (Nevill Holt), or the township itself, e.g. *the towne hadland* (Great Easton, Great Glen). A locational prefix is sometimes used, e.g. *bruke hadland* (Glooston), *Debdale hadland* (Gumley), *Estmerishauedlond* (Great Easton).

hēah[1] (**hēan** wk. obl.) OE, **hēh** (Angl), **high** ModE, adj., 'high, tall; important; lying high up, standing in a high place'. Highcroft Lodge, High Leas. Highfields (f.n. Great Glen), *High gate* (f.n. Frisby), *highloes* (f.n. Husbands Bosworth), High St (Evington, Hallaton, Market Harborough), *Highwood* (f.n. Hallaton), *Hyeblakemylde*, *Hyewulldale* (f.ns. Billesdon). The weak oblique form may be present in *Hendoe* (f.n. Houghton).

hēahfore OE, 'a heifer'. *Heffer Gutter* (f.n. East Langton).

hēah-weg OE, 'a highway, a main road'. *the highe waie* (with various spellings in Burton Overy, Cranoe, Great Glen, Mowsley, Tur Langton), Highway Cl (f.n. Blaston, Evington, Lubenham), Highway Park (f.n. Evington), *holgate hyway* (f.n. Gumley), *the Kings highway* (Kibworth Beauchamp).

heard OE, adj., 'hard; hard to till; uncomfortable, cheerless'. *Josiah Bents hard Layes* (f.n. Cranoe), *le Hardgore*, *Hardmydo* (f.ns. Stoughton), *Hardhill* (f.n. Houghton, Husbands Bosworth).

hearpe OE, 'a harp'; used topographically of something resembling a harp in shape. Harps (f.n. Houghton).

hecg OE, 'a hedge'. Freq. used in f.ns. with reference to boundary hedges between townships, e.g. *Holte hedge* (Drayton, Great Easton, Medbourne), *Ingarsbye Hedge* (Houghton), *Sibbertoft ~*, *Sulby ~*, *Thedingworth Hedge* (Husbands Bosworth), *Stretton hedge* (Great Glen), *Wellham hedg* (Cranoe). A surn. may be prefixed indicating hedges of private property, e.g. *Alynehegg'*, *Bayes hedge* (Great Easton), *Andrews ~*, *Chapman ~*, *Rowlotts ~*, *Woodfords hedge* (Husbands Bosworth). Topographical features may be prefixed, e.g. *le Cowelhegg'* (Hallaton), *Ridgeway hedge* (Great Glen), *Scockrill hedge* (King's Norton), Would Hedge (Billesdon), *the Wyer hedge* (Kibworth Beauchamp). *Wolfhegys* (*Prestgrave*) alludes to early response to wild animals. Some modern forms with *hedge* may conceal an original **edisc** or **etisc** (*q.v.*), as ?*the double hedge* (King's Norton), ?Green Hedges (Evington), ?Three Hedges (Husbands Bosworth).

hēg OE (Angl), 'hay, mowing grass'; in late forms sometimes difficult to distinguish from **hēah**[1] when compounded with **gata**. Heygate St. Hayfield (f.n. Saddington), Hay Gate (f.n. Bushby, Evington, Gumley, Houghton), *le Hayeleyis*, *Heyford*, ?*High gates* (f.ns. Great Bowden), *Hay Meadow* (f.n. Evington, Great Bowden), *Haysicke* (f.n. Smeeton Westerby), *Heiford way* (f.n. Theddingworth), Heyfords (f.n. Laughton), *heygatepol*, ?Higate (f.ns. Slawston), ?*High gate* (f.n. Frisby).

hegning ON, 'enclosed land'. *Hecyning* (f.n. Carlton Curlieu).

heiward ME, 'an officer in charge of fences and enclosures'; distinguishing the sb. from its surn. reflex is difficult. *hauards dole* (f.n. Burton Overy), *Hawards forlonge* (f.n. Husbands Bosworth), ?*Haywards hill* (f.n. Kibworth Beauchamp), ?*Hewedesmedowe* (f.n. Houghton).

helde OE, 'a slope, a declivity'. *the Butholde* (f.n. Noseley), *Helthirne* (f.n. Great Bowden).

hell OE, 'hell'. *Hellholes* (f.n. Husbands Bosworth).

helm OE, 'a helmet; the summit of a hill'; later 'a cattle shelter'. *Helmpittis* (f.n. Stoughton).

henn OE, 'a hen (esp. of wild birds); a water hen', etc. *Hen Acre* (f.n. East Langton), *Hendicke* (f.n. Saddington), ?*Hendoe* (f.n. Houghton), Hen Fd (f.n. Rolleston, Smeeton Westerby), Hen Mdw (f.n. Cold Overton), Hen Plot (f.n. Stoughton), *Hensick* (f.n. Frisby).

heorde-wīc OE, 'a herd farm'. Hardwick. *Hardwykeslade* (f.n. Mowsley).

heort OE, 'a hart, a stag, a grown male deer'. ?Hartwell Cl (f.n. Cold Overton), *Hartshorne* (f.n. Great Glen).

***herse** OE, 'a hill top'. ?Barearse (f.n. Medbourne), ?*Barearse hill* (f.n. Goadby), ?*Barehers* (f.n. Drayton), ?*Bareherse* (f.n. Hallaton), ?*Wyndeshers* (f.n. Billesdon).

heyghoge ME, 'a hedgehog'. Hedge Hog Mdw (f.n. King's Norton).

hider ME, adj., 'nearer'. *Heather Scockerill* (f.n. King's Norton), *Hether dame* (f.n. Newton Harcourt), *Hiderpeislond* (f.n. Theddingworth), *Hither Cocklow* (f.n. Husbands Bosworth), *the hyther furlonge* (f.n. Knossington).

hīewet OE, 'a hewing, a cutting', i.e. 'a place where trees are cut down'. ?Hewitts Park (f.n. Cold Overton).

hirde OE, 'a herdsman'. ?*hird hill* (f.n. Bushby).

hive ME, 'a beehive'. The Hives (f.n. Knossington).

hlaða ON, 'a storehouse, a barn'. *Lathyard* (f.n. Stonton Wyville).

hlāw OE, 'a mound, a hill'. The Coplow. *Ashlow*, *Cockloe*, *Drihtburhlawe*, *highloes*, *Litlow*, *Redloe*, *Rushpittloe*, *spellow*, *Windloe* (f.ns. Husbands Bosworth), *Belteslowe*, *Wencelawedale* (f.ns. Medbourne), *Beneath the low*, *Gumley low* (f.ns. Laughton), *Lytlow* (f.n. Burton Overy), *Scutlows gate* (f.n. Glooston), *Tykmanlow* (f.n. Mowsley), *Wakelopittes* (f.n. Great Bowden), *Wakelow* (f.n. Saddington).

hlinc OE, 'a ridge, a bank, a ledge of ploughland on a hillside, an unploughed strip or step between fields'. *Linch* (f.n. Husbands Bosworth).

hlið[1] OE, **hlíð**[2] ON, 'a slope, a hillside'. Life Hill.

hlōse (hlōsan nom.pl.) OE, 'a pigsty', originally 'a shelter, a shed'. *Lose hill* (f.n. Bushby), *Loosehill* (f.n. Houghton), *Lowsden* (f.n. Frisby), *Lowson* (f.n. Husbands Bosworth).

hnutbēam OE, 'a nut-tree'. *Notebamhull* (f.n. Theddingworth).

hnutu OE, **hnot** ON, 'a nut', whence 'a nut-bearing tree'. Nut Bush. ?Nuts Cl (f.n. Foxton), ?Nutts Leys (f.n. Kibworth Beauchamp), ?*Nutts Nook* (f.n. Cranoe).

hobb(e) OE, ' a tussock, a hummock'. Hinckley's Hobbs (f.n. Nevill Holt).

hobgoblin ME, 'a hobgoblin'. The Hobgoblin (f.n. Laughton).

hōc OE, 'a hook, an angle, a bend in a river, a spit of land in a river-bend, a corner or bend in a hill'. Lewin's Hook. *the Bailey Hook* (f.n. Kibworth Beauchamp), *Bridghooks* (f.n. Laughton), Bull Hook, *le Lytylmedowhoke* (f.ns. Medbourne), *the Cunstables Hooks*, *mill dam hooks* (f.ns. Houghton), *Duehooke*, *Larin hoks* (f.ns. Great Bowden), Far ~, Near Hook, *Hamerill Hookes* (f.ns. Saddington), Hemp Hook (f.n. Marefield), *Hoctong'*, Wooden Hooks (f.ns. Hallaton), *the Hookes*, *Tyney hooke* (f.ns. King's Norton), *merehock* (f.n. Nevill Holt), *the parsons hooke* (f.n. Stockerston), *waterlagghook*, *willie hooke* (f.ns. Husbands Bosworth), *Watermill Hooke* (f.n. Tur Langton).

hōcede OE, adj., 'having a hook or a corner; curved'. *Hokedsti* (f.n. Medbourne).

hogg OE, ME, 'a hog, a pig'; also used in ME and later of a young sheep from the time it ceases to be a lamb till its first shearing. Hog Lane (Burton Overy, Hallaton, Kibworth Harcourt). Hog Bank Cl, *Hog tree* (f.ns. Burton Overy), *Hogges balke*, *Hogges Foarde* (f.ns. Great Bowden), *Hoggs holme* (f.n. Hallaton, Stonton Wyville), *the hoggs pasture* (f.n. East Langton), Hogpit (f.n. Foxton), ?*Noggesforde* (f.n. Burton Overy).

hǫgg ON, 'a cutting or felling of trees'. *atte Hagge* (p) (Stoughton), *the Haggs* (f.n. Cranoe, Kibworth Beauchamp, Stonton Wyville), *Tho. Haycocks Hags* (f.n. Hallaton), Middle Haggs (f.n. Houghton), Town Haggs (f.n. Little Stretton).

hōh (**hōs** nom.pl., **hōm** dat.pl.) OE, 'a hill; a hill-spur'; in the Danelaw, difficult to distinguish from **haugr**. Cranoe, ?Hothorpe, Houghton on the Hill, Lubenham; Hoeback Spinney, Wignell Hill. *Galhou* (f.n. Foxton), Gallow Cl, *Onowh* (f.ns. Great Bowden), High Howe (f.n. Little Bowden), *Hobrinckes* (f.n. Kibworth Harcourt), Hobrook Fd, ?Stainer (f.ns. Fleckney), *Hoo Baulk* (f.n. Glooston), *hose wey* (f.n. Frisby), *Houbrinkes* (f.n. Medbourne), ?*houdale*, *Howse*, *Onhou* (f.ns. Great Easton), *le houe* (f.n. Hallaton), *Houwisgate*, *Howeslonde*, *Howes* (f.ns. Drayton), ?*Howgate* (f.n. Stonton Wyville), *Lytulho*, *Rynkso* (f.ns. Mowsley), *Mathelou*, *Stapilhouhil'* (f.ns. Shangton), *Pissowe* (f.n. Houghton), Redow (f.n. East Langton), ?Ringshill, *Seueshouhille* (f.ns. Saddington), Starter, *Strutthou*, *Trumpeshou* (f.ns. Billesdon), *Wakoe* (f.n. Owston), *Watho*, *Worthohyll* (f.ns. Burton Overy).

hol[1] OE, **hol** ON, 'a hole, a hollow'. Freq. in f.ns.: alluding to mineral extraction, e.g. Gravel Hole(s) (Billesdon, Burton Overy, Fleckney, Frisby, Great Glen, Illston), *Lamholes* (Houghton), Sand Hole(s) (Fleckney, Hallaton, Houghton), Stone Hole (Billesdon); prefixed by a locational name, e.g. Carland Hole, *Cuttillhole*, *Ruspitt hole*, *Stonehill hole* (Husbands Bosworth); with wild fauna, e.g. *Catteholis* (Hallaton, Nevill Holt), Rabbit Holes (Burton Overy), or flora, e.g. *Blacthorne hole* (Billesdon), *Glaphole* (Great Glen). *Money hole* (Kibworth Beauchamp) perh. points to the discovery of a coin hoard, while *Harrow hole* (Houghton) may refer to a lost religious site.

hol[2] OE, **holr** ON, adj., 'lying in a hollow, running in a hollow; sunken (esp. in road-names and stream-names)'. Holloway Spinney. ?Hobrook Fd (f.n. Fleckney), *Holdale* (f.n. Stretton Magna), *Holefurew* (f.n. Drayton), *Holgate* (f.n. Gumley, Nevill Holt), Holloway (f.n. Husbands Bosworth), *the hollow way* (f.n. Glooston).

holegn OE, 'holly'. Holly Bush (f.n. Wistow).

holh OE, 'a hollow, a hole'. Blaston Hollows, Theddingworth Hollow Spinney. Big Hollows (f.n. Foxton), Hollow Back (f.n. Knossington), Hollow Banks, Hollow Cl (f.ns. Blaston), *the hollow forowes* (f.n. Saddington), Hollow Mdw (f.n. Husbands Bosworth), Hollows (f.n. Hallaton), *Holoforth* (f.n. Burton Overy), *Lawnde pound hollow* (f.n. Great Easton), *Stockuall Hollow* (f.n. Drayton).

holmr ON, 'a water meadow; a piece of drier ground amid marsh'. Collin's Holme. Very freq. in f.ns.: with a prefixed surn., e.g. *Alldridge Home* (Kibworth Harcourt), *Barrsholme*, *Bullymerysholme* (Hallaton), *Goodriche Holme* (Husbands Bosworth), *Maynardesholm* (Great Bowden); with wild flora, e.g. *Cerssholme* (Evington), *Dokholm* (Drayton, Houghton) *Reedeholme* (East Langton, Houghton), Rush Holme (Medbourne), *Starholmes* (Hallaton); with livestock, e.g. Bullholmes (Great Easton, Stockerston), *Hoggs holme* (Hallaton),

Steedholme (Owston); location may be indicated, e.g. *Bradgate holme* (Lubenham), *Cergatisholme* (Great Bowden), *Cotoneholme* (Nevill Holt), *halloughton home* (Blaston), *Stillepolholm* (Shangton). Recurring are *mylneholm* (Drayton, Galby, Great Bowden, Smeeton Westerby) and *Priest Home* (Husbands Bosworth, Kibworth Beauchamp). The el. may occur as the specific of a p.n., e.g. Home Bank (Burton Overy), *homes gate* (Frisby), *homesmeere* (Husbands Bosworth), *le Holmeswro* (Billesdon).

holt OE, ON, 'a small wood, a single-species wood'. Nevill Holt; Hillcroft Holt, The Holt, Shangton Holt. Ash Holt (f.n. Stoughton), Bottom Holts (f.n. Galby, Houghton), Great Holt (f.n. Frisby), Holt (f.n. Little Stretton, Mowsley), *Holt Piece*, Hot Thrawly (f.ns. Glooston), Iliffs Holt (f.n. King's Norton), Knossington Holt (f.n. Knossington), Upper Holt (f.n. Illston).

home ModE, adj., 'near home'. Goadby Home Fm, Home Cl, Home Fm (Billesdon, Blaston, Glooston, Gumley, Medbourne, West Langton), Home Plantation, Noseley Home Fm. Home Cleaves (f.n. Billesdon), Home Cl (f.n. Blaston, Burton Overy, Carlton Curlieu, Evington, Fleckney, Glooston, Great Easton, Gumley, Husbands Bosworth), Home Fd (f.n. Billesdon, Fleckney, Foxton, Glooston, Great Easton), Homehall Cl (f.n. Husbands Bosworth), *Homes Down* (f.n. Billesdon), *the Parsonage Home Close* (f.n. Galby).

***hōpere** OE, 'a cooper, a maker of barrels'. ?*Houperyng* (f.n. Nevill Holt).

***hopet** OE, ' a small enclosure'. Far Hoppett (f.n. Welham).

hoppe ME, 'the hop-plant'. Hop Cl (f.n. Carlton Curlieu), Hop Ground (f.n. Hallaton).

***hopping** OE, 'a hop garden'. Hoppers Hill (f.n. Goadby), *Hopping Way* (f.n. Theddingworth), Hoppins (f.n. Fleckney), *hopyng* (f.n.Great Easton), *Hopynges* (f.n. Billesdon).

hop-yard ModE, 'a hop-yard, a hop-garden, an enclosure where hops are grown'. Hopyard Spinney. Hop Yard (f.n. Blaston, King's Norton, Noseley, West Langton).

horn OE, ON, 'a horn; a projecting piece of land'. ?Horninghold. *Hartshorne* (f.n. Great Glen).

***horning** OE, 'a headland; something shaped like a horn, a bend' ?Horninghold.

hors, ***hross** OE, **hross** ON, 'a horse'. Horseclose Spinney, Horse Hill. Horse Cl (f.n. Billesdon, Blaston, Foxton, Little Bowden), *the Horse fair* (f.n. Hallaton), Horseheads Furlong (f.n. Little Stretton), Horse Pasture (f.n. Billesdon), *Horsepoole* (f.n. Glooston, *Prestgrave*, Theddingworth), Horse Slade (f.n. Great Bowden), Horsey Cl (f.n. East Langton), Horstead Cl (f.n. Foxton), (*the*) *Horsewell* (f.n. Hothorpe, Theddingworth), *Horsewood close* (f.n. Hallaton), Roseley (f.n. Thurnby), ?*Rose hadland* (f.n. Foxton), *Ross Leys* (f.n. Hallaton), *yommanyshorstede* (f.n. Illston).

horskepere ME, 'one who has the care of horses'. Horsekeeper's Yard (f.n. Market Harborough).

hospital ME, 'a hospital, a hospice'. Hospital Cl (f.n. Little Stretton), *the Hospitall Land* (f.n. King's Norton).

housles ME, adj., 'inhospitable', **houseless** ModE, adj., 'lacking in houses'. *Houseless Lane* (f.n. Lubenham).

hovel eModE, 'a hovel, a shed, a frame or stand on which a stack of corn is built'. Black Hovel (f.n. Rolleston), Cart Hovel (f.n. Stretton Magna), Cow Hovel, Hovel Close Mdw (f.ns. Evington), Hovel Buildings, Porters Hovel, Red Hovel (f.ns. Blaston), Hovel Cl (f.n. Billesdon, Blaston, Hallaton, Kibworth Beauchamp, Knossington, Scraptoft), Hovel Fd (f.n. Billesdon, Foxton), Hovel Mdw (f.n. Billesdon, Mowsley), Hovels Cl (f.n. Great Easton), Left of Hovel, Right of Hovel (f.ns. Theddingworth).

hræfn OE, **hrafn** ON, 'a raven'. ?*Rauenesthuett* (f.n. Noseley), ?*Ravensaker* (f.n. Great Glen).

hramsa OE, 'wild garlic'. ?Ramburrow Cl (f.n. Horninghold), Ramsbed (f.n. Glooston, Goadby), ?Ramsborough (f.n. Stockerston), ?Ramshead or Ramshill (f.n. King's Norton),

hrēac OE, 'a rick'. *Rike place* (f.n. Husbands Bosworth).

hrēod OE, 'a reed, a rush', prob. also 'a reed-bed'; sometimes difficult to distinguish from **rēad** OE, 'red'. *Redbrochforlang*, *Redgress*, *Redloe* (f.ns. Husbands Bosworth), *le Redehalfacris* (f.n. Billesdon), *Rede holme* (f.n. Houghton), *Redemore* (f.n. Burton Overy), *Redesdale* (f.n. Mowsley), Red Grass (f.n. Illston), ?Red Hill (f.n. Kibworth Beauchamp), ?Red Hound Cl (f.n. Owston), Redmire (f.n. Rolleston), Redmires (f.n. Little Stretton), *Redome gate* (f.n. Thorpe Langton), ?Redow Cl (f.n. East Langton), *reedland* (f.n. Gumley).

hring OE, 'a ring, a circle', used of something sweeping in a curve (as a hill). ?Ringshill (f.n. Saddington).

hrīs OE, **hrís** ON, 'shrubs, brushwood'. *Endries*, *Prestrees* (f.ns. Knossington), Prestress Cl (f.n. Owston), *Rysburgh* (f.n. Mowsley), *Wateris* (f.n. Lubenham).

hrōc OE, **hrókr** ON, 'a rook'. *Rokhyll* (f.n. Great Bowden), ?*Rokeswelle* (f.n. Drayton), ?Rookwell (f.n. Little Bowden).

hrycg OE, **hryggr** ON, 'a ridge'. Old Ridges Mdw (f.n. Theddingworth), *Rigges Feild* (f.n. Smeeton Westerby), *Three Roode Riggs* (f.n. Cranoe).

hrycgweg OE, 'a ridgeway'. *Ridgwaye* (f.n. Great Glen, Mowsley).

***hūc** OE, ***hūk** Scand, 'a hook, a promontory'. ?Hothorpe.

hund OE, **hundr** ON, 'a hound'. ?*Houndfeld'* (f.n. Stoughton), *Hundel* (f.n. Lubenham), *Hundhill* (f.n. Theddingworth).

hundred OE, num., 'one hundred', sb., 'an administrative division of a county, prob. consisting originally of 100 hides'. Gartree Hundred.

hūne OE, 'hoarhound'. ?*Houndfeld* (f.n. Stoughton).

hungor OE, 'hunger', usually an allusion in f.ns. to 'barren ground'. *Hungurhill* (f.n. Noseley, Stockerston).

hungrig OE, adj., 'hungry, poor'. *le Hungriaker* (f.n. *Prestgrave*).

hunig OE, 'honey'; in f.ns., usually alluding to places where honey was found or produced, or perh. to 'sweet land'; but sometimes also used of sites with sticky soil. Honey Pot Lane. Honey Acre (f.n. Medbourne), Honey Pots (f.n. Hallaton), Honey Spot (f.n. Goadby), *honypot* (f.n. Gumley), ?*Hunnies balke* (f.n. Great Bowden).

***hunte** OE, **hunte** ME, 'a hunt', later 'a hunting district'. ?Hunt Moor Cl (f.n. Marefield).

hūs OE, 'a house', usually a dwelling house, but sometimes used of a building for a special purpose. *Aldousdale* (f.n. *Prestgrave*), *le Burnt house yardeland* (f.n. Goadby), *Coxes howse*, *Fossells house*, *Knights house* (Husbands Bosworth), House Fd, Old House Cl (f.ns. Billesdon), House Orchard (f.n. Owston), *hushome* (f.n. Blaston), *Mundeshowse* (Nevill Holt), *le mylne howse* (Market Harborough), *the Overhouse* (Knossington), Swanshouse (Welham).

husband ME, 'a husbandman, a farmer'. Husbands Bosworth.

hut eModE, 'a hut, a shed'. Black Hut Fd, Bottom ~, Top Hut (f.ns. Great Glen), Hut Cl (f.n. Bushby, Foxton, Great Easton, Hallaton, Houghton, Mowsley), Little Hut Cl (f.n. Saddington), Pig Hut (f.n. Stoughton).

hváll ON, 'an isolated rounded hill'. ?Wall Gates (f.n. Little Stretton).

*__hvin__ ON, **whin** ME, 'whin, gorse'. *Ethwyn*, *winpooles* (f.n. Knossington), *whinell dole* (f.n. Husbands Bosworth), Whin Hill (f.n. Fleckney), *Windoles peece* (f.n. Great Bowden).

hwǣg OE, 'whey'. *Whaybrooke* (f.n. Theddingworth), *Whebrooke* (f.n. Husbands Bosworth).

*__hwæl__ OE, 'a hill'. ?Wall Gates (f.n. Little Stretton).

hwǣte OE (Angl), 'wheat'. ?Wadcombe, ?Wheatland Syke (f.ns. Laughton), *Wetehil* (f.n. Shangton), *Wetelond* (f.n. Illston), *Stony wheathill* (f.n. Houghton), Wheat Cl (f.n. Illston, Little Stretton, Noseley, Theddingworth), Wheat Hill (f.n. Billesdon).

hwēol OE, 'a wheel'; used topographically to denote 'a physical feature which wheels round'. *Whildik'* (f.n. Great Bowden).

hwerfel OE (Angl), 'a circle', used in p.ns. to denote something circular such as 'a round-topped hill'. *Hwerluedale* (f.n. Billesdon), *Wharle* (f.n. Bushby, Houghton), *the Whorle* (f.n. East Langton), *Whorle dikes* (f.n. Newton Harcourt).

hwet-stān OE, 'a whetstone', prob. alluding in p.ns. to places where stone for such implements was to be had. *Whatston haden* (f.n. Burton Overy), Whetstone Hill (f.n. Hallaton).

hwīt OE, **hvítr** ON, adj., 'white'; in eModE, *white* 'infertile' may be contrasted with *black* 'fertile', while dial. *white* may refer to 'dry open pasture'. Limestone or chalky soil is occasionally alluded to. White House Fm. *Long whites* (f.n. Laughton), *underwytkotes* (f.n. Illston), *Whitecross* (Kibworth Harcourt, Mowsley), White Hills (f.n. Great Easton), *White Stone* (f.n. with various spellings in Great Bowden, Lubenham, Theddingworth), *whitland(s)* (f.ns. Gumley, Saddington, Smeeton Westerby, Theddingworth), *Whitleyes* (f.n. Billesdon, Goadby), *Whittley Furlong* (f.n. Theddingworth).

*__hygel__ OE, 'a hillock'. ?The Isle (f.n. Horninghold).

hyll OE, 'a hill'. Houghton on the Hill, Illston on the Hill; Cote Hill Fm, Gallow Hill, Green Hill, Hillcroft Holt, Mill Hill, Old Hill, Peashill Fm. Very freq. in f.ns.: geology may feature, e.g. *Gravelhyll*, *Sandihillis* (Burton Overy), *calcyl* (Great Easton), *stonhill* (Burton Overy, Glooston, Great Glen, Husbands Bosworth); wild flora may be indicated, e.g. *Brackenhil* (Houghton), *Bromhyll* (Houghton), *Ferne hill* (Fleckney), Gorse Hill (Glooston), *Notebamhull* (Theddingworth), *Thornhill* (Gumley, Hallaton), *threthornehul*, *Thurnehill* (Frisby), *whinnill* (Fleckney, Husbands Bosworth); and wild fauna, e.g. *Cattsfurlong hill*, *Musehull* (Husbands Bosworth), Coningsgrave Hill (Blaston), Crow Hill (Billesdon, Nevill Holt), *Hawerkil* (Illston), *Hundhill* (Theddingworth), *Toadhill* (Houghton), *wolfhill* (Gumley). Hill sites were common for crops, e.g. Bannals (Hallaton), *Barlihull*, *Pessill* (Husbands Bosworth), *berhull* (Burton Overy, Houghton, Medbourne), *Flaxlondhyll* (Billesdon), *Peysehil* (Shangton), *Rye hil* (Hothorpe), *Wetehil* (Billesdon, Houghton, Shangton). Early owners may feature, e.g. *Burmans Hill* (Great Easton), *Inggulberdhille* (Hallaton), *Normanhill* (Burton Overy), *Symshyl*

(Illston), *walters hill* (Husbands Bosworth), *Wlstaneshil* (Nevill Holt); and peasant activities, e.g. *Buterhil*, *Twynymill hill* (Husbands Bosworth), *Cocsitehil* (Nevill Holt), *Loosehill* (Houghton), *potteres hul* (Great Easton), *Wyndmilnehyl* (Great Easton, Glooston). The shape or appearance of a hill is freq. specified, e.g. *Branthyll* (Gumley, Noseley), *Cophull* (Billesdon), *Coppydhyll* (Great Easton, Houghton), *Gallow hill* (Blaston, Great Easton), Langhill (Carlton Curlieu, Evington, Husbands Bosworth), *Scharphill* (Mowsley), Stepnals (Husbands Bosworth). Note the prob. early fortified site indicated by Buxtons Hill (Hallaton).

hyllig OE, adj., 'hilly'. Hilly Mdw (f.n. Galby, Gumley, Illston, Owston), Lower Hilly Cl (f.n. Saddington).

***hylloc** OE, **hillok**, **hullok** ME, 'a hillock'. Hillocky Cl (f.n. Marefield).

hyrne OE (Angl), 'an angle, a corner; a recess in a hill, a corner in a valley, a spit of land in a river-bend'. *Blakeheyrns*, *Etheherne* (f.ns. Noseley), *Cogermans Irones*, *Moyst Irons* (f.ns. Laughton), *le Hirnefurlongis* (f.n. Billesdon), *Hyrne lane* (f.n. Great Bowden), *of the hyrne* (p) (Stretton Magna).

hyrst OE (Angl), 'a hillock, a wooded hill'. Bringhurst. *Broadhurst* (f.n. Kibworth Beauchamp), *le Fordehurst* (f.n. Nevill Holt), *le Holdemulnehurst* (f.n. Medbourne).

īfig OE, 'ivy'. Ivy Lodge Fm. Ivy Cl (f.n. Blaston).

-ig[3] OE, suffix, mostly adj., **-ig**, **-i**(**e**), **-y**(**e**) ME, **-y** ModE, adj. suffix. ?*Shirtecoat*. Bankey Mdw (f.n. Carlton Curlieu), Banky Cl (f.n. Fleckney, Shangton), Dockey Cl (f.n. Cold Overton, Hallaton), Hillocky Cl (f.n. Marefield), Horsey Cl (f.n. East Langton), Peasey Cl (f.n. Thurnby), ?*Schyrdaycotis* (f.n. Newton Harcourt), ?*Shortecotes* (f.n. Horninghold).

in OE, prep., 'in', sometimes with the adj. force 'inner'. *Inhomes Meadow* (f.n. Lubenham), *Inlond* (f.n. Slawston), Inn Mdw (f.n. Carlton Curlieu), *ynnefurlong* (f.n. Billesdon).

inclosure eModE, 'an inclosing, an enclosure'; a variant form of *enclosure*, being the statutory form of reference to the inclosing of waste lands, commons etc. *the Old Inclosier* (f.n. Stretton Magna), *the Old Inclosure* (f.n. Goadby).

***ing** OE, 'a hill, a peak'. *Yngbarowefelde* (f.n. Great Bowden).

-ing[1] OE, noun-forming suffix. ?Horninghold.

-ing[2] OE, toponymic suffix. ?Horninghold, ?Knossington. *Duninge* (f.n. Great Glen), *Heringhegis* (f.n. *Prestgrave*), *Saltingham leaes* (f.n. East Langton), ?*standinge poole* (f.n. Gumley), *thachink* (f.n. Frisby), *Thakines Bushe* (f.n. Kibworth Harcourt).

-ing[3] OE, patronymic suffix. ?Theddingworth.

-inga- OE, gen.pl. of *-ingas*, in compound p.ns. denoting groups or associations of people. Bringhurst, ?Horninghold, ?Theddingworth.

-ingtūn OE, added to a pers.n. to denote an estate associated with that particular individual. Evington, ?Knossington, Saddington, Tur Langton.

***innām** OE, **innám** ON, 'a piece of land taken in or enclosed'. *Innam Close*, *Innam Leys* (f.ns. Cranoe).

inntak ON, 'a piece of land taken in or enclosed', **intack**, **intake** ModEdial., 'a piece of land enclosed from a moor or waste'. Intake (f.n. Bushby, Little Stretton, Thurnby).

into ME, prep., 'into, unto'. *Intoþedikes* (f.n. Stoughton).

island eModE, 'a piece of land completely surrounded by water, a piece of elevated land surrounded by marsh'; also 'a piece of woodland surrounded by open country'. Highland Close Spinney, Highland Spinney. Island Mdw (f.n. Saddington).

īw OE, 'a yew-tree'. ?Nacher (f.n. Kibworth Harcourt).

joynynge ME, ppl.adj., 'adjoining'. *Joyning the Churchyard* (f.n. Tur Langton).

karl (karla gen.pl) ON, 'a freeman of the lower class', corresponding to OE **ceorl**. Carlton Curlieu; King Charles Well (*Carles Trough*).

kenel ME, 'a kennel'; sometimes in later names relating to kennels in which hunting dogs were kept. The Boundary Kennel, Dog Kennel Spinney. Dog Kennel Cl (f.n. Evington, Husbands Bosworth, Stretton Magna), Dog Kennel Lane (f.n. King's Norton).

kide ME, 'a kid, a young goat'. ?Kidmonks Cl (f.n. Foxton).

king ME, 'a king'. King's Norton. *the kings high way* (Cranoe, Stretton Magna), *the Kings way* (Kibworth Beauchamp, Knossington, Stockerston).

kirkja ON, 'a church'. Church Langton (*Kirke Langeton*). *Kerkley* (f.n. Fleckney), *atte Kirke* (p) (Stretton Magna), *atte Kyrke* (p) (Billesdon), *kirkegates* (f.n. Great Bowden), *le Kirkehaued* (f.n. Drayton), *le Kirkehauedlond*, *Kyrkstede* (f.ns. Nevill Holt), *Kirke Lane* (f.n. Carlton Curlieu), *Kirkwood*, *le kyrkelane* (f.ns. Hallaton), *le Kyrkekroft* (f.n. Billesdon).

kjarr ON, 'brushwood', **ker** ME, 'a bog, a marsh, especially one overgrown with brushwood'. Carland Spinney, ?Carrygate. Care (f.n. Gumley), *the carr*, *Kergate* (f.ns. Shangton), *Carres* (f.n. Kibworth Harcourt), Cars (f.n. Kibworth Beauchamp), *Cergates* (f.n. Great Bowden), *Kergate* (f.n. Great Glen), *Kestie* (f.n. Galby), Ralliker (f.n. Saddington).

klint ODan, 'a rocky cliff', used of a steep bank overlooking a river. Clint's Crest. Clint (f.n. Great Easton).

knob ME, 'a knob', whence 'a knoll'. Knob Hill. Riddlety Knob (f.n. Saddington).

krákr (**kráka** gen.pl.) ON, **crake** ME, 'a crow, a raven'. *Crakergate* (f.n. Galby).

la OFr, fem. def.art., 'the'. To be found in medieval f.ns. throughout the text.

lacu OE, 'a stream, a watercourse; a pool, a pond'. ?*Broade lake*, *Lakefurlong*, *le Waterlakes* (f.ns. Great Bowden).

lād OE, 'a watercourse'. ?*lads willowes* (f.n. Blaston).

ladde ME, 'a servant, a man of low birth'. ?*lads willows* (f.n. Blaston).

ladi ME, 'a lady'; often referring to a dowager or to a female proprietor or to the lady of the manor. Our Lady, the Virgin Mary, may be alluded to, esp. with reference to rents for the upkeep of a chapel. Lady Wood. Ladies Mdw (f.n. Bushby), *Ladipole*, *Lady rodis* (f.ns. Burton Overy), *Lady Close* (f.n. Glooston), the Lady Cl (f.n. Hallaton), *Ladydole* (f.n. Fleckney), *Ladye grounds* (f.n. Horninghold), *Ladyes land* (f.n. Slawston), *Lady poole Leas* (f.n. Kibworth Harcourt), Lady's Mdw (f.n. Noseley), Lady Well (f.n. Market Harborough), *My Ladies hedge* (f.n. Mowsley), *Our Ladyes Meadow* (f.n. Great Easton).

***lagge** OE, probably 'a marsh' or the like. *waterlag* (f.n. Husbands Bosworth).

la(g)h ME, **low** ModE, adj., 'low, low-lying'. *Low way* (f.n. Fleckney).

lair ME, 'a place for animals to lie down in'. Cow Lair, The Lair (f.ns. Hallaton), Cow Lair Cl, The Lair (f.ns. Houghton), Cow Layer (f.n. Billesdon).

lairing ModEdial., ppl.adj., '(of animals) lying down, resting'. *the lairing place* (f.n. Great Glen), the Layering place (f.n. Houghton).

lake ME, 'a lake'. The Lake. Lake Mdw (f.n. Galby).

lām OE, 'loam, clay'. *Lamholes* (f.n. Houghton).

lamb (lambra gen.pl.) OE, 'a lamb'. Lamb Coat (f.n. West Langton), *Lambcome* (f.n. Laughton), Lambcot Hill (f.n. King's Norton), *Lambersicke* (f.n. Great Bowden), *Lambescoates* (f.n. Glooston), ?Lambs Cl (f.n. Stockerston).

lammas eModE, 'Loaf Mass'; the 1st of August, in the early English Church observed as a harvest festival at which loaves of bread made from the first ripe corn were consecrated. In f.ns., referring to land which was under cultivation until harvest and reverted to common pasture from Lammas-tide until the following Spring. Lammas Close. (*the*) *Lammas Close* (f.n. Bringhurst, Bushby, Carlton Curlieu, Great Glen, Illston, Knossington, Saddington), *Lammas Croft* (f.n. Smeeton Westerby), the Lammas Ground (f.n. Houghton).

lām-pytt OE, 'a loam-pit'. Limepit Fm. *lampittis* (f.n. Frisby), *Lamport Hill* (f.n. Hallaton).

land, **lond** OE, **land** ON, 'land', either in the general sense 'ground, part of the earth's surface' or 'an estate or small tract of land' or 'a selion, a strip of arable in a great open-field'. Ashlands, Carland Spinney, Scotland (Burton Overy, Houghton), Scotland End. Very freq. in f.ns.: crops may be alluded to, e.g. *Banlandes* (with various spellings in Burton Overy, Drayton, Galby, Glooston and nine other townships), *Flaxlandis* (with various spellings in Burton Overy, Frisby, Little Bowden, *Prestgrave*), *Peaselands* (with various spellings in Billesdon, Frisby, Little Bowden, Nevill Holt), *Oatelands* (Mowsley), Ryelands (Great Easton, Laughton, Little Bowden), *Wadland* (Blaston, Burton Overy, Knossington), *Wheatland* (Illston, ?Laughton); and wild flora, e.g. *Bracklands* (Great Glen), *Gaulond'* (Billesdon), *le Gosse lands* (Great Bowden), *Winilondys* (Burton Overy). The colour of the soil may be specified, e.g. *blacklandes* (Great Bowden, Knossington), *Redlandes* (Glooston, Great Easton, Frisby, Hallaton, Knossington, Nevill Holt) or its nature, e.g. *Sandlands* (Great Glen, Gumley, Hallaton, Smeeton Westerby), *Sandylands* (Burton Overy, Gumley), *Steinland* (Drayton), *Stonlondis* (Great Easton, Gumley), *Stony Lands* (Evington, Great Glen). Shape or extent are freq. specified, e.g. *Bradelandes* (Billesdon), *Little Land* (Hallaton), *Longlands* (Evington, Frisby, Great Easton), *Scortlondes* (Billesdon, Frisby, Great Glen), *Wranglandis*, *Ranglands* (with various spellings in Billesdon, Burton Overy, Great Bowden and six other townships). Ownership or tenure may be noted by a surn., e.g. *Burtons lands*, *Chambers londis*, *Lovetts land*, *Villers land* (Husbands Bosworth), *Coops land*, *Dunningtons land* (Great Bowden), *Gilmonlond*, *Siberdeslond* (Evington), *Pensonland*, *Taylloures land* (Market Harborough), or by an el. signifying rank, e.g. *Ladyes land* (Slawston), *le Lordes land* (Great Bowden), *maid landes* (Blaston). Disputed lands are signalled, e.g. *Flitlondis* (Billesdon, Great Easton). Land endowed for charity appears as Mountsorrel Land (Bushby), while that for the upkeep of local roads occurs as The Causeway Land (Husbands Bosworth). Church lands are occasionally specified, e.g. *the Glebe Land* (Burton Overy, Glooston). Land Cl (Blaston, Galby) record the enclosure of selions or 'lands' of former great open-fields.

land-(ge)mǣre OE, 'a boundary'. *landemeredale* (f.n. Great Easton, *Prestgrave*).

lane OE, 'a lane, a narrow road'. Hunt's Lane, Long Lane, Tugwell Lane. Freq. in f.ns.: with surns., e.g. *Blondes Lane*, *Martyn Lane* (Hallaton), *Ferrars lane* (Great Bowden), *Hunts lane* (Blaston); with farm animals, e.g. Cow Lane

(Billesdon), Hog Lane (Burton Overy, Kibworth Beauchamp); with an el. indicating wetness, e.g. *Daglane* (Market Harborough), *Froglane* (Great Easton), *Starr Lane* (Evington); or size, e.g. Broad Lane (Evington, Husbands Bosworth), ?*Dedelane* (Owston), *the long lane* (Evington). Bridges and churches feature, e.g. Leys Bridge Lane (Burton Overy), *stone brige lane* (Fleckney), *the Church lane* (Cranoe), *Kirke Lane* (Carlton Curlieu), *le kyrkelane* (Hallaton). Note the unusual *Nulane* of 1365 (Illston).

lane-ende ME, 'a lane-end; land at the end of the lane' (*v*. Löfvenberg 117 and Ch **5** (1.ii), 262–3). *Birds lane end* (f.n. Great Bowden), *Broad lane end* (f.n. Husbands Bosworth), *Church lane end* (f.n. Knossington), *Colepit lane end* (f.n. Kibworth Beauchamp), *Grays laine end*, *Hunts Laine End* (f.ns. Hallaton), *Hall Lane End*, *Jaqueses Lane End* (f.ns. Little Stretton), *the Hall lane end* (f.n. King's Norton), Lane End (f.n. Medbourne), *Leicester Lane End*, *Stonegate lane end* (f.ns. Glooston), *Short Lane end* (f.n. Stonton Wyville).

lang[1] OE, **langr** ON, adj., 'long'. East Langton, Church Langton, West Langton; Long Lane. Freq. in f.ns. with a range of aspects of agricultural land, e.g. *Langdike*, *langelond'* (Frisby), *langrass*, *Longe furlonge* (Husbands Bosworth), *longestonlondes* (Great Easton), *Longfield* (Evington), *Longhedole*, *les Longrodes* (Billesdon). Note also the element in compound with topographical features, e.g. *Langham* (Cranoe, Glooston, Great Glen), Langhill (Evington, Husbands Bosworth), *Langmore* (Carlton Curlieu), *Lankthorne* (Gumley), *Longemor* (Great Easton), Long Fern (Bringhurst), Longwood (Billesdon).

lang[2] ME, sb., 'a long strip of land'. East Long (f.n. Slawston), *Estlonge* (f.n. Great Bowden), Level Longs (f.n. Tur Langton), *Longbygate* (f.n. Stoughton).

***langet** OE, 'a long strip of land'. *longegatte* (f.n. Glooston), Long Guts (f.n. Fleckney), Long Yatts (f.n. Kibworth Beauchamp).

lappa OE, 'a lap, the skirt of a garment'; used topographically of a border, an edge, thus 'land at the edge of a parish or estate'. Laphole Cl (f.n. Stretton Magna).

larch eModE, 'the larch-tree'. Larch Plantation, Larch Spinney, Larchwood Rise.

large ME, adj., 'large, great'. *Large Bridge* (Great Bowden).

lasse ME, comp.adj., 'smaller'. *The Lasse Bouudon* (i.e. Little Bowden).

launde OFr, ME, 'an open space in woodland, a forest glade, woodland pasture'. The Lawn, Fair Lawn. *Catgrave Lawnde*, Cow Lawns, Lawn Cl (f.ns. Gumley), *Knoles Laund Close* (f.n. Thurnby), Lawn (f.n. Shangton), The Lawn (f.n. Great Glen, Husbands Bosworth, Medbourne, Stretton Magna), Lawn Bushes Cl (f.n. Hallaton), Lawn Fd, Lawn Mdw (f.ns. Stockerston), *lawnd pound hollow* (f.n. Great Easton).

lāwerce OE, 'a lark'. *Larkhey* (f.n. Nevill Holt), Larkley (f.n. Smeeton Westerby).

***læc(c)** OE, 'a stream, a bog', **lache** ME, 'a slowly moving stream, a stream flowing through boggy land'. *Larchwell* (f.n. Great Bowden).

lǣfer OE, 'a rush, a reed'; prob. also 'a reed bed'. *leathergraues* (f.n. Knossington), Level Longs (f.n. Tur Langton).

lǣs (**lǣswe** gen.sg., dat.sg.) OE, 'pasture, meadow'; very difficult to distinguish from the pl. of **lēah** (**lǣh** (**lǣs** nom.pl.) (Angl)) to which some of the following may rather belong, *v*. **leys**. *Bratlyse*, Saint Leys Mdw (f.ns. Laughton), *le Hayeleyis* (f.n. Great Bowden), *Horkeleyes* (f.n. Houghton), *Le Leys* (f.n. Nevill Holt), Lickleys (f.n. Kibworth Beauchamp), *le Mareleyus*, Mill Layes (f.ns. Medbourne), *Sauntleys* (f.n. Theddingworth), *Smeton leyes* (f.n. Market

Harborough), *Swarboro leyes* (f.n. Mowsley); *Brook Leasow* (f.n. Saddington), *leasure* (f.n. Gumley), *South Leasow* (f.n. Thurnby).

le OFr, masc. def.art., 'the'. To be found in medieval forms throughout the text.

lēac OE, 'a leek, garlic'. Lickleys (f.n. Kibworth Beauchamp).

lēac-tūn OE, 'a leek enclosure', hence 'a herb garden'. Laughton.

lēah OE, **lǣh (lǣs** nom.pl.) (Angl), 'woodland, a woodland glade, a clearing in a wood'; later, 'pasture, meadow', *v.* **leys**. Gumley, Mowsley, Noseley; Bradley Priory, Stackley Ho. Ashley (f.n. Carlton Curlieu), ?Ashley Hades Furlong, Catley, Long Brimley (f.ns. Little Bowden), Bontley, ?*Gosseley* (f.ns. Saddington), Brackley, Lankley (f.ns. Great Glen), Bradley (f.n. Theddingworth), Bradley Wood (f.n. Great Easton), Corkley, Creakley, Larkley (f.ns. Smeeton Westerby), *Kerkley* (f.n. Fleckney), *Okley* (f.n. Stoughton), Radley, *Thranghlie* (f.ns. Cranoe), Roseley (f.n. Thurnby), Stackley (f.n. Little Stretton), *Tasley* (f.n. Foxton), Thrawly (f.n. Glooston), *Wambeley* (f.n. Nevill Holt), *Willey* (f.n. Husbands Bosworth).

lēoht OE, **līht** (Angl), adj., 'light, light-coloured'; also used as a sb. 'a light place' (*v.* Löfvenberg 122). Bottom ~, Middle Light (f.ns. Newton Harcourt).

les, **lez** OFr, pl. def.art., 'the'. To be found in medieval forms throughout the text.

ley[1] ME, 'a pool'. *le leywong*, ?*lygard* (f.ns. Great Bowden).

ley[2] ModE, 'a meadow, a pasture', *v.* **leys**. *Edw. Iliffes ley* (f.n. Kibworth Beauchamp), *Monkes ley* (f.n. Stonton Wyville), *the Towne ley* (f.n. Houghton, Little Stretton).

leyne, **lain** ME, 'a tract of arable land'. ?*the Lanes*, ?Skeffington's First Lane (f.ns. Stockerston).

leys ModE, 'meadows, pastures; grassed-over selions of a common field (lying fallow)'. F.ns. with *leys* (spellings in Gartree Hundred also in *layes*, *lays*, *leas*, *lease*, *lees*, *leies*, *leyes*) may have developed variously from the pl. of **lēah (lǣh (lǣs** nom.pl. (Angl)) in its later sense 'pasture, meadow' and from **lǣs** 'pasture, meadow' and it is very difficult to assign with confidence an individual name to either source, except where forms with *leasow*, *leasure* (from **lǣswe**, gen.sg. of the latter) survive. Professor K. Cameron has argued that most later f.ns. with *leys* (*ley* sg.) are prob. from **lēah**, *v.* L **2** 66 *s.n.* Carr Leys Wood. However, the modern sg. form *ley* may also be the result of the reduction of *leys* (from **lǣs** 'pasture, meadow') as a perceived plural. High Leas, Sunny Leys. Very freq. in f.ns.: esp. with locations, e.g. *Beare hill leyes* (Glooston), Chain Bridge Leys, Clack Hill Leys, Dunslade Leys (Little Bowden), *holy rood leyes*, *Shuggborowe leys* (Burton Overy); and surns., e.g. *Bakon lays* (Gumley), *Chapmans Leys* (Horninghold), Hardy's Leys (Frisby), *Mawkyns leyes* (Burton Overy), *Palmers Leys* (Husbands Bosworth). Adjacent townships may feature, e.g. Keythorpe Leys (Goadby), Shangton Leys (Carlton Curlieu), *Stretton leyes* (Great Glen) and the nature of the leys, e.g. *Josiah Bents hard Layes* (Cranoe), Bastard Leys (Little Bowden), *Blackeleys* (East Langton), Clod Leys (Billesdon), Ferny Lees (Houghton), Sandy Leys (Knossington), *White leyes* (Billesdon, Goadby). The el. occasionally occurs as a simplex, e.g. The Leys (Billesdon, Carlton Curlieu). Recurring are Church Leys (Glooston, Great Glen), Park Leys (Evington, Great Easton), Washpit Leys (Burton Overy, Great Glen), *Willow lees* (Billesdon, Goadby). In compound with a numeral, *leys* represents grassland units of tenure corresponding to *lands* (i.e. selions or strips) similarly used of arable, e.g. *nyneteene leyes* (Burton Overy), *Seaven leyes* (Houghton).

lime ModE, 'the lime-tree, the linden'. Limes Fm.

lim-kilne ME, 'a lime-kiln'. *Limekiln cross* (f.n. Hallaton), Lime Kiln Mdw (f.n. Evington, Scraptoft).

līn OE, **lín** ON, 'flax'. Limborough (f.n. Saddington), *Lincroft Leys* (f.n. Scraptoft), *Lynfeild* (f.n. Houghton).

-ling OE diminutive suffix. Stripling (f.n. Houghton).

līnsǣd OE, **linsed** ME, 'linseed, the seed of flax used esp. as a source of linseed oil'. The Linseed Fds (f.n. Houghton).

loc OE, 'a lock, a bolt; a fold'. *lokhawe* (f.n. Stockerston).

lock ModE, 'a canal lock; an enclosed section of a waterway which has gates at each end and in which the water level can be raised or lowered to move boats from one level to another'. Crane's Lock, Foxton Locks, The Lock Ho., Newton Bottom Lock, Pywell's Lock, Second Lock, Taylor's Turnover Lock, Top Lock.

loge OFr, **log(g)e** ME, 'a hut, a small house'; later 'a house in a forest for temporary use (a forester's house or hunting lodge), a house at the entrance of a park'. Freq. in modern house-names as a pretentious term for a country villa, often prefixed by an older p.n. by analogy with names of genuine hunting-lodges, forest-houses or manorial estate-houses. America Lodge, Amys ~, Belcher's ~, Belvoir ~, Billesdon ~, Blaston ~, Bosworth ~, Bradley ~, Buffalo Lodge, Cedar Lodge Fm, Coplow Lodge, Cranoe ~, Crick's ~, Elkington ~, Evington ~, Fleckney ~, Foxton ~, Frisby ~, Gallow ~, Glooston ~, Gore ~, Great Easton ~, Gumley ~, Hardwick ~, Highcroft ~, Houghton ~, Holyoaks ~, Illston Lodge, Ivy Lodge Fm, Knossington Lodge Fm, Little Bowden Lodge, The Lodge (Burton Overy, King's Norton, Laughton, Lubbenham), Lodge Fm (Billesdon Lodge South), Lower Lodge, Lyndene ~, Lyndon ~, Marefield ~, Muckleborough ~, Owston ~, Pastures ~, Preston ~, Riddlestone Lodge, Rolleston Lodge Fm, Saddington Lodge, Scraptoft ~, Selby's ~, Shangton ~, Snow's ~, Southfield ~, Springfield ~, Stoughton ~, Swains ~, Theddingworth ~, Thorne ~, Top ~, Tur Langton ~, Wade ~, Welham ~, West Langton ~, Wheler ~, White ~, Windmill Lodge. Lodge Cl (f.n. Billesdon, Illston), Lodge Fd (f.n. Nevill Holt), New Lodge Cl (f.n. Blaston).

lopping eModE, vbl.sb., 'the action of cutting off branches, the cutting away of the superflouous growth of trees'. Lawponsale, Little Lawpon (f.ns. Great Easton).

lord ME, 'a lord'. *the Lords close* (f.n. Great Bowden, Kibworth Beauchamp).

lundr ON, 'a small wood'. *Beylund* (f.n. *Prestgrave*), *Lundhul* (f.n. Shangton).

lūs-þorn OE, 'a spindle-tree; any of a genus of small trees or shrubs having a hard wood, formerly used for spindle making'. *lusthornebroc* (f.n. Drayton).

lyme-pytt ME, 'a lime-pit'. *Lime Pitt Cross* (f.n. Hallaton).

lȳtel, **lītel** OE, **lítill** ON, adj., 'little, small'. Little Bowden. Freq. in f.ns., e.g. *Lituldale* (Burton Overy, Hallaton), *Litle Hill* (Evington, Gumley), *Lytelyerd* (Great Glen), *Lytlow* (Burton Overy, Husbands Bosworth), *Lyttelyolwell'* (Illston) etc.

malt-kylne eModE, 'a malt-kiln'. the Old Malt Kiln (f.n. Hallaton).

malting ModE, 'a malt-house'. The Maltings (f.n. Mowsley).

malu** (malwe** dat.sg.) OE, 'a gravel ridge'. ?Mallow (f.n. Tur Langton).

maner ME, 'a manor (house), a mansion'. Great Glen Manor, Hallaton Manor, Manor Fm (Cold Overton, Drayton, Laughton, Marefield, Mowsley, Owston, Saddington), Manor Ho. (Blaston, Foxton, Galby, Goadby, Illston, Kibworth

Harcourt, Knossington, Lubbenham, Tur Langton), Manor House Fm (Burton Overy, Horninghold, King's Norton, Marefield), Manor Rd, Medbourne Manor. *the Mannor House* (Husbands Bosworth).

mansion eModE, 'a manor-house'. *the Mansion place* (f.n. Hallaton).

mansion-house eModE, 'the house of a lord of the manor; an official residence, esp. that belonging to the benefice of an ecclesiastic'. *the Mansion house* (Bringhurst, Burton Overy, Cranoe, East Langton, Great Glen, Knossington).

mare ME, a mare, the female of the domestic horse'. *the Mare Close* (f.n. Goadby).

market ME, 'a market, a market-place'. Market Harborough; Cattle Market, Market Place. *The Butter market*, *Sheep market* (Market Harborough), ?*Market sicke* (f.n. Stockerston).

marle ME, 'marl'. Marl Cl (f.n. Stoughton).

marle-pytt ME, 'a marl-pit'. *Comyn' Marlepyttes* (f.n. Great Bowden), *Marlepittes* (f.n. Laughton), *maulpates* (f.n. Knossington).

marr[1] ON, 'a fen, a marsh'. Great Marr (f.n. King's Norton), *le Mares* (f.n. Welham), ?Margraves (f.n. Hallaton), Marland (f.n. Theddingworth), Marr Fd (f.n. Fleckney), Nether Marr (f.n. Knossington).

maða OE, **math(e)** ME, 'a maggot, a grub; an earthworm', **mad** eModE, ModEdial. 'a maggot'. ?*Madback* (f.n. Lubenham).

matines ME, 'matins, one of the canonical hours of the breviary, sometimes recited at daybreak'. ?Mattin Cl (f.n. Glooston).

mægd OE, 'a maiden'. *maid landes* (f.n. Blaston), *Maidewell'* (f.n. Nevill Holt).

mægden OE, 'a maiden'. *Maidenewell* (f.n. Husbands Bosworth).

mægðe OE, 'may-weed'. ?Medbourne. ?*Madback* (f.n. Lubenham).

mǣl[2] OE, 'speech'. ?*Mallow* (f.n. Tur Langton).

(ge)mǣne OE, adj., 'common'; in p.ns., denoting land held or used communally. *Menegate* (f.n. *Prestgrave*).

(ge)mǣnnes OE, 'a community'; in p.ns., used of 'common land, a common holding'. Mans Horns (f.n. Fleckney).

(ge)mǣre OE, 'a boundary, a border; a strip of land forming a boundary'; often difficult to distinguish from **mere**[1]. Mere Rd. Freq. in f.ns.: most often with the name of an adjoining township, e.g. *Burton mere* (Great Glen), *Foxton Meare* (Gumley), *Galby Meere*, *Ilston Meere* (Frisby), *Horningold Meere* (Hallaton), *Lubnam mere* (Foxton). Boundary markers occasionally feature, e.g. *Meare Copp* (Evington), *Merehegg* (Great Easton).

mæðel OE, 'speech, assembly, council'. *Mathelou*, *Mathelehougate* (f.ns. Shangton).

mealt OE, 'malt'. Malt Adland (f.n. Great Easton).

mealt-hūs OE, 'a malt-house'. Malthouse Yard (f.n. Medbourne).

mearð OE, 'a marten, a weasel'. Marefield, *Old Marefield*.

mēd (**mēdwe** obl.sg.) OE (Angl), 'a meadow'. ?Medbourne. Examples in f.ns. from the nom.sg. are comparatively few; early instances are *Silkinemede* (1200 Drayton), *Medelond'* (1328 Shangton), *the Meade close* (1638 Saddington), *Millfield meade* (1653 Carlton Curlieu), while post-1750 examples are Far Mead, Great ~, Harp's ~, Long ~, Pride Mead (Houghton), Kestens Mead (Great Bowden). Freq. in the obl.sg.: early instances are *Litlemedwe* (e.13 Nevill Holt), *shouelebrodemedue*, *smethemedwe* (both c.1250 Frisby), *le Oldhulmedewe* (Edw 1 (1467 x 84) Billesdon), *Medewelondis* (l.13 Shangton), *Smethmedewe* (1383 Great Bowden), *Folkatmedowe*, *le Mermedewe* (both 1392 Hallaton), *Smethe*

Medewe 1397 (Illston). Note *Our Ladyes Meadow* (1587 Great Easton).

mere[1] OE, 'a pool, a lake', also 'wetland'; difficult to distinguish from **(ge)mǣre**. *Addemermedwe* (f.n. Stretton Magna), *Cranmer* (f.n. Husbands Bosworth), The Mear in Leicester Fd (f.n. Evington). The following are uncertain: *Carrs Meeres*, *dale meare*, *Pepin Meare*, *Reddle meare*, *the Mearis*, *Millmeare* (f.ns. Kibworth Beauchamp), *Davis meer*, The Meers (f.ns. Newton Harcourt), *Langham meere*, *myddle mere* (f.ns. Great Glen), Little Mere, *le mermedewe* (f.ns. Medbourne), *the Meyre* (f.n. Mowsley), *Schortesmere* (f.n. Theddingworth).

mere-stall OE, 'a (stagnant) pool, a pond' (*v*. Ch **3** 158–9). *Marstall* (f.n. Laughton).

mersc OE, 'a marsh, watery land'. *Anlong Brodmersche* (f.n. Illston), Braymish (f.n. Little Bowden), Bremish (f.n. Kibworth Harcourt, Smeeton Westerby), *Green Martch* (f.n. Kibworth Harcourt), *broad marche* (f.n. Tur Langton), Great Marsh (f.n. Owston), March Mdw (f.n. Hallaton), Marsdale (f.n. Frisby, Medbourne, Slawston), The Marshes (f.n. Great Easton, Slawston), *le Mersch* (f.n. Stretton Magna), Wood Marsh (f.n. Billesdon).

meðal ON, adv., 'among, between'; in p.ns. with adj. function 'middle', influencing or replacing OE **middel** in the Danelaw. *le medelfourlonge* (f.n. Great Easton).

micel, **mycel** OE, **mikill** ON, adj., 'big, great'; the OE el. is much influenced by the ON el. in the Danelaw and is difficult to distinguish. *Mikell Bowdon* (Great Bowden); Muckleborough Fm. Freq. in f.ns., e.g. *Mikelacr'* (Bringhurst), *Mikelbergh* (Great Bowden), *Muckledale* (Great Glen), *Myckle dale* (Great Easton).

middel OE, adj., 'middle. Freq. in f.ns., e.g. *le medelfourlonge*, *Midle gate* (Great Easton), *Middelfurlong* (Bringhurst), *le Middelstimoorsyke* (Billesdon), *Middle Close* (Billesdon, Burton Overy, Evington), Middle Fd, *the Middle Slade* (Great Glen), *midle hill* (Fleckney).

midwinter OE, 'the middle of winter'. *Midewinter stickes* (f.n. Stoughton).

milking eModE, vbl.sb., ppl.adj., 'the drawing of milk from the udders of cows and other animals'; 'concerned with lactation', i.e. a place for milch cows. Milking Pens Spinney. Milking Cl (f.n. Houghton).

millere ME, 'a miller'. Millerdale. Millers Acre (f.n. Smeeton Westerby).

mīl-stān OE, 'a mile-stone'. Milestone (f.n. Kibworth Beauchamp).

mirable ME, adj., 'wonderful, marvellous'; and as a sb., 'something wonderful, a wonder'. Great Merrible Wood, Little Merrible Wood.

mǫl ON, 'gravel' *Mealebecke* (f.n. Galby).

moldhille ME, 'a molehill, a small mound of earth thrown up by a mole in burrowing near the surface of the ground'. *Moldhils* (f.n. Saddington).

moneye ME, 'coin, money'. *Money hole* (f.n. Kibworth Beauchamp).

mont, **munt(e)** ME, 'a mount, a hill'. Mill Mound, The Mount (Billesdon, Market Harborough, Scraptoft, Wistow), The Munt. Mill Mount (f.n. Glooston, Great Bowden, Hallaton), *Milne mounte* (f.n. East Langton), Mount Cl (f.n. Gumley), *Mounthill* (f.n. Carlton Curlieu), Roly Mount (f.n. Saddington).

mōr[1] OE, **mór** ON, a moor; marshland, barren wasteland, barren upland'. Moorbank Fm, Moor Hill, The Moors. Andrews ~, Berry ~, Drany Moor, *Ghenderismore*, *le Middelstimoorsyke*, Moor Plot, New ~, Orchard Moor, *Pippiswellemore*, *Prestemor*, *Shouelbrodemoor*, West Moor (f.ns. Billesdon), Bartmore, *the more meadow* (f.ns. Fleckney), Blackmoor (f.n. Owston), *Blackmore*, *Redesmore*, *Skegesmore*, *Watmore* (f.ns. Houghton), *Bukwelmore*, *Foxton Moore*,

Hauerberghemore (f.ns. Great Bowden), *Buston hill ~*, *Little dale ~*, *St Morills more* (f.ns. Hallaton), *Caldewelmore*, *Flascemore*, *Hernoldismor*, *Tommor* (f.ns. Great Easton), *Copedmore* (f.n. Mowsley), *Cotemore*, *Steppmill more* (f.ns. Husbands Bosworth), Far Moor (f.n. Great Glen), *Houghton more*, *morrill sike*, *Wheate more* (f.ns. Frisby), *the Langmore Closes* (f.n. Carlton Curlieu), *longemur* (f.n. Galby), *Long Moor Close*, *Moor Field* (f.ns. Horninghold), *May Moore* (f.n. Kibworth Harcourt), Moor Cl, *Redemore* (f.ns. Burton Overy), Moore Hill, Spinney Moore (f.ns. Evington), *le Moorfeld* (f.n. Bringhurst), *the Moors* (f.n. Drayton), *Morewell'* (f.n. Nevill Holt), The Mowwell (f.n. Illston), Wildmore (f.n. Tur Langton). *Dead Moor* occurs with various spellings in Blaston, Frisby, Horninghold, Husbands Bosworth, Little Bowden and Lubenham.

mos OE, **mosi** ON, 'moss, lichen', also 'a bog, a swamp'. Moss Fm. *moserne* (f.n. Gumley), *Mosewellehyl* (f.n. East Langton), *Mussell seeke* (f.n. Knossington), *Muswell Hill* (f.n. Thorpe Langton), Muzzle Hole (f.n. Tur Langton), *Waueremos* (f.n. Frisby).

mōt OE, 'a meeting, a moot'. ?Moat Cl (f.n. Scraptoft), *mothoryn* (f.n. Illston).

mote ME, 'a moat, a protective ditch filled with water around a building'. The Mot. *the mill moote* (f.n. Cranoe), *the milne mote* (f.n. Glooston), Moat Cl (f.n. Evington), ?Moat Cl (f.n. Scraptoft).

moyst ME, adj., 'damp. slightly wet'. *Moyst Irons* (f.n. Laughton).

muche ME, adj., 'great'. *Much Bowden* (Great Bowden), *Much Stretton* (Stretton Magna).

***muddig** OE, adj., 'muddy'. ?Moody Syke (f.n. Cold Overton).

muk ME, 'dung, muck, dirt'. Muck Hill (f.n. Kibworth Beauchamp).

mūs OE, 'a mouse'. Mowsley. Mouses Quick (f.n. Little Bowden), *Musdale* (f.n. Little Stretton), *Musehull* (f.n. Husbands Bosworth), *Musfurlong* (f.n. Great Bowden).

***mylde** OE (Angl), 'soil, earth'. Black Miles (f.n. Husbands Bosworth, Medbourne, Tur Langton), *Blakemilde* (f.n. Billesdon, Nevill Holt), *Blakmylland* (f.n. Mowsley), *rademylde* (f.n. Great Bowden).

myln OE, 'a mill', cf. **water-mylne**, **wind-mylne**. Burnmill Lane, Mill Hill (Laughton, Market Harborough, Lubenham), Mill Ho., Mill Lane, Mill Mound, Old Mill Barn. Specified mills are: *Burnt Mill*, *Dunmoors Mill* (Hallaton), *William Campion his mill*, *Robert Freeman his mill* (Burton Overy), Easton Mill (Great Easton), Foxton Mill (Foxton), *le gatemyll'*, *Packes Mill* (Great Bowden), *the Milne* (Great Glen). Freq. in f.ns.: *the Mill balke* (Glooston, Nevill Holt)), *Mill Close* (Billesdon, Blaston), *Mill Dam* (Burton Overy), *the mill dore* (Husbands Bosworth), *Mill feild* (with various spellings in Blaston, Burton Overy, Carlton Curlieu, Cranoe, Foxton, Great Easton, Great Glen, Gumley, Horninghold, Nevill Holt), *Milnegate* (Gumley, Nevill Holt), Mill Hill (Fleckney, Great Glen), Mill Mdw (Great Glen), Mill Mount (Glooston, Hallaton), Mill Pits Cl (Foxton), Mill Slade (Husbands Bosworth), Mill Stede (Fleckney), *Milne Holme* (Drayton, Galby), *le mylne howse* (Market Harborough), *le mylnewong* (Drayton), Old Mill Cls (Gumley), *Twynymill hill* (Husbands Bosworth).

myngled eModE, ppl.adj, 'put together so as to make one'. *Myngde Feilde* (f.n. Little Stretton, Stretton Magna).

mýrr ON, 'a mire, a bog, swampy ground'. Blackmire (f.n. Houghton) *Carrs Mire* (f.n. Kibworth Beauchamp), *Fullwell meires* (f.n. Thorpe Langton), *Meires* (f.n. Tur Langton), Mire Cl (f.n. Little Stretton), The Mires (f.n. Billesdon, Cold Overton, Husbands Bosworth), ?Pisamire (f.n. Fleckney), *Redmires* (Little Stretton, Rolleston), *Brian Saterthwaite his myres* (f.n. Goadby).

myry ME, adj., 'miry, muddy'. *Merihegg* (f.n. Great Easton), *merimedowe* (f.n. Gumley), Mirey Hill (f.n. Goadby), Mirey Mdw (f.n. Billesdon, Bushby), Mirey Plantation, Mirey Spinney (f.ns. Thurnby).

nān-mann OE, 'no man, nobody'. *No mans Bush* (f.n. Tur Langton), *no mans butt* (f.n. Great Easton), *nomans leys* (f.n. Glooston).

nattok ME, of unknown origin and meaning, but poss. the name of a marsh plant; related to OE ***næt** 'wet' in formation with the noun suffix **-uc**. *Water Nattocke* (f.n. Thorpe Langton).

nearu OE, adj., 'narrow'. Narrow Cl (f.n. Billesdon), Narrow Croft (f.n. Smeeton Westerby), *Narrow Pike* (f.n. Frisby); used as a sb. in *Grannam Narrowe* (f.n. Great Bowden).

nēat OE, 'cattle'. ?Nacher (f.n. Kibworth Beauchamp), *Neates Leys* (f.n. Bushby), *the neates pasture* (f.n. Blaston, Hallaton), *Neatshead* (f.n. Frisby), *by Neyton* (f.n. Great Easton), *Mr Roberts neatespen*, *Mr Streetes Neets pen* (f.ns. Thorpe Langton).

neetherd ME, 'a cow-herd'. *the Neatheards baulke* (f.n. King's Norton).

neoðera OE, adj., 'lower'. Nether Hall. Freq. in f.ns., e.g. *Nederblakebroc* (Husbands Bosworth), *le Netherbaukes*, *Nethere Grenehil* (f.n. Billesdon), *the Netherfeild* (Cranoe), *le Netherforth* (Houghton), *Netherfurlong* (Burton Overy), *le Nether heth*, *le Nethersty* (Evington), Nether Mdw (Great Easton, Frisby), *le Netherorchard* (Nevill Holt), *Nethirbanlont* (Illston), *Nethir Wylardisgate* (Great Bowden).

nese ME, 'the nose', hence 'a headland, a promontory, a projecting piece of land in the bend of a river'. ?*Clarness* (f.n. East Langton), *Nise* (f.n. Foxton).

nest OE, 'a nest'; used figuratively for a comfortable, safe place or sometimes, in the type *crow's nest*, for the highest place in a district. ?*Niste hill* (f.n. Newton Harcourt), Norman's Nest (f.n. Theddingworth).

netel(e) OE, 'a nettle'. *netle dole* (f.n. Gumley), Nettle Cl (f.n. West Langton).

nexte ME, prep., 'adjacent to, nearest to'. *next the Sonne* (f.n. Houghton).

nigon OE, num., 'nine'. *the 9 foot dole* (f.n. Stonton Wyville).

nīwe OE, adj., 'new'. Newbold, Newton Harcourt. *le Newe close* (f.n. Burton Overy, Nevill Holt, Owston), *Newdole* (f.n. Houghton), *New Pool Leys*, *le upper newe close* (f.ns Horninghold), *Newstede* (f.n. Evington), *Nulane* (f.n. Illston).

nōk ME, 'a nook; a nook of land, a triangular plot of ground'. The Nook (Great Glen, West Langton). Bushy Nook, Cherry Tree Nook (f.ns. Owston), *the Church nook* (f.n. Great Glen), Codham Nook, Three Nooks (f.ns. Evington), *Hallaton Nookes*, *Nook End*, *Nutts Nook*, *Wellham Nook*, *Wood Nook* (f.ns. Cranoe), *Hewards nooke* (f.n. Kibworth Beauchamp), Nook, Wood Nook (f.ns. Knossington), Nooke Cl (f.n. Bushby), The Nooks (f.n. Wistow), Rookery Nook (f.n. Foxton).

Norman ME, 'a Norman of Normandy'. ?*Normantoftes* (f.n. Great Glen).

norð OE, ON, adj., 'northern, north'. King's Norton, *Northmardefeld'* (*Old Marefield*); North Lane. Freq. in f.ns., e.g. *Northlangfurlang* (Drayton, Great

Easton), *Northfeld* (Billesdon, Blaston, Burton Overy, Cranoe, Foxton, Great Bowden, Great Easton, Husbands Bosworth), *the North hill* (Bringhurst), *le northsike* (Horninghold).

Norðman late OE, 'a Norwegian'. ?*Normantoftes* (f.n. Great Glen).

norðweard OE, adj., adv., 'northern, northward, to the north'. ?Northward Cl (f.n. Shangton), *Northwardehyll* (f.n. Noseley).

nōs(e) OE, 'a promontory, a headland'. *Noston'* (f.n. Mowsley).

nursery eModE, 'a piece of ground in which young plants or trees are reared until fit for transplantation; a nursery garden'. (The) Nursery (f.n. Fleckney, King's Norton).

nyentene ME, num., 'nineteen'. *ouer nynetene leyes* (f.n. Burton Overy).

odde ME., adj. 'odd, single'. the Odd Willow (f.n. Medbourne).

***ofer**[2] OE, 'a slope, a hill, a ridge'. Cold Overton; Overclose Spinney. ?Far Over Hill (f.n. Goadby), ?*Ortondale* (f.n. Burton Overy).

ofer[3] OE, prep., 'over, above'; difficult to distinguish from **uferra**. *Ouerclyftherne* (f.n. Great Easton), *ouergoseacur*, *Ouergrymeswonge* (f.ns. Great Bowden), *ouer nynetene leyes* (f.n. (Burton Overy), ?*Ouertwel* (f.n. Theddingworth), Over Barn Cl (f.n. Billesdon).

ofer-þwart ME, adj. adv., 'across, lying across'. *ouerwharte greene seeke* (f.n. Knossington), *the overthwart hill* (f.n. Great Easton).

open OE, adj. 'open, unenclosed'. *Open Close* (f.n. East Langton), *the Open Doke* (f.n. Gumley).

orceard, **ort-geard** OE, 'a garden'; later in OE, 'an orchard'. Orchard Lane. Back ~, Evington ~, King's Orchard (f.ns. Evington), Back ~, Front Orchard (f.ns. Glooston), Barn's ~, Cleave ~, Harry's ~, Old Hall Orchard, Orchard Moor (f.ns. Billesdon), *Bernorcharde* (f.n. Nevill Holt), Bullsholme ~, Old Orchard (f.ns. Lubenham), *Canuilesorchard* (f.n. Medbourne), Crow ~, House Orchard (f.ns. Owston), Folly Orchard (f.n. Welham), *le Netherorcherd* (f.n. Nevill Holt), The Orchard (f.n. Foxton), Orchard Cl (f.n. Burton Overy, Evington, Illston), Rhodes Orchard (f.n. West Langton), Wad Orchard (f.n. Blaston), Widow Knight's Orchard (f.n. Husbands Bosworth).

ord OE, 'a point, a corner or spit of land, a projecting ridge of land'. *Ordalys* (f.n. Nosley), ?Orids (f.n. Frisby).

oter OE, 'an otter'. *Otter Brook* (f.n. Hallaton).

overte ME, adj., 'open, laid open, uncovered'. ?*Ouertwel* (f.n. Theddingworth).

oxa (**oxna** gen.pl.) OE, 'an ox'. *Goodinges oxe* (f.n. Great Bowden), Oxall (f.n. Fleckney), *Oxe close* (f.n. Husbands Bosworth), *Oxepol* (f.n. Shangton), *Oxhed* (f.n. East Langton), *Oxundal* (f.n. Burton Overy).

oyser, **osyer** ME, 'osier, willow'. *le Osiereswell* (f.n. Billesdon), Ozier Bed (f.n. Knossington, Little Stretton), Ozier Beds (f.n. Smeeton Westerby).

***padde** OE, **padda** ON, 'a toad'. ?Padgate Cl (f.n. Scraptoft), ?Pad Lands (f.n. Little Stretton, Stoughton), Padwell (f.n. Bushby).

paddock eModE, 'a small field or enclosure; a plot of pasture land usually adjoining a house or stable'. Chestnuts Paddock, Paddock (f.ns. Foxton), Fred Claypole's ~, H. Craythorne's ~, Mrs Miller Bakewell's Paddock (f.ns. Great Easton), Dents Paddocks (f.n. Blaston), Home ~, Little ~, Swinglers Paddock (f.ns. Lubenham), Home Paddock (f.n. Knossington), Jackson's Paddock (f.n. Medbourne), Johnson's First ~, Rand's ~, Stokes ~, Top Paddock (f.ns. Great Easton), Knight

Paddock (f.n. Billesdon), The Paddock (f.n. Billesdon, Illston, Nevill Holt), The Paddocks (f.n. Blaston, Great Glen), Yard Paddock (f.n. Shangton).

***padduc** OE, **paddok** ME, 'a frog'. *Paddockis Pyltche* (f.n. Great Bowden), *Paddock well* (f.n. East Langton), *Paddockwell Stile* (f.n. Thorpe Langton), *Podocks Pit* (f.n. Gumley).

pāl OE, **pole** ME 'a pole, a long slender piece of wood'; later 'a pole of definite length used as a measure', hence a lineal measure, esp. for land; as a measure of area, 30¼ square yards. Ashpole Spinney (f.n. Nevill Holt), ?Ashpools (f.n. Kibworth Beauchamp), ?Pole Cl (f.n. Nevill Holt).

palis ME, 'a palisade'. Palace Hill.

paradis ME, 'a garden, an enclosed pleasure ground'. Paradise (f.n. Glooston, Hallaton).

park ME, 'an enclosed tract of land for beasts of the chase'; later also 'an enclosed plot of ground, a field'. Cold Overton Park Wood, Cottage Park, Evington ~, Great Easton ~, Old ~, Welland Park, Park Wood. Fairly freq. in f.ns., e.g. America Park (Great Easton), Glen Hall ~, Manor Park (Great Glen), *Hall Park* (Hallaton), Longwood ~, Pigs ~, Reap ~, Shippen ~, Small ~, Town Park (Billesdon), *Parke wonge* (Knossington), The Park (Billesdon, Carlton Curlieu, Foxton, Great Glen, Laughton, Welham), Wood Meadow Park (Rolleston).

part ME, 'a part, a portion'. Bottom ~, Top Part (f.ns. Hallaton), Far Part (f.n. Illston), *the Mill parte* (f.n. King's Norton).

pasture ME, 'a pasture, a piece of pasture-land'. Blaston Pastures. Fairly common in f.ns.: Borsdens Pasture Cl (Blaston), the Bridge ~, the Cottiers ~, the Meadow Pasture (Lubenham), *Calfes paster* (Lubenham), Calves ~, Horse Pasture (Billesdon), *Cow Pasture* (Blaston, Burton Overy, Cranoe, Glooston, Great Bowden, Great Glen, Gumley, Husbands Bosworth), *the Common Cow Pasture* (Foxton), *Harborough Pastures* (Great Bowden), *the hoggs pasture* (East Langton), *Jenkynnes pasture* (Evington), the Neats Pasture, *Pastare Gapp* (Hallaton), *the Pasture*, Pasture Cl (Bringhurst).

patche eModE, 'a patch; a small piece of ground'. the Patches (f.n. Great Glen).

patched eModE, ppl.adj., 'patched, repaired'. ?*le Patched close* (f.n. Great Bowden).

***pat(t)e** OE, 'mud, marsh'. *Patrick* (f.n. Great Bowden).

pæð OE (Angl), **pad** ModEdial., 'a path, a track'. *Bradley pathe* (f.n. Medbourne), Stoney Path (f.n. Kibworth Beauchamp); Beggars Pad Cl (f.n. Owston), ?Pad Lands (f.n. Little Stretton, Stoughton).

***pēac** OE, 'a knoll, a hill, a peak'. *Peck field* (f.n. Blaston).

pece ME, 'a piece; a piece or plot of land'. Freq. in f.ns.: with a surn. indicating ownership, e.g. Ashby's Piece (Great Easton), Burnaby's Piece (Evington), *Dysons Peece* (Husbands Bosworth), *Wm. Worths Piece* (Cranoe); with a common building, e.g. *Cotes peice* (Drayton), Cottage Piece (Saddington), *Hall piece* (Glooston, Husbands Bosworth); with farm animals, e.g. *the Bull peice* (Hallaton, Houghton), *Cowpiece* (Evington); with crops, e.g. Crab Piece (East Langton), the Potatoe Piece (Hallaton); with an el. indicating the quality/nature of the ground, e.g. *Barearse Peice*, *Rushy Peice* (Hallaton), Hassocks Piece (Great Bowden), Rough Piece (Billesdon), *stonpeices* (Gumley); with location, e.g. Red House Piece (Medbourne), Road Piece (Illston), *Round Hill piece* (Glooston), Wash-pit Piece (Horninghold). Recurring is *Cheiscake peece* (Glooston, Great Bowden, Hallaton, Houghton). Note *Deadman peece* (Gumley) and Accommodation Piece (Medbourne).

pecock ME, 'a peacock'. *Pecocroft* (f.n. Billesdon).

pejon ME, 'a (young) dove, a pigeon'. ?Piggens Croft (f.n. Scraptoft).

peni ME, 'a penny'; used in f.ns. for something paying a penny rent. ?*Penytherne* (f.n. Great Bowden), ?*Pennythorne* (f.n. Lubenham).

penn[2] OE, 'a small enclosure, a fold'. Milking Pens Spinney. Fairly freq. in f.ns., esp. with the names of owners, e.g. *Harpers penn* (Great Bowden), *Thomas Hobsons pen* (Great Glen), *Mr Roberts neatspen*, *Mr Streetes Neets pen* (Thorpe Langton); with reference to cattle, e.g. *Stephensons Bullock Pen Close* (Hallaton), Cow Pen Cl (Evington, Glooston). Recurring is *Penn Close* (Billesdon, Carlton Curlieu, Fleckney, Goadby, Great Glen, Laughton) and Pen Yard (Illston, Owston).

personage ME, 'a parsonage'. *Blaston parsonage* (Blaston), *the Parsonage* (Stonton Wyville), *the Parsonage House* (Billesdon, Burton Overy, Carlton Curlieu, Cold Overton, Cranoe, Galby, Glooston, Great Bowden, Gumley, Hallaton, Houghton, Husbands Bosworth, Kibworth Beauchamp, Knossington, Shangton), *the Parsonage Bushe*, *Parsonage Leys*, *the Parsonage Sicke*, *the Parsonage whomsted* (f.ns. Hallaton), *the Parsonage Close* (f.n. Galby, Stretton Magna), *the Parsonage Dole* (f.n. Tur Langton), *the Parsonage Great Close* (f.n. Stockerston), *the Parsonage ground* (f.n. Houghton), *the Parsonage ground*, *the Parsonage meadow* (f.ns. Cranoe), *the Parsonage Land* (f.n. Great Bowden), *the Parsonage sicke* (f.n. Stonton Wyville), *Stonton Parsonage Close* (f.n. Glooston).

persone ME, 'a parson, a beneficed cleric'. Big Parsons (f.n. Slawston), Parson's Acre (f.n. Kibworth Harcourt), *Parsons bush*, Parsons Leas, *Parsons sicke* (f.ns. Hallaton), *the Parsons chiskeck*, *the Parsons tippitt dole* (f.ns. Glooston), Parsons Cl (f.n. Blaston, Great Easton, Scraptoft, Stockerston, Stretton Magna), *the parsons gore* (f.n. Frisby), *Parsons hedge* (f.n. Burton Overy), Parson's Mdw (f.n. Carlton Curlieu), *the Parsons Platts* (f.n. Stretton Magna), *the Parsons willowes* (f.n. Gumley), *the persons balke*, *the persons cloase* (f.ns. Tur Langton).

pertre ME, 'a pear-tree'. The Pear Tree. *Payretree Croft* (f.n. Carlton Curlieu), Pear Tree (f.n. Smeeton Westerby), Pear Tree Mdw (f.n. Stoughton).

peterstone eModE, 'a fossil encrinite, a small marine arthropod such as a trilobite'. Peter Stone Bridge (f.n. Lubenham).

pīc OE, 'a point; a pointed hill'. *Picke medewe* (f.n. Glooston), *the Pikes* (f.n. Cranoe, Hallaton), *Narrow Pike* (f.n. Frisby).

***pigga** OE, **pigge** ME, 'a young pig', **pig** ModE, 'a pig'. Pig Fd (f.n. Newton Harcourt), Pig Hut (f.n. Stoughton), Pigs Park (f.n. Billesdon).

piked ME, adj., 'tapering to a point'. Piked Mdw (f.n. Glooston).

pilche ME, 'a rough outer garment or rug'; in f.ns., prob. used figuratively for a patch of rough ground.

píll ON, 'a willow'. ?*Pylland* (f.n. Theddingworth).

***pinc** OE, 'a minnow'. Pinkwell Cl (f.n. Evington).

***pinca** OE, 'a finch'. Pincham (f.n. Scraptoft).

pinder ME, 'a pinder, an officer of a manor or township who impounded stray beasts'. *Pindermedow* (f.n. Houghton).

pingel ME, 'a small plot of ground'. Pingle (f.n. Knossington), *the Pingle* (f.n. Houghton, King's Norton, Owston), Church Pingle, Wilcox Spinney Pingle (f.ns.

Evington), Pingle Mdw (f.n. Billesdon).

pīpe OE, 'a conduit'. ?Bumpipe Cl (f.n. Saddington), *Pippiswell* (f.n. Billesdon).

***pipere** OE, 'a spring, a stream'. ?Pepper Hill Mdw.

pirige OE, 'a pear-tree'. *Perwickes Close* (f.n. Lubenham).

pise OE, 'pease'. Peace Hill, Peashill Fm. Freq. in f.ns., esp. in the compounds *Peaseland*(*s*) (with various spellings in Billesdon, Frisby, Goadby, King's Norton, Little Bowden, Medbourne, Nevill Holt, Slawston, Stoughton, Theddingworth) and *pesehylle* (with various spellings in Husbands Bosworth, Laughton, Saddington, Shangton, Slawston); Peas Cl (Knossington), *Peascroft Meare* (Kibworth Harcourt), *Pissowe* (Houghton).

pisse ME, 'urine'. ?Pisamire (f.n. Fleckney).

pissemyre ME, 'an ant'. ?Pisamire (f.n. Fleckney).

place ME, 'an area surrounding by buildings'; later 'a plot of land' and 'a residence'. Market Place. *Bernardisplace*, *Caundeleynysplace*, *Copsyesplace*, *Cretonesplace* (Medbourne), *le ferme place*, the Layering place (f.ns. Houghton), *the Gospell place* (f.n. Stonton Wyville), *Halleplace* (Little Stretton), *the lairing place* (f.n. Great Glen), *the Mansion place* (Hallaton), *Rike place* (f.n. Husbands Bosworth), *the Watering place* (f.n. Burton Overy).

plain ME, ''a great open tract'; also 'a piece of flat meadowland'. *Stockerston Plaine* (f.n. Stockerston).

planke ME, 'a plank, a plank bridge'. *Caudwell planke* (f.n. East Langton), Plank Cl (f.n. Smeeton Westerby, West Langton), Planks (f.n. Saddington).

plantation ModE, 'a wood of planted trees'. Blenheim Plantation, Cotton's Field ~, Dog Kennel ~, Elizabeth ~, Home ~, Larch ~, Laughton Brook ~, Long ~, Muckleborough Plantation. Freq. in f.ns.: *Ash Plantation*, Lower ~, Upper Plantation (Little Stretton), Banks Plantation, *Cranes Close Plantation*, Dungeon ~, Hill End ~, Little ~, Mason's Close ~, Wad Orchard ~, Watsons Acre Plantation (Blaston), Belt Plantation (Cold Overton), Cross Burrow Hill ~, Long Plantation (Glooston), Fir Hill ~, Gall Hill ~, Holme ~, Wisp Plantation (Knossington), Fish-pond Plantation (Great Glen), Holt Plantation (Nevill Holt), Mirey Plantation (Thurnby), Old Orchard Plantation (West Langton), Plantation Cl (Illston).

planting ModE, vbl.sb., 'a plantation'. Woolpits Planting.

plat[2] ME, 'a plot, a small piece of ground'. Boare Platt Cl (f.n. Gumley), *Calves platt* (f.n. Houghton), Coopers Meadow Platt (f.n. West Langton), Far Platt (f.n. Goadby), *Medow plattes* (f.n. Laughton), *the Parsons Platts*, Top Platt (f.ns. Stretton Magna), *Piners Platt* (f.n. Kibworth Harcourt), *Woostinsplat* (f.n. Husbands Bosworth).

plega OE, **plaga** (Angl), 'play, sport'; 'a place for games'. Play Cl (f.n. Horninghold).

pleg-stōw OE, 'a place where people gathered for play'. *Playstow*, *Westerplaystowe* (f.ns. Drayton).

plōg OE, **plógr** ON, 'a plough'. Little Plough Cl (f.n. Houghton), Long Plough (f.n. Wistow), The Old Plough Fd (f.n. Saddington), Plough Cl (f.n. Foxton, Frisby, Galby, Knossington, Slawston, Smeeton Westerby), Plough Fd (f.n. Frisby, Glooston), Plow Cl (f.n. Billesdon).

plot late OE, ME, 'a small piece of ground'. *the Bayleys Plott* (f.n. Houghton), Calves ~, Colt's ~, Moor ~, Potatoe Plot (f.ns. Billesdon), Dunmore's Plot (f.n.

Knossington), Hen Plot (f.n. Stoughton), *hyllynges plott* (f.n. Great Bowden), Meadow Plotts (f.n. Laughton), *the Parsons plott* (f.n. Blaston), the Plot (f.n. Medbourne, Welham), *Plottesgate* (f.n. Great Easton), *Woostons Plott* (f.n. Husbands Bosworth).

plūm-trēow OE, 'a plum-tree'. *Plumbetree Sicke* (f.n. Hallaton).

pode ME, 'a toad'. Podehill (f.n.Mowsley), Podell (f.n. Saddington).

poket ME, 'a pocket'; in f.ns., often alluding to a round field with a narrow entrance. Pocket Mdw (f.n. Cold Overton).

pōl[1] OE, 'a pool'. Freq. in f.ns.: *alby poyl* (Illston), *Beles Poole*, *Lady poole Leas* (Kibworth Harcourt), Bell Pool, *Ladipole* (Burton Overy) *Cleypole* (Great Bowden), *dodspole*, *Ripepoole*, *rutpoole* (Husbands Bosworth), *heygatepol* (Slawston), *horsepul* (Glooston), *horspol* (*Prestgrave*), *Milnepol* (Saddington), *Oxepol*, *Stillepol* (Shangton), *the pole* (Great Glen), *Poles Slade* (Great Bowden), Pool Cl, Two Pool (Scraptoft), *standinge poole*, *Stanypoole* (Gumley), *Stanipoll* (Foxton), *Swans poole* (King's Norton), *Washpoole* (Houghton), *winpooles* (Knossington), *Wylspole* (Goadby).

ponde ME, 'a pond, an artificial or natural pool'. Old Pond Wood. The Folly Pond (f.n. Great Bowden), (*the*) *Pond Close* (f.n. Galby, Horninghold, Husbands Bosworth, Noseley, Rolleston, Saddington).

pony ModE, a pony, a horse of any small breed'. Pony Cl (f.n. Fleckney), Pony's Fd (f.n. Billesdon).

poplere ME, 'a poplar, a tree of the genus *Populus*'. Poplar Spinney.

port[2] OE, 'a market-town, a market'. Port Bridge. ?*Porters hill* (f.n. Bringhurst), *Portgarth* (f.n. Husbands Bosworth), *Port hedge*, *Porthyll* (f.ns. Burton Overy), Port Hill (f.n. Kibworth Beauchamp), Portland Mdw (f.n. Saddington).

port-gate ME, 'a road to a (market-) town, a road to a market'. *Portegate* (Great Bowden, Shangton), ?*Portgarth* (f.n. Husbands Bosworth), (*le*) *Portgate* (Billesdon, Evington, Slawston, Stoughton), Purgate (Gumley).

port-wey ME, 'a road to a (market-) town, a road to a market'. ?*Porters hill* (f.n. Bringhurst), ?Port Hill (f.n. Kibworth Beauchamp), *Portway* (Billesdon, Great Glen), (*le*) *Portwey* (Burton Overy, Slawston, Stoughton).

post OE, 'a post, a pillar'. Post Cl (f.n. Fleckney).

potato eModE, 'the potato'. Potatoe Ground, the Potatoe Piece (f.ns. Hallaton), Potatoe Plot (f.n. Billesdon).

pot(t) late OE, 'a pot'. Honey Pot Lane. Honey Pots (f.n. Hallaton), ?Honey Spot (f.n. Goadby), *honypot* (f.n. Gumley).

potte ME, 'a deep hole, a pit'. ?Bluepott Cl (f.n. Burton Overy).

***pottere** OE, 'a pot-maker'. ?*Porters hill* (f.n. Bringhurst), *potteres hul* (f.n. Great Easton), *Potterisherþe* (f.n. Medbourne), Potters Croft, *Pottersholme* (f.ns. Great Bowden).

pouer(e) ME, adj., 'poor'; in modern f.ns., 'poor' (for 'the poor') alludes to land dedicated to poor-law relief or charity. Poor Close Spinney. Poor Cl (f.n. Illston, Saddington), Poor Mdw (f.n. Laughton), Poors Cl (f.n. Billesdon, Great Easton), The Poor's Land (f.n. Newton Harcourt), Poors Piece (f.n. Billesdon), Seaton Poor Cl (f.n. Blaston), *Uppingham Poors Close* (f.n. Horninghold).

prēost OE, 'a priest'. *Prestgrave*. *Presborowe feld* (f.n. Thorpe Langton), *Presborowe Hill*, *Prescott hill*, *Prestcroft*, *Prestwell'* (f.ns. East Langton), Pressgate Cl (f.n. Burton Overy), *Prestemor*, *le Prestisbring'* (f.ns. Billesdon),

Prestmedwe (f.n. Theddingworth), *Prestrees* (f.n. Knossington), Prestress Cl (f.n. Owston), Priest Holm (f.n. Kibworth Beauchamp), *Priest-home* (f.n. Husbands Bosworth), ?Priest Mdw (f.n. Fleckney).

pric(c)a OE, 'a prick, a prickle', used to form plant- and tree-names. *Prikeputes* (f.n. Medbourne).

primerose ME, 'the primrose' (*Primula vulgaris*). Primrose Mdw (f.n. Laughton).

prior ME, 'the prior of a religious house'. *the pryer wood* (f.n. Knossington).

pumpe ME, 'a pump'. Pump Fd (f.n. Saddington, Theddingworth).

pund ME, 'a pound, an enclosure into which stray cattle were put'. *lawnd pound hollow* (f.n. Great Easton), the Parish Pound (f.n. Medbourne), The Pound (f.n. Cranoe).

pūr OE, 'a bittern, a snipe'. ?Purgate (f.n. West Langton).

pyll OE, 'a pool in a river; a small stream'. ?*Pylland* (f.n. Theddingworth), *Pyllok* (f.n. Medbourne), *the Pylloke* (f.n. Evington), ?*Pyllokesholme*, ?*Pylwelfurlonge* (f.n. Great Bowden).

pynd OE, 'a pound, an enclosure'. *Pinslade* (f.n. Husbands Bosworth, Mowsley).

***pynd-fald** OE, 'a pinfold'. Pinfold Ho. Pinfold (f.n. Illston, Mowsley, Newton Harcourt), Pinfold Cl (f.n. Goadby, Gumley), *Pinfolde leies* (f.n. Glooston).

pyrige OE, 'a pear-tree'.?Purgate (f.n. West Langton).

pytt OE, 'pit, a natural hollow, an excavated hole'. Gravel Pit Spinney, Woolpits Planting. Freq. in f.ns.: recurring are *Blackpitt* (Gumley, Theddingworth) Gravel Pit(s) (Fleckney, Frisby, Great Bowden, Great Easton, Laughton, Hallaton, Nevill Holt), Gravel Pit Cl (Billesdon, Burton Overy, Carlton Curlieu), Wash Pit(s) (Houghton, Husbands Bosworth, Rolleston), Washpit Cl (Nevill Holt, King's Norton), Washpit Leys (Burton Overy, Great Glen). Surns. feature, e.g. *Glouers Pitt* (Husbands Bosworth), *Reynoldespyt* (Medbourne), *Wyllerspyttis* (Great Bowden); wild flora, e.g. *Hespitte* (Smeeton Westerby), *Rushpittloe*, *Willow Pit* (Husbands Bosworth), *Withy pittes* (Laughton); farm creatures, e.g. *Gasling pits* (King's Norton), Hogpit (Foxton). Note *Thyrspyt* (Nevill Holt) and Salt Pits (West Langton).

quagmire eModE, 'a piece of wet and boggy ground, too soft to sustain the weight of men and larger animals; a quaking bog'. *the Coggemire* (f.n. Great Glen), *the Quagmire* (f.n. Glooston, Medbourne).

quake ME, 'a stretch of quake-fen'. ?Quakers (f.n. Stretton Magna).

quarrelle ME, 'a quarry'. *Quarelpyttes* (f.n Burton Overy).

quarrere ME, 'a quarry'. Quarry Cl, Quarry Mdw (f.ns. Billesdon).

quarterne ME, 'a quarter, a fourth part, a division of a larger area'. Quartern Cl (f.n. Smeeton Westerby, Tur Langton), *the Quartorne land* (f.n. Houghton).

quyk ME, 'a hedge planted with one species, esp. whitethorn'. *Colsis Quick* (f.n. Great Bowden), Great Quick, Mouses Quick (f.ns. Little Bowden), Three Quick Mdw (f.n. Bringhurst).

quykset ME, 'a quickset hedge'. *the farr quicksett* (f.n. Great Bowden).

rá[2] ON, 'a boundary'. Rocott Spinney (f.n. Cold Overton).

rabet ME, 'a rabbit'. Rabbit Holes (f.n. Burton Overy), The Rabbit Warren (f.n. Nevill Holt).

ragu OE, 'moss, lichen'. Rags Cl (f.n. King's Norton).

raile ME, 'a fence, a railing'. ?Rales (f.n. Hallaton).

rake ME, 'a narrow path' (often up a hill, or leading upland and inland from a village to its pastures, and so often denoting a drove or a 'back-lane'). Raikes

Baulk (f.n. Theddingworth).

ramm OE, 'a ram'. ?Ramburrow Cl (f.n. Horninghold), Ram Cl (f.n. Gumley, Lubenham, Nevill Holt, Owston), *the Ram Close meadow* (f.n. Noseley), Ram Mdw (f.n. Illston, King's Norton), ?Ramsborough (f.n. Stockerston), ?Ramshead or Ramshill (f.n. King's Norton).

rand OE, 'an edge, a border, a brink'. ?Roundrick (f.n. Lubenham).

rāw OE, 'a row', of trees, etc., but esp. of houses, whence the sense 'a range of buildings, a street lined with houses'. Peep Row, Union Row. *Bates' row* (Market Harborough), *Nordrow* (f.n. Lubenham), *Vytharowe* (f.n. Medbourne).

ræsn OE, 'a plank', prob. sometimes in the sense 'a plank-bridge'. *Rassynhil* (f.n. King's Norton).

rēad OE, adj., 'red', in allusion to the colour of soil, rocks, water (esp. peat-stained); in f.ns., often difficult to distinguish from **hrēod**. ?Redbanks, Red Hovel. *radelond* (f.n. Frisby), *rademylde* (f.n. Great Bowden), Radley Fd (f.n. Cranoe), Ratcliffe Cl, *le Redehalfacris* (f.ns. Billesdon), Red Furlong, *Red hill* (f.ns. Laughton), *Redgate* (f.n. Hallaton), Red Hill (f.n. Kibworth Beauchamp), *Redland(es)* (f.n. Glooston, Great Easton, Hallaton, Houghton, Nevill Holt), ?Redon Cl (f.n. East Langton), ?*reedland* (f.n. Gumley).

rectory ModE, 'the residence pertaining to a rector'. (The) Old Rectory (Cranoe, Saddington), Old Rectory Ho., The Rectory (Burton Overy, Carlton Curlieu, Church Langton, Cold Overton, Galby, Glooston, Gumley, Houghton, Husbands Bosworth, Kibworth Beauchamp, Laughton, Medbourne, Mowsley, Shangton, Stonton Wyville), Rectory Ho., Rectory Lane. Rectory Fd (f.n. Smeeton Westerby).

rectour ME, 'a rector, a parson or incumbent of a parish whose tithes are not impropriate'. Rectors Cl (f.n. Gumley).

rein ON, 'a boundary strip'. *hilrene* (f.n. Great Bowden), *Rainbysleyde* (f.n. Goadby).

reke-yard ME, 'an enclosure containing ricks, a stackyard'. Rickyard (f.n. Newton Harcourt).

rennyng ME, 'a watercourse, a channel'. *renyngdale* (f.n. Slawston), ?*the running brooke* (f.n. Knossington).

***resbery** ME, 'a raspberry'. *Respyrys* (f.n. Burton Overy).

respis ME, 'a raspberry'. Rice Piece (f.n. Burton Overy).

***ric** OE, 'a narrow strip of land; a ditch'. *Patrick* (f.n. Great Bowden), ?Roundrick (f.n. Lubenham).

rickstead ModE, 'an enclosure containing ricks, a stackyard'. *Cooks Ricksted*, *Swans Ricksted* (f.ns. Hallaton), *Hang-mans Rickstead* (f.n. Husbands Bosworth), *the Rickstead* (f.n. King's Norton), *Rickstides* (f.n. Laughton).

rinc OE, 'a warrior'. *Rynkso* (f.n. Mowsley).

***rip** OE, 'an edge, a slope'. ?Reap Park (f.n. Billesdon), *Ripepoole* (f.n. Husbands Bosworth).

ripe ME, 'reaping, harvest'. ?Reap Park (f.n. Billesdon).

risc, ***rysc** OE, 'a rush'. Rushes Lane. *Rushbedds* (f.n. Houghton), Rush Cl, Russells Mdw (f.ns. Laughton), *Rushdale* (f.n. Slawston), *Rushes* (f.n. Wistow), the Rushes, Rush Holme (f.ns. Medbourne), *Rushpittloe* (f.n. Husbands Bosworth), *Rushwell* (f.n. Gumley), *Russewong* (f.n. Nevill Holt), *russhe farrgatts* (f.n. Tur Langton), *Ryschfurlong'* (f.n. Stretton Magna).

***riscig** OE, **rushy** ModE, adj., 'rushy, growing with rushes'. *rushie medowe* (f.n. Frisby), Rushy Cl (f.n. Bushby, King's Norton), Rushy Ham (f.n. Billesdon), Rushy Mdw (f.n. Foxton), *Rushy Peice* (f.n. Hallaton), *Russhygore* (f.n. Great Bowden).

rise ModE, 'a piece of rising ground'. Larchwood Rise, Scraptoft Rise, Sherwood Rise.

***rod**[1] OE, 'a clearing'. *le Rode* (f.n. *Prestgrave*), ?*Rodehill* (f.n. Hallaton).

rōd[2] OE, 'a cross'. *holy roode leyes* (f.n. Burton Overy), ?*Rodehill* (f.n. Hallaton).

rōd[3] OE, 'a rood of land, a rood measure'. Ban Roods Cl (f.n. Owston), *le Broderodes*, *Croumbehalfrodes*, *le Falshalfrodes*, *les Garbrodrodes*, *les Longrodes* (f.ns. Billesdon), *Curst Roods* (f.n. Theddingworth), *Fyuerodesty* (f.n. Bringhurst), *Lady rodis* (f.n. Burton Overy), *Long roods* (f.n. Saddington), *the old rood*, the Ten Roods (f.ns. Houghton), *Old Roods* (f.n. Fleckney), *The Seven Rood Peece* (f.n. Little Stretton), *Three Roode Riggs* (f.n. Cranoe), *The Three Roods* (f.n. Great Glen), *the Town roodes* (f.n. Hothorpe).

rookery ModE, 'a colony of rooks'. The Rookery (f.n. Hallaton), Rookery Nook (f.n. Foxton).

rose OE, 'a rose (flower); a shrub of the genus *Rosa*'. ?*Rose Lane* (f.n. Horninghold).

***roð** OE, 'a clearing'. *rotcom* (f.n. Gumley).

round ME, adj., 'round'; in modern f.ns., sometimes describing fields not necessarily circular, but equilateral rather than oblong or irregular polygons. *Priors Round Hill* (f.n. Great Glen), *the Round Acre*, Round Hill (f.ns. Hallaton), Round Cl (f.n. Stretton Magna), Round Hill (f.n. Great Easton, Little Bowden, Shangton, Smeeton Westerby, Stonton Wyville, West Langton), *Round Hill piece* (f.n. Glooston), Roundhills (f.n. Saddington).

roundabout eModE, 'a circle, a circular object'; in f.ns., often alluding to a piece of land surrounded by streams, trees or roads' and sometimes 'a piece of land with an isolated clump of trees within its bounds'. *Roundabout* (f.n. Husbands Bosworth).

rūh OE, adj., 'rough'. Rough Spinney. Great Roby, Rough Cl (f.ns. Frisby), *Robalk* (f.n. Illston), *Robrechesyke* (f.n. Noseley), Rough Cl (f.n. King's Norton), Rough Piece (f.n. Billesdon), Row Acre (f.n. Saddington), *Rowdikes*, *Rusyk* (f.ns. Mowsley), *le Rowehegges* (f.n. Drayton), *Rowlands* (f.n. Hallaton), *Ruf sick* (f.n. Gumley), *ruland* (f.n. Frisby).

rūm[1] OE, **rúm** ON, 'an open space, a clearing'. Deep Room (f.n. Knossington).

runlet ModE, 'a little stream, a runnel'. *the Runlett* (f.n. Knossington).

runnyng eModE, ppl.adj., 'flowing'. ?*the running brooke* (f.n. Knossington).

rūt OE, 'rough ground'. *rutpoole* (f.n. Husbands Bosworth).

***ryde** OE (Angl), 'a clearing'. *Rudde* (f.n. Medbourne).

***ryding** OE, vbl.sb., 'a clearing'. *Short Ridings* (f.n. Glooston).

ryge OE, 'rye'. *Ryecroft* (f.n. Blaston), *Rye furlong* (f.n. Houghton), *Rye hil* (f.n. Hothorpe), Ryelands (f.n. Little Bowden), *Ryland* (f.n. Laughton), Rylands (f.n. Great Easton).

rynel OE, **rundle** ModEdial., 'a runnel, a small stream'. ?Randall Walls (f.n. Galby), Rundell (f.n. Little Stretton), *Rundells* (f.n. West Langton), *waterrendeles* (f.n. Slawston).

sale eModE, 'a division or "quarter" of a wood, of which the underwood is cut down and sold' (*v.* Nth 157 and EDD *s.v.*). Lawponsale, Oaksale (f.ns. Great Easton).

salh, **salig** OE, 'a willow, a sallow'. *Sallow pitt* (f.n. Little Stretton), *Sawbrooke* (f.n. Fleckney), *Sawgate* (f.n. Goadby).

salt[1] OE (Angl), 'salt'. *Salgate* (f.n. Billesdon), *Saltingham leaes* (f.n. East Langton), Salt Pitts (f.n. West Langton), The Saltway (f.n. Cranoe).

saltere OE (Angl), 'a salt-merchant'. *Salteresgate* (f.n. Drayton, Nevill Holt), *Salters gate* (f.n. Cranoe), *salters peece* (f.n. Tur Langton), Salter's Way (f.n. Slawston).

sand OE, **sandr** ON, 'sand'. Bottom Sand Holes, *Sandlandes* (f.ns. Hallaton), Saint Leys Mdw, Sand Holes (f.ns. Laughton), Sand Acres (f.n. Billesdon), *Sandefurlong* (f.n. Great Bowden), *Sandelands* (f.n. Great Glen), Sand Hole, Sand Mdw (f.ns. Fleckney), *Sandhole*, *the Sand Sick* (f.ns. Houghton), Sandholes (f.n. Great Easton), *the Sands* (f.n. Burton Overy), *Sandwell* (f.n. East Langton), *Sauntcliff* (f.n. Mowsley), *Sauntleys* (f.n. Theddingworth).

sandig OE, adj., 'sandy'. *Sandie* (f.n. Wistow), *Sandihillis*, The Sandilands (f.n. Burton Overy), Sandy Brook (f.n. Hallaton), *Sandyhoke* (f.n. Theddingworth), *Sandylands* (f.n. Great Glen, Gumley), Sandy Leys (f.n. Knossington).

sand-pytt OE, 'a sand-pit, a place from which sand is extracted'. *Sandepittes* (f.n with various spellings in Great Bowden, Great Easton, Gumley, Hallaton, Laughton), Sand Pit Cl (f.n. Wistow), *Sandpytwong* (f.n. Nevill Holt), *Smeeton sandpittes*, Top Sandpit Mdw (f.ns. Saddington).

saw-pytt ME, 'a sawpit'. *Sawpittes* (f.n. Saddington), *Sawpitwong* (f.n. Nevill Holt).

sǣd OE, 'seed; sowing'; in modern f.ns., used of grasses sown for one year's mowing or grazing as distinguished from permanent pasture. Big Seeds (f.n. Billesdon, Great Easton), Folly ~, Horse Slade ~, New Seeds (f.ns. Great Bowden), Little Seeds (f.n. Billesdon), (The) Old Seeds (f.n. Billesdon, Evington, Great Bowden), Seed Fd (f.n. Glooston), (The) Seeds (f.n. Burton Overy, Foxton, Frisby, Great Easton).

scanca OE, 'a shank, a leg'; in p.ns., used figuratively of a shank of land or narrow hill-spur. Shangton.

sceaga, **scaga** OE, 'a small wood or copse'. ?Ringshill (f.n. Saddington), *del Shawe* (p) (King's Norton).

scearp OE, adj., 'sharp, pointed'. *Scharphill* (f.n. Mosley).

***scearpol** OE, 'a place characterized by some pointed feature; a pointed hill'. *le Scharpel* (f.n. Drayton).

scearu OE, 'a share, a division; a boundary'. Sharfoot Mdw, *Scerdyk* (f.ns. Husbands Bosworth).

scēað OE, **skeið** ON, 'a boundary'. *skeveland* (f.n. Gumley).

scelf OE, 'a ledge, shelving terrain'. ?Shellands (f.n. Little Bowden).

***sc(e)orf**, **scurf** OE, 'scurf, scum'. ?*Scurvey* (f.n. Noseley).

sc(e)ort OE, adj., 'short'. *Schorddall'* (f.n. Goadby), *le schortbrod* (f.n. Illston), *Schortefurlongis* (f.n. Shangton), *Schortpeselonde*, *Scortlondes* (f.ns. Billesdon), *schortstonlondes* (f.n. Great Easton), *Schortwranglondis* (f.n. Burton Overy), *shortcroftes* (f.n. Gumley), *Shortebanham*, *Shortwonge* (f.ns. Great Bowden), *shortebuttis*, *Shorte Tofts*, *shortland sike* (f.ns. Frisby), *the shorte fridayes*, *short hedge* (f.ns. Glooston), Shotten Slade (f.n. Great Glen).

***scēot**[3] OE, 'a steep slope'. ?*Scortecotes* (f.n. Horninghold).

scēp OE (Angl), 'a sheep'. Sheepthorns Spinney. Sheep Cl (f.n. Nevill Holt), *Sheepe Close* (f.n. Great Easton), *Sheep Dyke* (f.n. Horninghold), *Sheep market* (Market Harborough), the Sheep Pasture (f.n. Medbourne), Sheep Skirt Cl (f.n. Billesdon).

scēp-cot OE (Angl), 'a shelter for sheep'. *Goodmans sheepe coate*, *Shipcoates* (f.ns. Houghton), *Sheepecoate leyes* (f.n. Thurnby).

scēp-hirde OE (Angl), 'a shepherd'. ?Shepherd's Mdw (f.n Glooston).

scēp-wæsce OE (Angl), 'a place for dipping sheep, a sheep-wash'. *Sheepwash* (f.n. Houghton), *the Sheep Wash Close* (f.n. Newbold).

***scille** OE (Angl), adj., 'noisy'. ?Shillshanks (f.n. Houghton).

scinn(a) OE, 'a spectre, a phantom'. ?Shinnel (f.n. Burton Overy).

scīr[1] OE, 'a shire, a jurisdiction, an administrative district'. *the Sheire brooke* (f.n. Theddingworth).

scīr[2] OE, adj., 'bright'; also, when referring to plots of ground, 'clear of weeds'. ?*Shirtecoat*. ?*Schortecotes* (f.n. Horninghold), ?*Schyrdaycotis* (f.n. Newton Harcourt), ?*Shurly croftes* (f.n. Knossington).

***scirde** OE adj., perh. 'broken, derelict'. ?*Shirtecoat*. ?*Schortecotes* (f.n. Horninghold), ?*Schyrdaycotis* (f.n. Newton Harcourt), ?*Shurly croftes* (f.n. Knossington).

scite OE, 'dung, shit'. *Schythaysfurlonges* (f.n. Illston), *Sytforde* (f.n. Nevill Holt), *Upper Shittis acer* (f.n. Kibworth Harcourt).

scofl OE, 'a shovel'. Shovels (f.n. Wistow).

scofl-brǣdu OE, 'a shovel's breadth', in early f.ns., alluding to a narrow strip of land. *Shelboards* (Little Stretton), Shellbard (Fleckney), *Shil-board* (Lubenham), *Shouelbrodemoor*, *Souelbrod* (Billesdon), *shouelebrodemedue* (Frisby), *Shoulbrede* (Houghton), *Shouldbreads* (King's Norton), *shoulderbrod* (Gumley), *Shovellbroades* (Tur Langton), *Shuflebrode* (Great Bowden).

sconse, **skance** eModE, 'a shelter'. ?Sconsborough Hill.

scot ME, 'a payment, a tax'. Scotland (Burton Overy, Houghton), Scotland End. Scotches (f.n. Frisby), ?*Scotosyke* (f.n. Stretton Magna).

Scot(t) (**Scotta** gen.pl.) OE, 'a Scot, an Irishman', **Skottar** (**Skotta** gen.pl.) ON, 'the Scots'. ?*Scotosyke* (f.n. Stretton Magna).

***scrubb** OE, 'a shrub, brushwood, a place overgrown with brushwood'. Shrubs (f.n. Slawston), *the Shrubs* (f.n. Frisby).

scucca OE, 'an evil spirit, a demon'. *Shuggborowe leys* (f.n. Burton Overy).

scut ME, 'a hare'. ?*scutlows gate* (f.n. Glooston).

scylfe OE (Angl), 'a ledge, shelving terrain'. ?Shillshanks (f.n. Houghton).

scypen, **scipen** OE, 'a cow-shed'. Shippen Park (f.n. Billesdon).

seavy ModEdial., adj., 'rushy' (from ON **sef**). Savie Fd (f.n. Bringhurst), *Seavybroke* (f.n. Hallaton).

seeder ModE, 'a sower of seed'; also 'a mechanical contrivance for sowing seed'. Seeders Cl (f,n, Burton Overy).

sef ON, 'a rush'. Sea Brook (f.n. Burton Overy).

senna ON, **sænna** ODan, 'a dispute'. Senholme (f.n. Cold Overton).

seofon OE, num., 'seven'. *Seaven acres* (f.n. Husbands Bosworth), *Seaven leyes* (f.n. Houghton), *Seaven Wells* (f.n. Lubenham), *Seuenewell* (f.n. Great Bowden), Seven Acres (f.n. Slawston), Seven Oaks (f.n. Nevill Holt), *The Seven Rood Peece* (f.n. Little Stretton).

seolcen OE, adj., 'silken'. ?*Silkinemede* (f.n. Drayton).

seolfor OE, 'silver'. *Silver hill* (f.n. Great Glen), Silver Hill (f.n. Theddingworth).

(ge)set OE, 'a dwelling; a place for animals, a fold, a stable'. ?Setcroft Mdw (f.n. Burton Overy).

***set-copp** OE, 'a hill with a fold', poss. also 'a seat-shaped hill', i.e. a flat-topped hill'. *Sedcop* (f.n. Husbands Bosworth), *Setcupp* (f.n. Laughton), *settecuppe* (f.n. *Prestgrave*), ?Setcroft Mdw (f.n. Burton Overy).

severall eModE, adj., 'privately owned', alluding to land in individual ownership as opposed to common land. *Severalland* (f.n. Saddington).

shady ModE, adj., 'affording shade, shaded' Shady Lane.

sheep-dip ModE, 'a place for washing sheep'. Sheep Dip Mdw (f.n. Theddingworth).

shilling ModE, 'an English coin of the value of twelve pence'. Five Shilling Mdw (f.n. Evington).

***shingel**[2] ME, 'shingle, large gravel, small stones'. Shinnel (f.n. Burton Overy).

shrubbery ModE, 'a planting or growth of shrubs'. Long Shrubbery (f.n. Thurnby).

sīc OE, 'a small stream' (often used of a stream which formed a boundary), **siche** ME, 'a piece of meadow along a stream'. Bartmore Sytch (f.n. Fleckney), *calcylsyche* (f.n. Great Easton), *Maydewelle siche* (f.n. Nevill Holt), *Paynisich* (f.n. Mowsley), ?Shillshanks (f.n. Houghton), Swineherds Sitch (f.n. Marefield).

sīde OE, 'a side; the long side of a slope or hill, a hill-side, the land alongside a stream, a village, a wood etc.'. *Ayshewell' sydelondes*, *Sidelond* (f.ns. Nevill Holt), *Cheapside* (Market Harborough), *the Church side*, *the East feilde side*, *the Towne syde*, *Wayn Way side* (f.ns. Great Glen), Issets Side, Wood Side (f.ns. Hallaton), *Middow side*, Side Mdw (f.ns. Husbands Bosworth), *Sideholm* (f.n. *Prestgrave*), *Sideholme* (f.n. Great Easton), Townside Fd (f.n. Cranoe), *the West side Rundles* (f.n. West Langton).

***sīdling** OE, ME, 'a strip of land lying alongside a stream or some other piece of land'. *Jakson' sydling* (f.n. Mowsley), Siddling (f.n. Owston), Sideling (f.n. Smeeton Westerby), *Sidlyng'* (f.n. Billesdon).

sík ON, 'a ditch'; later 'a piece of meadow along a stream'. Freq. in f.ns.: esp. with a minor locational name, e.g. *Chaulcdalsyke* (Goadby), *Galutresike*, *Hernotehulsyke* (Billesdon), Horstead Sick (Foxton), *litloe sicke* (Burton Overy), *Ridgwaye sycke* (Great Glen), or with simple directional elements, e.g. *le northsike* (Horninghold), Sow Sick (Billesdon). Woodland clumps feature, e.g. *Brake sicke* (Tur Langton), *Grauesyke*, *Woodsike* (Billesdon), *Holt sicke* (Blaston); and streams, e.g. *Caldewellesike* (Great Easton), *Cawdell Seike* (Carlton Curlieu), Scamwell Sike (Billesdon), *Well sick* (Goadby). Pers.ns. and surns. indicate ownership, e.g. *Herewardissike* (Drayton), *Knightons sicke* (Burton Overy), *Orlokisseik* (Billesdon), *Tocharsike* (Shangton), while occasionally, birds record waterside fauna, e.g. *enedesike*, *Hensick* (Frisby). Local buildings appear, e.g. *Castle Scyke* (Hallaton), *Stanybryggesyk* (Nevill Holt). Recurring are Foul Syke (Evington, Frisby, Great Glen, Gumley, Hallaton), *Willow sick* (Cranoe, Frisby, Glooston, Hallaton).

sīma OE, 'a band, a rope, a chain'. ?Simborough (f.n. Little Bowden).

sinke ME, 'a bog, a sump, a cesspool'. Sinkhole (f.n. Stoughton), Sink Hole Mdw (f.n. Little Stretton).

***sīoluc** OE, 'a gulley'. ?*Silkinemede* (f.n. Drayton).

six OE, num., 'six'. Six Cocks (f.n. Kibworth Beauchamp).

skáli ON, 'a temporary hut or shed'. Gumskull (f.n. Medbourne).

skammr ON, adj., 'short'. *Scamdale* (f.n. Stretton Magna), Scamwell Sike (f.n. Billesdon).

skarð ON, 'an opening, an open place in the edge of something, a gap'. *le Skarthe* (f.n. Billesdon).

skeið ON, 'a boundary', *v.* **scēað** *supra*.

skirt ModE, 'the edge, the outskirts'. Sheep Skirt Cl (f.n. Billesdon).

skógr ON, **scoe** ME, 'a wood'. Scoborough.

skrap ON, 'scraps, scrapings'. ?Scraptoft.

slang eModE, 'a long narrow (sometimes sinuous) piece of land; the ground beside a (winding) stream'. (The) Slang (f.n. Billesdon, Evington, Houghton, Saddington, Smeeton Westerby, Stretton Magna, Welham), Garden Close Slang, Glovers Close Slang, Pond Close and Slang (f.ns. Noseley), Pitts Slang (f.n. Wistow), Thistly Field Slang (f.n. Theddingworth).

slæd OE (Angl), 'a valley, a hollow; a breadth of greensward in ploughed land'. Very common in f.ns., e.g. *Burnetts Slade*, *Grimeslade*, *Slimeslade*, *Stone Slade*, *Willow Sink Slade*, *Wood Close Slade* (Glooston), Dexter Slade, Far Slade, *Gilbertes Slade*, *Hauerbergh Slade*, Horse Slade, *Poles Slade* (Great Bowden), *hareslade*, *Holewelslade*, Mill Slade, *Pinslade*, *sneald slade*, *Stanslade*, *Swartingslade*, *Warclingesslade* (Husbands Bosworth).

***slæf** OE, 'mud'. *Slaf Medow* (f.n. Kibworth Harcourt).

***slæget** OE, 'a sheep pasture'. *Slatborow* (f.n. Burton Overy), *the Sleites* (f.n. King's Norton).

slide ModE, 'a landslip, a place on a hillside where an earth-slip has occurred'. *the slide* (f.n. Great Bowden), *Slide* (f.n. Husbands Bosworth).

slidor OE, adj., 'slippery'. *Slether Hill* (f.n. Little Stretton).

***slif(u)** OE, 'a slippery place'. *Sliffurlong* (f.n. Kibworth Beauchamp).

slīm OE, 'slime, mud'. *slimeslade* (f.n. Glooston).

sling ModEdial., 'a long narrow piece of land'. *the Sling pits* (f.n. King's Norton).

slipe ME, 'a slip, a long narrow piece of ground'. The Slip (f.n. Great Bowden, Medbourne, Slawston).

sludge ModE, 'mud'. Sludge Hall.

smæl OE, adj., 'narrow, thin'. *Smalehauedys* (f.n. Nevill Holt), *Smalehill*, *Smalewood* (f.ns. Hallaton), *Smalelongelond* (f.n. Illston), *þe smalesike* (f.n. Shangton), *Smalethorne* (f.n. Saddington), *small meadowe* (f.n. Husbands Bosworth), Small Park (f.n. Billesdon), Small Piece (f.n. Frisby), *Smalltoaftes* (f.n. Foxton), *Smalstret* (f.n. Mowsley), *Smalthornes* (f.n. Frisby, Great Bowden, Great Easton), *Smalthorngate* (f.n. Stoughton).

smeoru OE, 'fat, grease, lard', **smjǫr** ON, grease, butter'; in f.ns., alluding to rich pasturage, productive of milk and butter. *Smerclif'* (f.n. Billesdon).

smēðe[1] OE, adj., 'smooth'. *Smethemedewe* (f.n. Billesdon, Great Bowden, Illston), *Smethemeduis* (f.n. Shangton), ?Smith Mdw (f.n. Medbourne, Owston), *Smith Wonge* (f.n. King's Norton).

***smīte** OE, 'a dirty stream'. ?*Smitoft* (f.n. Newton Harcourt).

smið (smeoða gen.pl.) OE, 'a smith'. Smeeton Westerby. ?*Smeton leyes* (f.n. Market Harborough), ?Smith Hill (f.n. Evington), ?Smith Mdw (f.n. Medbourne, Owston), ?*Smitoft* (f.n. Newton Harcourt), ?Smith's Cl (f.n. Goadby).

smiððe OE, 'a smithy, a metal worker's shop'. *the Smythie* (f.n. Hallaton), ?Smithy Mdw (f.n. Medbourne).

smyther ME, 'a smith, a hammerman'. ?Smithers Green (f.n. Slawston).

snaca OE, 'a snake, a serpent'. Snake Spinney (f.n. Nevill Holt), *Snakesyke* (f.n. Great Bowden).

snap ON, 'poor pasture'; difficult to distinguish from **snæp**. ?*le Hawesnap* (f.n. Nevill Holt).

snægel, **snegel** OE, 'a snail'. *Snayllewelle* (f.n. Great Bowden), *sneald slade* (f.n. Husbands Bosworth).

***snæp**, ***snapa** OE, prob.'a boggy piece of land'; difficult to distinguish from **snap**. ?*le Hawesnap* (f.n. Nevill Holt).

socen OE, pa.part., 'wet, saturated'. ?*Soken acr'* (f.n. Nevill Holt).

sōcn OE, **soke** ME, 'jurisdiction, the district over which a right of jurisdiction is exercised'. *Barnesdale Soke* (f.n. Great Easton), ?*Soken acr'* (f.n. Nevill Holt).

spa eModE, 'a spa, a mineral medicinal spring'. Holt Spa.

spell OE, 'speech' is used in p.ns. esp. of places where speeches were made in assemblies and freq. denotes a hundred- or other meeting-place; it is often found compounded with words for 'hill'. ?Spell Cl (f.n. Scraptoft), *spellow* (f.n. Husbands Bosworth).

spinney ME, 'a copse, a small plantation'. Aqueduct Spinney, Ash ~, Barn Close ~, Bassett's Hill ~, Bath ~, Beech ~, Black ~, Bon Hills ~, Brickfield ~, Bull ~, Cambridge ~, Carland ~, Cheseldyne ~, Conduit ~, Cranesclose ~, Dent's Spinney (Blaston, Medbourne), Dick Hills Spinney, Fishpond ~, Fourteen Acre ~, Foxhole ~, Frisby's ~, Gravel Pit ~, Gunpowder ~, Heg ~, Highland ~, Hoeback ~, Holloway ~, Hopyard ~, Horseclose ~, Hubbard's ~, Lane's ~, Larch ~, Lodge ~, Milking Pens ~, New Southfield ~, New York ~, Oak ~, Overclose ~, Philip ~, Pope's ~, Poplar ~, Rough ~, Round ~, Scraptoft Long ~, Sheepthorns ~, Southfield Spinney, The Spinney, The Spinneys, Square Spinney (Great Glen, Scraptoft), Sturrad Spinney, Townsend Close ~, Washpit ~, Waterman's ~, Whinney Pit ~, Wingfield Spinney; Blackspinney Lane, Spinney Close, Spinney Hill, Spinney Ho. Common in f.ns.: Ashpole ~, Crow ~, Snake Spinney, Spinney Fd (Nevill Holt), Ash Spinney (Goadby), Banland ~, Stonyland Spinney (Great Glen), Bottom Stocks ~, Brook ~, Dungeon ~, Mill Field ~, Porters Spinney (Blaston), Fishponds Spinney (Galby), Illston ~, Long Close Spinney (Illston), Oak Spinney (Houghton), Old Spinney (Goadby), *Henry Palmers Spinay*, Wilcox Spinney (Evington), The Spinney (Burton Overy, Carlton Curlieu), Spinney Cl (Billesdon, Blaston, Fleckney, Houghton, Lubenham), Spinney Corner (Husbands Bowsorth), Spinney Gardens (Glooston), Spinney Mdw (Shangton), Steppings Spinney (Great Easton).

spong ModEdial., 'a long narrow strip of land'. *the Sponges* (f.n. Newton Harcourt).

***spot** OE, 'a small piece, a bit'; **spotte** ME, 'a small plot of ground'. ?Honey Spot (f.n. Goadby), Mill Spot (f.n. Knossington), Spots (f.n. Slawston).

spoute ME, 'a spout, a gutter', **spout** ModEdial., 'a spring of water'. *Spoutehome* (f.n. Stockerston).

spring[1] OE, 'a spring, a well, the source of a stream'. Springfield, Springfield Fm, Springfield Lodge, Springs Fm. Spring Cl (f.n. Carlton Curlieu, Knossington, Lubenham, Stretton Magna), Spring Fd, *Wellespring* (f.ns. Billesdon), Springfield (f.n. Rolleston), Springfield Mdw (f.n. Evington), Spring Lane (f.n. Houghton), Spring Leys Cl (f.n. West Langton), Springs Lane (f.n. Little Stretton), *Spryngwelle* (f.n. Great Easton), *welspringes* (f.n. Gumley).

spring[2] ME, 'a young plantation, a copse'. Spring Hill (f.n. Illston).

sprynkil ME, 'a sprinkler; that which sprinkles'. *Sprynkelwell* (f.n. Great Easton).

squar(e) ME, adj., 'square'. Square Spinney (Great Glen, Scraptoft). Square Cl (f.n. Little Stretton, Owston, Thurnby, Welham), Square Mdw (f.n. Evington).

squire ModE, 'a country gentleman, esp. one who is the principal landowner in a village or district'. *The Squires Spinney* (Square Spinney, Scraptoft). Squires Park (f.n. Nevill Holt).

stable ME, 'a building in which horses are kept'. the Stable Fd (f.n. Medbourne).

staca OE, 'a stake'. Stackley Ho. Bullstake Cl (f.n. Scraptoft), Stackley (f.n. Little Stretton), the Stake Mdw (f.n. Lubenham).

stackyard ModE, 'an enclosure for ricks'. Stackyard (f.n. Smeeton Westerby), Stackyard Cl (f.n. Stoughton).

stakkr ON, 'a stack, a rick'. Stack Garth (f.n. Nevill Holt).

stall OE (Angl), 'a place', esp. 'a standing place, a stall for cattle etc.', 'a site (of a building or other object or feature)', *v.* Sandred 37–41. ?Stalland Leys (f.n. Great Bowden).

stallion ME, 'an uncastrated male horse'. Stallion Cl (f.n. Wistow).

stān OE, 'a stone, stone'; when used as a first el., often has the adj. function 'stony', esp. in the names of roads, streams, fords and plots of ground; or may refer to something stone-built. Stonton Wyville; Horston Hill. Very freq. in f.ns.: referring to standing stones, boundary stones etc., e.g. *Greyston'* (Illston), *hoarestone* (Husbands Bosworth), King's Stone (Kibworth Beauchamp), *Watho Stones* (Burton Overy), *le Whiteston* (Great Bowden, Lubenham, Theddingworth); to stone bridges, e.g. Stone Bridge (Blaston), Stonebridge Cl (Evington), *stone brige lane* (Fleckney). *Stonehill* recurs (Burton Overy, Glooston, Great Bowden, Great Glen, Husbands Bosworth), as do *Stonland* (Great Bowden, Great Easton, Gumley), *stanmedowe* (Foxton, Glooston) and *Stone Slade* (Glooston, Husbands Bosworth).

standing ME, vbl.sb., ppl.adj., 'a place where cattle or horses may stand under shelter'. ?*standinge poole* (f.n. Gumley).

stān-(ge)delf OE, 'a stone-quarry'. *Standelfs* (f.n. Medbourne).

stānig OE, adj.,'stony, made of stone'. *Staneibrigge* (f.n. Nevill Holt), *Stanipoll* (f.n. Foxton), *Stany hill*, *Stonyforth*, *Stony wheathill* (f.ns. Houghton), *Stanyhull* (f.n. Great Bowden), *Stanypoole* (f.n. Gumley), *Stoney* (f.n. Mowsley), Stoney Furlong (f.n. Hallaton), Stoney Path (f.n. Kibworth Beauchamp), *Stonie* (f.n. King's Norton), *Stoniwelleslade* (f.n. Great Easton), *Stonney holes*, *stonye slade* (f.ns. Husbands Bosworth), *Stonnydale*, Stonyland (f.ns. Great Glen), *Stonyforth* (f.n. Goadby), *stonyforthe*, *stonymyddilyl* (f.ns. Illston), *Stonyhull* (f.n. Stockerston), *Stony Lands* (f.n. Evington).

***stān-pytt** OE, ***stan(e)pytt** ME, **stone-pit** ModE, 'a stone-pit, a quarry'. *Stonpit* (f.n. Billesdon, Burton Overy, Glooston, Medbourne), Stonepit Cl (f.n. Cranoe, Cold Overton, Hallaton), Stone-pit Six Acres (f.n. King's Norton), *Stonepits* (f.n. Husbands Bosworth, Owston).

stapol OE, 'a pillar, a post'. ?Stable Gate Way (f.n. Little Bowden), *Stapilhouhil'* (f.n. Shangton).

stæf OE, 'a staff, a stave, a rod'. *Stavesacre* (f.n. Bushby, Houghton).

***stæfer** OE, 'a polc, a stakc'. ?Sturrad Spinney.

stǣner OE, 'stony ground'. G. Redmonds, *Names and History* 2004, 77–79, defines ModEdial. *steaner*, *stayner* as 'the debris cast up by a river in flood, composed of sand, stones and gravel, or a piece of land covered with debris that had been isolated by a change in the course of the river'. ?Stainer (f.n. Fleckney), ?*Sternedale* (f.n. Mowsley), *Stearne*, *Sturnewood* (f.ns. Hallaton).

stær(e) OE, 'a starling'. ?Sturrad Spinney.

stēap (**stēapan** wk.obl.) OE, adj., 'steep'. *the Steeple End* (f.n. Great Glen), Stepnals (f.n. Husbands Bosworth).

stēda OE, 'a steed, a stallion'. Steedholme Cl (f.n. Owston).

stede OE, 'a place, a site, a locality'. ?Horseheads Furlong (f.n. Little Stretton), Horstead Cl (f.n. Foxton), Mill Stede (f.n. Fleckney), *Netherstedeyerd'* (f.n. Medbourne), *Newstede* (f.n. Evington), *Tongstede* (f.n. Great Bowden), *yommanys horstede* (f.n. Illston).

steinn ON, 'stone'; also used as 'stony'. Steen Hill. *Stainingges* (f.n. Billesdon), *Steinland* (f.n. Drayton), *Steyndale* (f.n. Great Glen).

stēor OE, 'a steer, a bullock, a young cow'. Stear Hill (f.n. Little Stretton), Stearwong (f.n. Knossington).

steort OE, 'a tail', used in p.ns. of 'a tail or tongue of land, the end of a piece of land, a projecting piece of land'. ?Great ~, Little Starter (f.ns. Billesdon).

stepping-stone ME, 'a stone on which to step' as in the kind of ford made of a row of stones. *the Stepping Stones* (f.n. Great Bowden).

***sterne** OE, poss. 'property'. ?Kingster (f.n. Smeeton Westerby).

stīg OE, **stígr** ON, 'a path, a narrow road, an upland path' (*v.* **sty-gate**); almost impossible to distinguish formally from **stig** 'a sty, a pen', and as in some cases the el. develops late as *stile*, it thus may be confused also with names formed with **stigel**. In f.ns., the el. is best recognized when combined with names of townships, e.g. Foxon Stiles (Lubenham), *Haloughton Sties* (Blaston), *Horninghold Stile* (Hallaton), *Ingwardbysti* (Billesdon), *Knaptoft Stile* (Mowsley), *Sirestonsty* (Stoughton). While *Croudonsty* (Evington), *Fyuerodesty* (Bringhurst), *Gardisty* (Billesdon), *Hokedsti* (Medbourne), *Kestie* (Galby), *Styfurlong* (Noseley), *Swannestyle* (Houghton), *under le sty* (Shangton) and *Wodesty* (Great Easton) may be safely assigned here, *Corts stile*, *Jonsty* (Great Bowden) and *le Nethersty* (Evington) are less certain.

stig OE, 'a sty' a pen'. ?*le Nethersty* (f.n. Evington), ?*Jonsty* (f.n. Great Bowden), *le Styh*, *le Sty versus Longlond'* (f.ns. Stoughton), *Suinsti* (f.n. Horninghold), *Swinsty* (f.n. Mowsley).

stigel OE, 'a stile'. *against Home Close stile* (f.n. Theddingworth), ?*Corts stile* (f.n. Great Bowden), *the newclose stile* (f.n. Shangton), ?*Swannestyle* (f.n. Houghton).

stille OE, adj., 'still, peaceful, quiet'. *Stillepol* (f.n. Shangton).

***stint** OE, 'a sand-piper, a dunlin'. Stinford Hill (f.n. Little Bowden), ?Stinkley (f.n. Smeeton Westerby).

stoc OE, 'a religious place; a place where cattle stand for milking in outlying pastures; a cattle farm; a dairy farm (esp. an outlying one); a secondary settlement'. ?Stockerston, Stoughton. *Kingstocke Bridge* (f.n. Kibworth Beauchamp), *Neather Stock*, *the Stockefielde* (f.ns. Little Stretton), Stock Cl (f.n. Stretton Magna), ?Stocker Hill, Stock Mdw, ?Stockwell Cl, *Stokfeld* (f.ns. Houghton), *Stokenol* (f.n. Nevill Holt), *Stokewong* (f.n. Drayton), *Thurstanestok* (f.n. Noseley).

stocc OE, **stokkr** ON, 'a tree-trunk, a stump, a stock, a log'. ?Stockerston. *Stocdole* (f.n. Billesdon), *Stockacre Streame* (f.n. Smeeton Westerby), ?Stocker Hill, ?Stockwell Cl (f.ns. Houghton), *Stockes*, *Stockuall Hollow* (f.ns. Drayton),

Stockewell (f.n. Saddington), Stock Hill (f.n. Cold Overton), Stocklands (f.n. Great Easton), ?Stock Mdw (f.n. Welham), Stockwell (f.n. Billesdon, Frisby, Smeeton Westerby), *Stockwell Hill* (f.n. Tur Langton), *Stocwellelane* (f.n. Nevill Holt), *Stokkis* (f.n. *Prestgrave*), ?*Thurstokys* (f.n. Noseley), Top Stocks (f.n. Blaston).

***stoccing** OE, **stocking** ME, 'a piece of ground cleared of stumps'. *Bernakestockyng*, *le Stockyng'* (f.ns. Nevill Holt), *le Stocking* (f.n. Medbourne), Stocking Cl (f.n. Hallaton), Stockings (f.n. Stonton Wyville).

stock eModE, 'livestock'. ?Stock Mdw (Welham), Stockhold Cl (f.n. West Langton).

stōd OE, 'a stud, a herd of horses'. The Stud Fm. Steedholme Cl (f.n. Owston), *Stodwoldhull* (f.n. Stretton Magna).

stōd-fald OE, 'a horse-enclosure'. *Long Steadfold* (f.n. Smeeton Westerby), *Stodfold* (f.n. Husbands Bosworth), *Stotfold* (f.n. Houghton).

stolpe, **stulpe** ME, 'a stake, a stump, a post'. ?Stopars (f.n. Smeeton Westerby).

stǫng ON, 'a pole, a stave'; also used in ME as a standard of measure, 'a pole'. *harbroue stong*, *stong* (f.ns. Gumley), *Threstonkys* (f.n. Billesdon).

stoppa OE, 'a bucket', in p.ns. used of something resembling a bucket, hence 'a hollow'. *Smeeton Stopers* (f.n. Gumley).

stor ME, 'livestock'. Store Cl (f.n. Blaston, Hallaton).

stǫrr[2] ON, **star** ODan, 'sedge, bent-grass'. *Starholmes* (f.n. Hallaton), *Starr Lane* (f.n. Evington).

storð ON, 'a young wood, land growing with brushwood'. *Prestgraue storte* (f.n. *Prestgrave*), *le Storth* (f.n. Billesdon).

stōw OE, 'a place, a place of assembly, a holy place'. Wistow. *le Hallestou* (f.n. Medbourne), Stowe Cl, *Stowe Welle* (f.ns. Hallaton), *the Stow Meadow* (f.n. Kibworth Beauchamp).

strang OE, **strangr** ON, adj., 'strong'; used of firm, compact soil. *Strongland* (f.n. Goadby).

strǣt OE, **strēt** (Angl), 'a Roman road, a paved road, a street'. Little Stretton, Stretton Magna; High St, Main St (Fleckney, Laughton). *Barnsdale strete* (Great Easton), *Burton streete* (King's Norton), *Skeftington strete* (Billesdon), *Smalstret* (Mowsley), *the Town Street* (Galby); *Streete furlong* (f.n. Smeeton Westerby), *Stretefurlonge* (f.n. Great Bowden).

strēam OE, 'a stream'. Stream (f.n. Smeeton Westerby), Three Streams (f.n. Medbourne).

***strīp** OE, 'a narrow tract of land'. Hallaton Road Strips (f.n. Medbourne), Stripe (f.n. Blaston), Stripling (f.n. Houghton).

***strūt** OE, 'strife, dispute; struggle'. *Strutholegate* (f.n. Horninghold), *Strutthou* (f.n. Billesdon).

stubb OE, 'a stub, a tree-stump'. *eldern stubb* (f.n. Knossington), *elder stubb* (f.n. Husbands Bosworth), *Elderstubs* (f.n. King's Norton), *Eldurstobe* (f.n. Mowsley), *elrenestub* (f.n. Frisby), *Elrenstub'* (f.n. Saddington), *heldyrstubb* (f.n. Smeeton Westerby), *Stubston Feild* (f.n. Kibworth Beauchamp).

***stubbing** OE, 'a place where trees have been stubbed, a clearing'. *Brinynghurst Stubbyng* (f.n. Bringhurst).

stump ME, 'a tree-stump; a broken-off stump of something'. *Stump Cross* (Hallaton).

***stybbing** OE, 'a place with tree-stumps, a clearing'. *Steppings* (f.n. East Langton, Great Easton, Stockerston).

***sty-gate** ME, 'a pathway, a narrow road, a footpath' (*v.* **stīg**, **stígr**, **gata**), cf. ***sty-way**. Stygates (f.n. Great Glen).

stykke ME, 'a stick, a stave, a stake'. *Midewinter stickes*, *le Mikel stikes* (f.ns. Stoughton).

***stynt** OE, 'stint, limit'. ?Stinkley (f.n. Smeeton Westerby), *the Stint* (f.n. Slawston).

***sty-way** ME, 'a pathway, a narrow road, a footpath', cf. ***sty-gate**. ?*Hasty way* (f.n. Theddingworth).

suer ME, 'an artificial watercourse for draining marshy land and carrying off surface water to a river'. *atte Syrwys* (p) (Glooston).

sugere ME, 'sugar'; in f.ns., alluding to 'sweet land'. Sugar Hill (f.n. Scraptoft), *Suger leaes* (f.n. Tur Langton).

sumor OE, **sumarr** ON, 'summer'; in p.ns., usually alluding to fords, roads, land etc. which were used or could be used only in summer months. *Somergate* (f.n. Burton Overy), *Sumebrygge* (f.n. Great Easton), Summer Fd (f.n. Little Stretton), Summers Land (f.n. Billesdon).

sunne OE, 'the sun'; in f.ns., alluding to ground which catches the best of the sun. *ageynst the Sunne* (f.n. Houghton), *under the Sunne* (f.n. Gumley).

sunni ME, **sunny** ModE, adj., 'sunny'. Sunny Leys. *the Sonney Close* (f.n. Houghton).

sūr OE, adj., 'sour, damp, coarse' (of land). *Sauerland* (f.n. Saddington).

sūð OE, adj., 'south, southern'. *Suthmardefeld* (Marefield); Southfield Lodge. *the Southbrook*, *South hill* (f.ns. Knossington), South End Fds (f.n. Great Glen), *the South Feild* (with various spellings in Billesedon, Blaston, Bringhurst, Burton Overy, Frisby, Galby, Great Bowden, Husbands Bosworth), *Sowbarow* (f.n. Tur Langton), *the sow meadow close* (f.n. Thurnby), *Sowtorp'* (f.n. Great Bowden), Sow Sick, *le Suthbreche* (f.ns. Billesdon).

sūðer OE, adj., 'south, southern'. *Sutherhil* (f.n. Nevill Holt).

sūðweard OE, adj., adv., 'southern, southward, to the south'. ?Southward Cl, Southward Twofields (f.ns. Shangton).

***swalg** OE (Angl), 'a pit, a pool'. ?Swallow Thorn (f.n. Owston).

swalwe[1] OE, 'a swallow'. ?Swallow Thorn (f.n. Owston).

swan[1] OE, 'a swan'. Swan Furlong (f.n. (Foxton), *Swans poole* (f.n. King's Norton).

swan[2] OE, 'a herdsman, a swine-herd, a peasant'. ?*Swannestyle* (f.n. Houghton).

swathe ME, 'a strip of grassland'. *the Church Swath*, *the School Swathes*, *the Swathes* (f.ns. Kibworth Beachamp), *the Swathes* (f.n. Kibworth Harcourt).

sweart OE, **svartr** ON, adj., 'black, dark'. *Swardboro* (f.n. Mowsley).

***swelle**, **(ge)swell** OE, 'a swelling'; used topographically of a hill or a ridge. *Swelles* (f.n. Billesdon).

sweord OE, 'a sword'; poss. used topographically of 'a narrow strip of land of the shape of a sword, a headland', or in allusion to places where swords were found or made. ?Swadborough (f.n. Stoughton), ?*Sword Croft* (f.n. Hallaton).

swēte OE, adj., 'sweet, pure, pleasant'. *Sweetehedge Feilde* (f.n. Stockerston).

swīn OE, **svín** ON, 'a swine, a pig'. *Joneswynesgore* (f.n. Stretton Magna), *Suinsti* (f.n. Horninghold), Swine Balk (f.n. Evington), Swinnel Cl (f.n. Carlton Curlieu), Swinny Mdw, *Swynemeadowe* (f.ns. Hallaton), *Swinsty* (f.n. Mowsley).

swing-gate ModE, 'a gate constructed to swing closed or shut of itself'. Swing Gate (f.n. Houghton).

swyneherd ME, 'a swine-herd'. Swineherds Sitch (f.n. Marefield).

***tagga**, ***tegga** OE, 'a teg, a young sheep'. ?*Tagyllisdyke* (f.n. Great Bowden).

tarbarelle ME, 'a barrel containing or that has contained tar, esp. as used for making a large fire (as in siege warfare); also for the carrying out of capital punishment by burning'. Alluding in f.ns. to dark, boggy ground. Tar Barrell (f.n. Houghton).

targett ME, 'a light round shield'; poss. used topographically of a small and round plot of land. Target Fd (f.n. Newton Harcourt), *Targett holme* (f.n. Great Bowden).

tægl OE, **taile** ME, 'a tail', used topgraphically of 'a tail of land, a piece of land projecting from a larger piece'; also 'the bottom end of a pool'. *Tayle bush* (f.n. Smeeton Westerby), *tybstayle* (f.n. East Langton).

tæppere OE, 'a tapper (of casks), a tapster'. *Teperwellesik* (f.n. Medbourne).

tǣse OE, adj., 'useful, convenient'. ?*Tasholm* (f.n. Drayton).

tǣsel OE, 'a teasel'. ?*Tasholm* (f.n. Drayton), *Tasley* (f.n. Foxton), *Tassel Sick* (f.n. Theddingworth).

tēn OE, num., 'ten'. *greate ten hades* (f.n. East Langton), *Teneacres*, the Ten Roods (f.ns. Houghton).

tentour ME, **teyntree** eModE 'a tenter, a frame for tenting cloth'. Tenter House (Hallaton), *the Tenters* (f.n. Husbands Bosworth), Tentery Cl (f.n. Little Stretton).

***tēo** OE, 'a boundary'. Tythorn Hill.

tēoða OE, 'a tithe, a tenth'. The Great Tythes (f.n. Little Stretton), *the Tythe Barne* (Fleckney), *the Tythe barne yarde* (f.n. Thurnby), *the Tythe Close* (f.n. Laughton), *Tythemedow* (f.n. Theddingworth), *Tythesykys* (f.n. Billesdon), Upper Tythe (f.n. Smeeton Westerby).

terrace ModE, 'a raised level place for walking; a horizontal shelf on the side of a hill; a row of houses on a level above the general surface, a row of houses of a uniform style'. *Railway terrace* (Market Harborough).

thing ME, 'property'. *Barnakerthyng*, *Bascotesthyng*, *le halle thing* (f.ns. Drayton), *bolton thynge* (f.n. Marefield), *Chapelenesthing* (f.n. Great Bowden), *Evington thynge* (f.n. Evington), *Humberston thyng'*, *Dame Margarete thyng* (f.ns. Medbourne).

thist(e)ly ME, adj., 'thistly, a bounding with thistles'. Thistley Close Cottages. Thistly Fd (f.n. Theddingworth), *Thistlyholm* (f.n. Houghton).

three-corner ModE, adj., 'having three corners, triangular'. Three Corner (f.n. Smeeton Westerby), Three Corner Bit (f.n. Shangton), Three Corner Cl (f.n. Husbands Bosworth), Three Corner Fd (f.n. Billesdon, Newton Harcourt, Theddingworth), Three Corner Piece (f.n. Gumley).

three-cornered ModE, adj., 'having three corners, triangular'. Three Cornered Cl (f.n. Evington, Lubenham, Stoughton), Three Cornered Cross Leys (f.n. Stretton Magna), Three Cornered Fd (f.n. Billesdon, Saddington), Three Cornered Mdw (f.n. Great Glen, Stretton Magna).

thride ME, adj., 'third, the last of three'. *the thirde feilde* (f.n. Shangton).

tilð OE, 'tilth, land under cultivation'. Tilt Fd, Tilt Mdw (f.ns. Carlton Curlieu).

***todd** OE, 'a fox'. *Toadhill* (f.n. Houghton).

toft ODan, late OE, 'a curtilage, a messuage, a plot of land in which a dwelling stands'. Scraptoft. *Blaktoftes* (f.n. Burton Overy), Grubtoft (f.n. Little Stretton), *hameltoft* (f.n. Frisby), *Knaptoft*, *Normantoftes* (f.ns. Great Glen), *Nethertoftes*, *Ouertoftes* (f.ns. Noseley), Old Tafts Grass, Tafts Plowed (f.ns. Husbands

Bosworth), *Ouertoftys* (f.n. Great Bowden), *Shorte Tofts*, *Tofts Gate* (f.ns. Frisby), *Smalltoaftes* (f.n. Foxton), *Smitoft* (f.n. Newton Harcourt), *Snelistoft* (f.n. Saddington), *taftes* (f.n. Knossington), *Toftes* (f.n. Billesdon, Lubenham, Nevill Holt, Theddingworth, Welham).

tōh OE, adj., 'tough, sticky, hard'. Towcroft (f.n. Great Bowden).

toll-bar ModE, 'a toll-bar, a toll-gate, a turnpike'. Houghton Tollbar. Toll Bar (f.n. Billesdon).

toll-gate ModE, 'a toll-gate, a toll-bar, a turnpike'. Tollgate Cl (f.n. Billesdon).

top ModE, adj., 'topmost, uppermost'. Top Cl (f.n. East Langton, Great Easton, Smeeton Westerby), Top Fd (f.n. Kibworth Beauchamp, Houghton), Top Mdw (f.n. Evington, Fleckney, Illston), Top Paddock, Top Town (f.ns. Great Easton), Top Town Cl (f.n. Houghton), Top Townsend (f.n. Great Glen).

topp OE, 'the top, the top of a bank or hill'. Far Meadow Top (f.n. Scraptoft), Kuffers Top, Life Hill Top (f.ns. Billesdon), *the Topp of Barlie hill*, *the Toppe of Burston hill*, *the Toppe of Fearne* (f.ns. Hallaton), Top of the Hill (f.n. Slawston, Stonton Wyville), Top o' the Lane (f.n. Great Glen), Topside (f.n. Smeeton Westerby).

***tōt-hyll** OE, 'a look-out hill'. *Totehille* (f.n. Mowsley).

tōweard OE, adj., prep., 'facing, towards'. *þe Broke toward Bylsdonfeld* (f.n. Houghton), *toward Lipping* (f.n. Shangton).

trēow OE, **tré** ON, 'a tree'. Gartree Hundred. *Coptree Furlong* (f.n. Hallaton), Crow Trees (f.n. Stonton Wyville), *Haltree moore* (f.n. Newton Harcourt), ?*Hectry Leys* (f.n. Horninghold), *Hog tree* (f.n. Burton Overy), Oak Tree (f.n. Medbourne), the Tree Fd (f.n. Houghton, Medbourne), Willow Tree (f.n. Houghton).

triangle ModE, 'a triangle', also used adj. as 'triangular'. *Triangle Meadow* (f.n. Glooston).

trog OE, 'a valley; a trough'. *the Abstrow Croft* (f.n. Lubenham), *Carles Trough* (f.n. Tur Langton).

trype ME, 'tripe, the stomach tissue of an ox, cow etc. for use as food'. *Tripe Alley* (Market Harborough).

tū OE, num., 'two'. *Thogates*, Twofields Mdw (f.ns. Shangton), *Towells* (f.n. Saddington), Two Cl (f.n. Burton Overy), *tuthorne* (f.n. Knossington), *Twodales* (f.n. Theddingworth).

tūn OE, 'a farmstead, a village, an estate', **tún** ON, 'a farmstead'. Blaston, Carlton Curlieu, Church Langton, Cold Overton, Drayton, East Langton, Foxton, Glooston, Great Easton, Hallaton, Houghton on the Hill, Illston on the Hill, King's Norton, Knossington, Little Stretton, Newton Harcourt, Owston, Rolleston, Shangton, Slawston, Smeeton Westerby, ?Stockerston, Stonton Wyville, Stoughton, Stretton Magna, West Langton; New Town, Town Close, Town End Cottage, Townsend Close Spinney. Lost farmsteads: *Bilton'* (Medbourne), ?*Bowghton* (Great Bowden), ?*Gunston*, ?*Heckston* (Houghton), *Neyton* (Great Easton), *Noston'* (Mowsley), ?*Orton* (Burton Overy), *Sireston* (Stoughton), ?*Smeton* (Market Harborough), *Stubston* (Kibworth Beauchamp). Common in f.ns.: e.g. Above Town (Billesdon), *Beneath the Towne* (Cranoe), Between Towns (Galby), *boueton* (Frisby), *by Neyton*, Top Town (Great Easton), *Ortondale* (Burton Overy), *Sirestonsty* (Stoughton). Town(s)end (Cl) recurs (Cold Overton, Cranoe, Foxton, Galby, Great Glen, Goadby, Gumley, Hallaton,

Houghton, Kibworth Beauchamp, Laughton, Nevill Holt), as do *the Towne syde* (Cranoe, Great Glen) and *the Town street* (Galby, Great Glen). Note also Town Adley (Fleckney), Town Cl (Illston), *the Towne Baulke* (Husbands Bosworth), *the Towne ley* (Houghton), Town Park, Town's Hill (Billesdon), Town Piece (Evington), Town Syke Mdw (Laughton).

tunge OE, **tunga** ON, 'a tongue', used in p.ns. of 'a tongue of land'. *Calewelletunge* (f.n. Illston), Fearn Tongue, *Hoctong'* (f.ns. Hallaton), *Grenehultunge* (f.n. Houghton), *Mr William Panes tonge* (f.n. Medbourne), *Tong* (f.n. East Langton), *atte Tonge* (f.n. Mowsley), *Tonghill* (f.n. Great Bowden, Husbands Bosworth), Tongs (f.n. Burton Overy), *the Tongs* (f.n. Tur Langton), *Tongs gate* (f.n. Frisby), *Tongstede* (f.n. Great Bowden), *Tongue* (f.n. King's Norton), *le Tunge* (f.n. Stoughton).

***tūn-stall** OE, 'the site of a farm, a farmstead'. *dunstall hill* (f.n. Knossington), The Dunstills (f.n. Gumley).

tup ME, 'a ram, a tup'. Tugwell Lane.

turf OE, 'turf, greensward'. The Torves (f.n. Burton Overy), Turf Cl (f.n. Tur Langton, West Langton).

turnepe eModE, 'a turnip'. Turnip Cl (f.n. Blaston, Laughton), Turnip Fd (f.n. Medbourne).

turnepike ME, 'a revolving pole bearing spikes and serving as a barrier', **turnpike** ModE, 'a road on which a toll is payable and along which movement is controlled by barriers'. the Turnpicke Road (f.n. Kibworth Harcourt), Turnpike Cl (f.n. Billesdon, Foxton, Houghton, Lubenham), Turnpike Spinney (f.n. Great Glen).

***twigen** OE, adj., 'covered with twigs or shoots'. ?*Twintill* (f.n. Theddingworth).

twinn OE, adj., 'double, twin'. Tween Dykes (f.n. Carlton Curlieu), ?*Twintill* (f.n. Theddingworth).

twisla OE, 'the fork of a river, the junction of two streams'. Twizzle Cl (f.n. Tur Langton), *Whistel Gate* (f.n. Kibworth, Harcourt).

twyn(n)y ME, adv., '(two) set apart'. *Twynymill hill* (f.n. Husbands Bosworth).

tynie eModE, adj., 'very small'. *Tyney hooke* (f.n. King's Norton).

typpett ME, 'a tippet, a long narrow slip of cloth forming part of a hood or sleeve'; poss. used topographically alluding to shape. *the Parsons tippitt dole* (f.n. Glooston).

þæc OE, **þak** ON, 'thatch, material for thatching'. Hack Moor (f.n. King's Norton), *Longthakholme* (f.n. Noseley), *thachink* (f.n. Frisby), *Thacholme* (f.n. Stockerston), *Thakines Bushe* (f.n. Kibworth Harcourt).

þe, **the** ME, def.art., 'the'. Early instances are *þe croftys* (f.n. Illston), *þe smalesike* (f.n. Shangton), *þe Wold* (f.n. Frisby). Modern instances as *the* are common throughout.

***þefa** OE, 'brushwood, bramble' or the like. *Thevdenes* (f.n. Gumley).

þicce[2] OE, adj., 'thick, dense'. *Thichethirne* (f.n. Saddington).

þiccett OE, 'a thicket, dense bushes or undergrowth'. *Sheepthorne thickett* (Sheepthorns Spinney).

þing OE, ON, 'an assembly, a council, a meeting'. ?Ting's Cl (f.n. Welham).

þistel OE, 'a thistle'. *Fisel Baulke*, *Thisseldale* (f.ns. Little Stretton), Thistle Fd (f.n. Stonton Wyville), Thistle Hill (f.n. Newton Harcourt), Thistles (f.n. Smeeton Westerby).

þorn OE, 'a thorn, a thorn-tree, the hawthorn'; perh. in some f.ns. collectively, 'a stand or thicket or a wood of thorn-trees'. Sheepthorns Spinney, Tythorn Hill. Fairly freq. in f.ns.: *Bikethorn*, *bygthoryn* (Illston), *Brethornhil*, *Crathornehull*, Thornwood (Billesdon), *Carriers Thorn* (Husbands Bosworth), *Caudell thornes* (Frisby), *Crowethornehyll* (Great Bowden), Crowthorn (f.n. Little Bowden), *Crowthornis* (Burton Overy), *Godiuethorn* (Drayton), *Lankthorne* (Gumley), Mans Horns (Fleckney), *Pennythorne* (Lubenham), *Smalthornes* (Frisby, Great Bowden, Great Easton, Saddington), Swallow Thorn (Owston), *the Thorn* (Stretton Magna), Thornborough (Little Bowden), Thorn Bush Cl, Thorncombe (Laughton), *thornhill* (Gumley, Hallaton, Houghton), Thorns (Hallaton), *tuthorne* (Knossington), *threthornehul* (Frisby).

þornig OE, adj., 'thorny, growing with thorns'. *Thorney baulke*, Thorney Leys, *Thorniwong* (f.ns. Houghton), *Thornie meddowe* (f.n. Cranoe), *Thorniholm* (f.n. Medbourne), Thorny Cl (f.n. Blaston, Burton Overy, Hallaton), *Thornydale* (f.n. Mowsley), *Thornygore* (f.n. Billesdon), Thorny Mason's Cl (f.n. Blaston), *Thorny medowe* (f.n. Glooston), *Thorny Pytt* (f.n. Theddingworth), *Thornye Way* (f.n. Hothorpe).

þorp ON, 'a secondary settlement, a dependent outlying farmstead or hamlet'. Hothorpe, Owthorpe, Thorpe Langton; *Godtorp* (*Gillethorp*). ?*Astrope hill* (f.n. Gumley), *Cawthorpe felde* (f.n. Thorpe Langton), Gold Thorpe (f.n. Blaston), *Oddestorp* (f.n. Medbourne), *Sowtorp'* (f.n. Great Bowden), Sybthorpe (f.n. Stoughton), ?*Thedyngesthorp* (f.n. Theddingworth), *Thorpewell* (f.n. Evington), *Thorphill* (f.n. Kibworth Harcourt).

þrang OE, sb., 'a throng, a crowd', **thrang** ME, adj., 'thick, dense'. *Thranghlie* (f.n. Cranoe).

þræl late OE, **þræll** ON, 'a thrall, a serf'. *Thralholm* (f.n. Medbourne), *Thrallhill* (f.n. East Langton), Thrawly (f.n. Glooston).

þrēo OE, num., 'three'. Three Bushes, Three Gates. *the Three Lands furlong* (f.n. Saddington), *Three Roode Riggs* (f.n. Cranoe), *The Three Roods* (f.n. Great Glen), *Threstonkys* (f.n. Billesdon), *threthornehul* (f.n. Frisby).

þriðing late OE, **þriðjungr** ON, 'a third part'. *Thirthyngys* (f.n. Nevill Holt).

þrop OE, 'a hamlet, an outlying farm'. ?*Astrope hill* (f.n. Gumley), ?*Thedyngesthorp* (f.n. Theddingworth).

þrūh OE, 'a conduit, a water-pipe'; sometimes figuratively alluding to 'a deep valley'. ?*Throwslade* (f.n. Frisby).

þūma OE, 'a thumb'; used topographically of something very small. *Thumbe home* (f.n. Hallaton), ?*Tommor* (f.n. Great Easton).

þurh OE, adv., prep., 'through'. ?*Throwslade* (f.n. Frisby).

þveit ON, **thwēt** ODan, 'a clearing, a meadow, a paddock'. *Rauenesthuett* (f.n. Noseley), *le Thwytelangelondes* (f.n. Medbourne).

þverr (**þvert** neut.) ON, adj., 'athwart, lying across'. *Thwerhull* (f.n. Billesdon), *Thwertforowes* (f.n. Stoughton), *Whart doles* (f.n. Great Bowden), *Whart gates* (f.n. Galby), *wharthill* (f.n. Knossington), Whartland (f.n. Slawston).

þwang OE, **þvengr** ON, 'a thong'; used topographically as 'a long strip of land'. *Edrichisthwong* (f.n. Stoughton), *Long thonge* (f.n. Houghton), *le Thwonge* (f.n. Great Bowden, Stoughton).

***þwīt** OE, 'a clearing, a meadow'. ?*le Thwytelangelondes* (f.n. Medbourne).

þyrne OE, **þyrnir** ON, 'a thorn-bush'. ?Thurnby. *Cliftherne*, *Helthirne*, *kyngestirne*, *Penytherne* (f.ns. Great Easton), *Thichethirne* (f.n. Saddington), *le Thirne* (f.n. Hallaton), *Thurn Close*, *Thyrnewong* (f.ns. Owston), *Thurnhill* (f.n. Frisby), Thyon Leys (f.n. Mowsley), *le Thyrne* (f.n. Wistow), Turn Back (f.n. Lubenham).

þyrni ODan, 'thorn-scrub'. ?Thurnby.

***þyrniht** OE, adj., 'growing with thorns'. *Thurney Pitt Leys* (f.n. Theddingworth).

þyrs OE, **þurs** ON, 'a demon, a giant'. *Thyrspyt* (f.n. Nevill Holt).

-uc, **-oc** OE, noun suffix. *Pyllok* (f.n. Medbourne), *the Pylloke* (f.n. Evington), ?*Pyllokesholme* (f.n. Great Bowden).

uferra OE, comp.adj., 'higher, upper'. *Vuerkibewrd* (Kibworth Harcourt); *Ouerhall* (The Hall, Houghton). Far Over Cl (f.n. Galby), *Litteldalesouerhende*, *Ouermore* (f.ns. Billesdon), *Ouer Ashes*, *Ouerblakbrok*, *Over Banlans*, *Over Coklow* (f.ns. Husbands Bosworth), *Ouerforth* (f.n. Houghton), *Ouertoftys*, *The Over Field* (f.ns. Great Bowden), *the Over Church furlong*, *the over end meer* (f.ns. Great Glen), Over Cl (f.n. Burton Overy), Over Cross Hill Mdw, *Overfield Close* (f.ns. Carlton Curlieu), *the Overhouse* (Knossington), *the over medow* (f.n. Great Easton), Over Old Fd (f.n. Goadby).

umber ME, 'shadow, shade'. ?*Umberbreche* (f.n. Nevill Holt).

under OE, adv., prep., 'under, beneath, below'. *Vnderlith* (Life Hill, Billesdon). *Under Gallow* (f.n. Great Bowden), Underhill Cl (f.n. Saddington), *under le sty* (f.n. Shangton), *Undersike* (f.n. King's Norton), *under Styopers*, *under the Sunne* (f.ns. Gumley), Under (the) Gorse (f.n. Billesdon), *underwytkotes* (f.n. Illston), *Vnderbretlond* (f.n. Bushby), *Vndurcrosse* (f.n. Noseley).

up, **uppe** ME, adv., prep., 'up, higher up, the higher one'. *atte Uphall* (p) (Carlton Curlieu Hall). *Vppewelcroft* (f.n. Stretton Magna).

upper ME, adj., 'higher'. *Upper Hall* (Scraptoft Hall). Common in f.ns., e.g. *the uper Cockland*, *uper hedge* (Husbands Bosworth), *Uper Lemonsong* (Fleckney), *Upper Church Furlong* (Great Glen), Upper Close Mdw (Evington), *the Upper Ground* (Blaston, Carlton Curlieu), *the Upper meadow* (Bringhurst, Cranoe, Great Easton).

ūt OE, **út** ON, adj., 'outer, on the outskirts'. Outwalks (f.n. Glooston).

val ME, 'a vale, a wide valley'. Vale Mdw (f.n. Rolleston).

vangr ON, 'an in-field'. Very freq. in f.ns.: esp. with pers.ns. or surns. indicating ownership, e.g. *Aylewordewong*, *Sirichiswong* (Shangton), *Grymyswong'* (Great Bowden), *Leamons wong* (Fleckney); *Abraham Woong* (Evington), *Fidelliswonge* (Great Bowden), *Flambuswong* (Husbands Bosworth), *Nicolswong* (Stoughton); or with locational names, e.g. *Dalewonge* (Hallaton), *Godiuethornwang* (Drayton), *Gorewong*, *maidewellewong*, *Sandpytwong*, *Sawpitwong* (Nevill Holt), *Parke wonge* (Knossington); or with livestock, e.g. Cow Wong (West Langton), *Goswong* (Billesdon), Stearwong (Knossington). Wild flora may feature, e.g. *Thyrnewong* (Newbold), *weythey wonge* (Gumley), *Willow Wong* (Tur Langton). As a simplex, e.g. *the Wong* (Evington, Great Glen, Houghton).

vápnatak ON, **wæpengetæc** late OE, **wapentac** ME, 'a wapentake, a sub-division of a county', corresponding to OE **hundred**. Gartree Wapentake.

vargr ON, 'a wolf'. ?*Warglondis* (f.n. Nevill Holt).

vengi ON, 'a field'. ?Wingfield Spinney. ?*Wingfeilds* (f.n. Scraptoft).

vestr ON, adj., 'west, westerly', **vestri**, comp., 'more westerly'. Smeeton Westerby.

vikerage ME, 'a vicarage'. The Vicarage (Billesdon, Evington, Fleckney, Great Easton, Great Glen, Horninghold, Lubenham, Slawston, Theddingworth, Thurnby), Vicarage Drive, Vicarage Ho. *the Vicarage grounde* (f.n. King's Norton), *Vicaridge Close* (f.n. Horninghold), the Vicaridge piece (f.n. Slawston).

vikere ME, 'a vicar'. *the Vicars peece* (f.n. Slawston).

village ME, 'a village'. Village Mdw (f.n. Glooston).

vinyerd ME, 'a vineyard'. *le Winyerd* (f.n. Stoughton).

víðir ON, 'a willow, a withy'. ?*Vytharowe* (f.n. Medbourne).

vrá ON, **wro** ME, 'a nook, a corner of land'. *in le Wro* (p) (Great Easton, Houghton, Scraptoft); *Gerardisvro* (f.n. Hallaton), *le Holmeswro* (f.n. Billesdon), *Sigrimeswro* (f.n. Drayton).

wacor OE, adj., 'watchful, vigilant'; poss. used also in p.ns. as a sb. with the meaning 'a watcher, a look-out'. ?Wakes Hill (f.n. Stoughton).

***wacu** OE, 'a watch, a wake'; poss. also in p.ns. with the meaning 'a watching-place'. *Wakelow* (f.n. Saddington), *Wakelopittes* (f.n. Great Bowden), *Wakoe* (f.n. Owston).

wād OE, 'woad'. The Wad Cabin (f.n. Evington), ?Wadcombe (f.n. Laughton), *Wadland* (f.n. Knossington), Wadlands Cl (f.n. Blaston, Burton Overy, Thurnby), Wadd Leys (f.n. Owston), Wad Orchard (f.n. Blaston), *le Wadsike* (f.n. Shangton), Woad Cl (f.n. Wistow), *the woad-ground* (f.n. Stonton Wyville).

wald OE (Angl), 'woodland, high forest land', **wald**, **wold** ME, 'an elevated stretch of open country or moorland'. Horninghold; Old Hill. Common in f.ns.: as a simplex in various guises, e.g. *the Olt* (Mowsley), *the Oult* (Little Stretton), *le Waud* (Shangton), *le Wold* (Billesdon, Frisby, Stretton Magna); recurring are *the Woolands* (Great Glen, East Langton, Mowsley, Newton Harcourt) and Old Hill (Burton Overy, Carlton Curlieu, Lubenham). Note also Gang Would (Marefield), *Hyewulledale*, *Woldegate*, *le Woldfurlong*, *Wooldales*, Would Hedge (Billesdon), *the olde brooke* (Little Stretton), *Stoctonwolde*, *Stodwoldhull* (Stretton Magna), *Wold Ditches* (Great Bowden), *Woldflaxlandis* (Mowsley), *Woldfurlong'* (Stoughton), *Woldmedow* (Burton Overy), Wooldale Mdw (Cold Overton).

walk ModE, 'a walking place; a path; a range of pasture'. Church Walk, Long Walk. *the Church Walk* (f.n. Carlton Curlieu), Long Walk (f.n. Stoughton), Outwalks (f.n. Glooston).

walu OE, 'a ridge of earth, a raised strip of ground, an embankment'. *Walewell* (f.n. Medbourne), *Walhill*, *Walsick* (f.ns. Fleckney).

wamb, **womb** OE, 'a womb, a belly', used topographically as 'a hollow'. ?*Wambeley* (f.n. Nevill Holt).

wand eModE, 'a measure of land, usually of about 30 acres'. High Wanfield (f.n. Evington).

wandale, **wandole** ME, 'a share of a great open-field', prob. consisting of a strip of land measured off with a specific wand or rod. *the Wandies* (f.n. Tur Langton), *le wandole* (f.n. Medbourne).

wareine ME, 'a game preserve; a piece of ground for breeding rabbits, a warren'. The Warren (Kibworth Beauchamp, Tur Langton). Holt Warren (f.n. Medbourne), ?*Warinwell* (f.n. Nevill Holt), *the Warren* (f.n. Nevill Holt, Stonton Wyville), Warren Cl (f.n. Lubenham).

water-mylne ME, 'a water-mill'. Glen Water Mill, Water Mill Ho. *Watermill Close* (f.n. Laughton), *watermill dore* (f.n. Husbands Bosworth), Watermill Hill (f.n.

Smeeton Westerby), *Watermill Hooke* (f.n. Tur Langton), *Water Mill Yard* (f.n. Mowsley), *Watermylhyll* (f.n. Saddington).

wateryng eModE, vbl.sb., ppl.adj., 'a place where cattle are taken to drink'. *Cow watering, New watering* (f.ns. Hallaton), *the Watering* (f.n. Kibworth Beauchamp, Mowsley), Watering Leys (f.n. Medbourne), *the watering place* (f.n. Burton Overy), *Wattering pitt furlonge* (f.n. Gumley), Well Wattering (f.n. Fleckney).

***wæccere** OE, 'a watchman, a look-out'. ?Wakes Hill (f.n. Stoughton).

wæfre OE, adj., 'unstable'. *Waueremos* (f.n. Frisby).

wægn, wægen OE, 'a waggon, a cart'. Wain Bridge. *Wayne waye* (f.n. Great Glen, Kibworth Harcourt), *Wayne Way Close* (f.n. Evington), *the Weyn Way* (f.n. Burton Overy).

wærg (Angl), adj., 'wretched'. ?*Warglondis* (f.n. Nevill Holt).

wæsce OE, 'a place for washing', of sheep, the wheels of carts etc. Washbrook Lane, Wash Dyke Bridge, Washdyke Rd, Washpit Lane. ?Wash Bit (f.n. Marefield), Washbrook Mdw (f.n. Foxton), Wash Pit (f.n. Houghton, Husbands Bosworth, Laughton, Little Stretton, Rolleston), Wash Pit Cl (f.n. King's Norton, Lubenham, Nevill Holt, Saddington), Washpit Leys (f.n. Burton Overy, Great Glen), Washpit Mdw (f.n. Evington, Scraptoft), Wash-pit Piece (f.n. Horninghold), *Washpoole* (f.n. Houghton), *Wassford* (f.n. Great Bowden).

***wæsse** OE, 'a wet place, a swamp, a marsh'. ?Wash Bit (f.n. Marefield).

wæter OE, 'water, an expanse of water, a lake or pool, a stream or river' or, as first el., 'near to a stream or pool; wet, watery'. *the water furrowes* (f.n. with various spellings (esp. *Water thorowes*) in Billesdon, Burton Overy, Fleckney, Goadby, Great Easton, Great Glen, Houghton, Husbands Bosworth, Illston, Laughton, Little Bowden, Mowsley), Water Furrows Cl (f.n. Owston), *waterlag* (f.n. Husbands Bosworth), *Waterlandes* (f.n. Goadby), *Wateris* (f.n. Lubenham), *le Waterlakes* (f.n. Great Bowden), *Watter moor* (f.n. Houghton).

wæter-(ge)fall OE, 'a rapid; a cascade, a waterfall; a stream', *v.* JEPNS **39**, 95. *le waterfall* (f.n. Billesdon), *at waterfal* (f.n. Horninghold), *on Waterfall* (f.n. Frisby, Husbands Bosworth), *Waterfalls* (f.n. Hallaton), *Watterfall Close* (f.n. Lubenham).

wæterig OE, adj., 'watery'; also used as a sb., 'a watery place'. *waterrey, Watry Balland* (f.ns. Gumley), Watery Cl (f.n. Foxton), Watery Mdw (f.n. Scraptoft), *le Watiri* (f.n. Nevill Holt).

wearm OE, adj., 'warm'. *Warmwelle* (f.n. Great Easton).

weax OE, 'wax'; in p.ns. prob. in allusion to where bees' wax was produced or found. *Waxland* (f.n. Gumley), *Waxlandes* (f.n. Burton Overy).

weg OE, 'a way, a road'. Holloway Spinney. Fairly freq., esp. with the name of a township, e.g. *Bilsdon way* (Frisby), *Harbarow Waye, Killworth way* (Husbands Bosworth), *Leicester way* (Burton Overy), *medburn waie* (Blaston); or prefixed by the name of a local feature, e.g. *Blackwell waye* (Glooston), *Dalewaye, Hogsdrift Way, March waye* (Hallaton), *hose wey* (Frisby). *Wayne waye* recurs (Burton Overy, Evington, Great Glen). Note The Saltway (Cranoe).

wella OE, **well(e)** (Angl), 'a well, a spring, a stream'. ?Welham; Bees Well Lane, Holy Well, Langton Caudle, St Ann's Well, Tugwell Lane. Freq. in f.ns.: with pers.ns., e.g. *Roger well* (Burton Overy), *Wulmereswell* (Billesdon), *yolwell'* (Illston); with wild fauna, e.g. *Buckwell* (Great Bowden), *Catwell* (Burton Overy,

Hallaton), *foxwellys* (Illston); with wild flora, e.g. *Hassewell* (Nevill Holt), *Mosewelle* (East Langton), *le Osiereswell* (Billesdon), *Rushwell* (Gumley); with livestock, e.g. *Cattelwell* (Saddington), *le Cowel* (Hallaton), *the Horsewell* (Hothorpe); with els. indicating particular aspects of the wells, e.g. *Drygwell* (Houghton), *Sprynkelwell*, *Warmwelle* (Great Easton). Sacred wells feature, e.g. *Holiewell* (Cranoe), *Maidewell* (Husbands Bosworth, Nevill Holt), *St Morrills well* (Hallaton), *Seaven Wells* (Great Bowden, Lubenham). Recurring are *Caldwell* (with various spellings in Carlton Curlieu, East Langton, Frisby, Hallaton, Horninghold, Laughton), *Fulwell* (with various spellings in Billesdon, Blaston, Burton Overy, Great Bowden, Hallaton, Illston) and *Stockwell* (with various spellings in Billesdon, Drayton, Frisby, Houghton, Little Bowden, Nevill Holt, Saddington).

*__wende__ OE, 'something which bends or winds'. *le Wendacre* (f.n. Evington).

wēod OE, 'a weed'; also 'a herb, grass'. *Wedefurlong'* (f.n. Goadby).

wer OE, 'a weir, a river-dam, a fishing enclosure in a river'. *Wey Brigg Weir* (f.n. Kibworth Harcourt).

*__werpels__ OE (Angl), 'a path, a cart-track, a track in the common field'. *Warpars* (f.n. Great Bowden).

west OE, **vestr** ON, adj., 'western, west'. West Langton, *Westnorton* (King's Norton). The great open-field name *Westfeld* recurs (with various spellings in Billesdon, Bringhurst, Burton Overy, Foxton, Great Easton, Husbands Bosworth). The minor f.n. West Mdw recurs (Billesdon, Burton Overy, Fleckney). Note *Westbury* (f.n. Husbands Bosworth), *Westcroftes* (f.n. Shangton).

*__wester__ OE, adj., 'west, western'. *le Westerplaystowe* (f.n. Drayton).

westerra OE, comp.adj., 'more westerly'. *Westere Langeton* (West Langton).

wēt OE (Angl), adj., 'wet, damp'. ?*Watho* (f.n. Burton Overy), *Watmore* (f.n. Houghton), *Wetland* (f.n. Smeeton Westerby), *Wheate more* (f.n. Frisby), ?Wheatland Syke (f.n. Laughton).

weðer OE, 'a wether, a castrated ram'. *Wether Close* (f.n. Houghton), Wethers Cl (f.n. Owston).

weyour ME, 'a pond'. Weir Fm, Weir Lane, Weir Rd. Weir Cl (f.n. Saddington), *Weyrdic* (f.n. Illston), The Wire (f.n. Hallaton), *the Wyer* (f.n. Laughton), *Wyregate close* (f.n. Mowsley).

wharf ModE, 'a structure built along waterways and railways so that barges and trucks may load and unload'. Debdale Wharf, North Kilworth Wharf, Station Wharf, Union Wharf, Welford Wharf.

whinny ME, adj., 'growing with whins and gorse-bushes'. Whinney Pit Spinney. Whinney (f.n. Little Stretton), *Whinney dole* (f.n. Husbands Bosworth), *Whynedolis* (f.n. Houghton), *Winilondys* (f.n. Burton Overy), Winney (f.n. King's Norton), Winnidoles (f.n. Houghton), Winnow Dale (f.n. Illston), *Wynnedoole* (f.n. Foxton).

wīc OE, 'a farm, a dairy farm, a building or collection of buildings for a special purpose'. *Bolewyk* (f.n. Hallaton), Creswick, *Perwickes Close* (f.ns. Lubenham), *Wikmedow* (f.n. Great Bowden).

wīc-stōw OE, 'a dwelling place'. *Wistowe Hill* (f.n. Hallaton).

wifel OE, 'a beetle, a weevil'. ?*Wylspole* (f.n. Goadby).

wilde OE, adj., 'wild, uncultivated, desolate'. *Wildemore* (f.n. East Langton), *Wildmore* (f.n. Tur Langton), *Wild Willows* (f.n. Evington).

wilder, **wild-dēor** OE, 'a wild beast, a deer'. Wild Harrey (f.n. Knossington).

wildernesse ME, 'a wilderness, a wild place'; in modern minor-names, sometimes a designed wild area in a constructed landscape or park. The Wilderness.

wīle OE, 'an engine, a mechanical contrivance'. ?*wilegate* (f.n. Slawston).

***wilig** OE (Angl), 'a willow'. Freq. in f.ns.: esp. with a prefixed surn. indicating ownership, e.g. *Judds willows* (Burton Overy), *Lads willows* (Blaston), *Parkers Willows* (Great Bowden), *Swansons Willows* (Hallaton). Church ownership features, e.g. *the Gleab Willows*, *the Parsons willowes* (Gumley). Willow-beds occur, e.g. Burton Willow Bed (Burton Overy), Willow Bed Cl (Scraptoft). Recurring is *Willow Sike* (Bushby, Cranoe, Frisby, Glooston, Hallaton, Houghton, Illston).

***wiligen** OE, adj., 'growing with willows'. ?*Wilughnegate* (f.n. Billesdon).

***wilign** OE, 'a willow copse'. ?*Wilughnegate* (f.n. Billesdon).

wince OE, 'a sharp bend in a river, a corner'. ?*Wencelawedale* (f.n. Medbourne).

***wincel** OE, 'a nook, a corner'. ?*Wencelawedale* (f.n. Medbourne).

wind[1] OE, **vindr** ON, 'wind'. *Windlowe* (f.n. Husbands Bosworth), *Wyndeshers* (f.n. Billesdon).

(ge)wind[2] OE, 'something winding, a winding path, a winding ascent'. *Wyndes willowes* (f.n. Laughton).

wind-mylne ME, 'a wind-mill'. Windmill Fm, Windmill Lodge. *Mr Vowes windmill* (Hallaton), *Windmill* (Carlton Curlieu, Market Harborough, Stonton Wyville), *the Wyndmylle* (Cranoe), Windmill Bank (f.n. Nevill Holt), Windmill Cl (f.n. Foxton, Great Glen, West Langton), Windmill Fd (f.n. Mowsley), *Windmill Furlong*, *Windmill Hill* (f.ns. Glooston), Windmill Hill (f.n. Slawston), ?*Whymmerhill* (f.n. Houghton), *Wyndmilnehyl* (f.n. Great Easton), *Wynd Myll Feilde* (f.n. Stonton Wyville).

***wisp** OE, 'a wisp' used of 'a thicket, brushwood'. Wisp (f.n. Knossington).

wīðig OE, 'a withy, a willow'. ?*Vytharowe* (f.n. Medbourne), *weythey wonge* (f.n. Gumley), *Withey poole* (f.n. Little Stretton), *Withy pittes* (f.n. Laughton).

***wīðign** OE, 'a willow, a willow copse'. *Wythenbuske* (f.n. Billesdon).

workhouse ModE, 'a workhouse, a place of public employment for the poor'. Union Workhouse. Glen Workhouse (Newton Harcourt), Workhouse (Smeeton Westerby), Workhouse Cl (f.n. Hallaton, Lubenham).

worð OE, 'an enclosure'. Husbands Bosworth, Kibworth Beauchamp, Kibworth Harcourt, Theddingwoth. *Cranesworth*, *Wineworth* (f.ns. Great Bowden).

wrang OE, adj., **vrangr** ON, adj., 'crooked, twisted in shape'. *le Wrange* (f.n. Drayton), *Wrangelondes* (f.n. with various spellings in Billesdon, Burton Overy, Fleckney, Foxton, Great Bowden, Gumley, Husbands Bosworth, Illston, Kibworth Beauchamp, Kibworth Harcourt, Laughton, Mowsley, *Prestgave*, Saddington, Theddingworth, Thorpe Langton), *Wranghadon* (f.n. Burton Overy), *le Wrongbroke* (f.n. Nevill Holt), *Wrongedoles*, *le Wrongesik* (f.ns. Medbourne), *Wrong gates* (f.n. Laughton), *Wronghenges* (f.n. Billesdon).

***wride** OE, 'a winding, a twist, a bend'. *Wride willowes* (f.n. Laughton).

wrīð OE, 'a bush, a thicket'. *Hopkin Wrytsmore* (f.n. Noseley).

wudu, earlier **widu** OE, 'a wood, a grove, woodland'. Bolt Wood, Glooston ~, Great Merrible ~, Gumley ~, Hallaton ~, Holt ~, Keythorpe ~, Lady ~, Noseley Wood,

Owston Woods, Sturrad Spinney. Black Dyke Wood, Bradley Wood, *forewodes*, *Powers Woode*, *Wodesty* (f.ns. Great Easton), *Brechewod* (f.n. Blaston), Drayton Wood, *Gongwode* (f.ns. Nevill Holt), Galby Wood Mdw (f.n. Galby), *Horsewood close*, *Kirkwood*, Smallwood (f.ns. Hallaton), Little Wood (f.n. Gumley), Longwood Park, Thornwood, Wood Marsh (f.ns. Billesdon), *Wodegate* (f.n. Drayton, Great Easton, Little Bowden, Nevill Holt), *wodegatehul* (f.n. Frisby), *Wodesyke* (f.n. Billesdon, Nevill Holt), Wood Breach (f.n. Little Bowden), *the Wood Close* (f.n. Blaston, Cranoe, Nevill Holt), *Woode feilde*, *Woodhome* (f.ns. Knossington), *the Wood Nook* (f.n. Cranoe), *Wydfeld'* (f.n. Noseley).

wulf (**wulfa** gen.pl.) OE, 'a wolf'. Woolpits Planting. ?*Wolfawell* (f.n. Theddingworth), *Wolfhegys* (f.n. *Prestgrave*), ?*wolfhill* (f.n. Gumley).

wyrm, **wurm** OE, 'a reptile, a snake', also 'a dragon', **worm** ME, 'an earthworm, an insect'. ?*Wormhill* (f.n. Husbands Bosworth).

wyrt OE, 'a plant, a vegetable'. *Worthohyll* (f.n. Burton Overy).

yerdland ME, 'a square measure of about 30 acres'. *le Burnt house yardeland* (f.n. Goadby), *Gowyneyerdeland* (f.n. Billesdon), *John Jolly's Quarter of a Yard Land* (f.n. Evington).

yoman ME, 'an attendant in a royal or noble household, an attendant or assistant to an official'. ?*yommanyshorstede* (f.n. Illston).

INDEX OF THE PLACE-NAMES OF GARTREE HUNDRED

This index includes all the major names and minor names in the Introduction and in the main body of the work but not in the section The Elements in Gartree Hundred's Place-Names. Field-names in lists (a) and (b) are not indexed. The names of the townships are printed in capitals. Lost names are printed in italic.